International Review of
RESEARCH IN
MENTAL RETARDATION

VOLUME 4

Contributors to This Volume

NORMAN R. ELLIS

MARY ANN FISHER

LAIRD W. HEAL

ARTHUR R. JENSEN

JOHN T. JOHNSON, JR.

LYLE L. LLOYD

GILBERT W. MEIER

A. B. SILVERSTEIN

WARNER WILSON

DAVID ZEAMAN

International Review of
RESEARCH IN
MENTAL RETARDATION

EDITED BY

NORMAN R. ELLIS

DEPARTMENT OF PSYCHOLOGY
UNIVERSITY OF ALABAMA
UNIVERSITY, ALABAMA

VOLUME 4

CONSULTING EDITORS FOR THIS VOLUME

Paul S. Siegel **Ivar Arnljot Björgen**
UNIVERSITY OF ALABAMA   UNIVERSITY OF OSLO
UNIVERSITY, ALABAMA   OSLO, NORWAY

Neil O'Connor
THE MAUDSLEY HOSPITAL
LONDON, ENGLAND

1970

ACADEMIC PRESS   New York and London

Copyright © 1970, by Academic Press, Inc.
ALL RIGHTS RESERVED
NO PART OF THIS BOOK MAY BE REPRODUCED IN ANY FORM,
BY PHOTOSTAT, MICROFILM, RETRIEVAL SYSTEM, OR ANY
OTHER MEANS, WITHOUT WRITTEN PERMISSION FROM
THE PUBLISHERS.

ACADEMIC PRESS, INC.
111 Fifth Avenue, New York, New York 10003

United Kingdom Edition published by
ACADEMIC PRESS, INC. (LONDON) LTD.
Berkeley Square House, London W1X 6BA

LIBRARY OF CONGRESS CATALOG CARD NUMBER: 65-28627

PRINTED IN THE UNITED STATES OF AMERICA

List of Contributors

Numbers in parentheses indicate the pages on which the authors' contributions begin.

NORMAN R. ELLIS, *University of Alabama, University, Alabama* (1)

MARY ANN FISHER, *University of Connecticut, Storrs, Connecticut* (151)

LAIRD W. HEAL, *George Peabody College for Teachers, Nashville, Tennessee* (107)

ARTHUR R. JENSEN, *University of California, Berkeley, California* (33)

JOHN T. JOHNSON, JR., *Memphis State University, Memphis, Tennessee* (107)

LYLE L. LLOYD, *Gallaudet College, Washington, D. C.* (311)*

GILBERT W. MEIER, *George Peabody College, Nashville, Tennessee* (263)

A. B. SILVERSTEIN, *Pacific State Hospital, Pomona, California* (193)

WARNER WILSON, *University of Alabama, Tuscaloosa, Alabama* (229)

DAVID ZEAMAN, *University of Connecticut, Storrs, Connecticut* (151)

*Present address: Mental Retardation Research and Training Committee, National Institute of Child Health and Human Development, National Institutes of Health, Bethesda, Maryland.

Preface

The contents of this volume, like the three previous ones, range widely — a theory of memory function in retardates, a theoretical conception of two behavioral types of retardation; reviews of research on inhibitory mechanisms in retardates, social-psychological research, audiology, research on mental retardation in animals, and psychometric characteristics; and a study of the growth and decline of intelligence in institutionalized retardates. These papers all attempt to contribute to our knowledge of the behavior of the mentally retarded through the vehicle of interpretive reviews and theoretical invention.

In the main, these materials deal with human (and animal) *laboratory* behavior. The extent to which these findings can be generalized to the real world of the retardate remains largely unexplored. However, much of the research described here does have important implications for understanding the retardate in his natural habitat, e.g., Jensen's research and theory point clearly to application. As noted in the preface to the previous volume, operant conditioning (or behavior modification) continues to dominate "behavioral engineering" in this field. Unfortunately, this "movement" appears to be in serious need of hard empirical evidence as to the validity of its methods and their economic feasibility with this population.

The derivation of principles for changing behavior in the home, classroom, or institution would appear to be a useful and rewarding endeavor. The seemingly erudite behavior theories, along with the research they generate, may well yield information for application. This series of volumes offers a fertile source for such efforts.

The overall objective of this series, as previously noted, is to provide current information on behavioral research and theory in mental retardation, both applied and basic. Though most materials for the series are invited, unsolicited manuscripts that "fit" the format and objectives of the series will be considered.

University, Alabama
January, 1969

Norman R. Ellis

Contents

List of Contributors v
Preface vii
Contents of Previous Volumes xiii

Memory Processes in Retardates and Normals
NORMAN R. ELLIS

I. Introduction 1
II. The Task 3
III. Theoretical 5
IV. Experimental 8
V. Motivational Effects 26
VI. Cultural Differences 28
VII. Summary and Discussion 28
References 31

A Theory of Primary and Secondary Familial Mental Retardation
ARTHUR R. JENSEN

I. Diagnosis and Taxonomy of Mental Retardation 33
II. Mental Retardation and Social Class 37
III. Theory of Primary and Secondary Retardation 51
IV. Evidence for the Level I-Level II Hypothesis 66
V. Implications for Education 97
References 100

Inhibition Deficits in Retardate Learning and Attention
LAIRD W. HEAL AND JOHN T. JOHNSON, JR.

I. Definitions and Rationale 107
II. The Inhibition of Learned Responses and Internal Inhibition ... 111
III. Inhibition of Attention to Stimulus Input and External Inhibition ... 130
IV. Conclusions and Speculations about Individual Differences in Learning Processes 141
References 144

Growth and Decline of Retardate Intelligence

Mary Ann Fisher and David Zeaman

I. Introduction 151
II. The Subject Population 156
III. Description of the Semi-longitudinal Method 156
IV. Results 159
V. Determination of K, a Constant Measure of Retarded Intelligence 167
VI. Summary and Conclusions 174
Appendix: Values of K as a Function of MA and CA 177
References 189

The Measurement of Intelligence

A. B. Silverstein

I. Introduction 194
II. Descriptions of the Tests 194
III. Validity 197
IV. Reliability 201
V. Short Forms 204
VI. Effects of Nonintellective Factors 207
VII. Modifications in Administration and Scoring 210
VIII. Factor Analyses 213
IX. Item Analyses and Pattern Analyses 214
X. Diagnostic Applications 218
XI. Conclusions 221
References 221

Social Psychology and Mental Retardation

Warner Wilson

I. Introduction 229
II. Retardation as a Social Problem 230
III. The Mental Retardate in His Social Environment 239
IV. Summary 255
References 256

Mental Retardation in Animals

Gilbert W. Meier

I. Introduction 263
II. Genetic Factors 265
III. Prenatal Factors 267
IV. Perinatal Factors 281
V. Postnatal Factors 284
VI. Multivariate Analysis 296

VII. Conclusion 299
    References 300

Audiologic Aspects of Mental Retardation
Lyle L. Lloyd

I. Introduction and Historic Perspective 311
II. Incidence of Hearing Impairment 313
III. Methodologic and Intermethod Research 334
IV. Intramethod Research 354
V. Habilitation 360
VI. Summary and Conclusions 361
    References 363

Author Index 375
Subject Index 387

Contents of Previous Volumes

Volume 1

A Functional Analysis of Retarded Development
SIDNEY W. BIJOU

Classical Conditioning and Discrimination Learning Research with the Mentally Retarded
LEONARD E. ROSS

The Structure of Intellect in the Mental Retardate
HARVEY F. DINGMAN AND C. EDWARD MEYERS

Research on Personality Structure in the Retardate
EDWARD ZIGLER

Experience and the Development of Adaptive Behavior
H. CARL HAYWOOD AND JACK T. TAPP

A Research Program on the Psychological Effects of Brain Lesions in Human Beings
RALPH M. REITAN

Long-Term Memory in Mental Retardation
JOHN M. BELMONT

The Behavior of Moderately and Severely Retarded Persons
JOSEPH E. SPRADLIN AND FREDERIC L. GIRARDEAU

Author Index — Subject Index

Volume 2

A Theoretical Analysis and Its Application to Training the Mentally Retarded
M. RAY DENNY

The Role of Input Organization in the Learning and Memory of Mental Retardates
HERMAN H. SPITZ

Autonomic Nervous System Functions and Behavior: A Review of Experimental Studies with Mental Defectives
RATHE KARRER

Learning and Transfer of Mediating Responses in Discriminative Learning
BRYAN E. SHEPP AND FRANK D. TURRISI

A Review of Research on Learning Sets and Transfer of Training in Mental Defectives
MELVIN E. KAUFMAN AND HERBERT J. PREHM

Programming Perception and Learning for Retarded Children
MURRAY SIDMAN AND LAWRENCE T. STODDARD

Programmed Instruction Techniques for the Mentally Retarded
FRANCES M. GREENE

Some Aspects of the Research on Mental Retardation in Norway
IVAR ARNLJOT BJÖRGEN

Research on Mental Deficiency During the Last Decade in France
R. LAFON AND J. CHABANIER

Psychotherapeutic Procedures with the Retarded
MANNY STERNLICHT

Author Index – Subject Index

Volume 3

Incentive Motivation in the Mental Retardate
PAUL S. SIEGEL

Development of Lateral and Choice-Sequence Preferences
IRMA R. GERJUOY AND JOHN J. WINTERS, JR.

Studies in the Experimental Development of Left–Right Concepts in Retarded Children Using Fading Techniques
SIDNEY W. BIJOU

Verbal Learning and Memory Research with Retardates: An Attempt to Assess Developmental Trends
L. R. GOULET

Research and Theory in Short-Term Memory
KEITH G. SCOTT AND MARCIA STRONG SCOTT

Reaction Time and Mental Retardation
ALFRED A. BAUMEISTER AND GEORGE KELLAS

Mental Retardation in India: A Review of Care, Training, Research, and Rehabilitation Programs
J. P. DAS

Educational Research in Mental Retardation
SAMUEL L. GUSKIN AND HOWARD H. SPICKER

Author Index – Subject Index

Memory Processes in Retardates and Normals[1]

NORMAN R. ELLIS

UNIVERSITY OF ALABAMA, UNIVERSITY, ALABAMA

I. Introduction	1
II. The Task	3
III. Theoretical	5
IV. Experimental	8
A. Study 1	8
B. Study 2	11
C. Study 3	13
D. Study 4	16
E. Study 5	20
F. Study 6	21
G. Study 7	23
H. Study 8	24
I. Study 9	25
J. Study 10	25
V. Motivational Effects	26
A. Study 11	26
B. Study 12	27
C. Study 13	27
VI. Cultural Differences	28
Study 14	28
VII. Summary and Discussion	28
References	31

I. INTRODUCTION

In 1963 I adduced evidence from a number of experimental sources indicating that mental retardates may have a deficiency in short term memory (STM). Even though the empirical basis was not substantial, a crude theoretical framework was attempted in order to stimulate and focus research in a promising area.

---

[1] All of the research upon which this paper is based was a collaborative effort. Three graduate students were centrally involved: Terry R. Anders (now a post-doctoral Fellow at Harvard Medical School), Jeanne Dugas Warrick, and Douglas Detterman. Another graduate student, Hugh Ashurst, assisted in data collection for one of the studies. Thanks are due Donald Baucum, an undergraduate, for data collection, statistical work, and drafting.

In brief, it was hypothesized that the retardate's inadequate behavior was *in part* due to a stimulus trace attenuated in amplitude and duration. The concept of stimulus trace was essentially that proposed by Hull (1952). From this premise, it could be predicted that when the performance of retardates and normals was compared on some task which depended upon bridging a temporal gap the retardate's behavior would suffer in comparison. Moreover, when the magnitude of temporal separation between events increased the retardate's performance would deteriorate even more. A number of tests of the hypothesis followed and these have been adequately reviewed by Scott and Scott (1968). Evidence both for and against the idea may be found in the literature. Some experimental studies are based on misconceptions of the hypothesis. The original formulation was based on comparisons between Ss of similar chronological age (CA), mainly adults. Therefore, derived predictions were valid for comparisons of retarded and normal Ss of equal CA only. Further, it was reasoned that normal children and older retardates of equal mental age (MA) may exhibit similar behavior, with the implication that STM may show developmental changes in the normal child as well as in the retardate. The empirical support for the STM deficit hypothesis as well as the logical basis for the "theory" has been questioned. Zigler (e.g., 1969) and his associates have attacked the "deficit theories," and the "stimulus trace theory" has not been slighted.

The rationale for the research strategy employed here seems clear. We wish to isolate differences and similarities in the behavior of retarded and normal human beings of similar chronological age. These differences and similarities seem most appropriately analyzed and defined in terms of the behavior of normal organisms. This position has been described and defended recently (Ellis, 1969a).

Contemporary research on STM is generally viewed as beginning with the work of such theorists as Hebb (1949), Broadbent (1958), and Peterson and Peterson (1959). Earlier research used the classic methods of digit span or delayed response, principally. But, the renewed interest in the retention of information over a brief interval stimulated the development of new methodologies. The technique of assessing memory for a single item (nonsense syllable or paired-associate, for example) devised by Peterson and Peterson (1959) had far-reaching implications for research in this area, theoretically as well as methodologically.

Most studies of STM in the retardate have relied principally upon delayed response, digit span, or some type of learning task in which time relations were varied. Much of the research since the stimulus trace hypothesis (Ellis, 1963) has also employed questionable methodologies. Whether or not these studies measured the same processes as those investigated by theorists concerned with normal human beings could be questioned. Moreover, the need for a systematic series of studies adopting a standardized laboratory procedure, with high face validity as a measure of STM was clearly indicated for investigating the hypothesized deficit in the retardate. The present paper describes a series of studies which bear on the long-term memory–short-term memory (LTM-STM) distinction as well as on normal-retardate differences in STM.

Extensive preliminary research in our laboratory led to the development of a methodology deemed suitable for measuring STM in Ss of widely differing ability level. The task, along with several studies of STM in normal Ss, has been reported by Ellis and Hope (1968). The present paper describes the experimental model, methodological studies, a theoretical schema, and a series of studies. These studies provide evidence for two STM processes in normal and retarded Ss as well as evidence that retardates suffer a deficit in rehearsal strategies, a mechanism of central importance to short-term storage. The order of presentation of these studies approximates the chronological course of our investigation, which in retrospect does not always appear to be a rational sequence.

II. THE TASK

The experimental paradigm may best be described by reference to the apparatus shown in Fig. 1. This is one of several pieces of apparatus in our laboratory. Others provide variation in number of positions, nature of stimuli, etc. The S console consists of the horizontal row of nine projectors (one-plane digital display units, Industrial Electronics, North Hollywood, California) and a tenth "probe" projector mounted above the row. Plexiglass response keys are mounted over the nine projectors and S can see the stimuli through the keys. In the particular apparatus shown, any projector can display any number (about 1 inch high) 1 through 9. The task is programmed so that S sees a random series of numbers exposed one after the other in order from left to right. After exposure of the ninth position, the probe is presented and S's task is to press the *position* where the probe number was seen. A correct response is signaled by a door bell chime. In practice we have used a procedure in which S responds until correct. E presets one of a random series of the numbers, a probe number, and the correct response position before each trial. After the initiation of a trial, all stimulus events occur automatically. E records manually the position of all responses; in some studies this is accomplished with a printout counter. Selection of probe numbers is on a random basis except that over trials the positions are

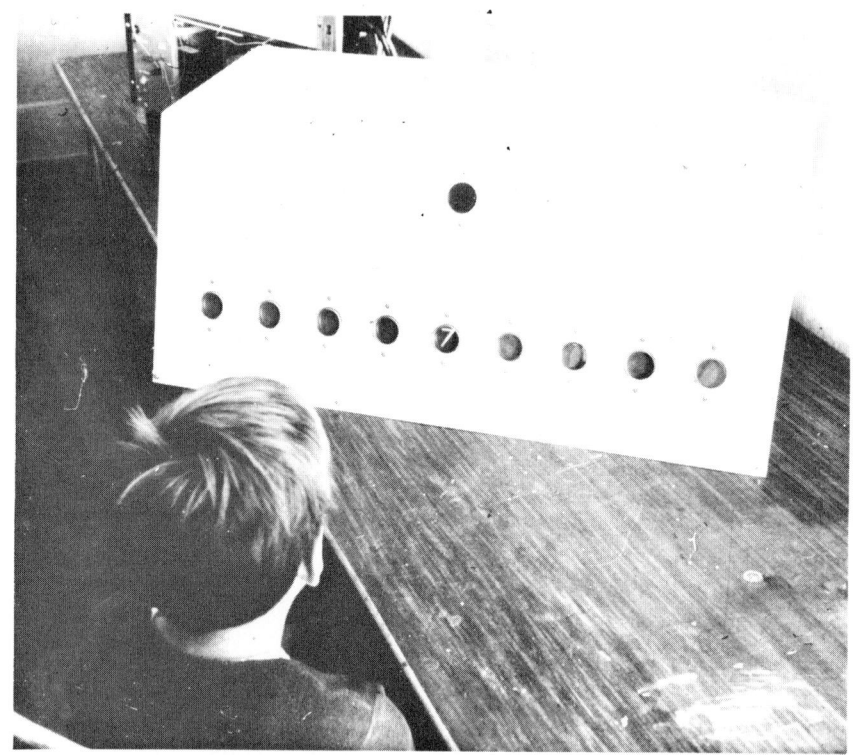

FIG. 1. The subject console of the 9-position memory apparatus.

probed equally often. More recently, a 16-mm movie projector programmed for single frame presentation has been used. Stimuli are presented in several horizontal rows and S points to the position believed to be correct. This technique yields similar data.

This model offers a number of advantages, both practical and conceptual. (a) Many aspects of the task may be varied, including item exposure duration, interitem interval, interval between last item and probe, and stimulus materials (numbers, letters, pictures, etc.). (b) Time relations are precisely controlled. (c) The partial report or probe technique provides an evaluation of short-term retention with the interfering effects of the recall process minimized. (d) The recall is a "key press" which seems less complex than an oral or written response. (e) The scale of measurement permits the assessment of the behavior of Ss differing widely in ability level. (f) Conceptually, the model has high face validity as a measure of STM, yielding a serial position effect similar to that found in immediate free recall and other STM tasks.

The supraspan input model (input of a sequence of information exceeding the "span of attention") would appear to be most representative of real life information processing by the human being. One is expected to retain momentarily an entire sentence, even a paragraph rather than a single word. For example, a child in the classroom must remember a series of steps involved in the solution of a mathematical problem. From a theoretical standpoint, the retention of supraspan information may involve process(es) in addition to those involved in memory for a single item.

III. THEORETICAL

The results of our early experiments with normal Ss supported a multi-process conception of retention of supraspan information even for brief time intervals (seconds). In three experiments (Ellis & Hope, 1968), rate of presentation was varied in a 9-digit task. Slower presentation rate (longer item exposure and/or interitem intervals) facilitated primacy but did not affect recency performance. In a fourth experiment, S performed under two rates of presentation and a 0-second, 10-second unfilled or a 10-second filled delay between the last item and the probe. The task included 12 positions, with letters as stimuli. The interpolated task was counting backwards by 3's from a 3-digit number. Again rate of presentation affected primacy and not recency. Delay led to marked decrements in the recency effect with a filled delay producing the larger effect. Delay had no effect upon primacy and the middle of the curve except when rate of presentation was fast. In this case, an unfilled delay, but not a filled delay, facilitated primacy performance.

These results suggested the presence of two memory processes operative in the retention of supraspan information over intervals as brief as five seconds. The recency and primacy segments of the serial position curve (SPC) appeared to be discontinuous processes. Primacy could be influenced by rate of presentation, or when presentation rate was fast, by a delay prior to recall. It was hypothesized that rehearsal strategies was the mechanism responsible for facilitating primacy performance. Opportunity for rehearsal may be provided during (rate effect) or immediately after (delay effect) presentation. Rehearsal appeared to have no substantial effect upon recency. Instead, memory for the terminal items in the series seemed transient, to decay rapidly with time (experimentally filled or unfilled). The filled delay did produce a greater decrement, perhaps by preventing rehearsal or by interference.

On the basis of these results, along with a substantial literature compatible with a two-process or multi-process interpretation of memory, we postulate a conceptual framework within which to analyze and compare memory functions in retardates and normals. The reader will recognize a strong kinship with a number of two-process (or multi-process) interpretations, notably those of Broadbent (1958), Waugh and Norman (1965), Hebb (1949), Atkinson and associates (e.g., see Atkinson & Shiffrin, 1965), and Bower (1967). The position advanced here amounts to a generalized model, and perhaps may best be described as a modified version of the Waugh and Norman theoretical conceptions. The model is presented schematically in Fig. 2. Though it borrows conceptually from each of those cited, it differs from them.

External stimulation is sensed through an attention (A) process and fed directly into the primary memory (PM). PM is viewed as a limited capacity system, capable of retaining only a few items which are quite transient, either as a result of decay with time per se or as a result of interference. Information is being constantly replaced in PM by new information. We assume that older items are lost first. PM is viewed as the most inefficient storage with much information being forgotten [indicated by the three-line arrow as contrasted with the two- and one-line arrows of secondary memory (SM) and tertiary memory (TM), respectively.] The rehearsal strategy (RS) is viewed as the mechanism transferring information from PM to SM and to TM. The RS is represented by dashed lines in the schematic. RS involves the focus of attention upon information being lost from PM, upon SM, or upon TM. Thus, RS is in

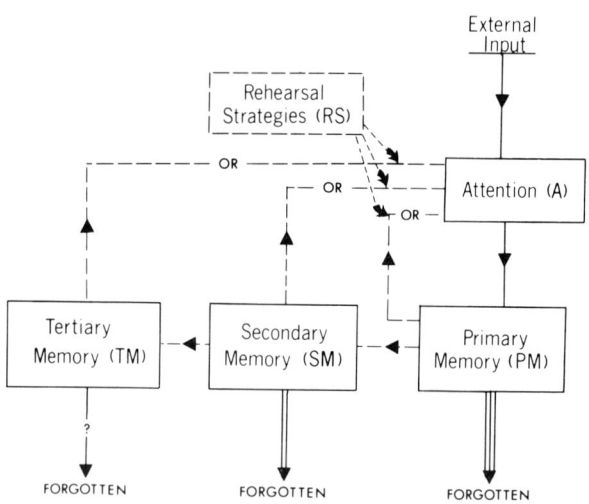

FIG. 2. The multi-process memory model.

part a loop wherein information is fed back through A and PM. No doubt, it involves considerably more such as chunking strategies, other grouping and organization devices, and encoding (a transduction of information, from visual to an auditory code, for example). Set or instruction may affect either the amount or nature of RS, thereby determining whether information is committed to SM only or on to TM. It is likely that meaningfulness facilitates the transfer of information from PM to SM. An S faced with storing a series of nine digits for immediate recall may, under certain instructions, remember the series several days, even a month later, i.e., store the information in TM. On the other hand, under other instructions or under conditions where the capacity to store information in TM is exceeded by high input rate (particularly under multiple trial conditions) only SM is involved and the information is forgotten following a brief (seconds or at most several minutes) interval. TM is synonymous with LTM as conventionally defined, i.e., retention over days, months, or longer. On the basis of previous research, which has been summarized by Belmont (1966), we assume that TM is "normal" in the retardate and this process receives no further attention in this paper. A question mark has been placed beside the forgetting process in TM, for some evidence suggests that memories in TM may be permanent. Psychoanalytic reports as well as the classic studies of Penfield and associates with neurosurgical research provide suggestive evidence on this issue. Attention may prove to be a superfluous construct. Rehearsal strategy is a key construct. However, at this stage of analysis, it is poorly defined and is perhaps credited with too many functions.

The above conceptual scheme is proposed as a frame of reference for research in this area. The terms A, PM, SM, TM, and RS are presented as logical constructs and have reference to, and will require operational definition by molar behavior in relation to a stimulus situation. The empirical underpinnings for the constructs vary considerably. Much of the experimental data deriving from STM research could be reasonably fitted into this rubric. Perhaps, from the plethora of research reports on the topic, some evidence would be in direct contradiction.

For the present purposes, the theoretical framework provides a vehicle for comparing the performance of retarded and normal Ss on a STM-type task. Moreover, it provides conceptual anchors for a specific analysis of processes involved in information storage and transmission in these Ss. It is not offered as a new "theory" of memory functions. A number of experiments using the probe digit model with retarded and normal Ss will be described and discussed in relation to the conceptual analysis presented above.

IV. EXPERIMENTAL

A. Study 1

This initial study compared normals and retardates under two presentation rates. A slower presentation rate was expected to increase the amount of rehearsal and therefore facilitate performance in the primacy segment of the serial position curve. Insofar as normal-retardate comparisons were concerned, no formal predictions were made.

The Ss were 32 retardates with a mean IQ of 60.8, range 50–82; mean CA 20 years, range 15–33 years and 32 undergraduate college students. The retardates were from a state residential institution; the undergraduates participated in order to fulfill a course requirement. The Ss were tested individually. The retardates received a monetary reward. The following instructions were given:

> This is a memory task. You are going to see some numbers in this row. These numbers will be shown briefly one at a time beginning in this window. After the last number has gone off in *this* window, a number will come on up here. This number will be the same as one you saw in this row. Your task is to remember in which window the number appeared and press the button underneath that window. You are to remember the place or location of the numbers. If you press the correct button, a chime will sound. If you press the wrong button, nothing will happen. You must continue to respond until you have located the correct position. Of course, you should try to make a correct response the first time. Now, let's have a few practice runs.

Following the instructions, Ss were given 2 practice trials, or more if he did not appear to understand the task. Ss were given 36 trials at 1 rate of presentation and then 36 at another rate in 1 session lasting around 1 hour. After the initial 36 trials, S was told that the rate would be different for the remaining trials, and he was given 2 practice trials at a new rate. A "crossover" type design permitted testing each S under the 2 rates. The rates were a .5-second item duration with a 0.0-second or a 2.0-second interitem interval, i.e., each of the 9 numbers was exposed one after the other, for .5 second, and for the 0.0-second condition the offset of one was contiguous with the onset of the next. For the other condition, 2.0 seconds intervened between the offset of one and the onset of the next. The onset of the probe was contiguous with the offset of the last number of the series in both rate conditions, and the probe remained on until S responded.

The stimuli were the numbers one through nine. A randomly determined series was preset by the E before each trial. Eighteen different random orders were used. The probe number and the correct response position for each trial was also preset by E. S continued to respond until the door chime signaled the correct response. E recorded the responses manually and reset the apparatus during the intertrial interval, requiring approximately four to six seconds.

An estimate of total amount retained can be determined by summing the proportions of correct responses for each of the nine positions. The retardates under the massed condition (0.0-second interitem interval) retained an average of 2.37 digits and under the spaced condition (2.0-second interitem interval) 2.58 digits. The normal Ss retained an average of 4.33 digits under the massed condition and 6.12 under the spaced condition. Obviously, retention in these Ss is quite different in total amount.

Figure 3 depicts performance for each of the four groups over the nine positions. The large differences in retention between the retardates and normals results mainly from primacy and middle positions. The recency effect appears to be rather similar in these groups, at least, at the

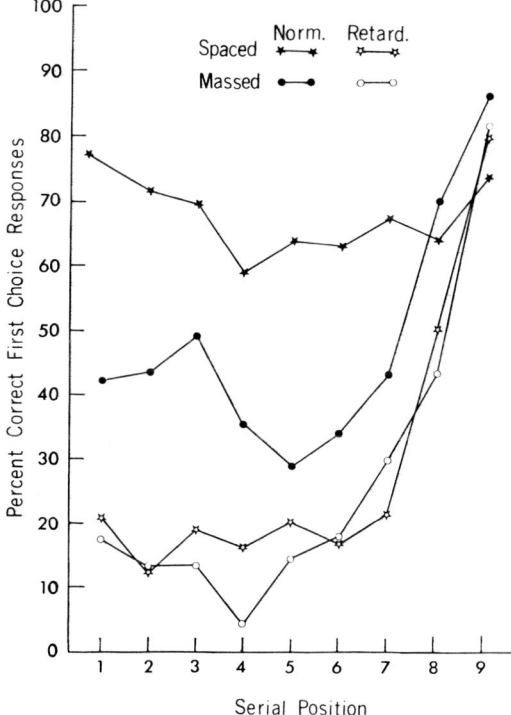

Fig. 3. Performance of normals and retardates under massed (0.0-second interitem interval) and spaced (2.0-second interitem interval) conditions on the 9-position task.

terminal position. Differences at positions seven and eight may reflect genuine changes in PM or they may be due to larger stores in SM superimposed on PM. This possibility may best be described graphically and Fig. 4 shows hypothetical functions for PM and SM. Only one function is shown for PM though it may be affected by variables such as perceptual clarity, attention, and motivation, and further research may show that a family of curves can be drawn for PM. A number of curves are shown for the SM function. Some evidence is presented in Fig. 3 that ability level and rate of presentation affect SM.

In terms of the model, these results suggest that PM in the retardate and normal may not differ. The major behavioral differences lie clearly in the primacy and middle portions of the SPC. Moreover, performance of the normal Ss, but not that of the retardates, can be influenced by rate of presentation. In view of the extensive literature suggesting that rehearsal facilitates performance in the primacy segment of the SPC (dating back to Welch & Burnett, 1924) along with the findings in the Ellis and Hope (1968) studies, we favor an "RS deficiency hypothesis" to account for the retardate-normal differences rather than an SM deficit. It would appear that the retardate does not rehearse, even under spaced conditions, therefore his memory for items exceeding the limited capacity of PM is poor.

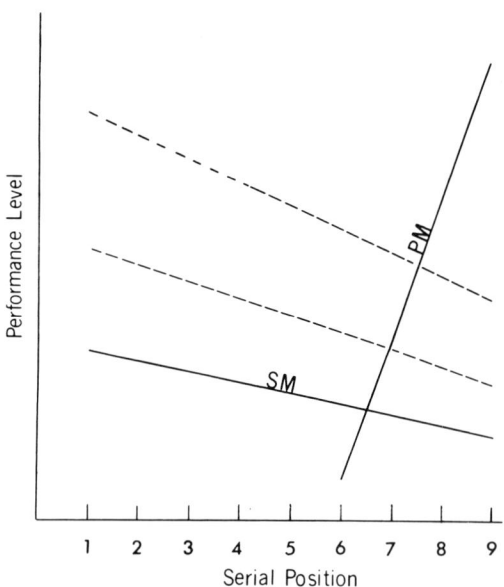

FIG. 4. Hypothetical functions for storage in PM and SM.

B. Study 2

This study was designed to provide a more definitive test of the effects of rate of presentation in the retardate. Performance of the retardates on primacy items in Study 1 is only slightly above chance (see Fig. 3) and it is possible that differences under massed and spaced conditions could have been obscured. Also, we wished to observe behavior under chronic testing conditions for methodological reasons, as well as to assess practice effects.

The 9 adult Ss (mean IQ = 62.4) were tested for 12 consecutive weekdays, 36 trials per daily session. Each S received 3 presentation rates, 0.5-second, 1.0-second, and 2.0-second item duration with no interitem interval. All 36 trials on a given day were at 1 presentation rate, all 3 rates were tested within each 3-day block (randomly arranged), and over the 12 days an S received 2 practice trials at the beginning of each session at the rate to be used on that day.

Figure 5 presents the averaged performance curves for the three rates. These curves are quite similar in form to those of Study 1, but in this case, primacy is substantially above the chance level. Obviously, rate has no appreciable effect, either in the recency or in the primacy segments of the curve. Again, the terminal points in recency are essentially identical to those for normal Ss and for the retardates in Study 1. Rate does appear to change the slope of the recency segment for normals but not for retardates. We are inclined to interpret these changes as due to rehearsal which tends to facilitate performance in increasing amounts from positions eight to one, and with no effects upon nine. Thus, recency performance may reflect a rather invariate PM process plus a superimposed SM process, especially in the normal S.

A comparison of Figs. 4 and 5 shows that performance of the retardate is slightly better in the chronic testing procedure. Figure 6 compares performance over the three 4-day blocks of trials. Even though there are changes in recency, the most substantial improvement occurs in primacy. Changes in primacy would be expected theoretically since the commitment of information to SM is viewed as a process similar to that occurring in learning. Conceptually, improvement in PM per se would be ascribed to changes in attention (A), motivation, or to some process other than PM.

Further analyses of these data were made to show individual differences. Figure 7 presents individual performance curves (solid lines) with days and rate collapsed. Performance varied markedly from the average curve for only two Ss, S_4 and S_8. The others showed a pronounced recency effect, and a lower, but variable, primacy effect. In an attempt to account for some of the variability in these data, we tallied frequency of

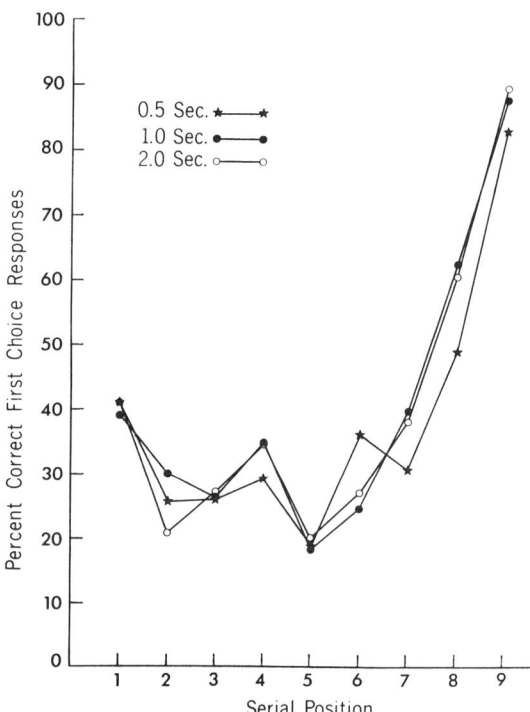

FIG. 5. Averaged performance curves showing percent correct first choice responses for the three presentation rates.

first choice responding at each of the nine positions and these (combining R+ and R−) are shown as (□) lines in Fig. 7. These findings are quite revealing; most of the Ss develop idiosyncratic response strategies which are maladaptive. For example, even though a position is correct only 11.1% of the time, S_5 responds initially to positions eight and nine 84% of the time and S_7 responds to position one 34% of the time. It would appear that when the retardate is faced with an extremely difficult task, he develops a response strategy even though it is a maladaptive one. The behavior may result from a reinforcement contingency during the early trials, from some task characteristic, or from some set he brings to the task with him. Of course, it should be noted that the response pattern even in these instances may not be independent of memory, and adjustments in the retention curves for differential response probabilities would seem inappropriate. In spite of this finding, the generalized retention curves are valid. The idiosyncratic responding merely contributes to error variance.

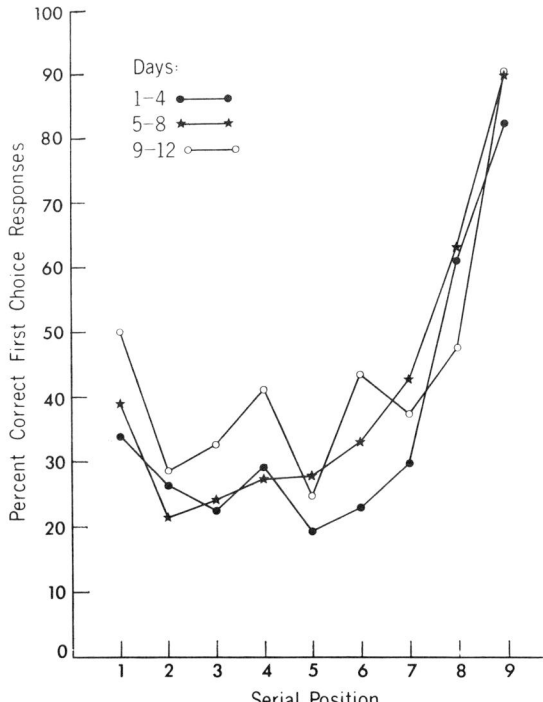

Fig. 6. Averaged performance curves showing percent correct first choice responses for three 4-day blocks with rate of presentation ignored.

C. Study 3

The purpose of Study 3 was to explore a method of "graduated difficulty" which seemed likely to be more conducive to the development of adaptive rehearsal strategies, thus facilitating primacy performance. Moreover, this procedure was expected to minimize idiosyncratic responding.

The Ss were 14 retardates with IQs ranging from 50 to 70, and a mean of 59.6. Their CAs ranged from 15 to 22 years with a mean of 17 years 8 months.

The Ss were given 36 trials on each of 7 days at a 1 digit per second rate. On the first day, Ss received a 3-digit series, on the second, a 4-digit series, and so on to the seventh day on which they received a 9-digit series.

Figure 8 presents averaged performance curves for each of the seven days. These results are quite orderly, showing increasing decrements in primacy with increase in series length, and with substantially no change

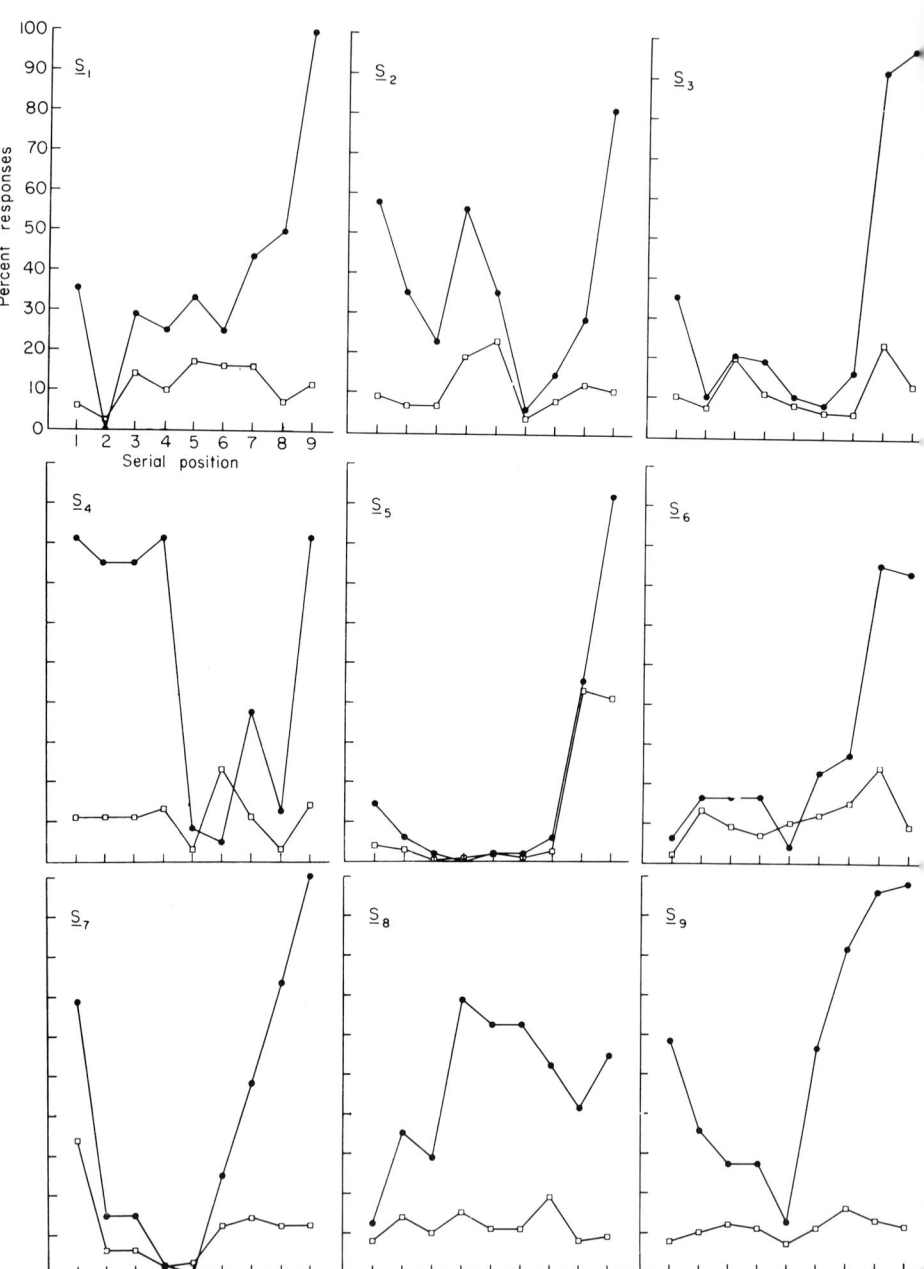

Fig. 7. Individual performance curves depicting percent correct first choice responses and total percent responses (correct and incorrect) over the nine positions. Key: Total percent first choice responses □ – □; percent correct first choice responses ● – ●.

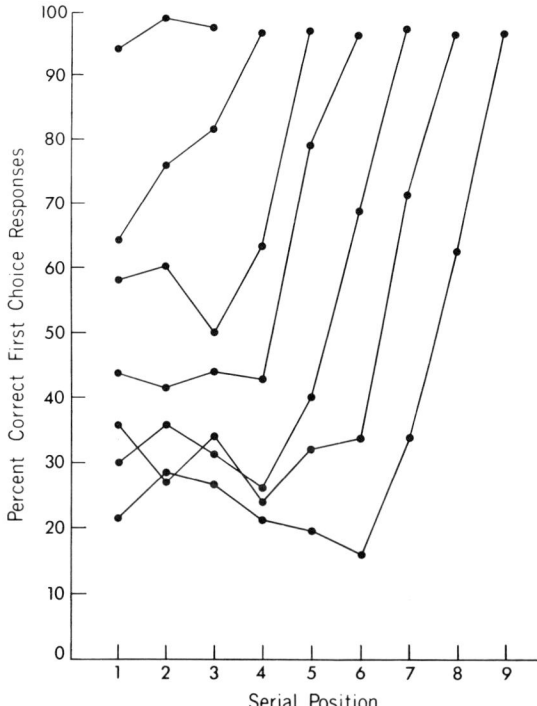

FIG. 8. Averaged performance curves for each of the seven days with increasing length of digit series.

in the recency effect. The performance on positions one through five in the 9-digit series is similar to data in the previous studies. Thus, this method did not seem to lead to the development of appreciable rehearsal strategies. Although there is not enough data on a single S to make a thorough analysis of idiosyncratic rehearsal strategies, inspection of the data indicates that Ss were more likely to distribute responses evenly over all positions.

The most interesting aspect of the data is the constancy in total amount retained with increasing list lengths. Figure 9 shows response probabilities summed over positions, providing an estimate of total items retained for each task. Recency is invariate and for the retardate the memory process, PM, underlying recency almost entirely accounts for retention irrespective of task length. The amount stored in recency can be estimated by fitting a straight line to these slopes and summing response probabilities under these functions. This was done by visual inspection and approximately 2.4 items were judged to be stored in recency.

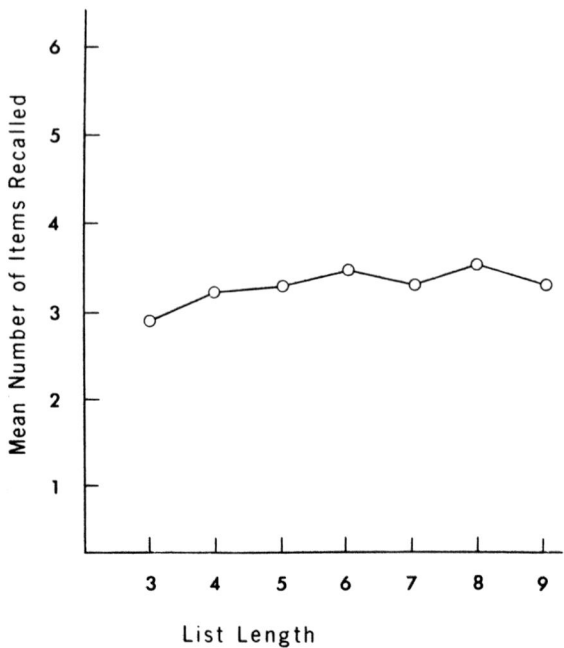

FIG. 9. Total retention for retardates over tasks of varying length.

In summary, it would appear that information in the short task, falling within the S's "memory span," can be stored in PM. As greater demands are made on the system, by increasing task length, PM continues to store the same amount of information. When this system is maximally loaded, SM serves to store the "overload." However, in the case of the retardate, this system fails. Therefore, the retardate's storage capacity reflects mainly PM. We have hypothesized that his rehearsal strategies are inadequate. These results support such a view.

D. Study 4

Study 4 provides more information on the phenomena found in Study 3. Ten college students and 10 retardates (CA, 15–28, IQ, 46–67) were tested on tasks varying from 3 to 12 items (letters of the alphabet) in length. Ss received 2 lists per day over a 5-day period with lists assigned on a random basis (note that Ss did not begin on the shortest list and advance to the longest list as in Study 3). The number of trials necessary to probe each serial position 4 times was given. Task presentation rate was 1 item per second with an immediate probe.

The main findings are presented in Figs. 10, 11, and 12. The results of Study 3 on retardates are clearly confirmed. Indeed, the performance levels over varying task lengths are quite similar even though the stimuli are numbers in one instance and letters in the other. Moreover, Study 3 used the increasing difficulty procedure and in Study 4, task difficulty (length) was randomly arranged within the series. Again, storage in the retardate is determined mainly by PM. As message length increases beyond the capacity of PM, SM fails to function adequately, and information in the message other than the terminal items is lost. On the other hand, the SM system in the normals accounts for storage of primacy items (in the 12-item task, approximately 55% of the first 6 items). Retention of the terminal items is approximately equal in the retardates and normals. However, the slopes of the recency function appear to be

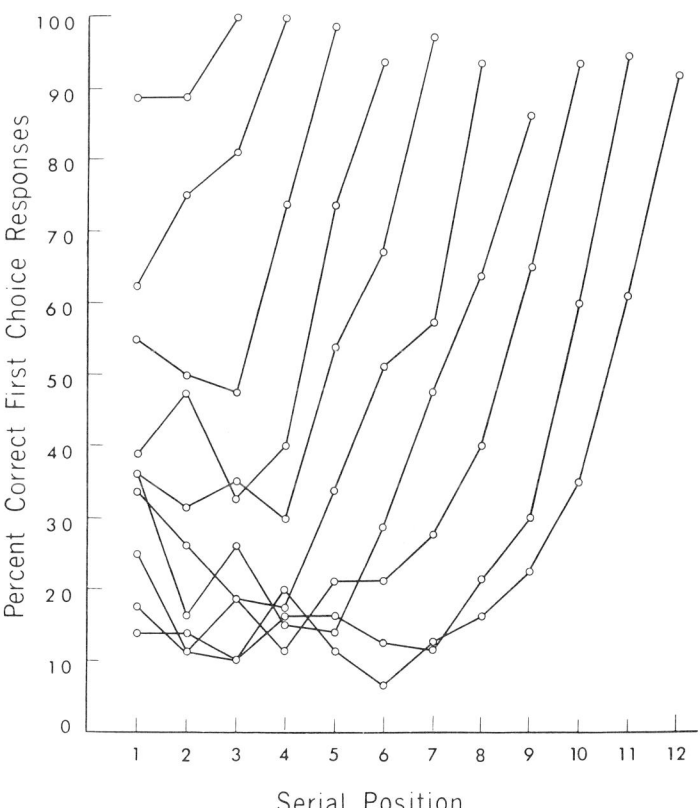

FIG. 10. Retention in the retardate over serial positions for tasks of varying length.

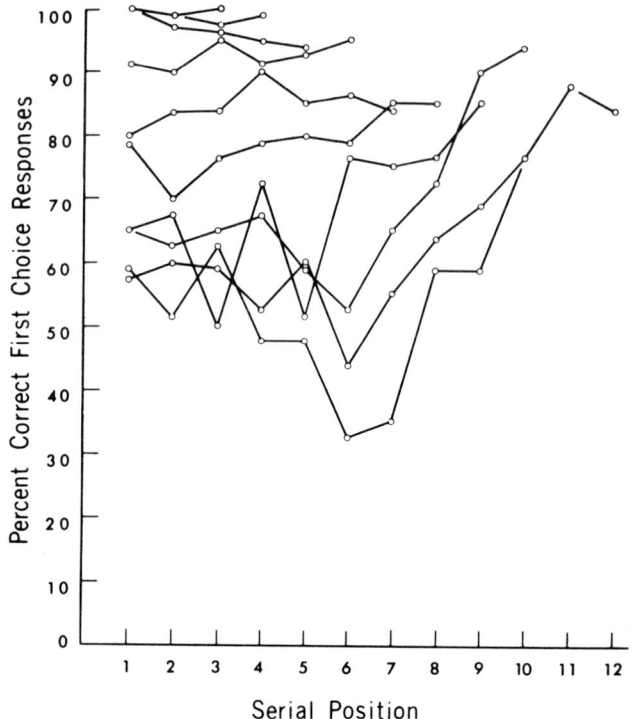

Fig. 11. Retention for normals over serial positions for tasks of varying length.

different, suggesting that PM has a greater capacity in the normals. Nevertheless, these possible differences in PM do not contribute substantially to the normal-retardate storage differences. It should be noted that performance of the normal Ss does not reach an asymptote on the 12-item task. Their storage is 7 of the 12 items, though an extrapolation of the curve suggests that they are far from maximal storage capacity.

At this stage of experimentation, it seemed clear that retardates and normals differed markedly in SM. We believed this to be due to inadequate rehearsal strategies rather than to the storage mechanism per se. Evidence for the last statement consisted of the following: (a) Spacing of items in the message facilitated normals' performance and not that of the retardates. (b) The initial studies with normals showed that a delay interval after stimulus presentation facilitated primacy if the rate of presentation had been rapid. (c) Normals' verbal reports indicated that they were rehearsing; retardates reported minimal rehearsal activity. This facilitation did not occur if the delay interval was filled with some activity designed to prevent rehearsal. An unanswered question was: Is the PM mechanism different in retardates and normals? And, does rehearsal reflect PM plus an additional storage increment due to rehearsal? In several studies, and particularly in Study 4, the slope of recency seemed related to the performance level in primacy. Moreover, the slope of the recency function seemed to vary from study to study in the normal Ss but remained essentially invariate in the retardates. These considerations led us to believe that recency performance was mainly determined by PM, viewed as a sensory, echoic memory dependent upon attention to the stimuli only. As a working hypothesis, these processes were viewed as identical in normals and retardates. Further, rehearsal seemed to contribute to recency performance. Waugh and Norman (1965) hypothe-

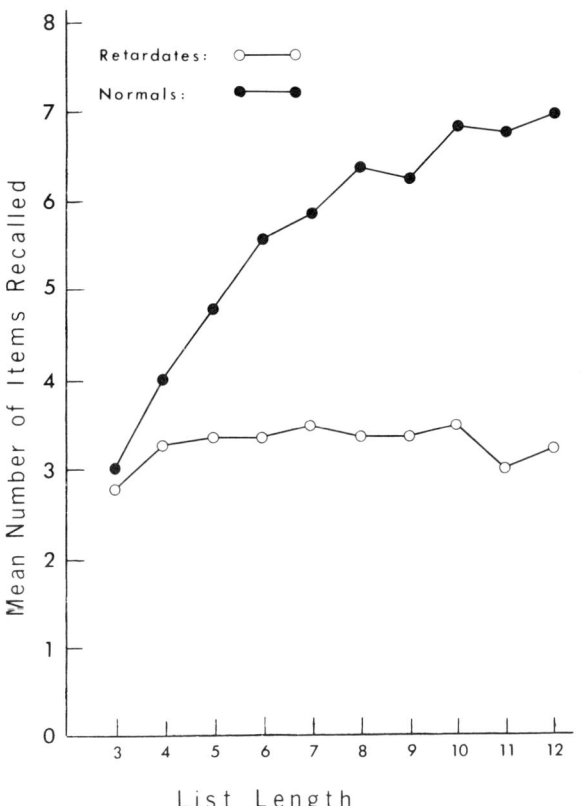

FIG. 12. Total retention for retardates and normals over tasks of varying length.

sized that rehearsal recirculated items in PM. Therefore, on this basis we could expect recency performance to be facilitated in the normal Ss over that of retardates.

E. Study 5

A study conducted prior to studies 3 and 4 examined the effects of rehearsal instructions upon performance of normal Ss and provides information on the possible effects of rehearsal upon PM. Twelve college students were assigned equally to three groups. Those in one group (no rehearsal) were instructed to "think only of the letter while it is visible and not of any previous letters." Those in another group were told, "As you are seeing the letters, think of them in groups of threes. This has been shown to be the most efficient method of performing this task." A third group did not receive any instructions pertaining to rehearsal.

The experimental design included 10 daily tests of 48 trials each. For 5 of these (alternate days) the presentation rate was .75 second, and for the other 5, 1.50 seconds. The task was 12 items (letters) in length with an immediate probe.

Figure 13 depicts the findings of most interest. Instruction to rehearse should have facilitated performance maximally under the slower rate. This did not occur. The rate by serial position interaction did occur, as in our other experiments. Instructions to rehearse affected performance except in the last few recency positions as expected.

Perhaps the best evidence for a rehearsal effect in primacy is shown by the patterning in the performance curve of the rehearsal group. These Ss were instructed to rehearse in threes. This chunking is clearly evident, particularly in recency. Moreover, the slope of recency has been affected by rehearsal instructions. Of course it could be argued that recency is determined solely by rehearsal and/or the same processes determining primacy (a single process memory). Although it is extremely difficult to eliminate rehearsal (perhaps even impossible) on the basis of verbal report, it seemed minimal in the no rehearsal Ss which leads us to believe that the main component of recency is due to PM. The Ellis and Hope (1968) study indicated that recency performance in normals deteriorated rapidly with the passage of time, with or without interpolated activity. Primacy performance was unaffected by delay intervals. Studies 4 and 5 provided further information about recency performance. The main purpose of Studies 6 and 7 was to assess differences in rate of decay of recency performance in retardates and normals and to shed light on the issue of whether or not PM in these Ss is similar or different.

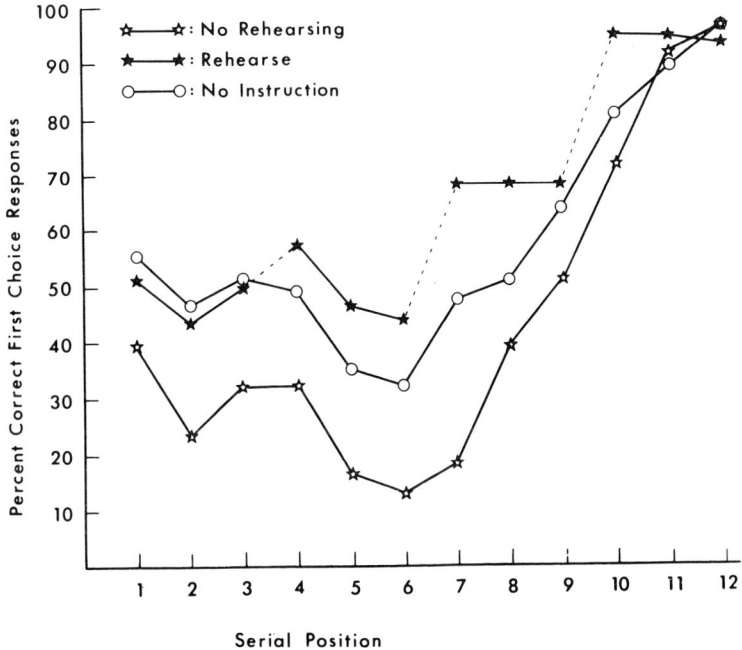

FIG. 13. Retention in normals as a function of type of instruction.

F. Study 6

This study was in collaboration with Terry R. Anders and presented in his doctoral dissertation as a preliminary study.

The Ss were 72 retardates with IQs of 50 or more and ranging in CA from 15 to 30 years. The normal Ss were 36 students recruited from undergraduate psychology courses.

The retardates were assigned to 4 groups of 18 Ss each and the normals to 4 groups of 9 Ss each. The 4 conditions were delays between the offset of the ninth number and the onset of the probe of 0, 5, 10, and 15 seconds. The Ss were given 36 trials and the rate of presentation was 1 second per item.

The main findings are depicted in Fig. 14. The performance curves for the retardates are typical with a marked recency effect and a negligible primacy effect. The delay effect is in the expected direction, though that for the 5- and 10-second conditions does not differ on the terminal point. An analysis of variance of the retardate data yielded a significant

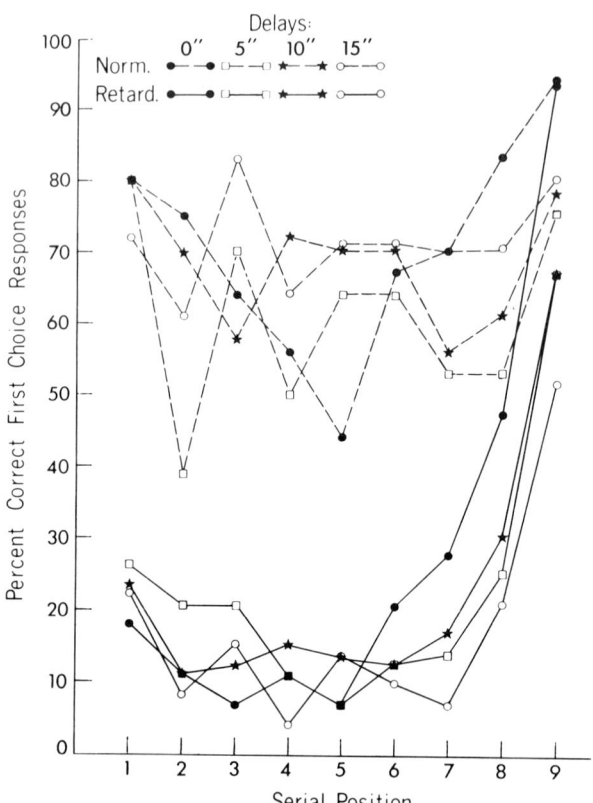

FIG. 14. Averaged performance curves for normals and retardates under four delay conditions. (N of 18 in each retardate group; 9 in each normal group.)

main effect for the serial position ($p < .001$) and for the interaction of delay by serial position ($p < .001$).

The data on the normal Ss are variable with only nine Ss per group, but the trend in the delay effect is of considerable interest. If valid, it may suggest a reminiscence effect not present in the retardate results. This is expected on the basis of the rehearsal strategy deficit hypothesis. Given unfilled delays, the normal Ss may engage in rehearsal which serves to reinstate memories in SM as well as PM. In the Ellis and Hope (1968) study, 10-second unfilled delays did lead to a facilitation of primacy performance. The study did not use other delay intervals so a reminiscence effect in PM could not be assessed. These data indicate that recency may decay more rapidly in the retardate, probably as a result of an absence of rehearsal which may serve to reinstate items in PM. This possible contamination precludes a definitive statement regarding the nature of PM in retardates and normals. Incidentally, half the retardates were diagnosed cultural-familial and half, brain-injured. However, there were no differences in the data attributable to these etiological categories.

G. Study 7

This study was carried out by Terry R. Anders and served as the basis for his doctoral dissertation (1968). Again, the main purpose was to probe characteristics of PM in normals and retardates. The Ss were 32 undergraduate college students and 32 retardates (CA $\overline{X} = 21.6$ years, IQ $\overline{X} = 69.7$). The normals were tested on a 12-letter task and the retardates on an 8-letter task which yielded similar performance levels in these Ss. The design was a $2 \times 2 \times 4 \times 2$ factorial including normals and retardates, filled and unfilled retention intervals, 0.-, 5.-, 10- and 20-second delays, and 2 serial positions, recency and primacy. The last dimension was for the statistical analysis only. The "filler" task for the normals was counting backwards by threes and that for the retardates, counting backwards by one. These tasks also proved approximately equally difficult for these Ss. All Ss were given 5 daily test sessions of 48 trials each, with the first being a familiarization session. The presentation rate was 1 item per second.

Figure 15 depicts the decay of recency in these Ss over the 4 retention intervals for the filled and unfilled conditions. Rate of decay is more rapid in retardates. However, this is apparently due to the marked reminiscence effect in the normal Ss, which does not occur in the retardates. Note the significant gain in retention following the 20-second interval over that after 10 seconds. The steeper slopes of the curves for the retardates over the shorter delays suggest more rapid decay prior to the reminiscence effect. However, this is not statistically significant.

Even though recency performance varies (in slope) over differing experimental conditions in normals and retardates and also decays more rapidly in the retardate, we are reluctant to conclude that these findings reflect PM differences in these Ss. Instead, the performance differences appear to be attributable to rehearsal strategy differences superimposed on performance due fundamentally to PM. No differences between retardates and normals appeared in primacy performance. These data are only suggestive, however, and the definitive experiment is yet to be done.

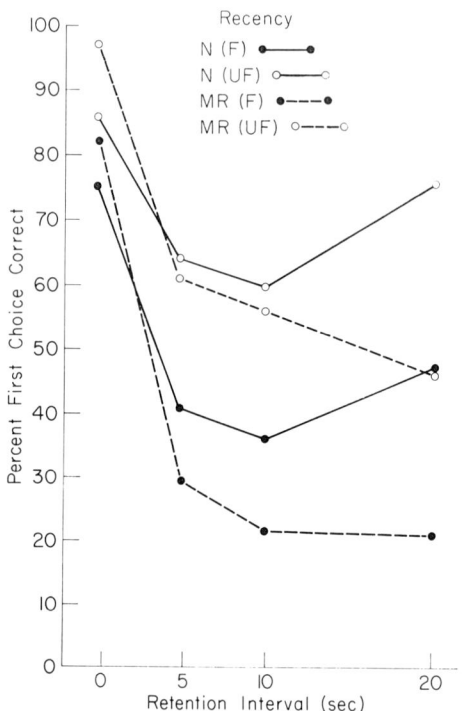

FIG. 15. Recency performance of retardates and normals (from Ander's doctoral dissertation).

H. Study 8

Further evidence from our laboratory points to the role of rehearsal in primacy performance, supporting the two-process conception of short-term memory, and indirectly, the retardate rehearsal deficit hypothesis. Ellis and Dugas (1968) compared the performance of college students under E- and S-paced conditions on a 9-position task with CVCs as stimuli. S-paced subjects pressed each position, one after the other from left to right and the stimulus in the position pressed came on for .75 second. Interresponse times (latencies) were recorded. E-paced Ss were presented the stimuli in the usual manner at a .75-second rate with no interitem interval.

The latency data yielded a serial position effect with the longest latencies occurring at positions three and four. Pattern of latencies over positions was highly consistent for individual Ss and there were no systematic changes over trials. The accuracy of performance was significantly and substantially higher for the S-paced subjects, though this difference obtained only in primacy and not in recency. Another analysis divided Ss with long and short latencies. Those with long latencies were more accurate in primacy but not in recency. These results are similar to those under E-paced massed and spaced presentation rates, and our interpretation is also similar. The long latencies presumably reflect extent of rehearsal mainly occurring during primacy and reaching a peak at the end of the first chunk (three or four items). Apparently, Ss rehearsed minimally, if at all, in recency. Although they did not appear to rehearse these terminal items when given the opportunity, this does not necessarily indicate that rehearsal would not have influenced accuracy on these items. This "natural strategy" may have maximized total performance on the task, however.

I. Study 9

In another study, Ellis and Anders (1969) evaluated the effects of an interpolated recall (probe) upon a second recall. The 9-position apparatus was modified so that immediately after the 9-number series, one position was probed and then another. For a control condition, a probe was given after a 7.5-second delay omitting the interpolated probe. The 7.5-second delay equated time relations for the two conditions. If the same memory process serves both primacy and recency performance, the interpolated recall should have similar detrimental effects in these portions of the curve. If, on the other hand, SM is the mechanism for primacy and PM for recency, interference should have a more profound disruptive effect upon transient PM. The more stable SM should be affected little, if at all.

Overall performance was significantly lower as a result of the interpolated probe. As expected, recency performance deteriorated significantly more than did primacy, supporting the hypothesis that recent memory in this task is less stable than that for earlier parts of the message.

J. Study 10

The hypothesis that rehearsal strategies underlie the transfer of information from PM to SM, and the hypothesis that the retardate suffers a deficit in rehearsal strategies, provides a rich source from which to derive *a priori* predictions. One such study (Ellis, 1969b) involved predictions based on both hypotheses. Twenty-four undergraduate college students were assigned to 2 groups of 12 each and tested on the 9-position task (digits). One group was instructed to "say the numbers aloud as they are presented." The other group remained silent, i.e., they followed the usual procedure. It was predicted that oral verbalization would be an activity preempting time normally used for covert rehearsal and, therefore, primacy performance would be depressed. On the other hand, such activity might provide additional (or stronger) sensory cues and strengthen recency performance. This prediction was fully supported. Performance curves for these treatment groups cross over between positions 5 and 6 with significant and substantial separations on both ends of the curve. The study was replicated with 22 retardates (CA, 13–24 years; IQ 50–75, $\overline{X} = 61.5$) using a 7-position (digit task). They were expected to rehearse minimally given the opportunity and primacy performance should not have been appreciably different under the two conditions. However, effects similar to those found for normals should have obtained in recency. In brief, the results were markedly similar to those for the normals! At this time no explanation for this effect is offered.

V. MOTIVATIONAL EFFECTS

Three studies assessed the effects of incentive upon performance. Although they are mainly of methodological interest, they do provide information of theoretical significance on the relationship of SM, PM, and incentive. Since SM is viewed as an activity under the control of instruction and other variables similar to those affecting performance on learning tasks, incentive is expected to affect SM. On the other hand, incentive would not be expected to affect PM, per se. It may influence attention and through this mechanism affect overall performance.

A. Study 11

Twenty college students performed on the 12-position (letters) tasks. Each S received three 24-trial blocks in 1 session. Within each 24-trial block, Ss received 1 cent for each correct response on 8 trials, 5 cents on 8 trials, and 25 cents on the remaining 8 trials. Incentive condition was randomly arranged within each 24-trial block. Ss could earn a maximum of $7.44 over the 72 trials. Twelve of the 24 Ss were given a .75-second rate and the other 12, a 1.5-second rate. The probe followed immediately. At the beginning of a trial, S was told the value of a correct response.

Analysis of variance showed the main effects of rate and serial position to be statistically significant, which was expected on the basis of previous studies. The main effect for motivation did not reach statistical significance. The rate by incentive interaction was significant ($p < .05$). Further analysis revealed that performance improved with higher incentives within the 1.50-second rate group. The difference between 5 and 25 cents was significant; that between 1 and 5 cents was not, though it was in the expected direction. For the .75-second rate, group performance deteriorated with higher incentives, with statistically significant differences between all three incentive amounts.

It is important to note that incentive did not differentially affect primacy and recency portions of the SPC. The rate by incentive interaction may be an example of the Yerkes-Dodson law. The 1.50-second rate is considerably easier than the .75-second rate. Of course, the facilitation of performance by incentive in the 1.50-second rate could be expected on the basis of the theory presented here. However, it would not predict the decrement with higher incentives in the .75-second group.

B. Study 12

Using a design similar to that of Study 11, 36 college students performed for 0, 1, or 10 cent rewards for correct responses. All other aspects of the study were similar. Only the main effects of rate and serial position were significant. None of the interactions were significant, nor were there any apparent trends.

C. Study 13

Thirty-six mildly retarded institutionalized Ss were tested on a 5-position task. The experimental design included the 5 serial positions, patterns versus colors as stimuli, 0-, 10-, and 20-second delays prior to the onset of the probe and 3 incentives for correct responses, 0, 1, or 10 cents. Each S received 30 trials in each of 2 daily sessions. Within a session, each 10-trial block was given under a different incentive condition. For 1 daily session, the stimuli were colors and for the other, patterns. The presentation rate was .75-second.

The incentive main effect was significant ($p < .05$). The mean percent correct responses for the 0, 1, and 10 cent conditions were 46.33, 51.75, and 54.40, respectively. The position by incentive interaction was also significant ($p < .01$). The main difference is the higher performance of the 10 cent condition over that of the other 2 in recency, an unexpected result. Both the 1 and 10 cent groups are higher than the 0 group in primacy, though the differences are small.

We conclude that these three experiments provide no definitive evidence that motivation affects memory processes. There is some suggestive evidence that incentive facilitated performance in Study 11, though this is not supported by Study 12. There is more substantial evidence that the retardate's performance was facilitated by incentive. However, in view of the effect over serial positions, we are inclined to attribute these differences to attention to the task rather than to effects upon memory per se.

VI. CULTURAL DIFFERENCES

Study 14

In this study, children from middle and upper socioeconomic classes were compared with lower socioeconomic children selected from a Head Start summer program. No specific predictions were made, though possible differences in language skills between these groups were recognized.

The original groups consisted of 34 (31 Negroes, 3 whites) from the Head Start group and 20 whites from a church-affiliated kindergarten and from the first grade of an elementary school. Twelve from the Head Start and 2 from the kindergarten groups were eliminated as a result of response bias (50% or more of total responses occurring at 1 serial position). An attempt to match Ss for CA on an individual basis was fairly successful (Kindergarten $\overline{X}$ CA = 72.7 months, Head Start = 74.0 months), though the elimination of Ss complicated this somewhat. The mean IQ (Peabody Picture Vocabulary) of the kindergarten Ss was 102.6 and that for the Head Start children was 85.5.

The 6-position task used pictures of objects judged to be approximately equally familiar to both groups—house, ball, tree, etc. Each stimulus was exposed for 1 second. Testing was conducted on 2 successive days, 36 trials per day. Figure 16 depicts percent correct responses for the 2 groups and it is apparent that the differences are negligible. No evidence for differences in memory between these Ss is found. Of course, it should be recalled that 12 Head Start Ss were eliminated as a result of performance on the dependent measure as compared to 2 kindergarten children. The mean CA of the 12 Ss was 69.2 months with a mean IQ of 75.5. For the 2, the CAs were 68 and 72 months and the IQs were 105 and 142! The eliminated Ss may or may not have had memory defects. They did develop maladaptive position habits which precluded further evaluation. It seems likely that the technique of increasing task length, beginning with a 2-position task, for example, will eliminate the position habit. Further studies involving these children will employ this method. Moreover, less familiar stimuli may well lead to differences in secondary memory storage by these Ss. Primacy performance may have been similar in these Ss in the current study as a result of the high familiarity of the stimuli for both groups. Given labels or names for stimuli, the culturally retarded, non brain-injured child may store information in SM in a normal fashion.

VII. SUMMARY AND DISCUSSION

These studies lead to three main conclusions: (a) two processes are

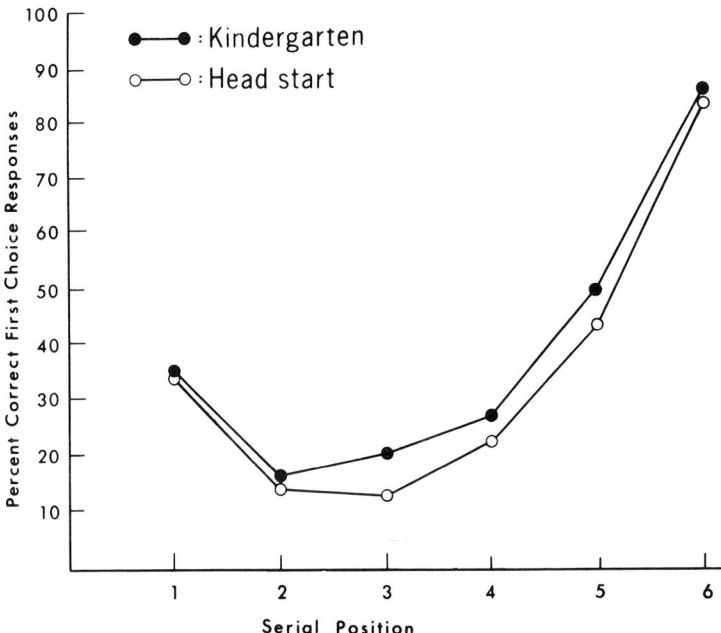

FIG. 16. Performance of kindergarten and Head Start children on six-position task.

involved in the short-term storage of supraspan messages, (b) in institutionalized retardates, one of these processes is defective, i.e., fails to function in a normal fashion, and (c) active rehearsal strategies are necessary for one of the storage processes but apparently not for the other. Another, less firm, conclusion is that the retardate's deficiency is due to a failure of the rehearsal mechanism(s). Evidence throughout the paper bearing on these conclusions will not be restated here.

Obviously, there are many gaps in our knowledge of these processes. Several studies now in progress in our laboratory should shed light on key issues. One of these will investigate the role of language in rehearsal strategies in normals and retardates. Possibly the retardate fails to store information in SM as a result of inadequate language skills which attenuate his capacity to rehearse. Another study will attempt to teach retardates how to rehearse. And still another will focus exclusively on possible retardate-normal differences in PM. Such a comparison will depend upon the development of a task which precludes the effects of rehearsal, i.e., performance must depend entirely upon the sensory or echoic memory. This may not be possible. It would be important to show that PM is either similar or different in these Ss. We are convinced that SM functions differently in retardates and normals. Further analysis will attempt to show why SM is inadequate.

The clinician may draw parallels between our findings and his own clinical observations. Retardates instructed to repeat a message, sentence or phrase, for example, often repeat only the last few words. (Recently, I observed a teacher instructing a retarded child to repeat her name. The teacher would say "Car-o-line." The child continued to say "line.") This is particularly true of the profoundly and severely retarded child. It also occurs in very young normal children. It seems likely that PM which subserves this function may remain fairly invariate over a wide range of intellectual differences. Moreover, PM may appear intact in the very young child and show no developmental changes. Of course, this is highly speculative, though it is testable. On the other hand, we suspect that SM will show developmental changes. Also, SM may well prove to be an important aspect of intelligent behavior, perhaps necessary for more abstract behaviors. George Miller (1956) states

> The intimate relation between memory and the ability to reason is demonstrated every time we fail to solve a problem because we fail to recall the necessary information. Since our capacity to remember limits our intelligence, we should try to organize material to make the most efficient use of the memory available to us. We cannot think simultaneously about everything we know. When we attempt to pursue a long argument, it is difficult to hold each step in mind as we proceed to the next, and we are apt to lose our way in the sheer mass of detail [p. 3].

and he goes on to note

> From the first it was obvious that this span of immediate memory was intimately related to general intelligence. Jacobs reported that the span increased between the ages of 8 and 19, and his test was later incorporated by Alfred Binet, and is still used, in the Binet Intelligence Test. It is valuable principally because an unusually short span is a reliable indicator of mental deficiency; a long span does not necessarily mean high intelligence [p. 4].

Our results show that the "span of attention" consists of the processes SM and PM and, apparently, that SM only varies with intelligence. Since retardates differ from normals mainly in more abstract behavior, it seems likely that SM (or an RS deficiency) may be central to their intellectual inadequacy.

The study of memory processes in the culturally deprived certainly warrants further investigation. On the basis of our initial study, it would appear that cultural retardation may not relate to SM. We were not able to assess memory in 14 of the 34 children in this sample, however. Also, it must be noted that the stimulus materials were quite familiar and both the deprived and middle class children knew names for all of them. With less meaningful stimuli which taxes language skills of the deprived child, differences may appear. However, such differences would not be attributable to memory per se. A future study will use an "increasing difficulty" procedure in an attempt to eliminate stereotyped position responding. Moreover, stimulus items varying in familiarity will be included.

Finally, the developmental aspects of PM and SM deserve attention. At this stage of knowledge, we suspect that SM parallels general mental development, though "mental development" in normal middle class children, culturally deprived children, and institutionalized retardates may reflect the interplay of different variables. The role of memory processes in the development of intelligent behavior seems crucial to all three groups.

ACKNOWLEDGMENTS

We are indebted to Dr. T. H. Patton, superintendent, Mrs. Marilyn Methvin, and James Price, psychologists, and Mrs. Mildren McLendon, chief nurse, all of Partlow State School, Mr. Gordon Crawford, principal of Skyland Elementary School, Mrs. Olivia Brantley, principal of Stafford Elementary School and Director of the Tuscaloosa Head Start Program in the Summer of 1968, and Mrs. Emmet R. Gribbin, Directoress of Canterbury Nursery and Kindergarten. All were instrumental in making children available as research subjects. The research was supported by Grants MH 10724 and HD 124 from the National Institute of Health, U. S. Public Health Service.

REFERENCES

Anders, T. R. Short-term memory for serially presented supraspan information in normal and mentally retarded individuals. Unpublished doctoral dissertation, University of Alabama, 1968.

Atkinson, R. C., & Shiffrin, R. M. Mathematical models for memory and learning. Technical Report No. 79, Institute for Mathematical Studies in the Social Sciences, Stanford University, 1965.

Belmont, J. M. Long-term memory in mental retardation. In N. R. Ellis (Ed.), *International review of research in mental retardation*. Vol. 1. New York: Academic Press, 1966.

Bower, G. A multicomponent theory of the memory trace. In K. W. Spence & M. T. Spence (Eds.), *Advances in the psychology of learning and motivation research and theory*. Vol. 1. New York: Academic Press, 1967. Pp. 229–325.

Broadbent, D. E. *Perception and communication*. New York: Macmillan (Pergamon), 1958.

Ellis, N. R. The stimulus trace and behavioral inadequacy. In N. R. Ellis (Ed.), *Handbook of mental deficiency*. New York: McGraw-Hill, 1963. Pp. 134–158.

Ellis, N. R. A behavioral research strategy in mental retardation: Defense and critique. *American Journal of Mental Deficiency*, 1969, 73, 557–566. (a)

Ellis, N. R. Evidence for two storage processes in short-term memory. *Journal of Experimental Psychology*, 1969, 80, 390–391. (b)

Ellis, N. R., & Anders, T. R. Effects of interpolated recall upon short-term memory. *Journal of Experimental Psychology*, 1969, 79, 568–569.

Ellis, N. R., & Dugas, J. The serial position effect in short-term memory under E- and S-paced conditions. *Psychonomic Science*, 1968, 12, 55–56.

Ellis, N. R., & Hope, R. Memory processes and the serial position curve. *Journal of Experimental Psychology*, 1968, 77, 613–619.

Hebb, D. O. *The organization of behavior*. New York: Wiley, 1949.

Hull, C. L. *A behavior system.* New Haven: Yale University Press, 1952.
Miller, G. A. Information and memory. *Scientific American,* 1956, **195**, 42–46.
Peterson, L. R., & Peterson, M. J. Short-term retention of individual verbal items. *Journal of Experimental Psychology,* 1959, **58**, 193–198.
Scott, K. G., & Scott, M. S. Research and theory in short-term memory. In N. R. Ellis (Ed.), *International review of research in mental retardation.* Vol. 3. New York: Academic Press, 1968. Pp. 135–162.
Waugh, N. C., & Norman, D. A. Primary memory. *Psychological Review,* 1965, **72**, 89–104.
Welch, D. B., & Burnett, C. T. Is primacy a factor in association formation? *American Journal of Psychology,* 1924, **35**, 396–401.
Zigler, E. Developmental versus difference theories of mental retardation and the problem of motivation. *American Journal of Mental Deficiency,* 1969, **73**, 536–556.

A Theory of Primary and Secondary Familial Mental Retardation

ARTHUR R. JENSEN
UNIVERSITY OF CALIFORNIA, BERKELEY, CALIFORNIA

I. Diagnosis and Taxonomy of Mental Retardation 33
   A. Established Diagnostic Categories 34
   B. Cultural-Familial Retardation 35
II. Mental Retardation and Social Class 37
   A. Genetic and Environmental Factors 38
   B. Motoric Precocity and Later Intelligence 49
III. Theory of Primary and Secondary Retardation 51
   A. A Hierarchy of Abilities 51
   B. Correlation between Level I and Level II 61
   C. Relationship of Levels I and II to Mental Retardation 64
IV. Evidence for the Level I-Level II Hypothesis 66
   A. General Observations 66
   B. Psychometric Evidence 68
   C. Memory Span 71
   D. Associative Learning and Intelligence 78
   E. Paired-Associate Learning 85
   F. Rote Learning, IQ, and Socioeconomic Status 86
   G. Free Recall and Associative Clustering 90
V. Implications for Education 97
   References 100

I. DIAGNOSIS AND TAXONOMY OF MENTAL RETARDATION

Recent evidence derived from experimental studies of learning in mentally retarded children and adults leads to a hypothesis of a hierarchy of mental abilities. The hypothesis has important implications for the taxonomy and diagnosis of mental retardation. This paper explicates the hypothesis and reviews some of the relevant experimental evidence. The implications of the hypothesis for the education of the retarded are also indicated.

A. Established Diagnostic Categories

Two broad categories of mental retardation are now generally recognized. The first category is diagnostically the most obvious; it is the variety of severe mental defects resulting in IQs for the most part below 50 and accompanied by physical abnormalities or clear signs of neurological damage. This category of mental deficiency forms a distribution of ability which, in a sense, stands apart from the normal distribution of mental abilities in the general population. Most of these severe defects appear to be due to (*a*) single mutant genes, often labeled "major gene" defects, (*b*) chromosomal defects, and (*c*) brain damage. Examples of *a* are recessive genetic defects such as phenylketonuria, galactosemia, amaurotic family idiocy, microcephaly, and hypertelorism, to name but a few. Examples of *b* are Down's syndrome (mongolism), due to triplication of chromosome 21, giving the child 47 rather than the normal 46 chromosomes; Kleinfelter's syndrome, due to an extra female sex chromosome in the male (XXY); and Turner's syndrome, a marked deficiency in spatial ability due to a missing sex chromosome in the female (XO instead of the normal XX). Examples of *c* are birth trauma, kernicterus due to prematurity or to rhesus incompatibility, and brain damaging diseases such as maternal rubella (German measles), neonatal septicemia, meningitis, and encephalitis.

The majority of persons with IQs below 50 are included in these diagnostic categories. Studies in England have found that among individuals in this severely subnormal range of IQ no specific causal factor was identifiable in about 30% of the cases (Kushlick, 1966, p. 130).

In the IQ range from 50 to 70, on the other hand, at least 75% of the individuals included therein appear clinically normal, evincing no signs of neurological damage, sensory defects, or physical stigmata. In fact, a report of the National Institute of Neurological Diseases and Blindness states that in 75 to 80% of *all* cases of mental retardation there is no specific identifiable cause such as those found in the categories outlined above (Research Profile No. 11, 1965).

These cases of retardation with no clinically identifiable cause are now commonly labeled cultural-familial retardation. The vast majority bearing this designation fall in the IQ range from 50 to 70. The evidence seems quite clear that these clinically normal persons are a part of the normal distribution of intelligence in the population, a distribution which is determined mainly by polygenic inheritance—that is, the influence of a large number of genes each of which contributes a small increment to mental ability (Gottesman, 1963). Familial retardation represents the bottom 2 to 3% of the lower tail of this normal distribution.

Some 70 to 80% of all persons identified as retarded at some point in their lives are in the familial category (Heber, Dever, & Conry, 1968).

The well-known excess or bulge at the lower end of the IQ distribution is attributable to major gene defects and brain damage which override normal polygenic determinants of intelligence. A study in England based on a complete sample of 3361 children showed actual frequencies not in excess of the frequencies expected from the normal or Gaussian distribution *above* IQs of 45. But the frequency of IQs *below* 45 was almost 18 times greater than would be expected (Roberts, 1952).

The most convincing evidence that the severely subnormal and the mildly subnormal familial retardates are different distributions and not different parts of a single underlying continuum of causal factors is the differences in amount of regression toward the mean IQ of the general population seen in the siblings of two types of retarded children. The siblings of familial retardates, on the average, have an IQ about half-way between the IQ of their retarded sib and the mean of the general population, an amount of regression that is rather precisely predictable from a polygenic model of the inheritance of intelligence. The very same amount of regression toward the mean is found in siblings of gifted children. On the other hand, the siblings of retardates with extremely low intelligence (IQs below 45 or 50) have an average IQ which is the same as the mean for the general population. In other words, the mental defect of the retarded sibling is superimposed upon and overrides the normal polygenic basis for intellectual development. Presumably the majority of the severely retarded would have been of normal or superior intelligence were it not for the devastating effect of a mutant gene, an abnormal chromosome, or brain damage (Shields & Slater, 1961).

It is still uncertain whether the normal distribution of polygenically determined intelligence extends below IQ 50 or thereabouts. The determination of this is made extremely difficult by the very small proportion of all retardates below IQ 50 that would be expected at this extreme of the normal curve. It is entirely possible, however, that some proportion of the 30% of the severely subnormal for whom no clinically identifiable etiology can be found are actually the lowest extreme of the normal distribution.

B. Cultural-Familial Retardation

Having now made this basic distinction between subnormality due to major genetic defects and neurologic damage, on the one hand, and cultural-familial retardation, on the other, the remainder of this paper is concerned with taking a diagnostically more analytic look at the cultural-familial category of mental retardation. This is not a sharply defined category. Traditionally the criteria for the diagnosis of cultural-familial includes IQs in the range from 50 to 70 or 75 and to this criterion is generally added some assessment of social competence. Persons not deficient in social competence are seldom regarded as retarded, despite a low IQ, except within the traditional school setting. From an educational standpoint and in terms of the scholastic requirements for entry into an ever increasing proportion of today's occupations, IQs below 85 are usually associated with educational retardation within the context of ordinary schooling, and consequently also with limited occupational opportunities. In preliterate and preindustrial societies most persons in the IQ range from 70 to 85 would not be perceived as retarded or occupationally disadvantaged, but in today's technological society they are at a marked disadvantage. More occupations today call for a higher level of developed skills than was true for past generations. Largely for this reason the American Association on Mental Deficiency has changed the intelligence test part of the criterion for retardation from two standard deviations (IQ 70) below the population mean to only one standard deviation (IQ 85) below the mean.

Edgerton (1968), an anthropologist who has studied mental retardation in primitive tribes, has expressed the doubt that the persons he has observed in industrial societies with the diagnosis of retardation in the IQ range 50 to 70 would be competent even in simpler, preliterate societies. Edgerton claims that the demands of life in African tribal society, for example, involve an amount of learning of customs, knowledge, and skills that is more than could be coped with by most persons regarded as mildly retarded by the usual IQ criterion. This is an important observation in the light of the major hypothesis put forth in this paper, for it falls in line with the observations that initially led to the studies which form the basis for our hypothesis, namely, the observation that some, perhaps many, of the children found to be retarded in school performance and on IQ tests appear to be normal and even bright in terms of a variety of criteria that clearly lie outside the scholastic realm.

The most likely reason that students of mental retardation have in the past failed to note or to emphasize this observation is that the criterion of social incompetence, as well as low IQ and poor scholastic performance, has determined the diagnosis of retardation and, even more than the intelligence test or scholastic criteria, has been the chief basis for admission to institutions for the retarded. A much broader spectrum of mental retardation is to be found in the public schools than in special residential institutions, and it would be difficult, if not impossible, to observe in institutions one type of retardation we have seen frequently in public schools—a "bright" child with a presumably valid low IQ (i.e., 50–75) which, in addition to his low scholastic performance, often results in his being placed in a special class for the retarded or for "slow learners."

A reformulation of the classification of cultural-familial retardation would therefore seem to be in order. A monolithic conception of this category, for example, has led to disputes over the claim that many persons are retarded only during their school years and once they leave school they become non-retarded. Mental retardation is thus viewed as a condition that results largely from the imposition of middle class standards and values by the schools. However, Heber et al. (1968) have noted that this interpretation fails to consider that the opportunities and criteria for evaluating mental retardation are very different for the preschool and postschool populations. Assessment based on clinical psychological tests have shown approximately the same incidence of retardation in the pre- and post-school population as are found in school, which only means that the criteria used in the psychological clinic are much the same as those used in schools. In the pre- and post-school years the IQ is less important and behavioral maturity and social competence are more important criteria in the assessment of retardation. Despite the general stability of the IQ throughout and beyond the school years, there are marked differences among children classed by the school as retarded. They differ in their social and occupational competence after leaving school, and these differences are only slightly correlated with IQ and scholastic performance. Some other important dimensions of ability, not assessed by the usual IQ tests nor highly correlated with scholastic performance, would seem to be involved in this phenomenon. We are concerned to find the nature of these non-IQ abilities and their educational and social implications.

II. MENTAL RETARDATION AND SOCIAL CLASS

Kushlick (1966, p. 130) has pointed out the fact that parents of severely subnormal children are evenly distributed among all the social strata of industrial society. Cultural-familial retardation, on the other hand, is predominantly concentrated in the lower social classes. On the basis of a number of surveys made largely in England, Kushlick concludes that "mild subnormality in the absence of abnormal neurological signs (epilepsy, electroencephalographic abnormalities, biochemical abnormalities, chromosomal abnormalities, or sensory defects) is virtually confined to the lower social classes." He goes on to say "there is evidence that almost no children of higher social class parents have IQ scores of less than 80, unless they have one of the pathological processes mentioned above." The same conclusion has been drawn by other investigators (e.g., Hardy, 1965) and is entirely consistent with the writer's experience gained in conducting studies in schools in lower class and middle class neighborhoods. The incidence of mild retardation is undoubtedly strongly associated with socioeconomic status (SES). Anyone who has attempted to do research on the relationship between retardation and SES knows the extreme difficulty in finding subjects in the IQ range from about 50 or 60 up to about 80 or 85 in the middle and especially upper-middle class segment of the population. Conversely, it has been our experience that it is not nearly as difficult to find gifted children (IQs above 130) in the lower classes as it is to find mildly retarded children in the upper classes. The Scottish National Survey established on a large scale that *high* intellectual ability is more widely distributed over different social environments than is low intellectual ability (Maxwell, 1953). This finding, of course, reflects the increasing *range* of mental test scores that we find as we move from the upper to the lower levels of occupational status. The upper bound of the IQ range changes relatively little going down the occupational scale, while the lower bound of the IQ range decreases markedly in going downward from the professions to unskilled labor (Tyler, 1965, pp. 338–339).

The association of the incidence of retardation with SES is also entirely consistent with the results of research on the relationship of SES to intelligence over the entire range of IQs. Correlations between the occupational status of adults and their IQs range between .50 and .70 (Tyler, 1965, p. 343) and between parents' occupation and children's IQ the correlations are, of course, lower than this—half of all such correlations reported in the literature are between .25 and .50 (Jensen, 1968c).

A. Genetic and Environmental Factors

The correlation between IQ and SES has led some writers to attribute the cause of this association strictly to environmental factors associated with SES. Neff (1938), for example, concluded from his extensive review of the evidence that environmental factors alone were sufficient to account for the observed relationship between SES and IQ. This conclusion, however, is decisively contradicted by evidence found in Neff's own review. If Neff accepts as valid the correlations he cites between the IQs of pairs of identical and fraternal twins, he must acknowledge the conclusion derived from these correlations, namely, that individual differences in intelligence have a genetic component. Once this is accepted, Neff's argument collapses unless it could be shown that there is no correlation whatsoever between the genetic component of intelligence variance and persons' occupational and educational status, which are the chief indices of SES. Similarly, a recent textbook states: "Inborn or biological differences in intelligence exist, but between individuals, not between large social or racial groups [Havighurst & Neugarten, 1967, p. 159]." For this statement to be true it would have to mean that all the factors involved in social mobility, educational attainments, and the selection of persons into various occupations have managed scrupulously to screen out all variance associated with genetic factors among individuals in various occupational strata. The possibility that the selection processes lead to there being only environmental variance among various socioeconomic groups and occupations—a result that could probably not be accomplished even by making an explicit effort toward this goal—is so unlikely that the argument amounts to a *reductio ad absurdum*. If individual differences in intelligence are due largely to genetic factors, then it is virtually impossible that average intelligence differences between social classes (based on educational and occupational criteria) do not include a genetic component.

This argument goes as follows. Twin studies and other methods for estimating the heritability of intelligence have yielded heritability values for the most part in the range from .70 to .90, with a mean value of about .80 (Jensen, 1967). Heritability (H) is a technical concept in quantitative genetics, referring to the proportion of variance in a metric characteristic, such as height and intelligence, that is attributable to genetic factors. $1 - H = E$, the proportion of variance due to non-genetic or environmental factors, which of course include prenatal as well as postnatal influences. The correlation between phenotypes (the measureable characteristic) and genotypes (the genetic basis of the phenotypes) is the square root of the heritability, i.e., $\sqrt{H}$. An average estimate of $\sqrt{H}$ for intelligence is .90, which is the correlation between phenotype and genotype. An average estimate of the correlation between occupational status and IQ (i.e., phenotypic intelligence) is .50. What Neff (1938) and Havighurst and Neugarten (1967) are saying, essentially, is that the correlation between IQ and occupation (or SES) is due entirely to the environmental component of IQ variance. In other words, their hypothesis requires that the correlation between the genotypes and SES be zero. So we have three correlations between three sets of variables: (*a*) between phenotype and genotype, $r_{pg} = .90$; (*b*) between phenotype and status, $r_{ps} = .50$; and (*c*) the hypothesized correlation between genotype and status, $r_{gs} = 0$. The first two correlations (r_{pg} and r_{ps}) are determined empirically, and are represented here by average values reported in the research literature. The third correlation (r_{gs}) is hypothesized to be zero by those who, like Neff and Havighurst and Neugarten, believe genetic factors play a part in individual differences but not in group differences. The question then becomes: is this set of correlations possible? The first two correlations we know are possible, because they are empirically obtained values. The correlation seriously in question is the hypothesized $r_{gs} = 0$. We know that mathematically the true correlations among a set of variables, 1,2,3, must meet the following general requirement: $r^2_{12} + r^2_{13} + r^2_{23} - 2r_{12}r_{13}r_{23}$ cannot have a value greater than 1.00. The fact is that when the values of $r_{ps} = .50$ and $r_{gs} = 0$ are inserted in the above formula, they yield a value greater than 1. This means that r_{gs} must in fact be greater than zero.

Perhaps an even simpler way of regarding this problem is as follows: if only the E (environmental) component determined IQ differences between status groups, then the H component of IQs would be regarded as random variation with respect to status. Thus, in correlating IQ with status, the IQ test in effect is like a test with a reliability of $1 - H = 1 - .80 = .20$. That is to say, only the E component of variance is not random with respect to indices of SES. Therefore the theoretical maximum correlation that IQ could have with SES would be $\sqrt{.20} = .45$. This value is very close to the obtained correlations between IQ and SES. So if we admit no genetic component in SES differences, we are forced to conclude that persons have been fitted to their socioeconomic status (meaning largely educational attainments and occupational status) almost *perfectly* in terms of their environmental advantages or disadvantages. In other words, it must be concluded that persons' innate abilities, talents, and proclivities play no part in their educational and occupational placement. This seems a preposterous conclusion. The only way one can reject the conclusion that there are genetic intelligence differences between SES groups is to reject the evidence on the heritability of individual differences in intelligence. But the evidence for a substantial genetic component in intellectual differences, is among the most consistent and firmly established research findings known in the fields of psychology and behavioral genetics. Much of the relevant evidence has been reviewed in detail elsewhere (Burt, 1955, 1958, 1959, 1961a, 1966; Eckland, 1967; Erlenmeyer-Kimling & Jarvik, 1963; Fuller & Thompson, 1960; Gottesman, 1963, 1968; Huntley, 1966; Jensen, 1967, 1968a, 1969; Jones, 1954).

More direct lines of evidence for SES genetic intelligence differences are also available. For example, the weak effect of SES as a causal factor in intellectual differences is seen in studies of identical twins separated shortly after birth and reared in different homes. The most valuable of these studies is by Sir Cyril Burt (1966), since the 53 pairs of identical twins in his study were separated at birth or within the first 6 months after birth and were reared apart in families that ranged across all the SES categories of the British census. Furthermore, there was a slightly negative but nonsignificant correlation between co-twins with respect to the SES of the homes in which they were reared. Yet the correlation between the Stanford-Binet IQs of co-twins at about 10 years of age was .87, which corresponds to an average difference of about 6 points on the IQ scale. (Corrected for attenuation, i.e., test unreliability, the difference is about 4 points.) Not all of even this small difference is due to social environmental factors; some of the difference, perhaps as much as half, is probably attributable to prenatal factors. Co-twins are not equally advantaged with respect to intrauterine space and prenatal nutrition; this is reflected in inequalities in their birth weights, inequalities which are correlated (positively) with their later IQs (Willerman & Churchill, 1967).

Another line of evidence is from studies of adopted children. The correlation between their IQs and the educational level of their biological parents is about the same as for children reared by their biological parents, while the correlation beween the adopted children and the education of the adopting parents is close to zero (Honzik, 1957). Children reared from infancy in an orphanage, and with no knowledge of their biological parents, show nearly the same correlation (about .25) between IQ and father's occupational status (graded into five categories) as is found for children reared by their parents (Lawrence, 1931). Also, adopted children show a smaller dispersion of mean IQ level as a function of SES of the adopting parents than do children reared by their own parents. Leahy (1935) matched two sets of parents on a number of SES indices — parents rearing their own children and foster parents of adopted children. Table I shows the mean IQs of the adopted and control children as a function of the father's or foster father's occupation.

TABLE I
IQs of Adopted and Control (own) Children in Homes of Different Occupational Categories[a]

Occupation of father	Adopted children			Control (own) children		
	N	Mean IQ	SD	N	Mean IQ	SD
Professional	43	112.6	11.8	40	118.6	12.6
Business manager	38	111.6	10.9	42	117.6	15.6
Skilled trades	44	110.6	14.2	43	106.9	14.3
Farmers	—	—	—	—	—	—
Semi-skilled	45	109.4	11.8	46	101.1	12.5
Slightly skilled, Day labor	24	107.8	13.6	23	102.1	11.0
General mean	194	110.6		194	109.7	

[a]Taken from Leahy (1935).

The variance among the occupational means for the control children's IQs is 15 times greater than among the mean IQs for adopted children (56.24 vs. 3.72).

Siblings have on the average only half of their genes in common, and show an average correlation of .5 for intelligence and other highly heritable traits. The average absolute intelligence difference between sibs reared together is about 12 IQ points on the Stanford-Binet. Most of the intelligence difference between siblings reared together is attributable to their genetic differences. There is evidence that when siblings reared in the same family move into different social strata, the sibs with IQs above the family average are more likely to move to a SES above that of their family and sibs with IQs below the family average are more likely to move down in SES (Young & Gibson, 1965). This condition would, of course, cause the gene pools for intelligence to differ among SES levels.

Since the mean IQ differences between SES categories reflect some combination of genetic and environmental determinants of intelligence, and since there is a broad spread of IQs about each category mean, as shown by the standard deviations of 10 to 12 points *within* SES categories, there should be increasing proportions of children falling below IQ 75, the borderline of mental retardation, in the IQ distribution of each SES category from the highest to the lowest. If genetic factors are predominant, the increasing proportion of IQs below 75 as we move down the scale of SES, should be in evidence throughout the scale, even between the higher SES categories in which there is no environmental disadvantage or deprivation in the usual sense of the term. Even the most disadvantaged environments found in industrial society, short of rare cases of almost total social isolation, do not produce IQs below 75 in the majority of children reared in such deprived environments. Thus genetic factors are almost certainly implicated in this degree of retardation, even when it occurs at the lowest end of the SES continuum. On the basis of large normative studies of the Stanford-Binet, Heber *et al.* (1968) have estimated the prevalence of IQs below 75 as a function of SES and race, as shown in Table II. It should be kept in mind that the estimates in Table II are based on Stanford-Binet IQs. We now have good reason to believe that on some other tests of mental ability, to be described shortly, the percentages for whites and Negroes would be much more similar than those in Table II, and SES differences would be very much smaller.

All this is quite consistent with what is known about polygenic inheritance. If we accept the polygenic theory of the inheritance of intelligence, which is strongly supported by the evidence, it follows that a certain proportion of the population will have relatively low intelligence. Furthermore, if we recognize the fact of what geneticists call assortative mat-

TABLE II
Estimated Prevalence of Children with IQs Below 75,
by Socioeconomic Status (SES) and Race Given
as Percentages[a]

SES	White	Negro
High 1	0.5	3.1
2	0.8	14.5
3	2.1	22.8
4	3.1	37.8
Low 5	7.8	42.9

[a]Taken from Heber et al. (1968).

ing — the tendency for like to marry like — we should expect that the frequency of genes for intelligence would become unequally assorted in different families and groups in the population. If persons were mated on a purely random basis, the average absolute difference in IQ between husbands and wives would be about 18 IQ points.[1] The degree of assortative mating in our society, however, is such that the average absolute difference between husbands and wives is actually between 10 to 13 IQ points, according to various studies. Thus, in terms of the polygenic theory the binomial expansion of $(\frac{1}{2}A + \frac{1}{2}a)^{2n}$ (where A and a represent intelligence enhancing and non-enhancing genes, respectively, and n is the number of gene loci) must be regarded as representing only the relative frequencies of these genes in the population. On the average, the frequencies of A and a genes in the population are assumed to be equal. Within a group selected for intelligence, however, the relative frequencies of A and a genes may be quite different, say, 20% A and 80% a, so that the binomial expansion of $(.2A + .8a)^{2n}$ will yield a skewed distribution of values, in this case having a preponderance of low values. The normal distribution of phenotypes in the total population should be thought of as the average of many differently skewed distributions for various "breeding groups." A variety of social, ethnic, educational, and economic factors in our society insures a high degree of assortative mating with respect to intelligence.

Given this polygenic model, plus the fact of assortative mating, we should predict that mental retardation would not occur in all families with equal probability. From this model it would be estimated that at least 25% of retarded persons would have one or both parents retarded. A corollary of this is that if none of the retarded reproduced, there

---

[1]The mean absolute difference between all possible pairs of scores in a normal distribution is equal to $2\sigma/\sqrt{\pi}$. For the Stanford-Binet test $\sigma = 16.4$.

would be a substantial reduction in the frequency of retardation in the next generation.

The most monumental study of this matter has been carried out by two geneticists, Elizabeth and Sheldon Reed, and their colleagues, at the University of Minnesota (Reed & Reed, 1965). They began with 289 retarded persons (IQ below 70) who were resident in a state institution for the retarded at some time during the years 1911 to 1918. From this nucleus of 289 retardates, the investigation branched out to include the study of 82,217 of their relatives. Practically all the descendants of the grandparents of the probands (i.e. the originally selected retardates) were included. Family pedigrees were traced over as many as seven generations, the primary aim being to determine as accurately as possible the mental status of all persons in the study. This involved searching school records for the subjects' grades and IQ scores and following their occupational histories. Analysis of these massive data lead to some clear conclusions.

First, it should be pointed out that in the following discussion of the Reeds' study the term "retarded" always means an IQ below 70. Since such individuals constitute about 3% of the white population, it means there are close to 6 million retardates in the white population of the United States.

The Reeds found that only 0.5% of children of normal parents (i.e. IQs above 70) with normal siblings were retarded.[2] The remaining 2.5% of the population who are retarded, therefore, have at least one parent or an aunt or uncle who is retarded. In other words, some 5 million of the 6 million retardates in the United States have a retarded parent or a normal parent who has a retarded sibling. Among 15,000 unselected retardates 48.3% had one or both parents retarded. The belief that the retarded of one generation contribute only a negligible proportion of the retarded of the next generation is therefore patently false.

Assortative mating occurred to a very high degree in families with a high incidence of retardation; retardates rarely marry anyone much above their own level. However, it is of some interest that 30% of illegitimate children born to the 289 probands were retarded, while only 11% of legitimate children were retarded. One might expect just the oppo-

---

[2] It is of interest that this is close to the percentage of retarded found among the offspring of Terman's gifted group. These were 1528 school children selected for IQs over 135 (mean IQ of entire group = 152). Their development has been followed into adulthood (most of them are now in their fifties). Among the 2452 children born to gifted parents, only 13 or 0.53% were retarded. Most of these cases were probably due either to major gene defects or brain damage rather than to polygenic inheritance. The average IQ of all the offspring of the gifted group was 132.7 when they were last tested (Terman & Oden, 1959, p. 404).

site. The explanation is that a high percentage of illegitimate children in this group were the product of incestuous relationships which would, of course, increase the probability of producing genotypes in the retarded range.

It is certainly true that the children of retarded parents are often subjected to a culturally and intellectually impoverished environment that would tend to depress their mental development. Yet, it is most important to note that of the children of retarded parents fewer than half are retarded. This would be difficult to explain strictly in terms of environmental influence. But it is what we should expect in terms of the polygenic theory. Although nearly all the children born into subnormal homes are presumably subjected to influences unfavorable to intellectual development, the fact that more than half of such children are not mentally retarded suggests that the more intelligent children must have received more desirable gene combinations.

Another striking finding is that retardation was extremely rare in some families. For example, in 37 of the families of the 289 cases, the only retardate was the proband. In some large families comprising over 2400 persons there were less than 1% retarded.

It is instructive from the standpoint of genetics to note the frequency of retardation among relatives of the probands as the distance of relationship increases. The results of such an analysis are shown in Table III. The probands were classified on the basis of case histories into one of four categories describing the most likely cause of retardation. The percentage of retarded relatives for three degrees of relationship was also determined, as shown in Table III. First degree relationships are those with whom the proband has one-fourth of his genes in common: mother, brothers, sisters, and children. Second degree relationships are those with whom the proband has one-fourth of his genes in common: grandparents, uncles, aunts, half-siblings, nephews, nieces, and grandchildren. Relatives of the third degree are those with whom the proband has one-eighth of his genes in common: half-uncles and aunts, half-nephews and nieces, great-nephews and nieces, and first cousins.

The point of primary interest in Table III is the rapid drop in the incidence of retardation as we go from first to second to third degree relatives. (Recall that the incidence of retardation in the general population is about 3%.) Note also that the etiological categories differ in the percentage of retarded relatives and in the rate of decline as the degree of relationship becomes more distant. Why should the category "primarily genetic" have fewer retarded relatives than the "probably genetic" category? First, because the "primarily genetic" category included some probands with major gene defects about which there was no doubt concerning genetic origin (and, as was pointed out earlier, these defects are very

TABLE III
The Percentages of Retardation in the Relatives of the
Probands According to Degree of Relationship and Category of Classification[a]

Category	First degree	Second degree	Third degree	Average percentage retarded
Primarily genetic	33.6	9.2	3.7	8.8 (452 of 5149)
Probably genetic	50.7	16.8	5.3	13.2 (496 of 3759)
Environmental	21.4	2.0	1.1	3.3 (60 of 1831)
Unknown	15.6	2.6	2.1	3.7 (275 of 7327)
All categories Percentages Totals	28.0 (532 of 1897)	7.1 (434 of 6070)	3.1 (317 of 10,099)	7.1 (1283 of 18,066)

[a]Taken from Reed and Reed (1965).

rare); second, because the chief criterion for classification into the category "probably genetic" was that the proband have retarded relatives in the first degree of relationship.

Table IV indicates the IQ frequency distributions of children resulting from various matings in which either one or both parents were retarded. It is most interesting that a number of bright (IQs 111–130) and definitely superior (131+) children resulted from such matings, despite

TABLE IV
IQ Range of Tested Children of Retardate Unions[a]

| Type of union | IQ range | | | | | | Total | Average IQ | Percent retarded |
	0–49	50–69	70–89	90–100	111–130	131+			
Retardate × retardate	6	29	36	17	1	0	89	74	39.4
Male retardate × normal	0	12	41	75	24	1	153	95	7.8
Female retardate × normal	6	15	32	43	10	1	107	87	19.6
Male retardate × unknown	3	16	68	80	20	1	188	90	10.1
Female retardate × unknown	10	29	64	79	22	2	206	87	19.0
Total	25	101	241	294	77	5	743	86	17.0

[a]Taken from Reed and Reed (1965).

the fact that some of these children came from what the Reeds described as "extremely impoverished environment." The largest number (294) of children from retardate unions was found in the average range of IQs from 90 to 110, again despite impoverished environment. Note, however, the skew of the overall distribution (i.e. the bottom "Total" line).

Another interesting feature of these data is that the mating of male retardate × normal female results in a significantly lower percentage of retarded offspring than the mating of a female retardate × normal male. Two hypotheses are suggested by this: (*a*) When the mother is retarded, the child's early environment may be more severely lacking in the kinds of mother-child interaction that promote mental development; (*b*) the retardate mothers may provide a poor *prenatal* environment for the developing fetus. Adverse intrauterine conditions could also have a genetic basis.

Table V shows the results of various retardate matings in more precise terms, made possible by having IQ scores on both parents.

Like low IQs, high IQs tend to cluster in particular families, rather than occurring in random distribution among families. In one family where the parents had IQs of 157 and 151, the three children had IQs of 132, 134, and 149. An unusual union in which one parent had an IQ of 135 and the other an IQ of 67 resulted in five children with IQs of 112, 115, 113, 97, 131 (average IQ of parents = 101, average IQ of children = 114).

All these findings taken together would seem to provide a more than adequate answer to the view expressed in a well-known book on mental subnormality by Masland, Sarason, and Gladwin (1958, p. 196): "We do not propose to *deny* that heredity is a factor, particularly in mental deficiency, but rather that we should leave it out of our accounting until it is supported by more than speculation and bias." The hereditary aspect of mental retardation is obviously now supported by more than "speculation and bias."

Furthermore, there would seem to be some eugenic implication in the Reeds' conclusion that

> ... the one to two percent of our population composed of fertile retardates produced 36.1 percent of the retardates of the next generation, while the other 98 to 99 percent of the population produced only 63.9 percent of the retarded persons in the next generation [p. 48].

The fact that the majority of the mildly retarded (IQs 50–70) are found in the lowest socioeconomic classes means that the majority of the mildly retarded children are born to parents who have the least to offer their children. The Reeds do not believe that social deprivation is a primary cause of retardation in the IQ range below 70. They state:

TABLE V
IQ Range of Tested Children of Retardate Unions in Which Both
Parents Had Been Tested[a]

Type of union	IQ range						Total	Average IQ of children	Percent retarded
	0-49	50-69	70-89	90-100	111-130	131+			
Both parents IQ 60 or below; average IQ 60 (12)	5	23	12	6	0	0	46	67	60.9
Father IQ 69 or below, average IQ 62; mother IQ 70 or above, average IQ 92 (26)	3	3	20	43	12	1	82	94	7.3
Mother IQ 69 or below, average IQ 63; father IQ 98 (15)	0	9	18	20	2	0	49	86	18.4
Total (53)	8	35	50	69	14	1	177	82	24.3

[a]Taken from Reed and Reed (1965).

We must assume that some cases of mental retardation are due primarily to social deprivation, but we don't find a large proportion of our probands who are available for this classification after an allocation has been completed for the causes which appear to have been present [p. 75].

They proceed to say: "One inescapable conclusion is that the transmission of mental retardation from parent to child is by far the most important *single* factor in the persistence of this social misfortune [p. 48]." The problem is how to prevent the approximately 6 million retarded persons in the United States from transmitting it genetically or environmentally. The Reeds conclude:

The transmission of mental retardation from one generation to the next, should, therefore, receive much more critical attention than it has in the past. It seems fair to state that this problem has been largely ignored on the assumption that if our social agencies function better, that if everyone's environment were improved sufficiently, then mental retardation would cease to be a major problem. Unfortunately, mental retardation will never disappear, but it can be reduced by manipulating the genetic and environmental factors involved . . . When voluntary sterilization for the retarded becomes a part of the culture of the United States, we should expect a decrease of about 50 percent per generation in the number of retarded persons, as a result of all methods combined to reduce retardation [p. 77].

An important point, in terms of the theory of primary and secondary retardation proposed in this paper, must be made concerning the interpretation and conclusions of the Reeds' study of familial retardation. It should especially be noted that all the retardates in this study were found by tracing down the more than 82,000 "blood" relationships of the 289 *institutionalized* probands. As will be shown in a later section, there is good reason to believe that institutionalized retardates differ in important ways from many individuals with IQs in the 50 to 70 range who do not become institutionalized. It seems very likely that a high proportion of the institutionalized retarded are the result of different genetic factors than those involved in the majority of noninstitutionalized persons with IQs below 70–75. Study of the relatives of institutionalized persons is also likely to give a much stronger weight to hereditary than to environmental and educational factors in the causation of retardation. We have found that there are some psychologically fundamental differences in the patterns of mental abilities between (*a*) institutionalized retardates, (*b*) non-institutionalized retardates from socially deprived backgrounds, and (*c*) retardates from non-deprived or middle-class backgrounds.

B. Motoric Precocity and Later Intelligence

Another interesting and important fact in terms of its diagnostic implications in the light of our theory of primary and secondary retardation is the low but significant negative correlation generally found between performance on infant mental tests, such as the Bayley Scales, and later IQ. Infant tests for children under 2 years of age yield a Developmental Quotient (DQ), as distinguished from the IQ, which can be obtained beyond 2 years of age by means of tests such as the Stanford-Binet. Bayley (1965b) has shown that it is the motor subtests rather than the perceptual-attentional subtests that largely account for the slightly negative correlation between DQ and IQ. Furthermore, up to about 1 year of age, the DQ—largely due to the motoric items—has a negative correlation with the SES level of the infants' parents. This inverse relationship between DQ and parental SES is much more marked in boys than in girls, for whom the correlation is close to zero. Bayley believes that genetic factors are involved in these relationships, and the pronounced sex difference at this early age would support this view. Beyond 2 years of age, on the other hand, boys and girls both show an increasingly positive correlation between IQ and SES. Bayley's results are shown in Fig. 1. Bayley (1965a) has also found that Negro infants up to 15 months of age perform better on the Bayley Scales, especially on the motor items, than white infants of comparable age. The highest mean scores on the Bayley Scales for any sizeable group that I have found reported in the literature were obtained on Negro infants of about 6 months of age living in the poorest neighborhoods of Durham, North Carolina (Durham Education Improvement Program, 1966–1967a,

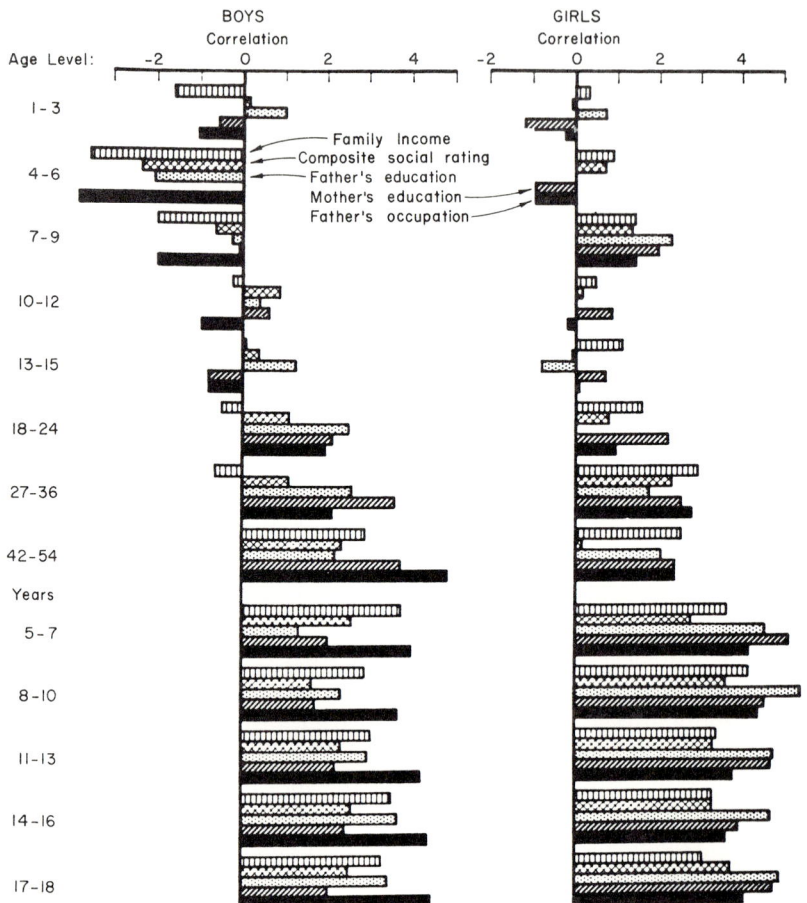

Fig. 1. Correlations between children's mental test scores, at 1 month to 18 years, and five indicators of parents' socioeconomic status at the time the children were born (from Bayley, 1966).

1966-1967b). These infants obtained Developmental Quotients on the motor items of the Bayley Scale averaging about 1 standard deviation above white norms. (On non-motor items they averaged half of a standard deviation above white norms.) The older siblings of these infants, by contrast, had IQs averaging about 1.3 standard deviations below white norms. Thus the negative correlation between DQ and IQ appears very marked in this segment of the Negro population. Similar findings have been reported in at least five other studies (Bayley, 1965a; Curti,

Marshall, Steggerda, & Henderson, 1935; Geber & Dean, 1966; Knoblock & Pasamanick, 1958; Walters, 1967).

When the test employed involves strictly cognitive rather than motoric aspects of development, negative correlations between performance and SES are found in children even below 12 months of age. For example, Kagan (1966) reports that on certain laboratory tests of cognitive functioning

> lower-class children, as early as 8 to 12 months of age, show slower rates of information processing than middle-class children of the same ordinal position. Lower-class children show less rapid habituation, less clear differentiation among visual stimuli, and, in a play situation, show a high threshold for satiation. The latter measure is obtained by placing the child in a standard playroom with a standard set of toys (quoits on a shaft, blocks, pail, mallet, peg board, toy lawn mower, and toy animals) and by noting the time involved in each activity. Some children play with the blocks for 10 seconds and then skip to the quoits or the lawn mower, playing only 10-20 seconds with each individual activity before shifting to another. A second group of children, called "high threshold for satiation infants," spends 1 or 2 minutes with an activity without interruption before changing. We do not believe the latter group of infants is taking more from the activity; rather it seems that they are taking longer to satiate on this action. It is important to note that the observation that lower-class infants show high threshold for satiation contrasts sharply with the observation that 4-year-old lower-class children are distractable and hyperkinetic. We believe both descriptions. The paradox to be explained is why these lower-class children are pokey and lethargic and nondistractible at 12 months of age, yet display polar-opposite behavior at 48 months of age.

III. THEORY OF PRIMARY AND SECONDARY RETARDATION

The empirical findings on which our hypothesis of primary and secondary retardation is based can be more easily summarized and their relevance more readily indicated if the hypothesis is described first in general terms.

A. A Hierarchy of Abilities

There is much evidence that mental abilities stand in some hierarchical relationship to one another. A number of factor analytic models have yielded results consistent with a hierarchical hypothesis (Vernon, 1950), but, as pointed out by Guilford (1967), the hierarchical factor model is as much a product of the particular method of factor analysis as of the raw data that go into it, and other models than hierarchical ones are possible. However, there are other lines of support for a hierarchical view of abilities which stem from experimental studies of the learning process, such as Gagné's (1962, 1968) work on learning hierarchies, and from studies of the developmental aspects of cognitive processes, such as those reviewed by White (1965). Both lines of evidence indicate that for many abilities there is a natural order of acquisition or emergence, such that when ability B is found, ability A will always be found, but not the reverse. Deficiencies in a lower level ability almost always imply deficiency in some higher level ability, but the reverse need not be the case. Some aspects of the ability hierarchy are attributable to the learning of specific subskills which stand in some hierarchical relationship to one another; these aspects are usually more closely related to the individual's grade in school and to the nature of the instruction he has received up to that point. Learning various operations and concepts in arithmetic is a good example. Other abilities are of a more maturational or developmental nature and are practically impossible to explain in terms of previous learning of specific subskills. The emergence of such abilities is apparently more dependent upon the growth of brain structures than upon learning and experience. Experience may be necessary but it is far from sufficient for certain abilities to become manifest in performance. Abilities that depend upon the maturation of neural structures can also be hierarchical, in the sense that normal maturation of a lower level does not necessarily insure maturation of higher levels in the hierarchy. Failure of maturation at lower levels, on the other hand, will result in some deficiency or impairment of the emergence of higher level functions in behavior, even if their neural substrate is normal.

The essential characteristic that most generally describes the levels of this mental maturation hierarchy is the degree of correspondence between "input" and "output." Lower levels of the hierarchy involve relatively little processing or transformation of the informational input; the stimulus-response correspondence is relatively simple and direct. Higher levels of the mental ability hierarchy depend upon elaborations and transformations of informational input, and upon comparisons of the informational input with previously stored information. Various cognitive tasks can be hypothetically placed along this continuum, from low to high: simple reaction time, Pavlovian conditioning, instrumental conditioning, complex reaction time, pursuit-rotor learning, discrimination learning, immediate memory span for digits (forward), immediate memory span for digits (backward), memory span for digits after a brief delay (i.e., 5-15 seconds) between presentation and recall, serial rote learning, free-recall of uncategorized word lists, paired-associate learning, free-recall of categorized word lists, complex concept learning and problem solving (e.g., verbal analogies, arithmetic "thought" problems, Raven's *Progressive Matrices*). It should be noted that this continuum is not one of increasing task difficulty per se. A digit span test can be made more difficult than a *Progressive Matrices* problem in terms of percentage of the population "passing" the items. Neither does the continuum necessarily represent one of increasing stimulus (input) complexity. The continuum seems to be best described in terms of the amount of transformation of the input—the amount and complexity of "mental" activity —called forth in the subject in the process of his responding to the stimulus in order to learn, retain, recall, or produce the correct response to a problem.

1. LEVEL I AND LEVEL II ABILITIES

Although up to now we have regarded these tasks as ranging along a single continuum, our hypothesis, for reasons that will become apparent, holds that the continuum is the resultant of at least two types of ability, which we shall call Level I or "associative ability" and Level II or "cognitive" ability.

Levels I and II are viewed as being qualitatively different, as existing in parallel, but as having quite different developmental rates. Individual differences in Levels I and II may in fact be correlated, but not because they are different manifestations of the same underlying structures or processes. That the underlying processes are essentially different and are not inherently correlated could be shown by obtaining groups of persons in whom the correlations are zero or even negative between tests that are highly loaded on Level I and tests loaded on Level II functions, such tests, for example, as digit span (Level I) and the *Progressive Matrices* (Level II). Probably no test on the behavioral level is completely free of both Levels I and II, but different tests can have markedly different loadings on each Level.

Correlation between tests of Level I and tests of Level II can occur in a given population mainly for three reasons:

(a) The essentially independent genetic factors determining individual differences in Level I and Level II may become associated through assortative mating. That is to say, persons who are below average in, say, scholastic ability, whether because they are below average in Level I or in Level II, or in both, have a greater probability of marrying one another than of marrying someone who is markedly different in ability. This tends to bring together in their offspring poor genetic potential for both Level I and Level II abilities. In the previous section in the review of the research of Reed and Reed (1965) on the genetic transmission of mental retardation, it was shown in Table IV that more retarded children resulted from matings of a retarded mother with a normal father than from a retarded father and a normal mother. While the explanation in terms of quality of the maternal environment offered by the Reeds is quite possibly sufficient, it is not the only possible explanation. A possible explanation in terms of the theory here proposed is that more of the retarded mothers than of the retarded fathers in the Reeds' sample had genotypes for deficiency in Level I abilities. Because of the demands of earning a living, mentally deficient men are less apt to be able to marry than retarded women, especially if the man's deficiency is in basic Level I processes, which would be a handicap in almost any line of work. Most standard intelligence tests are heavily loaded on Level II ability, and because of the hierarchical dependence of Level II on Level I for its manifestation in performance, a person who is deficient in Level I will also show some deficiency in behavioral indices of Level II. If Level I and Level II are under independent genetic control, and granting the hierarchical relationship between Levels I and II, one would predict that a normal person (i.e., average or above on Levels I and II) mated with a person genetically deficient in Level I would produce a higher proportion of phenotypically retarded children than a normal person mated with a person who is genetically deficient only in Level II abilities.

(b) The second basis for correlation between Levels I and II is already evident from the preceding discussion, viz., the functional dependence of the behavioral expression of Level II processes on Level I. The degree of this dependence is not yet completely known, but the evidence suggests that the degree of dependence may become increasingly weak above some "threshold" value of Level I; higher correlations between Level I and Level II tests would therefore be expected in the average to below average range of the distributions than in the above average ranges.

(c) Some of the information processing skills involved in Level II tests depend not only on the normal functioning of the neural substrate of Level I but also upon the prior learning of certain skills. The speed and thoroughness of acquisition of these skills depend also upon Level I associative learning ability. Thus there comes about a correlation between measures of Levels I and II.

2. INTELLIGENCE TESTS

Most standard intelligence tests are made up of items that are a mixture of Level I and Level II functions. Partly for this reason, it has been difficult to infer the two types of processes from total scores on these tests; the scores are too much an amalgam of Level I and Level II functions. Most intelligence tests that are heavily loaded with what Spearman characterized as the g factor—a capacity for abstract reasoning—are mainly indices of Level II functioning. Among standardized tests, Raven's *Progressive Matrices* and Cattell's *Culture-Fair Tests* are perhaps the purest measures of Level II ability. The Stanford-Binet and Wechsler tests have slightly lower g loadings than the Raven and Cattell tests and also contain subtests which are relatively pure measures of Level I abilities, such as the digit span and digit symbol tests of the Wechsler. Moreover, these conventional IQ tests contain informational items, such as vocabulary and general information, which depend upon previous learning. The low conceptual quality of the definitions required for passing, especially for the easier, more concrete words, and the simple factual content of the general information items, would involve Level I ability as well as Level II. The net effect is that these tests order individuals along a general, crude continuum of intellectual ability, somewhat more heavily weighted with Level II ability, but without making any clear distinction between individuals' relative strength or weakness in Level I and in Level II.

Some children who obtain seemingly valid low IQs in the range 50 to 80 on these tests appear to be socially bright and do not seem in the least retarded in learning the names of classmates, in acquiring playground skills and the practical knowledge of getting along with their neighborhood playmates. For many such children, who usually come from the lower classes, the IQ test is commonly presumed to be invalid because of the cultural loading of its item content. While some of the items in such tests as the Stanford-Binet and Wechsler have an obvious cultural element, as have also many of the group tests used in schools, it has been found that these items are not necessarily those on which lower-class children with low IQs do the most poorly. These children generally do no better, and often they do worse, on the less culturally loaded subtests such as block designs, and on tests like Raven's *Progressive Matrices* and the *Culture-Fair Tests* of Cattell (see Jensen, 1968c). Something besides cultural bias of test items is clearly involved. Eells *et al.* (1951), in their famous study of cultural bias in standard intelligence tests, found that the one characteristic that distinguished most between items showing a large social class difference in the probability of giving the correct answer was the degree of *abstractness* of the test items. This attribute of test items is a more important factor in determining disparity of test scores between upper and lower classes than the factor of cultural content per se. Examination of items in standard tests, moreover, supports the conclusion that the more culturally loaded items in tests are also among the least abstract. "Who wrote *Faust*?" (an item in the Wechsler-Bellevue), for example, is more culturally biased, but also less abstract or conceptual, than some other less cultural items from the same test, such as "In what way are an *egg* and a *seed* the same?" and "If seven pounds of sugar cost twenty-five cents, how many pounds can you get for a dollar?" Probably it was largely because of this inverse relationship between the cultural loading and the abstractness of intelligence test items that it was possible for McGurk (1967) to show that Negro children performed better (relative to whites) on the more culturally loaded items than on the less cultural questions of an intelligence test.

The cultural loading of test items is best regarded as essentially orthogonal to the Level I–Level II dimension along which various tests may range. The writer has argued the point elsewhere that the most objective index of a test's culture-fairness is its heritability coefficient (h^2) in the normative population (Jensen, 1968c). The two-dimensional space which must be hypothesized in order to comprehend the facts of SES differences in measured intelligence is shown in Fig. 2. The hypothetical positions of various mental tests in this space are indicated.

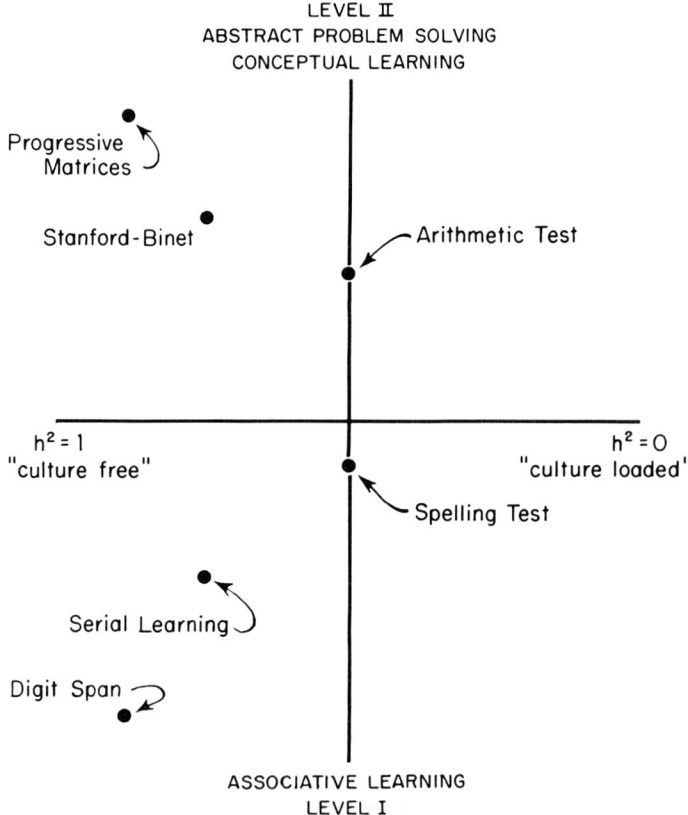

FIG. 2. The two-dimensional space required for comprehending social class differences in performance on tests of intelligence, learning ability, and scholastic achievement. The locations of the various "tests" are hypothetical.

Although various tests and forms of learning may differ in the extent to which they actually *require* Level II processes, there is little way to prevent Level II processes from entering into a subject's performance on tasks that require no more than Level I. Subjects tend to use whatever abilities they have at their command in approaching a learning or problem solving situation. Some tasks, however, minimize the usefulness of Level II processes. Mnemonic elaboration, coding, or other mediational processes are more often likely to hinder than to aid digit span memory, for example, and therefore digit span tests tap mostly Level I processes. Paired-associate (PA) learning, on the other hand, can be accomplished with Level I abilities, but Level II can also play a large role in PA learning. Thus, for individuals who are well endowed with Level II ability, such as college students, individual differences in PA learning may be determined largely by Level II, which will largely override individual differences in Level I. In young children, in whom Level II processes are still rudimentary, on the other hand, PA learning would be more a manifestation of Level I ability. Consequently, the correlation among tasks that can potentially involve both Level I and Level II but for which only Level I is essential should decrease with increasing age of the subjects from preschool to adolescence.

3. Relationship of Level I and II to "Fluid" and "Crystallized" Intelligence

Cattell (1963) has proposed a distinction between what he calls *fluid* and *crystallized* general intelligence.

Fluid intelligence is a basic capacity for learning and problem solving, a general "brightness" that is manifested in new learning, novel problem solving, and general intellectual adaptibility. It is independent of education and experience but is invested in the particular opportunities for learning afforded by the circumstances of the individual's life. Tests designed to minimize the importance of cultural and educational advantages, such as Cattell's *Culture-Fair Tests* and Raven's *Progressive Matrices*, are the best measures of fluid intelligence. Fluid intelligence reaches the peak of its growth curve in late adolescence, and thereafter reaches a plateau and begins gradually to decline in middle age, thus paralleling physical structures and functions such as brain weight and vital capacity.

Crystallized intelligence consists of learned knowledge and skills. It has been characterized as a "precipitate out of experience"—the resultant of the interaction of the individual's fluid intelligence and his culture. It increases throughout most of a person's life, depending upon the amount of his fluid intelligence and his opportunities for learning and new experience. From an operational standpoint, the difference between fluid and crystallized intelligence really amounts to the difference between culture-fair and culture-loaded tests.

Levels I and II are seen as being essentially orthogonal to fluid and crystallized intelligence. While many of the tests that characterize Level I processes, such as digit span, are also those that characterize tests of fluid intelligence, not all tests of fluid intelligence are confined to Level I functions. The *Progressive Matrices* and *Culture-Fair Tests*, for instance, are tests of fluid intelligence and are also among the best measures of Level II ability.

4. Relationship of Socioeconomic Status to Levels I and II

As shown in Fig. 3, individual differences in Level I and Level II abilities are hypothesized as having different distributions as a function of SES. The distribution of Level I abilities is shown as independent of SES. This may or may not, in fact, be true, but so far we have found little or no evidence that would contradict this simple assumption. When large, truly random samples of the population are tested however, it should not be surprising to find some difference between SES groups in the distribution of Level I abilities, especially in adults and in children beyond 8 to 10 years of age, for two reasons: (*a*) because of the hierarchical (but not complete) dependence of Level II on Level I ability we should expect assortative mating to affect gene pools for Level I in a manner similar to Level II, though to a much lesser degree, and (*b*) beyond 8 or

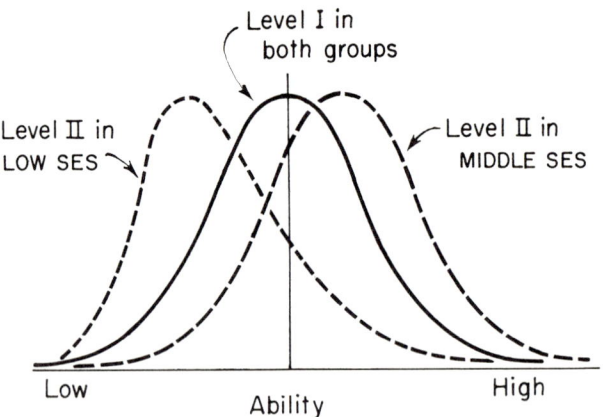

Fig. 3. Hypothetical distributions of Level I (solid line) and Level II (dashed line) abilities in middle-class and lower-class populations.

10 years of age, when both Level I and Level II processes are already clearly established in children's intellectual performance, it seems doubtful that Level II functions would not enter into performance on tasks that are intended as predominantly Level I, especially for children who are well-endowed in Level II ability. When performance on a Level I task is further facilitated by bringing Level II processes to bear upon it, upper SES children will show an advantage over lower SES children even in Level I tasks. Provided a sufficient number of different Level I and Level II tasks have been administered, factor analysis can aid in distinguishing the extent of involvement of Level I and Level II processes in the various tests, and factor scores representing Level I and Level II should show greater differences between lower and upper SES groups for the Level II factor and smaller differences for the Level I factor.

Why should Level II ability be different in upper and lower classes, while Level I is hypothesized as having little if any relationship to SES? One of the main factors determining an individual's SES is occupation or the occupation of the spouse. Occupation in turn is related to the individual's ability and educational attainments. Scholastic performance under traditional methods of instruction is heavily dependent upon Level II abilities. This is mainly why IQ tests, which were expressly devised to predict scholastic performance, are largely measures of Level II ability. Since individuals select mates of similar education and occupational status, the genetic component of Level II becomes segregated in the population. The greater the social mobility that is permitted by the society, the greater will be the segregation of genetic factors associated with social mobility, the chief factors in which are educational and occupational attainments in modern industrial society. In the course of generations there will be a gradual elimination of genetic factors making for poor Level II ability in the upper classes. Also, since there is some dependence of Level II upon Level I ability, low grades of Level I ability would also tend to be eliminated from the upper classes. In lower SES groups, on the other hand, education is not the chief means of succeeding, and small demands are made on abstract, conceptual ability, that is, the Level II processes. Level I abilities, however, are required to succeed in many manual occupations, and others' perception of the individual's intelligence or "wits" is based largely on his Level I ability when indices of scholastic attainments are lacking, are not valued, or are more or less uniformly meager among members of the group. In such cases, assortative mating will take place in terms of practical intelligence, "wits," cleverness, shrewdness, and the like. The Negro vernacular has its own term for this kind of intelligence: "mother wit."

High Level I ability is of value in any society or walk of life, and in primitive cultures it is probably of much more importance to survival than Level II ability. When there is little or no division of labor, except by sex role, every individual needs the ability to learn a large variety of facts and practical skills in order to fulfill his adult role in the society. Therefore there should be positive selection for Level I ability in all strata of all societies. The only condition under which one might expect a diminution of selection against low Level I ability is under circumstances in which no significant economic disadvantage is attached to relative inability to compete and in which vocational ineptitude is no barrier to mating, as might be the case when a society assumes complete support of its least able members and takes no measures to reduce their fecundity.

5. Levels I and II and the Focus of Attention

Rimland (1964), in his book on *Infantile Autism*, proposed a two-factor theory of mental functioning which bears considerable resemblance to the present distinction between Levels I and II. Rimland conceives of this difference as having to do largely with the focus of attention. He postulates that the brain contains a mechanism which focuses attention in a manner analogous to the operation of certain kinds of electronic equipment. His information-theory model of this aspect of brain function states, simply, that there is ordinarily a trade-off between fidelity and bandwidth in human attention. According to Rimland, the bandwidth aspect of mental functioning corresponds to Level II. It permits the individual to view, attend to, and recall specific experiences with respect to a larger context of associations, generalizations, and broad transfer from other experiences, to see differences and similarities between situations, and therefore to be able to deal with abstractions. "Fidelity," corresponding to Level I, permits an individual to deal in detail with the immediately given physical attributes of stimuli. Rimland believes that persons are capable of trading-off fidelity for bandwidth in their cognitive contact with the world, but each person has his own modal configuration of these capacities which characterizes his cognitive style and his pattern of mental capabilities. Rimland believes that persons whose main strength is Level I, or fidelity-reproductive processes, have a focus of attention that is largely *extracerebral*, that is, focused on real-world events taking place in the here and now of the person's environment. Such persons learn mainly by looking and doing. Unless they are also high in Level II, they are at a disadvantage in the traditional academic realm, which depends heavily upon learning from symbolic or abstract representations in the form of lectures and books. The person whose major strength is Level II, in contrast, directs more of his attention to intracerebral events a good part of the time. In the extreme, such individuals can become "lost in thought," which can at times put the individual at a disadvantage in dealing with many of the immediate exigencies of practical life. For example, it was said of Ernest O. Lawrence, the Nobel Prize-winning inventor of the cyclotron, that his tendency to become "lost in thought" while driving his car made him an unsafe driver to such an extent that he found it necessary to employ a chauffeur to drive him to and from work.

An important feature of Rimland's (1964) formulation of a two-process theory of cognitive functioning is that he cites cases in which Level II is almost entirely lacking despite apparently very superior Level I functioning, as found in some autistic children and so-called idiot savants. These observations support the notion that quite distinct brain processes are involved in these two types of ability, and thus they cannot be conceived of as simply different parts of a single underlying continuum of general mental ability. Just the opposite condition is found in Korsakoff's syndrome, in which some but not all Level I functions, such as the consolidation of short-term memory traces, are markedly deficient, although the victim retains the ability for normal performance on Level II tests (Talland, 1965).

B. Correlation between Level I and Level II

At present our hypothesis regards individual differences in Level I and Level II abilities as uncorrelated genotypically (i.e., in terms of their underlying mechanisms) but correlated phenotypically, because Level II functions have some degree of hierarchical dependence on Level I. [For example, solving an orally presented "thought problem" in arithmetic involves Level II, but also requires that the subject have sufficient short-term memory (Level I) to retain the elements of the problem in mind long enough to solve it. It is possible to retain the problem in mind without being able to solve it, but the reverse cannot be true.]

Tests of Level I and Level II, should, according to our hypothesis, produce correlation scatter diagrams like those shown in an exaggerated clear-cut form in Fig. 4. Level I is represented by tests of associative learning ability and Level II by intelligence tests with a high g loading. Because low Level II ability is not a crucial disadvantage in the lower SES groups, there is not much selection against it, while it tends to be eliminated from the upper SES groups. Thus the scatter diagrams for lower and upper SES groups differ mostly in the proportion of persons falling into the upper left quadrant. Because of the dependence of Level II on Level I in actual test performance, few if any authentic cases should be found in the lower right quadrant of either SES group. But if there is some fairly low threshold value of Level I above which any amount of

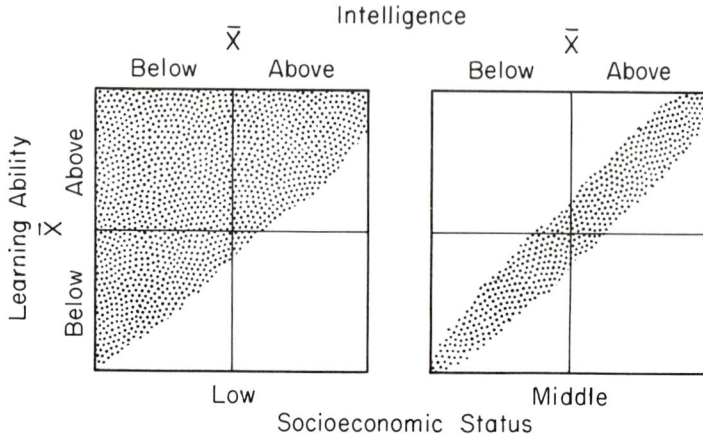

Fig. 4. Schematic illustration of the form of the correlation scatter-diagram for the relationship between associative learning ability and IQ in low SES and Upper-Middle SES groups.

Level II can be fully manifested, there may be more cases in the lower right quadrant than is depicted in Fig. 4. So far we have not found individuals who are superior in Level II tests and are also authentically deficient in Level I abilities. A few pseudo-deficient Level I cases with high IQs seem to be due to some fluke in the Level I testing, such as failure to understand instructions, excessive anxiety in the laboratory testing situation, etc. However, older brain-damaged and senile subjects could very probably be found in the lower right quadrant of the scatter diagram.

The hypothesized characteristics of the scatter diagram for lower and for upper SES groups implies much higher correlations between tests of Level I and Level II in high than in low SES groups. In fact, it was the finding of this difference in correlations between learning tests and IQ tests for lower and upper SES groups that initially prompted the formulation of this dual-process hypothesis of cognitive functioning.

1. Hypothetical Growth Curves of Levels I and II as a Function of SES

These are shown in Fig. 5. Since most of the child's behavioral development up to about 4 years of age is attributable, according to this hypothesis, to the growth of Level I, and since SES groups do not differ appreciably in Level I, there should be little or no differences between SES groups in early childhood. Children who appear retarded during this early stage of development are regarded as very probably retarded in Level I ability. If the degree of retardation is only slight, and if the child possesses normal or superior Level II ability, he will appear to be a "late bloomer" and during the early school years will come up to par intellectually. Thus, there is a near zero correlation (in fact, a low *negative* correlation for boys) between indices of early development and later IQ.

Figure 5 also illustrates a possible basis for the so-called "cumulative deficit" generally found in low SES children, that is, the fact that scholastically they tend to lag further and further behind their middle-class age mates as they go through school. As the content of the school's curriculum becomes increasingly abstract and conceptual with advancing grades, the child with below-average Level II ability, regardless of his status on Level I, will be at an increasing disadvantage. The cumulative deficit effect will then snowball because of the child's discouraging experience of diminishing returns from his efforts in school. The most important reinforcement in school learning is probably the student's perception of his own success and progress in learning, and when this reinforcement diminishes, the child is, in effect, on an extinction schedule with respect to the behaviors involved in classroom learning. This results in some children's appearing to be unable to learn even the simplest things taught in the classroom, despite the fact that outside the classroom they may learn more difficult things quite readily. Such extinction of school learning behavior could probably be prevented by conducting instruction in the basic school subjects more in accord with Level I processes rather than by means of techniques that maximize the role of Level II abilities in classroom instruction.

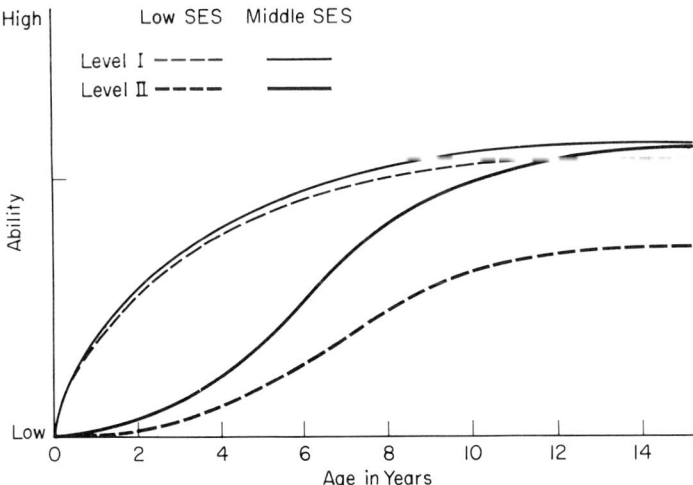

FIG. 5. Hypothetical growth curves for Level I and Level II abilities in middle SES and low SES populations.

2. The Heredity-Environment Aspects of Levels I and II

The previous review of the genetic aspect of mental retardation and of SES differences in intelligence bears directly on the question of the sources of individual differences in Levels I and II. Those who argue from the cultural deprivation hypothesis of SES intelligence differences would claim that Level I tests reflect more nearly the individual's genetic potential, and that tests of Level II reflect the individual's cultural acquisitions. According to this view, the basic source of individual differences in mental ability is seen as consisting of Level I processes, while Level II processes are regarded as the resultant of the interaction of the individual's Level I processes and the opportunities for learning afforded by his environment.

The present theory, on the other hand, postulates separate genetic mechanisms for Level I and Level II abilities. Although the development and manifestation in performance of Level II abilities doubtless depends upon experience and learning (the capability for much of which, in turn, depends upon Level I), experience and learning are regarded as *necessary but not sufficient* for the development of Level II. The idea that individual differences in Level II ability are largely determined by environmental factors, even granted a largely genetic determination of Level I, is contradicted by the evidence on the inheritance of intelligence, most of which is based upon tests that largely measure Level II functions. The purest Level II tests, such as Raven's *Progressive Matrices*, yield heritability estimates as high or higher than are found for omnibus intelligence tests like the Stanford-Binet (e.g., Shields, 1962). There have been no comparable studies of the heritability of Level I per se, but there is no reason to believe that Level I abilities are not fully as heritable as Level II. For example, pursuit-rotor learning—a form of perceptual-motor learning in which the subject practices keeping a stylus on a moving metal disc (or "target")—would seem to be a relatively pure type of Level I ability. Analysis of the correlations between sets of identical and fraternal twins for total time "on target" in the course of acquiring the pursuit-rotor skill yielded a heritability coefficient of .88, which is close to the heritability of physical stature (Bilodeau, 1966, Ch. 3).

C. Relationship of Levels I and II to Mental Retardation

Severe grades of mental defect due to mutant genes, chromosomal abnormalities, and brain damage probably always involve a marked deficiency in Level I; consequently Level II will also be deficient. Even in the severely retarded, however, the most elemental Level I functions are often prominent, such as high-fidelity transmission of stimulus inputs as commonly seen in the echolalia and echopraxia of imbecile children — in many cases these are their only signs of learned behavior, a high-fidelity "echoing" of what they see and hear (O'Connor & Hermelin, 1961). But here we are not primarily concerned with this category of severe mental deficiency. Rather, our present concern is with the milder forms of mental retardation associated with normal polygenic inheritance and due to the fact that polygenic characteristics assume a "normal" distribution of values in the population and such a distribution has a lower "tail." We have postulated two such distributions representing different genetically conditioned aspects of mental development: Level I and Level II. Because there are two underlying distributions, there are theoretically three ways that an individual can be retarded, but phenotypically two of these three "types" may look much alike from the standpoint of diagnosis. An individual may be diagnosed as retarded because (*a*) he is low on Level I but not on Level II; or because (*b*) he is low on Level II but not on Level I; or because (*c*) he is low on both Level I and Level II. Individuals in the categories *a* and *c* are probably the least distinguishable in performance and at present we do not know any means for clearly differentiating these groups, since normal Level II ability seems not to be manifested when Level I is very low.

Primary retardation here refers to a deficiency in Level I. *Secondary retardation* refers to a deficiency in Level II. This diagnostic distinction, we believe, has important implications for education and for occupational selection and training. While retardation generally refers to individuals who are more than two standard deviations below the general population mean on conventional IQ tests, there is a substantial segment of the population, largely among the groups now called culturally disadvantaged, who fall in the IQ range from 70 to 85 and might be regarded as of "borderline" intellectual ability in terms of conventional test scores and scholastic performance. The *primary* versus *secondary* distinction would seem especially important with respect to this group. Approximately half the Negro population of the United States, for example, is below IQ 85 on standardized tests, and approximately six times as many Negroes as whites are classified as mentally retarded by traditional criteria (Shuey, 1966). We do not know what proportions are below the average range in the *primary* or in the *secondary* sense, but from the evidence we have gathered so far, it appears that comparatively little of the intellectual retardation found in low SES groups is of the primary type. It is unfortunate that the label "retarded" is ever used in connection with individuals who are of average ability in Level I processes although they are quite far below average in Level II. Most such individuals are not perceived as retarded once they leave school, and, unless they show emotional instability or other severe behavior problems, they do not become institutionalized. Accurately speaking, they are not "slow-learners." Neither is their particular pattern of abilities primarily the result of cultural deprivation, in the majority of individuals. Some children with exceptionally high Level II ability come from a culturally deprived background (for some striking examples, see Burt, 1961b). Barrett, a student of mental retardation, has stated that "Perhaps the major obstacle to analysis and habilitation of retarded behavior is the paucity of measurement methods that amplify rather than homogenize the parameters of individual behavior [Barrett, undated, p. 16]." The differential assessment of Level I and Level II abilities is a step toward the more refined diagnosis of familial retardation, and it is a diagnostic approach based on a theoretical conception of the development and structure of mental abilities.

IV. EVIDENCE FOR THE LEVEL I–LEVEL II HYPOTHESIS

A. General Observations

The observations that initially gave rise to the studies that led to the dual-process hypothesis proposed here were brought to the writer's attention by school psychologists and teachers in classes for the educable mentally retarded (EMR, with Stanford-Binet IQs between 50 and 75) in schools that contained a large proportion of children called culturally disadvantaged. It was the teacher's impression, confirmed by the writer's own observations made in the classroom, on the playgrounds, and in laboratory testing, that low SES children in the EMR groups appeared in many ways to be much less retarded, and in fact usually appeared quite normal, as compared with middle-class children of the same IQ, even excluding those with sensorimotor disabilities or signs of neurological impairment. The same held true in observations of children not in EMR classes but in the "slow learner" category of IQs from 75 to 85 or 90. The low SES children, whether white, Negro, or Mexican-American, appeared more mature and capable in social interactions and in activities on the playground than middle SES children, despite very similar scores on a variety of intelligence tests, both verbal and nonverbal, and very similar performance in school subjects such as reading and arithmetic.

We found it possible to devise special tests, which we call "direct learning tests," that measure how fast the child could learn something new right in the test situation itself. Such tests are much less tests of achievement than the ordinary intelligence tests. Direct learning tests depended relatively little on knowledge or specific skills that have been acquired prior to being tested. The "direct learning tests" consist of measures of short-term memory and rote associative learning; they minimized conceptual learning. In brief, it was found that the low SES children in EMR classes and in the IQ range from 75 to 85 performed on the average much better on these learning tests than their middle-class counterparts of similar IQ. Low SES children of average or above average IQ, however, were found not to perform any differently on the learning tests than middle SES children of the same IQ. This finding suggested that the low SES versus middle SES difference was not simply due to the IQ tests' being more culturally loaded than our learning tests, such that the IQ underestimated the intelligence of the low SES group. It appeared that two different kinds of ability were being assessed — associative learning abilities, to which we later gave the general label of Level I, and conceptual or cognitive abilities, which we have labeled Level II. The typical results of several of these studies are summarized by Fig. 6.

It later became apparent that selecting subjects only from EMR classes actually biased our experimental results *against* the hypothesis. In many schools in low SES neighborhoods, it was found that the majority of children with IQs in the 50 to 75 range are not found in EMR classes but are in the regular classes, although their scholastic achievement is usually commensurate with their low IQs. The low SES children who are placed

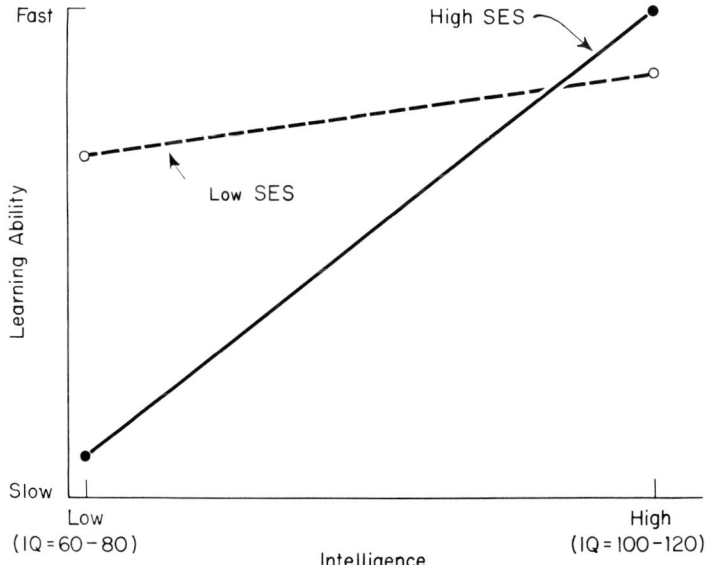

FIG. 6. Summary graph of a number of studies showing relationship between learning ability (free recall, serial and paired-associate learning) and IQ as a function of socioeconomic status (SES).

in EMR classes are more likely to resemble middle SES children of the same IQ than are low SES children in the regular classes despite IQs in the EMR range. On the other hand, we have found no middle SES children with IQs between 50 and 75 in regular classes. When such children are found, they are in the special EMR classes. The great majority of low SES children in regular classes but with low IQs and with scholastic achievement 2 or 3 years below grade level perform in the same average range as the majority of average IQ middle SES children on our Level I learning tests.

The literature on mental retardation frequently notes that many retardates are regarded as retarded only during their school years and make a normal social and vocational adjustment once they are out of school. From then on most are rarely perceived as retarded (Robinson & Robinson, 1965; Tyler, 1965, pp. 370-377). Only a small minority of individuals diagnosed as retarded while in school are ever placed in institutions or sheltered workshops for the retarded.

We have tested institutionalized familial retardates, as well as those in sheltered workshops, on some of our direct learning tests. We find that almost without exception these individuals are as deficient on our learning tests as on conventional IQ tests, and this is true even when we rule out individuals with any suspicion of organic impairment. (Retardation due to single gene and chromosomal defects has never formally entered into our research, but the several such cases that have been tested showed marked deficiency on the Level I tests.) It seems clear that among groups diagnosed as familial retarded, especially when social incompetence is part of the diagnostic criterion, there is a preponderance of primary retardation.

There is an indication that primary and secondary retardation can exist in different siblings reared together in the same family. Barnett (undated) studied four brothers, 8 to 14 years of age, diagnosed as familial retarded, with both parents also retarded, in an instrumental discrimination learning situation. Instrumental learning clearly qualifies as a Level I process. Two of the brothers (IQs 72 and 55) were grossly superior to the other two (IQs 63 and 48) in instrumental learning. One of the brothers (IQ 72), in fact, performed like a normal adult. All were markedly retarded in school work, although the two showing the better instrumental conditioning were also somewhat better in scholastic performance.

B. Psychometric Evidence

1. MA, IQ, AND COGNITIVE DEVELOPMENT AND LEARNING RATE

As illustrated in Fig. 5, different developmental curves are hypothesized for Level I and Level II processes, with Level II becoming increasingly prominent beyond the preschool years. Mental Age (MA), as derived from tests such as the Stanford-Binet, is an index of the individual's status in this form of cognitive development. But it is also an index of the amount of learning, as represented by the acquisition of knowledge and skills, that has taken place up to the chronological age at which the child is tested. Some part of this knowledge acquisition depends mainly on the child's associative learning ability, which is a Level I process. Thus, MA is a composite index representing both cognitive developmental status and amount of learning. The IQ, being a ratio of MA/CA, is an index of the rate of cognitive development and of the rate of learning. Culture-fair tests tap cognitive development more than learning.

2. HETEROGENEITY OF FAMILIAL RETARDATION

If the relationship between Level I and Level II performance is as shown in the correlation scatter diagrams in Fig. 4, we should expect to find greater heterogeneity in associative learning abilities among a group of retarded than among average or gifted children, even though all three groups have much the same variance on the IQ (or Level II) measure. Jensen (1963) tested all the children in EMR classes (IQs 50-75) in an urban junior high school on a trial-and-error selective learning task and compared their performance with representative samples of average (IQs 90-110) and gifted children (IQs 135 and above) in the same school. The groups all differed significantly from one another, in the expected direction. But the most striking finding was the extreme hetergeneity of the EMR group on the learning task. Although the standard deviation of their IQs was 7.13 as compared with 8.06 for the average and 4.94 for the gifted, the EMR's variance on various trial and error selective learning tests was from 2 to 5 times greater than the variance of the average group, and from 10 to 25 times greater than the variance of the gifted group. Several of the EMR children performed above the mean level of the gifted group. Interestingly enough, the two fastest learners in the study had IQs of 147 and 65! On the other hand, none of the average or gifted subjects had scores as low as the mean for the retarded. None of the gifted, in fact, was below the mean of the average group. These results are highly consistent with our dual process formulation. Virtually the full range of Level I ability was found among the EMR, though all were deficient in Level II. Also, the lowest part of the range of Level I ability was not found in the average and gifted IQ groups.

If (a) there are two underlying ability distributions, Level I and Level II, and if (b) omnibus intelligence tests like the Stanford-Binet contain items that measure both Levels to some extent, and if (c) one distribution (Level II) but not the other (Level I) is correlated with SES, then we should predict an *increase* in the population variance and an increase in the mean SES difference on tests which are more pure measures of Level II. This is exactly what Cattell (1934) found with a "culture-fair" measure of g, a test which taps Level II almost exclusively. When IQ is derived from Cattell's test in the same fashion that it is derived from the Stanford-Binet, by taking MA/CA, the standard deviation of the Cattell test is 50% greater than for the Stanford-Binet (i.e., 24 vs. 16), and SES IQ differences are greatly magnified by the Cattell test, despite the fact that it contains much less cultural content than the Stanford-Binet. This would be expected from our hypothesis.

A similar finding is that of Higgins and Sivers (1958), who found that large groups of 7- to 9-year-old low SES Negro and white children who did not differ on Stanford-Binet IQ showed a significant difference, with Negroes scoring lower, on Raven's *Colored Progressive Matrices*, a relatively pure test of g or abstract reasoning. Sperrazzo and Wilkins (1958, 1959) (also see Jensen, 1959) found similar Negro-white differences in each of three subgroups on the SES scale.

The Porteus mazes test, often regarded as one of the most culture-free tests and recognized for its sensitivity to brain damage, appears to be more a test of Level I processes than of g or Level II. The test apparently correlates with other intelligence tests because of their partial dependence on Level I functions, not because it measures Level II functions directly. Its lack of loading on Level II makes it particularly suited to distinguishing primary and secondary familial retardation, as shown in a study by Cooper, York, Daston, and Adams (1967). They were led to the use of the Porteus test by their impression that the Wechsler and Stanford-Binet tests often result in misleading and erroneous decisions when applied to a population of lower-class Southern Negro adolescents. They state:

> We were first led to question these procedures through observations of Southern Negro adolescents committed to a state institution for the mentally retarded. In the judgment of their teachers, nurses, social workers, and attendants a substantial number of these adolescents were functioning socially and vocationally at levels far above those to be expected of persons mentally retarded.

They point out that "extended retesting [on Wechsler and Stanford-Binet] failed to produce any reliable discrimination between the adolescents who appeared behaviorally nonretarded and those who were grossly deficient in effective and adaptive social behavior." Here, then, appears to be a clear-cut example of the failure of IQ tests, which tap mainly Level II, to discriminate between primary and secondary retardation. The Porteus test apparently made this discrimination. Subjects were divided into 2 groups—those for whom judges gave the answer "yes" to 6 or more of the following questions and those for whom they answered "no" to 6 or more:

> Is he socially alert?
> Is he socially effective?
> Is his general activity level high?
> Is he mentioned more often?
> Is his vocational ability high?
> Does he have sports ability?
> Is his physical appearance good?
> Is his social judgment accurate?

Although these 2 groups had mean Wechsler IQs of 56.0 and 63.1, respectively, their mean IQs on the Porteus were 63.6 and 121.7. None of the primary retardates scored above 84 on the Porteus and none of the secondary retardates scored below 102; the highest scored 132.

C. Memory Span

Tests of immediate memory span are among the best indices of Level I ability.

Memory span for digits has been underrated as a psychometric test by most clinical psychologists. The main reasons for the depreciation of the digit span test as it is generally used by clinicians are (a) its relatively low reliability as compared with most other subtests, and (b) the fact that in some cases it yields results that are highly discrepant from other subtests, as when a person with a very low IQ obtains an average or superior score on digit span. Poor performance on digit span, however, is rarely found in persons of average or superior IQ, unless there is evidence of extreme anxiety, an organic brain condition, or other pathologic disturbance. Wechsler (1958) has stated that "Except in cases of special defects or organic disease, adults who *cannot* retain 5 digits forward and 3 backward will be found, in 9 cases out of 10, to be feeble minded or mentally disturbed [p. 71]." He adds, "Rote memory more than any other capacity seems to be one of those abilities of which a certain absolute minimum is required, but excesses of which seemingly contribute relatively little to the capacities of the individual as a whole." This view probably underrates the importance of individual differences in the ability assessed by digit span in the region above the minimum requirement Wechsler speaks of.

The relationship of memory span to general intelligence is actually greater than is generally believed. Memory span for digits formed a part of the original Binet intelligence scale and has been included in all the revisions of the test. It is also among the subtests of the Wechsler Adult Intelligence Scale (WAIS) and the Wechsler Intelligence Scale for Children (WISC). The low reliability of the very brief digit span (DS) test as used in these batteries is probably what misled Wechsler to state that ". . . as a test of general intelligence it [digit span] is among the poorest [Wechsler, 1958, p. 70]." This statement, however, is belied by the massive normative data presented in Wechsler's own book.

First of all, it must be noted that the reliability of the DS test of the WAIS is between .66 and .71 for various age groups. The WISC Manual reports DS reliabilities between .50 and .60 for various age groups (Wechsler, 1949). By comparison, the reliability of the Full Scale IQ on both the WAIS and the WISC is between .92 and .97. Vocabulary has the highest reliability (.95) of any of the single scales. But low reliability is no real problem with the DS test. Its reliability can be boosted to any desired level simply by increasing the number of series presented. It also helps to standardize the procedure as much as possible, by presenting the digits at a metronomic 1 second rate by means of a tape recording for auditory digit span or an automatic projector for visual digit span. We obtain reliabilities above .90 under these conditions, and a reliability as high as .96 has been obtained even among a relatively homogeneous group of university students.

The correlation between DS and Full Scale IQ (minus DS) on the WISC, after correction for attention, ranges between .60 and .70, and for the WAIS it is .75. These correlations compare favorably with those of other individual scales after they are corrected for attenuation. The ability to repeat two digits at age 2½ correlates .62 with Stanford-Binet IQ at that age (Terman & Merrill, 1960, p. 342).

Of further interest is Wechsler's claim that DS correlates very little with g, the general factor common to all the WAIS subtests. Yet Wechsler (1958, p. 122) presents a factor analysis (Holzinger's bi-factor method) of the WAIS in which a large g factor, accounting for some 50% of the total variance, was extracted. The DS test has a loading of .63 on g in the age group 18–19, which is the peak age for DS performance. Corrected for attenuation, this factor loading becomes approximately .80, which is a very substantial loading as compared with the g loadings of other subscales. Wechsler's notion that DS ceases to correlate significantly with other measures of intelligence once DS exceeds a certain minimal threshold would seem to be further belied by the correlation of .60 (.73 corrected for attenuation) between the DS and Vocabulary subtests of the WAIS in the normative population. It appears that seemingly small individual differences in immediate memory span, when multiplied over a lifetime of experiences, make for highly significant differences in such acquired indices of intelligence as vocabulary. A person with good short-term memory span plus rapid consolidation of the memory traces would learn more per unit of time from his experience than a person with a shorter span or slower trace consolidation. This seems a reasonable explanation for the substantial correlation between DS and Vocabulary in Wechsler's normative population. Another line of evidence that rote memory abilities do not cease to be important above a minimal threshold was obtained by Jensen (1965b), who derived 12 factor scores from a battery of memory span and serial rote learning tasks administered to university students. The multiple correlation between the 12 factors and students' college grade point average was .76 (.68 after correction for shrinkage).

The reader should not gain the impression that memory span is a unitary ability. There is ample evidence, for example, that the abilities to repeat digits forward and backward are not entirely the same. Korsakoff patients, for instance, show far greater than the normal discrepancy between forward and backward digit span (Wechsler, 1958, p. 71). And factor analyses of the intercorrelations among a variety of tests including forward and backward span have shown that they have different factorial compositions (Jensen, 1965b; Osborne, 1966). From these analyses repeating digits forward can be interpreted as an almost pure measure of Level I ability, while repeating digits backward involves some Level II ability. This is in line with the fact that backward span calls for a transformation of the input, which brings some Level II elements into play. Forward digit span, for example, correlates more with the WISC Information subtest than with Arithmetic "thought" problems, while backward digit span is just the opposite. Also, backward digit span is more highly correlated with Block Design than is forward digit span, and Block Design is the best measure of g among the Performance tests.

Other procedural variations of the digit span task, such as requiring a 10-second delay between presentation and recall of the digit series, introduce further individual differences factors. Subjects do not remain in the same rank-order of ability on immediate and delayed recall (Jensen, 1965b).

The argument that digit span is positively correlated with IQ mainly because more intelligent subjects are capable of more sophisticated strategies for encoding strings of digits is not very convincing. For one thing, digit span correlates at least as highly with IQ at 2½ years of age as at any later ages. Furthermore, digit span reaches a peak at around 19–20 years of age and shows a relatively early gradual decline, following much the same curve as brain weight and vital capacity. This seems hard to account for in terms of conscious strategies for remembering digits. It is more likely that digit span is closely tied to very basic brain functions. Intensive training of digit span ability has been shown not to produce any permanent increase in children's digit span over what would be normal for their mental age (Gates & Taylor, 1925).

1. Short-term Memory and Retardation

Ellis (1963) has proposed the hypothesis that the mentally retarded are essentially characterized by a deficit in short-term memory (STM). He has postulated that the retardate is deficient in both the strength and duration of the stimulus trace. There is considerable support for this theory, most of it based on studies of institutionalized retardates. The position of the present paper is that Ellis' theory applies only to primary retardation as here defined. It is hypothesized that secondary retardation does not involve a STM deficit but depends upon a specific deficiency in Level II, i.e., abstract and conceptual processes. We also believe that the majority of low SES children with IQs in the range from 50 to 85 are intellectually retarded only in the secondary sense and do not evince a STM deficit.

2. Interaction of Digit Span, IQ, and SES

We have found that the substantial correlation between DS and IQ in the normative population of the Wechsler and Stanford-Binet intelligence tests breaks down completely in low SES segments of the population (Jensen, 1968b). The reason for the low or negligible correlation between DS and IQ in low SES groups is attributable, according to our theory, to a deficiency in Level II mechanisms. We hypothesize that there is too little variance in Level II potential in low SES groups for even quite large individual differences in Level I to make any substantial difference in tests of Level II.

If digit span correlated as highly with IQ in the low SES population as it does in the middle-class population, we could claim to have a culture-free test of general intelligence in the form of digit span. But we have found that DS and IQ are much less correlated in low than in middle SES groups. The fact that the low correlation in the low SES group is found even for the most status-fair tests, such as the *Progressive Matrices*, indicates that the phenomenon we are observing is not a result of DS and IQ differing in culture-fairness, but rather is a result of their measuring quite different mental abilities.

In one study (Jensen, 1968b), children from grades 4 to 6 in an all-Negro school in a low SES neighborhood and children in an all-white school in an upper-middle-class suburban neighborhood were given an auditory digit span test and Raven's *Colored Progressive Matrices*. (The mean IQ difference between the two schools is approximately 2 standard deviations.) The nonparametric correlation (phi coefficient) between digit span and *Progressive Matrices* was 0.33 for the low SES ($N = 60$) and 0.73 for the upper-middle SES ($N = 60$). The idea that STM as indexed by DS may be necessary but is certainly not sufficient for performance on a highly g-loaded test such as the *Progressive Matrices* is supported by a comparison of the 30 *highest*-scoring children on DS in the Negro ghetto school (the upper 7.9% in DS in grades 4, 5, 6) with the 30 *lowest*-scoring children on DS in the white suburban school (the lower 6.1% in DS in grades 4, 5, 6). The mean DS scores (expressed as percent of the maximum possible score) were 65.3 for the ghetto group and 38.7 for the suburban group. Yet the corresponding *Progressive Matrices* scores (expressed as percent of possible maximum score) were 64.7 and 72.6, respectively.

A more detailed analysis of auditory digit memory in relation to IQ in low and high SES groups was performed on groups of preschool children between 3 and 5 years of age. The low SES group ($N = 100$) was predominantly Negro children attending day-care centers; in all cases their parents were receiving public welfare assistance. The upper-middle SES group ($N = 100$) was composed of white children in private nursery schools. The mean ages of the high and low SES groups were 50 and 52 months, respectively. All the children were administered a battery of tests composed of auditory digit series of from 2 to 9 digits, the Binet and Wechsler digit span tests, serial and paired-associate learning of pictures of common objects, and the Peabody Picture Vocabulary Test (PPVT). The various tests yielded 26 variables in all. The intercorrelations among the variables were factor analyzed (i.e., a varimax rotation of the 5 principal components having Eigenvalues greater than 1) separately for the low and high SES groups. The results of the factor analysis were quite different for the two groups. Although the groups differed by 19 points in PPVT IQ (an average mental age difference of 16 months), they showed no appreciable differences in the digit span and serial and paired-associate learning tests. The pattern of intercorrelations among tests differed, however, in the low and the high SES groups, and these differences were, of course, reflected in the factor analyses. In the high SES group a single factor accounted for most of the variance on all the tests; the intelligence test and the digit series and learning tests were all substantially intercorrelated, yielding a large general factor common to all. In the low SES group, on the other hand, there was a clear separation of the intelligence factor from the factor representing the digit series and learning tests.

The results are shown in Table VI. It is especially instructive to examine the intelligence factor in detail. The intelligence factor is so defined because it is the only factor with a high loading on PPVT mental age. Digit span on both the Binet and Wechsler is defined as the longest series of digits the subject can recall perfectly (after a single auditory presentation at a rate of 1 second per digit) on 50% of the trials. As shown in Fig. 6, the low and high SES groups do not differ significantly in means or standard deviations on either the Binet or the Wechsler digit span tests, despite a 16 months difference between the mean mental ages of the groups. Also note that DS has nonsignificant loadings on the intelligence factor in the low SES group and very substantial loadings in the high SES group.

The digit series test, comprised of series of from 2 to 9 digits, were administered in the same manner as the DS test from the Binet and Wechsler, but they are scored differently. Two different scores were obtained. The *position* (Pos.) score is the number of digits recalled in the correct absolute position. The *sequence* (Seq.) score is the number of digits correct in forward adjacent sequence, regardless of absolute position. Since the maximum possible sequence score is necessarily 1 less than the maximum possible position score for a given series length, +1 is added to

TABLE VI
MEANS, STANDARD DEVIATIONS, AND CORRELATIONS WITH INTELLIGENCE FACTOR IN LOW AND HIGH SOCIOECONOMIC GROUPS ($N = 100$ IN EACH GROUP)[a]

Variable	Mean		Standard deviation		Factor loadings	
	low SES	high SES	low SES	high SES	low SES	high SES
Mental age (mo.)	48.41	64.46	22.67	19.16	.504	.512
Binet digit span	3.72	3.63	1.05	1.07	.047	.482
WISC digit span	3.99	4.12	1.02	1.12	.073	.613

	low SES		high SES		low SES		high SES		low SES		high SES	
	Pos.	Seq.	Pos.	Seq.	Pos.	Seq.	Pos.	Seq.	Pos.	Seq.	Pos.	Seq.
Digit series 2	1.99	1.99	1.99	1.99	.05	.05	.09	.05	.032	.032	.023	.023
3	2.82	2.85	2.88	2.91	.40	.31	.38	.29	.138	.181	.214	.210
4	3.06	3.20	3.02	3.13	1.13	.88	1.15	.95	.023	.010	.877	.870
5	2.00	2.46	1.83	2.42	1.32	.98	1.58	1.21	.157	.156	.563	.511
6	1.02	2.01	1.05	1.95	1.03	.83	1.03	.90	.340	.478	.372	.273
7	.54	1.53	.56	1.63	.65	.63	.84	.88	.325	.534	.072	.017
8	.41	1.66	.38	1.46	.49	.71	.60	.65	.138	.698	.057	.020
9	.26	1.71	.28	1.71	.37	.83	.49	.91	.148	.760	.133	.194

[a]Factor loadings significant beyond .001 level are underscored.

TABLE VII
CORRELATION BETWEEN POSITION AND SEQUENCE SCORING
OF DIGIT SERIES TEST

	Series length							
SES	2	3	4	5	6	7	8	9
High	1.00	.98	.93	.93	.85	.60	.47	.39
Low	1.00	.95	.91	.90	.83	.29	.16	−.01

the sequence score to make it equivalent to the position score. The reason that the two types of scores were used is that it had been found in a previous study of digit memory in college students that in supraspan series (i.e., series lengths beyond the subject's memory span) the two scores cease to be highly correlated and apparently measure different factors (Jensen, 1965b). In supraspan series the subject seems to retain pair-wise associations between adjacent digits in the series rather than some mental representation of the series as a whole, in which absolute position is retained. Table VII shows the correlations between position and sequence scores for different series lengths.

Note again in Table VI that the low and high SES groups do not differ significantly in means or standard deviations on any series by either form of scoring. The loadings on the intelligence factor, however, are entirely different for the low and high SES groups. The low SES group has no appreciable loadings on any series for position scoring. The high SES group has very high loadings for series of 4 and 5 digits, which are the series lengths near the threshold of subjects' memory span at this age. For the high SES group the loadings are approximately the same for position and sequence scores. This is not so for the low SES group, which has its only sizeable digit series of lengths 7, 8, and 9, the clearly supraspan series which more or less force subjects to learn only adjacent associations. This strongly suggests that the intelligence test (PPVT) is measuring different mental processes in the high and low SES groups. It is hard to characterize psychologically the processes of the high SES group, but those of the low SES group appear to be of an associative nature, since their sequence scores are the only ones that correlate with the intelligence factor. These different patterns of correlations within the digit series tests would be most difficult to account for in terms of culture influences, especially in view of the fact that the distributions of scores in the low and high SES groups are indistinguishable. The different correlation patterns more likely reflect fundamental differences in neurological organization.

D. Associative Learning and Intelligence

Some of the most puzzling research in all of psychology is concerned with the relationship between psychometric intelligence and learning ability. An enormous range of correlations between various learning measures and intelligence test scores has been found, leading to a diversity of conclusions and disputes about the relationship between learning ability and intelligence (Rapier, 1962). Reviews of studies of learning ability in the mentally retarded show that this field is also characterized by similar conflicting findings (Goulet, 1968; Prehm, 1968; Zeaman & House, 1967).

Much of the puzzlement in the research findings is probably due to the failure, first, to distinguish between subjects on the basis of primary and secondary retardation and, second, to pay sufficient attention to the properties of the learning task with respect to its position on the Level I–Level II continuum. If one makes some judgment about whether the subjects of the study were predominantly primary or secondary retardates, and about whether the learning tasks were most heavily dependent on Level I or Level II processes, a considerable degree of order emerges from the various findings. For example, there is no disagreement among various researches that persons called retarded by any criteria are deficient on tests involving abstract and conceptual abilities. This characterizes both primary and secondary retardates. But as we get into the realm of associative learning tasks, the findings appear confusing, because it is in this type of learning that primary and secondary retardates show divergent abilities. The results will depend largely upon the proportions of primary and secondary retardates in the investigator's sample. If the subjects have IQs below 50, they will almost always be primary retardates, and the evidence is quite clear that these subjects are markedly below average in associative learning. If the subjects have IQs in the range 50 to 75 and are institutionalized, the chances are great that most of them are primary retardates, for we know that the vast majority of persons in this IQ range are never institutionalized. Thus, institutionalized subjects usually show a severe deficiency in learning ability. When the subjects are school children with IQs between 50 and 75 and are in special classes for the educable mentally retarded, there will be a considerable mixture of primary and secondary types of retardation, so that great variance will be found on rote learning tasks, and often the group's mean on such tasks will differ little from that of children with average IQs. When the subjects are children of low SES with IQs between 50 and 80, and are in regular classes, there will be little or no evidence of deficiency in associative learning as compared with the performance of middle-class children of average IQ.

Extremely simple forms of learning, which require no discriminations and involve no competition among multiple response alternatives — for example, classical conditioning — do not distinguish even between primary and secondary retardates or between retardates and persons of average or superior IQ. It is only when discriminative features enter the conditioning procedures that some correlation with intelligence is manifested (Zeaman & House, 1967, pp. 195-197).

In general, the evidence leads to the conclusion that there is a moderate correlation between IQ and learning ability for simple discrimination learning, for paired-associate and serial learning, and in learning-set formation (Zeaman & House, 1967). Our theory would predict that these correlations should be higher in groups containing fewer secondary retardates. A test of this hypothesis that does not require the diagnosis of primary and secondary retardation would be to obtain the correlation between IQ and associative learning ability (or any Level I test) in random samples of school children, one group with IQs from 60 to 95, the other group with IQs from 105 to 140. All the instances of secondary retardation could be presumed to be in the 60 to 95 IQ range. The correlation between associative learning and IQ in this range should be lower than in the range 105 to 140. This test of the hypothesis has not yet been made, although some evidence to be reviewed shortly comes very close to it and is consistent with the hypothesis.

Prehm (1968, pp. 37-38), in reviewing the research on rote verbal learning in the retarded, has drawn 12 conclusions from the evidence:

[1] The rote verbal learning performance of the retarded is considerably more variable than that of Ss of normal intelligence.

This is what should be expected when the retardate groups are a mixture of primary and secondary types.

[2] The rote learning performance of the retarded is inferior to that of normal Ss. *This is most true when the materials are more abstract than pictures of common objects.*

We would expect that more abstract items would depend more upon Level II processes.

[3] The serial learning performance of the retarded seems to be subject to the same principles (invariance of the serial position curve, isolation effects, etc.) governing the serial performance of Ss of normal intelligence.

In a later section we will mention some important exceptions to this generalization which are predictable from our theory.

[4] When compared to massed practice, distributed practice enhances the learning performance of the retarded to a greater extent than it does for normal Ss.

This conclusion supports the hypothesis that primary retardates have a slower rate of consolidation of short-term memory traces, which, prior to consolidation, are easily interfered with or "erased" by new input; distributed practice allows more time for consolidation and freedom from input and output interference, to the relatively greater advantage of retardates than of normals. It is hypothesized from the present theory that this generalization applies only to primary retardates.

[5] Retardates learn a list of paired associates more readily when the stimulus and response items are the actual objects rather than a picture of that object and when they can pronounce a CVC trigram as a word as opposed to spelling the response.

Paired associate learning tasks can differ in their relative dependence on Level I and Level II processes. Less abstract materials depend less upon Level II processes.

[6] The exposure of stimulus items for longer (four to seven seconds) intervals enhances the learning performance of the retarded.

Again, more consolidation time is of relatively greater advantage to the primary retardate.

[7] The retarded use high level mediational strategies in paired-associate learning to a lesser degree than do Ss of normal intelligence.

This conclusion should hold for both primary and secondary retardates, since mediational strategies are examples of Level II processes.

[8] When non-meaningful and meaningful materials are equated for degree of difficulty, retardates exhibit a learning deficit on both types of material.

[9] The retarded exhibit both a short- and a long-term retention deficit.

This, again, theoretically applies only to primary retardates. There is no question of their STM deficit. Long-term deficit is more difficult to prove, since it depends upon equating groups for degree of original learning, which is rarely accomplished. Zeaman (1965) has concluded on the basis of the present evidence, such as it is, that long-term retention is good even in primary retardates.

[10] The retention deficit of the retarded can be minimized by instituting overlearning procedures. The relationship between amount of overlearning and the amount of retention loss is, however, unclear.

[11] Although associative clustering [in free recall of verbal materials] occurs in the retarded, their performance on tasks of this type is inferior to that of the normal Ss.

Recent experiments from our laboratory, to be reported in a following section, indicate that free recall per se is a Level I ability and that clustering is a Level II process. Our theory thus mediates certain predictions about the relationships among the variables of age, IQ, free recall, and clustering tendency.

[12] The retention performance of the retarded is impaired as a function of both proactive and retroactive inhibition, with the unlearning of OL [original learning] associations accounting for the effects of retroactive inhibition (RI). Overlearning during OL significantly reduces the effects of RI.

Conflicting Evidence

So far in his search of the literature the writer has found only one experimental result which is unequivocally in conflict with the major hypothesis set forth here. Pursuit-rotor learning would seem to be an even purer form of Level I ability than digit span, serial, and paired-associate learning. So we should expect pursuit-rotor learning to show little if any difference between groups of school children who presumably differ in IQ but not in Level I ability. In fact, in one study of the relationship between pursuit rotor learning ability and MA, the correlation was only .17 (McNemar, 1933). Wright and Hearn (1964) found a large, significant difference in pursuit rotor learning between a group of 20 institutionalized mental defectives and a group of 20 high-school and college students, which is consistent with the idea that institutionalized retardates are usually deficient in Level I. The evidence that appears to be in direct conflict with our theory is from a recent experiment by Noble (1968, pp. 230–232), who found highly significant differences among a sample of 500 rural school children of white (W) and Negro (N) ancestry. The groups were matched for age, sex, and conditions of practice (L vs. R hand). The outcome was $WR > WL > NR > NL$. When whites, mulattoes (M), and Negroes, similarly matched on age and sex, were compared, the results were $W > M > N$. As Noble points out, it is hard to know how to interpret these results. Since we have found no difference between Negro and white children on such Level I measures as digit span and serial learning, though they differ by 15 to 20 points in IQ (mostly Level II), it is puzzling why Negro children should perform less well than white children on pursuit rotor learning, which seems to be a purely Level 1 task. One likely hypothesis is that pursuit rotor learning involves a form of work inhibition ("reactive inhibition" in Hullian terminology) which is absent in STM and verbal learning tasks. There could well be racial differences in rates of build-up and dissipation of reactive inhibition, just as there are highly reliable individual differences within races. Pursuit rotor experiments manipulating distribution of practice, the measure of reminiscence, and other measurements of reactive inhibition such as those described by Jensen (1966), should provide the means for testing this hypothesis.

Goulet (1968) has reviewed the research on serial rote learning in the retarded and concluded that these studies show "unequivocal findings of superior learning for normal Ss." He goes on to state that these studies, however, "have not provided insight into the specific process or factor responsible for the retardate deficit."

According to our theory, the serial learning deficit should be found only in primary retardates, since serial learning is a Level I ability closely related to memory span. All of the studies of serial learning reviewed by Goulet were based on groups of retardates among whom could be expected a preponderance of primary retardates. The one study which probably had a relatively smaller proportion of primary retardates was one by Cassell (1957). Cassell selected from a population of 152 retardates the 52 subjects who could read; non-readers were excluded. The 52 retarded Ss who could read showed only a marginal difference from a group of normal children in serial learning ability. Among the retardates, the readers did not differ from the non-readers in IQ. We conjecture that while all were more or less equally deficient in Level II ability, more of the readers were not deficient in Level I ability (i.e., they were secondary retardates) and therefore were of normal ability in serial learning. There can be little doubt that authentic primary familial retardates are markedly deficient in serial learning ability. A study by Jensen (1965a), for example, showed that institutionalized young adult familial retardates were markedly inferior in serial rote learning compared with normal children matched for Stanford-Binet mental age.

Two main types of evidence support the contention that serial learning is essentially a Level I ability. In the first place, normal subjects, when questioned after a serial learning experiment, claim not to resort to the use of strategies, mnemonic devices, mediational techniques, or other "higher level" mental processes in serial rote learning. Their subjective reports of how they learned the serial list are in marked contrast to their reports on paired-associate learning, in which verbal mediational processes play a prominant role in normal adult subjects. Furthermore, neither normals nor retardates show an improvement in serial learning when given special instructions to use verbal mediators in learning the serial list. The same type of instructions, however, greatly facilitate paired-associate learning, relatively more in retardates than in normals (Jensen & Rohwer, 1963a, 1963b). Paired-associates can be learned by means of Level I associative processes, but they also permit the greater play of Level II elaborative processes for subjects who possess these abilities.

Second, Jensen (1965b) has found that individual differences in serial learning are highly correlated with STM for digit series. When a battery of 14 different memory span tests and 17 serial learning measures were factor analyzed together, the loadings of both the memory span and serial learning measures were of approximately the same magnitude on the general factor common to all tests in the battery. Between 67 and 78% of the variance in the various serial tasks and between 67 and 82% of the variance on the memory span tasks was accounted for by the communalities (i.e., the common factor variance).

A series of experiments by Jensen and Roden (1963) showed a relationship between memory span and the degree of skewness of the serial position curve in normal subjects. Subjects with longer memory spans made relatively fewer errors in the first half of the serial position curve than did subjects with shorter memory spans. Since the degree of skewness (i.e., the piling up of errors more toward the end of the serial list during the learning trials prior to mastery) is related to memory span, we should expect from our theory that primary retardates should not only be slower in learning a serial list, but should produce a less skewed serial position curve. Consistent with this prediction, Barnett, Ellis, and Pryer (1960) found a tendency for normal high school students to make relatively more errors for middle items and fewer errors for the beginning items than retarded subjects. The writer tested this hypothesis further by administering an 8-item serial list composed of pictures of familiar objects (i.e., comb, spoon, house, dog, shoe, etc.) to a group of 20 familial mentally retarded (Stanford-Binet IQs between 50 and 70, with a mean of 58) young adults in a state institution for the retarded. No subjects with sensorimotor handicaps or a history or signs of neurological abnormality were included in this sample. Subjects learned by the usual anticipation method. Since the absolute speed of learning was not the essential point of the study, in order to maximize the number who would attain the criterion of mastery (one errorless trial), the serial presentation was subject-paced and subjects were encouraged to guess rather than fail to respond in anticipating each item. Four of the 20 Ss had to be dropped for failure to attain criterion; their repeated failures and mounting frustration after a reasonable length of time made it inadvisable to continue the task. The serial position curve for the remaining 16 Ss who attained criterion, plotted as the mean percentage of total errors occurring at each position, is shown in Fig. 7. This serial position curve is extremely atypical from that of normal subjects. It is quite unlike

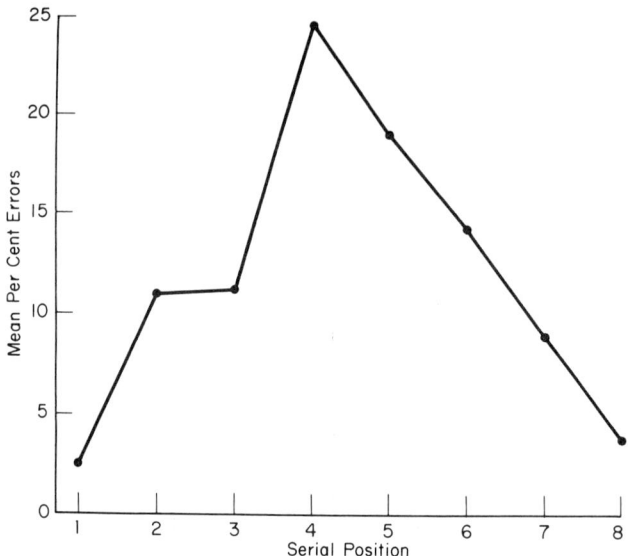

FIG. 7. Serial position curve for 16 primary mentally retarded young adults (IQ 50-70). Note the lack of skewness typically found in the serial position curve of normal subjects.

any the writer has seen in his serial learning experiments with normal subjects or any of the 70 serial position curves he has found in the literature and which closely fit the idealized serial position curve predicted by a theoretical model of serial learning (Jensen, 1962). The serial position curve of the retardates shows none of the skewness of normal serial position curves; the peak of errors comes before the middle of the series rather than just past the middle (i.e., position 4 rather than position 5). It is interesting to note that the best-fitting model of the serial position curve predicts a relative decrease in skewness as the length of the list increases even for normal Ss (Jensen, 1962). An 8-item list for primary retardates is probably the equivalent of a list of 20 or more items for normal Ss. For lists of this length the skewness of the serial position curve even for normal subjects would be hardly perceptible.

One serial learning experiment with retardates used the von Restorff effect (also called the isolation effect) to introduce a Level II factor into the serial learning. It is a well-established phenomenon that causing one item in the middle of a serial list to stand out from the others by making it distinctive in some way results in fewer errors on this distinctive item than if it had not been made distinctive. McManis (1966) made an item distinctive by printing it in red, while the remaining items in the serial list were printed in black. Both retarded and normal subjects showed a reduction of errors on the item isolated by this means. When the item in the same serial position was isolated by making it distinctly different in meaningfulness (inserting a low-meaningful item in a list of high-meaningful items), however, only the normal subjects showed the isolation effect—the retardates did not. The registration of the item's meaningfulness is mainly a Level II process, involving the arousal of the subjects' network of verbal associations. Since these spontaneous associative processes are notably deficient in retardates, this form of item distinctiveness in serial learning did not affect their performance.

E. Paired-Associate Learning

Paired associate (PA) learning apparently differs from serial learning mainly in benefiting to a larger degree from past verbal experience. PA learning can be more influenced by verbal mediational processes than serial learning (Jensen & Rohwer, 1963a). Also, the developmental growth curves for serial and PA learning appear to be markedly different. Serial learning ability reaches an asymptote much earlier in life than PA learning. Jensen and Rohwer (1965), in comparing serial and PA learning in children from kindergarten to twelfth grade, found little improvement in serial learning ability beyond 8 or 9 years of age, while PA learning ability showed improvement up to 18 years of age. Beyond 7 or 8 years of age serial learning is more highly correlated with IQ than with mental age, while the reverse is true for PA learning, which suggests that PA learning benefits more from cumulated past verbal experience. Four out of 7 studies of PA learning in which retardates were compared with normals of the *same mental age* showed no significant difference in learning rate; and 4 out of 9 studies in which the retarded and normal groups were of equal chronological age (and therefore differed both in IQ and MA) showed no significant difference in PA learning (Goulet, 1968). Furthermore, all but one of the studies showing retarded subjects to be inferior to normals in PA learning used institutionalized retardates. These findings support the notion that PA learning is largely a Level I function which is facilitated by amount of prior verbal experience largely associated with age, and may also involve Level II processes (mediational strategies, mnemonic elaboration, etc.) when the learning materials are of an abstract nature or are otherwise such as to evoke Level II processes in the learner. The evocation of Level II processes, however, can hinder as well as facilitate PA learning. Wallace and Underwood (1964) found, for example, that retardates do not suffer interference from *conceptual* similarity among items in the PA list, as do subjects of normal intelligence. This type of interference is clearly associated with Level II processes. Other things being equal, however, *abstractness* of the items in PA learning causes greater difficulty in learning for retardates relative to matched MA normals, for example, paired-pictures versus paired-objects (Iscoe & Semler, 1964; Semler & Iscoe, 1965).

F. Rote Learning, IQ, and Socioeconomic Status

A number of studies by the writer and some of his colleagues and graduate students at Berkeley are explicitly relevant to the theory outlined previously.

The first study in this series (Jensen, 1961) compared groups of Mexican-American and Anglo-American fourth and sixth grade school children of different levels of IQ ranging from 60 to 120 on a number of learning tasks consisting of immediate free recall of a dozen familiar objects, serial learning and paired-associate learning of familiar and abstract objects. On these measures of learning ability, Mexican-American children of low IQ (Mean IQ = 82.89, SD = 5.82) were much faster learners than Anglo-Americans of the same IQ (Mean IQ = 81.78, SD = 3.93). Bright Mexican-Americans (Mean IQ = 117.33, SD = 4.27), on the other hand, showed little difference in learning ability. The relationships for all learning tasks are essentially those summarized in Fig. 6. Teachers of the children in this study remarked that the low IQ Mexican-American children seemed much brighter on the playground than the Anglo-American children of similar IQ, although both low IQ groups performed equally poorly in scholastic subjects. Our interpretation is that most of the Mexican-American group in this range of IQs (73 to 89) are somewhat retarded only in Level II functions, while the Anglo-American group in this IQ range is retarded in both Level I and Level II. (The Level II retardation may be either direct or indirect, that is, due to the functional dependence of Level II processes on the more basic Level I processes.)

Rohwer and Lynch (1968) administered a paired-associate test consisting of 24 picture pairs presented 2 times at a rate of 3 seconds per pair to groups of low SES and middle SES children from kindergarten to sixth grade. More than 90% of the low SES children were Negro; all of the middle SES children were white. The low and middle SES groups have an average IQ difference at the various grade levels of between 15 and 20 points. The difference in their scholastic achievement is even more striking. Many children of the low SES group are described by their teachers as "nonlearners" in the classroom, and the majority of these children lag 2 or 3 grade levels behind middle SES children on standard achievement tests. The performances of these groups on PA learning are shown in Fig. 8. Analysis of variance showed no significant differences between the low and middle SES groups. (The difference between grade levels was significant.) The fact that these 2 groups which differ so markedly in IQ and scholastic performance do not differ on this paired-associate learning task leads to the interpretation that the groups differ in Level II but not in Level I abilities. To check this interpretation, Rohwer and Lynch administered the test under the same conditions to a group of retarded young adults in a state institution for the retarded. All were familial retardates without a history or signs of neurological impairment. The fact that they were in an institution is regarded as indicative that most, probably all, are primary retardates. Their average Stanford-Binet MA of 9.70 (IQ of 59) is equivalent to that of normal children

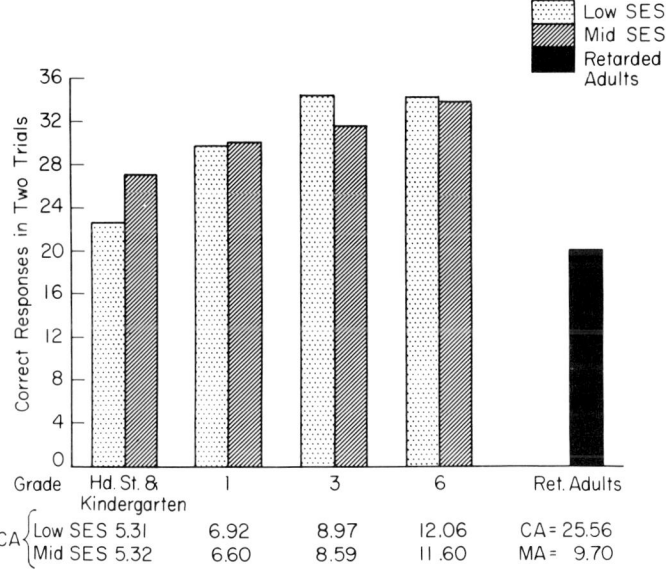

FIG. 8. Comparisons of low and middle socioeconomic groups at various ages with retarded adults on a paired-associate task (24 picture pairs presented two times at a rate of 3 seconds per pair) (from Rohwer, 1967).

in the fifth grade. Yet these retardates showed poorer paired-associate learning ability than the 5-year-old children in Head Start and kindergarten. Also consistent with our hypothesis is the fact that the correlation between PA learning scores and MA (with CA partialed out) is .51 for the middle SES group and .10 for the low SES group. The correlation scatter diagrams of the 2 SES groups show the characteristics depicted in Fig. 4.

In a more recent experiment, Rohwer (1968a) administered four 25-item PA tests (picture-pairs) to groups (total $N = 288$, with 48 in each group) of low SES Negro and upper-middle SES white children in grades K, 1, and 3. These SES groups at all grade levels differed by from about 1.5 to 2 standard deviations (20 to 30 IQ points) on the Peabody Picture Vocabulary IQ and on Raven's *Colored Progressive Matrices*. On the total PA learning score a significant difference between the lower and upper SES groups was found only for the kindergarten children. Rohwer comments

> ... these results suggest that in the development of the kind of learning ability assessed by the PA test, the discrepancy between upper-strata white children and lower-strata Negro children progressively narrows with succeeding grade levels.

Rohwer goes on to note that this is in marked contrast with the results obtained with the PPVT and the Raven, which show increasing divergence between the SES groups from grades K to 3. This is just what would be predicted from the hypothesized growth curves for Level I and Level II processes (depicted in Fig. 5). This is the only study so far that has failed to show a significant SES difference in the correlations between associative learning ability and psychometric intelligence, although the differences are in the predicted direction. The MA correlated with total PA score .64 in the high SES and .52 in the low SES group; IQ correlated with PA .27 and .22 in high and low SES groups, and the corresponding correlations for Raven raw scores were .44 and .41.

A study by Rapier (1968) helps to establish the phenomenon described in Fig. 6 as a function mainly of social class rather than of race, as might be incorrectly interpreted from the fact that most of our experiments have confounded race and SES. When school children are retested on the basis of SES, there will be a preponderance of Negro and Mexican-American children, 8 to 12 years of age, in public schools. She compared low and middle SES children in special classes for the educable mentally retarded (mean Stanford-Binet IQs for low SES was 70.20, SD = 3.64, range = 63–68, and for middle SES 71.45, SD = 4.95, range = 63–78) and low and middle SES children of above-average intelligence in regular classes (IQ for SES 104.5, SD = 3.23, range 100–110, and for middle SES 105.1, SD = 3.70, range = 100–110). There were 20 Ss in each of the 4 groups. All children whose records indicated any sensorimotor, neurological, or emotional disabilities were excluded. (It is an interesting point that Rapier was able to obtain the 20 low SES retarded children from three special classes in one school district but had to canvass 10 special classes in 4 school districts to locate 20 middle SES retarded children.) Serial and PA learning tasks (using pictures of familiar objects) were given to all subjects: 1 serial list and 3 different PA lists administered on 3 different days. (Other experimental variables manipulated in this experiment, involving special instructions to prompt verbal mediation of PA learning, are not central to our present hypothesis.) Rapier's overall results reveal the same relationships as shown in Fig. 6, but, unlike the other studies in our series, the results were in the predicted direction but not significantly so on the first day's serial and PA learning tests. IQ showed a significant effect, but SES and the interaction of IQ × SES were non-significant. On the second day's tests, however, there was a significant IQ × SES interaction, with the low SES retardates and normals showing no appreciable difference in trials to criterion in PA learning (4.6 vs. 4.9) and the middle SES retardates and normals showing a large difference in PA learning trials to criterion 7.7 vs. 4.0). SES, IQ, and SES × IQ were all significant beyond the .01 level on the third day of testing. The normal subjects of the low and middle SES groups did not differ significantly in trials to criterion in PA learning (5.95 vs. 5.10), but the low and middle SES retarded groups differed markedly in learning trials (6.6 vs. 10.1). The learning-to-learn effects of 3 daily sessions on these rote-learning tasks mainly brought about a divergence of the middle and low SES retardates because the middle SES retarded group showed relatively little learning-to-learn (i.e., generalized practice effect).

Also consistent with our hypothesis were Rapier's findings concerning the difference in correlations between IQ and the learning scores for the middle and low SES groups. The average r between intelligence and the learning tests was .44 for the middle SES and .14 for the low SES group; in terms of variance in PA learning accounted for by the variance in the psychometric tests, this represents 19% vs. 2%.

Rohwer, Lynch, Levin, and Suzuki (1968) compared large groups (total $N = 432$) of first, third, and sixth grade children from greatly contrasting high- and low-strata schools. The high-strata school's population was white; the low-strata school's population was Negro. The modal occupational category of fathers of the students in high-strata schools was professional whereas that of fathers of students of low-strata schools was semi-skilled or unskilled manual. The children in the two schools differed widely in psychometric intelligence and achievement. Yet total scores on a variety of PA learning tasks showed no significant difference ($F<1$) between school strata. Rohwer *et al.* state ". . . the average performance of children from low-strata schools was virtually the same as that of children from high-strata schools [p. 19]." This is especially interesting in view of the fact that the relatively low IQs of the low-strata children are commensurate with their generally poor scholastic performance as assessed by standardized tests and the fact that the teachers of these children describe them generally as being "slow to learn and difficult to teach." The PA learning task involves largely Level I ability while the schools' instructional methods apparently rely heavily on Level II abilities—those abilities measured by intelligence tests with a high g loading.

In a study by Jensen and Rohwer (1969), 100 low SES Negro preschool children in day care centers and 100 upper-middle SES white children in private nursery schools, all between 3 and 5 years of age, were given digit span tests, a serial learning test, and four paired-associate learning (both using pictures of familiar objects), along with the Peabody Picture Vocabulary Test as the measure of IQ. The correlation between MA and serial learning was .49 for the high SES and .27 for the low SES; the correlation between MA and the total of four PA tests was .58 for high SES and .20 for low SES. The multiple correlation was determined between MA, on the one hand, and CA, serial learning, PA learning, and digit span, on the other. Corrected for shrinkage, the multiple-R was .66 for the high SES and .42 for the low SES group. This corresponds to 44% and 18% of the variance, respectively. In other words, the Level I tests—learning and memory span (plus CA)—predict more than twice as much of the variance in MA for high SES as for low SES children.

G. Free Recall and Associative Clustering

The technique of free recall as a measure of learning and STM especially lends itself to the investigation of the Level I–Level II distinction. In the free recall of uncategorized lists (abbreviated as FR_u), the subject is presented briefly with a number of items (words, pictures, or objects) and then is asked to recall as many of the names as possible within some specified time limit. A number of experimental parameters can be varied

—the number of items, the types of items, the method and rate of presentation. Usually the items are presented in a new randomized order on each trial. Uncategorized lists are composed of items which are relatively unrelated to one another by any supraordinate concept or category labels. The procedures for free recall of categorized lists (FR_c) is the same as FR_u except that the list is composed of items which can be grouped into two or more perceptual or conceptual categories, usually categories that can be readily given a supraordinate category label, like furniture, musical instruments, food, etc. Perceptual categories are those based on resemblance among items on the basis of qualities that range along various dimensions of primary stimulus generalization, such as color, size, and shape. Conceptual categories are mediated by semantic associations, usually of a hierarchical type involving indirect associations among items via their supraordinate category labels.

Comparisons of the amounts of free recall of categorized and uncategorized lists are most valuable from the standpoint of our theory. It has been argued that the reason that low SES children perform so much better on our Level I learning tasks than would be predicted from their IQs and scholastic performance is that our Level I learning tasks (e.g., digit span, serial and PA learning) are less academic, more "interesting," more "relevant," and therefore more motivating to low SES children than are the usual intelligence tests. To rule out this motivational hypothesis as the explanation for our findings, we need two tasks that are essentially indistinguishable in general appearance and procedure, and thus will not elicit different motivational sets, but also which differ clearly in the extent to which performance on the tasks depends upon Level I and Level II abilities. Free recall of uncategorized and categorized lists meets these requirements. FR_u taps mainly Level I ability, or at least requires nothing more than Level I ability, involving simply the reproduction of the input. FR_c also requires nothing more than Level I ability, but it can also reflect Level II ability, i.e., the transformation of the random order of input into conceptual categories as reflected in the order of the subject's output of the items—the phenomenon known as "clustering." Thus, the random imput may be *chair, shoe, bed,* and *hat*; and if there is clustering according to the supraordinate categories of furniture and clothing, the output order will be *chair bed, shoe hat.* The rearrangement of the random input order on the basis of hierarchically arranged verbal mediators is clearly an abstract, conceptual process of the type that characterizes Level II. The amount of material recalled is increased when clustering is possible. Thus, more material is recalled from categorized than from uncategorized lists, and persons who are high on Level II ability should presumably have a relatively greater advantage over persons with low Level II ability in FR_c as compared with FR_u.

1. ASSOCIATIVE CLUSTERING IN THE MENTALLY RETARDED

Studies of free recall and associative clustering in the retarded have been reviewed by Goulet (1968) and Prehm (1968). Three facts are well established both for normal and for retarded subjects: (*a*) perceptual and conceptual clustering both increase with age; (*b*) there is an increase both in the number of items recalled and in the degree of associative clustering over repeated trials; and (*c*) there is a positive correlation between individual differences in the amount of associative clustering and the number of items recalled.

A number of conclusions can be drawn from studies of the retarded. Retardates show less clustering and poorer recall than normals of the same CA. The results for comparisons of retardates and normals of equal MA are more ambiguous, but most studies indicate that MA is a chief source of variance in clustering; retardates and normals matched on MA show similar degrees of clustering (Goulet, 1968). One study, by Rossi (1963), suggests, however, that the level of MA at which retardate versus normal comparisons are made is an important factor, since clustering tendency increases with increasing MA at a faster rate in normals than in retardates. In general, we have claimed that above 5 or 6 years of age, MA, as measured by standard tests such as the Stanford-Binet, is essentially an index of the individual's developmental status in Level II functioning, and these results of equal-MA comparisons reflect just what we should expect according to this formulation.

Compared with normal persons of equal CA, retardates are found to show not only *quantitative* differences in clustering but also *qualitative* differences (Prehm, 1968). Normal subjects cluster items mainly by supraordinate categories; retardates show more pair-wise coordinate groupings, often of an idiosyncratic nature. For example, *bed* and *shoe* may be recalled together consistently on repeated trials. Other items in the list would usually lead to *bed* and *shoe* being separated by normal subjects into the clusters of *furniture* and *wearing apparel.* The retardates' basis for clustering is a coordinate association rather than hierarchical conceptual associations; for example, he will say *bed* and *shoe* go together because "you put your shoes under your bed."

2. SOCIAL CLASS DIFFERENCES IN ASSOCIATIVE CLUSTERING

How do groups of children differing markedly in Level II ability (e.g., IQ) but not differing appreciably in Level I (e.g., digit span and serial learning) compare in free recall and associative clustering? This question has been investigated in two studies in our laboratory, using subjects drawn from the same subject pool as that used in our other studies comparing low and middle SES groups in Level I and Level II performance. The prediction from our theory was that low and high SES children would differ little in FR_u but would differ markedly in FR_c, and that the SES difference between FR_u and FR_c would be greater with increasing age of the subjects. These predictions, of course, follow directly from the theory of the relationship between SES and Levels I and II.

Glasman (1968) used several 20-item lists of 4 categories each, with 5 items per category. The categories were: animals, foods, furniture, musical instruments, jobs, eating utensils, clothing, and vehicles. The items consisted of models, toys, or other three-dimensional representations of real objects. The 20 items were presented singly for 3 seconds each, in a random order, for 5 trials. After every trial subjects were allowed 2 minutes to verbally recall the items in any order; the S's output was tape-recorded. There were 32 Ss in each of the 4 groups formed by the 2×2 design; Kindergarten vs. 5th Grade and low SES vs. high SES. The low SES group was composed of Negro children from a school in a low SES neighborhood; the high SES group was drawn from an all white school in an upper-middle-class neighborhood. Thus social class and race are confounded in this experiment. The mean IQs (PPVT) of the groups were 90 for low SES and 120 for high SES. The grade levels were matched on IQ. The main results of the study are shown in Figs. 9 and 10. The measure of clustering (Fig. 10) is the one most commonly used in studies of clustering, and is described by Bousfield and Bousfield (1966). A cluster is defined as a sequence of two responses from the same category which are immediately adjacent. The Bousfield formula corrects this value by subtracting the expected value for a random sequence of the items recalled. The results shown in Tables X and XI clearly bear out our theoretical predictions. At Grade 5 the low SES and high SES groups differ by approximately 1 standard deviation, both in recall and in clustering. (The Grades × SES interaction is statistically significant beyond the .05 level for recall and beyond the .001 level for clustering.)

Since FR_c is essentially a Level II function, it should be correlated with MA about equally in both the low and high SES groups. This was what Glasman found. Correlation between MA and amount of *recall* was .62 for low SES and .72 for high SES; the correlation between MA and amount of *clustering* was .76 for low SES and .77 for high SES. The correlations are much higher for fifth Graders than for Kindergartners, who show very little clustering and are presumably still operating in this

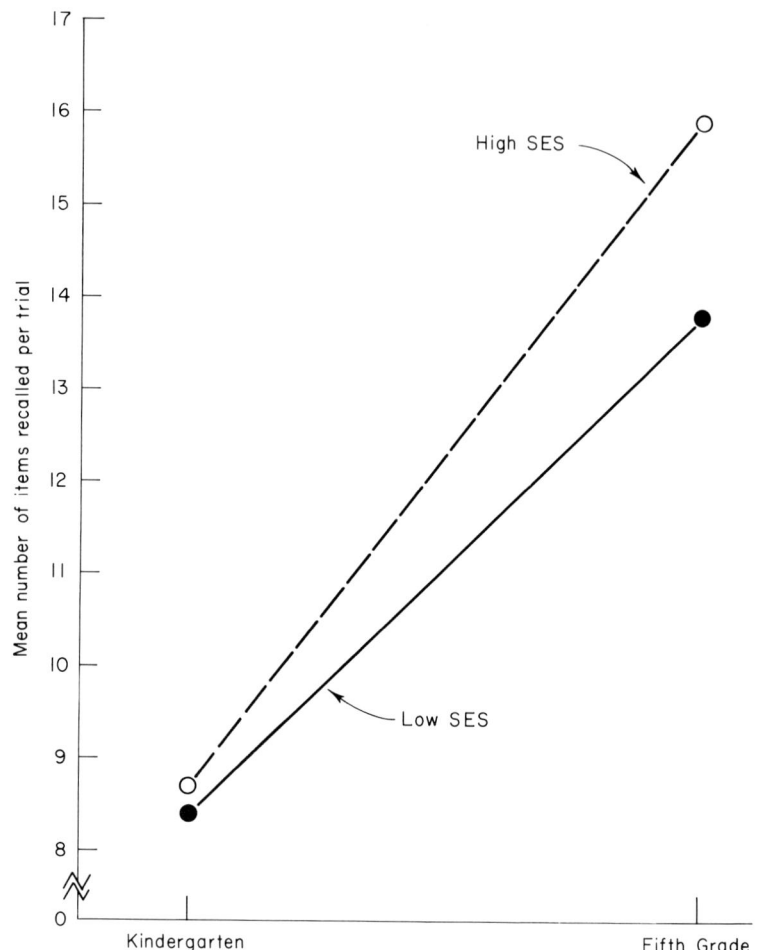

FIG. 9. Mean number of items per trial (over 5 trials) in free recall of a categorized list, as a function of Grade and Socioeconomic Status (SES) (from Glasman, 1968).

task by a Level I process. (The correlation of MA and recall is .06 at Kindergarten and .59 at Grade 5; the correlation between MA and clustering is .02 at Kindergarten and .68 at Grade 5.) These results are highly consistent with predictions based on the hypothetical growth curves for Level I and Level II abilities as a function of SES, shown in Fig. 5. FR_c performance is so strongly related to MA that when the data of Tables X and XI were subjected to an analysis of covariance, with MA as the control variable, all the main effects and the interactions were completely wiped out.

Although Glasman's study demonstrated age and social class differences in the free recall of *categorized* lists, it was not designed to study age and SES differences in performance on the free recall of categorized versus noncategorized lists. A noncategorized list is made up of unrelated or remotely associated items which cannot be readily grouped according to supraordinate categories. Subjective organization of the items in the list is likely to consist of pairs of items related on the basis of pri-

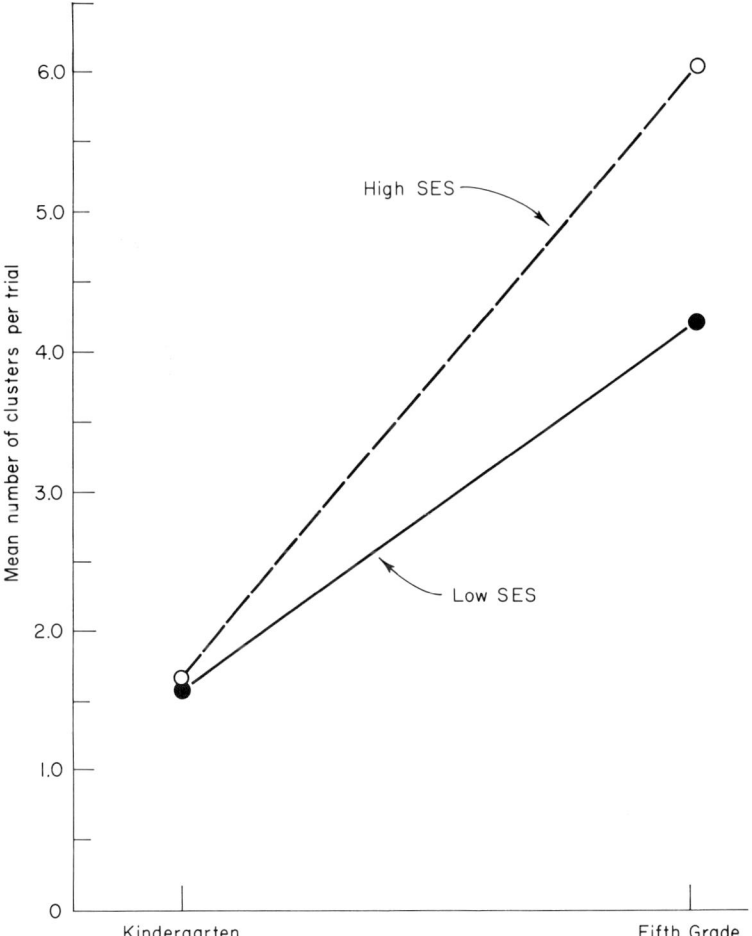

FIG. 10. Mean number of associative clusters per trial (over 5 trials) in the free recall of a categorized list, as a function of Grade and Socioeconomic Status (SES) (from Glasman, 1968).

mary generalization, clang association, or functional relationship. A noncategorized list therefore lends itself less than a categorized list to evoking Level II processes. Consequently, subjects differing in Level II ability (but not in Level I) should show less difference in FR_u than in FR_c.

Jensen and Frederiksen (in press) tested this prediction directly. The low SES and high SES groups were drawn from essentially the same populations as those in the Glasman study, i.e., lower-class Negro and middle- to upper-middle-class white children. The age factor was again investigated by comparing grades 2 and 4. Sets of 20 objects were used for the noncategorized and categorized lists; the 4 categories of the latter were: clothing, tableware, furniture, and animals. Forty Ss received the noncategorized list, consisting of 20 common but unrelated objects, including 1 object from each of the 4 categories of the categorized lists. Forty Ss received the categorized list with the items presented in a random order, and another 40 Ss had the same categorized lists with the items presented in a "blocked" fashion, i.e., all items within a given category are presented in immediate sequence—a procedure which prompts clustering and facilitates recall. Five trials of presentation followed by free recall were given in all conditions. For the categorized lists, the results were essentially the same as those of the Glasman experiment: Grade 4 was superior to Grade 2 under all conditions, and the SES differences were greater at Grade 4 than at Grade 2. Whereas at Kindergarten there was no difference between SES groups, a difference in free recall clearly emerges by Grade 2, in favor of the high SES group. At Grade 4 there is a large interaction between SES level and FR_u vs. FR_c for both random and blocked lists, although the blocked condition reduces the SES difference by boosting the recall performance of the low SES group. In other words, when the input is already categorized and therefore no transformation of the input is called for, the output is facilitated in the low SES group. The high SES group, on the other hand, spontaneously transforms the random input into clustered (i.e., categorized) output and obtains approximately the same facilitation as when the input is already blocked into categories. Recall of the noncategorized list showed a relatively small difference in favor of the high SES group at both second and fourth grades. Also, for the noncategorized list there is no significant interaction between SES and grades—the SES difference is nearly the same at Grades 2 and 4. This is in marked contrast to the categorized lists, which show a large SES × Grades interaction.

All of these findings on free recall are highly consistent with our theory that social class differences in ability involve mainly Level II processes rather than Level I.

V. IMPLICATIONS FOR EDUCATION

If the theory of primary and secondary retardation becomes fully substantiated by further research, it should raise important questions for educational practices. The first question concerns whether different approaches to instruction can yield more optimal effects if they take account of the differences between primary and secondary retardation. It would seem that this distinction should imply quite different techniques and goals of instruction.

Why has traditional schooling been so unsuccessful in teaching children with low IQs but with quite normal Level I learning ability? Many such children do not acquire the basic scholastic skills even in 12 years of schooling. How can one account for this in cases where the child has normal learning ability? One hypothesis is that basic skills are generally taught in such a manner as to make their acquisition heavily dependent upon abstract, conceptual abilities. The criterion of learning in the eyes of many teachers, and the types of pupil performance on which reinforcements from the teacher are contingent, often emphasize the signs of Level II competence—evidence of broad transfer, of broad conceptual generalization of specific learning, of the ability to perform verbal transformations and elaborations on what has been learned, such as being able to "tell it back in your own words" and the ability to say something formally different but conceptually similar. Teachers look for these signs of Level II performance in their pupils. Teachers encourage it, and reward it. The manifestation of Level I ability in its own right is not encouraged or rewarded. It is viewed only as a means to Level II performance. Consequently, the children with the better than average IQs experience a schedule of reinforcements from the teacher and from their perception of their own progress, a schedule of reinforcements which is quite ample for sustaining the behaviors that promote further learning. The low IQ child, on the other hand, even though he may be average or above in Level I learning ability, experiences, in effect, a schedule of non-reinforcement, which results in the experimental extinction of the behaviors that promote learning. One of the major tasks of future research is to determine the full extent to which Level I abilities can be capitalized upon in the teaching of scholastic skills. When Level II performance is made (a) the criterion of learning, (b) the basis for teacher dispensed reinforcement, and (c) the demonstration of having learned by passing achievement tests, the child who is deficient in Level II ability will fail to learn much that could easily be learned by means of Level I.

The writer observed one first grade class of presumably "slow-learning" children called culturally disadvantaged. The majority of these children could not say the alphabet or name the letters of the alphabet. Many apparently could not even discriminate the letters of the alphabet, despite the fact that their teacher had spent part of every school day for 6 months in trying to impart a knowledge of the letters to these children. In their ability to learn school subjects, these children appeared so extremely retarded that the writer suspected primary retardation. The writer's colleague, Dr. William Rohwer, offered to test these children individually on a picture paired-associates learning test which had already been shown to differentiate primary and secondary retardation (see Fig. 9). The children in this class learned, on the average, 16 of the 24 paired-associates in 1 presentation of the list, presented at the rate of 3 seconds per pair. Their performance was completely on a par with that of middle-class children of comparable age in another school who were making normal progress scholastically. Why, then, were the disadvantaged children not learning even letters and simple number facts, to say nothing of reading and writing? Some hours spent in systematic observation of this class and similar classes have led to some psychological speculations that might help to explain these phenomena.

First of all, it was quite apparent that the children's exceedingly poor scholastic performance could not be attributed to any lack of good will, dedication, or effort on the part of the teachers. Furthermore, the teachers had learned well the principle of reinforcement, and readily dispensed encouragement and approval. However, what seemed to be getting reinforced more than anything else was the child's *efforts* rather than his successes. Reinforcing the behaviors that are signs of effort, when the effort does not eventuate in success, indeed increases motivation—but it also leads to frustration. Probably the most potent reinforcement for learning is the child's self-perception of his own *success*, that is, of his own increasing mastery of whatever it is he is attempting to do. Much too few of these instances of success were in evidence in the classes I observed, although the children's effortful but failing attempts at teacher-determined tasks were frequently reinforced by the teacher's well-intentioned praise and approval. Why were there so few opportunities for success? Partly because some of the things being taught were too far beyond the children's present capabilities, but mostly because the teachers seemed to be operating under a preconception of what kinds of behavior constitute learning and should be shaped through reinforcement—it is mainly the child's verbal behavior which evinces Level II processes. Since at the beginning of the term the children were good at Level I associative learning, the teachers tend not to want to "waste their time" on rote activities but instead try to elicit and reinforce almost exclusively those forms of behavior, mostly verbal, which are most characteristic of children with superior IQs. Conceptual brightness, verbally expressed, is the supreme value, even to many devoted teachers who pride themselves on being specialists in teaching the culturally disadvantaged. A child's learning of $2 + 2 = 4$ is perceived as being inferior to learning to solve $2 + ? = 4$. The school places excessive valuation and emphasis on what Sheldon White (1965) has called cognitive learning as contrasted with associative learning. Is this possibly the cause of the seemingly poor scholastic potential of many "disadvantaged" children with normal Level I abilities?

Is there a failure to capitalize on existing Level I abilities? To reinforce effort but not success? To make success dependent on Level II abilities when these are meager or undeveloped in some children? These are the conditions that could produce behavioral consequences reminiscent of phenomena described by Pavlov: experimental extinction, conditional inhibition, and experimental neurosis. Accordingly, when the behaviors that are necessary for learning are repeatedly unreinforced, the behaviors extinguish. In addition, the stimulus conditions under which such extinction takes place become conditioned inhibitors. Not only are conditioned inhibitors the stimuli for not responding, but conditioned inhibitors also become aversive stimuli, from which the subject turns away, either passively or actively. Unresponsiveness, drowsiness, inattentiveness, as well as aimless hyperactivity are some of the symptoms of conditioned inhibition. Nearly all the stimuli in the classroom, and especially the teacher and all those things on which the child must focus his attention—books, papers, pencils, and blackboards—all can become conditioned inhibitors for the kinds of behavior essential for learning. Pavlov found in his attempts to establish differential conditioned responses in dogs that when the discriminative stimuli were so similar as to be beyond the dog's capacity to discriminate them, the dog's behavior deteriorated, a condition that Pavlov called "experimental neurosis." It is a condition that can occur without there being any punishment. It occurs simply by withholding reinforcements when the animal fails to make impossibly difficult discriminations. The dog's behavior becomes unstable, hyperactive, and highly resistant to further training. After an experimental neurosis has developed, even the simplest discriminations, which the dog could normally have learned without difficulty, become inordinately difficult or even impossible for the dog to learn. Itard observed manifestations of this condition in Victor, the wild boy of Aveyron, while training him in color and form matching tasks. When the required discriminations were made too difficult, Victor's once normal responding turned to violent anger (Broadhurst, 1961, p. 728). The writer has observed children's behavior in some elementary school classes that closely resembles the manifestations of extinction, conditioned inhibition, and experimental neurosis as described by Pavlov.

Being importuned simply to "try harder" also could be expected to hinder the emergence of whatever Level II processes the child might otherwise evince in learning and problem solving. The well-established Yerkes-Dodson principle states that the optimum level of motivation for performance on complex tasks is lower than for performance on simple tasks. Consequently, if relatively complex learning and problem solving require Level II processes, and if the degree of motivation and arousal is beyond the optimum level for these complex processes, performance will be hindered, and the less complex Level I processes, being nearer their optimal level of motivation, will predominate over Level II. Since the relationship of the Yerkes-Dodson principle to Level I and Level II functions remains speculative, it points to an important area for future research, viz., the relationship of drive states to the potentiation of Level I and Level II functions.

Undoubtedly the most urgent research for its implications for education concerns the question of the extent to which Level II processes can be acquired through appropriate instruction by children of normal Level I ability. The fact that siblings and unrelated children reared in the same family can differ markedly on measures of Level II ability strongly suggests that individual differences in Level II are not solely a product of environmental influences but probably have a substantial genetic component. But this should not rule out the possibility that at least some aspects of Level II functioning can be learned through Level I processes, especially when these are average or above. Some of the cognitive strategies that can facilitate learning and can be acquired by all children of normal Level I ability have been described by Rohwer (1968b), who is conducting an extensive program of research on instructional methods for inculcating, stimulating, or simulating Level II processes in children who do not evince them spontaneously. It is most important that the many children of seemingly meager educational potential in terms of the traditional criteria, but who evince normal Level I abilities, should be given every opportunity to use these abilities in acquiring the basic skills and in achieving realistic educational and vocational goals. Among the important tasks for future research is the further investigation of the theory here proposed and the discovery of means for making the most of Level I abilities in the educational process.

REFERENCES

Barnett, C. D., Ellis, N. R., & Pryer, M. W. Serial position effects in superior and retarded subjects. *Psychological Reports*, 1960, 7, 111–113.

Barrett, B. H. Behavioral individuality in four cultural-familially retarded brothers. Mimeo, undated.

Bayley, N. Comparisons of mental and motor test scores for ages 1-15 months by sex, birth order, race, geographical location, and education of parents. *Child Development*, 1965, **36**, 379-411. (a)
Bayley, N. Research in child development: A longitudinal perspective. *Merrill-Palmer Quarterly*, 1965, **11**, 183-208. (b)
Bayley, N. Learning in adulthood: The role of intelligence. In H. J. Klausmeier & C. W. Harris (Eds.), *Analyses of concept learning*. New York: Academic Press, 1966. Pp. 117-138.
Bilodeau, E. A. (Ed.) *Acquisition of skill*. New York: Academic Press, 1966.
Bousfield, A. K., & Bousfield, W. A. Measurement of clustering and of sequential constancies in repeated free recall. *Psychological Reports*, 1966, **19**, 935-942.
Broadhurst, P. L. Abnormal animal behavior. In H. J. Eysenck (Ed.), *Handbook of abnormal psychology*. New York: Basic Books, 1961. Pp. 726-763.
Burt, C. The evidence for the concept of intelligence. *British Journal of Educational Psychology*, 1955, **25**, 158-177.
Burt, C., The inheritance of mental ability. *American Psychologist*, 1958, **13**, 1-15.
Burt, C. Class differences in general intelligence: III. *British Journal of Statistical Psychology*, 1959, **12**, 15-33.
Burt, C. Intelligence and social mobility. *British Journal of Statistical Psychology*, 1961, **14**, 3-24. (a)
Burt, C. The gifted child. *British Journal of Statistical Psychology*, 1961, **14**, 123-139. (b)
Burt, C. The genetic determination of differences in intelligence: A study of monozygotic twins reared together and apart. *British Journal of Psychology*, 1966, **57**, 137-153.
Cassell, R. H. Serial verbal learning and retroactive inhibition in aments and children. *Journal of Clinical Psychology*, 1957, **13**, 369-372.
Cattell, R. B. Occupational norms of intelligence and the standardization of an adult intelligence test. *British Journal of Psychology*, 1934, **25**, 1-28.
Cattell, R. B. Theory of fluid and crystalized intelligence: A critical experiment. *Journal of Educational Psychology*, 1963, **54**, 1-22.
Cooper, G. D., York, M. W., Daston, P. G., & Adams, H. B. The Porteus Test and various measures of intelligence with Southern Negro adolescents. *American Journal of Mental Deficiency*, 1967, **71**, 787-792.
Curti, M., Marshall, F. B., Steggerda, M., & Henderson, E. M. The Gesell schedules applied to one-, two-, and three-year old Negro children of Jamaica, B. W. I. *Journal of Comparative and Physiological Psychology*, 1935, **20**, 125-156.
Durham Education Improvement Program, Duke University, 1966-1967. (a)
Durham Education Improvement Program, Research. Durham, North Carolina, 1966 -1967. (b)
Eckland, B. K. Genetics and sociology: A reconsideration. *American Sociological Review*, 1967, **32**, 173-194.
Edgerton, R. B. Anthropology and mental retardation: A plea for the comparative study of incompetence. In H. J. Prehm, L. A. Hamerlynck, & J. E. Crosson (Eds.), *Behavioral research in mental retardation*. Eugene, Oregon: University of Oregon Press, 1968. Pp. 75-87.
Eells, K., Davis, A., Havighurst, R. J., Herrick, V. E., & Tyler, R. *Intelligence and cultural differences*. Chicago: University of Chicago Press, 1951.
Ellis, N. R. The stimulus trace and behavioral inadequacy. In N. R. Ellis (Ed.), *Handbook of mental deficiency*. New York: McGraw-Hill, 1963. Pp. 134-158.

Erlenmeyer-Kimling, L., and Jarvik, L. F. Genetics and intelligence: A review. *Science*, 1963, 142, 1477-1479.
Fuller, J. L., and Thompson, W. R. *Behavior genetics.* New York: Wiley, 1960.
Gagné, R. M. The acquisition of knowledge. *Psychological Review*, 1962, 69, 355-365.
Gagné, R. M. Contributions of learning to human development. *Psychological Review*, 1968, 75, 177-191.
Gates, A. I., & Taylor, G. A. An experimental study of the nature of improvement resulting from practice in mental function. *Journal of Educational Psychology*, 1925, 16, 583-593.
Geber, M., & Dean, R. F. A. Precocious development in newborn African infants. In Y. Brackbill & G. Thompson (Eds.), *Readings in infancy and childhood.* New York: Free Press, 1966.
Glasman, L. D. A social-class comparison of conceptual processes in children's free recall. Unpublished doctoral dissertation, University of California, 1968.
Gottesman, I. I. Genetic aspects of intelligent behavior. In N. R. Ellis (Ed.), *Handbook of mental deficiency.* New York: McGraw-Hill, 1963. Pp. 253-296.
Gottesman, I. I. Biogenetics of race and class. In M. Deutsch, I. Katz, & A. R. Jensen (Eds.), *Social class, race, and psychological development.* New York: Holt, Rinehart & Winston, 1968. Pp. 11-51.
Goulet, L. R. Verbal learning and memory research with retardates: An attempt to assess developmental trends. In N. R. Ellis (Ed.), *International review of research in mental retardation.* Vol. 3. New York: Academic Press, 1968.
Guilford, J. P. *The nature of human intelligence.* New York: McGraw-Hill, 1967.
Hardy, J. B. Perinatal factors and intelligence. In S. F. Osler & R. E. Cooke (Eds.), *The biosocial basis of mental retardation.* Baltimore: Johns Hopkins Press, 1965. Pp. 35-60.
Havighurst, R. J., & Neugarten, B. L. *Society and education.* (3rd ed.) Boston: Allyn & Bacon, 1967.
Heber, R., Dever, R., & Conry, J. The influence of environmental and genetic variables on intellectual development. In H. J. Prehm, L. A. Hamerlynck, & J. E. Crosson (Eds.), *Behavioral research in mental retardation.* Eugene, Oregon: University of Oregon Press, 1968. Pp. 1-23.
Higgins, C., & Sivers, C. A comparison of Stanford-Binet and Colored Raven Progressive Matrices IQ's for children with low socioeconomic status. *Journal of Consulting Psychology*, 1958, 22, 465-468.
Honzik, M. P. Developmental studies of parent-child resemblance in intelligence. *Child Development*, 1957, 28, 215-228.
Huntley, R. M. C. Heritability of intelligence. In J. E. Meade & A. S. Parker (Eds.), *Genetic and environmental factors in human ability.* New York: Plenum Press, 1966. Pp. 201-218.
Iscoe, I., & Semler, I. J. Paired-associate learning in normal and mentally retarded children as a function of four experimental conditions. *Journal of Comparative and Physiological Psychology*, 1964, 57, 387-392.
Jensen, A. R. A statistical note on racial differences in the Progressive Matrices. *Journal of Consulting Psychology*, 1959, 23, 272.
Jensen, A. R. Learning abilities in Mexican-American and Anglo-American children. *California Journal of Educational Research*, 1961, 12, 147-159.
Jensen, A. R. An empirical theory of the serial-position effect. *Journal of Psychology*, 1962, 53, 127-142.
Jensen, A. R. Learning abilities in retarded, average, and gifted children. *Merrill-Palmer Quarterly*, 1963, 9, 123-140.

Jensen, A. R. Rote learning in retarded adults and normal children. *American Journal of Mental Deficiency*, 1965, **69**, 828–834. (a)
Jensen, A. R. Individual differences in learning: Interference factor. Cooperative Research Project No. 1867, U.S. Office of Education, 1965. (b)
Jensen, A. R. The measurement of reactive inhibition in humans. *Journal of General Psychology*, 1966, **75**, 85–93.
Jensen, A. R. Estimation of the limits of heritability of traits by comparison of monozygotic and dizygotic twins. *Proceedings of the National Academy of Sciences, U.S.*, 1967, **58**, 149–157.
Jensen, A. R. Social class, race, and genetics: Implications for education. *American Educational Research Journal*, 1968, **5**, 1–42. (a)
Jensen, A. R. Patterns of mental ability and socioeconomic status. *Proceedings of the National Academy of Sciences, U.S.*, 1968, **60**, 1330–1337. (b)
Jensen, A. R. Another look at culture-fair testing. In *Western regional conference on testing problems, proceedings for 1968. Measurement for educational planning.* Berkeley, Calif.: Educational Testing Service, Western Office, 1968. Pp. 50–104. (c)
Jensen, A. R. How much can we boost IQ and scholastic achievement? *Harvard Educational Review*, 1969, **39**, 1–123.
Jensen, A. R., & Frederiksen, J. Social-class differences in free recall learning. *Journal of Educational Psychology*, in press.
Jensen, A. R., & Roden, A. Memory span and the skewness of the serial-position curve. *British Journal of Psychology*, 1963, **54**, 337–349.
Jensen, A. R., & Rohwer, W. D., Jr. Verbal mediation in paired-associate and serial learning. *Journal of Verbal Learning and Verbal Behavior*, 1963, 1, 346–352. (a)
Jensen, A. R., & Rohwer, W. D., Jr. The effect of verbal mediation on the learning and retention of paired-associates by retarded adults. *American Journal of Mental Deficiency*, 1963, **68**, 80–84. (b)
Jensen, A. R., & Rohwer, W. D., Jr. Syntactical mediation of serial and paired-associate learning as a function of age. *Child Development*, 1965, **36**, 601–608.
Jensen, A. R., & Rohwer, W. D., Jr. Mental retardation, mental age, and learning rate. *Journal of Educational Psychology*, 1968, **59**, 402–403.
Jensen, A. R., & Rohwer, W. D., Jr. Experimental analysis of learning abilities in culturally disadvantaged children. Final Report on OEO Project No. 2404, U.S. Office of Economic Opportunity, 1969.
Jones, H. E. The environment and mental development. In L. Carmichael (Ed.), *Manual of child psychology.* (2nd ed.) New York: Wiley, 1954. Pp. 631–696.
Kagan, J. A developmental approach to conceptual growth. In H. J. Klausmeier & C. W. Harris (Eds.), *Analyses of concept learning.* New York: Academic Press, 1966. Pp. 97–115.
Knobloch, H., & Pasamanick, B. The relationship of race and socioeconomic status to the development of motor behavior patterns in infancy. *Psychiatric Research Reports*, 1958, **10**, 123–133.
Kushlick, A. Assessing the size of the problem of subnormality. In J. E. Meade & A. S. Parkes (Eds.), *Genetic and environmental factors in human ability.* New York: Plenum Press, 1966. Pp. 121–147.
Lawrence, E. M. An investigation into the relation between intelligence and inheritance. *British Journal of Psychology, Monograph Supplement*, 1931, **16**, No. 5.
Leahy, A. M. Nature-nurture and intelligence. *Genetic Psychology Monographs*, 1935, **17**, 241–305.

Masland, R. L., Sarason, S. B., and Gladwin, T. *Mental subnormality.* New York: Basic Books, 1958.
Maxwell, J. *Social implications of the 1947 Scottish Mental Survey.* London: University of London Press, 1953.
McGurk, F. C. J. The culture hypothesis and psychological tests. In R. E. Kuttner (Ed.), *Race and modern science.* New York: Social Science Press, 1967. Pp. 367-381.
McManis, D. L. The von Restorff effect in serial learning by normal and retarded subjects. *American Journal of Mental Deficiency,* 1966, **70,** 569-575.
McNemar, Q. Twin resemblances in motor skills, and the effect of practice thereon. *Journal of Genetic Psychology,* 1933, **42,** 70-97.
Neff, W. S. Socioeconomic status and intelligence: A critical survey. *Psychological Bulletin,* 1938, **35,** 727-757.
Noble, C. E. The learning of psychomobar skills. *Annual Review of Psychology,* 1968, **19,** 203-250.
O'Connor, N., & Hermelin, B. Like and cross modality recognition in subnormal children. *Quarterly Journal of Experimental Psychology,* 1961, **13,** 48-52.
Osborne, R. T. Stability of factor structure for the WISC for normal Negro children from pre-school level to first grade. *Psychological Reports,* 1966, **18,** 655-664.
Prehm, H. J. Rote verbal learning and memory in the retarded. In H. J. Prehm, L. A. Hamerlynck, & J. E. Crosson (Eds.), *Behavioral research in mental retardation.* Eugene, Oregon: University of Oregon, 1968. Pp. 31-43.
Rapier, J. L. Measured intelligence and the ability to learn. *Acta Psychologica,* 1962, **20,** 1-17.
Rapier, J. L. The learning abilities of normal and retarded children as a function of social class. *Journal of Educational Psychology,* 1968, **59,** 102-119.
Reed, E. W., & Reed, S. C. *Mental retardation: A family study.* Philadelphia: Saunders, 1965.
Research Profile No. 11. Summary of progress in childhood disorders of the brain and nervous system. U.S. Public Health Service, Washington, D.C., 1965.
Rimland, B. *Infantile autism.* New York: Appleton-Century-Crofts, 1964.
Roberts, J. A. F. The genetics of mental deficiency. *Eugenics Review,* 1952, **44,** 71-83.
Robinson, H. B., & Robinson, N. M. *The mentally retarded child. A psychological approach.* New York: McGraw-Hill, 1965.
Rohwer, W. D., Jr., Social class differences in the role of linguistic structures in paired associate learning. Cooperative Research Project No. 5-0605, U.S. Office of Education, 1967.
Rohwer, W. D., Jr., Socioeconomic status, intelligence and learning proficiency in children. Paper read at the annual meeting of the American Psychological Association, San Francisco, August, 1968. (a)
Rohwer, W. D., Jr. Mental mnemonics in early learning. *Teachers College Record,* 1968, **70,** 213-226. (b)
Rohwer, W. D., Jr., & Lynch, S. Retardation, school strata, and learning proficiency. *American Journal of Mental Deficiency,* 1968, **73,** 91-96.
Rohwer, W. D., Jr., Lynch, S., Levin, J. R., & Suzuki, N. Grade level, school strata, and learning efficiency. *Journal of Educational Psychology,* 1968, **59,** 26-31.
Rossi, E. L. Associative clustering in normal and retarded children. *American Journal of Mental Deficiency,* 1963, **67,** 691-699.
Semler, I. J., & Iscoe, I. Concept interference and paired-associates in retarded children. *Journal of Comparative and Physiological Psychology,* 1965, **60,** 465-466.
Shields, J. *Monozygotic twins brought up apart and brought up together.* London: Oxford University Press, 1962.

Shields, J., & Slater, E. Heredity and psychological abnormality. In H. J. Eysenck (Ed.), *Handbook of abnormal psychology.* New York: Basic Books, 1961. Pp. 298–343.
Shuey, A. M. *The testing of Negro intelligence.* (2nd ed.) New York: Social Science Press, 1966.
Sperrazzo, G., & Wilkins, W. L. Further normative data on the Progressive Matrices. *Journal of Consulting Psychology,* 1958, **22,** 35–37.
Sperrazzo, G., & Wilkins, W. L. Racial differences on Progressive Matrices. *Journal of Consulting Psychology,* 1959, **23,** 273–274.
Talland, G. A. *Deranged memory: A psychonomic study of the amnesic syndrome.* New York: Academic Press, 1965.
Terman, L. M., & Merrill, M. A. *Stanford-Binet Intelligence Scale: Manual for the third revision, Form L-M.* Boston: Houghton Mifflin, 1960.
Terman, L. M., & Oden, M. *The gifted group at mid-life.* Stanford: Stanford University Press, 1959.
Tyler, L. E. *The psychology of human differences.* (3rd ed.) New York: Appleton-Century-Crofts, 1965.
Vernon, P. E. *The structure of human abilities.* New York: Wiley, 1950.
Wallace, W. P., & Underwood, B. J. Implicit responses and the role of intralist similarity in verbal learning by normal and retarded subjects. *Journal of Educational Psychology,* 1964, **55,** 362–370.
Walters, C. E. Comparative development of Negro and white infants. *Journal of Genetic Psychology,* 1967, **110,** 243–251.
Wechsler, D. *Manual of the Wechsler Intelligence Scale for Children.* New York: Psychological Corporation, 1949.
Wechsler, D. *The measurement and appraisal of adult intelligence.* (4th ed.) Baltimore: Williams & Wilkins, 1958.
White, S. H. Evidence for a hierarchical arrangement of learning processes. In L. P. Lipsitt & C. C. Spiker (Eds.), *Advances in child development and behavior.* Vol. 2. New York: Academic Press, 1965. Pp. 187–220.
Willerman, L., & Churchill, J. A. Intelligence and birth weight in identical twins. *Child Development,* 1967, **38,** 623–629.
Wright, L., & Hearn, C. B., Jr. Reactive inhibition in normals and defectives as measured from a common performance criterion. *Journal of General Psychology,* 1964, **71,** 57–64.
Young, M., and Gibson, J. B. Social mobility and fertility. In J. E. Meade & A. S. Parkes (Eds.), *Biological aspects of social problems.* Edinburgh: Oliver & Boyd, 1965.
Zeaman, D. Learning processes of the mentally retarded. In S. F. Osler & R. E. Cooke (Eds.), *The biosocial basis of mental retardation.* Baltimore: Johns Hopkins Press, 1965. Pp. 107–127.
Zeaman, D., & House, B. J. The relation of IQ and learning. In R. M. Gagné (Ed.), *Learning and individual differences.* Columbus, Ohio: Merrill, 1967.

Inhibition Deficits in Retardate Learning and Attention

LAIRD W. HEAL
GEORGE PEABODY COLLEGE FOR TEACHERS, NASHVILLE, TENNESSEE

AND

JOHN T. JOHNSON, JR.
MEMPHIS STATE UNIVERSITY, MEMPHIS, TENNESSEE

I. Definitions and Rationale 107
  A. Definition of Inhibition 108
  B. Contrast Groups and the Assessment of Inhibitory Deficits 109
II. The Inhibition of Learned Responses and Internal Inhibition 111
  A. Extinction 111
  B. Differentiation 113
  C. Inhibition of Transfer or Transfer Suppression 119
III. Inhibition of Attention to Stimulus Input and External Inhibition .. 130
  A. The Orienting Reflex (OR) and Inhibition of Attention to Stimuli 130
  B. Satiation Phenomena 133
  C. Distraction (External Inhibition) in Instrumental Learning 136
IV. Conclusions and Speculations about Individual Differences in Learning Processes 141
  A. Response Inhibition 141
  B. Stimulus Inhibition 142
  C. Abstraction 143
  D. Encoding 143
  E. Rigidity 143
  References 144

I. DEFINITIONS AND RATIONALE

The question in mental retardation research that is probably generic to all others is, "How are retardates abnormal?" This question immediately suggests the research strategy of comparing "retardates" and "normals" in order to see how they differ. The implicit, if not explicit, goal of this developmental-comparative strategy is to identify basic learning processes that correlate with intellectual development [mental age (MA) and/or intelligence quotient (IQ)]. The usual procedure has been to compare "retardates" and "normals" on a class of tasks that appear on a priori grounds to require the same learning process. If performance on a class of these tasks bears a consistent relationship to MA or IQ (i.e., if retardates and normals differ) then the underlying learning process is assumed to be a crucial component of intellectual development.

One such process is inhibition. Over the past decade, several investigators have attempted to relate this construct to intellectual development (Denny, 1964; Diamond, Balvin, & Diamond, 1963; Heal, Ross, & Sanders, 1966; Luria, 1963; Ross, 1966; Scott, 1969; Siegel & Foshee, 1960). As is the case with many verbal labels that serve as pretheoretical constructs, the speculations regarding the role of inhibition in mental retardation vary broadly. At the extreme Diamond, Balvin, and Diamond argue that inhibition is a global manifestation of the underlying neurophysiology of the organism, and that it is *the* mechanism that modulates all intelligent behavior. A neural deficiency would, they argue, result in an organism with global behavioral inhibition deficits. Conversely, the organism with global behavioral deficits must necessarily be deficient in his inhibitory neural processes.

In contrast to Diamond *et al.*, the present paper avoids neurophysiological speculation and also resists temptation to consider a priori that all facets of inhibition are necessarily correlated. Instead, classes and subclasses of research operations are considered separately. Evidence for an inhibitory deficit in the retarded is considered for each of these.

A. Definition of Inhibition

For present purposes inhibition is defined as withholding a response or suppressing stimulus input when such action is adaptive. Four clarifications of this definition should be made. First, inhibition is a hypothetical construct to be defined in terms of antecedent and consequent events. Inhibition itself is not observable: it must be inferred from a change in behavior that is occasioned by a change in the environment. In contrast to the usual learning constructs, the change is not an increase in the measured responsiveness but rather a decrease. Second, inhibition is defined as adaptive. For present purposes behavior is regarded as adaptive if it maximizes the amount of reward per unit of response output. Since inhibition is usually studied in some kind of extinction paradigm, this adaptiveness is usually defined in terms of the reduction in response output when the reward is reduced to zero. Third, this definition implies that there is a baseline against which any reduction (inhibition) of behavior is assessed. Furthermore, there must be a baseline of normal inhibitory behavior to which the retardates' "non-inhibitory" behavior can be compared. The determination of this baseline will be discussed in Section I,B.

Fourth, stimulus inhibition is distinguished from response inhibition, but it is defined in very similar terms. Attention to a stimulus must be inferred from a publicly observable behavioral index and inhibition of attention must be inferred from a decrease in this index. For instance, one problem is to assess the degree to which a subject inhibits attention to stimuli that are extraneous to the task before him. The study of figural aftereffects offers one solution to this problem, if it can be assumed that the subject who shows figural aftereffects is one who is successful in inhibiting such maladaptive attention to distracting stimuli.

B. Contrast Groups and the Assessment of Inhibitory Deficits

Inhibition has been defined as an adaptive reduction in responding. The first step in assessing an inhibitory deficit in a particular setting is to establish the amount of inhibition that is considered normal. The retardate would be considered deficient in inhibition if he failed to achieve this level.

1. RATIONALE FOR THE MENTAL AGE (MA) OR EQUAL-ABILITY CONTROL POPULATION

The position of the present paper is that if the goal of a research effort is to identify the learning processes that are crucial to an overall intellectual deficit, then the deficient organism should be compared to his non-deficient peer who is at the same overall level of intellectual development (i.e., at the same MA). If MA can be conceived as a composite of learning processes and learning products, then retardates and their MA peers would be expected to differ on the composition of their overall MA scores. The retardate, with his greater experience, would be expected to score relatively high on those tasks that tap products of experience; the normal MA peer, on the other hand, would be expected to score relatively low on the products tasks and relatively high on tasks that depend upon learning processes. If the performance of the MA peer surpasses that of the retardate, then the task is believed to tap some crucial learning process.

The use of MA as a matching measure for a learning task is, of course, very crude. It is much more desirable to match populations on an index that has a closer correspondence to the task that will be used to compare them. For instance, if the dependent variable of interest is the number of errors on a discrimination transfer task, then populations should probably be matched on a discrimination task that closely resembles the one on which they will be compared. This kind of matching tends to equate populations on incentive value of the reward used and motivation in the laboratory setting in addition to the ability to perform the experimental task and experience with such a task. A matching variable should always be used as a covariate in the analysis of covariance in order to eliminate the bias against the experimental hypothesis that is inherent in matched groups designs (Stanley, 1967).

The interpretation of retardate-normal differences seems quite straightforward in the case of the MA or ability match. If the populations differ on some task despite such matching, it is concluded that retardates are deficient in the learning process(es) required by the task. For example, if retardates match normals' performance on a two-choice discrimination, but do more poorly on a reversal of the discrimination, it can be argued that retardates are less able than normals to inhibit a habit when such inhibition is required to maximize reward. Furthermore, it can be argued that this deficit is specific to the transfer task and cannot be attributed to a deficit in overall learning ability, motivation, or other factors that are peculiar to the testing situation. A corollary of this interpretation is that a process found to be deficient in the retardate is important for learning in the normal subject.

It is important to realize that there is an alternative to this interpretation of the performance of ability-matched populations. Groups matched on MA or ability, but differing in IQ, must necessarily differ on a number of dimensions that have nothing to do with what is usually called intelligence. For instance, retardate and normal MA peers would be expected to differ on shoe size; yet few would insist that shoe size be taken as an index of some crucial learning process. This ludicrous example points out the weakness of the assumption that is usually made in the interpretation of performance differences in ability-matched groups. It is always possible that retardate-normal differences might be a function of differential experience or physical development and not a function of differential intelligence.

2. Relevance of the Chronological Age (CA) Match

The "shoe size" phenomenon makes clear the necessity of comparing retardates to their CA peers as well as their MA peers in cases where the behavior in question might be a characteristic of general development or experience rather than intellectual development per se. If retardates are found inferior to both their MA and CA peers on some task, then it is no longer possible to argue that observed differences are due to the immaturity of the MA peers.

This consideration prompted the inclusion in the current review of much research for which a comparison was made or implied between retardates and their CA peers as well as their MA peers.

II. THE INHIBITION OF LEARNED RESPONSES AND INTERNAL INHIBITION

This review is divided into two major divisions: inhibition of learned responses and inhibition of attention to extraneous stimuli. Historically these have close ties, respectively, to the internal and external inhibition of Pavlov. Internal inhibition was learned to stimuli that were a part of the learning situation; external inhibition was occasioned by the introduction of stimuli that were extraneous to the conditioning stimuli. Response inhibition is discussed in the present section; stimulus inhibition is discussed in Section III.

Two classes of internal inhibition identified by Pavlov, extinction and differentiation, serve as points of unification of a considerable body of literature. A third class, inhibition of transfer or transfer suppression, is closely related to the inhibition of extinction. Transfer suppression refers to the suppression of old learning that is no longer maximally rewarded. In other words, transfer suppression is to transfer learning what extinction is to simple learning.

A. Extinction

Extinction or partial reinforcement effects in classical conditioning are embarrassing to the Pavlovian concept of internal inhibition. The extinction curves obtained in eyelid conditioning, instead of demonstrating the gradual decline indicative of the accumulation of inhibition, show precipitous drops after three or four trials. The finding that groups receiving partial reinforcement are more resistant to extinction than those receiving continuous reinforcement creates similar problems.

A series of studies (e.g., Spence & Platt, 1967) provided evidence that the inferior performance under partial reinforcement in acquisition and the precipitous drop of extinction curves were a function of the formation of a cognitive inhibitory set based on the discriminability of nonreinforced trials from reinforced trials. Thus a cognitive inhibitory set, not Pavlovian conditioned inhibition, was used to explain the effects of partial reinforcement in both acquisition and extinction. While the above definition of inhibition (Section I,A) did not distinguish between inhibition that was under verbal control and inhibition that was not, it will probably be useful to make this distinction as our sophistication with the construct develops.

The literature comparing retardates and normals tends to support the hypothesis that retardates are poor inhibitors. Mateer (1918), as reported by Denny (1964), compared 50 normals (CA = 2 to 7) and 14 retardates (CA = 3 to 7.9; MA = 1 to 7) on classical conditioning.

> The simple, even crude, conditioning set-up consisted of sliding a blindfold over the subject's eyes (CS), waiting 10 seconds and placing a small piece of chocolate candy in his mouth (US), and recording kymographically the CR (opening of the mouth before the ten seconds had elapsed) . . . . The criterion of conditioning was two CR's in succession. Twenty-four hours later, conditioning was given to the same criterion . . . (relearning, which was . . .) followed immediately by extinction to a criterion of failing to make the CR twice in a row, followed terminally by reconditioning to the original criterion [Denny, 1964, p. 102].

While there was no difference in acquisition, the retardates extinguished more slowly than the normals, indicating a slower development of inhibition.

This finding of slower retardate extinction has held up fairly well over the years. Ross, Koski, and Yaeger (1964) compared 48 college students and 40 institutionalized retardates in an eyelid situation under conditions of partial ($\overline{MA} = 35.0$; $\overline{CA} = 23.6$; $\overline{IQ} = 19.9$) and continuous ($\overline{MA} = 34.2$; $\overline{CA} = 17.2$; $\overline{IQ} = 18.0$) reinforcement. Each subject was given 110 acquisition trials and 40 extinction trials over a period of 3 days. Retardate performance was not different under the two reinforcement contingencies in either acquisition or extinction, while normals showed the better acquisition and faster extinction that is usually associated with continuous reinforcement. There is a striking parallel between retardates' performance in this study and normals' performance in the Spence and Platt study, where inhibitory set was presumably controlled by disguising the task.

Ross, Headrick, and MacKay (1967) compared two CA levels ($\overline{CA} = 50.6$; $N = 10$ and $\overline{CA} = 93.2$; $N = 10$) of institutionalized Mongoloid children on acquisition and extinction of the conditioned eyelid response. Half the subjects in each group were conditioned with a 500 millisecond (msec) interstimulus interval (ISI) and the other half with a 3000 msec ISI. Each subject was given 80 continuously reinforced acquisition trials followed by 25 extinction trials. The trials were spread over a 6-day period. The only acquisition occurred under the 5000 msec ISI, with the older group reaching a superior level. There was some indication that the younger group extinguished more slowly. However, due to the presence of non-learners, who created a floor effect for the younger group, this difference could not be satisfactorily analyzed.

Johnson (1968) examined the correlation between IQ and performance in classical eyelid conditioning. Children of fourth grade age were randomly selected for either continuous ($N = 30$; $\overline{CA} = 134.9$; $\overline{IQ} = 92.9$)

or partial ($N = 30$; $\overline{CA} = 136.7$; $\overline{IQ} = 86.7$) reinforcement. Each subject was given 60 acquisition trials followed by 30 extinction trials. No significant correlations with IQ were found for either group in acquisition or extinction.

Baumeister, Beedle, and Urquhart (1964) compared 40 institutionalized retardates ($\overline{IQ} = 48.7$; $\overline{CA} = 42.4$) and 29 normals ($\overline{CA} = 29.2$) on galvanic skin response (GSR) conditioning. Ten habituation trials (tone alone) were followed by 20 trials in which a tone was followed by shock, and 10 extinction (tone alone) trials. The analysis revealed no difference between normals and retardates in the number of GSRs given in extinction.

Lobb (1967) compared acquisition and extinction of the GSR in 110 institutionalized retardates (CA = 18 to 30) and 110 institutional personnel of presumed normal intelligence. Each subject was given 32 acquisition trials for which the CS was a 4000 Hz (or cps) tone. Half of these were reinforced with a shock. Acquisition was followed in 24 hours by 20 extinction trials. It was found that while normals responded more in acquisition, the retardates extinguished more slowly. However, in a later paper, Lobb (1968) pointed out that the extinction differences could have been due to acquisition differences or lack of recognition of non-reinforcement as well as an inhibitory deficit.

In conclusion, there is good evidence that retardates extinguish a classically conditioned eyelid response more slowly than normals. However, this extinction appears to be a function of an inhibitory set based on recognition of non-reinforcement rather than classical Pavlovian internal inhibition. It appears that retardates do not form this set as readily as normals. At least two factors could contribute to this deficiency: failure to recognize stimulus change, a topic to be discussed in Section III, or failure to withhold a response. The studies in GSR conditioning failed to provide any impressive support for a retardate inhibitory deficiency. It should be noted that none of the studies in classical conditioning was conducted with subjects who were matched on MA.

Two studies (Johnson, 1966; Semler, 1965) indicated that the retardate has no decrement in the ability to extinguish an instrumental habit. However, more evidence is required to establish the generality of this conclusion.

B. Differentiation

1. DIFFERENTIAL CLASSICAL CONDITIONING

In differential classical conditioning, the subject is given successive presentations of two conditioning stimuli, one of which (the CS+) is always followed by a stimulus (the US) that unconditionally elicits a known response.

Gynther (1957) demonstrated in a series of studies of differential eyelid conditioning that an important factor in differentiation is the accumulation of inhibition to the CS—. This inhibition is not only evidenced by differentiation, but, as the CS+ and CS— are brought closer together, by a decrease in level of responding to the CS+, presumably due to generalization of inhibition from the CS—. The ultimate case of closeness of the stimuli is partial reinforcement, in which the role of inhibition has been previously discussed. Classical differential conditioning, therefore, should detect a difference in the inhibitory processes in the retardate.

Ohlrich and Ross (1968) examined acquisition and differentiation of the eyelid response in 32 normal ($\overline{MA} = 84$; $\overline{CA} = 83$) and 32 retarded ($\overline{MA} = 84$; $\overline{CA} = 159$) children matched on MA. Each subject was given a sequence of 60 single-cue, continuously reinforced acquisition trials; 90 trials of differential conditioning; and 30 trials after the cue values were reversed. Half of the subjects in each group were conditioned under an ISI of 500 msec, and the other half under 800 msec. Both the retardate and normal 800 ISI groups responded differentially, but only the normals appeared to have *learned* the differentiation. The response decrement of the normals to the CS— developed gradually over trials, suggesting that these subjects increasingly inhibited their responding to the CS— as differential learning progressed. The corresponding decrement of the retardates appeared full-blown on the first block of CS— trials, suggesting that their "inhibition" was primarily an artifact of the generalization decrement from the CS+ to the CS—. No reversal was shown by any group. The same procedures with adults have yielded both differentiation and reversal. The authors suggested that the results of the study demonstrated that the presumed inhibitory processes necessary for differentiation and reversal are lacking in normal children relative to adults and in retardates relative to normals of the same MA.

A series of studies reported by Ohlrich (1968) indicated that the classical differential eyelid conditioning of retardates is inferior to that of normals. The CSs were tones and the US was a puff of air delivered to the eye. Thirty-six institutionalized retardates ($\overline{MA} = 84.3$; $\overline{CA} = 188.8$) were given 60 trials of differential eyelid conditioning with an ISI of 500, 800, or 1100 msec. No differential conditioning was obtained at any interval. Even when these subjects were given 200 additional trials, the differential conditioning which was obtained at the 800 and 1100 ISIs was inferior to that of a group of college students given 100 trials.

Ohlrich's (1968) failure to find differential eyelid conditioning in retardates is in essential agreement with the results of Johnson and Heal (1967). Forty-eight institutionalized retardates ($\overline{MA} = 143$; $\overline{CA} = 348$; $\overline{IQ} = 38$) were given 100 trials of differential conditioning using tone CSs and airpuff USs. Twelve subjects were conditioned under each of four

CS-UCS ISIs (500, 800, 1100, or 1400 msec), six with a 1000 Hz tone reinforced and six with a 2000 Hz tone reinforced. When the ISI was 500 msec and the 1000 Hz tone positive, significant differentiation was obtained. Differentiation was not significant under any other conditions.

It must be concluded that differentiation of the eyelid response in retardates is obtained only under optimal conditions. Even if obtained, the differentiation is inferior to that of CA and MA peers. This failure to differentiate is consistent with the hypothesis that the retardate is deficient in the ability to inhibit his response to the unreinforced CS.

2. INSTRUMENTAL DISCRIMINATION LEARNING

The most popular variation of instrumental discrimination learning is the two-choice simultaneous discrimination, for which the choice of one cue is associated with reward and the choice of the other with nonreward or with punishment. The usual interpretation of the learning that occurs in the simultaneous discrimination is that the subject learns to excite a response to the rewarded cue and inhibit a response to the nonrewarded cue. Zeaman and House (1962, Experiment 3) suggested that this interpretation is indeed the appropriate one. Nineteen institutionalized retardates (MA = 20 to 72; CA = 81 to 179), only two of whom were experimentally naive, were tested on a Wisconsin General Test Apparatus (WGTA) with common objects as stimuli. All subjects were tested under two conditions. For both conditions three two-choice problems were given simultaneously. One of these conditions required the subject to respond to cue configurations rather than to "positiveness" and "negativeness" of cues. That is, the subject was required to select cue A when it appeared with cue B, select B when it appeared with C, and select C when it appeared with A. The second (control) condition was an ambiguous cue problem that will be described below. Zeaman and House found that none of the 19 subjects scored above chance on the configurational problems while 13 scored above chance on at least one of the control problems. While a more appropriate control condition could be proposed, the conclusion to be drawn from this experiment is difficult to challenge: retardates are able to solve three problems simultaneously when the approach and avoidance tendencies learned to specific cues do not interfere with one another in the different problems, but they are unable to do so when these tendencies conflict with one another in the different problems. There seems to be no alternative to the explanation that a subject learns a two-choice discrimination by selection of the rewarded cue and/or inhibiting selection of the nonrewarded cue.

If this interpretation is correct, then an inhibitory deficit could result in a discrimination learning deficit. It should be quickly noted that a discrimination deficit does not necessarily imply an inhibition deficit. Indeed, many plausible explanations are available. A discrimination deficit might imply: a disposition to attend to stimulus classes other than the one that is correlated with reward and nonreward (Zeaman & House, 1963); a state of social deprivation that makes the subject more interested in interacting with the experimenter than with the task (Harter, 1967); a state of social discomfort that prevents maximal performance (Boice, 1966); a low drive to work for the incentives of the task (Zigler & deLabry, 1962); etc. Furthermore, it is possible that an organism with an inhibitory deficit would develop compensatory mechanisms in order to cope with the multitude of different discriminations that are required in daily living. Nevertheless, the most straightforward assumption is that if an organism has an inhibitory deficit, he will be deficient in solving simultaneous discrimination problems, which depend in part on the inhibition of one or more responses. Recent reviews of retardate discrimination learning (Denny, 1964; House & Zeaman, 1960; Stevenson, 1963) preclude an extensive review here. Suffice it to say that these reviewers concluded (Stevenson with reluctance, Denny with assurance, and House and Zeaman with enthusiasm) that the retardate lags behind his normal MA peer in the ability to perform two-choice simultaneous discrimination problems, and therefore may be deficient in his inhibitory learning processes.

3. Role of the Negative Cue in the Instrumental Discrimination Deficit of Retardates

If the retardate is deficient in instrumental discrimination learning, then the next step is to investigate the possibility that this deficit results from his failure to avoid the negative (non-rewarded) cue. While this question is simple conceptually, its translation into operation is fraught with problems.

a. Cue-Substitution Paradigms. Most research that has attempted to deal with this question has compared a task for which the positive (rewarded) cue has been replaced with a task for which the negative (nonrewarded or punished) cue has been replaced. The non-replaced cue has usually been kept intact. If the intact positive is associated with a smaller decrement in performance than the intact negative, then approach processes are assumed to dominate in the discrimination solution. However, there is an inevitable confound in every cue-substitution study. The replacing or novel cue is positive when it replaces the positive cue and negative when it replaces the negative. If this novel cue affects performance in its own right, then it will have an indeterminate but differential effect in the intact-positive as opposed to the intact-negative condition. An experiment by Heal *et al.* (1966) illustrates this confounding more clearly. Thirty-six retardates ($\overline{\text{MA}} = 6\text{-}4$, $\overline{\text{CA}} = 14\text{-}3$) and 36 normals ($\overline{\text{MA}} = 6\text{-}4$;

CA = 5-4) were compared on three two-stage transfer problems: positive-cue-retained-and-reversed, negative-cue-retained-and-reversed, and a standard reversal. Colors were projected from the rear onto two 3-inch-square screens. Subjects were instructed to move a response lever in a horizontal slot toward the color that was rewarded with an M&M, and away from the one that was punished with a loud buzzer. The results showed that while the retardates generally performed more poorly than the normals, the impairment was not diminished under the negative reversal. (It should have been according to the inhibition deficit hypothesis.) However, these results were made difficult to interpret by the significant number of correct responses on the first Stage 2 trial of the partial reversals. These spontaneous reversals tended to be made more by retardates than normals and more under the positive-cue-reversed (novelty chosen) than under the negative-cue-reversed (novelty not chosen) condition. Thus, the novel cue seemed to influence performance in a way that would minimize retardates' apparent inhibitory deficit.

A review of the cue substitution literature[1] lends little support to the hypothesis that retardates learn less about the negative cue (inhibit less) than normals in a simultaneous discrimination. The studies showing less effective use of the negative cue by retardates (Eimas, 1964; House & Zeaman, 1963) had no normal comparison groups and the studies that had normal comparison groups (Heal, 1966; Heal *et al.* 1966) failed to show differential cue utilization for either population. The only evidence that retardates might be deficient in learning to avoid the negative cue is based on a comparison across two studies (Eimas, 1964, 1965) that differed procedurally. On the other hand, a study by Spence (1966), which compared correct-response feedback with incorrect-response feedback, provided support for the hypothesis that normals make better use of negative feedback than do their retarded MA peers.

b. The Ambiguous Cue Problem. A second paradigm to study approach and avoidance in retardates' discrimination learning, the ambiguous cue paradigm, was first used by Zeaman and House (1962). Twenty-two institutionalized retardates (MA = 32 to 72; CA = 106 to 219; IQ = 17 to 60) were tested on a WGTA with colored geometric forms or common objects as stimuli. Each subject was required to solve a problem for which three cues were used: the positive, the negative, and the ambiguous. A third of the trials featured two additional cues in a standard two-choice discrimination. On another third of the trials the ambiguous cue was paired with the positive, and on a final third it was paired with the nega-

---

[1] This detailed review was cut from an earlier draft of this chapter and is available on request from the first author under the title, "Inhibitory Deficits in the Discrimination Learning of Retardates."

tive. Finding that retardates did better on negative-cue-present trials than on positive-cue-present, the Zeamans concluded, somewhat paradoxically, that their retardates depended more on approach than avoidance tendencies. They reasoned that if the retardate lacks inhibition, then he must learn to approach the ambiguous cue on negative-cue trials and the positive on positive-cue trials. Thus, positive-cue trials constitute an approach-approach conflict. These trials would tend to be harder than the negative-cue trials, which contrast a sometimes-rewarded ambiguous and a neutral (non-inhibited) negative cue. Zeaman and House noted marked individual differences with some subjects making fewer errors on negative-cue trials, some on positive-cue trials, and some making equal numbers of errors on the two types of trials. Unfortunately, no correlations with MA or IQ were reported.

Support for the Zeamans' interpretation that superior negative cue performance is indicative of inhibitory weakness is given by Heal, Kral, and Headrick (1968) who replicated the ambiguous cue problem using culturally deprived 5-year-olds (MA = 40 to 75; CA = 62 to 72; IQ = 58 to 114) from a preschool enrichment program. White geometric forms and their colored backgrounds were projected from the rear onto 3- by 4-inch screens, which the subject was instructed to press. Correct responses were rewarded with a doorchime, and incorrect responses were punished with a buzzer. The results were very similar to those of Zeaman and House. Negative-cue-present trials were significantly easier than positive-cue-present trials, and there were very large individual differences in the relative difficulty of the two kinds of trials. To improve interpretability, all three stimuli were presented for a non-feedback choice on every seventh trial. From the Zeamans' conclusion that better negative-cue performance implied a weakness of inhibitory processes, it would follow that the difference between negative-cue and positive-cue trials should correlate with the proportion of ambiguous cue choices: the approach learner should see the positive-cue-present trial as an approach-approach conflict and should often choose the ambiguous cue on choice trials. The avoidance learner should see the negative-cue-present problem as an avoidance-avoidance conflict and should seldom choose the ambiguous cue on choice trials. Heal, Kral, and Headrick found that the ambiguous cue choices correlated significantly with the difference between negative-cue and positive-cue errors (.69 uncorrected for attenuation) indicating that the Zeamans were correct in their interpretation. Having established that the superiority of negative-cue trials was probably an indicator of relative inhibitory weakness, Heal et al. correlated this superiority with mental age to see if there was a relationship between intelligence and this inhibitory weakness. Finding a correlation of .02, they concluded that there was no evidence to support the proposed association between inhibition and intelligence.

These two studies must be interpreted as detrimental to the inhibitory deficit hypothesis. First, despite differences in apparatus and procedures, the results are very similar for the Zeamans' institutionalized retardates and the MA-matched 5 year olds of Heal *et al.* Second, and more important, MA was not correlated with the difference between negative-cue-present and positive-cue-present trials within the 5-year-old group. While the narrow MA range would tend to restrict the size of the correlation, there is no suggestion that the low correlation in the present case would increase appreciably with an extended range.

Despite the failure of the ambiguous cue problem to reveal differences in inhibition that could be attributed to intelligence, it is clearly a reliable measure of a subject's tendency to approach or avoid during the learning of a two-choice simultaneous discrimination problem. It appears to offer much as a methodology for the study of individual differences in inhibitory processes, whether or not these processes are correlated with intelligence.

In summary, there is only meager evidence of a retardate deficit in the ability to inhibit responding to the negative cue. When the negative and positive cues are replaced by novel cues, the results tend to show that retardates rely more on the positive than on the negative cue, but the data showing that their reliance is greater than normals' are inconsistent at best.

C. Inhibition of Transfer or Transfer Suppression

Considerable evidence has accumulated over the last decade to suggest that the ability to suppress transfer is crucial for much learning. That is to say, much learning requires the learner to ignore prior learning; much learning can proceed only if prior learning is abandoned. Gonzalez, Behrend, and Bitterman (1967), for instance, have shown that a major difference between pigeons and phylogenetically inferior goldfish is that pigeons forget from one day to the next which cue has been rewarded while goldfish remember. (Successive discrimination reversals were given on successive days.) Similarly, Riopelle (1953) presented very convincing evidence that as a monkey develops learning set, it increasingly suppresses transfer ("forgets" which cue is rewarded) from one problem to the next. It is somewhat ironic that transfer suppression should be considered an adaptive process. However, in situations where there is likely to be negative transfer, it is important that the subject be able to inhibit his prior learning and begin his new learning from zero rather than "in the hole." Several subclasses of experiments seem relevant to this topic.

1. TRANSFER SUPPRESSION IN DISCRIMINATION LEARNING

If retardates have difficulty suppressing transfer in discrimination shifts, then they should show greater evidence of original learning than normals when they are transferred to a new problem. In negative transfer paradigms the retardate, with his presumed inhibitory deficit, should consistently show greater negative transfer than his normal MA peer.

a. Response-Defined Strategies and Transfer Suppression. Perhaps the most direct assessment of discrimination learning and transfer can be done by monitoring a subject's responding during the pre-solution period of a learning task. It has long been known that this responding is not random, but indeed shows systematic patterns from which a subject's hypotheses or strategies can be inferred (Krechevsky, 1938; Levine, 1963).

The importance of these strategies cannot be stressed too much. In the first place, it is only through these that inhibition, as it is defined in the present paper, can be examined in the instrumental learning situation. If the research goal is to test the retardate's ability to inhibit or suppress transfer, then the dependent variable should be the occurrence of response-defined strategies that are appropriate to the pre-transfer task. Errors or trials to criterion communicate little about the rate at which these are inhibited during the course of transfer learning.

b. Discrimination Reversal. One of the most direct tests of the transfer suppression hypothesis is the comparison of retardates and normals on discrimination reversal. The learning of a reversal necessarily requires the subject to abandon the performance of his old habit. There are, of course, several processes other than inhibition that are assumed to influence reversal learning. It might be that retardates are less frustrated by nonreward than normals (see Longstreth, 1966, for a study of the application of frustration theory to extinction in retarded and normal children). Or it might be that retardates are more rigid than normals (Kounin, 1941). In contrast to the transfer suppression hypothesis, which states that retardates are less able than their MA peers to inhibit one habit after they have learned another, the Lewin-Kounin hypothesis is that retardates are less likely to slip spontaneously from a current habit into a prior one. Thus Kounin would predict that retardates would take longer than their MA peers to make the first correct reversal response, but once they had learned a reversal they would be less likely to show pre-reversal strategies and make errors. Finally, discrimination reversal is, after all, a special case of discrimination learning. All the alternatives (attention, motivation, etc.) that might account for the discrimination learning deficit (Section II,B,2) might be invoked to account for a discrimination reversal deficit unless populations are matched on a discrimination learning task rather than on MA.

Table I presents the 12 studies of discrimination reversal in which subjects were matched on MA. Inspection of this table leads to several interesting conclusions. First, there is persuasive evidence that the retardate is inferior to his MA peer in the ability to perform a discrimination reversal. Of the 12 studies shown in Table I, 8 showed some evidence that the normals were superior (Balla & Zigler, 1964; Heal, 1966; Heal et al., 1966; Heal & Johnson, 1968; Penney, Croskery, & Allen, 1962; Plenderleith, 1956; Sanders, Ross, & Heal, 1965; Yaeger, 1964); 2 failed to find a significant difference between the two populations (Milgram & Furth, 1964; Stevenson & Zigler, 1957); and 2 suggested that the retardates were superior (Kounin, 1941; O'Connor & Hermelin, 1959). Of the 25 specific comparisons made in these studies 9 found evidence for normal superiority, 13 found evidence for no difference between the two populations, and 3 showed the retardates to be superior.

While the transfer suppression hypothesis is supported most strongly by a finding of normal superiority on a discrimination reversal, failure to find retardate-normal differences is no particular embarrassment, since it could be blamed on insufficient technical precision (a Type II error). However, the finding of retardate superiority (Kounin, 1941; O'Connor & Hermelin, 1959) cannot be rejected so glibly.

The Kounin study was especially interesting in that it was the only one for which the transfer suppression hypothesis and the Lewin-Kounin rigidity hypothesis made different predictions. Kounin assumed that a subject who had been instructed to reverse would replace his prior habit with a new one. He reasoned that the instructed retardate would be less likely than the instructed normal to slip back into his pre-reversal behavior. Thus, Kounin was able to account for the apparent paradox that his retardates did better than normals when they were instructed to reverse, but more poorly than normals on a classification shift (see Section II,C,1,c) for which the instructions to shift did not explicitly provide a new habit.

Unlike Kounin, O'Connor and Hermelin (1959) did not instruct their subjects to reverse. The significant superiority of retardates in this study is therefore embarrassing to Kounin's rigidity hypothesis as well as the transfer suppression hypothesis. However, Balla and Zigler (1964) followed the procedures of O'Connor and Hermelin in considerable detail and found that the normals did significantly better, suggesting that the anomalous finding of the prior study was not reliable.

It is noteworthy that both two-choice studies (Heal, 1966; Heal & Johnson, 1968) which manipulated levels of prereversal training found some evidence that the normal superiority is enhanced by increasing

TABLE I
DISCRIMINATION REVERSAL STUDIES IN RETARDATES AND THEIR NORMAL MA PEERS

Author	N	Group	MA	CA	Results		Interpretation		Relevant stimuli
					Stage 1	Stage 2	Stage 1	Stage 2	
Kounin (1941)	21	OR	69 to 94	29-3 to 53-9		24		N>YR≥OR	Position
	21	YR	72 to 96	10-10 to 17-0		57			
	21	N	72 to 96	6-0 to 7-9		140			
Plenderleith	15	R−1	71.0	122.7	27.4	7.2	N=R	N=R	Picture pairs
(1956)	15	N−1	69.7	62.1	21.9	6.9			
	15	R−42	68.8	128.6	27.4	13.1	N=R	N<R	
	15	N−42	66.4	62.5	24.8	6.7			
Stevenson	10	OR−5	5.2 to 7.0	19.8 to 54.0	24.0	18.6			Black blocks
& Zigler (1957)	10	OR−5+30			21.3	16.3			(size)
	10	YR−5	4.9 to 7.0	8.8 to 14.3	22.7	18.4	N=YR=OR	N=YR=OR	
	10	YR−5+30			23.7	22.1			
	10	N−5	4.7 to 7.6	4.6 to 5.8	20.0	15.5			
	10	N−5+30			21.0	21.0			
O'Connor	10	R	58	11.5	39.6	11.0			Black
& Hermelin	10	RV	58	11.5	25.1	39.6	N=RV=R	N=RV>R	squares (size)
(1959)	10	N		5.1	31.5	25.4			
Penney et al.	12	R100	8.4	11.1		50.8		N100<R100	Projected
(1962)	12	R50				52.5			forms
	12	N100	8.5	8.4		73.3		N50=R50	
	12	N50				50.4			
Balla & Zigler	5	FR5	5.0	11.2	4.13	4.51	N=FR=BD	N<FR≤BD	Black
(1964)	5	FR6	6.5	14.1	2.76	2.86			squares (size)
	5	BD5	5.0	15.6	5.03	4.98			
	5	BD6	6.4	18.2	2.45	4.99			
	5	N5	5.1	4.6	2.47	1.87			
	5	N6	6.4	6.0	2.16	2.13			
	5	FR5	5.1	12.5	2.57	3.92	N=FR=BD	N=FR=BD	Black
	5	FR6	6.6	13.5	2.46	3.71			blocks (size)
	5	BD5	5.2	13.6	3.24	3.64			
	5	BD6	6.3	13.6	4.97	4.41			
	5	N5	5.1	4.8	3.03	4.07			
	5	N6	6.4	6.4	4.71	3.91			
Milgram	≈12	R6P	5.5 to 7		≈1.20	2.64	N=R	N=R	Size, color,
& Furth (1964)	≈12	R9P	8.5 to 10		≈1.68	2.12	N=R	N=R	or shape of
	≈12	N6P		6 to 7	≈1.20	2.45			blocks and
	≈12	N9P		8 to 10	≈1.68	2.23			position
	≈12	R6D	5.5 to 7		≈1.20	4.42	N=R	N=R	
	≈12	R9D	8.5 to 10		≈1.68	2.61	N=R	N=R	
	≈12	N6D		6 to 7	≈1.20	2.91			
	≈12	N9D		8 to 10	≈1.68	1.94			
Yaeger (1964)	10	RL	40.6	250.7	≈87	≈29	NL≥RL	N<R	Light-on or
	10	RNL			≈69	≈50			light-off
	10	NL	60.3	49.8	≈68	≈66	NNL=RNL		
	10	NNL			≈60	≈62			
Sanders, Ross,	16	R	115.5	($\overline{IQ}$=70.7)	≈24	≈15.0	N=R	N≤R	Color or
& Heal (1965)	16	N	124.4	($\overline{IQ}$=110.4)	≈23	≈7.5			form blocks
Heal et al.	36	R	6-4	14-3	2.52	5.36	N=R	N<R	Colored
(1966)	36	N	6-4	5-4	1.61	2.28			panels
Heal (1966)	24	R6	Matched on	16-5 to 28-6	2.46	9%	N=R	N6=R6	Color or
		R6+40	discrimi-			10%			form
	24	N6	nation	5-4 to 6-4	2.46	11%		N+<R+	
		N6+40	learning			2%			
Heal &	10	R5	(IQ=31 to 64)	14-8 to 53-8	45.5	48		N5=R5	Form
Johnson	10	R20				53			
(1968)	14	N5	5-1 to 12-4	6-6 to 9-6	50.4	36	N=R	N20<R20	
	14	N20				22			

Key: FR = Familial Retardates; BD = Brain damaged Retardates; OR = Old Retardates; YR = Young Retardates; V = Verbalization of relevant cue required; N<R = Normals' performance is superior to retardates' on the reversal task at the .05 level; ≤ = .1

Irrelevant stimuli	Reward (punishment)	Method	Stage 1 (learning) criterion	Stage 2 (reversal) criterion	Dependent variable
None	Marbles	Lever pressed down as fast as possible for marble reward. Correction. Lever was pulled up for reversal	90 resp.	60 resp.	Errors
Position	Charms	Simultaneous discrimination of picture pairs. Retrained and reversed after 1 or 42 days. Noncorrection	5 consec. corr. on trials 2-6 of 3 successive problems	Same criterion as St. 1	Errors
Position	Paper tokens	Simultaneous 3-choice size discrimination using wooden blocks. Noncorrection	5 consec. corr. or 5 corr. + 30 trials overtraining	30 trials	Corr. resp. (10 = chance)
Position	Candy	Choice of 1 of 2 cards to uncover candy in ash tray. Noncorrection. Gp RV required to verbalize during learning. Institutionalized retardates	10 consec. corr.	10 consec. corr.	Trials
Position	Marbles	Single cue rewarded 50% for half the Ss. Form cues projected onto panels which the subject pressed. Novel positive cue added for reversal.	20 resp.	20 resp.	% corr. (50 = chance)
Position	Marbles	Replication of O'Connor & Hermelin (1959). 2-choice simultaneous discrimination. Noncorrection. Institutionalized retardates	8 consec. corr.	8 consec. corr. or 90 trials	$\sqrt{\text{Errors}}$
Position	Marbles	Replication of Stevenson & Zigler (1957). 3-choice simultaneous discrimination. Noncorrection. Institutionalized retardates	5 consec. corr.	5 consec. corr. or 90 trials	$\sqrt{\text{Errors}}$
The two that were not relevant.	Verbal feedback regarding right and wrong	3-choice simultaneous discrimination. Position and a cue from 1 dimension were redundant in St. 1. Either the position or the redundant cue was reversed in St. 2, the nonreversed cue becoming irrelevant. Correction procedure. Noninstitutionalized retardates	6 consec. corr. or 72 trials	6 consec. corr. or 72 trials	$\sqrt{\text{Errors}}$
None	Cocoa Puffs	S raised a lever when light-on (L) or light-off (NL) occurred in St. 1. Reverse contingency in St. 2. Free responding situation	15 min 1st day 5 min 2nd day	10 min 2nd day	(a) % corr. resp. (b) Resp. amplitude (see Sect. II,B,2)
Position and form or color	Cocoa Puffs	2-choice simultaneous discrimination. Noncorrection. Institutionalized and noninstitutionalized retardates	10 consec. corr.	15 consec. corr.	Errors
Position	M&Ms (buzzer)	Lever was moved horizontally toward correct cue. 1/3 of Ss had positive cue replaced; 1/3 had negative replaced; and 1/3 had neither replaced for the reversal problem. Noncorrection. Institutionalized retardates	6 consec. corr.	17 trials	Errors on trials 2-17
Position and form or color	Doorchime (buzzer)	Cues were projected onto panels which S pressed. Each S was given both the 6-criterion and the 6 + 40 overtraining condition. Institutionalized retardates	6 consec. corr.	20 trials	Stage 1: $\sqrt{\text{Errors}+.5}$ St. 2: % errors on trials 4-20
Color and position	Doorchime (buzzer)	Cues were projected onto panels which S pressed. Half of each group was given an OL criterion of 5 and half a criterion of 20. Noncorrection. Institutionalized retardates	5 consec. corr. 20 consec. corr. 5 consec. corr. 20 consec. corr.	10 consec. corr. or 100 trials	St. 1: Trials to last error St. 2: Total trials

level; = = Not significantly different; ≈ = Data are approximate, estimated from figures, etc.; consec. corr. = consecutive correct; corr. = correct; resp. = responses.
Note: The meaning of numbers following a group label is implied under Method.

amounts of this training. One interpretation of this finding is that the retardate finds it harder to suppress or inhibit a habit that has been overtrained.

The go:no-go discrimination of Yaeger (1964) should have been especially sensitive to an inhibitory deficit, since the correct response during negative-cue (S-delta) periods was to *withhold* a response. Yaeger's retardates were clearly inferior to her normals despite the fact that retardates were, if anything, superior in learning the original discrimination.

Several tentative conclusions are suggested by this review. First, there seems to be ample evidence that normals perform a two-choice discrimination reversal more easily than their retardate MA peers. Furthermore, most of the studies that showed a reversal decrement did not show a decrement on the pre-reversal problem. Thus, it is unlikely that motivation, cue differentiation, social interaction, incentive, etc., are crucial factors in the reversal deficit. Instead, it must be assumed that some process crucial to reversal learning is deficient in the retardate. Second, there is some suggestion that this deficit is in flexibility rather than inhibition. While these notions have never been explicitly pitted against one another, the study for which they make different predictions (Kounin, 1941, instructed reversal) favored a flexibility deficit.

c. Shifts in Categorizing Stimuli from one Stimulus Class to Another. Another negative transfer paradigm that has received considerable attention is the extra-dimensional shift. This shift requires the subject to classify or sort stimuli on the basis of one dimension (e.g. form) after he has been trained to classify or sort them on the basis of a different dimension (e.g. color). For instance, a subject might be given colored shapes and asked to put all the red objects in one pile and all the green in another (Stage 1) and then asked to put all the square objects in one pile and the round ones in another (Stage 2). For maximum interference between the two stages, it is critical that the same cues be used for the pre-shift and the post-shift problems. According to the transfer suppression hypothesis, retardates would have difficulty inhibiting Stage 1 learning as they learn Stage 2.

A review of the classification shift literature (see footnote 1, p. 117) indicates greater difficulty for the retardate than his normal MA peer in shifting the dimension by which he classifies stimuli (Bolles, 1937; Heal, 1964, 1966; Kounin, 1941; Zigler & deLabry, 1962, verbal feedback condition), although there have been several failures to replicate this finding (Kern, 1967; Sanders, Ross, & Heal, 1965; Stevenson & Zigler, 1957, Experiment 2; Weaver & Dixon, 1965; Zigler & deLabry, 1962, token reward condition; Zigler & Unell, 1962). The Sanders *et al.* finding that retardates surpassed normals is especially perplexing. Her study differed from the others in that it was a simultaneous two-choice discrimination using stereo-metric cues that were both replaced at the time of the shift; whereas the other studies had three choices (Stevenson & Zigler, 1957), used planometric stimuli that were not both replaced (Heal, 1964, 1966), or employed a sorting task (all others). It may be critical that both of Sanders' relevant cues were replaced at the time of the shift. If the retardate tends to respond primarily on the basis of the global cue compounds and not on the basis of attention to the relevant component attributes of cues, then cue replacement would free him from the negative transfer that would impair the shift performance of his normal MA peer, who would presumably be disposed to attend to the originally relevant dimension regardless of whether or not cues had been replaced. This interpretation must be regarded as speculative, however, especially since Heal (1964, 1966) replaced one of his cues (either the positive or negative) at the time of the shift and found normal superiority.

2. Proactive and Retroactive Inhibition

Proactive and retroactive inhibition paradigms seem ideally suited for the investigation of an inhibition deficit in the retardate. An impairment in current learning that can be attributed to some prior learning is called proactive inhibition. An impairment in current relearning that can be attributed to some learning that has followed original learning is called retroactive inhibition. Proactive inhibition is perhaps the more interesting of the two. According to Briggs (1954), List 1 responses are unlearned or extinguished as List 2 responses are learned. If unlearning, like extinction in classical conditioning, is a function of inhibition, then a deficit in the retardate should be reflected in less unlearning of, and greater interference by, the List 1 responses in List 2. The paradox resulting is that the retardate's proactive inhibition should be greater than the normal's because of his poor unlearning.

Johnson and Blake (1960) compared 80 public school retardates ($\overline{MA}$ =111.6; $\overline{CA}$=164.8; $\overline{IQ}$=68) with 80 normals ($\overline{MA}$=111.6; $\overline{CA}$=107.3; $\overline{IQ}$ =104.4). The original task was the pairing of the first 9 letters of the alphabet with randomly assigned numerals 1 through 9. The intervening list consisted of the same letters and numbers re-paired. The lists were presented in a booklet with 9 lists per page and a total of 10 pages. The subject was allowed 45 seconds per page and 30 seconds between pages. Half of the subjects in each group were given the intervening list and half were read a story before relearning the original lists. No difference was found in the proactive inhibition of the normals and retardates when the analysis was made on the difference between the rates of learning the original and intervening lists. When the difference score was computed by subtracting the control groups' relearning scores from the experimental groups' intervening learning scores, the normals, but not the retardates, demonstrated proactive interference. Both results were in opposition to the hypothesis of greater proactive interference in the retardate.

Iscoe and Semler (1964) compared 48 normals ($\overline{MA}$=6.47; $\overline{CA}$=5.93) and 48 institutionalized retardates ($\overline{MA}$=6.64; $\overline{CA}$=12.19) on the learning of 6 pairs that were conceptually compatible (e.g., banana-orange; glove-shoe) or incompatible (e.g., banana-shoe; glove-orange). The paired associates were learned by the anticipation method to a criterion of two perfect recitations of the list or 12 total list presentations. It was found that when pairs were incompatible the retardates' rate of learning over trials was impaired more than normals'. This result indicates an inability in the retardate to break or inhibit familiar associations.

In a similar study, Milgram and Furth (1966) compared 20 non-institutionalized educable retardates (MA=5.5 to 6.0; CA=8 to 11; IQ=60 to 75) with 40 of their MA peers (CA=6 to 7) as well as 51 trainable retardates (MA=4 to 7; CA=11 to 25; IQ=25 to 45) with 20 of their MA peers (CA=3 to 5) on a four-item paired-associates task. For each pair, the stimulus was a colored rectangle and the response was the selection of one colored toy from among the four that appeared on every trial. About half of each population learned a list of incompatible associates (e.g., black-green tree, green-black locomotive) and the other half a list of compatible associates. A correction procedure was used. With the incompatible pairs, the four populations took about the same number of trials to learn. With the compatible pairs, the low-MA retardates and the younger normals did about the same as they had with the incompatible pairs, but the high-MA retardates and older normals did significantly better. It is a little troublesome that the interference errors (color-compatible responses on the incompatible list) were not significantly greater than the non-interference errors. These results suggest that the higher MA groups (1) were better learners and (2) were more influenced by the compatibility of stimuli and responses. This second finding appears to contradict that of Iscoe and Semler, which indicated more interference from incompatible associations in subjects having lower intelligence. This contradiction is perhaps resolved by Milgram and Furth's proposal that their low-MA subjects, whose MA's were well below those of Iscoe and Semler's subjects, had not reached the level of development required for them to use the colors as mnemonic learning tools.

Borkowski (1965) divided a group of females in a maternity ward into two groups, one with IQs above 95 (N=30; $\overline{CA}$=33.7; $\overline{IQ}$=102.8) and another with IQs below 91 (N=30; $\overline{CA}$=24.7; $\overline{IQ}$=81.9). Immediate recall for individual items was tested using a list of six trigrams, three with a retention interval of 3 seconds and three with an interval of 15 seconds. Subjects read two-digit numbers between presentation and recall to prevent rehearsal. The low group's accuracy of recall declined steadily with increasing items (increasing proactive interference) at the 15-second interval but improved at the 3-second interval. The high group's overall accuracy of recall at either interval approximated that of the low group at the 3-second interval. At the longer interval, then, the low-IQ group demonstrated greater proactive interference than the high-IQ group. The differential increase in intrusion errors at 15 seconds in the low-IQ group was attributed to their inability to discriminate among items. In terms of the current review they could not inhibit previous items. Similar results were obtained from a second study which compared 30 retardates ($\overline{IQ}$=63.7; $\overline{MA}$=10.3; $\overline{CA}$=25.7) and 30 normals ($\overline{IQ}$=104.4; $\overline{MA}$=10.5; $\overline{CA}$=10.1) using lists of bigrams. At 4 seconds normals and retardates did not differ regardless of number of previous items. At 16 seconds normal-retardate differences increased with increases in number of proactive items. Again the number of intrusion errors appeared to be greater for retardates than for normals, indicating an inability to inhibit previously learned responses.

Briggs' (1954) study indicated that retroactive inhibition is a function of the extinction of List-1 responses as List-2 responses are learned. If the retardate has difficulty in inhibiting old associations, an equal number of trials on List 2 should result in less unlearning in retardates than in normals. Therefore, it might be expected that those studies which give a set number of trials on List 2 would demonstrate less retroactive inhibition in retardates. On the other hand, the studies which use the criterion of number of correct responses on List 2 would maximize the likelihood of showing greater retroactive inhibition in retardates.

Johnson and Blake (1960), in the study previously mentioned, also compared the normals and retardates in reference to differential effects of retroactive inhibition. No difference was found between the relearning slopes of the retardate experimental and control groups. For the normals, however, the experimental group relearned the list significantly slower than the control group. Thus, retroactive interference was demonstrated in normals but not retardates. Cassell (1957) tested three groups of 26 males, matched on mental age, using a memory drum to present serial lists of familiar words. The normal group had a mean CA of 9.4, and the organic and non-organic groups of retardates had mean CAs of 20. One hundred retardates were eliminated from the study because they could not read the list. Each subject learned the experimental list of six familiar words to a criterion of one perfect recitation. Then an interpolated list which had two new words and words from the original list was learned, also to a criterion of one perfect recitation. After learning the interpolated list, the original list was relearned. The results indicated significant retroactive inhibition for all subjects but no difference between normals and retardates or between the two groups of retardates in the amount of retroactive inhibition.

Fagan (1966) compared seven non-institutionalized retardates ($\overline{CA}$=137.7; $\overline{MA}$=103.3; $\overline{IQ}$=75.3) with seven normals ($\overline{CA}$=107.3; $\overline{MA}$=107.6; $\overline{IQ}$=100.3) on short-term retention and retroactive inhibition. Besides being matched on MA, the groups were also matched on sex and socioeconomic class (upper middle). Each child was given a four-digit sequence and asked to recall it after an interval that was either void or filled with an interpolated task. The interpolated task consisted of naming the colors of either four or eight cards. Five delay conditions were varied within subjects: no delay, a delay resulting from four interpolated cards, a blank interval comparable in time to four cards, a delay resulting from eight interpolated cards, and a void interval comparable in time to eight interpolated cards. Each child was given four different random sequences of these conditions for a total of 20 trials. In recall the subject was given one point for each correctly recalled digit and another point for each digit recalled in the correct position. Significant retroactive inhibition occurred for all subjects. However, normals and retardates did not differ in retroactive inhibition.

Fagan (1968) compared the effects of retroactive inhibition in non-institutionalized retardates ($\overline{CA}$=142.5; $\overline{MA}$=104.2; $\overline{IQ}$=73.9; N=13) matched on sex and MA with two groups of normals ($\overline{CA}$=102.5 and 101.2; $\overline{MA}$=104.4 and 104.0; $\overline{IQ}$=102.1 and 102.5; N=13 in each group). Each subject was given 24 trials on a digit span task. The length of the span for the retardates and one normal group was 5 digits. The other normal group had a 6-digit span in an attempt to equate the level of immediate recall with that of the retardates. The 24 trials were divided into 3 blocks of 8. For 1 block of trials the recall was requested 2 seconds after the presentation of the last digit. In the other 2 blocks recall was delayed 10 seconds and the last 8 seconds were filled with interference. The low interference consisted of a "humming" noise and the high interference consisted of the repetition of 4 "color words." Neither type of retroactive inhibition produced any differential effects among the IQ groups when item recall (correct serial position not scored) was the measure in analysis. When correctness of serial position was included in the recall measure, the retardates were found to be significantly superior to the normals under the low interference condition. A non-significant trend toward retardate superiority was also present in the high interference group. This evidence suggests that the retardates learned the material as well as the normals and showed less retroactive inhibition.

Three studies of interest compared the retroactive inhibition of normals and retardates matched on chronological age. Pryer (1960) in a serial learning task presented 10 highly familiar nouns to 75 institutionalized retardates ($\overline{CA}$=22.1; $\overline{IQ}$=59.5) and 75 high school students ($\overline{CA}$=16.1; $\overline{IQ}$=102.7). The subjects learned an original and an intervening list of 10 nouns to a criterion of one perfect recitation. The intervening list was presented either 30 seconds, 5 minutes, 30 minutes, or 2 hours following the original list. The first list was relearned 24 hours following the original learning. One group of subjects within each IQ range relearned the original list without any intervening list. After covariance adjustments for differences in original learning, the superiority of the normals' percent savings scores failed to reach significance. Thus, no difference in retroactive inhibition between the normals and their retarded CA peers was demonstrated.

Baumeister, Hawkins, and Holland (1967b) compared the retroactive inhibition of 24 institutionalized retarded women ($\overline{IQ}$=40.2; $\overline{CA}$=27) and 24 normal women ($\overline{CA}$=27.7). Each subject was presented with a list of digits whose length was one digit longer than the span that she could correctly recall 50% of the time. The interpolated task was the recall of either another digit (similar) or letter (dissimilar) list. The subject was given either 0, 1, 2, or 3 trials of interpolated material between each trial of learning. Each subject was given 25 trials under each condition. Neither the amount nor the type of retroactive interference was found to differentially affect the 2 intelligence groups.

In a study by McManis (1967) 32 institutionalized retardates ($\overline{IQ}$=73.2; $\overline{CA}$=17-4) and 32 college students (CA=17 to 21) learned a list of 8 paired associates (words) to a criterion of one perfect recitation. Both groups were then given 20 trials on a second list before relearning List 1 for 10 trials. Half of each group was given the list sequence, A-B, A-C, A-B, and the other half was given the sequence, A-B, C-D, A-B. The IQ by treatment interaction was not significant, indicating no difference between normals and retardates in retroactive inhibition. It is of interest that in the control groups only 6 of 16 normals but 13 of 16 retardates (p ≈.015 by a Fisher exact test) made List 1 intrusions in the learning of List 2. Thus, retardates appeared to have greater difficulty in inhibiting the List 1 responses during the learning of List 2, a condition indicative of proactive interference.

In conclusion, it appears that the retardates' short-term or long-term suppression of previously learned material seems to be deficient resulting in greater proactive interference with regard to either normal MA peers (Borkowksi, 1965, Experiment 2; Iscoe & Semler, 1964) or normal CA peers (Borkowski, 1965, Experiment 1). This is consistent with the greater number of retardates making errors that are intrusions from prior lists (Borkowski, 1965; McManis, 1967), although Milgram and Furth (1966) failed to find analogous intrusions in their paired associates task for which color stimuli were made incompatible with the colors of response items. A single study (Johnson & Blake, 1960) found some evidence to suggest that retardates show less proactive inhibition than their normal MA peers.

The evidence regarding retroactive inhibition is less clear. The retardate did not differ significantly from his MA peer in two studies (Cassell, 1957; Fagan, 1966), and showed less retroactive inhibition in two others (Fagan, 1968; Johnson & Blake, 1960). The retardate did not differ from his CA peer in three studies (Baumeister et al., 1967b; McManis, 1967; Pryer, 1960). There appears to be no ready explanation for these inconsistencies. However, it should be noted that only the study by Pryer required subjects to reach a criterion of learning on the interpolated task before proceeding to relearning. This requirement, as mentioned previously, is essential for interpreting retardate-normal differences in retroactive inhibition.

III. INHIBITION OF ATTENTION TO STIMULUS INPUT AND EXTERNAL INHIBITION

It is somewhat paradoxical that distractibility and inflexibility should be considered to result from the same underlying inhibition deficit. It would seem that either the retardate is rigid in his attention to a task and refuses to be distracted *or* he is distracted by stimuli that are extraneous to the task—surely not both. The apparent paradox can be resolved by making a distinction between stimulus inhibition and response inhibition. Stimulus inhibition involves inhibition of extraneous stimuli, an attention process. Response inhibition involves the suppression of a learned response, an instrumental process. To this point the review has concerned itself with response inhibition. In order to make the distinction between stimulus and response inhibition functional, one must be able to independently measure stimulus inhibition.

A. The Orienting Reflex (OR) and Inhibition of Attention to Stimuli

The orienting reflex has special relevance in defining the inhibition of attention to stimuli. This response has been a favorite topic of investigation in Russia in recent years (Razran, 1961). As defined by Sokolov (1963), who has been responsible for much of the research and theory, the OR is the organism's first reaction to any change in the stimulus situation. In effect, it is the organism's normal reaction to a novel stimulus.

The reaction appears to be a preparatory one, a focusing of attention, a getting ready to respond. It apparently tunes the organism to insure optimal reception of stimuli. According to Sokolov's theory, the OR occurs in the following manner. As a stimulus is repeated, a multidimensional neuronal model of it is established in the cortex. The dimensions include quality, intensity, frequency, and duration as well as more abstract and less well-defined aspects of the stimulus. Once the model is established, all succeeding stimuli are compared to it. If the stimulus is consonant with the model, the cortex does not emit the impulses which evoke an OR. If the stimulus is dissonant with the model, an OR occurs. The magnitude of the OR is directly proportional to the degree of stimulus discrepancy from the model.

Habituation occurs with repetition as the model develops to match all dimensions of the stimulus. The lessening discrepancy of the model from the stimulus is reflected in the decreased magnitude of the OR until the stimulus and model become congruent and no OR occurs. As in the case of an extinguished conditioned response, the extinguished OR can be disinhibited by the presentation of a novel stimulus. The findings that decorticated animals do not show habituation of the OR and that animals higher in the phylogenetic order habituate faster are the main support for the role of the cortex in the stimulus model (Sokolov, 1963; Razran, 1961).

Lynn (1966) lists the several components of the OR which have been differentiated. These components include the following: increase in receptor sensitivity; bodily orientation toward the stimulus; arrest of ongoing activity; increase in ongoing electromyographic activity; electroencephalographic (EEG) activation or a block in the "alpha" rhythms that are normally associated with a relaxed state; a divergent vasomotor response, cerebral vasodilation accompanied by peripheral vasoconstriction; decrease in skin resistance as measured by the galvanic skin response (GSR); decrease in respiration rate; and a change, probably deceleratory, in heartrate.

Several studies have compared the ORs of normals and their CA peers. A series of findings by Luria (1963) indicated that the retardates' OR is weak. Weak stimuli that evoked an OR in normal children frequently did not do so in retarded children of the same chronological age. If evoked, this OR habituated very rapidly. Also an OR was more likely to be evoked in a retarded than in a normal child by a stimulus which was extraneous to the problem solving task. This susceptibility to orient to extraneous stimuli would be synonymous with distractibility.

A study by Lobb, Moffitt, and Gamlin (1966) demonstrated the relevance of the OR for discrimination learning. Eighteen fast learners and 18 slow learners on a discrimination task were compared on GSR reaction to novel stimuli. The subjects were institutionalized retardates with MAs ranging from 2 to 4.5. It was found that the GSR of the fast learners habituated much more quickly than that of the slow learners. Lobb *et al.*, suggested that the inferior habituation of the slow learners could be indicative of weak neural inhibition.

Baumeister, Spain, and Ellis (1963) compared the alpha block duration of 10 institutionalized retardates ($\overline{CA}$ = 22.8; $\overline{IQ}$ = 54.2) and 7 normals ($\overline{CA}$ = 28.6) from the institution's staff. Each subject received from 10 to 15 presentations of a photic stimulus while alpha waves were present in his EEG reading. The normals were found to display a significantly longer block than were the retardates, indicating a weak OR in the retardate. It appears that the majority of the effect could be attributed to a large difference on the first trial. There was also graphic evidence which indicated that the normals habituated to the stimulus over trials while the retardates did not, although this might have been the result of a floor effect in the retardates.

Similar results were obtained by Vogel (1961), who examined the relationship between the GSR, pulse rate, and finger vasomotor response components of the OR as a function of age and intelligence in six retarded (IQ = 50 to 70), six normal (estimated IQ = 93 to 108), and six gifted subjects (estimated IQ = above 130). The stimuli were a tone and cold water. Each subject was given two presentations of each stimulus. Within a trial the responses of the retarded group were found to recover baseline faster than responses of the other groups. If this response duration is taken as an index of the strength of the OR, then it might be concluded that the retardate's OR was weaker.

Clausen and Karrer (1968) compared the divergent head-finger blood volume response, GSR, and systolic blood pressure response of normals, organic, and nonorganic retardates (N = 10 in each group). The subjects were presented with eight stimuli, five tones and three light flashes, on each of 2 days. The two sessions were 1 week apart. On Day 1, the normals made more ORs than the nonorganic retardates, who in turn made more ORs than the organic retardates. Day 2 showed a decrease in the normals' responding and an increase in retardates' responding, which eliminated any difference between the two groups. The GSR measure provided an exception to this general finding. It increased slightly in the normals and definitely decreased in the retardates from Day 1 to Day 2. The groups did not differ in habituation or in response to the change from tone to light.

The relationship of the OR to hyperactivity in retardates was investigated by Tizard (1968). GSR and EEG changes to 20 presentations of a tone were compared in eight hyperactive retardates ($\overline{CA}$ = 9-7; $\overline{IQ}$ = 20), eight normally active retardates ($\overline{CA}$ = 9-9; IQ = 30 to 39), and eight normal CA controls ($\overline{CA}$ = 9-8). It was expected that an inhibition deficit in the hyperactive retardates would be reflected in slower habituation of the OR in this group. The results indicated, however, that retardation rather than hyperactivity was the important factor in OR habituation. Both retardate groups failed to habituate to the tone.

Wolfensberger and O'Connor (1965) presented projected stimuli of three durations (.2, 3, 15 seconds) and two intensities to institutionalized retardates ($\overline{MA}$ = 8-5; $\overline{IQ}$ = 57; $\overline{CA}$ = 23; N = 36) and normals ($\overline{CA}$ = 23; N = 23). The GSR amplitude response of the retardates was found to be greater than that of the normals. While the normals demonstrated shorter alpha blocking latencies, an interaction indicated that at one duration (3 seconds) the retardates blocked longer. No difference between normals and retardates was found in habituation of either the GSR or alpha block response.

The bulk of the evidence indicates that the OR of the retardate is weak. With exceptions (Wolfensberger & O'Connor, 1965), a given stimulus was likely to evoke an OR of less magnitude in the retardate than in the normal (Baumeister et al., 1963; Clausen & Karrer, 1968; Luria, 1963; Vogel, 1961). The evidence is less clear concerning the habituation of the OR. Luria (1963) and Lobb et al. (1966) found that the OR tended to habituate more quickly in the retardate. On the other hand, Baumeister et al. (1963) and Tizard (1968) indicated that the retardate habituates more slowly than his normal CA peer. Finally, the retardate appears more likely to make an OR to stimuli that are extraneous to the task at hand, resulting in disrupted performance.

Partial resolution of these findings might be made by examining two measures of the OR, magnitude and probability of occurrence. The evidence indicates that while the retardate's OR to a given stimulus is weak, it is more likely to occur. The implication is that the smaller magnitude and slower habituation are both linked to the same retardate deficiency. The OR in the normal is seen to be sufficiently strong to filter extraneous stimuli. The OR in the retardate, on the other hand, appears to be too weak to filter similarly, and extraneous stimuli evoke their own ORs. Thus, the retardate is seen as (1) deficient in his ability to inhibit responding to extraneous stimuli because (2) his OR (attention) to relevant stimuli is weak.

The literature in this area leaves the reader with the feeling that any conclusions are premature because of the mysteries of the autonomic nervous system and psychologists' lack of sophistication in monitoring autonomic responses. Nevertheless, many researchers are convinced that there are lawful relationships between these responses and the subject's attention. It seems that the pursuit of these relationships should be encouraged, despite the low probability of an immediate payoff.

B. Satiation Phenomena

If the retardate's OR to novel stimuli is weak, then he might be expected to show weak satiation effects. He might be expected to show less stimulus satiation (i.e., less avoidance of familiar stimuli and preference for novel stimuli), less neural satiation (i.e., less perceptual distortion that occurs as a function of prolonged exposure to a stimulus), and less reactive inhibition (i.e., less tendency to avoid repeating a response).

1. STIMULUS SATIATION

Stimulus satiation is typically indexed by the degree to which a subject prefers a novel cue over a familiar cue. Effort is made to assure that the subject is not differentially set by instructions or reward contingencies to select one or the other.

Terdal (1967b) compared the stimulus satiation of institutionalized adult ($\overline{CA}$ = 20-5; $\overline{IQ}$ = 57) and pre-adolescent ($\overline{CA}$ = 11-4; $\overline{IQ}$ = 44) retardates, and adult ($\overline{CA}$ = 19-6; $\overline{IQ}$ = 104), pre-adolescent ($\overline{CA}$ = 10-8) and pre-school ($\overline{CA}$ = 4-8) normals. There were 20 subjects in each group. The pre-school and pre-adolescent normals served as MA controls for the pre-adolescent and adult retardates, respectively. The subject was shown a series of 24 slides, each of which contained 2 checkerboard-like designs. One design was constant from trial to trial and the other varied. A subject's stimulus satiation was indexed by the amount of time he spent looking at the constant design, the varied design, or neither. Terdal found that the adult and pre-adolescent normal populations spent significantly more time looking at the varied design than did the other three populations, whose times did not differ from one another. These differences were very consistent over the 24 trials, suggesting that satiation occurred very rapidly or not at all. The young normals ($\overline{MA} \approx 4.8$) and the adult retardates ($\overline{MA} \approx 10.3$) performed very similarly, and both spent less time than the pre-adolescent normals ($\overline{MA} \approx 10.3$) viewing the varied figure. These results indicate that stimulus satiation is weaker in the retardate than in either his CA or his MA peer.

In a second study, Terdal (1967a) tested the same subjects with the same apparatus. Instead of a single constant design, there were four in this study, two of which were rated to be simple and two to be complex. Each of the four was used for six different slides. The data were combined in a way that precluded the comparison of normals with their MA peers, but it is interesting to note that retardates and their normal CA peers satiated to the two types of constant designs at different rates. With more and more slides, the decrease in viewing time to the simple constant designs was much more rapid than the decrease to the complex constant designs for normals, but the rates of decrease for the two types of constant designs were about the same for retardates.

These two studies suggest that normals satiate to repetitive stimuli more extensively than retardates of a comparable CA or a comparable MA. This is regarded to be consistent with the retardates' weak orienting reflexes and weaker inhibition.

2. NEURAL SATIATION

If the retardate has a weak orienting reflex and a corresponding lack of stimulus satiation, then he should show a weakness in neural or cortical satiation, which is presumably occasioned by intense attention to a stimulus.

Spitz (1963), in his review of the literature and theory of cortical satiation, defined satiation as "auto-inhibition" resulting from repeated stimulation of the same area of the cortex. Satiation is indexed behaviorally by figural aftereffects, perceptual distortions that follow prolonged stimulation by a constant stimulus. For instance, prolonged observation of a bowed line makes a subsequently observed straight line appear to be bowed in the direction that is opposed to the bowing of the original line.

On the basis of his review, Spitz proposed four postulates of a cortical satiation theory to account for observed differences between retardates and their CA peers. The general point of these postulates was that cortical satiation builds up a slower rate and dissipates at a slower rate in retardates than in their normal CA peers and possibly their normal MA peers as well.

3. REACTIVE INHIBITION

Hullian theory proposes that reactive inhibition results from the energy lost in making a response. If responses are fairly well spaced, the inhibition from one response dissipates before another is made. If the responses are in close temporal proximity, however, the inhibition accumulates and impedes the performance of the response. If the retardate has a deficit in reactive inhibition, his performance under a massed-trials condition would not be impeded and would not differ from learning under a spaced-trials condition. Duncan (1956) suggested several similarities between reactive inhibition and neural satiation. They both arise from afferent stimulation and appear to be central, not peripheral, in origin. Both require some time to acquire minimum amounts; both have an asymptote; and both decay rapidly after stimulation ceases.

The correlation of these two types of inhibition, neural satiation and reactive inhibition, was examined by Lipman and Spitz (1961). On the basis of their ability to see figural aftereffects, retardates ($\overline{CA}= 17$; $\overline{IQ}= 72$) were divided into high ($N = 23$) and low ($N = 24$) satiation groups and then compared on their pursuit rotor performance. The pursuit rotor apparatus resembles a phonograph turntable. The subject's task is to hold a stylus on a small disk that is built into the rotating turntable. The high satiation subjects, those who easily saw figural aftereffects, were found to be significantly inferior to the low satiators in rotary pursuit performance under massed trials (20-second work periods alternated with 10-second rest periods). Lipman and Spitz concluded that the high satiators developed more reactive inhibition than the low satiators. When they were changed from massed to spaced practice (from 10- to 40-second rest periods between their 20-second work periods) the low satiators gained significantly more (showed more reminiscence) than the high satiators despite their higher performance prior to the change. Furthermore, their final performance was higher than that of the high satiators. Because reactive inhibition is theoretically required to dissipate rapidly with rest, Lipman and Spitz suggested that these last two findings resulted from the conditioning (learning) of inhibition to the stimuli of the task, and that a major difference between low and high satiators was the extent to which the conditioned inhibition as well as reactive inhibition developed in the latter. This suggestion was supported by a second study using female college students. Unfortunately, changes in procedure precluded any retardate-normal comparisons. However, the role of neural satiation appeared to be very similar in the two populations.

Four studies have compared the pursuit rotor performance of retardates and normals who were matched on CA. Two of these (Ellis, Pryer, & Barnett, 1960; Wright & Hearn, 1964) showed the reminiscence in normals to be greater than in their retarded CA peers, and one (Baumeister, Hawkins, & Holland, 1967a) found no difference. This reminiscence was taken as evidence for the dissipation of the reactive inhibition built up by the normals during training. Lipman and Spitz (1961) argued that the depressed reminiscence of poor learners in their study was due to the *conditioning* of inhibition for these subjects. The results from Jones and Ellis (1962), which seem to indicate retardate inferiority in conditioned rather than reactive inhibition, are consistent with this contention. Nevertheless, the evidence is persuasive that reactive inhibition is also more apparent in the pursuit rotor performance of normals than in that of their retarded CA peers. Unfortunately, no studies were found that compared the reactive inhibition of retardates and their MA peers.

C. Distraction (External Inhibition) in Instrumental Learning

Two conclusions were advanced regarding the OR. First, it was suggested that the OR is weaker in the retardate than in the normal. Following from this was the prediction that retardates' satiation effects would be less, a prediction that received considerable support in the preceding section (Section III,B). Second, it was suggested that the OR is more disinhibitable in the retardate — that the OR to novel stimuli is more likely to occur in the retardate. This second suggestion leads to the prediction that the retardate is more susceptible to distraction from the task at hand by extraneous stimuli. If the retardate's OR is easily disinhibited, then his instrumental behavior should be also. Researchers and teachers in retardation have long assumed that this was the case. Strauss and Lehtinen (1955) have described at length the hyperactive, brain-damaged retardate and his great susceptibility to disruption by extraneous stimuli. However, the data that would associate this distractibility with intelligence per se have been inconsistent, at best.

In the first place, it is doubtful that retarded individuals who are identified a priori to be brain-damaged can also be shown to be more distractible than their "non-brain-damaged" retardate peers. Cruse (1961) compared 24 familials ($\overline{CA} = 13.5$; $\overline{MA} = 6.2$) and 24 brain-damaged subjects ($\overline{CA} = 14.4$; $\overline{MA} = 6.6$) on a reaction time task under distraction (toys, a mirror, and balloons strung from the ceiling and blown by a fan) and no distraction. He found that both populations improved significantly when the distractor was removed, and that the brain-damaged had significantly longer reaction times. However, there was no indication that the impairment under the distraction condition was greater for the brain-damaged subjects than for the non-brain-damaged.

With this evidence to refute the position that brain-damaged and familial retardates are differentially distractible, the next question concerns whether retardates in general are more distractible than nonretardates of a comparable mental age. It is useful to divide the literature that deals with this question into two sections: research using novel or distracting cues that are extraneous to the learning task and research using novel cues that are embedded in the task. The review that follows will reveal that intelligence tends to correlate with distraction in the second case but not the first.

1. DISTRACTION BY CUES THAT ARE EXTRANEOUS TO THE LEARNING TASK

Two studies have addressed themselves directly to the comparison of retardates with their normal MA peers. Girardeau and Ellis (1964) Experiment 1 compared 60 retardates ($\overline{MA} = 100.6$; $\overline{CA} = 154.9$) and 60 normal MA peers ($\overline{CA} = 109.6$) on a 10-word serial learning task using tape recordings of "environmental sounds" to distract performance for half of each population. They found that the normals were superior to retardates, and that the distractor did not affect the performance of either population.

In the second study, Ellis, Hawkins, Pryer, and Jones (1963) gave 144 normals ($\overline{CA} = 87$; MA = 6 to 7, 7 to 8, 8 to 9) and 144 retardates ($\overline{CA} = 183$; MA = 6 to 7, 7 to 8, 8 to 9) a 100-trial oddity discrimination using a modified WGTA. Stimuli were common objects that were scaled for attention-attracting value. Two types of distraction were manipulated: (1) attention value of the stimulus objects and (2) mirror versus no mirror above the objects at the subject's eye level. They found that the attention value of the objects did not influence the performance of either population, and that the mirror had a paradoxical effect, facilitating the performance of the normals but not affecting the performance of the retardates.

These studies indicate that there is no evidence to suggest that the retardate is more distractible than his MA peer. Furthermore, the studies that follow suggest that the retardate is no more distractible than his CA peer either.

In a series of experiments comparing college students and their retardate CA peers, Belmont and Ellis (1968) investigated the influence of a distractor that followed knowledge-of-results feedback in a paired-associate task. The stimuli were the digits 1–9 projected from the rear onto a small screen, and the responses involved the selection of the correct geometric form from among the 9 that were projected onto a row of similar screens on every trial. The distractor, a 2-second presentation of a pair of 300-watt lights, was introduced simultaneously with the response for the 3 "immediate" pairs, delayed 5 seconds for the 3 "delayed" pairs, and not given at all for the 3 "control" pairs. The results showed that 24 college students (Experiment 2) performed as expected, with the poorest performance on immediate pairs, some decrement in the delayed pairs, and the best performance with the control pairs. All pairwise comparisons among the 3 conditions were significant. Eight retardates (CA = 16 to 23; IQ = 58 to 69), on the other hand, showed no significant treatment effects (Experiment 4), although there was a tendency for the poorest learning with the control pairs. In Experiments 5 ($N = 35$) and 6 ($N = 20$) Belmont and Ellis used a meaningful distractor (a projected picture of 2 seconds' duration) with a new group of retardates (CA = 15 to 26; IQ = 50 to 83). The subject's task was to select the correct member from each of 10 or 12 stimulus pairs that were presented as a single problem. Stimuli were nonsense line drawings. There was a tendency for the distractor to produce a greater decrement in performance as learning progressed in Experiment 5, and this decrement was significant in Experiment 6. The results of these experiments led the authors to conclude that the retardate is, if anything, less distracted than his CA peer and becomes distractible only with experience. Contrary to the inhibition deficit hypothesis, distractibility occasioned by extraneous stimuli appears to be adaptive behavior.

In contrast to Belmont and Ellis, Sen and Clarke (1968a,b) presented evidence to suggest that the retardate is more distractible than his CA peer. In their series, non-institutionalized retardates (CA = 17 to 33; MA = 2-6 to 11-4; N = 9 to 27 in the various experiments) were asked to name six outline pictures drawn on cardboard. Various distractors were presented through earphones. Performance decrement on the naming task appeared to be related to both task difficulty and ability (MA). (1) While both high- and low-MA subjects were distracted when the distractors were rapidly spoken names of pictures used, only the low-MA subjects were distracted when these words were irrelevant to the pictures. (2) The decrement in performance under the two conditions in which the distractors were rapidly spoken words correlated significantly (.45) with MA. (3) Random noise or background conversation did not significantly disturb performance in the low-MA subjects while relevant words, irrelevant words, and even nonsense syllables produced significant decrements. (4) When the pictures featured objects that were more familiar, significant decrements were not produced even by the most potent distractor. These results led to the conclusion that susceptibility to distraction is negatively correlated with mental age and/or task ease. This conclusion directly contradicted the results of Belmont and Ellis (1968), which indicated that distractibility is *positively* correlated with mental age and/or task ease. The operations that defined distraction were quite different in the two cases, but there is no apparent reason for the discrepancies in the two series of experiments.

In conclusion, there seems to be little evidence to support the suggestion from the OR literature and the Strauss statements that the retardate is more distracted by extraneous stimuli than either his MA or his CA peer. However, more favorable evidence for such a deficit can be found in experiments in which the novel cue is introduced to replace a training cue.

2. Distraction by Novel Cues That Are Embedded in the Training Task

In the cue-substitution studies reported above (Section II,B,3,a) a novel cue replaced one of the training cues. It is useful to reconsider these as distraction paradigms. If the retardate and the nonretardate are at a comparable level of learning (at criterion) when the novel cue is introduced, then their performance decrement should be the same when a novel cue replaces one of the training cues. However, several studies suggest that the retardate is more likely to show a performance decrement than the nonretardate under these circumstances. Heal (1966, 1967) and Heal *et al.* (1966) trained a total of 48 kindergartners and 48 retardates of comparable discrimination ability to a criterion of 6 consecutive correct or, in some cases, to a criterion of 6 plus 40 trials of overtraining. Cues were planometric colors or forms, which were projected from the rear onto panels that the subject either pressed (Heal, 1966) or selected with a lever movement (Heal et al., 1966). Immediately following criterion one of the cues (the positive for half the problems, the negative for the other half) was replaced by a novel cue for a single choice trial. Distraction by the novel cue was assumed if the subject responded in a way that was contrary to the value of his training cues. By this definition, significantly more responses were distracted in the retardates (41/120) than in the kindergartners (19/120).

Similarly, Bryant (1967a,b) found that the retardate's performance suffered greatly when he was given a new cue to sort in a card-sorting task. Bryant (1967a) matched 30 subnormals (MA = 48 to 75) with 30 normals (CA = 59 to 69) for a two-choice sorting task with 2-inch-square cards. The subject was faced with two boxes and trained to sort one color into the box at the left and the other into the box at the right. After a criterion of five consecutive correct was reached, one of the colors was replaced with a new one. While this procedure did not significantly affect the performance of the normals, who sorted the new card as though it were the replaced card, it resulted in significant deterioration in the performance of the retardates, especially with regard to the sorting of the novel cue. In criticism of this study, it must be noted that gross typographical errors in the tables of data and/or analyses made it impossible to check Bryant's verbal conclusions. Nevertheless, these results were replicated (Bryant, 1967b) in a task that required similar retardates (MA = 49 to 74) and normals (CA = 58 to 67) to sort one color into one box and two colors (half as many cards of each color) into the other box.

The results of all these experiments suggest that when novelty is embedded in the cues of the task, it is associated with greater performance decrement in retardates than in normals. These results stand in contrast to those cited in the previous section, which indicated that distractors which were extraneous to the cues of the task were not associated with differential normal-retardate performance. The theoretical meaning of this conclusion is not clear. It might be that the distinction between inhibition and generalization decrement is relevant here. Distractors that are extraneous to the subject's task appear to qualify as external inhibitors in the Pavlovian sense. Changes in the training cues themselves would be expected to occasion performance (generalization) decrements that would mirror the extent of stimulus change. Perhaps it is more difficult for the retardate to reconstruct an entire situation from its unchanged parts. Perhaps the retardate responds to global cue compounds, which he is unable to recognize when some of their component parts are changed. That is, perhaps the retardate shows a greater generalization decrement but not greater distractibility than the normal.

IV. CONCLUSIONS AND SPECULATIONS ABOUT INDIVIDUAL DIFFERENCES IN LEARNING PROCESSES

The review above and the speculations below imply that it is worthwhile to search for deficits in retardates' response-defined learning and attention processes. It seems that this search has two potential payoffs. First, it appears to be an efficient way to refine knowledge about these processes. If retardates and normals are found to differ with regard to some learning process such as inhibition, it is reasonable to infer that this process is important for individual differences in normal learning. Second, it provides descriptive information about retardates. It seems that this information is an essential prerequisite for any remediation or rehabilitation of the retardate. Before any dimensions of normality can be developed or identified in the retardate, it is necessary to describe accurately his current status with regard to his normal peers.

These positions require at least two qualifications. First, nothing here implies that there is a single behavioral deficit that distinguishes the retarded from the normal. Second, nothing implies that the retarded constitute a unitary population. These qualifications pose no great threat to the strategy of comparing the two populations. Even though all retardates are not inferior to all normals with regard to some particular learning process, significant differences between the two populations should obtain if the process influences individual differences in adaptive behavior. After a scientist discovers such a process, he can assess the individuals' differences with regard to it, thereby refining his description of their intellectual ability.

The speculation that follows examines several possible deficits. The constructs involved must be regarded as pre-theoretical and lacking any formal theoretical framework. This level of theorizing seems appropriate to the present understanding of individual differences in learning processes.

A. Response Inhibition

Table II shows that the review findings are reasonably supportive of a retardate deficit in response inhibition. While there were many contradictory findings, this support was especially firm in the case of transfer suppression, where discrimination reversal, classification shifts, and proactive interference paradigms all pointed to such a deficit. Extinction and differentiation paradigms also supported this conclusion. The only really troublesome result was the failure to find consistently that the retardate has more difficulty than the normal in learning to avoid the negative cue in a discrimination learning task.

B. Stimulus Inhibition

Table II shows reasonable support for the proposed retardate deficit in stimulus inhibition, although this evidence was found primarily in reference to the retardate's CA peer. Consistent with Sokolov's interpretation of the role of the OR in inhibition, the retardate's OR was weak and was disinhibited more easily than his CA peer's. Furthermore, retardates satiated to stimuli to a lesser extent than CA or MA peers. However, the most critical test, distraction by extraneous cues, was almost completely nonsupportive: retardates did not appear to be distracted

TABLE II
SUMMARY OF RESEARCH FINDINGS RELATING TO RETARDATES' INHIBITORY DEFICITS

Situation or task	MA peer	CA peer
Response inhibition		
Extinction: classical conditioning	–	N
Extinction: instrumental learning	I	–
Classical differential conditioning	N	NN
Instrumental simultaneous discrimination learning	N	(NN)
Avoidance of the negative cue	I	–
Perseveration of response-defined strategies	N	NN
Discrimination reversal: 2-choice	NN	(NN)
Discrimination reversal: 3-choice	I	–
Discrimination reversal: 2-choice instructed	R	–
Shift in the dimension by which cues are classified	N	–
Suppression of proactive transfer	N	N
Suppression of retroactive transfer	I	I
Stimulus inhibition		
Orienting reflex: strength	–	N
Orienting reflex: disinhibition	–	N
Stimulus satiation	N	NN
Neural satiation	–	N
Reactive inhibition	–	NN
Distraction by extraneous novel stimuli	I	I
Distraction by task-embedded novel stimuli	NN	–

Key: R = retardate shows better performance; N = normal shows better performance; I = results inconsistent or nonsignificant; – = no data available. Double letters indicate especially consistent findings. Parentheses indicate results for which this review provides no data.

any more than normals by stimuli that were extraneous to the learning task. On the other hand, retardates showed a greater performance decrement than normals when novel cues were embedded in the learning task.

It seems highly probable that the operations used in the studies of "external inhibition" did not tap a unitary construct. In fact, it would not be completely accurate to indicate that they attempted to do so, although their terminology often implied such a construct. Further research is needed to indicate more explicitly the conditions under which the retardate is more distractible than the normal and those under which he is not.

C. Abstraction

Some of the data reviewed above might be related to an abstraction deficit in the retardate. Perhaps the retardate responds to global compound cues and not to the abstract components of which they were composed. This explanation was invoked to account for the finding that retardate performance deteriorated when distractors were embedded in the cues of the task, but not when they were extraneous to these cues (Section III,C,2). While the distraction between concrete (attention to global, compound properties of cues) and abstract (attention to separable component properties of cues) perceptual attitude in the brain-injured has a long history, its recent application to interpreting behavioral deficits in the retarded has been neglected.

D. Encoding

The finding that retardates' OR is weaker than normals' leads to the possibility that their encoding is weaker. That is, perhaps maximum attention to a measured exposure of a stimulus provides the retardate with less information than the normal. This description is tantamount to his having a stimulus trace whose amplitude is less. In other words, it may be that there are individual differences in the total information that is encoded per unit of time.

Such a notion might account for retardate-normal differences in a number of areas. For instance, the retardate's tendency to perseverate abnormally to some strategy that is not maximally rewarded might mean that he is not receiving enough input to modify it. This is consistent with his transfer suppression weakness.

E. Rigidity

"Topological rigidity" was proposed by Lewin and Kounin to account for individual differences in the ability to change set. Lewin conceived of areas of experience (regions) that were separated by boundaries. These boundaries could vary in rigidity, brittleness, thickness, etc. Rigidity defined the degree of communication of one region with another and, therefore, the ease with which the individual "moved" from one region to another.

This construct seems especially viable in view of the data reviewed. First, it makes nearly all the predictions that would be made by the transfer suppression hypothesis. Furthermore, it can account for the retardate's superiority on the instructed reversal (Kounin, 1941) whereas the transfer suppression hypothesis can not. Second, rigid boundaries should protect the organism from distraction by extraneous stimuli. Data from Belmont and Ellis (1968) suggested that this might be the case. On the other hand, the decrement in performance associated with distraction by cues embedded in the learning task would be predicted from a rigidity position: the rigid person should be unable to respond to a partially changed situation as though it were unchanged.

In short, the rigidity hypothesis provides for the resolution of several paradoxes that cannot be resolved by other pre-theoretical constructs of individual differences in intelligence. Its reapplication to the study of the mentally retarded seems long overdue.

ACKNOWLEDGMENTS

The authors express gratitude to Barbara Grigsby and Mary Urda for their assistance in the typing of the final manuscript and especially to Patricia Frith Vaughan for her assistance in all phases of the preparation of this review. The helpful suggestions of Leonard E. Ross, Norman R. Ellis, and Alfred A. Baumeister are gratefully acknowledged.

This chapter was prepared with partial support from NICHHD grants HD-43 and HD-973.

REFERENCES

Balla, D., & Zigler, E. Discrimination and switching learning in normal, familial retarded, and organic retarded children. *Journal of Abnormal and Social Psychology*, 1964, **69**, 664–669.

Baumeister, A. A., Beedle, R., & Urquhart, D. GSR conditioning in normals and retardates. *American Journal of Mental Deficiency*, 1964, **69**, 114–120.

Baumeister, A. A., Hawkins, W. F., & Holland, J. Motor learning and knowledge of results. *American Journal of Mental Deficiency*, 1967, **70**, 590–594. (a)

Baumeister, A. A., Hawkins, W. F., & Holland, J. M. Retroactive inhibition in short-term recall in normals and retardates. *American Journal of Mental Deficiency*, 1967, **72**, 253–256. (b)

Baumeister, A. A., Spain, C. J., & Ellis, N. R. A note on Alpha block duration in normals and retardates. *American Journal of Mental Deficiency*, 1963, **67**, 723–725.

Belmont, J. M., & Ellis, N. R. Effects of extraneous stimulation upon discrimination learning in normals and retardates. *American Journal of Mental Deficiency*, 1968, 72, 525-532.
Boice, R. Methodological considerations and the discrimination deficit in the severely retarded. *Journal of Genetic Psychology*, 1966, 109, 163-167.
Bolles, M. M. The basis of pertinence: A study of the test performance of aments, dements, and normal children of the same mental age. *Archives of Psychology*, 1937, No. 212.
Borkowski, J. G. Interference effects in short-term memory as a function of level of intelligence. *American Journal of Mental Deficiency*, 1965, 70, 458-465.
Briggs, G. E. Acquisition, extinction, and recovery functions in retroactive inhibition. *Journal of Experimental Psychology*, 1954, 47, 285-293.
Bryant, P. E. The transfer of sorting concepts by moderately retarded children. *American Journal of Mental Deficiency*, 1965, 70, 291-300.
Bryant, P. E. Verbal labeling and learning strategies in normal and severely subnormal children. *Quarterly Journal of Experimental Psychology*, 1967, 19, 155-161. (a)
Bryant, P. E. Verbal labeling and the learning of complex discriminations by normal and severely subnormal children. *Language and Speech*, 1967, 10, 36-45. (b)
Cassell, R. H. Serial verbal learning and retroactive inhibition in aments and children. *Journal of Clinical Psychology*, 1957, 13, 369-372.
Clausen, J., &·Karrer, R. Orienting response-frequency of occurrence and relationship to other autonomic variables. *American Journal of Mental Deficiency*, 1968, 73, 455-464.
Cruse, D. Effects of distraction upon the performance of brain injured and familial retarded children. *American Journal of Mental Deficiency*, 1961, 66, 86-92.
Denny, R. Research in learning and performance. In H. A. Stevens & R. Heber (Eds.), *Mental retardation*. Chicago: University of Chicago Press, 1964. Pp. 104-142.
Diamond, S., Balvin, R. S., & Diamond, F. R. *Inhibition and choice*. New York: Harper & Row, 1963.
Duncan, C. P. On the similarity between reactive inhibition and neural satiation. *American Journal of Psychology*, 1956, 69, 227-235.
Eimas, P. D. Components and compounds in discrimination learning of retarded children. *Journal of Experimental Child Psychology*, 1964, 1, 301-310.
Eimas, P. D. Stimulus compounding in the discrimination learning of kindergarten children. *Journal of Experimental Child Psychology*, 1965, 2, 178-185.
Ellis, N. R., Hawkins, W. F., Pryer, M. W., & Jones, R. W. Distraction effects in oddity learning by normal and mentally defective humans. *American Journal of Mental Deficiency*, 1963, 67, 576-583.
Ellis, N. R., Pryer, M. W., & Barnett, C. D. Motor learning and retention in normals and defectives. *Perceptual and Motor Skills*, 1960, 10, 83-91.
Fagan, J. F., III. Short-term retention in normal and retarded children. *Psychonomic Science*, 1966, 6, 303-304.
Fagan, J. F., III. Short-term memory processes in normal and retarded children. *Journal of Experimental Child Psychology*, 1968, 6, 279-296.
Girardeau, F. L., & Ellis, N. R. Rote verbal learning by normal and mentally retarded children. *American Journal of Mental Deficiency*, 1964, 68, 525-532.
Gonzalez, R. C., Behrend, E. R., & Bitterman, M. E. Reversal learning and forgetting in birds and fish. *Science*, 1967, 158, 519-521.
Gynther, M. D. Differential eyelid conditioning as a function of stimulus similarity and strength of response to the CS. *Journal of Experimental Psychology*, 1957, 53, 408-416.
Harter, S. Mental age, IQ, and motivational factors in the discrimination learning set performance of normal and retarded children. *Journal of Experimental Child Psychology*, 1967, 5, 123-141.

Heal, L. W. Discrimination transfer in normal and mentally retarded children of comparable discrimination ability: Partial intradimensional shifts as a function of overtraining. Unpublished doctoral dissertation, University of Wisconsin, 1964.

Heal, L. W. The role of cue value, cue novelty, and overtraining in the discrimination shift performance of retardates and normal children of comparable discrimination ability. *Journal of Experimental Child Psychology*, 1966, 4, 126-142.

Heal, L. W. The role of cue novelty in the discrimination learning of subjects who differ in intellectual ability. Paper presented at the First Congress of the International Association for the Scientific Study of Mental Deficiency, Montpellier, September, 1967.

Heal, L. W., & Johnson, J. T., Jr. The role of cue familiarization in the discrimination performance of retardates, primary students, and college students. Institute on Mental Retardation and Intellectual Development (IMRID) Papers and Reports, 1968, Vol. 5, No. 16, George Peabody College for Teachers, Nashville, Tennessee.

Heal, L. W., Kral, P. A., & Headrick, M. The role of approach and avoidance in discrimination learning: A re-evaluation of the ambiguous cue technique. Unpublished manuscript, George Peabody College for Teachers, Nashville, Tennessee, 1968.

Heal, L. W., Ross, L. E., & Sanders, B. Reversal and partial reversal in mental defectives and normal children of a comparable mental age. *American Journal of Mental Deficiency*, 1966, 71, 411-416.

House, B. J., & Zeaman, D. Visual discrimination learning and intelligence in defectives of low mental age. *American Journal of Mental Deficiency*, 1960, 65, 51-58.

House, B. J., & Zeaman, D. Learning sets from minimum stimuli in retardates. *Journal of Comparative and Physiological Psychology*, 1963, 56, 735-739.

Iscoe, I., & Semler, I. J. Paired-associate learning in normal and mentally retarded children as a function of four experimental conditions. *Journal of Comparative and Physiological Psychology*, 1964, 57, 387-392.

Johnson, B. M. Reward schedules and instrumental conditioning in normal and retarded children. *Child Development*, 1966, 37, 633-644.

Johnson, G. O., & Blake, K. A. *Learning performance of retarded and normal children.* Syracuse: Syracuse University Press, 1960.

Johnson, J. T., Jr. Developmental aspects of inhibition and the orienting reflex. Unpublished doctoral dissertation, George Peabody College for Teachers, Nashville, Tennessee, 1968.

Johnson, J. T., Jr., & Heal, L. W. CS-UCS interval in differential eyelid conditioning with retardates. *Psychonomic Science*, 1967, 9, 327-328.

Jones, R. W., & Ellis, N. R. Inhibitory potential in rotary pursuit acquisition by normal and defective subjects. *Journal of Experimental Psychology*, 1962, 63, 534-539.

Kern, W. H. Negative transfer on sorting tasks, MA, and IQ in normal and retarded children. *American Journal of Mental Deficiency*, 1967, 72, 416-426.

Kounin, J. S. Experimental studies of rigidity: I. The measurement of normal and feeble-minded persons. *Character & Personality*, 1941, 9, 251-273.

Krechevsky, I. A study of the continuity of the problem-solving process. *Psychological Review*, 1938, 45, 107-133.

Levine, M. Mediating processes in humans at the outset of discrimination learning. *Psychological Review*, 1963, 73, 254-276.

Lipman, R. S., & Spitz, H. The relationship between kinesthetic satiation and inhibition in rotary pursuit performance. *Journal of Experimental Psychology*, 1961, 62, 468-475.

Lobb, H. Attenuation of trace electrodermal conditioning by benzedrine in mentally defective and normal adults. Paper presented at the annual convention of the American Association on Mental Deficiency, Denver, May, 1967.

Lobb, H. Trace GSR conditioning with benzedrine® in mentally defective and normal adults. *American Journal of Mental Deficiency*, 1968, **73**, 239-246.

Lobb, H., Moffitt, A., & Gamlin, P. Frustration and adaptation in relation to discrimination learning ability of mentally defective children. *American Journal of Mental Deficiency*, 1966, **71**, 256-265.

Longstreth, L. E. Frustration and secondary reinforcement concepts as applied to human conditioning and extinction. *Psychological Monographs*, 1966, **80**, 11 (Whole No. 619).

Luria, A. R. *The mentally retarded child*. New York: Macmillan (Pergamon), 1963.

Lynn, R. *Attention, arousal, and the orientation reaction*. New York: Macmillan (Pergamon), 1966.

Mateer, F. *Child behavior*. Boston: Gorham Press, 1918.

McManis, D. L. Retroactive inhibition in paired-associate learning by normals and retardates. *American Journal of Mental Deficiency*, 1967, **71**, 931-936.

Milgram, N. A., & Furth, H. G. Position reversal versus dimension reversal in normal and retarded children. *Child Development*, 1964, **35**, 701-708.

Milgram, N. A., & Furth, H. G. Response competition in paired-associate learning by educable and trainable retarded children. *American Journal of Mental Deficiency*, 1966, **70**, 849-854.

O'Connor, N., & Hermelin, B. Discrimination and reversal learning in imbeciles. *Journal of Abnormal and Social Psychology*, 1959, **59**, 409-413.

Ohlrich, E. S. The effect of CS-UCS interval on the single-cue and differential eyelid conditioning of retarded children. Unpublished doctoral dissertation, University of Wisconsin, 1968.

Ohlrich, E. S., & Ross, L. E. Acquisition and differential conditioning of the eyelid response in normal and retarded children. *Journal of Experimental Child Psychology*, 1968, **6**, 181-193.

Penney, R. K., Croskery, J., & Allen, G. Effects of training schedules on rigidity as manifested by normal and mentally retarded children. *Psychological Reports*, 1962, **10**, 243-249.

Plenderleith, M. Discrimination learning and discrimination reversal learning in normal and feebleminded children. *Journal of Genetic Psychology*, 1956, **88**, 107-112.

Pryer, R. S. Retroactive inhibition in normals and defectives as a function of temporal position of the interpolated task. *American Journal of Mental Deficiency*, 1960, **64**, 1004-1011.

Razran, G. The observable unconscious and the inferable conscious in current Soviet psychophysiology: Interoceptive conditioning, semantic conditioning, and the orienting reflex. *Psychological Review*, 1961, **68**, 81-147.

Riopelle, A. J. Transfer suppression and learning sets. *Journal of Comparative and Physiological Psychology*, 1953, **46**, 108-114.

Ross, L. E. Classical conditioning and discrimination learning: Research with the mentally retarded. In N. R. Ellis (Ed.), *International review of research in mental retardation*. Vol. 1. New York: Academic Press, 1966. Pp. 21-24.

Ross, L. E., Headrick, M. W., & MacKay, P. B. Classical eyelid conditioning of young Mongoloid children. *American Journal of Mental Deficiency*, 1967, **72**, 21-29.

Ross, L. E., Koski, C. H., & Yaeger, J. Classical eyelid conditioning of the severely retarded. *Psychonomic Science*, 1964, **1**, 253-254.

Sanders, B., Ross, L. E., & Heal, L. W. Reversal and nonreversal shifts in retardates and normal children of a comparable mental age. *Journal of Experimental Psychology*, 1965, **69**, 84-88.

Scott, K. G. Intelligence and learning. In H. C. Haywood (Ed.), *Psychometric intelligence.* New York: Appleton-Century-Croft, 1969, in press.

Semler, I. J. Selective learning in severely retarded children as a function of differential reaction to nonreward. *Child Development*, 1965, **36**, 143-152.

Sen, A., & Clarke, A. M. The effect of distraction during and after learning a serial recall task. *American Journal of Mental Deficiency*, 1968, **73**, 46-49. (a)

Sen, A., & Clarke, A. M. Some factors affecting distractibility in the mental retardate. *American Journal of Mental Deficiency*, 1968, **73**, 50-60. (b)

Siegel, D. S., & Foshee, J. G. Molar variability in the mentally defective. *Journal of Abnormal and Social Psychology*, 1960, **61**, 141-143.

Sokolov, E. N. *Perception and the conditioned reflex.* New York: Macmillan, 1963.

Spence, J. T. Verbal-discrimination performance as a function of instructions and verbal-reinforcement combination in normal and retarded children. *Child Development*, 1966, **37**, 269-281.

Spence, K. W., & Platt, J. R. Effects of partial reinforcement on acquisition and extinction of the conditioned eyeblink in a masking situation. *Journal of Experimental Psychology*, 1967, **74**, 259-263.

Spitz, H. H. Field theory in mental deficiency. In N. R. Ellis (Ed.), *Handbook of mental deficiency: Psychological theory and research.* New York: McGraw-Hill, 1963. Pp. 11-40.

Stanley, J. C. Problems in equating groups in mental retardation research. *Journal of Special Education*, 1967, **1**, No. 3.

Stevenson, H. W. Discrimination learning. In N. R. Ellis (Ed.), *Handbook of mental deficiency: Psychological theory and research.* New York: McGraw-Hill, 1963. Pp. 424-438.

Stevenson, H. W., & Zigler, E. Discrimination learning and rigidity in normal and feeble-minded individuals. *Journal of Personality*, 1957, **25**, 699-711.

Strauss, A. A., & Lehtinen, L. E. *Psychopathology and education of the brain-injured child.* New York: Grune & Stratton, 1955.

Terdal, L. G. Complexity and position of stimuli as determinates of looking behavior in retardates and normals. *American Journal of Mental Deficiency*, 1967, **72**, 384-387. (a)

Terdal, L. G. Stimulus satiation and mental retardation. *American Journal of Mental Deficiency*, 1967, **71**, 881-885. (b)

Tizard, B. Habituation of EEG and skin potential changes in normal and severely subnormal children. *American Journal of Mental Deficiency*, 1968, **73**, 34-40.

Vogel, W. The relationship of age and intelligence to autonomic functioning. *Journal of Comparative and Physiological Psychology*, 1961, **54**, 133-138.

Weaver, T. T., Jr., & Dixon, J. C. Comparison of mental defectives and normal children on simple and contingency problem solving. *American Journal of Mental Deficiency*, 1965, **70**, 585-589.

Wolfensberger, W., & O'Connor, N. Stimulus intensity and duration effects on EEG and GSR responses of normals and retardates. *American Journal of Mental Deficiency*, 1965, **70**, 21-37.

Wright, L., & Hearn, C. B., Jr. Reactive inhibition in normals and defectives as measured from a common performance criterion. *Journal of Genetic Psychology*, 1964, **71**, 57-64.

Yaeger, J. A. Instrumental selective learning and reversal in retarded and normal children. Unpublished bachelor of science thesis, University of Wisconsin, 1964.

Zeaman, D., & House, B. J. Approach and avoidance in the discrimination learning of retardates. *Child Development*, 1962, **53**, 355-372.

Zeaman, D., & House, B. J. The role of attention in retardate discrimination learning. In N. R. Ellis (Ed.), *Handbook of mental deficiency.* New York: McGraw-Hill, 1963. Pp. 159-233.

Zigler, E., & deLabry, J. Concept-switching in middle class, lower class, and retarded children. *Journal of Abnormal and Social Psychology*, 1962, **65**, 267-273.

Zigler, E., & Unell, E. Concept-switching in normal and feebleminded children as a function of reinforcement. *American Journal of Mental Deficiency*, 1962, **66**, 651-657.

Growth and Decline of Retardate Intelligence[1]

MARY ANN FISHER AND DAVID ZEAMAN
UNIVERSITY OF CONNECTICUT, STORRS, CONNECTICUT

I. Introduction 151
II. The Subject Population 156
III. Description of the Semi-longitudinal Method 156
IV. Results 159
    A. Growth Curve for the Entire Population 159
    B. Semi-longitudinal MA Growth, by Level 161
    C. Cross-sectional Growth, by Level 162
    D. Semi-longitudinal Growth, by Level and Sex 163
    E. Diagnostic Categories 163
    F. Age-Changes in IQ, by Level 165
V. Determination of K, a Constant Measure of Retarded Intelligence 167
    A. An Empirical Equation 167
    B. Goodness of Fit 168
    C. Interpretation of the Parameters 169
    D. A Simplification of Equation 1 171
    E. Reliability and Constancy of K, Compared to IQ 172
    F. Reliability of K and IQ Over Time 173
VI. Summary and Conclusions 174
    Appendix: Values of K as a Function of MA and CA 177
    References 189

I. INTRODUCTION

The major goal of this study is to analyze semi-longitudinally the growth and decline of Binet mental ages of a large institutionalized population of retardates. To our knowledge such a study has never been reported.

How does retardate intelligence grow? Traditional IQ theory says it

---

[1]The research reported in this paper has been supported by Grant M-1099 of the National Institute of Mental Health, and Research Career Program Award K6-HD-20,325 of the National Institute of Child Health and Human Development, U.S. Public Health Service.

grows just like normal intelligence, in that mental age grows linearly up to about 16 years of CA and then stops, the only difference being the rate at which it grows. The rate is, of course, the IQ. Higher grade retardates presumably have higher rates of MA growth, lower grades have lower rates. This relation is illustrated in Fig. 1(A-1).

Other simple relations are clearly possible, and it is instructive to consider their consequences. Four large categories of non-traditional growth rates are drawn in Fig. 1. Consider B-1; if retardates were deserving of their name and simply "retarded" in their development, their rates of MA growth would be retarded or slower. Given the fact of an upper limit of MA growth for normals, the subject with a lower IQ might simply take longer to reach this upper limit. They might, in other words, have a longer MA growing season. The result would be an increase in IQ after CA 16 as shown in B-2, using again the conventional upper limit of CA in the IQ formula. The idea of a slower maturational rate and longer period of development for the retarded coincides with the views of a number of writers (Eustis, 1947; Clarke & Clarke, 1954; Clarke, Clarke, & Reiman, 1958; Bell & Zubek, 1960).

It is perhaps equally intuitive that the retardate might have a shorter MA growing season, as depicted in C-1, with a consequent fall in IQ after CA 10, as drawn in C-2. A shorter growing season implies that retardates reach their peak relatively early. If this were found to be the case, retardates might more properly be called "mental accelerates."

A combination of slower growth rates and lower final level of MA for retardates is shown in D-1. The IQ rises after CA 16, but does not ever reach normal level.

In all the cases illustrated above, linear MA growth rates have been associated with constant IQs. That this is by no means a necessary consequence is shown in E-1 and E-2. The three retardate growth functions (a, b, and c) shown in E-1 are linear, but because they do not extrapolate back through the origin (MA = CA = 0), the MA/CA formula does not yield constant IQs, as indicated in E-2. A faulty zero point of the underlying scale has this effect.

In summary, a variety of possible and not unreasonable patterns of retarded MA growth rates could lead to nonconstant IQs. Ideally, it should be possible to go to the literature and find out which is true. There have been about three dozen reports on the constancy of retardate IQ, most of these reporting a spontaneous decline of IQ with age (Doll, 1920; Kuhlmann, 1921; Minogue, 1926; Cattell, 1931; Hoakley, 1932; Arthur, 1933; Engel, 1937; Strauss & Kephart, 1939; Kaplan, 1943; Sloan & Harmon, 1947; Guertin, 1950; Thompson, 1951; Zeaman

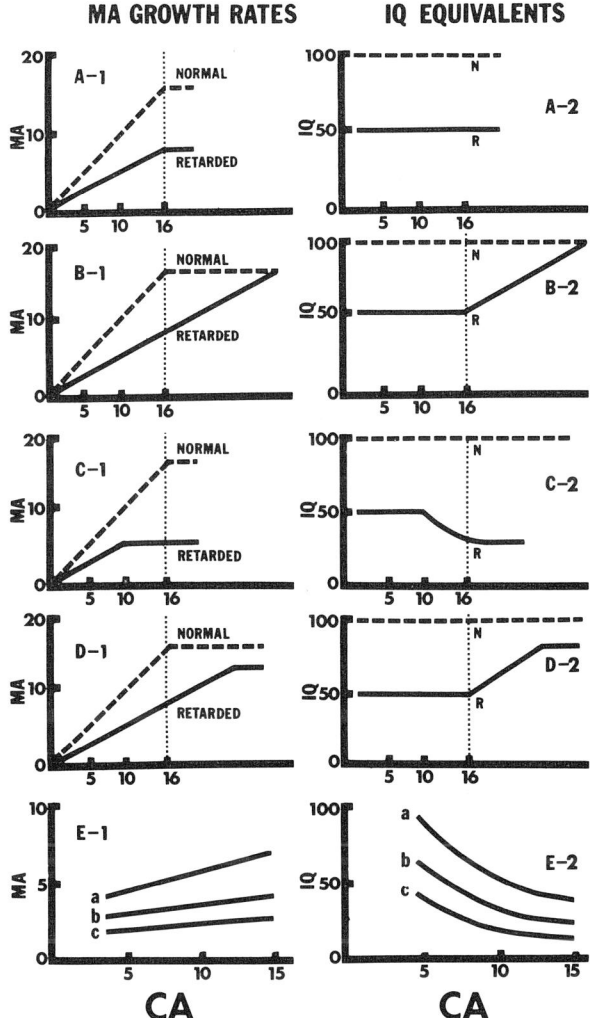

FIG. 1. Some alternative patterns of growth of mental age and associated changes in IQ (N = normal; R = retarded).

A-1 and A-2: Traditional view. Differences between normal and retardates in both rate and final level. Same growing season for all IQs. B-1 and B-2: Differences between normal and retardates in rate but not final level. Longer growing seasons for lower IQs. C-1 and C-2: Both rate and level differences, with shorter growing seasons for lower IQs. D-1 and D-2: Both rate and level differences, with longer growing seasons for lower IQs. E-1 and E-2: Linear growth functions which do not go through the origin.

& House, 1962; Earhart & Warren, 1964; Fishler, Graliker, & Koch, 1965; Silverstein, 1966; Erickson, 1968; White, 1969).

This fall in subnormal intelligence with age is not restricted to institutionalized populations. Mountain children in Tennessee and Kentucky have been reported to have, on the average, lower intelligence than normal; and their IQs have been found to fall spontaneously with age (Hirsch, 1928; Wheeler, 1932; Chapanis & Williams, 1945).

Loss in IQ with age is not the only effect found with subjects of subnormal intelligence. Spontaneous gains in retardate IQ have been reported by Poull (1929), Woodall (1931), Strauss and Kephart (1939), Clarke and Clarke (1954), Clarke *et al.* (1958), Ross (1962), Reger (1962), and Rosen, Stallings, Floor, and Nowakiska (1968).

To complete the picture, a half-dozen studies report no appreciable changes with age for retardate IQs. These include Crissey (1937), Whatley and Plant (1957), Collmann and Newlyn (1958), Alper and Horne (1959), Holowinsky (1962), and Throne, Schulman, and Kaspar (1962).

There is nothing necessarily contradictory about this array of quite different findings. Retardates of different ages, levels, and etiologies were examined, and the growth of intelligence could conceivably change with these variables. The only apparent rule that accounts for the bulk of these studies is quite simple: the younger the subjects (below 16), the greater the likelihood of a spontaneous decrease in IQ with age, the older the subjects, the greater the likelihood of an increase in IQ. This rule implies a nonmonotonic IQ vs. age function : falling at early ages, but rising later on. Retardate MA growth of the kind illustrated in Fig. 1 (E-1), coupled with the longer than normal growing season as in Fig. 1 (B-1), would account for this suggested IQ vs. age relation (fall then rise).

What is needed to confirm these suggestions from the literature is a study of the growth of retardate intelligence over a wide age range, with sizable groups at each of the five levels of retardation. Optimally such a study would be a longitudinal one. The heroic effort necessary for a longitudinal study of this type makes it unlikely. A cross-sectional study would be easier, but not worth the doing without adequate controls for the many factors confounding cross-sectional studies. Adequate controls here would make a cross-sectional study also assume heroic proportions. The literature reveals no heroes in this domain.

A less exacting method of growth study exists which is quicker to run than a longitudinal method, and easier to control than a cross-sectional study. This is a semi-longitudinal method. A brief comparison of the three methods of analysis follows.

For a cross-sectional study, each subject is measured just once, and an average taken of different subjects at different CA levels. Such data are often readily available, especially in institutions for the retarded, but the difficulties of control are obvious. The major variable of age is confounded with subject selection. Younger subjects, for instance, may not be selected from a population equal in all relevant respects to the older groups. In an institutionalized population, very young residents tend to be severely and profoundly retarded, otherwise they would not be recognized. And as the brighter subjects get older, they are often graduated out of the institution. Such factors confound a cross-sectional curve. Many other sources of bias could be cited such as: changes in institutional admissions and release policies, changes in diagnostic criteria, introduction of new drugs, differential death rates, or changes in socio-economic level of the general population.

The longitudinal method requires the repeated measurement of the same individuals for many years. Except for the bias introduced by repeated measurement (a practice effect) and a possible selection of subjects (not everyone will stay in a longitudinal study) this method is relatively unconfounded. The real trouble with the longitudinal method is that a lifetime of data collection is necessary.

A semi-longitudinal study, on the other hand, requires at most a few years for data collection, and provides controls for many of the factors confounding cross-sectional measurement. Each subject is tested at least twice over a period of years, but many repeated measurements are not required. The basic idea of a semi-longitudinal analysis is displayed in Fig. 2. Straight lines are used to connect adjacent measures of the same individual, as shown in the panel at left. The slopes of these lines are then averaged within each CA interval, as shown in the center panel. These average slopes are then made continuous and adjusted for level as

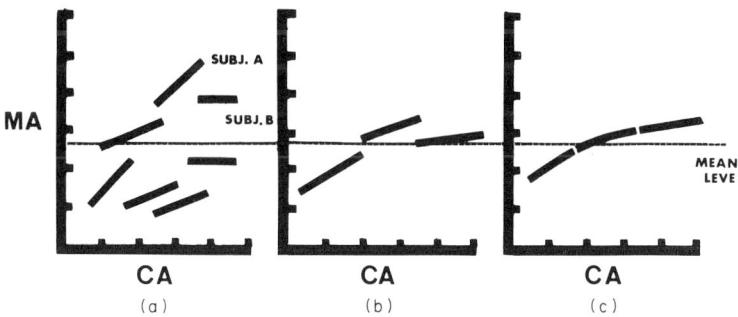

FIG. 2. Graphical illustration of the elements of semi-longitudinal method. (a) Semi-longitudinal raw data (each S measured at least twice); (b) averaging slopes within CA blocks (small blocks, linear slopes); (c) semi-longitudinal, corrected for level differences (easier than longitudinal, not as confounded as cross-sectional).

indicated in the last panel. The semi-longitudinal method has been described by Zeaman and House (1962), and will be reviewed in more precise detail presently.

The semi-longitudinal method affords some controls not provided by cross-sectional methodology. Since pairs of measures are considered for all subjects, the changes in performance from test to test cannot easily be attributed to sampling biases (i.e., getting different kinds of subjects at different ages). It must be admitted that the many forms of possible sampling bias are not perfectly controlled by semi-longitudinal measurement. If these biases are to have an effect on the form of the semi-longitudinal growth function, then the effect must be on the *rate of change of MA*, not the level of MA (or IQ). While such sources of confounding are certainly possible (e.g., subjects may be selected for retest who are changing in MA in some specific way), we judge them less likely than the biases affecting the *level* of response in cross-sectional measurement.

Despite the feasibility and advantages of the semi-longitudinal method, it has not been applied in any large-scale study of retardate intelligence. This is surprising since the data for such studies must already be available in many institutions for the retarded, where residents are retested with something greater than zero frequency. There were, for instance, available to us at Mansfield Training School several thousand retests of intelligence, recorded over the years for residents at all levels of retardation and over wide age ranges. These we have analyzed semi-longitudinally.

II. THE SUBJECT POPULATION

The numbers of retested subjects of both sexes at the five levels of retardation and in various diagnostic categories are given in Table I. There are approximately equal numbers of each sex and roughly the same proportion of cases at each level with the exception of the Borderline which is relatively smaller in size.

Table II presents further descriptive statistics on the subject population and indicates that each subject has been retested about four times at intervals of about five years. The total number of tests and retests is approximately 4700.

III. DESCRIPTION OF THE SEMI-LONGITUDINAL METHOD

Since the methods of semi-longitudinal analysis are not widely used, a detailed description will be given with numerical and graphical examples.

TABLE I

NUMBER OF MALE AND FEMALE SUBJECTS IN EACH OF SEVEN DIAGNOSTIC CATEGORIES FOR FIVE LEVELS OF RETARDATION

Diagnostic category	Level of Retardation										Total
	Borderline		Mild		Moderate		Severe		Profound		
	Male	Female	Male	Female	Male	Female	Male	Female	Male	Female	
Epilepsy	9	11	17	24	21	28	28	27	26	64	255
Cultural-familial	4	8	33	72	35	49	17	15	10	10	253
Congenital cerebral defect	15	17	53	35	57	72	37	23	46	28	383
Mongolism	0	0	0	0	3	2	18	24	27	28	102
Cranial anomalies	0	0	0	1	0	5	1	4	7	10	28
Motor defect	0	1	1	0	1	3	2	3	1	1	13
Miscellaneous	4	6	13	13	10	11	14	7	19	28	125
Subtotal	32	43	117	145	127	170	117	103	136	169	1159
Total	75		262		297		220		305		

Within each CA interval an average slope is taken of all the subjects having a measure within that interval. In the graphical display (Fig. 3), for example, the average slope within the first CA interval is unity, there being only one subject in that interval having that slope. In the second CA interval, there are two slopes, 1.0 and 2.8 which average to 1.9. In the third CA interval (between 2 and 3), the topmost function has two slopes, partly the CD slope and partly the DE slope. A weighted average of these two slopes is obtained by linearly connecting the two points at the beginning and end of the interval (shown in Fig. 3 by the dashed line

TABLE II

DESCRIPTIVE STATISTICS ON INTELLIGENCE AND AGE AT FIVE LEVELS OF RETARDATION, TOGETHER WITH NUMBER AND SPACING OF TESTS

Level	IQ Range	MA (yr) Mean	MA (yr) SD	CA (yr) Mean	CA (yr) SD	Months between tests Mean	Number tests per subject Mean
Borderline	83–68	10.0	1.5	28.0	13.4	55.1	3.8
Mild	67–52	8.2	1.4	26.5	13.1	58.6	4.1
Moderate	51–36	6.2	1.1	28.5	13.9	61.0	4.6
Severe	35–20	3.9	0.9	25.6	13.5	65.9	4.2
Profound	20–0	1.7	1.0	21.1	12.4	68.1	3.5

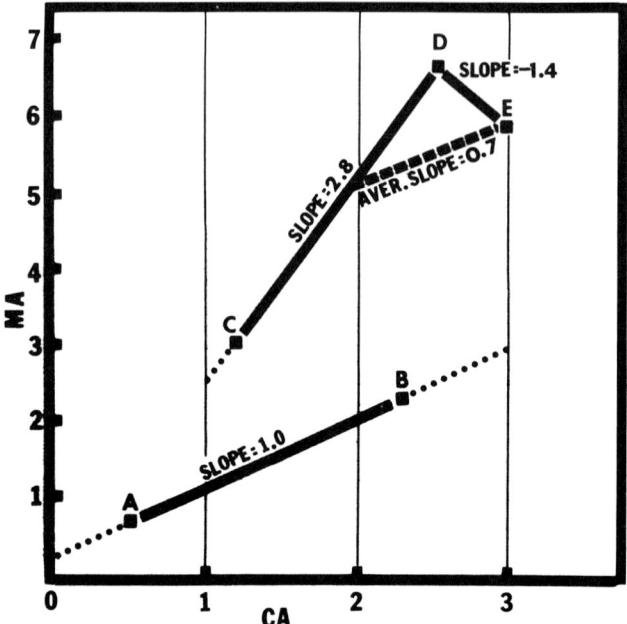

Fig. 3. Initial steps of semi-longitudinal analysis. Straight lines are used to connect adjacent test-retest data points for each subject (A-B, and C-D-E). The dotted lines show linear extrapolations within an interval. The dashed line in Interval 3 is an average slope.

with slope 0.7). The average slope for the third CA interval would therefore be 0.85. With actual data, of course, there are many slopes of varying signs and magnitudes to be averaged algebraically.

The result of this analysis is a series of average slopes or rates of MA change at each CA level. These rates can be integrated to yield a function relating MA to CA. In the example given above the average rates for the three intervals were 1.0, 1.9, and 0.85, respectively. A graphical integration of these is shown in Fig. 4. The rates are merely laid end to end.

The form of the integrated function is fixed by the integration procedure, but the function is left floating at an indeterminate level on the ordinate. To fix the level of the function, average MA values are found for all individual functions corresponding to the midpoint of the CA at each interval. In graphical terms, this would require a perpendicular line drawn at each CA interval midpoint of Fig. 3, and a measurement of the points of intersection of the perpendicular with each of the individual functions. The means of these points yield a new function relating CA and MA which is best regarded as a cross-sectional curve. It corresponds closely to a rolling average of an ordinary cross-sectional curve. Such a curve is drawn in Fig. 5. It is used to determine the level of the semi-longitudinal curve by a least-squares procedure. The semi-longitudinal curve is, in effect fitted to the cross-sectional curve by moving the semi-longitudinal curve up or down on the ordinate to minimize the squared ordinal discrepancies between the two curves. In this way, the form of the semi-longitudinal curve is preserved, and the level determined by the cross-sectional data.

The computations of a semi-longitudinal analysis are sufficiently tedious as to require computerization. A program for this purpose, written in Fortran IV, is available from the authors. The program has been used successfully on an IBM 7040 and IBM 360.

IV. RESULTS

A. Growth Curve for the Entire Population

A comparison of the average cross-sectional and semi-longitudinal curves is provided by Fig. 6. The semi-longitudinal curve has been purposely placed arbitrarily low on the ordinate to eliminate overlap of the two functions and facilitate a comparison of their forms. The cross-sectional curve appears to rise with only slight deceleration during 70 years of CA. The continued rise in this function is probably caused by differ-

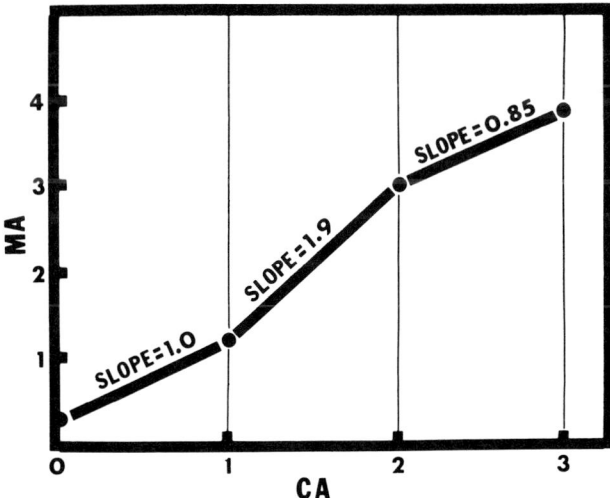

FIG. 4. A semi-longitudinal plot of average slopes within each interval connected to form a continuous function. The position of the curve on the ordinate is indeterminate.

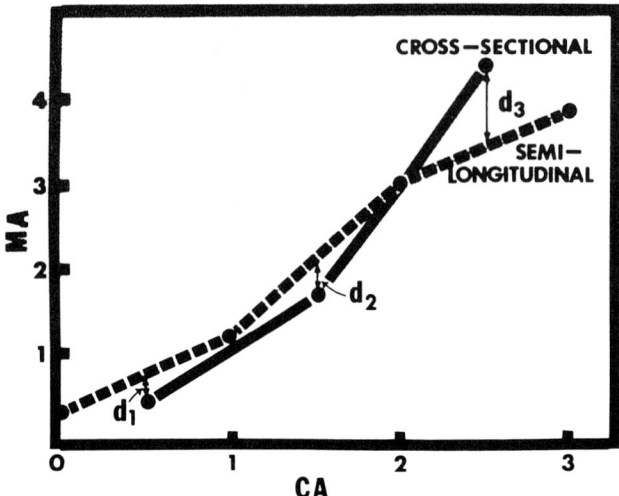

Fig. 5. The semi-longitudinal curve of Fig. 4 has been positioned on the ordinate so as to minimize the deviations (d_1, d_2, and d_3) from the cross-sectional curve.

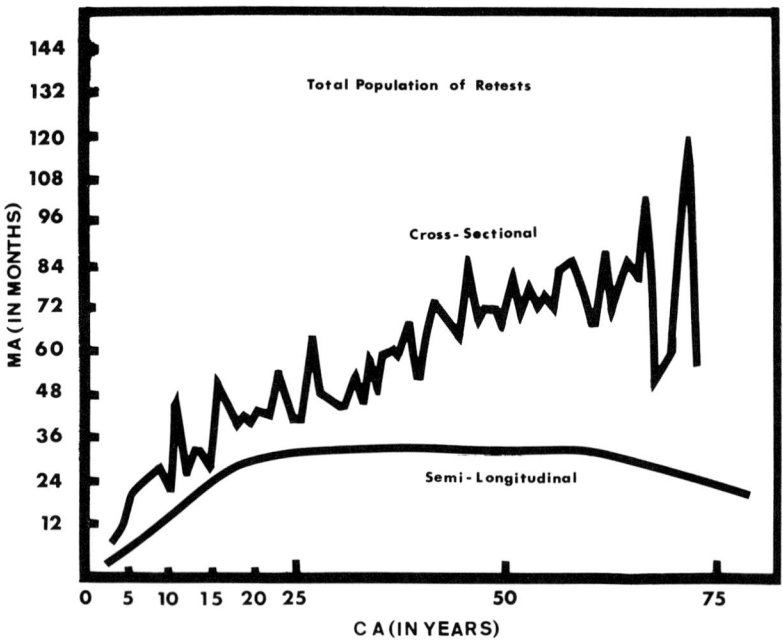

Fig. 6. MA growth functions for the entire population of retests computed cross-sectionally and semi-longitudinally. Level differences should be ignored.

ential death rate. The severe and profound tend to die earlier, leaving higher levels at the older ages.

In contrast, the semi-longitudinal function has the overall shape of the growth and decline of normal intelligence in that it grows initially with strong linear components (from 3 to 15 years), slopes off and becomes flat between 20 and 60 years, and then begins to taper off.

The variability around the semi-longitudinal function is graphed in Fig. 7. The standard deviation (SD) grows linearly up to about 12 years, and then decelerates, reaching a peak at about 20 years. The function then declines relatively steadily with age until CA 70. The SDs are noisy thereafter because of the small sample sizes. The overall shape of the SD function suggests that the underlying MA growth functions are linearly diverging up to about 12 years. The reasoning here is more of a best-guess nature than strictly deductive. It can be shown mathematically that if the underlying growth functions were linearly diverging from a common starting point, the SD of the group function would be linearly rising also. While other forms of underlying growth curves may also produce a linear SD function, these would have to be very special, that is, a tiny class compared to the function families that do not produce the linear SD growth. The presumption is therefore that the underlying curves are linearly diverging.

This inference for the SD curve can be seen to be substantially correct in Fig. 8, but another inference from the SD curve leads instead to a puzzle. This is the decline in SD from CA 20 to 60. It suggests that the lower IQ groups have longer growing seasons, and therefore a tendency to catch up somewhat with the higher groups. The result would be a shrinking group variability. The effect can be seen graphically in Fig. 1 (B-1 and B-2, or D-1 and D-2). Later analyses do not confirm this inference, so we must look elsewhere for an explanation of the declining SD with age. The most likely explanation comes from the fact that in later adult years, the extreme groups make up less and less of the sample. The Borderlines leave, the Profounds die.

B. Semi-Longitudinal MA Growth, by Level

The semi-longitudinal growth functions for five levels of retardation are depicted in Fig. 8. The following features are noteworthy.

(a) Initially, a strong linear component, with slopes clearly related to level. This feature, at least, is traditional. All slopes are less than normal.

(b) Higher levels have longer growing seasons. The Profounds flatten off before 15 years, the Severes continue to grow noticeably until 25, and the higher levels do not appear to reach their highest MA levels before 35. This feature is certainly not traditional.

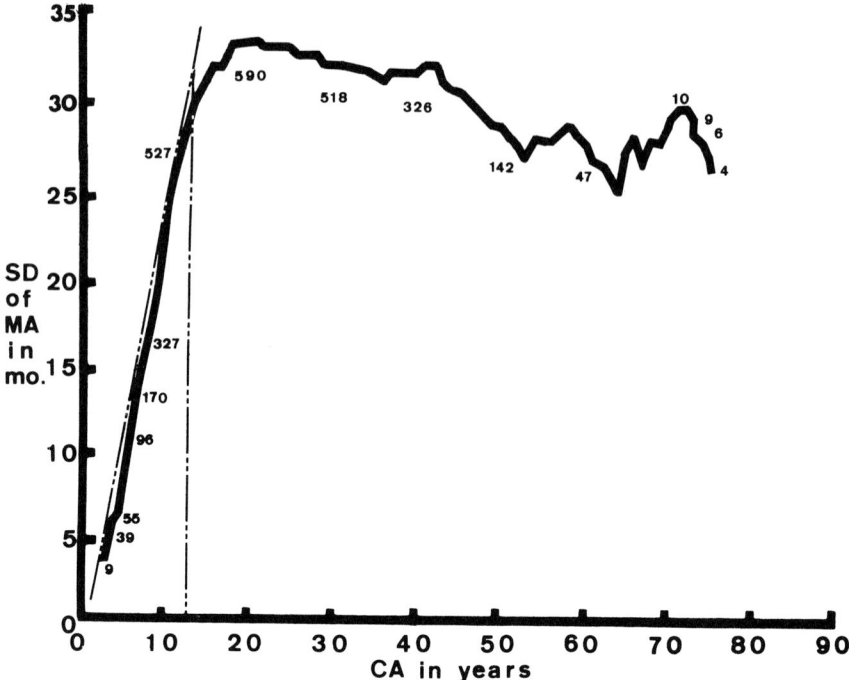

FIG. 7. Group variability of MA as a function of CA. The numbers of cases are indicated at various points on the function.

(c) All show some signs of decline after 60. There is a suggestion that the higher levels fall off the most (having more to lose) but the curves are noisy after 60 due to small Ns. A more detailed quantitative analysis of these functions presented here in a later section confirms the notion that the higher levels show greater decline at advanced ages.

(d) One important but not obvious feature of these functions is the extrapolation of the linear components of these functions backward toward the origin. The extrapolations would cross the ordinate at points higher than MA zero. The bearing this has on IQ constancy is shown in Fig. 1, E-1 and E-2. This property is also present in the data of the 1937 Stanford-Binet. Using these data, Pinneau (1961, p. 53) presents an MA growth curve for a group having a deviation IQ of 36. The linear extrapolation of this function crosses the ordinate in the neighborhood of 15 months MA, which accords well with the data of Fig. 8.

C. Cross-Sectional Growth, by Level

The cross-sectional curves corresponding to the semi-longitudinal functions are shown in Fig. 9. These show some but not all of the properties of the semi-longitudinal plots. The early linear components with slopes related to level are observable, but the shorter growing seasons for the lower levels are obscured, as are the old age declines.

D. Semi-Longitudinal Growth, by Level and Sex

The addition of the parameter of sex makes little difference in the forms of growth function for the various levels. Fig. 10 shows a slight tendency for the males to deteriorate more after 50 than the females, but the numbers of cases at the advanced ages are too small (especially in the Borderlines) to mean much. A statistical analysis of sex differences was performed showing these to be unreliable. The fact that the overall forms of the male and female functions match reasonably well provides a measure of reliability of the general findings.

E. Diagnostic Categories

Review of Table I indicates there are three groups, diagnosed as epileptic, cultural-familial, and congenital cerebral defect, which had

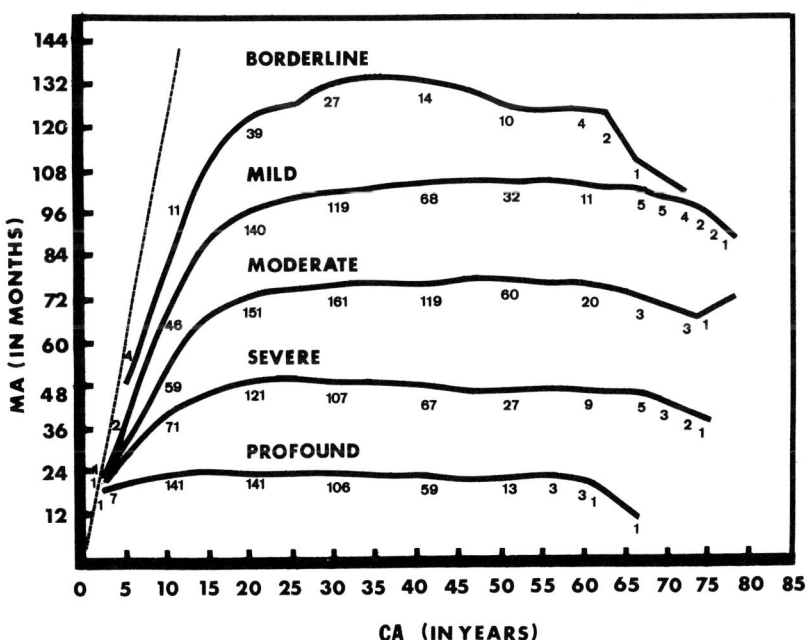

Fig. 8. Mean semi-longitudinal MA growth functions for the five levels of retardation. Numbers on the curves refer to number of subjects measured.

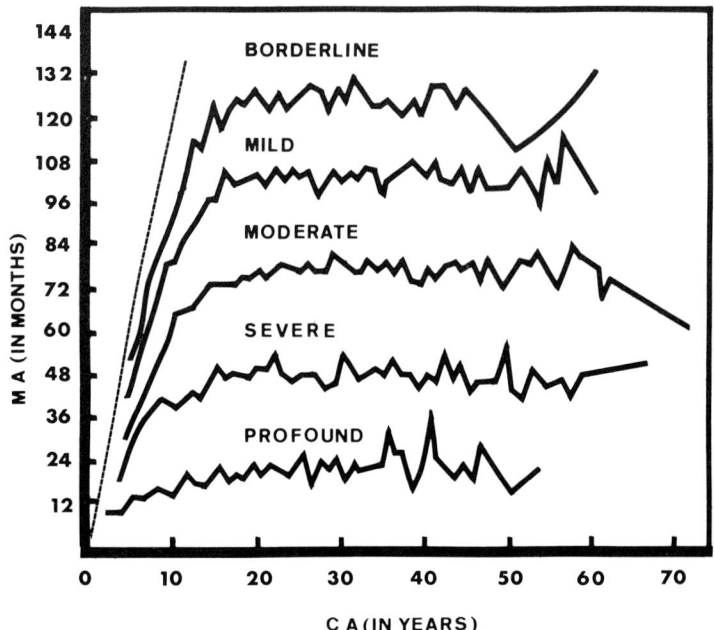

FIG. 9. Mean cross-sectional MA growth curves for the five levels of retardation.

enough cases at each level to permit a comparison with level controlled. This is done by calculating an average of the five levels (unweighted by the number of cases within a level) for each diagnostic category. The results are shown in Fig. 11. There are no apparent differences in growth of MA for these diagnostic categories when level is controlled. It does not appear to make any difference how one gets to be a retardate, whether through bad genes, brain pathology, or seizures, the maturational results are the same.

There is a tendency for the epileptics to decline more in old age, but the number of cases is too small to be sure. More data are needed here.

The mongoloids at the severe and profound levels had enough cases to be compared with cranial anomalies and other categories at the severe and profound levels. The semi-longitudinal functions for these groups are displayed in Fig. 12. The level differences are unimportant, since these are subject to cross-sectional biases, but the forms of the functions are important. They tell us that the mongoloids at the profound level have about the same growth function as the cranial anomalies. These could be super-imposed by elevating the bottom function slightly. The two "severe" functions are also roughly parallel.

The general conclusion is that diagnostic category is a weak variable in determining the form of growth of retarded intelligence, when level is controlled. Since subject variables such as sex and diagnostic category are not strong determinants of the growth of retarded intelligence in our sample, these variables have been ignored in our subsequent analyses.

F. Age-Changes in IQ, by Level

The same methods used for deriving semi-longitudinal MA functions have been applied to IQ measurements. Fig. 13 plots age changes in conventional Stanford-Binet IQs for the five levels of retardation. All levels fall precipitously from CA 2 to 16 years. Then, because CA is fixed at about 16 in the MA/CA formula, the IQ starts to rise for the higher levels (because the MA is still growing).

These data show that it is indeed possible to get either increases or decreases in IQ over time for retarded populations, depending upon what ages and levels are chosen. Very few of the apparently discrepant, published findings of IQ changes in the retardate are inconsistent with

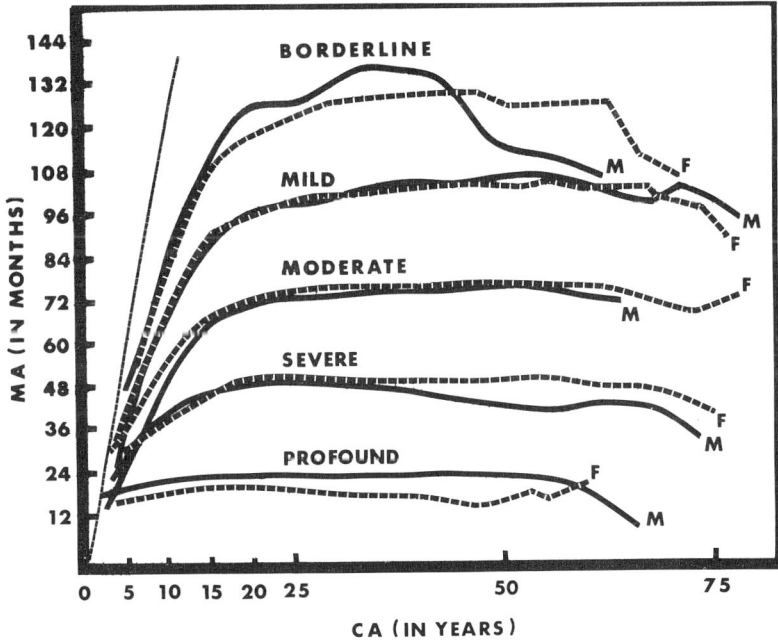

FIG. 10. Semi-longitudinal MA growth curves for both sexes at the five levels of retardation.

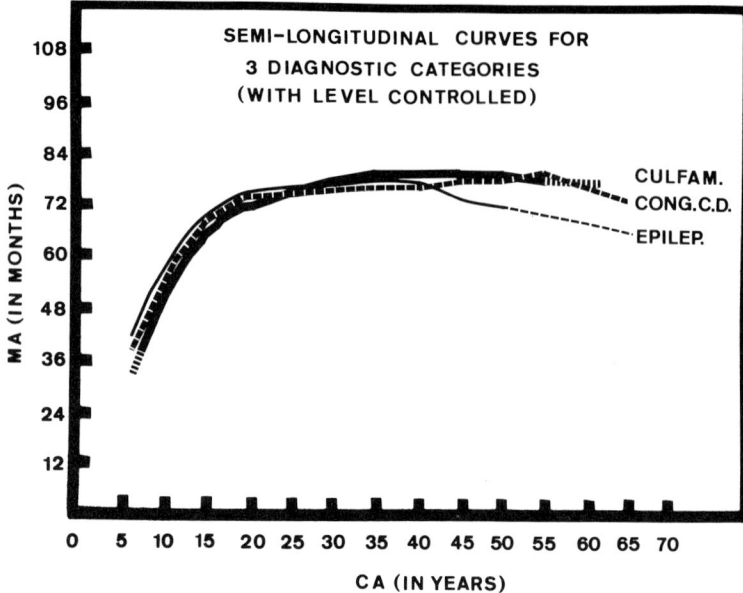

FIG. 11. Age changes in MA computed semi-longitudinally for three diagnostic categories (with level controlled), cultural-familial (culfam.), congenital cerebral defect (cong. c. d.), and epileptics (epilep.).

this general picture (a picture which we do not believe has been drawn before).

The same pattern of changes emerges from the cross-sectional measurements, as seen in Fig. 14, but with greater variability. Changing from a conventional Stanford-Binet IQ to a deviation IQ (using Pinneau's tables), does little to affect the overall forms of the IQ functions. This can be seen in Fig. 15.

We do not attach any profound psychological significance to these changes in IQ. The decline in IQ, for instance, is not easily attributable to institutionalization because the same effect has been shown for noninstitutionalized subnormal populations. A better scaling procedure with an adequate retarded standardization group might provide a zero point at zero CA (by extrapolation), which in turn might eliminate the initial fall in IQ.

Whatever interpretive significance attaches to these IQ changes, in practice they constitute a nuisance because of their inconstancy. Also, in a theoretical sense, if the test were aiming to measure a constant, genetically determined aspect of intelligence, it would be appropriate to try to find a transformation of the scale which would yield age-invariant scores. In other words, it would be nice if we could find for each retardate a number, representing his intelligence, which would remain constant over a lifetime and would predictively describe the growth and decline of mental age.

V. DETERMINATION OF K, A CONSTANT MEASURE OF RETARDED INTELLIGENCE

A. An Empirical Equation

To find such a number (a constant substitute for the inconstant IQ), we took the family of semi-longitudinal MA growth curves for the five levels of retardation (shown in Fig. 8), and fitted to these curves an equation of the form

$$MA = k_1 \ln CA + k_2 CA + k_3 \qquad (1)$$

Equation (1) was not arbitrarily chosen. Previous studies by Zeaman and House (1962), and by Silverstein (1966), had shown that mongoloid intelligence had a strong logarithmic growth component. To include

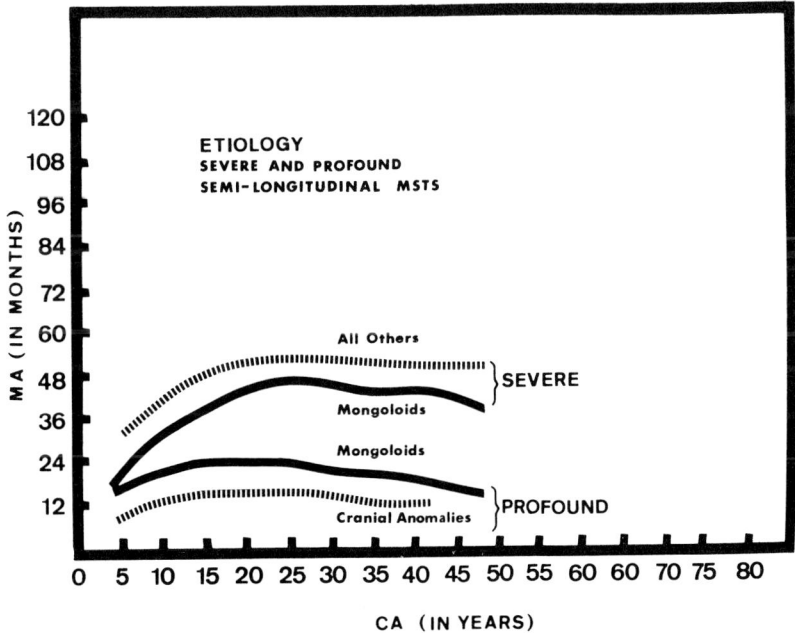

FIG. 12. Mongoloid MA growth compared with cranial anomalies at the Profound level and with a mean of all other diagnostic categories at the Severe level.

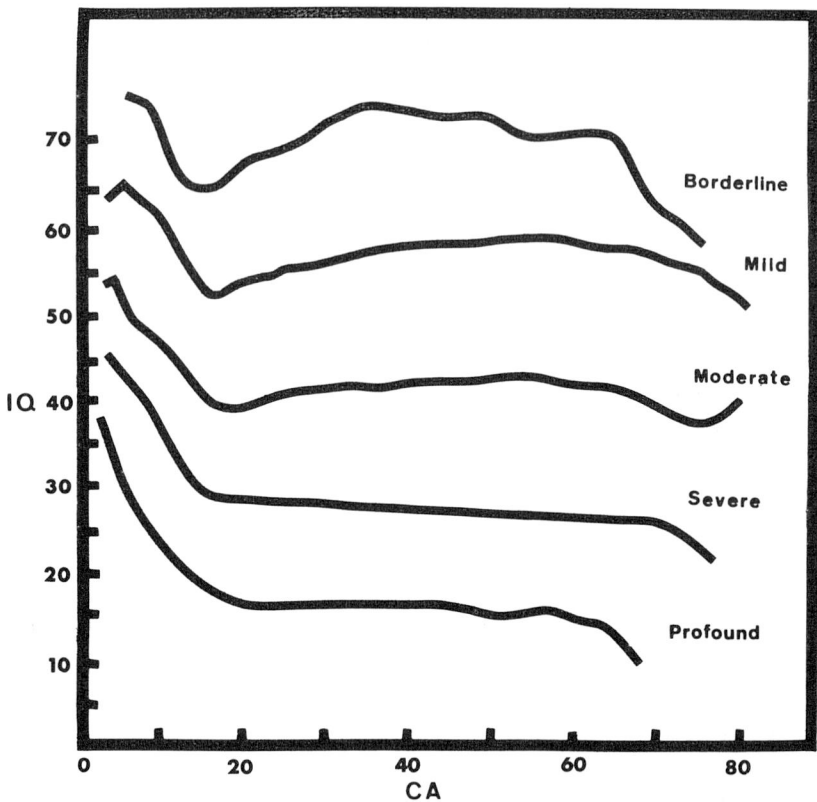

Fig. 13. Age changes in IQ for the five levels of retardation computed semi-longitudinally.

this, the first term of the equation is proportional to the natural logarithm of CA. The next term, k_2CA is a linear decay term, since k_2 is negative, and brings the function down when CA gets large. The k_3 parameter is a level factor. The k_1, k_2, and k_3 parameters vary from individual to individual and group to group.

B. Goodness of Fit

The results of multiple regression analyses for the five levels of retardation are shown in Table III. The best-fitting parameter values (by least-squares) are shown to vary widely and systematically for the five group functions. The correlation of data points and equation values is extremely high for all groups except the Profounds (which is a respectable +.78).

The goodness of fit is also measured by the standard error of estimate ($SE_{est.}$) which provides an index of the dispersion of individual empirical points around the mean value predicted by Eq. (1). Table III shows the $SE_{est.}$ to vary between 1.3 and 2.4 months of MA. The data points hug the equation.

C. Interpretation of the Parameters

The k_1 parameters control the initial growth rates most strongly because they are relatively large and positive multipliers of ln CA. This parameter increases sharply with intelligence level.

The effects of k_2 (algebraically negative) are felt mostly at the higher age levels, since the values of k_2 are relatively small and require multipli-

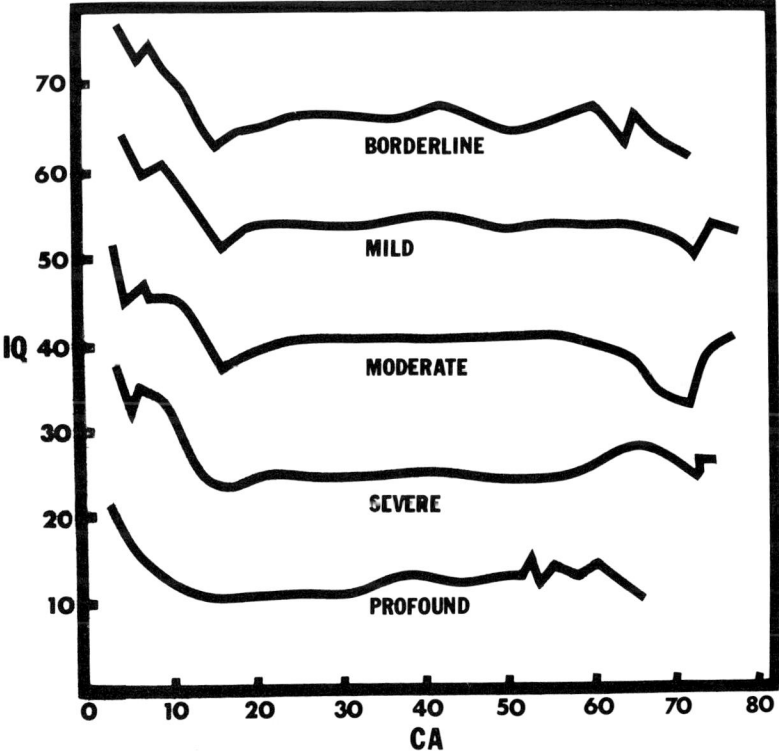

FIG. 14. Cross-sectional measurement of IQ age changes. These functions are not purely cross-sectional because each individual contributes to several consecutive CA intervals.

cation by large CAs to achieve an appreciable product. This parameter can be interpreted as a linear decay (or aging) factor which eventually overpowers the influence of the logarithmic growth parameter, k_1. The k_2 values are also related to level of retardation: higher levels show more decline than the lower.

The ratio of k_1 and k_2 in Table III has a special significance in terms of growth and decay. It is the CA (in years) at which MA ceases to grow and begins to decline. This can be shown by setting the first derivative of Eq. (1) ($dMA/dCA = k_1/CA + k_2$) equal to zero and solving for CA. This yields a maximum at $CA = -k_2/k_1$. The ratio $-k_2/k_1$ is best viewed as the growing season parameter, or the number of years it takes to hit an MA maximum.

It would appear that the shortest two growing seasons are displayed by the Profound and Severe levels. As indicated previously, these groups might be called "mental accelerates" in the sense that they peak up rela-

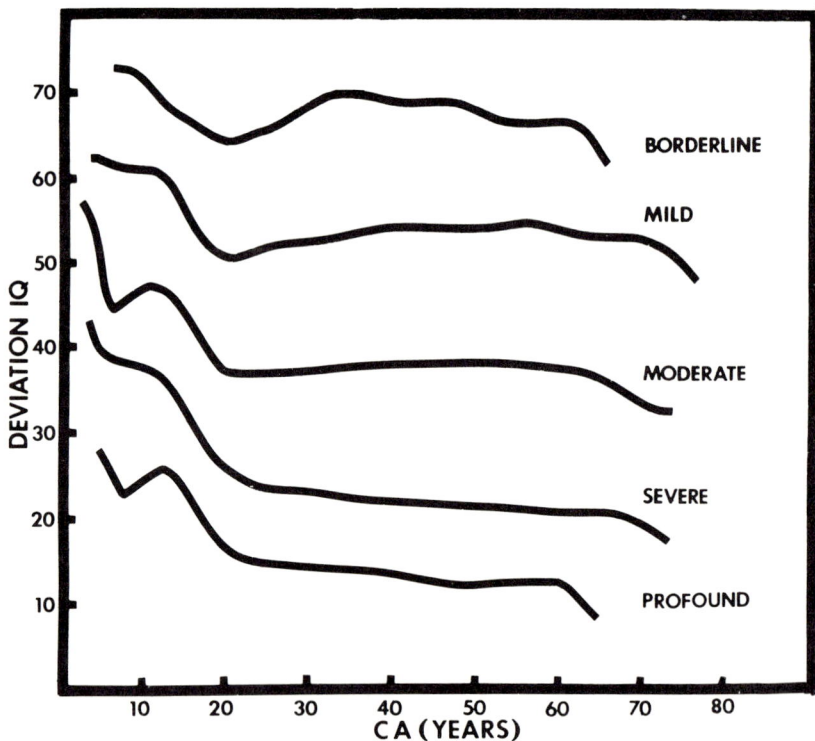

FIG. 15. The semi-longitudinal course of change of deviation IQs of the five levels of retardation.

TABLE III
Parameter Values and Measures of Goodness of Fit for the Equations
$MA = k_1 \ln CA + k_2 CA + k_3$ for Five Levels of Retardation

Level	Parameter values				Goodness of fit	
	k_1	k_2	k_3	$-k_2/k_1$	r	SE of est.
Borderline	83.1	−2.4	−80.0	35	.99	2.4
Mild	49.5	−1.2	−29.2	41	.99	2.0
Moderate	32.9	− .8	−10.6	41	.99	2.0
Severe	17.8	− .6	6.3	30	.97	1.3
Profound	4.3	− .2	15.7	22	.78	1.6

tively fast. The most surprising aspect of these growing season parameters is their size. The unit of CA is in *years*. These parameters tell us that most retardates continue to grow in MA until they are 30 to 40 years of age, even if the rates are not high.

The third parameter, k_3 is related to the first two. It is the mental age predicted by the curve at the CA for which $CA/\ln CA = -k_2/k_1$. This parameter controls the level but not the form of the MA growth functions.

D. A Simplification of Equation 1

Although Eq. (1) describes the growth and decline of retardate MA with precision, we were not particularly happy with it. Each retardate would have to be characterized by three numbers (k_1, k_2, and k_3) instead of the usual one (the IQ). Not only would it require several measures of MA at different ages to compute k_1, k_2, and k_3, but also a short course in mathematics to interpret them.

We observed in Table III that k_1, k_2, and k_3 were all closely related. The values of k_1 were roughly proportional to k_2, and k_3 was linearly related to k_2.

Since both k_1 and k_3 were thus functions of k_2, why not replace k_1 and k_3 with these functions, and reduce the number of parameters to just one? This was done, and the result was Eq. (2).

$$MA = -36 K \ln CA + KCA + 44.8 K + 27.1 \qquad (2)$$

Each subject can now be assigned a value of K by substituting his MA and CA at any age into this equation and solving for K. A table converting MA and CA to K has been included as an appendix to this chapter.

The value of K should remain constant from early childhood to old age, interpretable much as the IQ is interpreted—a measure of relative intelligence (although in this case the result of both growth and decay processes).

The MA growth functions implied by Eq. (2) are shown in Fig. 16. The higher the negative value of K the higher the level of the retardate. The values of K in Fig. 16 are those corresponding to the five levels of retardation (see also the k_2 column in Table III). A value of $K = 0$ means no growth of MA at all; positive values of K imply an initially declining MA. The goodness of fit of Eq. (2) to the data is not sufficiently different from that of Eq. (1) to warrant replacement of Table III. Other data on the constancy and reliability of K will be presented.

The empirical nature of Eq. (2) can be seen from the fact that it can generate irrational (negative) values of MA. It is not much good before CAs of 6 or 7 years, but then it stays fairly constant for the lifetime of the retardate.

E. Reliability and Constancy of K, Compared to IQ

The constancy of K can be seen graphically most easily by using a semi-longitudinal method to compute and plot the mean values of K for

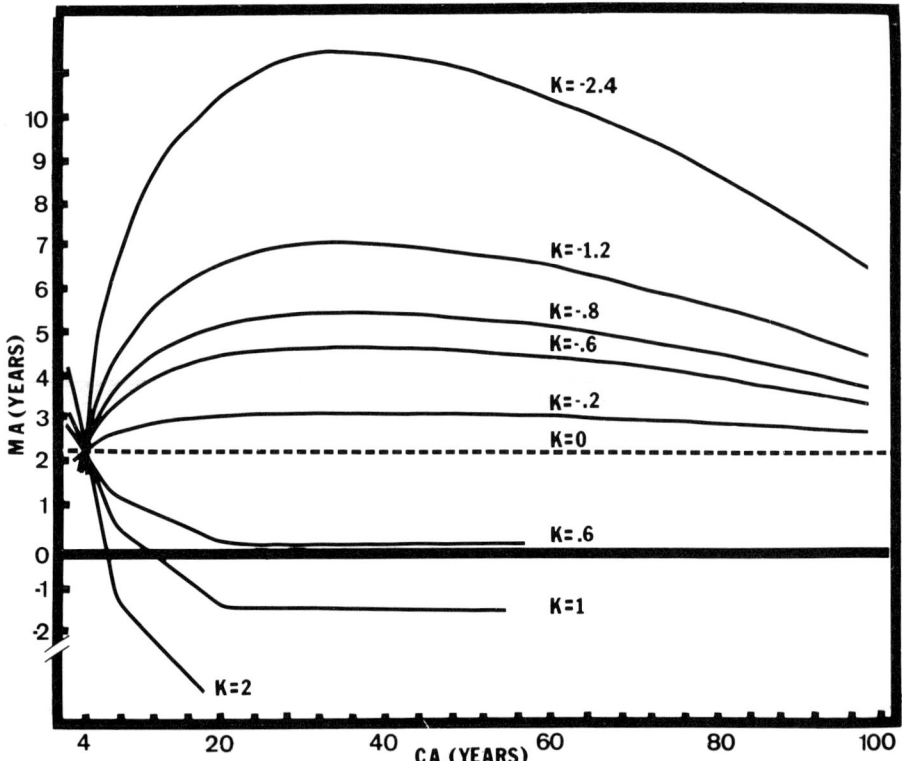

FIG. 16. Age changes in MA predicted by Eq. (2) (MA $=-36K$ in CA $+ KCA + 44.8K +$ 27.1). The negative parameter values of K ($-2.4, -1.2, -.8, -.6,$ and $-.2$) are those corresponding to the five levels of retardation (Borderline $= -2.4$, Mild -1.2, etc.) Tabulated values of K in the Appendix, have been made positive for convenience.

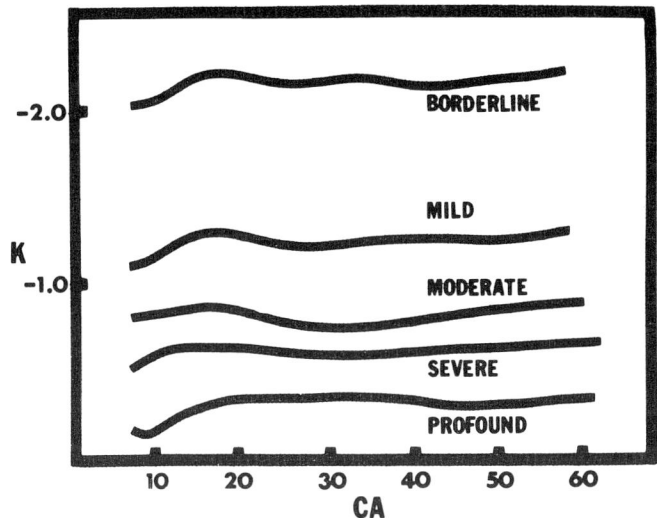

FIG. 17. The course of change in K over age for the five levels of retardation. Averages based on Ns under 5 have been excluded.

each level of retardation as a function of age. These are shown in Fig. 17. While not absolutely flat, these functions are far more stable than the corresponding age changes in IQ (cf. Fig. 13).

More stable indices of reliability and constancy of K values can be obtained by correlating all possible pairs of K values for each individual. There are over 8500 pairs of K values for our total population, disregarding the time intervals separating the measurements. Scatter-plots of such populations are too cumbersome to plot, so mean values over intervals have been calculated and graphed in Fig. 18 for both K and IQ. The linearity of the empirical points is some index of the test-retest correlation ($r = .961$ for K, $r = .864$ for IQ), while the deviation from the diagonal line in Fig. 18 is an index of nonconstancy. The IQ function deviates (downward) markedly from the 45° slope, showing the subsequent tests are on the average lower than preceding tests. The conclusions to be drawn from these comparisons of test-retest relations is that the K parameter is less subject to either variable errors or constant errors than is the IQ.

F. Reliability of K and IQ Over Time

The decline of test-retest correlations over time is a well-known phenomenon in the area of intelligence testing. It has been written about by Anderson (1939), and more recently by Bloom (1964) who has summarized the data on normals. Fig. 19 portrays the decline for our population of retardates. The correlation remains high for both K and IQ over intervals exceeding 15 years, with K showing the greater resistance to loss.

Interpretation of this general phenomenon has been the topic of some theoretical discussion, e.g., Anderson's (1939) Overlap Hypothesis, which relates the fall in reliability to underlying structure of the test. Data relevant to such theories can be obtained by generating families of correlational functions of the kind illustrated in Fig. 19, with the parameters of level of retardation, age at initial test, and MA. This remains to be done, and will be the subject of a further report using these retardate data. In the meantime it seems safe to make the simple empirical statement that the reliability of K holds up for long periods of time.

VI. SUMMARY AND CONCLUSIONS

Semi-longitudinal methods have been used to study the growth and decline of retardate intelligence. The basic data were provided by institutional records of Binet mental ages for a population of 1159 resident retardates, varying widely in age and intelligence, each of whom has been tested at least twice over a period of years. The following results (based on 4700 observations) were obtained.

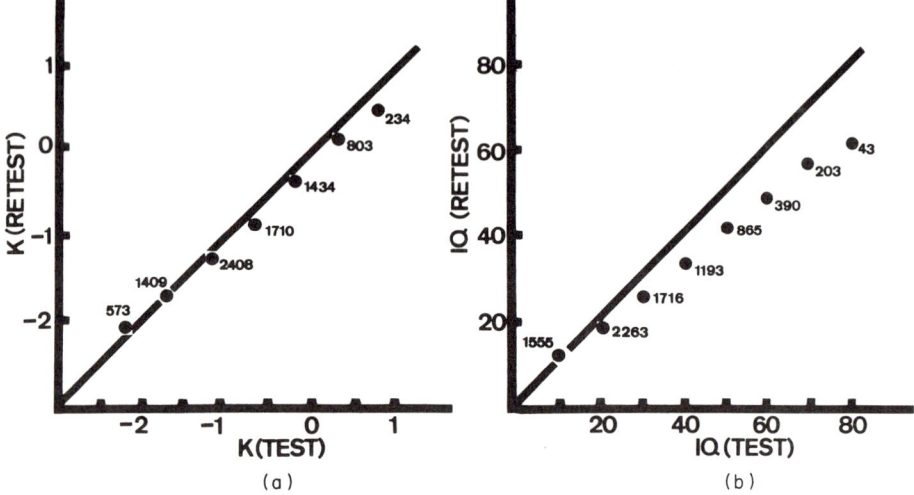

FIG. 18. The relation of test and retest scores for K and IQ (Fig. 18a, $r = .961$; Fig. 18b, $r = .864$). The figure should be read as follows: for the K function at left there were 573 cases of K values between -2 and -2.5; on subsequent retest these cases had an average K value of about -2.0; there is thus generated the first point on the K function. If the average test score (for K or IQ) equaled the average retest score, all points would fall on the diagonal line.

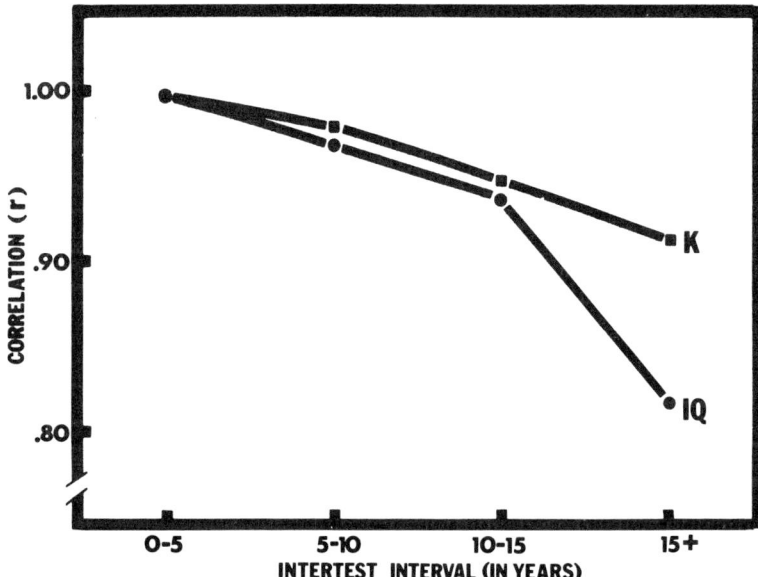

FIG. 19. The decline of test-retest correlations as a function of the time interval between tests. With intervals of 0–4.99 years, the test-retest correlations for both K and IQ are over +.99. With intervals of 15 years and more, the IQ reliability slopes off markedly.

1. The growth of MA of retardates is roughly linear between 5 and 16 years, regardless of level. Growth rate is directly related to level.
2. Higher level retardates continue to grow (although not linearly) in MA for longer periods of their life (at least until the late 30's). The MA growth functions for lower level subjects flatten off earlier.
3. MAs for all levels show a tendency to decline with advancing age (after CA 60).
4. Between 5 and 16 years, IQs of retardates fall precipitously despite their linear increase in MA. This is true for measurements made semi-longitudinally or cross-sectionally, and for deviation IQs as well as conventional IQs.
5. Between 16 and 60 years, retardate IQ is relatively stable, with higher levels showing some tendency to gain IQ points with age.
6. The subject variables of sex and diagnostic category had little effect on the growth of intelligence, when level was controlled.
7. A single equation fitted well the spontaneous growth and decline of retardate intelligence (MA) at all levels. A composite of a logarithmic growth factor, a linear decline, and a level factor yielded a close-fitting family of functions for the empirical, MA vs. CA curves.

8. The equation was simplified to contain a single parameter, K, which may be used to characterize individual retardates. This parameter is more reliable than IQ, and remains constant from childhood to old age. K may profitably replace the inconstant IQ for these subjects as an index of intelligence.

ACKNOWLEDGMENTS

We gratefully acknowledge the help of Betty House and Andrew S. Martin in the conduct of this research and preparation of the manuscript. The testing records of the Mansfield State Training School were provided by Charles Fonda and Superintendent Francis P. Kelley, without whose help this research would not have been possible.

APPENDIX
Values of K as a Function of MA and CA

The table values of K (K_t) were computed from a linear transformation on the K values described in the body of the report (K_r) such that $K_t = -K_r + 2$. The effect of the transformation in the retarded population is to make all table values positive numbers between 0 and 5 and to associate higher values of K with higher levels of intelligence.

The table may be used to find a K value for any subject whose MA and CA are known. MAs are listed in 2-month intervals. It is appropriate to use the mean of the values in successive rows (linear interpolation) to find a value corresponding to an MA not listed. CAs are given in 2-month intervals from 6 years through 21 years 10 months and in 1-year intervals from 22 to 57 years. Linear interpolation between 2 adjacent columns for CAs not listed is also appropriate. When both MA and CA fall between the numbers provided, the correct value is the mean of the 4 adjacent K values. Only MA-CA combinations corresponding to the study sample are presented.

	Chronological Age										
Mental Age	6-0	6-2	6-4	6-6	6-8	6-10	7-0	7-2	7-4	7-6	7-8	7-10
0- 1	0.10	0.20	0.30	0.38	0.45	0.51	0.57	0.62	0.67	0.71	0.75	0.78
0- 3	0.24	0.34	0.43	0.50	0.57	0.63	0.68	0.73	0.77	0.81	0.84	0.88
0- 5	0.39	0.48	0.56	0.63	0.69	0.74	0.79	0.83	0.87	0.91	0.94	0.97
0- 7	0.53	0.62	0.69	0.75	0.81	0.85	0.90	0.94	0.97	1.01	1.04	1.06
0- 9	0.68	0.75	0.82	0.87	0.92	0.97	1.01	1.04	1.08	1.11	1.13	1.16
0-11	0.83	0.89	0.95	1.00	1.04	1.08	1.12	1.15	1.18	1.20	1.23	1.25
1- 1	0.97	1.03	1.08	1.12	1.16	1.20	1.23	1.26	1.28	1.30	1.32	1.34
1- 3	1.12	1.17	1.21	1.25	1.28	1.31	1.34	1.36	1.38	1.40	1.42	1.44
1- 5	1.26	1.30	1.34	1.37	1.40	1.42	1.45	1.47	1.48	1.50	1.52	1.53
1- 7	1.41	1.44	1.47	1.50	1.52	1.54	1.56	1.57	1.59	1.60	1.61	1.62
1- 9	1.55	1.58	1.60	1.62	1.64	1.65	1.67	1.68	1.69	1.70	1.71	1.72
1-11	1.70	1.72	1.73	1.75	1.76	1.77	1.78	1.78	1.79	1.80	1.80	1.81
2- 1	1.85	1.86	1.86	1.87	1.88	1.88	1.88	1.89	1.89	1.90	1.90	1.90
2- 3	1.99	1.99	1.99	1.99	1.99	1.99	1.99	1.99	1.99	2.00	2.00	2.00
2- 5	2.14	2.13	2.12	2.12	2.11	2.11	2.10	2.10	2.10	2.09	2.09	2.09
2- 7	2.28	2.27	2.25	2.24	2.23	2.22	2.21	2.21	2.20	2.19	2.19	2.18
2- 9	2.43	2.41	2.39	2.37	2.35	2.34	2.32	2.31	2.30	2.29	2.28	2.27
2-11	2.58	2.54	2.52	2.49	2.47	2.45	2.43	2.42	2.40	2.39	2.38	2.37
3- 1	2.72	2.68	2.65	2.62	2.59	2.56	2.54	2.52	2.51	2.49	2.47	2.46
3- 3	2.87	2.82	2.78	2.74	2.71	2.68	2.65	2.63	2.61	2.59	2.57	2.55
3- 5	3.01	2.96	2.91	2.86	2.83	2.79	2.76	2.73	2.71	2.69	2.67	2.65
3- 7	3.16	3.09	3.04	2.99	2.94	2.91	2.87	2.84	2.81	2.79	2.76	2.74
3- 9	3.31	3.23	3.17	3.11	3.06	3.02	2.98	2.95	2.91	2.89	2.86	2.83
3-11	3.45	3.37	3.30	3.24	3.18	3.13	3.09	3.05	3.02	2.98	2.95	2.93
4- 1	3.60	3.51	3.43	3.36	3.30	3.25	3.20	3.16	3.12	3.08	3.05	3.02
4- 3	3.74	3.65	3.56	3.49	3.42	3.36	3.31	3.26	3.22	3.18	3.15	3.11
4- 5	3.89	3.78	3.69	3.61	3.54	3.48	3.42	3.37	3.32	3.28	3.24	3.21
4- 7	4.04	3.92	3.82	3.73	3.66	3.59	3.53	3.47	3.42	3.38	3.34	3.30
4- 9	4.18	4.06	3.95	3.86	3.78	3.70	3.64	3.58	3.53	3.48	3.43	3.39
4-11	4.33	4.20	4.08	3.98	3.90	3.82	3.75	3.69	3.63	3.58	3.53	3.49
5- 1	4.47	4.33	4.21	4.11	4.01	3.93	3.86	3.79	3.73	3.68	3.63	3.58
5- 3							3.97	3.90	3.83	3.77	3.72	3.67
5- 5							4.08	4.00	3.93	3.87	3.82	3.77
5- 7							4.19	4.11	4.04	3.97	3.91	3.86
5- 9							4.30	4.21	4.14	4.07	4.01	3.95
5-11							4.41	4.32	4.24	4.17	4.10	4.04

GROWTH AND DECLINE OF RETARDATE INTELLIGENCE

Chronological Age

Mental Age	8-0	8-2	8-4	8-6	8-8	8-10	9-0	9-2	9-4	9-6	9-8	9-10
0- 1	0.82	0.85	0.87	0.90	0.92	0.95	0.97	0.99	1.01	1.02	1.04	1.06
0- 3	0.91	0.94	0.96	0.98	1.01	1.03	1.05	1.07	1.08	1.10	1.11	1.13
0- 5	1.00	1.02	1.05	1.07	1.09	1.11	1.13	1.14	1.16	1.17	1.19	1.20
0- 7	1.09	1.11	1.13	1.15	1.17	1.19	1.21	1.22	1.24	1.25	1.26	1.27
0- 9	1.18	1.20	1.22	1.24	1.25	1.27	1.28	1.30	1.31	1.32	1.33	1.35
0-11	1.27	1.29	1.31	1.32	1.34	1.35	1.36	1.38	1.39	1.40	1.41	1.42
1- 1	1.36	1.38	1.39	1.41	1.42	1.43	1.44	1.45	1.46	1.47	1.48	1.49
1- 3	1.45	1.47	1.48	1.49	1.50	1.51	1.52	1.53	1.54	1.55	1.56	1.56
1- 5	1.54	1.55	1.56	1.57	1.58	1.59	1.60	1.61	1.62	1.62	1.63	1.63
1- 7	1.63	1.64	1.65	1.66	1.67	1.67	1.68	1.69	1.69	1.70	1.70	1.71
1- 9	1.72	1.73	1.74	1.74	1.75	1.75	1.76	1.76	1.77	1.77	1.78	1.76
1-11	1.81	1.82	1.82	1.83	1.83	1.83	1.84	1.84	1.84	1.85	1.85	1.85
2- 1	1.90	1.91	1.91	1.91	1.91	1.92	1.92	1.92	1.92	1.92	1.92	1.92
2- 3	2.00	2.00	2.00	2.00	2.00	2.00	2.00	2.00	2.00	2.00	2.00	2.00
2- 5	2.09	2.08	2.08	2.08	2.08	2.08	2.08	2.07	2.07	2.07	2.07	2.07
2- 7	2.18	2.17	2.17	2.16	2.16	2.16	2.15	2.15	2.15	2.15	2.14	2.14
2- 9	2.27	2.26	2.25	2.25	2.24	2.24	2.23	2.23	2.22	2.22	2.22	2.21
2-11	2.36	2.35	2.34	2.33	2.33	2.32	2.31	2.31	2.30	2.30	2.29	2.29
3- 1	2.45	2.44	2.43	2.42	2.41	2.40	2.39	2.38	2.38	2.37	2.36	2.36
3- 3	2.54	2.53	2.51	2.50	2.49	2.48	2.47	2.46	2.45	2.44	2.44	2.43
3- 5	2.63	2.61	2.60	2.59	2.57	2.56	2.55	2.54	2.53	2.52	2.51	2.50
3- 7	2.72	2.70	2.69	2.67	2.66	2.64	2.63	2.62	2.61	2.59	2.58	2.57
3- 9	2.81	2.79	2.77	2.75	2.74	2.72	2.71	2.69	2.68	2.67	2.66	2.65
3-11	2.90	2.88	2.86	2.84	2.82	2.80	2.79	2.77	2.76	2.74	2.73	2.72
4- 1	2.99	2.97	2.94	2.92	2.90	2.88	2.87	2.85	2.83	2.82	2.80	2.79
4- 3	3.08	3.06	3.03	3.01	2.98	2.96	2.94	2.93	2.91	2.89	2.88	2.86
4- 5	3.17	3.14	3.12	3.09	3.07	3.04	3.02	3.00	2.99	2.97	2.95	2.94
4- 7	3.26	3.23	3.20	3.18	3.15	3.13	3.10	3.08	3.06	3.04	3.03	3.01
4- 9	3.36	3.32	3.29	3.26	3.23	3.21	3.18	3.16	3.14	3.12	3.10	3.08
4-11	3.45	3.41	3.38	3.34	3.31	3.29	3.26	3.24	3.21	3.19	3.17	3.15
5- 1	3.54	3.50	3.46	3.43	3.40	3.37	3.34	3.31	3.29	3.27	3.25	3.23
5- 3	3.63	3.59	3.55	3.51	3.48	3.45	3.42	3.39	3.37	3.34	3.32	3.30
5- 5	3.72	3.67	3.63	3.60	3.56	3.53	3.50	3.47	3.44	3.42	3.39	3.37
5- 7	3.81	3.76	3.72	3.68	3.64	3.61	3.58	3.55	3.52	3.49	3.47	3.44
5- 9	3.90	3.85	3.81	3.76	3.73	3.69	3.66	3.62	3.59	3.57	3.54	3.52
5-11	3.99	3.94	3.89	3.85	3.81	3.77	3.74	3.70	3.67	3.64	3.61	3.59
6- 1	4.08	4.03	3.98	3.93	3.89	3.85	3.81	3.78	3.75	3.72	3.69	3.66
6- 3	4.17	4.12	4.06	4.02	3.97	3.93	3.89	3.86	3.82	3.79	3.76	3.73
6- 5	4.26	4.20	4.15	4.10	4.06	4.01	3.97	3.93	3.90	3.87	3.83	3.80
6- 7	4.35	4.29	4.24	4.19	4.14	4.09	4.05	4.01	3.98	3.94	3.91	3.88
6- 9							4.13	4.09	4.05	4.02	3.98	3.95
6-11							4.21	4.17	4.13	4.09	4.05	4.02
7- 1							4.29	4.24	4.20	4.16	4.13	4.09
7- 3							4.37	4.32	4.28	4.24	4.20	4.17
7- 5							4.45	4.40	4.36	4.31	4.28	4.24
7- 7							4.53	4.48	4.43	4.39	4.35	4.31

Mental Age	Chronological Age											
		10-0	10-2	10-4	10-6	10-8	10-10	11-0	11-2	11-4	11-6	11-8	11-10
0- 1	1.07	1.08	1.10	1.11	1.12	1.13	1.14	1.16	1.17	1.17	1.18	1.19
0- 3	1.14	1.16	1.17	1.18	1.19	1.20	1.21	1.22	1.23	1.24	1.25	1.25
0- 5	1.21	1.23	1.24	1.25	1.26	1.27	1.28	1.28	1.29	1.30	1.31	1.32
0- 7	1.28	1.30	1.31	1.32	1.32	1.33	1.34	1.35	1.36	1.36	1.37	1.38
0- 9	1.36	1.37	1.37	1.38	1.39	1.40	1.41	1.41	1.42	1.43	1.43	1.44
0-11	1.43	1.44	1.44	1.45	1.46	1.47	1.47	1.48	1.49	1.49	1.50	1.50
1- 1	1.50	1.51	1.51	1.52	1.53	1.53	1.54	1.54	1.55	1.55	1.56	1.56
1- 3	1.57	1.58	1.58	1.59	1.59	1.60	1.60	1.61	1.61	1.62	1.62	1.63
1- 5	1.64	1.65	1.65	1.66	1.66	1.66	1.67	1.67	1.68	1.68	1.68	1.69
1- 7	1.71	1.72	1.72	1.72	1.73	1.73	1.73	1.74	1.74	1.74	1.75	1.75
1- 9	1.78	1.79	1.79	1.79	1.79	1.80	1.80	1.80	1.80	1.81	1.81	1.81
1-11	1.85	1.86	1.86	1.86	1.86	1.86	1.87	1.87	1.87	1.87	1.87	1.87
2- 1	1.93	1.93	1.93	1.93	1.93	1.93	1.93	1.93	1.93	1.93	1.93	1.94
2- 3	2.00	2.00	2.00	2.00	2.00	2.00	2.00	2.00	2.00	2.00	2.00	2.00
2- 5	2.07	2.07	2.07	2.06	2.06	2.06	2.06	2.06	2.06	2.06	2.06	2.06
2- 7	2.14	2.14	2.13	2.13	2.13	2.13	2.13	2.13	2.12	2.12	2.12	2.12
2- 9	2.21	2.21	2.20	2.20	2.20	2.20	2.19	2.19	2.19	2.19	2.18	2.18
2-11	2.28	2.28	2.27	2.27	2.27	2.26	2.26	2.26	2.25	2.25	2.25	2.24
3- 1	2.35	2.35	2.34	2.34	2.33	2.33	2.32	2.32	2.32	2.31	2.31	2.31
3- 3	2.42	2.42	2.41	2.41	2.40	2.39	2.39	2.39	2.38	2.38	2.37	2.37
3- 5	2.49	2.49	2.48	2.47	2.47	2.46	2.46	2.45	2.44	2.44	2.43	2.43
3- 7	2.57	2.56	2.55	2.54	2.53	2.53	2.52	2.51	2.51	2.50	2.50	2.49
3- 9	2.64	2.63	2.62	2.61	2.60	2.59	2.59	2.58	2.57	2.57	2.56	2.55
3-11	2.71	2.70	2.69	2.68	2.67	2.66	2.65	2.64	2.64	2.63	2.62	2.62
4- 1	2.78	2.77	2.76	2.75	2.74	2.73	2.72	2.71	2.70	2.69	2.68	2.68
4- 3	2.85	2.84	2.83	2.81	2.80	2.79	2.78	2.77	2.76	2.76	2.75	2.74
4- 5	2.92	2.91	2.89	2.88	2.87	2.86	2.85	2.84	2.83	2.82	2.81	2.80
4- 7	2.99	2.98	2.96	2.95	2.94	2.93	2.91	2.90	2.89	2.88	2.87	2.86
4- 9	3.06	3.05	3.03	3.02	3.01	2.99	2.98	2.97	2.96	2.95	2.94	2.93
4-11	3.14	3.12	3.10	3.09	3.07	3.06	3.05	3.03	3.02	3.01	3.00	2.99
5- 1	3.21	3.19	3.17	3.16	3.14	3.12	3.11	3.10	3.08	3.07	3.06	3.05
5- 3	3.28	3.26	3.24	3.22	3.21	3.19	3.18	3.16	3.15	3.14	3.12	3.11
5- 5	3.35	3.33	3.31	3.29	3.27	3.26	3.24	3.23	3.21	3.20	3.19	3.17
5- 7	3.42	3.40	3.38	3.36	3.34	3.32	3.31	3.29	3.28	3.26	3.25	3.23
5- 9	3.49	3.47	3.45	3.43	3.41	3.39	3.37	3.36	3.34	3.32	3.31	3.30
5-11	3.56	3.54	3.52	3.50	3.48	3.46	3.44	3.42	3.40	3.39	3.37	3.36
6- 1	3.63	3.61	3.59	3.56	3.54	3.52	3.50	3.48	3.47	3.45	3.44	3.42
6- 3	3.71	3.68	3.66	3.63	3.61	3.59	3.57	3.55	3.53	3.51	3.50	3.48
6- 5	3.78	3.75	3.72	3.70	3.68	3.66	3.63	3.61	3.60	3.58	3.56	3.54
6- 7	3.85	3.82	3.79	3.77	3.74	3.72	3.70	3.68	3.66	3.64	3.62	3.61
6- 9	3.92	3.89	3.86	3.84	3.81	3.79	3.77	3.74	3.72	3.70	3.69	3.67
6-11	3.99	3.96	3.93	3.90	3.88	3.85	3.83	3.81	3.79	3.77	3.75	3.73
7- 1	4.06	4.03	4.00	3.97	3.95	3.92	3.90	3.87	3.85	3.83	3.81	3.79
7- 3	4.13	4.10	4.07	4.04	4.01	3.99	3.96	3.94	3.92	3.89	3.87	3.85
7- 5	4.20	4.17	4.14	4.11	4.08	4.05	4.03	4.00	3.98	3.96	3.94	3.92
7- 7	4.27	4.24	4.21	4.18	4.15	4.12	4.09	4.07	4.04	4.02	4.00	3.98
7- 9	4.35	4.31	4.28	4.25	4.22	4.19	4.16	4.13	4.11	4.08	4.06	4.04
7-11	4.42	4.38	4.35	4.31	4.28	4.25	4.22	4.20	4.17	4.15	4.12	4.10
8- 1	4.49	4.45	4.42	4.38	4.35	4.32	4.29	4.26	4.24	4.21	4.19	4.16
8- 3	4.56	4.52	4.48	4.45	4.42	4.39	4.36	4.33	4.30	4.27	4.25	4.22
8- 5	4.63	4.59	4.55	4.52	4.48	4.45	4.42	4.39	4.36	4.34	4.31	4.29
8- 7							4.49	4.46	4.43	4.40	4.37	4.35
8- 9							4.55	4.52	4.49	4.46	4.44	4.41
8-11							4.62	4.59	4.56	4.53	4.50	4.47
9- 1							4.68	4.65	4.62	4.59	4.56	4.53
9- 3							4.75	4.72	4.68	4.65	4.62	4.60

	Chronological Age										
Mental Age	12-0	12-2	12-4	12-6	12-8	12-10	13-0	13-2	13-4	13-6	13-8	13-10
0- 1	1.20	1.21	1.22	1.22	1.23	1.24	1.24	1.25	1.26	1.26	1.27	1.27
0- 3	1.26	1.27	1.28	1.28	1.29	1.30	1.30	1.31	1.31	1.32	1.32	1.33
0- 5	1.32	1.33	1.34	1.34	1.35	1.35	1.36	1.37	1.37	1.38	1.38	1.39
0- 7	1.38	1.39	1.40	1.40	1.41	1.41	1.42	1.42	1.43	1.43	1.44	1.44
0- 9	1.45	1.45	1.46	1.46	1.47	1.47	1.48	1.48	1.48	1.49	1.49	1.50
0-11	1.51	1.51	1.52	1.52	1.53	1.53	1.53	1.54	1.54	1.55	1.55	1.55
1- 1	1.57	1.57	1.58	1.58	1.58	1.59	1.59	1.60	1.60	1.60	1.60	1.61
1- 3	1.63	1.63	1.64	1.64	1.64	1.65	1.65	1.65	1.66	1.66	1.66	1.66
1- 5	1.69	1.69	1.70	1.70	1.70	1.71	1.71	1.71	1.71	1.71	1.72	1.72
1- 7	1.75	1.75	1.76	1.76	1.76	1.76	1.77	1.77	1.77	1.77	1.77	1.77
1- 9	1.81	1.82	1.82	1.82	1.82	1.82	1.82	1.82	1.83	1.83	1.83	1.83
1-11	1.87	1.88	1.88	1.88	1.88	1.88	1.88	1.88	1.88	1.88	1.89	1.89
2- 1	1.94	1.94	1.94	1.94	1.94	1.94	1.94	1.94	1.94	1.94	1.94	1.94
2- 3	2.00	2.00	2.00	2.00	2.00	2.00	2.00	2.00	2.00	2.00	2.00	2.00
2- 5	2.06	2.06	2.06	2.06	2.06	2.06	2.06	2.05	2.05	2.05	2.05	2.05
2- 7	2.12	2.12	2.12	2.12	2.11	2.11	2.11	2.11	2.11	2.11	2.11	2.11
2- 9	2.18	2.18	2.18	2.18	2.17	2.17	2.17	2.17	2.17	2.17	2.17	2.16
2-11	2.24	2.24	2.24	2.23	2.23	2.23	2.23	2.23	2.22	2.22	2.22	2.22
3- 1	2.30	2.30	2.30	2.29	2.29	2.29	2.29	2.28	2.28	2.28	2.28	2.28
3- 3	2.36	2.36	2.36	2.35	2.35	2.35	2.34	2.34	2.34	2.34	2.33	2.33
3- 5	2.43	2.42	2.42	2.41	2.41	2.41	2.40	2.40	2.40	2.39	2.39	2.39
3- 7	2.49	2.48	2.48	2.47	2.47	2.46	2.46	2.46	2.45	2.45	2.45	2.44
3- 9	2.55	2.54	2.54	2.53	2.53	2.52	2.52	2.51	2.51	2.51	2.50	2.50
3-11	2.61	2.60	2.60	2.59	2.59	2.58	2.58	2.57	2.57	2.56	2.56	2.55
4- 1	2.67	2.66	2.66	2.65	2.65	2.64	2.63	2.63	2.62	2.62	2.61	2.61
4- 3	2.73	2.72	2.72	2.71	2.70	2.70	2.69	2.69	2.68	2.68	2.67	2.66
4- 5	2.79	2.79	2.78	2.77	2.76	2.76	2.75	2.74	2.74	2.73	2.73	2.72
4- 7	2.85	2.85	2.84	2.83	2.82	2.81	2.81	2.80	2.79	2.79	2.78	2.78
4- 9	2.92	2.91	2.90	2.89	2.88	2.87	2.87	2.86	2.85	2.84	2.84	2.83
4-11	2.98	2.97	2.96	2.95	2.94	2.93	2.92	2.92	2.91	2.90	2.89	2.89
5- 1	3.04	3.03	3.02	3.01	3.00	2.99	2.98	2.97	2.97	2.96	2.95	2.94
5- 3	3.10	3.09	3.08	3.07	3.06	3.05	3.04	3.03	3.02	3.01	3.01	3.00
5- 5	3.16	3.15	3.14	3.13	3.12	3.11	3.10	3.09	3.08	3.07	3.06	3.05
5- 7	3.22	3.21	3.20	3.19	3.18	3.17	3.16	3.15	3.14	3.13	3.12	3.11
5- 9	3.28	3.27	3.26	3.25	3.23	3.22	3.21	3.20	3.19	3.18	3.17	3.17
5-11	3.34	3.33	3.32	3.31	3.29	3.28	3.27	3.26	3.25	3.24	3.23	3.22
6- 1	3.41	3.39	3.38	3.37	3.35	3.34	3.33	3.32	3.31	3.30	3.29	3.28
6- 3	3.47	3.45	3.44	3.42	3.41	3.40	3.39	3.38	3.36	3.35	3.34	3.33
6- 5	3.53	3.51	3.50	3.48	3.47	3.46	3.44	3.43	3.42	3.41	3.40	3.39
6- 7	3.59	3.57	3.56	3.54	3.53	3.52	3.50	3.49	3.48	3.47	3.45	3.44
6- 9	3.65	3.63	3.62	3.60	3.59	3.57	3.56	3.55	3.53	3.52	3.51	3.50
6-11	3.71	3.69	3.68	3.66	3.65	3.63	3.62	3.60	3.59	3.58	3.57	3.56
7- 1	3.77	3.76	3.74	3.72	3.71	3.69	3.68	3.66	3.65	3.64	3.62	3.61
7- 3	3.83	3.82	3.80	3.78	3.77	3.75	3.73	3.72	3.71	3.69	3.68	3.67
7- 5	3.90	3.88	3.86	3.84	3.82	3.81	3.79	3.78	3.76	3.75	3.74	3.72
7- 7	3.96	3.94	3.92	3.90	3.88	3.87	3.85	3.83	3.82	3.81	3.79	3.78
7- 9	4.02	4.00	3.98	3.96	3.94	3.92	3.91	3.89	3.88	3.86	3.85	3.83
7-11	4.08	4.06	4.04	4.02	4.00	3.98	3.97	3.95	3.93	3.92	3.90	3.89
8- 1	4.14	4.12	4.10	4.08	4.06	4.04	4.02	4.01	3.99	3.97	3.96	3.94
8- 3	4.20	4.18	4.16	4.14	4.12	4.10	4.08	4.06	4.05	4.03	4.02	4.00
8- 5	4.26	4.24	4.22	4.20	4.18	4.16	4.14	4.12	4.10	4.09	4.07	4.06
8- 7	4.32	4.30	4.28	4.26	4.24	4.22	4.20	4.18	4.16	4.14	4.13	4.11
8- 9	4.39	4.36	4.34	4.32	4.30	4.28	4.26	4.24	4.22	4.20	4.18	4.17
8-11	4.45	4.42	4.40	4.38	4.35	4.33	4.31	4.29	4.28	4.26	4.24	4.22
9- 1	4.51	4.48	4.46	4.44	4.41	4.39	4.37	4.35	4.33	4.31	4.30	4.28
9- 3	4.57	4.54	4.52	4.50	4.47	4.45	4.43	4.41	4.39	4.37	4.35	4.33
9- 5	4.63	4.60	4.58	4.55	4.53	4.51	4.49	4.47	4.45	4.43	4.41	4.39
9- 7	4.69	4.66	4.64	4.61	4.59	4.57	4.55	4.52	4.50	4.48	4.46	4.45
9- 9	4.75	4.73	4.70	4.67	4.65	4.63	4.60	4.58	4.56	4.54	4.52	4.50
9-11	4.81	4.79	4.76	4.73	4.71	4.68	4.66	4.64	4.62	4.60	4.58	4.56
10- 1	4.88	4.85	4.82	4.79	4.77	4.74	4.72	4.70	4.67	4.65	4.63	4.61
10- 3							4.78	4.75	4.73	4.71	4.69	4.67
10- 5							4.83	4.81	4.79	4.77	4.74	4.72
10- 7							4.89	4.87	4.84	4.82	4.80	4.78

	Chronological Age										
	14-0	14-2	14-4	14-6	14-8	14-10	15-0	15-2	15-4	15-6	15-8	15-10
0- 1	1.28	1.28	1.29	1.29	1.30	1.30	1.31	1.31	1.32	1.32	1.32	1.33
0- 3	1.33	1.34	1.34	1.35	1.35	1.36	1.36	1.36	1.37	1.37	1.38	1.38
0- 5	1.39	1.39	1.40	1.40	1.41	1.41	1.41	1.42	1.42	1.42	1.43	1.43
0- 7	1.44	1.45	1.45	1.46	1.46	1.46	1.47	1.47	1.47	1.48	1.48	1.48
0- 9	1.50	1.50	1.51	1.51	1.51	1.52	1.52	1.52	1.53	1.53	1.53	1.53
0-11	1.56	1.56	1.56	1.56	1.57	1.57	1.57	1.58	1.58	1.58	1.58	1.59
1- 1	1.61	1.61	1.62	1.62	1.62	1.62	1.63	1.63	1.63	1.63	1.63	1.64
1- 3	1.67	1.67	1.67	1.67	1.67	1.68	1.68	1.68	1.68	1.68	1.69	1.69
1- 5	1.72	1.72	1.72	1.73	1.73	1.73	1.73	1.73	1.74	1.74	1.74	1.74
1- 7	1.78	1.78	1.78	1.78	1.78	1.78	1.79	1.79	1.79	1.79	1.79	1.79
1- 9	1.83	1.83	1.83	1.83	1.84	1.84	1.84	1.84	1.84	1.84	1.84	1.84
1-11	1.89	1.89	1.89	1.89	1.89	1.89	1.89	1.89	1.89	1.89	1.89	1.89
2- 1	1.94	1.94	1.94	1.94	1.94	1.94	1.94	1.94	1.94	1.95	1.95	1.95
2- 3	2.00	2.00	2.00	2.00	2.00	2.00	2.00	2.00	2.00	2.00	2.00	2.00
2- 5	2.05	2.05	2.05	2.05	2.05	2.05	2.05	2.05	2.05	2.05	2.05	2.05
2- 7	2.11	2.11	2.11	2.11	2.10	2.10	2.10	2.10	2.10	2.10	2.10	2.10
2- 9	2.16	2.16	2.16	2.16	2.16	2.16	2.16	2.16	2.15	2.15	2.15	2.15
2-11	2.22	2.22	2.22	2.21	2.21	2.21	2.21	2.21	2.21	2.21	2.20	2.20
3- 1	2.27	2.27	2.27	2.27	2.27	2.26	2.26	2.26	2.26	2.26	2.26	2.26
3- 3	2.33	2.33	2.32	2.32	2.32	2.32	2.32	2.31	2.31	2.31	2.31	2.31
3- 5	2.38	2.38	2.38	2.38	2.37	2.37	2.37	2.37	2.36	2.36	2.36	2.36
3- 7	2.44	2.44	2.43	2.43	2.43	2.42	2.42	2.42	2.42	2.41	2.41	2.41
3- 9	2.49	2.49	2.49	2.48	2.48	2.48	2.47	2.47	2.47	2.47	2.46	2.46
3-11	2.55	2.55	2.54	2.54	2.53	2.53	2.53	2.52	2.52	2.52	2.52	2.51
4- 1	2.60	2.60	2.60	2.59	2.59	2.58	2.58	2.58	2.57	2.57	2.57	2.56
4- 3	2.66	2.66	2.65	2.65	2.64	2.64	2.63	2.63	2.63	2.62	2.62	2.62
4- 5	2.72	2.71	2.71	2.70	2.70	2.69	2.69	2.68	2.68	2.68	2.67	2.67
4- 7	2.77	2.77	2.76	2.75	2.75	2.74	2.74	2.74	2.73	2.73	2.72	2.72
4- 9	2.83	2.82	2.81	2.81	2.80	2.80	2.79	2.79	2.78	2.78	2.77	2.77
4-11	2.88	2.87	2.87	2.86	2.86	2.85	2.85	2.84	2.84	2.83	2.83	2.82
5- 1	2.94	2.93	2.92	2.92	2.91	2.91	2.90	2.89	2.89	2.88	2.88	2.87
5- 3	2.99	2.98	2.98	2.97	2.96	2.96	2.95	2.95	2.94	2.94	2.93	2.93
5- 5	3.05	3.04	3.03	3.03	3.02	3.01	3.01	3.00	2.99	2.99	2.98	2.98
5- 7	3.10	3.09	3.09	3.08	3.07	3.07	3.06	3.05	3.05	3.04	3.03	3.03
5- 9	3.16	3.15	3.14	3.13	3.13	3.12	3.11	3.10	3.10	3.09	3.09	3.08
5-11	3.21	3.20	3.20	3.19	3.18	3.17	3.16	3.16	3.15	3.14	3.14	3.13
6- 1	3.27	3.26	3.25	3.24	3.23	3.23	3.22	3.21	3.20	3.20	3.19	3.18
6- 3	3.32	3.31	3.30	3.30	3.29	3.28	3.27	3.26	3.26	3.25	3.24	3.23
6- 5	3.38	3.37	3.36	3.35	3.34	3.33	3.32	3.32	3.31	3.30	3.29	3.29
6- 7	3.43	3.42	3.41	3.40	3.39	3.39	3.38	3.37	3.36	3.35	3.34	3.34
6- 9	3.49	3.48	3.47	3.46	3.45	3.44	3.43	3.42	3.41	3.40	3.40	3.39
6-11	3.54	3.53	3.52	3.51	3.50	3.49	3.48	3.47	3.47	3.46	3.45	3.44
7- 1	3.60	3.59	3.58	3.57	3.56	3.55	3.54	3.53	3.52	3.51	3.50	3.49
7- 3	3.65	3.64	3.63	3.62	3.61	3.60	3.59	3.58	3.57	3.56	3.55	3.54
7- 5	3.71	3.70	3.69	3.67	3.66	3.65	3.64	3.63	3.62	3.61	3.60	3.60
7- 7	3.76	3.75	3.74	3.73	3.72	3.71	3.70	3.69	3.68	3.67	3.66	3.65
7- 9	3.82	3.81	3.79	3.78	3.77	3.76	3.75	3.74	3.73	3.72	3.71	3.70
7-11	3.88	3.86	3.85	3.84	3.82	3.81	3.80	3.79	3.78	3.77	3.76	3.75
8- 1	3.93	3.92	3.90	3.89	3.88	3.87	3.85	3.84	3.83	3.82	3.81	3.80
8- 3	3.99	3.97	3.96	3.94	3.93	3.92	3.91	3.90	3.88	3.87	3.86	3.85
8- 5	4.04	4.03	4.01	4.00	3.99	3.97	3.96	3.95	3.94	3.93	3.92	3.90
8- 7	4.10	4.08	4.07	4.05	4.04	4.03	4.01	4.00	3.99	3.98	3.97	3.96
8- 9	4.15	4.14	4.12	4.11	4.09	4.08	4.07	4.05	4.04	4.03	4.02	4.01
8-11	4.21	4.19	4.18	4.16	4.15	4.13	4.12	4.11	4.09	4.08	4.07	4.06
9- 1	4.26	4.25	4.23	4.22	4.20	4.19	4.17	4.16	4.15	4.13	4.12	4.11
9- 3	4.32	4.30	4.28	4.27	4.25	4.24	4.23	4.21	4.20	4.19	4.17	4.16
9- 5	4.37	4.36	4.34	4.32	4.31	4.29	4.28	4.27	4.25	4.24	4.23	4.21
9- 7	4.43	4.41	4.39	4.38	4.36	4.35	4.33	4.32	4.30	4.29	4.28	4.27
9- 9	4.48	4.47	4.45	4.43	4.42	4.40	4.39	4.37	4.36	4.34	4.33	4.32
9-11	4.54	4.52	4.50	4.49	4.47	4.45	4.44	4.42	4.41	4.40	4.38	4.37
10- 1	4.59	4.58	4.56	4.54	4.52	4.51	4.49	4.48	4.46	4.45	4.43	4.42
10- 3	4.65	4.63	4.61	4.59	4.58	4.56	4.54	4.53	4.51	4.50	4.49	4.47
10- 5	4.70	4.68	4.67	4.65	4.63	4.61	4.60	4.58	4.57	4.55	4.54	4.52
10- 7	4.76	4.74	4.72	4.70	4.68	4.67	4.65	4.63	4.62	4.60	4.59	4.57

Mental Age

GROWTH AND DECLINE OF RETARDATE INTELLIGENCE

		Chronological Age										
		16-0	16-2	16-4	16-6	16-8	16-10	17-0	17-2	17-4	17-6	17-8	17-10
Mental Age	0- 1	1.33	1.33	1.34	1.34	1.34	1.35	1.35	1.35	1.36	1.36	1.36	1.36
	0- 3	1.38	1.39	1.39	1.39	1.39	1.40	1.40	1.40	1.41	1.41	1.41	1.41
	0- 5	1.43	1.44	1.44	1.44	1.44	1.45	1.45	1.45	1.46	1.46	1.46	1.46
	0- 7	1.48	1.49	1.49	1.49	1.50	1.50	1.50	1.50	1.50	1.51	1.51	1.51
	0- 9	1.54	1.54	1.54	1.54	1.55	1.55	1.55	1.55	1.55	1.56	1.56	1.56
	0-11	1.59	1.59	1.59	1.59	1.60	1.60	1.60	1.60	1.60	1.60	1.61	1.61
	1- 1	1.64	1.64	1.64	1.64	1.65	1.65	1.65	1.65	1.65	1.65	1.66	1.66
	1- 3	1.69	1.69	1.69	1.69	1.70	1.70	1.70	1.70	1.70	1.70	1.70	1.71
	1- 5	1.74	1.74	1.74	1.75	1.75	1.75	1.75	1.75	1.75	1.75	1.75	1.75
	1- 7	1.79	1.79	1.79	1.80	1.80	1.80	1.80	1.80	1.80	1.80	1.80	1.80
	1- 9	1.84	1.84	1.85	1.85	1.85	1.85	1.85	1.85	1.85	1.85	1.85	1.85
	1-11	1.89	1.90	1.90	1.90	1.90	1.90	1.90	1.90	1.90	1.90	1.90	1.90
	2- 1	1.95	1.95	1.95	1.95	1.95	1.95	1.95	1.95	1.95	1.95	1.95	1.95
	2- 3	2.00	2.00	2.00	2.00	2.00	2.00	2.00	2.00	2.00	2.00	2.00	2.00
	2- 5	2.05	2.05	2.05	2.05	2.05	2.05	2.05	2.05	2.05	2.05	2.05	2.05
	2- 7	2.10	2.10	2.10	2.10	2.10	2.10	2.10	2.10	2.10	2.10	2.10	2.09
	2- 9	2.15	2.15	2.15	2.15	2.15	2.15	2.15	2.15	2.15	2.14	2.14	2.14
	2-11	2.20	2.20	2.20	2.20	2.20	2.20	2.20	2.20	2.19	2.19	2.19	2.19
	3- 1	2.25	2.25	2.25	2.25	2.25	2.25	2.25	2.25	2.24	2.24	2.24	2.24
	3- 3	2.31	2.30	2.30	2.30	2.30	2.30	2.30	2.29	2.29	2.29	2.29	2.29
	3- 5	2.36	2.35	2.35	2.35	2.35	2.35	2.35	2.34	2.34	2.34	2.34	2.34
	3- 7	2.41	2.41	2.40	2.40	2.40	2.40	2.40	2.39	2.39	2.39	2.39	2.39
	3- 9	2.46	2.46	2.45	2.45	2.45	2.45	2.45	2.44	2.44	2.44	2.44	2.44
	3-11	2.51	2.51	2.50	2.50	2.50	2.50	2.50	2.49	2.49	2.49	2.49	2.48
	4- 1	2.56	2.56	2.56	2.55	2.55	2.55	2.54	2.54	2.54	2.54	2.54	2.53
	4- 3	2.61	2.61	2.61	2.60	2.60	2.60	2.59	2.59	2.59	2.59	2.58	2.58
	4- 5	2.66	2.66	2.66	2.65	2.65	2.65	2.64	2.64	2.64	2.64	2.63	2.63
	4- 7	2.72	2.71	2.71	2.70	2.70	2.70	2.69	2.69	2.69	2.68	2.68	2.68
	4- 9	2.77	2.76	2.76	2.75	2.75	2.75	2.74	2.74	2.74	2.73	2.73	2.73
	4-11	2.82	2.81	2.81	2.81	2.80	2.80	2.79	2.79	2.79	2.79	2.78	2.78
	5- 1	2.87	2.86	2.86	2.86	2.85	2.85	2.84	2.84	2.84	2.83	2.83	2.83
	5- 3	2.92	2.92	2.91	2.91	2.90	2.90	2.89	2.89	2.89	2.88	2.88	2.87
	5- 5	2.97	2.97	2.96	2.96	2.95	2.95	2.94	2.94	2.93	2.93	2.93	2.92
	5- 7	3.02	3.02	3.01	3.01	3.00	3.00	2.99	2.99	2.98	2.98	2.98	2.97
	5- 9	3.07	3.07	3.06	3.06	3.05	3.05	3.04	3.04	3.03	3.03	3.02	3.02
	5-11	3.13	3.12	3.11	3.11	3.10	3.10	3.09	3.09	3.08	3.08	3.07	3.07
	6- 1	3.18	3.17	3.16	3.16	3.15	3.15	3.14	3.14	3.13	3.13	3.12	3.12
	6- 3	3.23	3.22	3.22	3.21	3.20	3.20	3.19	3.19	3.18	3.18	3.17	3.17
	6- 5	3.28	3.27	3.27	3.26	3.25	3.25	3.24	3.24	3.23	3.22	3.22	3.21
	6- 7	3.33	3.32	3.32	3.31	3.30	3.30	3.29	3.29	3.28	3.27	3.27	3.26
	6- 9	3.38	3.37	3.37	3.36	3.35	3.35	3.34	3.33	3.33	3.32	3.32	3.31
	6-11	3.43	3.43	3.42	3.41	3.40	3.40	3.39	3.38	3.38	3.37	3.37	3.36
	7- 1	3.48	3.48	3.47	3.46	3.45	3.45	3.44	3.43	3.43	3.42	3.42	3.41
	7- 3	3.54	3.53	3.52	3.51	3.50	3.50	3.49	3.48	3.48	3.47	3.46	3.46
	7- 5	3.59	3.58	3.57	3.56	3.55	3.55	3.54	3.53	3.53	3.52	3.51	3.51
	7- 7	3.64	3.63	3.62	3.61	3.60	3.60	3.59	3.58	3.58	3.57	3.56	3.56
	7- 9	3.69	3.68	3.67	3.66	3.66	3.65	3.64	3.63	3.62	3.62	3.61	3.60
	7-11	3.74	3.73	3.72	3.71	3.71	3.70	3.69	3.68	3.67	3.67	3.66	3.65
	8- 1	3.79	3.78	3.77	3.76	3.76	3.75	3.74	3.73	3.72	3.72	3.71	3.70
	8- 3	3.84	3.83	3.82	3.81	3.81	3.80	3.79	3.78	3.77	3.76	3.76	3.75
	8- 5	3.89	3.88	3.87	3.87	3.86	3.85	3.84	3.83	3.82	3.81	3.81	3.80
	8- 7	3.95	3.94	3.93	3.92	3.91	3.90	3.89	3.88	3.87	3.86	3.86	3.85
	8- 9	4.00	3.99	3.98	3.97	3.96	3.95	3.94	3.93	3.92	3.91	3.90	3.90
	8-11	4.05	4.04	4.03	4.02	4.01	4.00	3.99	3.98	3.97	3.96	3.95	3.94
	9- 1	4.10	4.09	4.08	4.07	4.06	4.05	4.04	4.03	4.02	4.01	4.00	3.99
	9- 3	4.15	4.14	4.13	4.12	4.11	4.10	4.09	4.08	4.07	4.06	4.05	4.04
	9- 5	4.20	4.19	4.18	4.17	4.16	4.15	4.14	4.13	4.12	4.11	4.10	4.09
	9- 7	4.25	4.24	4.23	4.22	4.21	4.20	4.19	4.18	4.17	4.16	4.15	4.14
	9- 9	4.30	4.29	4.28	4.27	4.26	4.25	4.24	4.23	4.22	4.21	4.20	4.19
	9-11	4.36	4.34	4.33	4.32	4.31	4.30	4.29	4.28	4.27	4.26	4.25	4.24
	10- 1	4.41	4.39	4.38	4.37	4.36	4.35	4.34	4.33	4.32	4.30	4.30	4.29
	10- 3	4.46	4.45	4.43	4.42	4.41	4.40	4.39	4.37	4.36	4.35	4.34	4.33
	10- 5	4.51	4.50	4.48	4.47	4.46	4.45	4.44	4.42	4.41	4.40	4.39	4.38
	10- 7	4.56	4.55	4.53	4.52	4.51	4.50	4.49	4.47	4.46	4.45	4.44	4.43

	Chronological Age										
Mental Age	18-0	18-2	18-4	18-6	18-8	18-10	19-0	19-2	19-4	19-6	19-8	19-10
0- 1	1.37	1.37	1.37	1.37	1.38	1.38	1.38	1.38	1.39	1.39	1.39	1.39
0- 3	1.42	1.42	1.42	1.42	1.42	1.43	1.43	1.43	1.43	1.43	1.44	1.44
0- 5	1.46	1.47	1.47	1.47	1.47	1.47	1.48	1.48	1.48	1.48	1.48	1.48
0- 7	1.51	1.51	1.52	1.52	1.52	1.52	1.52	1.53	1.53	1.53	1.53	1.53
0- 9	1.56	1.56	1.56	1.57	1.57	1.57	1.57	1.57	1.57	1.58	1.58	1.58
0-11	1.61	1.61	1.61	1.61	1.62	1.62	1.62	1.62	1.62	1.62	1.62	1.62
1- 1	1.66	1.66	1.66	1.66	1.66	1.66	1.67	1.67	1.67	1.67	1.67	1.67
1- 3	1.71	1.71	1.71	1.71	1.71	1.71	1.71	1.71	1.72	1.72	1.72	1.72
1- 5	1.76	1.76	1.76	1.76	1.76	1.76	1.76	1.76	1.76	1.76	1.76	1.76
1- 7	1.80	1.80	1.81	1.81	1.81	1.81	1.81	1.81	1.81	1.81	1.81	1.81
1- 9	1.85	1.85	1.85	1.85	1.85	1.85	1.86	1.86	1.86	1.86	1.86	1.36
1-11	1.90	1.90	1.90	1.90	1.90	1.90	1.90	1.90	1.90	1.90	1.90	1.90
2- 1	1.95	1.95	1.95	1.95	1.95	1.95	1.95	1.95	1.95	1.95	1.95	1.95
2- 3	2.00	2.00	2.00	2.00	2.00	2.00	2.00	2.00	2.00	2.00	2.00	2.00
2- 5	2.05	2.05	2.05	2.05	2.05	2.05	2.05	2.04	2.04	2.04	2.04	2.04
2- 7	2.09	2.09	2.09	2.09	2.09	2.09	2.09	2.09	2.09	2.09	2.09	2.09
2- 9	2.14	2.14	2.14	2.14	2.14	2.14	2.14	2.14	2.14	2.14	2.14	2.14
2-11	2.19	2.19	2.19	2.19	2.19	2.19	2.19	2.19	2.19	2.19	2.18	2.18
3- 1	2.24	2.24	2.24	2.24	2.24	2.24	2.23	2.23	2.23	2.23	2.23	2.23
3- 3	2.29	2.29	2.29	2.29	2.28	2.28	2.28	2.28	2.28	2.28	2.28	2.28
3- 5	2.34	2.34	2.33	2.33	2.33	2.33	2.33	2.33	2.33	2.33	2.32	2.32
3- 7	2.39	2.38	2.38	2.38	2.38	2.38	2.38	2.38	2.37	2.37	2.37	2.37
3- 9	2.43	2.43	2.43	2.43	2.43	2.43	2.42	2.42	2.42	2.42	2.42	2.42
3-11	2.48	2.48	2.48	2.48	2.47	2.47	2.47	2.47	2.47	2.47	2.47	2.46
4- 1	2.53	2.53	2.53	2.52	2.52	2.52	2.52	2.52	2.52	2.51	2.51	2.51
4- 3	2.58	2.58	2.57	2.57	2.57	2.57	2.57	2.56	2.56	2.56	2.56	2.56
4- 5	2.63	2.63	2.62	2.62	2.62	2.62	2.61	2.61	2.61	2.61	2.61	2.60
4- 7	2.68	2.67	2.67	2.67	2.67	2.66	2.66	2.66	2.66	2.65	2.65	2.65
4- 9	2.72	2.72	2.72	2.72	2.71	2.71	2.71	2.71	2.70	2.70	2.70	2.70
4-11	2.77	2.77	2.77	2.76	2.76	2.76	2.76	2.75	2.75	2.75	2.75	2.74
5- 1	2.82	2.82	2.82	2.81	2.81	2.81	2.80	2.80	2.80	2.80	2.79	2.79
5- 3	2.87	2.87	2.86	2.86	2.86	2.85	2.85	2.85	2.84	2.84	2.84	2.84
5- 5	2.92	2.92	2.91	2.91	2.90	2.90	2.90	2.89	2.89	2.89	2.89	2.88
5- 7	2.97	2.96	2.96	2.96	2.95	2.95	2.95	2.94	2.94	2.94	2.93	2.93
5- 9	3.02	3.01	3.01	3.00	3.00	3.00	2.99	2.99	2.99	2.98	2.98	2.98
5-11	3.06	3.06	3.06	3.05	3.05	3.04	3.04	3.04	3.03	3.03	3.03	3.02
6- 1	3.11	3.11	3.10	3.10	3.10	3.09	3.09	3.08	3.08	3.08	3.07	3.07
6- 3	3.16	3.16	3.15	3.15	3.14	3.14	3.14	3.13	3.13	3.12	3.12	3.12
6- 5	3.21	3.20	3.20	3.20	3.19	3.19	3.18	3.18	3.17	3.17	3.17	3.16
6- 7	3.26	3.25	3.25	3.24	3.24	3.23	3.23	3.23	3.22	3.22	3.21	3.21
6- 9	3.31	3.30	3.30	3.29	3.29	3.28	3.28	3.27	3.27	3.26	3.26	3.26
6-11	3.36	3.35	3.34	3.34	3.33	3.33	3.32	3.32	3.32	3.31	3.31	3.30
7- 1	3.40	3.40	3.39	3.39	3.38	3.38	3.37	3.37	3.36	3.36	3.35	3.35
7- 3	3.45	3.45	3.44	3.44	3.43	3.42	3.42	3.41	3.41	3.40	3.40	3.40
7- 5	3.50	3.49	3.49	3.48	3.48	3.47	3.47	3.46	3.46	3.45	3.45	3.44
7- 7	3.55	3.54	3.54	3.53	3.53	3.52	3.51	3.51	3.50	3.50	3.49	3.49
7- 9	3.60	3.59	3.58	3.58	3.57	3.57	3.56	3.56	3.55	3.55	3.54	3.54
7-11	3.65	3.64	3.63	3.63	3.62	3.61	3.61	3.60	3.60	3.59	3.59	3.58
8- 1	3.69	3.69	3.68	3.67	3.67	3.66	3.66	3.65	3.64	3.64	3.63	3.63
8- 3	3.74	3.74	3.73	3.72	3.72	3.71	3.70	3.70	3.69	3.69	3.68	3.68
8- 5	3.79	3.78	3.78	3.77	3.76	3.76	3.75	3.75	3.74	3.73	3.73	3.72
8- 7	3.84	3.83	3.83	3.82	3.81	3.81	3.80	3.79	3.79	3.78	3.77	3.77
8- 9	3.89	3.88	3.87	3.87	3.86	3.85	3.85	3.84	3.83	3.83	3.82	3.82
8-11	3.94	3.93	3.92	3.91	3.91	3.90	3.89	3.89	3.88	3.87	3.87	3.86
9- 1	3.99	3.98	3.97	3.96	3.95	3.95	3.94	3.93	3.93	3.92	3.91	3.91
9- 3	4.03	4.03	4.02	4.01	4.00	4.00	3.99	3.98	3.97	3.97	3.96	3.96
9- 5	4.08	4.07	4.07	4.06	4.05	4.04	4.04	4.03	4.02	4.01	4.01	4.00
9- 7	4.13	4.12	4.11	4.11	4.10	4.09	4.08	4.08	4.07	4.06	4.05	4.05
9- 9	4.18	4.17	4.16	4.15	4.15	4.14	4.13	4.12	4.12	4.11	4.10	4.09
9-11	4.23	4.22	4.21	4.20	4.19	4.19	4.18	4.17	4.16	4.16	4.15	4.14
10- 1	4.28	4.27	4.26	4.25	4.24	4.23	4.23	4.22	4.21	4.20	4.20	4.19
10- 3	4.32	4.32	4.31	4.30	4.29	4.28	4.27	4.26	4.26	4.25	4.24	4.23
10- 5	4.37	4.36	4.35	4.35	4.34	4.33	4.32	4.31	4.30	4.30	4.29	4.28
10- 7	4.42	4.41	4.40	4.39	4.38	4.38	4.37	4.36	4.35	4.34	4.34	4.33

Mental Age	Chronological Age 20-0	20-2	20-4	20-6	20-8	20-10	21-0	21-2	21-4	21-6	21-8	21-10
0- 1	1.39	1.40	1.40	1.40	1.40	1.40	1.40	1.41	1.41	1.41	1.41	1.41
0- 3	1.44	1.44	1.44	1.45	1.45	1.45	1.45	1.45	1.45	1.45	1.46	1.46
0- 5	1.49	1.49	1.49	1.49	1.49	1.49	1.50	1.50	1.50	1.50	1.50	1.50
0- 7	1.53	1.53	1.54	1.54	1.54	1.54	1.54	1.54	1.54	1.54	1.55	1.55
0- 9	1.58	1.58	1.58	1.58	1.58	1.59	1.59	1.59	1.59	1.59	1.59	1.59
0-11	1.63	1.63	1.63	1.63	1.63	1.63	1.63	1.63	1.63	1.64	1.64	1.64
1- 1	1.67	1.67	1.67	1.68	1.68	1.68	1.68	1.68	1.68	1.68	1.68	1.68
1- 3	1.72	1.72	1.72	1.72	1.72	1.72	1.72	1.72	1.73	1.73	1.73	1.73
1- 5	1.77	1.77	1.77	1.77	1.77	1.77	1.77	1.77	1.77	1.77	1.77	1.77
1- 7	1.81	1.81	1.81	1.81	1.81	1.81	1.82	1.82	1.82	1.82	1.82	1.82
1- 9	1.86	1.86	1.86	1.86	1.86	1.86	1.86	1.86	1.86	1.86	1.86	1.86
1-11	1.90	1.91	1.91	1.91	1.91	1.91	1.91	1.91	1.91	1.91	1.91	1.91
2- 1	1.95	1.95	1.95	1.95	1.95	1.95	1.95	1.95	1.95	1.95	1.95	1.95
2- 3	2.00	2.00	2.00	2.00	2.00	2.00	2.00	2.00	2.00	2.00	2.00	2.00
2- 5	2.04	2.04	2.04	2.04	2.04	2.04	2.04	2.04	2.04	2.04	2.04	2.04
2- 7	2.09	2.09	2.09	2.09	2.09	2.09	2.09	2.09	2.09	2.09	2.09	2.09
2- 9	2.14	2.14	2.14	2.14	2.14	2.14	2.13	2.13	2.13	2.13	2.13	2.13
2-11	2.18	2.18	2.18	2.18	2.18	2.18	2.18	2.18	2.18	2.18	2.18	2.18
3- 1	2.23	2.23	2.23	2.23	2.23	2.23	2.23	2.23	2.22	2.22	2.22	2.22
3- 3	2.28	2.28	2.27	2.27	2.27	2.27	2.27	2.27	2.27	2.27	2.27	2.27
3- 5	2.32	2.32	2.32	2.32	2.32	2.32	2.32	2.32	2.32	2.31	2.31	2.31
3- 7	2.37	2.37	2.37	2.37	2.37	2.36	2.36	2.36	2.36	2.36	2.36	2.36
3- 9	2.42	2.41	2.41	2.41	2.41	2.41	2.41	2.41	2.41	2.41	2.40	2.40
3-11	2.46	2.46	2.46	2.46	2.46	2.46	2.45	2.45	2.45	2.45	2.45	2.45
4- 1	2.51	2.51	2.51	2.50	2.50	2.50	2.50	2.50	2.50	2.50	2.49	2.49
4- 3	2.56	2.55	2.55	2.55	2.55	2.55	2.55	2.54	2.54	2.54	2.54	2.54
4- 5	2.60	2.60	2.60	2.60	2.59	2.59	2.59	2.59	2.59	2.59	2.59	2.58
4- 7	2.65	2.65	2.64	2.64	2.64	2.64	2.64	2.64	2.63	2.63	2.63	2.63
4- 9	2.69	2.69	2.69	2.69	2.69	2.68	2.68	2.68	2.68	2.68	2.68	2.67
4-11	2.74	2.74	2.74	2.73	2.73	2.73	2.73	2.73	2.72	2.72	2.72	2.72
5- 1	2.79	2.79	2.78	2.78	2.78	2.78	2.77	2.77	2.77	2.77	2.77	2.76
5- 3	2.83	2.83	2.83	2.83	2.82	2.82	2.82	2.82	2.82	2.81	2.81	2.81
5- 5	2.88	2.88	2.88	2.87	2.87	2.87	2.87	2.86	2.86	2.86	2.86	2.85
5- 7	2.93	2.92	2.92	2.92	2.92	2.91	2.91	2.91	2.91	2.90	2.90	2.90
5- 9	2.97	2.97	2.97	2.96	2.96	2.96	2.96	2.95	2.95	2.95	2.95	2.94
5-11	3.02	3.02	3.01	3.01	3.01	3.00	3.00	3.00	3.00	2.99	2.99	2.99
6- 1	3.07	3.06	3.06	3.06	3.05	3.05	3.05	3.05	3.04	3.04	3.04	3.03
6- 3	3.11	3.11	3.11	3.10	3.10	3.10	3.09	3.09	3.09	3.08	3.08	3.08
6- 5	3.16	3.16	3.15	3.15	3.15	3.14	3.14	3.14	3.13	3.13	3.13	3.12
6- 7	3.21	3.20	3.20	3.19	3.19	3.19	3.18	3.18	3.18	3.18	3.17	3.17
6- 9	3.25	3.25	3.24	3.24	3.24	3.23	3.23	3.23	3.22	3.22	3.22	3.21
6-11	3.30	3.29	3.29	3.29	3.28	3.28	3.28	3.27	3.27	3.27	3.26	3.26
7- 1	3.35	3.34	3.34	3.33	3.33	3.33	3.32	3.32	3.31	3.31	3.31	3.30
7- 3	3.39	3.39	3.38	3.38	3.38	3.37	3.37	3.36	3.36	3.36	3.35	3.35
7- 5	3.44	3.43	3.43	3.43	3.42	3.42	3.41	3.41	3.41	3.40	3.40	3.40
7- 7	3.48	3.48	3.48	3.47	3.47	3.46	3.46	3.45	3.45	3.45	3.44	3.44
7- 9	3.53	3.53	3.52	3.52	3.51	3.51	3.50	3.50	3.50	3.49	3.49	3.49
7-11	3.58	3.57	3.57	3.56	3.56	3.55	3.55	3.55	3.54	3.54	3.53	3.53
8- 1	3.62	3.62	3.61	3.61	3.60	3.60	3.60	3.59	3.59	3.58	3.58	3.58
8- 3	3.67	3.67	3.66	3.66	3.65	3.65	3.64	3.64	3.63	3.63	3.62	3.62
8- 5	3.72	3.71	3.71	3.70	3.70	3.69	3.69	3.69	3.68	3.67	3.67	3.67
8- 7	3.76	3.76	3.75	3.75	3.74	3.74	3.73	3.73	3.72	3.72	3.71	3.71
8- 9	3.81	3.80	3.80	3.79	3.79	3.78	3.78	3.77	3.77	3.76	3.76	3.76
8-11	3.86	3.85	3.84	3.84	3.83	3.83	3.82	3.82	3.81	3.81	3.81	3.80
9- 1	3.90	3.90	3.89	3.89	3.88	3.87	3.87	3.86	3.86	3.86	3.85	3.85
9- 3	3.95	3.94	3.94	3.93	3.93	3.92	3.92	3.91	3.91	3.90	3.90	3.89
9- 5	4.00	3.99	3.98	3.98	3.97	3.97	3.96	3.96	3.95	3.95	3.94	3.94
9- 7	4.04	4.04	4.03	4.02	4.02	4.01	4.01	4.00	4.00	3.99	3.99	3.98
9- 9	4.09	4.08	4.08	4.07	4.06	4.06	4.05	4.05	4.04	4.04	4.03	4.03
9-11	4.13	4.13	4.12	4.12	4.11	4.10	4.10	4.09	4.09	4.08	4.08	4.07
10- 1	4.18	4.17	4.17	4.16	4.16	4.15	4.14	4.14	4.13	4.13	4.12	4.12
10- 3	4.23	4.22	4.21	4.21	4.20	4.20	4.19	4.18	4.18	4.17	4.17	4.16
10- 5	4.27	4.27	4.26	4.25	4.25	4.24	4.24	4.23	4.22	4.22	4.21	4.21
10- 7	4.32	4.31	4.31	4.30	4.29	4.29	4.28	4.27	4.27	4.26	4.26	4.25

Chronological Age

Mental Age	22-0	23-0	24-0	25-0	26-0	27-0	28-0	29-0	30-0	31-0	32-0	33-0
0- 1	1.41	1.42	1.43	1.43	1.44	1.44	1.45	1.45	1.45	1.45	1.46	1.46
0- 3	1.46	1.47	1.47	1.48	1.48	1.49	1.49	1.49	1.49	1.50	1.50	1.50
0- 5	1.50	1.51	1.52	1.52	1.52	1.53	1.53	1.53	1.54	1.54	1.54	1.54
0- 7	1.55	1.55	1.56	1.56	1.57	1.57	1.57	1.58	1.58	1.58	1.58	1.58
0- 9	1.59	1.60	1.60	1.61	1.61	1.61	1.62	1.62	1.62	1.62	1.62	1.62
0-11	1.64	1.64	1.65	1.65	1.65	1.66	1.66	1.66	1.66	1.66	1.66	1.67
1- 1	1.68	1.69	1.69	1.69	1.70	1.70	1.70	1.70	1.70	1.71	1.71	1.71
1- 3	1.73	1.73	1.73	1.74	1.74	1.74	1.74	1.74	1.75	1.75	1.75	1.75
1- 5	1.77	1.78	1.78	1.78	1.78	1.78	1.79	1.79	1.79	1.79	1.79	1.79
1- 7	1.82	1.82	1.82	1.82	1.83	1.83	1.83	1.83	1.83	1.83	1.83	1.83
1- 9	1.86	1.86	1.87	1.87	1.87	1.87	1.87	1.87	1.87	1.87	1.87	1.87
1-11	1.91	1.91	1.91	1.91	1.91	1.91	1.91	1.91	1.91	1.91	1.91	1.91
2- 1	1.95	1.95	1.95	1.95	1.95	1.96	1.96	1.96	1.96	1.96	1.96	1.96
2- 3	2.00	2.00	2.00	2.00	2.00	2.00	2.00	2.00	2.00	2.00	2.00	2.00
2- 5	2.04	2.04	2.04	2.04	2.04	2.04	2.04	2.04	2.04	2.04	2.04	2.04
2- 7	2.09	2.09	2.09	2.08	2.08	2.08	2.08	2.08	2.08	2.08	2.08	2.08
2- 9	2.13	2.13	2.13	2.13	2.13	2.13	2.13	2.12	2.12	2.12	2.12	2.12
2-11	2.18	2.18	2.17	2.17	2.17	2.17	2.17	2.17	2.17	2.17	2.16	2.16
3- 1	2.22	2.22	2.22	2.21	2.21	2.21	2.21	2.21	2.21	2.21	2.21	2.21
3- 3	2.27	2.26	2.26	2.26	2.26	2.25	2.25	2.25	2.25	2.25	2.25	2.25
3- 5	2.31	2.31	2.30	2.30	2.30	2.30	2.29	2.29	2.29	2.29	2.29	2.29
3- 7	2.36	2.35	2.35	2.35	2.34	2.34	2.34	2.34	2.33	2.33	2.33	2.33
3- 9	2.40	2.40	2.39	2.39	2.39	2.38	2.38	2.38	2.38	2.37	2.37	2.37
3-11	2.45	2.44	2.44	2.43	2.43	2.42	2.42	2.42	2.42	2.42	2.41	2.41
4- 1	2.49	2.49	2.48	2.48	2.47	2.47	2.46	2.46	2.46	2.46	2.46	2.46
4- 3	2.54	2.53	2.52	2.52	2.51	2.51	2.51	2.50	2.50	2.50	2.50	2.50
4- 5	2.58	2.57	2.57	2.56	2.56	2.55	2.55	2.55	2.54	2.54	2.54	2.54
4- 7	2.63	2.62	2.61	2.61	2.60	2.60	2.59	2.59	2.59	2.58	2.58	2.58
4- 9	2.67	2.66	2.66	2.65	2.64	2.64	2.63	2.63	2.63	2.63	2.62	2.62
4-11	2.72	2.71	2.70	2.69	2.69	2.68	2.68	2.67	2.67	2.67	2.67	2.66
5- 1	2.76	2.75	2.74	2.74	2.73	2.72	2.72	2.71	2.71	2.71	2.71	2.71
5- 3	2.81	2.80	2.79	2.78	2.77	2.77	2.76	2.76	2.75	2.75	2.75	2.75
5- 5	2.85	2.84	2.83	2.82	2.82	2.81	2.80	2.80	2.80	2.79	2.79	2.79
5- 7	2.90	2.89	2.87	2.87	2.86	2.85	2.85	2.84	2.84	2.83	2.83	2.83
5- 9	2.94	2.93	2.92	2.91	2.90	2.89	2.89	2.88	2.88	2.88	2.87	2.87
5-11	2.99	2.97	2.96	2.95	2.94	2.94	2.93	2.93	2.92	2.92	2.92	2.91
6- 1	3.03	3.02	3.01	3.00	2.99	2.98	2.97	2.97	2.96	2.96	2.96	2.95
6- 3	3.08	3.06	3.05	3.04	3.03	3.02	3.02	3.01	3.01	3.00	3.00	3.00
6- 5	3.12	3.11	3.09	3.08	3.07	3.07	3.06	3.05	3.05	3.04	3.04	3.04
6- 7	3.17	3.15	3.14	3.13	3.12	3.11	3.10	3.09	3.09	3.09	3.08	3.08
6- 9	3.21	3.20	3.18	3.17	3.16	3.15	3.14	3.14	3.13	3.13	3.12	3.12
6-11	3.26	3.24	3.23	3.21	3.20	3.19	3.19	3.18	3.17	3.17	3.17	3.16
7- 1	3.30	3.28	3.27	3.26	3.25	3.24	3.23	3.22	3.22	3.21	3.21	3.20
7- 3	3.35	3.33	3.31	3.30	3.29	3.28	3.27	3.26	3.26	3.25	3.25	3.25
7- 5	3.39	3.37	3.36	3.34	3.33	3.32	3.31	3.31	3.30	3.29	3.29	3.29
7- 7	3.44	3.42	3.40	3.39	3.37	3.36	3.35	3.35	3.34	3.34	3.33	3.33
7- 9	3.48	3.46	3.44	3.43	3.42	3.41	3.40	3.39	3.38	3.38	3.37	3.37
7-11	3.53	3.51	3.49	3.47	3.46	3.45	3.44	3.43	3.43	3.42	3.42	3.41
8- 1	3.57	3.55	3.53	3.52	3.50	3.49	3.48	3.47	3.47	3.46	3.46	3.45
8- 3	3.62	3.60	3.58	3.56	3.55	3.53	3.52	3.52	3.51	3.50	3.50	3.50
8- 5	3.66	3.64	3.62	3.60	3.59	3.58	3.57	3.56	3.55	3.55	3.54	3.54
8- 7	3.71	3.68	3.66	3.65	3.63	3.62	3.61	3.60	3.59	3.59	3.58	3.58
8- 9	3.75	3.73	3.71	3.69	3.68	3.66	3.65	3.64	3.64	3.63	3.62	3.62
8-11	3.80	3.77	3.75	3.73	3.72	3.71	3.69	3.68	3.68	3.67	3.67	3.66
9- 1	3.84	3.82	3.80	3.78	3.76	3.75	3.74	3.73	3.72	3.71	3.71	3.70
9- 3	3.89	3.86	3.84	3.82	3.80	3.79	3.78	3.77	3.76	3.75	3.75	3.75
9- 5	3.93	3.91	3.88	3.86	3.85	3.83	3.82	3.81	3.80	3.80	3.79	3.79
9- 7	3.98	3.95	3.93	3.91	3.89	3.88	3.86	3.85	3.84	3.84	3.83	3.83
9- 9	4.02	3.99	3.97	3.95	3.93	3.92	3.91	3.90	3.89	3.88	3.87	3.87
9-11	4.07	4.04	4.01	3.99	3.98	3.96	3.95	3.94	3.93	3.92	3.92	3.91
10- 1	4.11	4.08	4.06	4.04	4.02	4.00	3.99	3.98	3.97	3.96	3.96	3.95
10- 3	4.16	4.13	4.10	4.08	4.06	4.05	4.03	4.02	4.01	4.01	4.00	3.99
10- 5	4.20	4.17	4.15	4.12	4.11	4.09	4.08	4.06	4.05	4.05	4.04	4.04
10- 7	4.25	4.22	4.19	4.17	4.15	4.13	4.12	4.11	4.10	4.09	4.08	4.08

GROWTH AND DECLINE OF RETARDATE INTELLIGENCE

		Chronological Age										
		34-0	35-0	36-0	37-0	38-0	39-0	40-0	41-0	42-0	43-0	44-0	45-0
Mental Age	0- 1	1.46	1.46	1.46	1.46	1.46	1.46	1.46	1.45	1.45	1.45	1.45	1.45
	0- 3	1.50	1.50	1.50	1.50	1.50	1.50	1.50	1.50	1.50	1.49	1.49	1.49
	0- 5	1.54	1.54	1.54	1.54	1.54	1.54	1.54	1.54	1.54	1.54	1.53	1.53
	0- 7	1.58	1.58	1.58	1.58	1.58	1.58	1.58	1.58	1.58	1.58	1.58	1.57
	0- 9	1.62	1.62	1.62	1.62	1.62	1.62	1.62	1.62	1.62	1.62	1.62	1.62
	0-11	1.67	1.67	1.67	1.67	1.67	1.67	1.66	1.66	1.66	1.66	1.66	1.66
	1- 1	1.71	1.71	1.71	1.71	1.71	1.71	1.71	1.71	1.70	1.70	1.70	1.70
	1- 3	1.75	1.75	1.75	1.75	1.75	1.75	1.75	1.75	1.75	1.75	1.74	1.74
	1- 5	1.79	1.79	1.79	1.79	1.79	1.79	1.79	1.79	1.79	1.79	1.79	1.79
	1- 7	1.83	1.83	1.83	1.83	1.83	1.83	1.83	1.83	1.83	1.83	1.83	1.83
	1- 9	1.87	1.87	1.87	1.87	1.87	1.87	1.87	1.87	1.87	1.87	1.87	1.87
	1-11	1.91	1.91	1.91	1.91	1.91	1.91	1.91	1.91	1.91	1.91	1.91	1.91
	2- 1	1.96	1.96	1.96	1.96	1.96	1.96	1.96	1.96	1.96	1.96	1.96	1.96
	2- 3	2.00	2.00	2.00	2.00	2.00	2.00	2.00	2.00	2.00	2.00	2.00	2.00
	2- 5	2.04	2.04	2.04	2.04	2.04	2.04	2.04	2.04	2.04	2.04	2.04	2.04
	2- 7	2.08	2.08	2.08	2.08	2.08	2.08	2.08	2.08	2.08	2.08	2.08	2.08
	2- 9	2.12	2.12	2.12	2.12	2.12	2.12	2.12	2.12	2.12	2.12	2.12	2.12
	2-11	2.16	2.16	2.16	2.16	2.16	2.16	2.16	2.16	2.17	2.17	2.17	2.17
	3- 1	2.21	2.21	2.21	2.21	2.21	2.21	2.21	2.21	2.21	2.21	2.21	2.21
	3- 3	2.25	2.25	2.25	2.25	2.25	2.25	2.25	2.25	2.25	2.25	2.25	2.25
	3- 5	2.29	2.29	2.29	2.29	2.29	2.29	2.29	2.29	2.29	2.29	2.29	2.29
	3- 7	2.33	2.33	2.33	2.33	2.33	2.33	2.33	2.33	2.33	2.33	2.34	2.34
	3- 9	2.37	2.37	2.37	2.37	2.37	2.37	2.37	2.37	2.37	2.38	2.38	2.38
	3-11	2.41	2.41	2.41	2.41	2.41	2.41	2.41	2.42	2.42	2.42	2.42	2.42
	4- 1	2.45	2.45	2.45	2.45	2.45	2.46	2.46	2.46	2.46	2.46	2.46	2.46
	4- 3	2.50	2.50	2.50	2.50	2.50	2.50	2.50	2.50	2.50	2.50	2.50	2.51
	4- 5	2.54	2.54	2.54	2.54	2.54	2.54	2.54	2.54	2.54	2.54	2.55	2.55
	4- 7	2.58	2.58	2.58	2.58	2.58	2.58	2.58	2.58	2.59	2.59	2.59	2.59
	4- 9	2.62	2.62	2.62	2.62	2.62	2.62	2.62	2.62	2.63	2.63	2.63	2.63
	4-11	2.66	2.66	2.66	2.66	2.66	2.66	2.66	2.67	2.67	2.67	2.67	2.68
	5- 1	2.70	2.70	2.70	2.70	2.70	2.70	2.71	2.71	2.71	2.71	2.71	2.72
	5- 3	2.75	2.74	2.74	2.74	2.75	2.75	2.75	2.75	2.75	2.75	2.76	2.76
	5- 5	2.79	2.79	2.79	2.79	2.79	2.79	2.79	2.79	2.79	2.80	2.80	2.80
	5- 7	2.83	2.83	2.83	2.83	2.83	2.83	2.83	2.83	2.84	2.84	2.84	2.84
	5- 9	2.87	2.87	2.87	2.87	2.87	2.87	2.87	2.87	2.88	2.88	2.88	2.89
	5-11	2.91	2.91	2.91	2.91	2.91	2.91	2.91	2.92	2.92	2.92	2.93	2.93
	6- 1	2.95	2.95	2.95	2.95	2.95	2.95	2.96	2.96	2.96	2.96	2.97	2.97
	6- 3	2.99	2.99	2.99	2.99	2.99	3.00	3.00	3.00	3.00	3.01	3.01	3.01
	6- 5	3.04	3.04	3.04	3.04	3.04	3.04	3.04	3.04	3.04	3.05	3.05	3.06
	6- 7	3.08	3.08	3.08	3.08	3.08	3.08	3.08	3.08	3.09	3.09	3.09	3.10
	6- 9	3.12	3.12	3.12	3.12	3.12	3.12	3.12	3.13	3.13	3.13	3.14	3.14
	6-11	3.16	3.16	3.16	3.16	3.16	3.16	3.16	3.17	3.17	3.17	3.18	3.18
	7- 1	3.20	3.20	3.20	3.20	3.20	3.20	3.21	3.21	3.21	3.22	3.22	3.23
	7- 3	3.24	3.24	3.24	3.24	3.24	3.25	3.25	3.25	3.25	3.26	3.26	3.27
	7- 5	3.29	3.28	3.28	3.28	3.29	3.29	3.29	3.29	3.30	3.30	3.31	3.31
	7- 7	3.33	3.33	3.33	3.33	3.33	3.33	3.33	3.33	3.34	3.34	3.35	3.35
	7- 9	3.37	3.37	3.37	3.37	3.37	3.37	3.37	3.38	3.38	3.38	3.39	3.40
	7-11	3.41	3.41	3.41	3.41	3.41	3.41	3.41	3.42	3.42	3.43	3.43	3.44
	8- 1	3.45	3.45	3.45	3.45	3.45	3.45	3.46	3.46	3.46	3.47	3.47	3.48
	8- 3	3.49	3.49	3.49	3.49	3.49	3.50	3.50	3.50	3.51	3.51	3.52	3.52
	8- 5	3.53	3.53	3.53	3.53	3.53	3.54	3.54	3.54	3.55	3.55	3.56	3.56
	8- 7	3.58	3.57	3.57	3.57	3.58	3.58	3.58	3.58	3.59	3.59	3.60	3.61
	8- 9	3.62	3.62	3.62	3.62	3.62	3.62	3.62	3.63	3.63	3.64	3.64	3.65
	8-11	3.66	3.66	3.66	3.66	3.66	3.66	3.66	3.67	3.67	3.68	3.68	3.69
	9- 1	3.70	3.70	3.70	3.70	3.70	3.70	3.71	3.71	3.71	3.72	3.73	3.73
	9- 3	3.74	3.74	3.74	3.74	3.74	3.74	3.75	3.75	3.76	3.76	3.77	3.78
	9- 5	3.78	3.78	3.78	3.78	3.78	3.79	3.79	3.79	3.80	3.80	3.81	3.82
	9- 7	3.83	3.82	3.82	3.82	3.83	3.83	3.83	3.84	3.84	3.85	3.85	3.86
	9- 9	3.87	3.87	3.86	3.87	3.87	3.87	3.87	3.88	3.88	3.89	3.90	3.90
	9-11	3.91	3.91	3.91	3.91	3.91	3.91	3.91	3.92	3.92	3.93	3.94	3.95
	10- 1	3.95	3.95	3.95	3.95	3.95	3.95	3.96	3.96	3.97	3.97	3.98	3.99
	10- 3	3.99	3.99	3.99	3.99	3.99	3.99	4.00	4.00	4.01	4.01	4.02	4.03
	10- 5	4.03	4.03	4.03	4.03	4.03	4.04	4.04	4.04	4.05	4.06	4.06	4.07
	10- 7	4.07	4.07	4.07	4.07	4.07	4.08	4.08	4.09	4.09	4.10	4.11	4.11

	Chronological Age												
Mental Age		46-0	47-0	48-0	49-0	50-0	51-0	52-0	53-0	54-0	55-0	56-0	57-0
	0- 1	1.45	1.44	1.44	1.44	1.43	1.43	1.43	1.42	1.42	1.41	1.41	1.40
	0- 3	1.49	1.49	1.48	1.48	1.48	1.47	1.47	1.47	1.46	1.46	1.45	1.45
	0- 5	1.53	1.53	1.53	1.52	1.52	1.52	1.51	1.51	1.51	1.50	1.50	1.49
	0- 7	1.57	1.57	1.57	1.57	1.56	1.56	1.56	1.55	1.55	1.55	1.54	1.54
	0- 9	1.62	1.61	1.61	1.61	1.61	1.60	1.60	1.60	1.60	1.59	1.59	1.59
	0-11	1.66	1.66	1.65	1.65	1.65	1.65	1.65	1.64	1.64	1.64	1.64	1.63
	1- 1	1.70	1.70	1.70	1.70	1.69	1.69	1.69	1.69	1.68	1.68	1.68	1.68
	1- 3	1.74	1.74	1.74	1.74	1.74	1.74	1.73	1.73	1.73	1.73	1.73	1.72
	1- 5	1.79	1.78	1.78	1.78	1.78	1.78	1.78	1.78	1.77	1.77	1.77	1.77
	1- 7	1.83	1.83	1.83	1.83	1.82	1.82	1.82	1.82	1.82	1.82	1.82	1.81
	1- 9	1.87	1.87	1.87	1.87	1.87	1.87	1.87	1.86	1.86	1.86	1.86	1.86
	1-11	1.91	1.91	1.91	1.91	1.91	1.91	1.91	1.91	1.91	1.91	1.91	1.91
	2- 1	1.96	1.96	1.95	1.95	1.95	1.95	1.95	1.95	1.95	1.95	1.95	1.95
	2- 3	2.00	2.00	2.00	2.00	2.00	2.00	2.00	2.00	2.00	2.00	2.00	2.00
	2- 5	2.04	2.04	2.04	2.04	2.04	2.04	2.04	2.04	2.04	2.04	2.04	2.04
	2- 7	2.08	2.08	2.08	2.08	2.08	2.09	2.09	2.09	2.09	2.09	2.09	2.09
	2- 9	2.13	2.13	2.13	2.13	2.13	2.13	2.13	2.13	2.13	2.13	2.13	2.13
	2-11	2.17	2.17	2.17	2.17	2.17	2.17	2.17	2.18	2.18	2.18	2.18	2.18
	3- 1	2.21	2.21	2.21	2.21	2.22	2.22	2.22	2.22	2.22	2.22	2.22	2.23
	3- 3	2.25	2.25	2.26	2.26	2.26	2.26	2.26	2.26	2.27	2.27	2.27	2.27
	3- 5	2.30	2.30	2.30	2.30	2.30	2.30	2.31	2.31	2.31	2.31	2.32	2.32
	3- 7	2.34	2.34	2.34	2.34	2.35	2.35	2.35	2.35	2.35	2.36	2.36	2.36
	3- 9	2.38	2.38	2.38	2.39	2.39	2.39	2.39	2.40	2.40	2.40	2.41	2.41
	3-11	2.42	2.43	2.43	2.43	2.43	2.44	2.44	2.44	2.44	2.45	2.45	2.45
	4- 1	2.47	2.47	2.47	2.47	2.48	2.48	2.48	2.49	2.49	2.49	2.50	2.50
	4- 3	2.51	2.51	2.51	2.52	2.52	2.52	2.53	2.53	2.53	2.54	2.54	2.55
	4- 5	2.55	2.55	2.56	2.56	2.56	2.57	2.57	2.57	2.58	2.58	2.59	2.59
	4- 7	2.59	2.60	2.60	2.60	2.61	2.61	2.61	2.62	2.62	2.63	2.63	2.64
	4- 9	2.64	2.64	2.64	2.65	2.65	2.65	2.66	2.66	2.67	2.67	2.68	2.68
	4-11	2.68	2.68	2.69	2.69	2.69	2.70	2.70	2.71	2.71	2.72	2.72	2.73
	5- 1	2.72	2.72	2.73	2.73	2.74	2.74	2.75	2.75	2.76	2.76	2.77	2.77
	5- 3	2.76	2.77	2.77	2.78	2.78	2.78	2.79	2.80	2.80	2.81	2.81	2.82
	5- 5	2.81	2.81	2.81	2.82	2.82	2.83	2.83	2.84	2.85	2.85	2.86	2.87
	5- 7	2.85	2.85	2.86	2.86	2.87	2.87	2.88	2.88	2.89	2.90	2.90	2.91
	5- 9	2.89	2.90	2.90	2.90	2.91	2.92	2.92	2.93	2.94	2.94	2.95	2.96
	5-11	2.93	2.94	2.94	2.95	2.95	2.96	2.97	2.97	2.98	2.99	3.00	3.00
	6- 1	2.98	2.98	2.99	2.99	3.00	3.00	3.01	3.02	3.02	3.03	3.04	3.05
	6- 3	3.02	3.02	3.03	3.03	3.04	3.05	3.05	3.06	3.07	3.08	3.09	3.09
	6- 5	3.06	3.07	3.07	3.08	3.08	3.09	3.10	3.11	3.11	3.12	3.13	3.14
	6- 7	3.10	3.11	3.11	3.12	3.13	3.13	3.14	3.15	3.16	3.17	3.18	3.19
	6- 9	3.15	3.15	3.16	3.16	3.17	3.18	3.19	3.19	3.20	3.21	3.22	3.23
	6-11	3.19	3.19	3.20	3.21	3.21	3.22	3.23	3.24	3.25	3.26	3.27	3.28
	7- 1	3.23	3.24	3.24	3.25	3.26	3.27	3.27	3.28	3.29	3.30	3.31	3.32
	7- 3	3.27	3.28	3.29	3.29	3.30	3.31	3.32	3.33	3.34	3.35	3.36	3.37
	7- 5	3.32	3.32	3.33	3.34	3.34	3.35	3.36	3.37	3.38	3.39	3.40	3.41
	7- 7	3.36	3.37	3.37	3.38	3.39	3.40	3.41	3.42	3.43	3.44	3.45	3.46
	7- 9	3.40	3.41	3.42	3.42	3.43	3.44	3.45	3.46	3.47	3.48	3.49	3.51
	7-11	3.44	3.45	3.46	3.47	3.48	3.48	3.49	3.50	3.52	3.53	3.54	3.55
	8- 1	3.49	3.49	3.50	3.51	3.52	3.53	3.54	3.55	3.56	3.57	3.58	3.60
	8- 3	3.53	3.54	3.54	3.55	3.56	3.57	3.58	3.59	3.60	3.62	3.63	3.64
	8- 5	3.57	3.58	3.59	3.60	3.61	3.62	3.63	3.64	3.65	3.66	3.68	3.69
	8- 7	3.61	3.62	3.63	3.64	3.65	3.66	3.67	3.68	3.69	3.71	3.72	3.73
	8- 9	3.66	3.66	3.67	3.68	3.69	3.70	3.71	3.73	3.74	3.75	3.77	3.78
	8-11	3.70	3.71	3.72	3.73	3.74	3.75	3.76	3.77	3.78	3.80	3.81	3.83
	9- 1	3.74	3.75	3.76	3.77	3.78	3.79	3.80	3.81	3.83	3.84	3.86	3.87
	9- 3	3.78	3.79	3.80	3.81	3.82	3.83	3.85	3.86	3.87	3.89	3.90	3.92
	9- 5	3.83	3.84	3.84	3.86	3.87	3.88	3.89	3.90	3.92	3.93	3.95	3.96
	9- 7	3.87	3.88	3.89	3.90	3.91	3.92	3.93	3.95	3.96	3.98	3.99	4.01
	9- 9	3.91	3.92	3.93	3.94	3.95	3.97	3.98	3.99	4.01	4.02	4.04	4.05
	9-11	3.95	3.96	3.97	3.98	4.00	4.01	4.02	4.04	4.05	4.07	4.08	4.10
	10- 1	4.00	4.01	4.02	4.03	4.04	4.05	4.07	4.08	4.10	4.11	4.13	4.15
	10- 3	4.04	4.05	4.06	4.07	4.08	4.10	4.11	4.12	4.14	4.16	4.17	4.19
	10- 5	4.08	4.09	4.10	4.11	4.13	4.14	4.15	4.17	4.19	4.20	4.22	4.24
	10- 7	4.12	4.13	4.15	4.16	4.17	4.18	4.20	4.21	4.23	4.25	4.26	4.28

REFERENCES

Alper, A. E., & Horne, B. M. Changes in IQ of a group of institutionalized mental defectives over a period of two decades. *American Journal of Mental Deficiency*, 1959, **64**, 472-475.

Anderson, J. E. The limitations of infant and preschool tests in the measurement of intelligence. *Journal of Psychology*, 1939, **8**, 351-379.

Arthur, G. The predictive value of the Kuhlman-Binet Scale for inmates of a state school for the feebleminded. *Journal of Applied Psychology*, 1933, **17**, 188-194.

Asher, E. J. The inadequacy of current intelligence tests for testing Kentucky mountain children. *Journal of Genetic Psychology*, 1935, **46**, 480-486.

Baller, W. R., Charles, D. C., & Miller, E. L. Mid-life attainment of the mentally retarded: A longitudinal study. *Genetic Psychology Monographs*, 1969, **75**, 235-329.

Barclay, A. Longitudinal changes in intellectual and social development of non-institutionalized retardates. *American Journal of Mental Deficiency*, 1969, **73**, 831-837.

Bayley, N. Consistency and variability in the growth of intelligence from birth to eighteen years. *Journal of Genetic Psychology*, 1949, **75**, 165-196.

Bell, A., & Zubek, J. P. The effect of age on the intellectual performance of mental defectives. *Journal of Gerontology*, 1960, **15**, 285-295.

Berman, P. W., & Waisman, H. A. Intelligence in treated PKU children. A developmental study. *Child Development*, 1966, **37**, 731-747.

Bloom, B. J. *Stability and change in human characteristics.* New York: Wiley, 1964.

Cattell, P. Constant changes in the Stanford-Binet IQ. *Journal of Educational Psychology*, 1931, **22**, 544-550.

Chapanis, A., & Williams, W. C. Results of a mental survey with the Kuhlmann-Anderson intelligence tests in Williamson county, Tennessee. *Journal of Genetic Psychology*, 1945, **67**, 27-55.

Clarke, A. D. B., & Clarke, A. M. Cognitive changes in the feebleminded. *British Journal of Psychology*, 1954, **45**, 173-179.

Clarke, A. D. B., Clarke, A. M., & Reiman, S. Cognitive and social changes in the feebleminded—three further studies. *British Journal of Psychology*, 1958, **49**, 144-157.

Collmann, R. D., & Newlyn, D. Changes in Terman-Merrill IQs of mentally retarded children. *American Journal of Mental Deficiency*, 1958, **63**, 307-311.

Crissy, O. L. Variations in the intelligence quotient of 105 children. *Child Development*, 1937, **8**, 217-220.

Doll, E. A. The growth of intelligence. *Princeton Contributions to Psychology*, 1920.

Earhart, R., & Warren, S. A. Long term constancy of Binet IQ in retardation. *Training School Bulletin*, 1964, **61**, 109-115.

Engel, A. M. Constancy of the IQ; experiments with mental defectives. *Nation's Schools*, 1937, **19**, 19-21.

Erickson, M. T. The predictive validity of the Cattell Infant Intelligence Scale for young mentally retarded children. *American Journal of Mental Deficiency*, 1968, **72**, 728-733.

Eustis, R. S. The primary etiology of the specific language disabilities. *Journal of Pediatrics*, 1947, **31**, 448-455.

Fishler, K., Graliker, B. V., & Koch, R. The predictability of intelligence with Gesell Developmental Scales in mentally retarded infants and young children. *American Journal of Mental Deficiency*, 1965, **69**, 515-525.

Guertin, W. H. Differential characteristics of the pseudofeebleminded. *American Journal of Mental Deficiency*, 1950, **54**, 394-398.

Hirsch, N. D. M. An experimental study of the east Kentucky mountaineers. *Genetic Psychology Monographs*, 1928, **3**, 183-244.

Hirschenfang, S., & Benton, J. Delayed intellectual development in cerebral-palsy children. *Journal of Psychology*, 1965, **60**, 235-238.

Hoakley, Z. P. The variability of intelligence quotients. *Proceedings of the American Association for the Study of Feeblemindedness*, 1932, **37**, 119-146.

Holowinsky, I. IQ constancy in a group of institutionalized mental defectives over a period of 3 decades. *Training School Bulletin*, 1962, **59**, 15-17.

Honzig, M. P., Macfarlance, J. W., & Allen, L. The stability of mental test performance between two and 18 years. *Journal of Experimental Education*, 1948, **4**, 309-324.

Hunt, J. McV. *Intelligence and experience*. New York: Ronald Press, 1961.

Jones, H. E., & Conrad, H. S. The growth and decline of intelligence: A study of a homogeneous group between the ages of 10 and 60. *Genetic Psychology Monographs*, 1933, **13**, 223-298.

Kaplan, O. Mental decline in older morons. *American Journal of Mental Deficiency*, 1943, **47**, 277-285.

Kuhlmann, F. The results of repeated mental re-examinations of 639 feebleminded over a period of ten years. *Journal of Applied Psychology*, 1921, **5**, 195-224.

Minogue, B. The constancy of the IQ in mental defectives. *Mental Hygiene*, 1926, **10**, 751-758.

Owens, W. A. Age and mental abilities: A longitudinal study. *Genetic Psychology, Monographs*, 1953, **48**, 3-54.

Pinneau, S. *Changes in intelligence quotient: Infancy to maturity*. Boston: Houghton Mifflin, 1961.

Poull, L. E. Constancy of IQ in mental defectives according to the Stanford revision of Binet tests. *Journal of Educational Psychology*, 1929, **12**, 223-234.

Reger, R. Brief tests of intelligence and academic achievement. *Psychological Reports*, 1962, **11**, 82.

Rosen, R., Stallings, L., Floor, L., & Nowakiska, M. Reliability and stability of Wechsler IQ scores for institutionalized mental subnormals. *American Journal of Mental Deficiency*, 1968, **73**, 218-225.

Ross, R. T. The mental growth of mongoloid defectives. *American Journal of Mental Deficiency*, 1962, **66**, 736-738.

Rushton, C. S., & Stockwin, A. E. Changes in Terman-Merrill IQs of educationally subnormal boys. *British Journal of Educational Psychology*, 1963, **33**, 132-142.

Silverstein, A. B. Mental growth in mongolism. *Child Development*, 1966, **37**, 725-729.

Sloan, W., & Harmon, H. H. Constancy of IQ in mental defectives. *Journal of Genetic Psychology*, 1947, **71**, 177-185.

Strauss, A. A., & Kephart, N. C. Role of mental growth in a constant environment among higher grade moron and borderline children. *Proceedings of the American Association of Mental Deficiency*, 1939, **44**, 137-142.

Thompson, C. W. Decline in limit of performance among adult morons. *American Journal of Psychology*, 1951, **64**, 203-215.

Thorndike, R. L. Constancy of the IQ. *Psychological Bulletin*, 1940, **37**, 167-186.

Throne, F. M., Schulman, J. L., & Kaspar, J. C. Reliability and stability of the Wechsler Intelligence Scale for Children for a group of mentally retarded boys. *American Journal of Mental Deficiency*, 1962, **67**, 455-457.

Vernon, P. E. Symposium on the effect of coaching and practice on intelligence tests. V. Conclusions. *British Journal of Educational Psychology*, 1954, **24**, 57-63.

Whatley, R. G., & Plant, W. T. The stability of the WISC IQ's for selected children. *Journal of Psychology*, 1957, **44**, 165-167.

Wheeler, L. R. The intelligence of East Tennessee mountain children. *Journal of Educational Psychology*, 1932, **23**, 351-370.

White, D. IQ changes in mongoloid children during post-maturation treatment. *American Journal of Mental Deficiency*, 1969, **73**, 809-813.

Woodall, C. S. Analysis of IQ variability. *Proceedings of the American Association for the Study of Feeblemindedness*, 1931, **36**, 247-262.

Zeaman, D., & House, B. J. Mongoloid MA is proportional to log CA. *Child Development*, 1962, **33**, 481-488.

The Measurement of Intelligence

A. B. SILVERSTEIN

PACIFIC STATE HOSPITAL, POMONA, CALIFORNIA

I. Introduction	194
II. Descriptions of the Tests	194
A. The Binet	194
B. The WISC and the WAIS	196
III. Validity	197
A. The Authors' Positions	197
B. The Reviewer's Position	197
C. Comparisons among the Tests	198
IV. Reliability	201
A. Test-Retest Reliability	201
B. Alternate-Form Reliability	202
C. Internal Consistency	202
V. Short Forms	204
A. The Binet	204
B. The WISC and the WAIS	206
VI. Effects of Nonintellective Factors	207
A. Age and Length of Institutionalization	208
B. Sex	209
C. Ethnicity	209
D. Anxiety	210
VII. Modifications in Administration and Scoring	210
A. Range of Testing	210
B. Severely Retarded Subjects	211
C. Physically Handicapped Subjects	211
D. Pseudo-Retarded Subjects	212
VIII. Factor Analyses	213
IX. Item Analyses and Pattern Analyses	214
A. The Binet	214
B. The WISC and the WAIS	215
X. Diagnostic Applications	218
A. The Binet	218
B. The WISC and the WAIS	219
XI. Conclusions	221
References	221

I. INTRODUCTION

The literature on the measurement of intelligence in the field of mental retardation is so extensive that a reviewer must set strict, and sometimes arbitrary, limits if the product of his labors is to be more than an annotated bibliography.

One restriction on the coverage of the present chapter concerns the tests to be considered. Some years ago, in a nationwide survey of psychological testing practices at state institutions for the retarded, Silverstein (1963b) found that the three intelligence tests most frequently used were the Stanford-Binet Intelligence Scale (Binet), the Wechsler Intelligence Scale for Children (WISC), and the Wechsler Adult Intelligence Scale (WAIS). More recently, an international survey by Stevens and Heber (1968) indicated that these same three tests are used with retardates around the world. Accordingly, this chapter is limited to a review of studies of the Binet, the WISC, and the WAIS.

A second restriction concerns the criterion of retardation to be applied, specifically the upper bound to be set on the retarded range. There are many systems for classifying the retarded, and something less than complete agreement among them on this point. However, it is one point on which the authors of the tests to be considered do agree: statistically, at least, the retardate is a subject whose IQ is below 70. Consequently, this chapter is limited to a review of studies with groups of subjects whose mean IQ is below 70. (In some sections, studies with the standardization samples are also cited, to provide a frame of reference.)

Even within these limits, the coverage is not exhaustive. For example, abstracts and unpublished materials are not included, nor are clinical case studies and articles in which no data are reported. The selection of studies for inclusion is based largely on the reviewer's personal preferences and prejudices, and since the nature of these will doubtless be apparent, no self-analysis is attempted here.

II. DESCRIPTIONS OF THE TESTS

For the benefit of those who may not be familiar with the Binet, the WISC, and the WAIS, this section presents brief sketches of the tests, including their underlying rationale, construction, standardization, and norms. More detailed information on each of these points can be found in the manuals.

A. The Binet

The second and third revisions of the Binet (Terman & Merrill, 1937, 1960) display the same features that marked not only the first revision, but also the original scale devised by Binet and Simon: the use of age standards of intellectual performance, the inclusion of a variety of items involving the more complex mental processes, and the reliance on a concept of general intelligence that is reflected in mental adaptability to new problems. On both revisions, intellectual level is expressed in terms of mental age. Both include a number of pictorial and manipulative items, but are heavily weighted with verbal ones. On neither is an attempt made to measure separate abilities.

The items on both revisions are arranged in order of difficulty by age levels, starting at Year II, with 6 items at all but one level. The second revision has two forms, L and M, each of which contains 122 items plus an alternate item at each of the preschool levels. The main criteria for selecting these items were an increase in the percentage of subjects passing at successive age levels, and a high correlation with the total score. The third revision has only one form, L-M, which contains the best 122 items from Forms L and M (65 from Form L, 39 from Form M, and 18 that appear on both forms) plus an alternate item at each level.

The standardization sample for the second revision consisted of 3184 native-born white subjects, equally divided between the sexes, and ranging in age from 1½ to 18. Precautions were taken to insure that a representative group of school children was tested, but the sample proved to be slightly higher in socioeconomic status than the general population, according to the 1930 census, and to include a disproportionate number of urban subjects.

The third revision did not involve a restandardization, but instead a check of existing standards against current empirical data. The records of 4498 subjects tested between 1950 and 1954 were compared with those of the subjects in the standardization sample, and items were retained as they were, or eliminated, relocated, or rescored, on the basis of this comparison. The subjects tested in the 1950's were not chosen to provide a representative sample of school children, but care was taken to avoid special selective factors.

On both revisions, mental age is found by adding to the basal age (the lowest level at which every item is passed) additional credits for all the items passed above that level. On the second revision, IQ is defined in terms of the ratio of mental age to chronological age, and IQ tables are provided for ages 2 to 16. On the third revision, IQ is redefined as a standard score with a mean of 100 and an SD of 16, and the IQ tables, adjusted for the sampling inadequacies of the standardization, are extended upward to age 18. Both sets of tables include IQs down to about 30.

B. The WISC and the WAIS

The WISC (Wechsler, 1949) is essentially a revision and restandardization of Form II of the Wechsler-Bellevue Intelligence Scale (Wechsler, 1944), and the WAIS (Wechsler, 1955) bears a similar relationship to Form I of that test. Thus it is only natural that the WISC and the WAIS have a number of features in common: the renunciation of mental age as the basic measure of intellectual level, although Wechsler (1951) subsequently presented methods for finding mental age on the WISC; the definition of IQ as a standard score with a mean of 100 and an SD of 15; and the deliberate attempt to take into account the nonintellective factors that contribute to the total effective intelligence of the subject. Both tests rely on Wechsler's concept of intelligence as the global capacity to act purposefully, think rationally, and deal effectively with one's environment.

The WISC contains 12 subtests, divided into 2 scales. Information, Comprehension, Arithmetic, Similarities, Vocabulary, and Digit Span comprise the Verbal Scale; Picture Completion, Picture Arrangement, Block Design, Object Assembly, Coding, and Mazes make up the Performance Scale. Only 10 subtests were used in establishing the IQ tables (Digit Span and Mazes are considered supplementary or alternate subtests), and so proration is required to find IQ when all the subtests are given. The WAIS contains 11 subtests, also divided into 2 scales. The composition of the Verbal Scale is the same as for the WISC; on the Performance Scale, Coding is replaced by Digit Symbol and Mazes is omitted.

The standardization sample for the WISC consisted of 2200 white children, equally divided between the sexes, and ranging in age from 5 to 15. The sample was stratified with respect to geographic region, urban-rural residence, and parental occupation, on the basis of the 1940 census. One noteworthy feature of the sample is that it contained 55 retardates, drawn from state institutions and special classes in public schools. Subjects whose retardation was due to postnatal disease or accident were excluded.

The WAIS was standardized on a sample of 1700 adults, equally divided between the sexes, and ranging in age from 16 to 64. The sample was stratified with respect to geographic region, urban-rural residence, race (white vs. non-white), occupation, and education, on the basis of the 1950 census. As with the WISC, roughly 2% of the subjects were retardates, drawn from state institutions. A separate standardization for older persons was based on a sample of 251 subjects, ranging in age from 65 to over 75, who were not chosen according to census specifications.

To find IQ on both the WISC and the WAIS, the raw score on each subtest is first translated to a scaled score with a mean of 10 and an SD of 3. On the WISC, tables for this purpose are provided for ages 5 to 16. On the WAIS, the corresponding table is based on the performance of subjects between the ages of 20 and 34, who generally obtained the highest scores. On both tests, the sums of scaled scores on the Verbal, Performance, and Full Scales are then converted to IQs with the aid of additional tables; on the WAIS, a set is provided for each age group. These tables include IQs down to about 45.

III. VALIDITY

The basic problem in seeking to assess the validity of the Binet, the WISC, and the WAIS is that—other than intelligence tests themselves—there is no existing measure to serve as a definitive criterion of intelligence. In this connection, it is instructive to consider the positions taken by the authors of the tests in regard to their validity.

A. The Authors' Positions

Terman and Merrill (1960) cited three types of evidence for the validity of the Binet: (a) the choice of items for Form L-M assures that it is measuring the same thing that is measured by Forms L and M, which in turn test the same kinds of mental functions that proved useful on the first revision; (b) there are regular increases in mental age from one chronological age to the next; and (c) each item is correlated with the test as a whole, even more highly on the third revision than on the second.

Wechsler (1958), too, mentioned three "criteria" that were met by the Wechsler-Bellevue Intelligence Scale, from which both the WISC and the WAIS were derived: (a) the scores agree with experts' ratings of intelligence; (b) performance shows increments with age paralleling those observed in normal growth curves of mental ability; and (c) the test effectively appraises mental retardation in subjects diagnosed as retarded by other means.

B. The Reviewer's Position

It is reasonable to expect performance on the tests to relate significantly to various other test and non-test behaviors that are themselves presumed to reflect intelligence, for example, measures of adaptive behavior, academic achievement, and learning ability; and this expectation is generally borne out, although the magnitude of the relationships is not impressively high. As a rule, however, these other measures have not been as well constructed and standardized as the tests under consideration, and so are unsatisfactory as criteria. The same can be said of most other intelligence tests. Therefore, at the risk of appearing to beg the question of validity altogether, this section concentrates on studies comparing the tests.

C. Comparisons among the Tests

Some problems inherent in any comparison between the Binet and the WISC or the WAIS may be noted before reviewing the pertinent studies. First, as mentioned earlier, the Binet is heavily weighted with verbal items, whereas both the WISC and the WAIS are about evenly divided between verbal and performance subtests. One might therefore expect the correlation of the Binet with the WISC or WAIS Verbal Scale to be higher than its correlation with the Performance and Full Scales. Second, the Binet has an SD of 16, whereas the WISC and the WAIS have SDs of 15. It might be expected, then, that even if the tests were perfectly correlated, the Binet mean would be somewhat lower than the WISC and WAIS means, the magnitude of the difference depending on the degree of retardation. For the same reason, one might expect the Binet SD to be somewhat larger than the WISC and WAIS SDs.

Table I summarizes the results of a number of studies comparing the tests. (Some of the statistics given in this table, and elsewhere in the chapter, were calculated or recalculated by the reviewer from data reported by the original investigators.) Only two of the three expectations put forth in the preceding paragraph are met. The correlation of the Binet with the WISC or WAIS Verbal Scale tends to be higher than its correlation with the Performance and Full Scales, and the Binet mean tends to be lower than the WISC and WAIS means. Contrary to expectation, the Binet SD tends to be lower than the WISC SDs, though not the WAIS SDs. In the case of the Performance Scale, at least, this result may be attributable to the prevalence of perceptual and motor handicaps among the retarded, and the heightened variability that that implies.

In evaluating the comparisons among the tests, it is useful to distinguish between two possible meanings of the term "equivalence" (Stephens & Crowne, 1964). *Conceptual* equivalence requires only that the correlation between two tests be sufficiently high to indicate that they are measuring the same thing. *Functional* equivalence demands that the correlation between them be so high that whatever variance remains unaccounted for is negligible; for some purposes, the tests must also have equal means and SDs. Conceptual equivalence is primarily of theoretical interest, whereas functional equivalence is a practical necessity if the tests are to be regarded as actually interchangeable.

TABLE I
Studies Comparing the Binet, the WISC, and the WAIS

A. Binet vs. WISC

Investigator	N	Age		Binet IQ	WISC VIQ	WISC PIQ	WISC FSIQ
Nale (1951)	104	9–16	Mean	55	—	—	58^a
			SD	10	—	—	10
			r		—	—	.91^a
Sloan & Schneider (1951)	40	9–16	Mean	56	60^a	65^a	58
			SD	5	6^a	13^a	10^a
			r		.75^a	.64^a	.76^a
Stacey & Levin (1951)	70	7–16	Mean	65	67^a	72	66
			SD	7	7	11	8
			r		.69^a	—	.68^a
Sandercock & Butler (1952)	90	10–16	Mean	58	63^a	63^a	59
			SD	9	10	12^a	12^a
			r		.80^a	.66^a	.76^a
Sharp (1957)	50	8–16	Mean	64	65	70^a	64
			SD	10	9	17^a	12
			r		.62^a	.57^a	.69^a
Rohrs & Haworth (1962)	46	9–16	Mean	57	56	58	53^a
			SD	6	9^a	11^a	10^a
			r		.72^a	.50^a	.69^a

B. Binet vs. WAIS

Investigator	N	Age		Binet IQ	WAIS VIQ	WAIS PIQ	WAIS FSIQ
Brengelmann & Kenny (1961)	75	M=37	Mean	51	60^a	62^a	58
			SD	12	8^a	14^a	11
			r		.79^a	.78^a	—
Fisher et al. (1961a)	180	18–73	Mean	44	—	—	60^a
			SD	10	—	—	9
			r		—	—	.69^a

C. WISC vs. WAIS

Investigator	N	Age		WISC VIQ	WISC PIQ	WISC FSIQ	WAIS VIQ	WAIS PIQ	WAIS FSIQ
Webb (1963)	20	WISC 13–16 WAIS 16–18	Mean	68	74	68	77^a	84^a	79^a
			SD	4	12	7	6^a	8^a	7
			r				.80^a	.91^a	.84^a
Webb (1964)	32	WISC Md=14 WAIS Md=17	Mean	69	74	68	78^a	83^a	79^a
			SD	5	11	8	7^a	10	8
			r				.85^a	.78^a	.82^a

^{a} Correlation, or difference between means or SDs, significant at .05 level.

The correlations among the tests are moderately high but, with few exceptions, they are not high enough to demonstrate functional equivalence; the variance that remains unaccounted for can hardly be considered negligible. It follows that the findings obtained with one test cannot safely be generalized to those with another, and that the results on two tests cannot legitimately be combined. On the other hand, the correlations are high enough to warrant a more positive evaluation of the conceptual equivalence of the tests; to a considerable extent, they do appear to be measuring the same thing.

It is appropriate at this point to consider Fisher's charge that the WAIS is not a valid measure of intelligence for the retarded. Fisher, Kilman, and Shotwell (1961a) compared the Binet and the WAIS performance of subjects between the ages of 18 and 73, and found that the WAIS mean was significantly higher than the Binet mean at all ages. Moreover, the difference was significantly greater for the older subjects than for the younger ones. The investigators observed that since the WAIS norms make an allowance for normal deterioration with age, it would be logical to assume that the WAIS is a more accurate measure of intelligence than the Binet. However, they also noted the possibility that this allowance might not be applicable to retardates, and called for studies, preferably of the longitudinal type, to resolve this issue.

Taking his own suggestion, Fisher conducted two such follow-up studies. In the first of these (Fisher, 1962c), he compared performance on the Binet and the WAIS with that on the Binet, given 20 to 26 years earlier. The two Binet means were quite comparable, but the WAIS mean differed markedly from that on the first Binet. Moreover, there was a correlation of .37 between age and the difference between the WAIS and the second Binet. Fisher concluded that the Binet is a reliable measure of intelligence for retardates over a long period of time, whereas the WAIS overestimates their intelligence, increasingly with advancing age, and is therefore of questionable validity.

Fisher's (1962b) second follow-up study compared performance on the WAIS with that on the WISC, given 6 years earlier. He predicted that the same degree of discrepancy would obtain between early WISC and later WAIS means as between early Binet and later WAIS means. Consistent with this prediction, the difference between the WAIS and WISC means was within one IQ point of that between the WAIS and Binet means for the same age group in the first follow-up study. Fisher took these results as additional evidence that the WAIS is not a valid measure of intelligence for retardates.

Fisher has provided a convincing demonstration that the WAIS is not functionally equivalent to the Binet and the WISC, and he has correctly pointed up the need for systematic exploration of the possibility that the rate of normal deterioration with age may vary as a function of intellectual level. However, functional equivalence is not synonymous with validity, and it is difficult to accept his conclusion that the WAIS is not valid without other sorts of evidence than that provided by comparisons among the tests.

IV. RELIABILITY

Most of the pertinent studies of the Binet and the WISC have dealt with test-retest reliability, but there have also been studies of the alternate-form reliability of the Binet, and the internal consistency of both tests. No pertinent studies of the WAIS were found. Note that both test-retest and alternate-form reliability imply functional equivalence; not only should the correlation be high, but the means and SDs should also be equal.

A. Test-Retest Reliability

A rather broad definition of test-retest reliability is employed in this section. Strictly speaking, reliability is more concerned with day-to-day variations than with relatively long-term changes, but there have been a number of studies dealing with the constancy of IQ over a period of years, and these, too, are reviewed here.

In order for a subject's IQ to indicate the same relative standing at different ages, the means and SDs in the standardization sample must be stable. Although it is generally assumed that the mean on the second revision of the Binet is 100 and the SD 16, the means in the standardization sample actually varied from 101 to 110, and the SDs from 12 to 21, at different ages. On the basis of his analysis of the standardization data, McNemar (1942) presented a corrected IQ table for those ages with the highest and lowest SDs, but his table is insufficiently detailed for practical purposes. Roberts and Mellone (1952) therefore conducted their own analysis of the standardization data and presented a more elaborate table of corrections for ages 5 to 14.

Scarr (1953) tested the Roberts-Mellone adjustments by comparing observed IQ changes with those "predicted" on the basis of Roberts and Mellone's table, using a test-retest interval of 1 year. She concluded that the adjustments were inapplicable to IQs below 40, but that above this level, the predicted changes were closely realized up to age 12. Collmann and Newlyn (1958) conducted a very similar study, and their findings essentially confirmed Scarr's. In a related study, Hiskey and Sadnavitch (1958) compared changes in IQ defined as a ratio, with those in IQ defined as a standard score, using a test-retest interval of 3 years. Both the means and SDs of the ratio IQs differed significantly, whereas those of the standard-score IQs did not. The investigators concluded that the definition of IQ as a standard score is essential.

The adoption of such a definition on Form L-M would appear to have solved the problem with which these studies were concerned. The new IQ tables are also applicable to Forms L and M, and it is strongly recommended that these tables be used routinely, with the second revision as well as with the third.

Table II summarizes the results of a number of studies of the test-retest reliability of the Binet. In what is apparently the only pertinent study of the WISC, Throne, Schulman, and Kaspar (1962) found reliabilities of .92, .89, and .95 for the Verbal, Performance, and Full Scales with a test-retest interval of 3 or 4 months. Neither the means nor SDs differed significantly. Both the Binet and the WISC appear to have satisfactory test-retest reliabilities, but the evidence for long-term constancy of IQ is equivocal.

B. Alternate-Form Reliability

Terman and Merrill (1937) compared performance on Forms L and M in the standardization sample for the Binet, and found a reliability of .98 for retarded subjects; the difference between the means was less than 3 IQ points. The reliability was not estimated in the customary manner, by correlating the two forms, but by working backward from the difference between the means. Subsequently, McNemar (1942) presented a more detailed analysis of the same data that showed an increase in reliability as a function of age.

Budoff and Purseglove (1963) compared performance on the second and third revisions of the Binet, given in counterbalanced order with an interval of 1 month between tests. The correlation between Forms L and L-M was .90, and neither the means nor SDs differed significantly. The investigators concluded that the two forms are comparable and interchangeable, incidentally justifying the manner in which they are treated in this chapter.

C. Internal Consistency

Silverstein (1969b) studied the internal consistency of the Binet, and found a reliability of .95. This value corresponds to the average of the split-half correlations that would result from dividing the test in all possible ways, taking into account the fact that the items are arranged in order of difficulty by age levels. Silverstein concluded that the internal consistency of the test is satisfactorily high, and of a magnitude comparable

TABLE II
Studies of the Test-Retest Reliability of the Binet

Investigator	N	Age	Interval (yr)		Initial test	Retest
Spaulding (1946)	71	M=14	4	Mean	56	58
				SD	15	18[a]
				r		.91
Scarr (1953)	350	6–14	1	Mean	57	56[a]
				SD	14	—
				r		.96
Birch (1955)	225	5–16	3	Mean	64	63[a]
				SD	10	11
				r		.80
Walton & Begg (1957)	30	7–37	4	Mean	39	40
				SD	8	8
				r		.85
Collmann & Newlyn (1958)	182	6–15	1	Mean	68	68
				SD	—	—
				r		.93
Hiskey & Sadnavitch (1958)	201	3–10	3	Mean	65	68[a]
				SD	11	14[a]
				r		.74
Francey (1960)	42	6–12	2	Mean	44	45
				SD	6	8[a]
				r		.62
Rushton & Stockwin (1963)	111	7–13	6	Mean	71	66[a]
				SD	8	9[a]
				r		.63
Barclay & Goulet (1965)	36	M=5	1	Mean	50	57
				SD	14	16
				r		.62

[a] Difference between means or SDs significant at .05 level.

to that of the test-retest and alternate-form reliabilities reported by other investigators.

Davis (1966) studied the internal consistency of the WISC, using essentially the same procedure employed in the standardization of the test. Specifically, he determined the odd-even reliability of all the subtests except Digit Span, Coding, and Mazes, to which this procedure is not applicable, and also of the Verbal, Performance, and Full Scales, excluding these three subtests. The reliabilities averaged .92, .83, and .93 for the Verbal, Performance, and Full Scales, and showed a tendency to increase as a function of intellectual level. Davis concluded that the internal consistency of the test is satisfactory.

V. SHORT FORMS

Someone has observed, only half in jest, that psychologists have probably spent more time in devising short forms of the Binet, the WISC, and the WAIS than they have saved in using them, but studies of this type continue unabated. The validity of a short form is generally defined in terms of its correlation with the test from which it is taken, and this convention is followed throughout the present section.

A. The Binet

On both the second and third revisions, Terman and Merrill (1937, 1960) selected four items at each age level that are as representative as possible of the test as a whole with respect to variety, difficulty, interest to the subject, sex differences, and correlation with the total score. They suggested that when limitations of time make it necessary, these starred items may be used as a short form, and mental age estimated by redistributing the allotment of credits at each level. The authors cautioned, however, that despite the high validity of this short form, its use may result in substantial error in individual cases.

Wright (1942) rescored the records of a group of retardates to obtain scores on the Terman-Merrill short form, and found that 10% of the IQs differed from those on the original form by more than five points. As an alternative, she proposed that the basal age and ceiling (maximal) level be established by administering all the items, rather than the starred items only. When she rescored the records used in the previous analysis to obtain scores on this short form, she found that only 1% of the IQs differed from those on the original form by more than five points. Wright concluded that when time is at a premium, her short form can be used without unduly penalizing the subject.

Most of the pertinent studies have used the Terman-Merrill and/or Wright short forms, and Wright's procedure of rescoring the original form to obtain scores on the short form. Table III summarizes the results of a number of these studies. Both short forms not only have high validities, but are actually functionally equivalent to the original form. The statistically significant differences between the means and SDs are

TABLE III
Studies of the Terman-Merrill (T-M)
and Wright Short Forms of the Binet

Investigator	N	Age		Binet IQ	T-M IQ	Wright IQ
Wright (1942)	477	3–56	Mean	59	58	58
			SD	14	—	—
			r		—	—
			Saving		—	20%
Shotwell & McCulloch (1944)	100	16–49	Mean	49	49	49
			SD	—	—	—
			r		—	—
			Saving		47%	22%
Birch (1955)	225	5–16	Mean	64	63^a	—
			SD	10	10	—
			r		.95^a	—
			Saving		46%	
Silverstein & Fisher (1961)	160	18–73	Mean	44	43^a	43^a
			SD	9	10^a	10^a
			r		.98^a	.99^a
			Saving		39%	20%
Silverstein (1963a)	80	M=13	Mean	49	49	49
			SD	8	8	7
			r		.95^a	.98^a
			Saving		43%	19%

^{a} Correlation, or difference between means or SDs, significant at .05 level.

attributable to the very high correlations, and in any case are too small to be of any practical significance.

Birch (1955) and others have pointed out that rescoring results in spuriously high validities, since an item passed (or failed) on the original form must also be passed (or failed) on the short form. To deal with this problem, he suggested comparing the correlation between the short form and a retest with that between the original form and the retest. He found that the correlation between the Terman-Merrill short form and a retest, after an interval of 3 years, was .73; the correlation between the original form and the retest was .80. Even though this difference was significant, Birch concluded that the use of a short form seems advisable in clinical practice.

Birch's procedure does not provide a completely satisfactory solution to the problem raised by rescoring. Ideally, the original and short forms should be given independently, to control the effects of factors such as set, practice, fatigue, and disruption of the continuity of item difficulty. No study using this ideal procedure was found.

B. The WISC and the WAIS

Wechsler's tests contain nothing analogous to the starred items on the Binet, but their very format suggests that short forms can be devised by reducing the number of subtests. McNemar (1950) and Doppelt (1956) have even presented formulas that make it possible to determine the validities of a number of such short forms without having to obtain the sum of scaled scores on each of them separately. Instead, these formulas rely primarily on the intercorrelations among the subtests, and in the case of Doppelt's formula, on the correlation of each subtest with the Full Scale.

Unlike short forms of the Binet, which provide a direct means of estimating mental age, short forms of the WISC and the WAIS do not provide a direct means of estimating the sum of scaled scores on the Full Scale. The literature has little to say on this point, but since the validity of a short form is generally defined in correlational terms, it would seem that the sum of scaled scores on the Full Scale should be estimated from the sum of scaled scores on the short form by means of a regression equation, rather than by proration.

Maxwell (1957) and Silverstein (1967) have determined the validities of all possible WISC and WAIS short forms of from two to five subtests, using portions of the standardization data. No similar studies of WAIS short forms with retardates were found, but Carleton and Stacey (1954) conducted such a study of WISC short forms, and found validities ranging from .80 for the best dyad to .88 for the best pentad. Osborne and Allen (1962) focused on WISC short forms of three subtests, and found a number of triads with validities of .87 and .88. Presumably because of the limited variability of the retarded groups in IQ, these values are lower than the corresponding values in the standardization sample, but they are still respectably high.

On the basis of his analysis of the standardization data for the WAIS, Doppelt (1956) proposed a short form comprised of Arithmetic, Vocabulary, Picture Arrangement, and Block Design, for which he found a validity of .96. Fisher and Shotwell (1959) used this short form with a group of retardates, and found a validity of .93. The short form mean was significantly higher than the original form mean, but the difference was too small to be of any consequence.

The short forms considered up to this point require only the simple summation of scaled scores, but a short form that entails the differential weighting of scaled scores may be expected to afford something of an advantage, in terms of a higher validity. Finley and Thompson (1958) proposed such a short form of the WISC, comprised of Information, Picture Completion, Picture Arrangement, Block Design, and Coding, especially for use with the retarded. They found a validity of .89 for this short form, and in subsequent studies, Kilman and Fisher (1960) and Thompson and Finley (1962b) both found validities of .86. However, Silverstein (1968b) reanalyzed Finley and Thompson's data using simple summation, and found a validity of .88 for their short form. He concluded that the advantage of differential weighting was minimal.

One negative feature of short forms that reduce the number of subtests is that they sacrifice the variety of functions tapped by the Full Scale. To deal with this problem, Satz and Mogel (1962) and Yudin (1966) suggested a new approach to the design of short forms, by reducing the number of items within subtests. Silverstein (1968c) determined the validities of these short forms using portions of the standardization data, and found average validities of .89, .83, and .91 for the WISC Verbal, Performance, and Full Scales, and .91, .91, and .94 for the corresponding WAIS scales. These values were corrected statistically for the bias introduced by rescoring.

Reid, Moore, and Alexander (1968) studied the Yudin short form of the WISC with a group of retardates, and found validities of .93, .85, and .92 for the Verbal, Performance, and Full Scales. They concluded that this short form is useful, since it includes all the subtests and thereby avoids the possibility of unduly penalizing a subject who has marked deficits in certain abilities.

Silverstein (1968a) studied a "split-half" modification of the Satz-Mogel short form of the WAIS with a group of retardates, using the procedure that Birch (1955) had suggested for short forms of the Binet. He found validities of .96, .86, and .92 for the Verbal, Performance, and Full Scales. The correlations between the short form and a retest, after an interval of 4 years, were .76, .75, and .81; the correlations between the original form and the retest were .79, .71, and .78. None of these differences was significant, and Silverstein concluded that the new approach appears promising.

VI. EFFECTS OF NONINTELLECTIVE FACTORS

The results of studies of the effects of nonintellective factors on performance are often difficult to interpret, since factors other than the one under investigation may operate to create spurious effects or mask true ones. Moreover, the customary procedure of equating groups or matching subjects to control the effects of such nuisance factors may not only be ineffective, but even misleading. In the light of these observations, either the presence or absence of significant effects in the results of the studies reviewed in this section must be interpreted with caution.

A. Age and Length of Institutionalization

Traditionally, there are two methods for tracing developmental changes. In the longitudinal approach, each subject is tested a number of times, with the same group of subjects represented at each point in time. In a study using this approach, Sternlicht and Siegel (1968) investigated the Binet performance of subjects between the ages of 5 and 11, who were tested initially within 2 months of admission to an institution, and at 3 yearly intervals thereafter. The results demonstrated an average decrement of 10 IQ points over this period, confirming the investigators' hypothesis that institutionalization results in a lowering of the level of intellectual functioning.

In the cross-sectional approach, each subject is tested just once, with different groups of subjects represented at each point in time. The obvious problem with this approach is that the changes found from test to test may actually be due to differences among the groups in factors other than age and length of institutionalization. To illustrate this point, consider a study by Bensberg and Sloan (1950), who investigated the Binet performance of subjects between the ages of 30 and 55 and found what appeared to be a progressive decline in the means with age. The average decrement over a period of 20 years was 13 IQ points. However, they found very similar differences in the means on the first revision of the Binet, given when the subjects were between the ages of 15 and 24. In interpreting this finding, the investigators suggested that brighter subjects fail to remain in the institution and so are not included in the older groups.

In another study using the cross-sectional approach, Silverstein (1962) investigated the WAIS performance of subjects ranging in age from 16 to 59, and in length of institutionalization from 0 to 39 years. He found uniformly negative, but nonsignificant, correlations between both of these factors and the Verbal, Performance, and Full Scales, but it is impossible to determine to what extent these findings may have been affected by differential release rates.

Zeaman and House (1962) have proposed an alternative to the two traditional methods for tracing developmental changes. In their semilongitudinal approach, each subject is tested at least twice, but the same group of subjects need not be represented at each point in time. This approach provides a solution to the problem noted previously with the cross-sectional approach, since the changes found from test to test cannot be due to differences among the groups.

Using both the semilongitudinal and cross-sectional approaches, Silverstein (1969a) studied the Binet performance of subjects ranging in length of institutionalization from 0 to 30 years. The results of the two methods agreed in demonstrating a progressive decline, but whereas the average decrement over a period of 25 years was 15 IQ points according to the cross-sectional approach, it was only 8 points according to the semilongitudinal approach. In interpreting this difference, Silverstein suggested that subjects who are still available for testing 20 to 30 years after admission are likely to have lower IQs than those who have been released some time prior to that.

B. Sex

The over-all sex differences in IQ in the standardization samples were negligible, although differences were found at various ages and on individual items or subtests (McNemar, 1942; Seashore, Wesman, & Doppelt, 1950; Wechsler, 1958).

In studies with retardates, Finley and Thompson (1959) and Gainer (1965) found nonsignificant sex differences on the WISC. On the other hand, Alper (1967) found significant differences on all but one of the WISC subtests, and with a single exception, these favored the male subjects. Fisher, Risley, and Silverstein (1961b) equated male and female subjects on the WAIS Full Scale, and found significant sex differences on several of the subtests, generally paralleling those found in the standardization sample.

Note that the standardization samples were selected so as to be representative of the general population, whereas samples consisting of consecutive admissions to a state institution, a cross-section of the residents of such an institution, or members of special classes may be biased by differential referral, admission or selection, and release rates.

C. Ethnicity

In considering the results of the following studies with retardates, it should be borne in mind that the standardization sample for the WISC consisted of white subjects only, whereas that for the WAIS consisted of both white and non-white subjects in the proportions found in the 1950 census.

Webb (1964) compared the performance of Negro and white subjects on the WISC and the WAIS, and found nonsignificant differences on both tests. Silverstein, Shotwell, and Fisher (1962) compared the performance of Mexican-American and control subjects on the WAIS, and found nonsignificant differences on the Verbal and Full Scales, but a significant difference on the Performance Scale, in favor of the Mexican-American subjects. Kaback (1965) compared the WAIS performance of subjects born in Puerto Rico with that of subjects born in New York, and found significant differences in favor of the subjects born in Puerto Rico.

In none of these studies can the possibility be ruled out that the observed differences or lack of differences are actually due to factors other than ethnicity.

D. Anxiety

In studies concerned with *general* anxiety, as measured by the Children's Manifest Anxiety Scale (Castaneda, McCandless, & Palermo, 1956), Carrier, Orton, and Malpass (1962) found a significant negative correlation with the WISC Full Scale, and Malpass, Mark, and Palermo (1960) and Feldhusen and Klausmeier (1962) found negative but nonsignificant correlations with the same measure.

In studies concerned with *test* anxiety, as measured by the Test Anxiety Scale for Children (Sarason, Davidson, Lighthall, & Waite, 1958), Knights (1963) found negative correlations with Binet, but they were significant only for the female subjects. Silverstein, Mohan, Franken, and Rhone (1964) compared subjects who were high and low in anxiety, and found nonsignificant differences on the Binet and the WISC Verbal and Full Scales. However, they did find significant differences in favor of the low-anxiety subjects on a set of "non-verbal" items on the Binet, and the WISC Performance Scale.

The results of these studies are quite consistent in indicating a negative relationship between anxiety and intelligence test performance, but the effects are not sufficiently marked to be of any practical significance.

VII. MODIFICATIONS IN ADMINISTRATION AND SCORING

Psychologists have encountered a variety of problems in using the Binet, the WISC, and the WAIS with retardates. Some of these they have attempted to solve by making modifications in the administration and scoring of the tests. This section reviews studies of these modifications and their effects on performance.

A. Range of Testing

According to Terman and Merrill (1937), little error will result in using the Binet with normal subjects by testing no farther down than the first level at which all the items are passed, and no farther up than the first level at which all are failed. In the interest of greater thoroughness, accuracy, or fairness to the subject, however, some psychologists using the test with retardates have proposed that the range of testing be extended.

Carlton (1940) investigated the effects of extending the upper limit to three levels at which every item is failed. Considering the bias introduced by not extending the lower limit in the same way, the effects were minimal, the average gain being less than ½ IQ point. Presumably, if the lower limit were similarly extended, the gains and losses would cancel out altogether.

B. Severely Retarded Subjects

A problem arises with the Binet when every item is not passed at Year II, the lowest level, so that a basal age cannot be established. When this occurs, common practice is to switch to a test whose norms extend lower, such as Kuhlmann's (1939) Tests of Mental Development. Sternlicht (1965) sought to determine whether in such cases it is valid to assume a basal age of 1½ years, adding credits for all the items passed at and above Year II. He found that the correlation between Kuhlmann's test and the Binet, based on this assumption, was .90, and that neither the means nor SDs differed significantly. These findings support the validity of Sternlicht's procedure.

A related problem arises with the WISC and the WAIS when the sum of scaled scores is too low to be converted to IQ with the aid of the tables provided, since only those for the WAIS Verbal and Performance Scales cover the full range of possible sums of scaled scores. Working backward from the table for the WISC Full Scale, Ogdon (1960) derived a regression equation for IQ in terms of the sum of scaled scores, and presented a table of extrapolated IQs extending down to a scaled score of one. Silverstein (1963c) used essentially the same procedure to prepare tables of extrapolated IQs on the WISC Verbal and Performance Scales, and the WAIS Full Scale. Of course, all extrapolations entail some risk of error, and in the present case, the reliability of the extrapolated IQs is attenuated by the small number of items on which they are based. Consequently, Ogdon's and Silverstein's tables should be used with caution.

C. Physically Handicapped Subjects

The prevalence of perceptual and motor handicaps among the retarded poses a problem in the use of tests designed primarily for use with physically normal subjects. Katz (1956) provided a method of selecting items from the Binet for use with cerebral palsied and other handicapped subjects, and presented a table showing whether vision, hearing, speech, sitting balance, arm-hand use, and walking are required to perform each item on Forms L and M. Allen and Jefferson (1962) have presented a similar, but somewhat more elaborate, table for the items on Form L-M. This table not only shows whether vision, hearing, speech, and arm-hand use are required, but also indicates whether the item can be adapted in order to circumvent a given requirement.

D. Pseudo-Retarded Subjects

Bijou (1939) suggested a modification in the scoring of the Binet to deal with the problem of pseudo-retardation. Specifically, he proposed that instead of defining the basal age as the lowest level at which every item is passed, it be defined as the level immediately below the highest one at which any item is passed. On the assumption that the truly retarded subject can only pass items in the retarded range, whereas the pseudo-retarded subject can also pass items above this range, the "upper IQ" found on the basis of this procedure would then provide an index of intellectual potential. Bijou found that half the subjects in a group with IQs between 50 and 70 had "upper IQs" above 70, and concluded that his procedure could distinguish these pseudo-retarded subjects from truly retarded subjects.

In reply, Speer (1940) argued that while Bijou's procedure increased the differences between subjects, it did not change their relative standings, and in support of this argument he presented data that reflect a correlation of .85 between "upper IQ" and IQ. Speer pointed out that the procedure for finding "upper IQ" gives the subject credit for the things he cannot do and penalizes him for those he can do. He also noted that there is no justification for retaining the criterion for the diagnosis of retardation (IQ below 70) and changing the procedure for arriving at this criterion.

Like Bijou, Jastak (1949) maintained that a subject's level of performance may be depressed by the effects of nonintellective factors. He criticized IQ as a misleading "average" of the scores on different tasks, and suggested the altitude quotient (AQ), defined in terms of the subject's highest score, as an index of intellectual potential. He also advocated that the diagnosis of retardation be made only if the subject's scores on every task are within the retarded range.

Fisher (1960a, 1961a) conducted two studies of a variant of Jastak's AQ on the WISC and the WAIS. He determined AQ by prorating the sum of scaled scores on the two subtests with the highest scaled scores and then converting to AQ with the aid of the IQ tables. He found that the correlation between AQ and IQ was .78 on the WISC and .90 on the WAIS. In a related study of AQ on the Wechsler-Bellevue Intelligence

Scale, from which both the WISC and the WAIS were derived, Silverstein, Fisher, and Owens (1963) found correlations between AQ and IQ ranging from .85 to .89. On the basis of these results they raised the question of whether AQ is measuring anything that is not measured by IQ.

VIII. FACTOR ANALYSES

In their review of the role that factor analysis can play in research on mental retardation, Dingman and Meyers (1966) observed that tests like the Binet, the WISC, and the WAIS provide thin soil for the discovery of factors, since they were not designed for this purpose, but they raised no objection to finding out what structure may exist in these tests. McNemar (1942) and Cohen (1957, 1959) have investigated the factor structure of the tests, using portions of the standardization data. No similar studies of the Binet with retardates were found, but there have been several of the WISC and at least one of the WAIS.

In two related studies, Baumeister and Bartlett (1962a,b) investigated the factor structure of the WISC for three groups of retardates and a group of normals from the standardization sample, equated for age with one of the retarded groups. They found a general factor, a verbal factor, and a performance factor for all groups, and a fourth factor, interpreted as short-term memory or stimulus trace, for the retarded groups only. The investigators concluded that these results supported the hypothesis that the mental abilities of retardates differ qualitatively from those of normals.

Belmont, Birch, and Belmont (1967) also factored the WISC subtest intercorrelations for a group of retardates, and compared their results with those for two groups of normals of comparable age from the standardization sample. They found a verbal factor, a performance factor, and a third factor, interpreted as attention, freedom from distractibility, or memory, for all groups, but the third factor had its highest loadings for the retarded group. The investigators concluded that their results were similar to those of Baumeister and Bartlett.

Sprague and Quay (1966) factored the WAIS subtest intercorrelations for a group of retardates and a group of normals of comparable age from the standardization sample. They found a general factor, a verbal factor, and a performance factor for both groups, and a fourth factor, interpreted as stimulus trace, for the retarded group only. The investigators noted the strong similarities between these results and those of Baumeister and Bartlett, but they also pointed out some differences, presumably due to differences in the subjects and/or tests.

Considering the differences among the studies, there is a high degree of similarity in their findings. A factor loaded most consistently by Arithmetic, Digit Span, and Coding invariably appears for retarded subjects, but not (or not as prominently) for normal subjects. Of course the appearance of a short-term memory or stimulus-trace factor for retardates implies not that they possess some ability lacking in normals, but that they are more variable in this ability.

IX. ITEM ANALYSES AND PATTERN ANALYSES

Most of the studies reviewed up to this point were of "general intelligence" or intelligence as a "global capacity." However, in principle it is also possible to analyze performance to assess the relative intellectual strengths and weaknesses of a given subject or group of subjects. Because of differences in the format of the tests, item analysis serves this purpose for the Binet, whereas pattern analysis serves much the same purpose for the WISC and the WAIS.

A. The Binet

Rautman (1942) analyzed the performance of a group of retardates to determine the relative difficulty of the items, and found that items such as Verbal Absurdities, Memory for Sentences, Finding Reasons, and Picture Completion: Man were consistently more difficult than Vocabulary and Comprehension items. He concluded that a complete evaluation of performance must consider the relative difficulty of the items passed and failed.

Sloan and Cutts (1947) conducted a similar study, and found that Verbal Absurdities, Memory for Sentences, and Opposite Analogies were among the more difficult items, and that Definitions, Vocabulary, and Picture Absurdities were among the easier ones. They concluded that the essential difference between the two sets of items was their degree of concreteness or abstractness.

The two previous studies were limited to retarded subjects, but there have also been studies in which the performance of retardates has been compared with that of normal or superior subjects, equated for mental age.

Thompson and Magaret (1947) set out to test the hypotheses that the items that discriminate retarded from normal subjects differ with respect to their dependence on (a) past experience or (b) rigidity. They compared the performance of a group of retardates with that of a group of normals from the standardization sample, and found no support for either of the initial hypotheses. They then hypothesized that the items that were more difficult for the retardates would have higher loadings on the general, first factor that McNemar (1942) had found in his factor analyses of the standardization data. This hypothesis was confirmed, and the investigators concluded that it is "brightness" that accounts for the differences in the performance of retardates and normals.

In a second study, based in part on the same data, Magaret and Thompson (1950) added a group of superior subjects from the standardization sample. The findings of the first study were generally confirmed when the performance of the retarded and superior subjects was compared. The investigators reasoned that since the subjects were equated for mental age, and the contribution of McNemar's first factor was less for retarded than for normal and superior subjects, the contribution of some other factor or factors must be greater for the retardates. They found that the items that were easier for the retarded subjects did indeed tend to have higher loadings on McNemar's second factor, but unfortunately the nature of this factor was not clear in the original analyses. The investigators concluded that retardates differ from normal and superior subjects not only in being less bright, but also in possessing other abilities to a greater degree. These other abilities remain to be identified.

B. The WISC and the WAIS

Baroff (1959) analyzed the performance of a group of retardates on the WISC, and found that 45% of the subjects showed a pattern in which Similarities was among the most difficult subtests, and Object Assembly and Block Design among the easiest. He also ranked the subtests from easiest to most difficult for each subject, and found that although the average correlation among the rankings was statistically significant, it was very low. Baroff concluded that pattern analysis is a self-limiting procedure, in part because of the unreliability of the subtests.

Fisher (1960b) attempted to cross-validate Baroff's pattern, but found that only 8% of his subjects showed this pattern, whereas 33% showed a pattern in which Arithmetic was among the most difficult subtests, and Picture Completion and Object Assembly among the easiest. The average correlation among the subjects' rankings was again statistically significant but very low. The correlation between Fisher's average ranking and Baroff's was .63.

Table IV summarizes the results of a number of pattern analytic studies of the WISC and the WAIS. Since Digit Span and Mazes are considered supplementary or alternate subtests on the WISC, they are omitted from the rankings, although they were included in some of the studies cited. There is a fair amount of agreement in the results of studies of the

TABLE IV
Pattern Analytic Studies of the WISC and the WAIS

A. WISC

Investigator	N	Age	FSIQ Mean	SD	I	C	A	S	V	PC	PA	BD	OA	CO
Sandercock & Butler (1952)	90	10–16	59	11	9	5	7	4	8	1	6	3	2	10
Vanderhost et al. (1953)	38	11–16	62	7	7	9	8	3	10	2	4	6	1	5
Stacey & Carleton (1955)	150	7–16	68	12	8	7	10	4	9	2	5	6	1	3
Finley & Thompson (1958)	309	8–14	68	7	9	4	10	6	8	1	7	3	2	5
Baroff (1959)	53	9–16	63	10	8	5	7	10	9	2	6	2	1	4
Fisher (1960b)	100	8–16	57	8	7	3	10	5	9	1	6	4	2	8
Webb (1963)	20	13–16	68	7	8	6	7	10	9	2	5	4	3	1
Gainer (1965)	200	6–14	67	8	10	4	7	6	9	2	8	5	3	1
Alper (1967)	713	5–16	63	10	8	6	9	4	10	2	5	3	1	7
Belmont et al. (1967)	71	8–10	61	10	7	9	8	4	10	3	6	2	1	5

B. WAIS

Investigator	N	Age	FSIQ Mean	SD	I	C	A	S	D	V	DS	PC	BD	PA	OA
Fisher (1961b)	436	16–44	61	11	4	3	11	7	9	5	10	1	6	8	2
Kaback (1965)	39	17–21	63	8	3	2	10	11	4	9	4	1	7	8	6
Sternlicht, Siegel, & Deutsch (1968)	509	16–63	60	—	4	1	9	10	5	7	11	2	6	8	2

Note: Subtests ranked from easiest (1) to most difficult (10).

WISC, in that Vocabulary, Arithmetic, and Information are consistently among the most difficult subtests, whereas Object Assembly and Picture Completion are consistently among the easiest. In the results of studies of the WAIS, Arithmetic is consistently among the most difficult subtests, whereas Picture Completion and Comprehension are among the easiest.

The studies reviewed in the previous paragraphs were limited to retarded subjects, but there have also been studies in which the patterns of retardates have been compared with those of normal and/or superior subjects.

Gallagher and Lucito (1961) analyzed the patterns of retarded, normal, and superior subjects, all from the standardization sample for the WISC, and found that Vocabulary, Information, and Picture Arrangement were the most difficult subtests for retardates, whereas Object Assembly, Digit Span, and Picture Completion were the easiest. The correlations between the average rankings for the retardates and those for the normal and superior subjects were .02 and −.57. The investigators concluded that the retarded subjects appeared strongest on those subtests requiring perceptual organization and weakest on those relating to verbal comprehension, and that this pattern was almost the mirror image of that of the superior subjects.

Thompson and Finley (1962a) compared the performance of retarded and superior subjects on the WISC, and found a correlation of −.15 between the average rankings for the two groups. They concluded that while generalizations may be made as to the relative strengths and weaknesses of groups, their application to individual subjects is highly questionable, because of the overlap in the distributions of subtest scores and their unreliability.

Belmont et al. (1967) compared the performance of retarded and normal subjects on the WISC, and found a correlation of .12 between the average rankings for the two groups. When they scored each subtest in terms of its deviation from the mean for the group and used the pattern of the normals as a baseline, they found that the retardates were relatively strong on four of the subtests on the Performance Scale, and relatively weak on five of the subtests on the Verbal Scale. The investigators concluded that the retardate is not only a subject with a low IQ, but also one with a different pattern of strengths and weaknesses.

There is one type of pattern that merits special consideration, and that is the relation of Verbal IQ (VIQ) to Performance IQ (PIQ). Seashore (1951) analyzed VIQ-PIQ differences for retarded subjects from the standardization sample for the WISC, and found that the average difference was two IQ points in favor of the Performance Scale. He concluded that it would be unsafe to accept the generalization that retardates are less retarded on performance tasks. Similarly, Wechsler (1958) analyzed VIQ-PIQ differences in the standardization sample for the WAIS. He noted that one might expect that subjects with low IQs would do better on the Performance Scale than on the Verbal Scale, but this expectation was not borne out; the average difference was almost two points in the "wrong" direction.

Although the findings in the standardization samples were hardly encouraging, there have been a number of other studies of VIQ-PIQ differences with retardates. In studies of the WISC, Sloan and Schneider (1951), Stacey and Levin (1951), Vanderhost, Sloan, and Bensberg (1953), and Alper (1967) all found significant differences in favor of the Performance Scale, while Baroff (1959) found a nonsignificant difference in the same direction. However, Young and Pitts (1951), Atchison (1955), and Hughes and Lessler (1965) all found significant differences in the opposite direction for Negro retardates. In studies of the WAIS, Warren and Kraus (1961) found a significant difference in favor of the Performance Scale, while Brengelmann and Kenny (1961) found a non-significant difference in the same direction. The findings of these studies are quite consistent, but the differences are generally too small to be of any practical significance.

X. DIAGNOSTIC APPLICATIONS

Some of the topics considered previously have, or are commonly believed to have, relevance to the problem of diagnosis, but there have also been a number of studies dealing specifically with diagnostic differences in performance. Almost all of these were with "organic" and "non-organic" retardates, although the terminology differed from study to study. In studies of the Binet, the groups were usually matched or equated for mental age; in studies of the WISC and the WAIS, for performance on the Full Scale.

A. The Binet

Hoakley and Frazeur (1945) compared the performance of endogenous and exogenous retardates, using as a measure of scatter the number of levels between the basal age and ceiling level. Contrary to expectation, they found that the endogenous retardates tended to show more scatter, although the difference was not significant. They also compared the performance of the two groups on three sets of items, requiring visual-motor, verbal, and memory ability, and found a significant difference on only one item. The investigators concluded that psychologists should use diagnostic patterns with extreme caution.

Berko (1955) hypothesized that brain-injured, aphasic retardates would show more scatter than non-brain-injured retardates. He compared the performance of the two groups, using as a measure of scatter the number of items failed between the basal age and ceiling level, and found a significant difference in the predicted direction. Berko concluded that his initial hypothesis had been confirmed, and posed the question of whether scatter may have prognostic, as well as diagnostic, significance.

Satter (1955) compared the performance of familial and organic retardates with that of normal subjects. He used still another measure of scatter, calculated by arbitrarily giving no credit for the items passed at the basal age, and credits of 1, 2, 3, and so on, for the items passed at successively higher levels. He found that the organic retardates showed significantly more scatter than the normal subjects, whereas the familial retardates did not differ significantly from either of the other groups. Satter concluded that the difference between the two retarded groups was not sufficiently pronounced to provide more than a supplementary diagnostic sign.

Gallagher (1957) compared the performance of brain-injured and non-brain-injured retardates, using a measure of "total scatter" not further specified, and found a nonsignificant difference. He also compared the performance of the two groups on 30 individual items, and found significant differences on only 2 of them. Gallagher concluded that the similarities between the groups seemed more striking than the differences.

Rohrs and Haworth (1962) compared the performance of familial and organic retardates, equated for age and performance on an earlier Binet. They used the same measures of scatter employed by Hoakley and Frazeur and by Berko, and found that the organic retardates showed significantly more scatter on both measures. They also compared the performance of the two groups on 24 individual items, and found a significant difference on only 1 of them. The investigators concluded that further research with larger groups of subjects was called for to verify their results.

B. The WISC and the WAIS

Beck and Lam (1955) attempted to find a pattern characteristic of organic retardates on the WISC. For each subject they calculated the difference between the scaled score on every subtest and the mean score on all the subtests, and then they averaged these differences across subjects. However, only 1 of their 27 organic retardates showed the pattern that appeared in the group data. The investigators concluded that there is no pattern for organics that is representative of the individual subjects' patterns.

Birch, Belmont, Belmont, and Taft (1967) compared the performance of brain-damaged and non-brain-damaged retardates on the WISC, and found that (a) subjects with either soft or hard neurological signs of central nervous system abnormality had significantly lower means than subjects with no such signs; (b) in groups equated for performance on the Full Scale, subjects with hard signs showed significantly greater variability in subtest scores than subjects with soft signs or no signs; (c) when the subtest scores were expressed as ranks, the groups showed highly similar patterns. The investigators concluded that either the test is insensitive to etiological differences, or that brain damage may constitute the etiological basis for retardation even in those subjects with no neurological signs.

Friedman and Barclay (1963) compared the performance of brain-damaged and non-brain-damaged retardates on the WAIS, and found nonsignificant differences on a set of "organic indices" (Digit Span, Digit Symbol, and Block Design), and the remaining subtests as well. They concluded that the factor of limited intelligence appeared stronger than any other factor, and overshadowed any slight differences that might characterize the groups.

In the first of a series of studies, Fisher, Dooley, and Silverstein (1960) compared the performance of familial and undifferentiated retardates on the WAIS, and found no significant differences. They concluded that these results provided some empirical justification for combining the two groups in psychological studies. In the second study, Fisher (1961b) compared the performance of the endogenous retardates from the previous study with that of exogenous retardates, and found only negligible differences. He concluded that attempts to differentiate such groups on the basis of patterns appear futile. This conclusion was presumably reinforced by the results of the third study, in which Fisher (1962a) compared the performance of endogenous and exogenous retardates using the Hewson (1949) ratios, which are based on various combinations of subtest scores. He found that the two groups did not differ in the percentage of subjects who obtained organic diagnoses by these criteria.

In a study of diagnostic differences in the relation of VIQ to PIQ on the WISC, Newman and Loos (1955) found significant differences in favor of the Performance Scale for familial and undifferentiated retardates, but a nonsignificant difference for subjects whose retardation was due to trauma or infection. In a similar study, Birch *et al.* (1967) found nonsignificant differences for both brain-damaged and non-brain-damaged retardates, although they tended to be in favor of the Performance Scale. In a related study of the WAIS, Fisher (1960c) found significant differences in favor of the Verbal Scale for subjects whose retardation was due to infection or organic nervous disease, but nonsignificant differences for a number of other diagnostic groups, including familial and undifferentiated retardates.

The results of studies comparing the performance of "organic" and "non-organic" retardates has not been particularly rewarding. A basic flaw in most of these studies has been the implicit assumption that organicity is a unitary concept. On the premise that there is some value in being able to make diagnostic differentiations along such lines, future investigators would do well to take into account the factors on which organics differ from one another, for example, the nature of the lesion, its location and extent, and the age at which it was incurred.

XI. CONCLUSIONS

There have been many indications in recent years that workers in the field of mental retardation are not satisfied with the measurement of intelligence as we know it. In the same nationwide survey that suggested that the coverage of this chapter be limited to the Binet, the WISC, and the WAIS, more than 20% of the respondents mentioned improved intelligence tests as the greatest need in psychological testing for the retarded. Others cited the need for improved tests for infants and the severely retarded, improved non-verbal tests, improved tests for subjects with physical handicaps, and improved culture-free or culture-fair tests. Each of these responses reflects some degree of dissatisfaction with the present state of affairs.

Among a number of possible alternative approaches to the measurement of intelligence, two may be singled out for brief mention, although neither is yet ready to replace the approach represented by the tests considered in this chapter. First, attempts are being made to develop standardized tests within the framework of Piaget's developmental psychology. This research raises the prospect of a psychometrics based on a theory of cognitive development, something that has been notably lacking in the past. Second, attempts are also being made to develop tests for the retarded within the framework of Guilford's structure of intellect. Eventually, instead of a single all-purpose test, this research may provide a pool of factor-pure tests from which batteries can be selected for particular purposes.

The direction of future developments in this area is not yet clear, but of one thing the reviewer is sure: the last chapter on the measurement of intelligence in the field of mental retardation has not yet been written.

REFERENCES

Allen, R. M., & Jefferson, T. W. *Psychological evaluation of the cerebral palsied person: Intellectual, personality, and vocational applications.* Springfield, Ill.: Thomas, 1962.

Alper, A. E. An analysis of the Wechsler Intelligence Scale for Children with institutionalized mental retardates. *American Journal of Mental Deficiency*, 1967, 71, 624–630.

Atchison, C. O. Use of the Wechsler Intelligence Scale for Children with eighty mentally defective Negro children. *American Journal of Mental Deficiency*, 1955, 60, 378–379.

Barclay, A., & Goulet, L. R. Short-term changes in intellectual and social maturity of young non-institutionalized retardates. *American Journal of Mental Deficiency*, 1965, 70, 257–261.

Baroff, G. S. WISC patterning in endogenous mental deficiency. *American Journal of Mental Deficiency*, 1959, **64**, 482-485.

Baumeister, A. A., & Bartlett, C. J. A comparison of the factor structure of normals and retardates on the WISC. *American Journal of Mental Deficiency*, 1962, **66**, 641-646. (a)

Baumeister, A., & Bartlett, C. J. Further factorial investigations of WISC performance of mental defectives. *American Journal of Mental Deficiency*, 1962, **67**, 257-261. (b)

Beck, H. S., & Lam, R. L. Use of the WISC in predicting organicity. *Journal of Clinical Psychology*, 1955, **11**, 154-158.

Belmont, I., Birch, H. G., & Belmont, L. The organization of intelligence test performance in educable mentally subnormal children. *American Journal of Mental Deficiency*, 1967, **71**, 969-976.

Bensberg, G. J., & Sloan, W. A study of Wechsler's concept of "normal deterioration" in older mental defectives. *Journal of Clinical Psychology*, 1950, **6**, 359-362.

Berko, M. J. A note on "psychometric scatter" as a factor in the differentiation of exogenous and endogenous mental deficiency. *Cerebral Palsy Review*, 1955, **16**, 20.

Bijou, S. W. The problem of pseudo-feeblemindedness. *Journal of Educational Psychology*, 1939, **30**, 519-526.

Birch, H. G., Belmont, L., Belmont, I., & Taft, L. T. Brain damage and intelligence in educable mentally subnormal children. *Journal of Nervous and Mental Disease*, 1967, **144**, 247-257.

Birch, J. W. The utility of short forms of the Stanford-Binet tests of intelligence with mentally retarded children. *American Journal of Mental Deficiency*, 1955, **59**, 462-484.

Brengelmann, J. C., & Kenny, J. T. Comparison of Leiter, WAIS, and Stanford-Binet IQ's in retardates. *Journal of Clinical Psychology*, 1961, **17**, 235-238.

Budoff, M., & Purseglove, E. M. Forms L and LM of the Stanford-Binet compared for an institutionalized adolescent mentally retarded population. *Journal of Clinical Psychology*, 1963, **19**, 214.

Carleton, F. O., & Stacey, C. L. Evaluation of selected short forms of the Wechsler Intelligence Scale for Children (WISC). *Journal of Clinical Psychology*, 1954, **10**, 258-261.

Carlton, T. Performances of mental defectives on the Revised Stanford-Binet, Form L. *Journal of Consulting Psychology*, 1940, **4**, 61-65.

Carrier, N. A., Orton, K. D., & Malpass, L. F. Responses of bright, normal, and EMH children to an orally-administered children's manifest anxiety scale. *Journal of Educational Psychology*, 1962, **53**, 271-274.

Castaneda, A., McCandless, B. R., & Palermo, D. S. The children's form of the manifest anxiety scale. *Child Development*, 1956, **27**, 317-326.

Cohen, J. The factorial structure of the WAIS between early adulthood and old age. *Journal of Consulting Psychology*, 1957, **21**, 283-290.

Cohen, J. The factorial structure of the WISC at ages 7-6, 10-6, and 13-6. *Journal of Consulting Psychology*, 1959, **23**, 285-299.

Collmann, R. D., & Newlyn, D. Changes in Terman-Merrill IQs of mentally retarded children. *American Journal of Mental Deficiency*, 1958, **63**, 307-311.

Davis, L. J., Jr. The internal consistency of the WISC with the mentally retarded. *American Journal of Mental Deficiency*, 1966, **70**, 714-716.

Dingman, H. F., & Meyers, C. E. The structure of intellect in the mental retardate. In N. R. Ellis (Ed.), *International review of research in mental retardation*. Vol. 1. New York: Academic Press, 1966. Pp. 55-76.

Doppelt, J. E. Estimating the full scale score on the Wechsler Adult Intelligence Scale from scores on four subtests. *Journal of Consulting Psychology*, 1956, **20**, 63-66.

Feldhusen, J. F., & Klausmeier, H. J. Anxiety, intelligence, and achievement in children of low, average, and high intelligence. *Child Development*, 1962, **33**, 403–409.

Finley, C. J., & Thompson, J. An abbreviated Wechsler Intelligence Scale for Children for use with educable mentally retarded. *American Journal of Mental Deficiency*, 1958, **63**, 473–480.

Finley, C., & Thompson, J. Sex differences in intelligence of educable mentally retarded children. *California Journal of Educational Research*, 1959, **10**, 167–170.

Fisher, G. M. The altitude quotient as an index of intellectual potential: I. WAIS data for familial and undifferentiated mental retardates. *American Journal of Mental Deficiency*, 1960, **65**, 252–255. (a)

Fisher, G. M. A cross-validation of Baroff's WISC patterning in endogenous mental deficiency. *American Journal of Mental Deficiency*, 1960, **65**, 349–350. (b)

Fisher, G. M. Differences in WAIS Verbal and Performance IQ's in various diagnostic groups of mental retardates. *American Journal of Mental Deficiency*, 1960, **65**, 256–260. (c)

Fisher, G. M. The altitude quotient as an index of intellectual potential. II: WISC data for familial and undifferentiated mental retardates. *Journal of Psychological Studies*, 1961, **12**, 126–127. (a)

Fisher, G. M. A comparison of the performance of endogenous and exogenous mental retardates on the Wechsler Adult Intelligence Scale. *Journal of Mental Deficiency Research*, 1961, **5**, 111–114. (b)

Fisher, G. M. The efficiency of the Hewson ratios in diagnosing cerebral pathology. *Journal of Nervous and Mental Disease*, 1962, **134**, 80–83. (a)

Fisher, G. M. Further evidence of the invalidity of the Wechsler Adult Intelligence Scale for the assessment of intelligence of mental retardates. *Journal of Mental Deficiency Research*, 1962, **6**, 41–43. (b)

Fisher, G. M. A note on the validity of the Wechsler Adult Intelligence Scale for mental retardates. *Journal of Consulting Psychology*, 1962, **26**, 391. (c)

Fisher, G. M., Dooley, M. D., & Silverstein, A. B. Wechsler Adult Intelligence Scale performance of familial and undifferentiated mental subnormals. *Psychological Reports*, 1960, **7**, 268.

Fisher, G. M., Kilman, B. A., & Shotwell, A. M. Comparability of intelligence quotients of mental defectives on the Wechsler Adult Intelligence Scale and the 1960 revision of the Stanford-Binet. *Journal of Consulting Psychology*, 1961, **25**, 192–195. (a)

Fisher, G. M., Risley, T. R., & Silverstein, A. B. Sex differences in the performance of mental retardates on the Wechsler Adult Intelligence Scale. *Journal of Clinical Psychology*, 1961, **17**, 170. (b)

Fisher, G. M., & Shotwell, A. M. An evaluation of Doppelt's abbreviated form of the WAIS for the mentally retarded. *American Journal of Mental Deficiency*, 1959, **64**, 476–481.

Francey, R. E. Psychological test changes in mentally retarded children during training. *Canadian Journal of Public Health*, 1960, **51**, 69–74.

Friedman, E. C., & Barclay, A. The discriminative validity of certain psychological tests as indices of brain damage in the mentally retarded. *Mental Retardation*, 1963, **1**, 291–293.

Gainer, W. L. The ability of the WISC subtests to discriminate between boys and girls classified as educable mentally retarded. *California Journal of Educational Research*, 1965, **16**, 85–92.

Gallagher, J. J. A comparison of brain-injured and non-brain-injured mentally retarded children on several psychological variables. *Monographs of the Society for Research in Child Development*, 1957, **22**(2, Whole No. 65).

Gallagher, J. J., & Lucito, L. J. Intellectual patterns of gifted compared with average and retarded. *Exceptional Children*, 1961, **27**, 479-482.

Hewson, L. R. The Wechsler-Bellevue Scale and the Substitution Test as aids in neuropsychiatric diagnosis. *Journal of Nervous and Mental Disease*, 1949, **109**, 158-183.

Hiskey, M. S., & Sadnavitch, J. M. Minimizing exaggerated changes in Binet ratings of retarded children. *Exceptional Children*, 1958, **25**, 16-20.

Hoakley, Z. P., & Frazeur, H. A. Significance of psychological test results of exogenous and endogenous children. *American Journal of Mental Deficiency*, 1945, **50**, 263-271.

Hughes, R. B., & Lessler, K. A comparison of WISC and Peabody scores of Negro and white rural school children. *American Journal of Mental Deficiency*, 1965, **69**, 877-880.

Jastak, J. A rigorous criterion of feeblemindedness. *Journal of Abnormal and Social Psychology*, 1949, **44**, 367-378.

Kaback, G. R. A comparison of WAIS, Binet, and WISC test results of mentally retarded young adults born in New York City and Puerto Rico. *Training School Bulletin*, 1965, **62**, 108-112.

Katz, E. A method of selecting Stanford-Binet Intelligence Scale test items for evaluating the mental abilities of children severely handicapped by cerebral palsy. *Cerebral Palsy Review*, 1956, **17**, 13-17.

Kilman, B. A., & Fisher, G. M. An evaluation of the Finley-Thompson abbreviated form of the WISC for undifferentiated, brain-damaged and functional retardates. *American Journal of Mental Deficiency*, 1960, **64**, 742-746.

Knights, R. M. Test anxiety and defensiveness in institutionalized and noninstitutionalized normal and retarded children. *Child Development*, 1963, **34**, 1019-1026.

Kuhlmann, F. *Tests of Mental Development: A complete scale for individual examination*. Minneapolis: Educational Test Bureau, 1939.

Magaret, A., & Thompson, C. W. Differential test responses of normal, superior and mentally defective subjects. *Journal of Abnormal and Social Psychology*, 1950, **45**, 163-167.

Malpass, L. F., Mark, S., & Palermo, D. S. Responses of retarded children to the children's Manifest Anxiety Scale. *Journal of Educational Psychology*, 1960, **51**, 305-308.

Maxwell, E. Validities of abbreviated WAIS scales. *Journal of Consulting Psychology*, 1957, **21**, 121-126.

McNemar, Q. *The revision of the Stanford-Binet Scale*. Boston: Houghton Mifflin, 1942.

McNemar, Q. On abbreviated Wechsler-Bellevue scales. *Journal of Consulting Psychology*, 1950, **14**, 79-81.

Nale, S. The childrens-Wechsler and the Binet on 104 mental defectives at the Polk State School. *American Journal of Mental Deficiency*, 1951, **56**, 419-423.

Newman, J. R., & Loos, F. M. Differences between Verbal and Performance IQ's with mentally defective children on the Wechsler Intelligence Scale for Children. *Journal of Consulting Psychology*, 1955, **19**, 16.

Ogdon, D. P. WISC IQs for the mentally retarded. *Journal of Consulting Psychology*, 1960, **24**, 187-188.

Osborne, R. T., & Allen, J. Validity of short forms of the WISC for mental retardates. *Psychological Reports*, 1962, **11**, 167-170.

Rautman, A. L. Relative difficulty of test items of the Revised Stanford-Binet: An analysis of records from a low intelligence group. *Journal of Experimental Education*, 1942, **10**, 183-194.

Reid, W. B., Moore, D., & Alexander, D. Abbreviated form of the WISC for use with brain-damaged and mentally retarded children. *Journal of Consulting and Clinical Psychology*, 1968, **32**, 236.

Roberts, J. A. F., & Mellone, M. A. On the adjustment of Terman-Merrill I.Q.s to secure comparability at different ages. *British Journal of Psychology, Statistical Section*, 1952, **5**, 65-79.

Rohrs, F. W., & Haworth, M. R. The 1960 Stanford-Binet, WISC, and Goodenough tests with mentally retarded children. *American Journal of Mental Deficiency*, 1962, **66**, 853-859.

Rushton, C. S., & Stockwin, A. E. Changes in Terman-Merrill I.Q.s of educationally subnormal boys. *British Journal of Educational Psychology*, 1963, **33**, 132-142.

Sandercock, M. G., & Butler, A. J. An analysis of the performance of mental defectives on the Wechsler Intelligence Scale for Children. *American Journal of Mental Deficiency*, 1952, **57**, 100-105.

Sarason, S. B., Davidson, K., Lighthall, F., & Waite, R. A test anxiety scale for children. *Child Development*, 1958, **29**, 105-113.

Satter, G. Psychometric scatter among mentally retarded and normal children. *Training School Bulletin*, 1955, **52**, 63-68.

Satz, P., & Mogel, S. An abbreviation of the WAIS for clinical use. *Journal of Clinical Psychology*, 1962, **18**, 77-79.

Scarr, E. H. Changes in Terman-Merrill I.Q.s with dull children: A test of the Roberts-Mellone adjustments. *British Journal of Statistical Psychology*, 1953, **6**, 71-76.

Seashore, H. G. Differences between Verbal and Performance IQs on the Wechsler Intelligence Scale for Children. *Journal of Consulting Psychology*, 1951, **15**, 62-67.

Seashore, H., Wesman, A., & Doppelt, J. The standardization of the Wechsler Intelligence Scale for Children. *Journal of Consulting Psychology*, 1950, **14**, 99-110.

Sharp, H. C. A comparison of slow learners' scores on three individual intelligence scales. *Journal of Clinical Psychology*, 1957, **13**, 372-374.

Shotwell, A. M., & McCulloch, T. L. Accuracy of abbreviated forms of the Revised Stanford-Binet Scale with institutionalized epileptics. *American Journal of Mental Deficiency*, 1944, **49**, 162-164.

Silverstein, A. B. Length of hospitalization and intelligence test performance in mentally retarded adults. *American Journal of Mental Deficiency*, 1962, **66**, 618-620.

Silverstein, A. B. An evaluation of two short forms of the Stanford-Binet, Form L-M, for use with mentally retarded children. *American Journal of Mental Deficiency*, 1963, **67**, 922-923. (a)

Silverstein, A. B. Psychological testing practices in state institutions for the mentally retarded. *American Journal of Mental Deficiency*, 1963, **68**, 440-445. (b)

Silverstein, A. B. WISC and WAIS IQs for the mentally retarded. *American Journal of Mental Deficiency*, 1963, **67**, 617-618. (c)

Silverstein, A. B. Validity of WISC short forms at three age levels. *Journal of Consulting Psychology*, 1967, **31**, 635-636.

Silverstein, A. B. Evaluation of a split-half short form of the WAIS. *American Journal of Mental Deficiency.*, 1968, **72**, 839-840. (a)

Silverstein, A. B. Simple summation vs. differential weighting in the construction of WISC short forms. *Psychological Reports*, 1968, **23**, 960. (b)

Silverstein, A. B. Validity of a new approach to the design of WAIS, WISC, and WPPSI short forms. *Journal of Consulting and Clinical Psychology*, 1968, **32**, 478-479. (c)

Silverstein, A. B. Changes in the measured intelligence of institutionalized retardates as a function of hospital age. *Developmental Psychology*, 1969, **1**, 125-127. (a)

Silverstein, A. B. The internal consistency of the Stanford-Binet. *American Journal of Mental Deficiency*, 1969, **73**, 753-754. (b)

Silverstein, A. B., & Fisher, G. M. An evaluation of two short forms of the Stanford-Binet, Form L-M, for use with mentally retarded adults. *American Journal of Mental Deficiency,* 1961, **65**, 486-488.

Silverstein, A. B., Fisher, G. M., & Owens, E. P. The altitude quotient as an index of intellectual potential: III. Three studies of predictive validity. *American Journal of Mental Deficiency,* 1963, **67**, 611-616.

Silverstein, A. B., Mohan, P. J., Franken, R. E., & Rhone, D. E. Test anxiety and intellectual performance in mentally retarded school children. *Child Development,* 1964, **35**, 1137-1146.

Silverstein, A. B., Shotwell, A. M., & Fisher, G. M. Cultural factors in the intellectual functioning of the mentally retarded. *American Journal of Mental Deficiency,* 1962, **67**, 396-401.

Sloan, W., & Cutts, R. A. Test patterns of mental defectives on the Revised Stanford-Binet Scale. *American Journal of Mental Deficiency,* 1947, **51**, 394-396.

Sloan, W., & Schneider, B. A study of the Wechsler Intelligence Scale for Children with mental defectives. *American Journal of Mental Deficiency,* 1951, **55**, 573-575.

Spaulding, P. J. Retest results on the Stanford L with mental defectives. *American Journal of Mental Deficiency,* 1946, **51**, 35-42.

Speer, G. S. The problem of pseudo-feeblemindedness: A reply. *Journal of Educational Psychology,* 1940, **31**, 693-698.

Sprague, R. L., & Quay, H. C. A factor analytic study of the responses of mental retardates on the WAIS. *American Journal of Mental Deficiency,* 1966, **70**, 595-600.

Stacey, C. L., & Carleton, F. O. The relationship between Raven's Colored Progressive Matrices and two tests of general intelligence. *Journal of Clinical Psychology,* 1955, **11**, 84-85.

Stacey, C. L., & Levin, J. Correlation analysis of scores of subnormal subjects on the Stanford-Binet and Wechsler Intelligence Scale for Children. *American Journal of Mental Deficiency,* 1951, **55**, 590-597.

Stephens, M. W., & Crowne, D. P. Correction for attenuation and the equivalence of tests. *Psychological Bulletin,* 1964, **62**, 210-213.

Sternlicht, M. A downward application of the 1960 Revised Stanford-Binet with retardates. *Journal of Clinical Psychology,* 1965, **21**, 79.

Sternlicht, M., & Siegel, L. Institutional residence and intellectual functioning. *Journal of Mental Deficiency Research,* 1968, **12**, 119-127.

Sternlicht, M., Siegel, L., & Deutsch, M. R. WAIS subtest characteristics of institutionalized retardates. *Educational and Psychological Measurement,* 1968, **28**, 465-468.

Stevens, H. A., & Heber, R. An international review of developments in mental retardation. *Mental Retardation,* 1968, **6**(2), 4-23.

Terman, L. M., & Merrill, M. A. *Measuring intelligence: A guide to the administration of the new revised Stanford-Binet tests of intelligence.* Boston: Houghton Mifflin, 1937.

Terman, L. M., & Merrill, M. A. *Stanford-Binet Intelligence Scale: Manual for the third revision, Form L-M.* Boston: Houghton Mifflin, 1960.

Thompson, C. W., & Magaret, A. Differential test responses of normals and mental defectives. *Journal of Abnormal and Social Psychology,* 1947, **42**, 285-293.

Thompson, J. M., & Finley, C. J. A further comparison of the intellectual patterns of gifted and mentally retarded children. *Exceptional Children,* 1962, **28**, 379-381. (a)

Thompson, J. M., & Finley, C. J. The validation of an abbreviated Wechsler Intelligence Scale for Children for use with the educable mentally retarded. *Educational and Psychological Measurement,* 1962, **22**, 539-542. (b)

Throne, F. M., Schulman, J. L., & Kaspar, J. C. Reliability and stability of the Wechsler Intelligence Scale for Children for a group of mentally retarded boys. *American Journal of Mental Deficiency*, 1962, **67**, 455–457.

Vanderhost, L., Sloan, W., & Bensberg, G. J., Jr. Performance of mental defectives on the Wechsler-Bellevue and the WISC. *American Journal of Mental Deficiency*, 1953, **57**, 481–483.

Walton, D., & Begg, T. L. Cognitive changes in low-grade defectives. *American Journal of Mental Deficiency*, 1957, **62**, 96–102.

Warren, S. A., & Kraus, M. J., Jr. WAIS Verbal minus Performance IQ comparisons in mental retardates. *Journal of Clinical Psychology*, 1961, **17**, 57–59.

Webb, A. P. A longitudinal comparison of the WISC and WAIS with educable mentally retarded Negroes. *Journal of Clinical Psychology*, 1963, **19**, 101–102.

Webb, A. P. Some issues relating to the validity of the WAIS in assessing mental retardation. *California Journal of Educational Research*, 1964, **15**, 130–135.

Wechsler, D. *The measurement of adult intelligence.* (3rd ed.) Baltimore: Williams & Wilkins, 1944.

Wechsler, D. *Wechsler Intelligence Scale for Children: Manual.* New York: Psychological Corporation, 1949.

Wechsler, D. Equivalent test and mental ages for the WISC. *Journal of Consulting Psychology*, 1951, **15**, 381–384.

Wechsler, D. *Manual for the Wechsler Adult Intelligence Scale.* New York: Psychological Corporation, 1955.

Wechsler, D. *The measurement and appraisal of adult intelligence.* (4th ed.) Baltimore: Williams & Wilkins, 1958.

Wright, C. A modified procedure for the abbreviated Revised Stanford-Binet Scale in determining the intelligence of mental defectives. *American Journal of Mental Deficiency*, 1942, **47**, 178–184.

Young, F. M., & Pitts, V. A. The performance of congenital syphilitics on the Wechsler Intelligence Scale for Children. *Journal of Consulting Psychology*, 1951, **15**, 239–242.

Yudin, L. W. An abbreviated form of the WISC for use with emotionally disturbed children. *Journal of Consulting Psychology*, 1966, **30**, 272–275.

Zeaman, D., & House, B. J. Mongoloid MA is proportional to log CA. *Child Development*, 1962, **33**, 481–488.

Social Psychology and Mental Retardation

WARNER WILSON

UNIVERSITY OF ALABAMA, TUSCALOOSA, ALABAMA

    I. Introduction 229
    II. Retardation as a Social Problem 230
    III. The Mental Retardate in His Social Environment 239
        A. The Retardate's Social Success 239
        B. The Retardate's Vocational Success 242
        C. The Retardate's Self-Concept 245
        D. The Public's View of the Mental Retardate 247
        E. The Retarded Child and His Family 250
    IV. Summary 255
        References 256

I. INTRODUCTION

This first section considers the extent to which a social psychology of mental retardation does or does not exist. The second section treats retardation as a social problem which may be alleviated by a eugenics program. The third considers the retardate's social success, his vocational success, his self-concept, his image in the eyes of the layman, and his relation to his family.

No body of information exists that can meaningfully be called the social psychology of mental retardation. In order to document this assertion, this writer undertook a survey which, though quite informal, seems thoroughly convincing. The survey covered 41 texts, books of readings, and handbooks of social psychology. The 41 included 2 volumes on the social psychology of education. Mental retardation appeared in the subject index of only 2 volumes (Hartley & Hartley, 1952; Lindesmith & Strauss, 1968, pp. 94-95, 428-429). A smaller survey of 7 general texts in the related fields of sociology and anthropology included no references to retardation; so at least to the extent that such literature defines social psychology, it does not include much on retardation. Kurtz (1964) and Katz (1964) seemed to agree that there is little in the way of a social psychology of mental retardation. Edgerton (1968) commented that the anthropological study of mental retardation for all practical purposes did not exist. Dexter (1959) stated that sociological interest was actually considerable from 1910 to 1925, but fell off to virtually no interest by 1949, and later began to revive.

Granted the dearth of comments on retardation in the social psychological literature, this writer turned to the retardation literature in search of articles of special relevance from a social-psychological point of view. Many of the contributers to this literature (for example, Dexter, Edgerton, Farber, and Perry) do, it may be noted, have backgrounds in sociology, social psychology, and anthropology. Social psychologically oriented contributions by these writers and others seem to have been considerable, especially in very recent years, and indeed, are contributions to a social psychology of mental retardation. The point is that a social psychology of mental retardation seems to be emerging as a development within the field of mental retardation—not as a development within the field of social psychology. No doubt the coverage of this literature is incomplete and inadequate in many ways, and for these limitations apologies are offered.

II. RETARDATION AS A SOCIAL PROBLEM

The incidence of mental retardation, and its seriousness as a social problem, has increased in the past and will increase in the future—not necessarily because the genetic potential of the population is decreasing or because opportunities for developing one's potential are decreasing, but because *the demands of society are increasing and are destined to outstrip an ever-increasing percentage of the total population*—unless a eugenics program is adopted.

This view of retardation contrasts with positions taken by several mental retardation experts. Perry (1966) emphasized, from a sociological point of view, the cultural arrangements that produce mental retardation. If clinicians wish to,

> Prevent the greatest number of cases from ever happening, they must, as clinicians, become concerned with radical changes in the social order . . . This order produces mental deficiency by poverty; racial discrimination; tax protection of the advantaged classes to the handicap of the disadvantaged; public school programs designed, not for the culturally deprived, but only for the articulate and influential families of the middle class and the rising members of the working class; and all other public programs of little meaning within the subculture of the lower class [p. 173].

Perry's call for better social services to enable the whole population to develop its potential to the fullest deserves the warmest endorsement. One may still disagree with his apparent assumption that the lower class is genetically equivalent to the other classes. This paper is enthusiastically in favor of every possible environmental enrichment—but with proviso that environmental enrichment alone will not be adequate to prevent a steady increase in retardation.

Dexter (1956, 1958, 1960, 1964) has suggested that the problems of the retardate are in large part a function of the fact that he is labeled retarded and then must carry the onus of this label which becomes a sort of self-fulfilling prophecy of difficulty in social adjustment, employment, and so on. Again, partial agreement is willingly offered. As this paper will document, attitudes toward the retardate are not favorable, and these unfavorable attitudes can only add to the retardate's problems. The issue would seem to be which comes first, the inappropriate behavior or the onerous label. To be fair to Dexter it is conceded that he says that the label is applied on the basis of irrelevant criteria (such as reading, writing, and calculating), and then acts to interfere with other more important activities such as getting a job and earning a living. The irrelevance of the criteria for labeling, however, is simply not quite obvious.

Dexter actually seems to suggest that an identity as a retardate is a necessary condition for retarded behavior, at least he has been so interpreted (Albizu-Miranda, Matlin, & Stanton, 1966 p. 9). The findings of Albizu-Miranda *et al.* should perhaps be considered further in regard to the question of the effects of labeling. This study reported that 31.6% of all Puerto Ricans were retarded according to psychometric tests (pp. 23, 31). Yet, the great majority of these 31.6% are indistinguishable from the rest of the poor (p. 13), and have no special difficulties. Needless to say, the neighbors of this 31.6% do not single them out for any special labeling or treatment.

Some may wish to interpret these results as showing that retardation really is no special problem, and becomes so only if society ferrets out its existence, labels it, and arbitrarily defines it as a disability. Such an interpretation would be most inappropriate. As Albizu-Miranda *et al.* (1966) themselves point out (p. 13), a psychometric definition of retardation is meaningless in an underdeveloped country. Most of Albizu-Miranda *et al.*'s 31.6% score low on tests because they have had little opportunity, need, desire, or encouragement to acquire relevant skills. The 3% of the United States population who score low do not do so for these same reasons. The fact that the unlabeled 31.6% in Puerto Rico with low test scores get on well is no sign at all that the labeled 3% in the United States with low test scores would get along well if only they were not labeled. Indeed, Albizu-Miranda *et al.* did find some relationship between test scores and success, the relationship being stronger in the more urbanized communities.

Edgerton (1967) has provided a most readable and informative account of the day-to-day life of 48 retardates (IQ range 85 to 47) released from an institution as able to care for themselves. It is hard to see how anyone can read this account (sympathetic and humanitarian though its writer may be) and maintain that these retardates would have little difficulty had not society ferreted out their disability, labeled it, and arbitrarily defined it as important. Especially impressive is Edgerton's indication that people who have no way of knowing about the retardation beforehand readily detect it, and react negatively (pp. 215–217). Edgerton also notes that the retardate's difficulties with space, time, and numbers obtrude into his social interactions as well as into his practical workaday affairs.

A book by Farber (1968a) has as its most original contribution the notion that the mentally retarded are a "surplus" population. Farber suggests that major social institutions—education, social service, and especially industry—not only help create retardates but also profit from their presence (pp. 13–15). For example, the presence of retardates is said to be important in maintaining the existing social structure (p. 242).

So far as the assertion that basic institutions, especially industry, need a retarded surplus is concerned, it is readily apparent that this is a difficult position. It is hard to see how a retarded surplus can be of much benefit to industry which needs fewer and fewer unskilled people and more and more skilled people. Paradoxically, Farber (1968a) also says that surplus groups inhibit the smooth operation of institutions (p. 106) and that through their contributions to the surplus population the retarded threaten the social structure (p. 261). The problem is perhaps one of confusing surplus in the sense of "reject," with surplus in the sense of being "extra." It is true that industry, for example, prefers to have a surplus of applicants for any position, so that it can pick those most exactly qualified for particular jobs, but a retarded surplus composed of persons hardly qualified for any job is no asset, but rather a nuisance.

The assertion that industry and other institutions somehow cause retardation, if true, can only be true in a rather special sense. It is true that most institutions, including industry and education, are not committed to include everyone. Institutions reject certain individuals who then acquire a certain label, and in this way institutions "cause" retardation. In this regard Farber's (1968a) position is much like that of Dexter (1956, 1958, 1960), but once again it is necessary to ask if individuals become retarded because they are rejected or if they get rejected because they are retarded.

Farber's (1968a) solution is for social institutions to base participation not on ability and test scores but on the capacity for personal, intellectual, and emotional growth (pp. 116, 269). This humanitarian sentiment deserves the warmest approval. Policy based on such sentiment, however, might not help the retardate as much as it might seem. Certainly the retardate has the ability to grow and develop. It would seem, however, that normal and superior people have this capacity to a much larger degree, and one might argue that industry, for example, would be better advised to spend its money upgrading the skills of the already successful employees rather than spending comparable resources trying to upgrade retardates to the point of employment.

This writer is less inclined to see the problem as one of hard-hearted employers and educators refusing to include certain individuals, and is more inclined to see the problem as one of certain individuals having minimal qualifications for inclusion no matter how benign the social order. Another aspect of the view of retardation taken by this writer makes the matter of prevention seem perhaps especially urgent. If retardation is seen as something like dwarfism, something which affects a constant proportion of the population, the problem would not be expected to become critical, even if efforts at prevention showed no progress indefinitely. Likewise one may be optimistic if he believes retardation can be banished by changing people's attitudes or renovating slums. On the other hand, if the incidence of retardation is a measure of where the population stands relative to cultural demands, and if these are inexorably increasing, as this writer believes, then efforts at remediation seem much more urgent.

This position leads to several specific questions: First, has society increased in complexity and in the demands it makes on the individual? Second, has retardation increased over the centuries, as the above analysis would indicate? And third, would a eugenics program, even if adopted, be a feasible solution?

Few will quarrel with the assertion that society has become more complex. Several experts in retardation have noted this trend and explicitly recognized its implications for retardation. Robinson and Robinson (1965, pp. 42-45) note that whether or not a person is considered retarded is very much a matter of the attitude of the community. Wolfensberger (1967b, pp. 234-235) says that self-service laundries and elevators, automats and even traffic cloverleafs are, in a social and habitational sense, causes of retardation.

Goldstein (1964) notes that the occupational adjustment of retardates has not been improved in recent years by the great proliferation of services for the retarded. His interpretation is that good effects of these services have only enabled the retardate to keep pace with rising job requirements.

In regard to the assertion that retardation has increased in prevalence in correspondence with the increase in cultural complexity, one can suggest several lines of evidence. One is the apparent increase in recognized prevalence over the centuries.

Evidence of an accelerating increase in recognized prevalence just in recent years is impressive. Clausen (1967) indicates that an increase in prevalence is to be expected as a function of the broadening of the definition of retardation and cites a number of estimates of prevalence from 1890 to the present.

Farber (1968a, p. 66) apparently concludes that an increase has occurred since the early 1900's and suggests that this increase may be due to the greater degree of intellectual competence required to comprehend the workings of contemporary society.

Data on military rejects offers an empirical line of evidence with very practical implications. Ginzberg (1965) points out that in World War II the armed forces required roughly a fifth-grade literacy level, and that 1 person in 25 failed to reach this criterion. By 1963 the military required roughly a ninth-grade literacy level, and 1 person in 6 failed. Ginzberg notes that the failure rate in different parts of the country correlates strongly with educational expenditures, per capita income, degree of rurality, Negro racial extraction, and family size. In South Carolina, and Mississippi, for example, the overall rejection rate is 1 out of 2, while the rejection rate for Negroes is said to be possibly 4 out of 5 (Ginzberg, 1965, p. 4). The most vivid datum here is the fact that in roughly 20 years, from World War II to 1963, the number of retardates increased from 4% to 16%. Apparently the rejection rate in World War I was only .9%.

Most people in the field of mental retardation seem almost violently opposed to eugenics as a means of slowing the apparent increase in retardation.

Many discussions of eugenics do it a disservice by focusing on negative eugenics in the narrowest sense, that is, a negative eugenics which concerns itself mainly with known deleterious recessives (Day, 1966, pp. 196–197; Dunn & Dobzhansky, 1946; Robinson & Robinson, 1965, p. 76). This is not to say that such a negative eugenics would not be worthwhile, but it is emphasized that this narrow approach offers far less than other eugenics approaches.

Reed and Reed (1965) have reported a massive study of retarded persons and their relatives, and on the basis of their evidence have urged negative eugenics of a broader and potentially more valuable sort. They conclude that a conservative estimate indicates that 1 or 2% of the population composed of fertile retardates produces 36% of the retardates of the next generation. Reed and Reed then emphasize a point that is usually overlooked—when a trait is passed on from parent to offspring, sterilization or other eugenic precautions will work, and it is irrelevant whether the basis of the trait is genetic or environmental. This writer believes that retarded persons subject their children to a "double jeopardy" by providing both an inadequate genetic endowment and an impoverished environment. But whether one thinks parents transmit bad genes, bad environments, or both, the logic used by Reed and Reed seems inescapable—if the retarded of this generation do not reproduce, far less retarded will be present in the next generation. The same reasoning would seem to apply to poverty and crime and everything else that tends to run in families.

In support of the acceptability and feasibility of negative eugenics, Reed and Reed make several points: (a) Some types of retardation depend not on single recessives but on a frequently occurring, transmissible polygenic trait in which assortive mating is high. (b) Even if such a trait has no genetic basis, sterilization will have an important effect which will be greatest in the first generation. (c) Kemp (1957) estimated that in Denmark voluntary sterilization and related efforts were reducing the frequency of retardation by about 50% each generation.

In commenting on sterilization in this country (which has been quite limited) Goldstein (1964) says that follow-up studies: "Generally indicate that the operation results in an improvement in the social adjustment in the parolee [p. 219]." The remarkable thing about this seemingly emphatic statement is that it occurs in the context of a literature that is usually reluctant to concede anything. One might expect, for example, that special classes would do a person more good than sterilization; yet, there is no agreement at all that special classes have been proven beneficial (Guskin & Spicker, 1968). Yet it seems that many writers recommend special classes and almost none recommend sterilization. It is noted, however, that Edgerton (1967, pp. 153–156) reported that most of his subjects (who had been sterilized) held strongly negative feelings about sterilization. Many of these subjects desired children; however, when one notes the many problems that beset these subjects, it is hard to imagine that the addition of child rearing responsibilities would have been any great blessing.

For those who, despite this evidence, find sterilization offensive, it is fully conceded that, except for the greater surety of sterilization, it makes no difference at all if some other contraceptive technique is used. Currently contraceptives are maximally available to those who are unlikely to have retarded children, and minimally available to those who are most likely to have retarded children—an ironic state of affairs from a eugenic point of view. It seems that mothers of low socioeconomic status are often eager for birth control assistance which the powers that be, in their wisdom and compassion, choose not to make available. A passage in the report by the Southern Regional Council (1967) reads as follows: "No program of birth control is available to the poor, although every mother with whom I talked expressed a desire for help in limiting her family [p. 17]." This report entitled "Hungry Children" starkly documents the grim fate in store for those children who are not prevented. The great majority of them will be retarded, but retardation will be the least of their problems. The Report of the National Advisory Commission on Civil Disorders (1968, pp. 465–466) also documents the poors' desire for contraception. Since the poor are the high risk group, for retardation as well as many other misfortunes, any increased use of contraception by this group can only be salutary. Since the poor themselves seem to want contraception, the chief problem seems to be the attitude of officialdom which withholds contraception from them. Mental retardation experts are urged to do what they can—in classes, public address, and publications—to promote more constructive attitudes and practices where contraception is concerned.

Although negative eugenics, as envisioned by Reed and Reed (1965, p. 77), seems eminently worthwhile, even greater gains might be had from positive eugenics. Positive eugenics, as envisioned by this writer, would work through sperm donorship which could be utilized by interested couples on a voluntary basis. Sperm could be made available by physicians, other individuals, and hopefully, eventually by government agencies.

Such a positive eugenics program would require selecting only a relatively *few* critical positive traits: such as longevity, general good health throughout the life span, high intelligence, emotional stability, good character, and physical prowess. The consistent presence of such traits as these, of course, attests to the virtual absence of any negative genetic material, since even a few deleterious genes of any sort would be incompatible with the constellation of traits suggested. This approach, of course, requires the assumption that, directly or indirectly, good traits have *some* genetic basis.

One may expect that if the practice of utilizing donated sperm ever got started, it would catch on quickly as eugenic off-spring captured the bulk of honors in intellectual and athletic endeavors. Some geneticists, for example, Lerner (1968, esp. p. 271) apparently have a limited enthusiasm for eugenics because they assume that only a small percent of the population would practice eugenics, and that only occasional utilization of superior donors would have little effect on the total gene pool. It is, of course, conceded that the national average cannot be changed much by eugenics unless a substantial percent participates. One admittedly cannot, therefore, be optimistic about eugenics as a solution to retardation on a national scale unless he believes, as the present writer does, that eugenics can potentially appeal to a substantial percentage of the population.

Something has happened in the United States, and presumably still is happening, which amounts almost to a natural experiment in just the sort of positive eugenics being advocated. This "experiment" apparently is yielding encouraging results. An article by Kleegman (1963) discusses artificial insemination which is apparently available in this country as a medical service. It is, of course, expected at this time that this service will be sought only by those couples who cannot conceive by themselves. Kleegman states that donors must be of superior intelligence, and that their family histories are examined conscientiously for any adverse genetic history that would disbar them. Most donors are medical students. It may be noted that medical students, due to the demands of the medical curriculum, can be expected to be above average in intelligence, emotional stability, and stamina. What is more, medical students are very well qualified to present the type of history which would reveal any disqualifying family traits. This article by Kleegman is summarized in the *Sociological Abstracts* (Kleegman, 1964). The Abstract, for some reason, seems to contain information not included in the article itself. In particular, it mentions follow-up observations which apparently are not discussed in the main article, and perhaps were done after the main article was written. The abstract states that on the basis of the follow-up, the resulting babies were the finest seen in medical practice. This outcome was attributed to the superior genetic composition of the donors, the careful selection of the couples, and the great love which the much wanted babies enjoyed. Further follow-up studies of such off-spring would seem to be a research endeavor of utmost priority!

Haller (1963) relates an even bolder experiment initiated by John Humphrey Noyes. Noyes founded a religious community in 1848, and in 1869 he initiated efforts to match those most advanced in health and perfection. The founder's son reported the subsequent children to be far above normal. The community, however, dissolved in 1880.

If intelligence and other good qualities are genetically based, a positive eugenics program should succeed in raising the endowment of the average individual. What relevance does such a program have, however, to mental retardation, which concerns the lower end of the curve—a population whose imagination may not be easily fired by the prospect of seeking sperm donors? This question may be answered by recapitulation of the three-variable model of retardation being offered in this paper.

In planning for the future, mental retardation experts should consider three factors: the genetic endowment of the population, the ability level, and the demands of the society. The genetic endowment is now changing little. [Reed and Reed (1965) suggest that it may be rising slightly, but for practical purposes, it is probably not changing much.] The ability level is going up slowly. These small gains are due to changes in such things as nutrition, hygiene, and teaching techniques. The best that can be expected from such gains is a slow linear trend. The demands of society, on the other hand, are increasing at a rapid and accelerating rate. As endowment remains constant and ability increases slowly, the rapid acceleration of demands will create a growing ability gap. The percentage of retarded in the population is merely a reflection of the size of this gap. This gap could, in a very short time, overtake the population average, not just the lower end! If a rapid increase in retardation is to be avoided in the next few generations, the development of society will have to be slowed or reversed (perhaps through wars, riots, and other dislocations) or else the ability level will have to be raised through a eugenics program, preferably a positive eugenics program. In the long run, man might be well advised to make deliberate efforts to moderate the natural increase in social demands, so that too large a percentage will not be left behind.

Haller (1963) says that after 1930 eugenics rapidly lost favor. He does say, however, that today a cautious and scientific eugenics is struggling for attention (p. 7). It apparently will not be welcomed with open arms, however.

Albizu-Miranda and Matlin say: "We are losing little in substantially ignoring the effect of heredity [1968, p. 28]." An article by the American Eugenics Society expresses the opinion that "The majority of geneticists . . . would not at present give scientific support to a program of positive eugenics [1953]." Perry (1966, p. 358) reflects what seems to this writer to be a virtual concensus when he says "Measures of positive and negative eugenics . . . offer relatively little hope."

Many of the articles covered by this writer conjure up a picture of a steady stream of retardates emerging from hospitals and special classes to take their rightful place as fully participating members of society. This "sweetness and light" syndrome is well illustrated by Stevens who says:

> Concerted action is required for these (retarded) individuals to take their rightful place in our society, and, more important, to assume their full share of responsibilities in support of our democratic way of life [Stevens, 1964, p. 2].

This writer, however, is not particularly reassured by all this sweet optimism, and will leave it up to these anti-eugenics optimists to explain why hospitals hold more patients now than they did five years ago, and why the military in 1963 rejected 4 times the proportion of men they rejected during World War II, and over 16 times the proportion they rejected in World War I.

III. THE MENTAL RETARDATE IN HIS SOCIAL ENVIRONMENT

This section considers the social success of the retardate, his vocational success, his self-concept, the public's conception of him, his family and family relationships, and his life as it is affected by institutions.

A. The Retardate's Social Success

Several studies reviewed by Dentler and Mackler (1962) show moderate relationships between ability and sociometric status among normal children. The correlations range from .28 to .45. Likewise, studies of institutionalized retarded children show correlations from .34 to .50.

Dayan (1964) has reported one of the few studies that does not show a definite relationship between sociometric status and intelligence per se. His study involved sociometric data on mental retardates living in seven different cottages. Dayan's data did show a positive relationship between intelligence and acceptance in all seven cottages, but it is significant in the case of only one. Dayan found that adaptive behavior, as measured by the Gardner behavior chart, was a better predictor of popularity than was the IQ. The relevant correlations were not very high, but were predominantly positive in the case of acceptance and predominantly negative in the case of rejection.

It is important to note that studies done on normal children in school and on retarded children in institutions are both dealing with restricted ranges. The results of these studies lead one to suspect that retarded children in a normal school environment, where they have to compete for popularity with normal and superior children, are likely to be very rejected, indeed. This expectation is firmly supported by several studies (Turner, cited by Dentler & Mackler, 1962; Johnson, 1950; Johnson & Kirk, 1950; Baldwin, 1958; Miller, 1956; Diggs, 1963). Other studies showed that when retarded subjects spent part of their time in regular classes and part of their time in special classes, they received more acceptance from their special class peers (Diggs, 1964).

Another investigation, Meyerowitz (1967b), studied acceptance by other children in the neighborhood, rather than other children in the school. The retarded children were actually more salient, in the sense of being better known; but in spite of this greater salience the retarded children were disregarded, that is, they were social isolates, accepted less often and also rejected less often than their normal peers.

In the light of this impressive evidence that the retarded pupil is poorly accepted by his normal classmates, the previously cited study by Diggs (1964) and a study by Chennault (1967) are of special interest. The main purpose of the Diggs study was to attempt to improve the status of the retarded child in regular classes by giving the teacher information about the social structure of the class, and instructions for attempting to change the structure. Unhappily, Diggs (1964) apparently obtained, at best, minimal evidence of any positive effect. Chennault was able to improve the sociometric standing of unpopular special class students by having them plan, rehearse, and present a dramatic skit.

Teachers trying to help retardates win better sociometric status will want to remember that retardates are generally unaccepted because of bothersome, inappropriate, or antisocial behavior, including bullying, fighting, misbehaving, showing off, swearing, lying, and cheating (Baldwin, 1958; Johnson, 1950; Johnson & Kirk, 1950); or simply an absence of positive likeable traits and behavior (Lapp, 1957; Meyerowitz, 1967b).

Retardates apparently continue to be social rejects in adulthood. Edgerton (1967, p. 214) indicates that retardates have a great need for affection, but that they are inept in seeking it and often drive away those who are kindly disposed to them. The ubiquitious effect of retardation on social interaction is shown by the fact that when normal persons become aware of incompetence, they modify their verbal interaction markedly. They talk more loudly, condescendingly, simply, and slowly. "The result is a slowing down of interaction to the point of virtual cessation [p. 216]." Although retardates have few friends, they do typically have one or more benefactors on whom they depend for assistance and without whose help they could not manage.

The retardate also apparently encounters social rejection on the job. Goldstein (1964) cited Peckham (1951) and Brainerd (1954) to indicate that the most frequent reason given for job termination by clients of vocational rehabilitation was that they were the targets of teasing, ridicule, and practical jokes on the part of their fellow workers, and that it sometimes took as long as two years for the retarded workers to be accepted as regular employees by their fellow workers.

These data suggest that one should consider segregating retardates, if only to protect them from rejection. Children (and adults) will apparently segregate themselves informally on the basis of IQ even if there is no formal segregation.

Evidence of the difficulty of integrating children with wide IQ differences comes from a study by Kahn (1965). She reported that since 1961 normal and retarded teenagers have been placed together in a social and camping program sponsored by a Young Men's–Young Women's Hebrew Association. It was concluded, however, that the integration of retardates and normals was unrealistic. The normals recognized the limits of the retardates and developed a strong sense of pity, but although the youngsters were in close proximity and engaged in identical programs, the desired interaction was lacking.

Another study (Laing & Chazan, 1966) suggested that when retarded children are segregated, typical sociometric patterns and a normal degree of group cohesion does develop. Farber (1968a) and Cleland and Dingman (1970) in commenting on a number of articles, also suggest that social opportunities are available in some institutions. Patients in some hospitals apparently form cliques and differentiate among themselves in regard to status, talk about sex, and so on. Edgerton's (1963) description of patient social life in one co-educational hospital gives the impression that social opportunities, even "dates," are not necessarily lacking, especially if a patient is fortunate enough to belong to the "elite group." In this hospital, elite patients, patients with high social status, were predominantly Negro or Mexican-American, of slightly lower IQ than non-elite but 'high grade' patients, Catholic rather than Protestant, and likely to have been apprehended in law violation necessitating police action, the respective percentages being 90 and 5 in this last case. In accordance with this last observation, it may be noted that the patient elite apparently modeled itself after its conception of the non-institutionalized delinquent. A major prerequisite for elite membership, for example, was fighting ability. This requirement applied to females as well as males.

Quay (1963), however, has indicated the complexity of the issue of segregating retardates for the sake of their social adjustment, suggesting, among other things, that retardates might prefer to be rejected in regular classes to being segregated in special classes.

Some studies, indeed, do not reassure one that segregation will in any sense guarantee retardates a good social life. A study by Dentler and Mackler (1964) concerned 29 new arrivals at a state institution. These arrivals, apparently, all took up residence with each other in one or more cottages. Initially group status correlated highly with mental ability, social initiative (frequency of observed contact attempts with peers), and restriction of conduct (frequency of aide disciplinary measures). In the second month the abler boys experienced a decline in status and were more frequently restricted. Social status, Dentler and Mackler suggested, was progressively associated with compliance to institutional norms as rigorously applied by cottage aides. Although a low, but still significant, correlation persisted between social status and mental ability, the apparent function of the institution was to cause social and mental ability to be a disability. One gets the impression that it makes a lot of difference what particular institution an individual goes to.

B. The Retardate's Vocational Success

Several studies estimate that some 96% of retarded individuals reside outside of institutions (Clarke, Clarke, & Reiman, 1958; Stevens, 1964, p. 2; United States Department of Health, Education, and Welfare, 1966). Goldstein (1964, p. 233), however, estimates 90%. Many retardates, of course, are dependent on parents and relatives, but a great many eventually make successful independent adjustments to society, both vocationally and otherwise. Studies of variables predictive of an ability to manage outside an institution have not led to agreement on many points. About the most that can be concluded is that retarded individuals do not succeed as well as normals.

1. Variables Predicting Successful Adjustment

A classic review in this area by Windle (1962) has now been augmented by Goldstein (1964) and Eagle (1967). Eagle's article indicates that the results are conflicting in relation to most variables. The most definite conclusions following a review of data from 47 studies involving more than 40 release characteristics was that favorable conditions in the placement home are predictive of success. Madison (1964) concluded that professional staff agreement concerning suitability for work placement is predictive of success. This conclusion seems encouraging and at least has apparently not been contradicted, as yet. Another uncontradicted finding seems to be that if failure is to occur it tends to occur relatively soon (Madison, 1964; Windle, 1962, p. 21). One reason it has been so hard to find variables predictive of success is that relevant variables are taken into account before releases are granted. It is this selection factor that prevents intelligence, for example, from being consistently predictive of success among releasees. Patients with very low intelligence are unlikely to be released in the first place. Windle (1962) was quite aware of this selection problem and suggested that it also operated in the case of personality traits.

Eagle (1967) evaluated the results reported in 36 follow up studies on institutionalized retardates published between 1941 and 1965. Among the 7436 releases the overall failure rate was 39.6%. Eagle considered only those who failed in the community and were returned to the institution; partial successes, partial failures, the undefined, etc. were not considered to be failures in these calculations. This suggests that the 39.6% figure may be a rather minimal one. Among the releasees studied by Edgerton (1967), for example, apparently hardly any achieved on their own an adjustment which could be called successful by middle class standards. The majority maintained their marginal adjustments only with the aid of normal benefactors.

Eagle (1967) indicated that the 11 studies since 1960 showed a failure rate of 50%, and calculations by this writer suggest that the failure rate in the earlier 25 studies must have been 36%. This difference, between 36% and 50%, certainly does not prove anything, but it does seem to be compatible with the position expressed in section II.

As noted, the results of studies of institutional releasees are clouded by selection factors. Another line of evidence comes from studies of children placed in special classes or otherwise identified as retarded, but not necessarily institutionalized. This type of study, of course, in no way avoids selection problems. Again a biased sample is involved, consisting of children bad off enough to be diagnosed, but not bad off enough to be immediately institutionalized. A classic study in this area was initiated by Baller (1936). The (apparently) same sample was reported on by Charles (1953, 1957). Baller, Charles, and Miller (1967) and Charles (1966) report longitudinal studies that include a low group, a middle group, and a high group. Baller *et al.* (1967) indicate that their low group compared favorably with the other two groups, though slightly lower in degree of social and recreational activity. Charles (1966) said that a great majority of persons known as mental retardates in early life prove to be, superficially at least, indistinguishable from the mass of men and women, in their fifties. He does mention, however, that in the low group 67% were self-supporting but 16% needed some help to get along, while in the other two groups almost everyone was employed. All groups were said to be law abiding. The studies just discussed paint a generally optimistic picture, and tend to deemphasize differences between retardates and others. Also an optimist is Kolstoe (1961) who said past research relating IQ scores to employability was equivocal and that any earned IQ from 40 up was sufficiently high not to interfere with employment, provided that job selection was carefully done.

A weighty body of evidence, not to mention common sense, seems to deny this optimism. A number of studies compared retarded to normals or to higher-grade retardates and found the upper groups more employable and/or better employed (Collmann & Newlyn, 1956, 1957; Durling, 1931; Kennedy, 1966). Also, studies covering only more seriously retarded subjects show a much lower degree of success than studies of the less seriously retarded (Bobroff, 1957; Delp & Lorenz, 1953; Hegge, 1944; Harding, Singer, & O'Hara, 1964). One recent report, which is not so optimistic even about the mildly retarded (Miller, 1966), found only 30% of a group of 50 working and only 5 making more than $40 per week.

Another recent follow-up study of interest is that reported by Kennedy (1966). Kennedy too stressed the similarities rather than the differences between the retarded group and a normal comparison group, but the retarded group were somewhat more often employed in unskilled and semiskilled jobs, were unable to earn as much money (a median of $88 vs. $102 per week), and were more often arrested.

In regard to the causes of job failure, Bloom (1967) cited research showing attitudinal and personality factors more often than lack of job skills to be the cause of failure. Bloom's article describes and evaluates a program that stressed efforts to instill desirable personality and attitudinal characteristics.

To close this section with a report that is recent, optimistic, and which reports on a very large sample—Strickland and Arrell (1967) made a survey of the records in the state office of the Division of Vocational Rehabilitation, to determine the extent to which educable retarded youth found employment on jobs for which they were trained in the Texas Statewide Cooperative Program for Special Education in public school: 80% out of a sample of 1405 secured employment on a job for which they were trained.

2. EMPLOYER RECEPTIVITY

Attitudes of employers toward the hiring of mentally retarded individuals are obviously crucial to the vocational success of retardates. The available studies show at best a moderate degree of receptivity.

Michal-Smith (1951) asked personnel directors and institutional directors whether retarded persons could be "successful" on eight types of jobs. Work and manual labor received the strongest endorsement: about 90% or more expected success; machine operation (mobile) and public contact jobs received the weakest endorsement: only about 45% or less expecting the retarded to be successful on such jobs. The institutional directors were somewhat more optimistic than the personnel directors.

In a study of employers (Cohen, 1963), roughly 65% said they would hire a mentally retarded person as readily as a normal person; only about 1% or 2% said they would not hire a mentally retarded person under any circumstance; and only about 22% said they would hire a mentally retarded person only on a temporary basis. Contrary to Cohen's expectation, a small but significant biserial correlation of −.23 indicated that the better educated employers were less willing to hire retardates. He found no significant correlation between a measure of realistic conception, or degree of knowledge, of mental retardates and willingness to hire them. He did find a significant correlation of .45 between knowledge, or realistic conception of retardates, and education.

A majority of employment counselors felt that their employment counseling experience with the mentally retarded had been unsuccessful most of the time (Smith, 1964). No relation was found between knowledge about retardation and attitudes toward retardates. Counselors that had had experience in working with the special class program for educables scored higher on a test of knowledge but no higher on the attitude scale. It was concluded that nearly all of the counselors had favorable attitudes toward the retarded but that the majority of them were not well informed about mental retardation. Phelps (1965) showed hospital and motel personnel managers to be more favorable toward hiring rehabilitated mentally retarded persons than hotel and laundry-cleaners managers, with restaurant and nursing home managers being least favorable of all. Greater favorability was associated with large organizations, much education, little experience, and college rather than business school training.

C. The Retardate's Self-Concept

Some writers claim that there is no clear evidence that retardates are generally maladjusted (Guskin & Spicker, 1968). Others say that it is uncommon to see a retarded child who presents no emotional maladjustment of moderate to severe degree (Phillips, 1966, p. 112). The predominance of evidence seems to be that retardates are more generally maladjusted (Beier, 1964, p. 459; Heber, 1964; Snyder, 1966). This paper limits itself to the self-concept, a traditional social psychological concern.

The literature seems to provide relatively little definite information about the retardate's self-concept (Heber, 1964, p. 147). Retardation, as such, has not been shown to have any definite effect. The same is true of institutionalization and special class placement. Some evidence does suggest that retardates with better self-concepts achieve better.

Two general studies suggest that retardates are perhaps not so very different from normals in regard to their concerns about themselves and in regard to the correlates of high self-esteem. Guthrie, Butler, Gorlow, and White (1964) found that retarded women were concerned about things that are also of concern to other women, such as popularity, sexual acceptability, compliance, and friendship, as well as fears of being ignored or rejected, giving and not receiving, and being angry with peers. Their ideals centered around themes of self-confidence, popularity, compliance, charity, loyalty, assertion, awareness of others, and avoiding involvement with peers. The authors concluded that these self-attitudes and ideals resulted from the need for protection against abuse which these women had suffered in past experiences. Gorlow, Butler, and Guthrie (1963) found small but significant positive relationships between self-acceptance and intelligence, school achievement, success in the institutional training program, and success on parole. This study also found that retardates who were separated from their parents at an early age were more negative in their self-attitudes. They also found that those expressing high degrees of self-acceptance tended to express less need for the support of others and to be more acceptant of their own hostility.

A number of writers apparently believe that there is a consistent relationship between low IQ and low self-appraisal (e.g., Bialer, 1968, p. 22), and some studies support this conclusion (e.g., Gorlow et al., 1963). The literature, however, does not seem to show any consistent relationship between favorability of self-concept and intellectual status. Ringness (1961) found that a retarded group generally tended to overestimate success more than an average or a bright group. At the same time bright children, in an absolute sense, rated themselves most highly, the retarded rated themselves next most highly, and average children rated themselves the lowest of all. Mentally retarded children, therefore, were shown to have less realistic self-concepts than either bright or average children. Fine and Caldwell (1967) found that educable mentally retarded students in the 9 to 13 range rated themselves as good or better than their classmates and other children their own age. From this the authors concluded that the self-perceptions of the retarded were inaccurate, inflated, and unrealistic. It is noted, however, that they were also, in some sense, favorable.

Piers and Harris (1964) did find that retardates had less favorable self-concepts as measured by their scale. Their assumption that this result validated their scale hardly seems warranted, however. Albizu-Miranda et al. (1966, pp. 49–55) reported rather strong evidence of unfavorable self-concepts among the retarded. Finally Edgerton (1967) stressed that retardates have a very strong need to deny that they are retarded and to pass as normal. He left the impression that their self-concept is, at best, precariously defended and vulnerable.

The effect of special classes on self-concept and adjustment generally has recently been reviewed by Guskin and Spicker (1968) and by Gardner (1968). Both seem to conclude that the results are equivocal; Guskin and Spicker conclude that there is no clear evidence that special classes have an effect one way or the other. They note, however, that a number of investigators have found some evidence of better adjustment among special class students. Meyerowitz (unpublished) apparently concluded that at the end of the second grade retarded children had more derogatory self-concepts than did normals, and that retarded children randomly assigned to special classes had more derogatory self-concepts than those assigned to regular classes.

The results on the effects of institutionalization are completely inconsistent. Guthrie, Butler, and Gorlow (1963) compared female retardates living in institutions versus at home and concluded that the girls in institutions had a much more negative set of self-attitudes. One's satisfaction with this conclusion is somewhat tempered by the fact that Gorlow et al. (1963) apparently found a slight trend in the direction of better self-concepts as a function of length of institutionalization. McAfee and Cleland (1965) found little relation between self-concept and length of institutionalization. They also found, it may be noted, little relation between self versus ideal-self discrepancies and other adjustment measures. Kniss, Butler, Gorlow, and Guthrie (1962) found self-attitudes to be independent of length of institutionalization and of age and IQ as well. The work by Guthrie and his associates has recently been summarized by Guthrie, Gorlow, and Butler (1967).

Snyder, Jefferson, and Strauss (1965) found favorability of self-concept to be strongly related to reading achievement and to favorable personality variables in general. Snyder (1966) also found that a high-achieving versus a low-achieving, mildly retarded group had a better self-concept, better personality scores, and lower anxiety scores. Snyder concluded that personality variables are highly important in determining the extent to which mental retardates will achieve their intellectual potential.

D. The Public's View of the Mental Retardate

Apparently, attitudes toward the retarded have varied enormously in the past. Currently, attitudes toward the retarded are at best moderately unfavorable, both absolutely and relative to attitudes toward other disabled groups. What is more, the few attempts to change attitudes have been unsuccessful, and may even have resulted in a worsening of attitudes.

1. ATTITUDES TOWARD THE RETARDATE

Wallin (1962) has provided a general comment on society's changing attitudes toward the retardate. He notes that the attitude of society toward the retarded child has changed considerably from time to time and from place to place. During ancient times retarded children apparently met with a variety of reactions ranging from indifference, contempt, cruelty, and even extermination, to superstitious reverence.

In more recent times, Guskin (1963a, 1963b) investigated the content of the stereotype of the retardate. He found considerable agreement that the defective 18-year-old boy is less assertive, less capable, and less normal than the average 18 year old.

Of special interest are the attitudes and misconceptions of parents of retardates. One study relevant to this issue is that of Olshansky and Schonfield (1965). The children in question had all graduated from special classes for the mentally retarded. Nonetheless, less than one third of the 105 parents and relatives, when asked about the mental status of the child, thought he was mentally retarded. About one third said they thought the child was normal; the remainder refused to make a judgment. This study suggests that parents and relatives of retardates may, not surprisingly, be reluctant to accurately perceive the child's disability.

Greenbaum and Wang (1965) classified their respondents into four groups: (a) parents; (b) professional experts: e.g., school psychologists, physicians, vocational counselors, and the like; (c) para-professionals who supervise the day-by-day care of retardates; and (d) business executives. Each respondent filled out a semantic differential.

The results show that the image of the mentally retarded is mainly a negative one. The mental retardate is seen as low on intelligence and social independence. The para-professionals had the most positive view, followed by the parent group, and then by the professionals and the employers.

Greenbaum and Wang note that even the parents, who had an average factor score of 4.37, apparently have an ambivalent attitude toward the mental retardate. Generally, all the groups viewed mental retardation more negatively than they did mental illness. Lower class respondents had a more positive conception of the mentally retarded than did either the middle class or upper class respondents ($p < .01$). Respondents with less than a high school education had a more positive conception than the other educational groups.

Meyers, Sitkei, and Watts (1966) studied the attitudes of a random sample of households in relation to those of a household group selected because a child at the address had been in a class for the retarded in the local public school. Special class families are more willing to keep retarded children at home rather than to send them away. Also, the special class families tend to be more supportive of public school provision for the retardates.

Jones, Gottfried, and Owens (1966) used an orthodox social distance questionnaire to explore attitudes toward 12 categories of exceptionality. On the item, "I would accept as close kin by marriage," the groups ranked as follows: average, gifted, speech-handicapped, partially seeing, chronically ill, deaf, blind, delinquent, emotionally disturbed, hard of hearing, crippled, mildly retarded, and severely retarded. The rankings were not exactly the same on all of the social distance items, but the rankings on this item are by no means atypical. Needless to say, this study shows all too well that attitudes toward the retarded are not outstandingly good.

2. ATTITUDE CHANGE

General experience in social psychology suggests that it is easy to obtain favorable changes in attitudes on paper and pencil tests as a function of brief exposure to the object in question or almost any other manipulation. This general expectation, apparently, is not supported by studies of attitudes toward mental retardates.

Cleland and Chambers (1959) and Cleland and Cochran (1961) investigated the effects of institutional tours upon attitudes. Cleland and Chambers summarized their results by saying that significant shifts in attitudes were induced by a guided tour, but that these shifts were not necessarily positive. The authors say that from a standpoint of institutional policy, it seems that the absence of a tour program would be inadvisable. On the other hand, as far as this writer can ascertain from the work of Cleland and his associates, the attitudes toward the hospital and the retarded apparently would be just as good, if not better, if tours could be avoided.

While the Cleland and Chambers and Cleland and Cochran studies showed a predominance of undesirable changes, the study by Quay, Bartlett, Wrightsman, and Catron (1961) apparently had little success changing attendants' attitudes one way or the other, even though they used three different persuasive techniques. Barnett (1964) was somewhat more successful in getting attendants to show favorable changes on information and attitudinal items. Butterfield (1967), in reviewing attempts to change attendants' attitudes, was not very optimistic about the effectiveness of such efforts, especially since no one had apparently even tried to determine whether or not attempts at changing attitudes influence subsequent behavior. On the other hand, one study showed positive attitude changes on the part of parents of educable retardates as a function of group discussions with their childrens' teacher (Bitter, 1963).

Kimbrell and Luckey (1964) found that following a tour, visitors were less likely to believe that a number of patients had normal intelligence or that mentally retarded individuals can be trained to make their own way in society. The visitors become more favorable toward the institution itself, however, being more inclined to believe that sanitary conditions were maintained and that patients were admitted only if they were retarded. Again, there is certainly no evidence here that institutional tours will generally produce favorable attitudes.

The somewhat pessimistic tone of the last few paragraphs can be climaxed by reference to a study by Warren, Turner, and Brody (1964). Their subjects were 80 sophomore students, enrolled at a college of education and registered for an integrated developmental psychology-education-sociology program oriented around the concept of the child in American culture. These subjects had opportunities to visit comparable institutions for the sight-handicapped, hearing-handicapped, and the mentally retarded. Their response measure was a pre-test versus post-test ranking of preference for working with seven areas of exceptionality. The various visits did not increase reported preferences for working with the retarded. The final rank order of preference was sight-handicapped, academically handicapped, mildly retarded, brain-injured, and severely retarded.

E. The Retarded Child and His Family

1. THE IMPACT OF THE RETARDED CHILD ON HIS FAMILY

Parental reactions to the retarded child range from viewing him as a pet, an inhuman monster, or a cross to bear (Eliot, 1932). Kramm (1963) has provided a very readable and informative report on the reactions of families. Some studies suggest that the parents of retardates overestimate their children, while other studies suggest a fairly realistic appraisal (Farber, 1968a, p. 153; Gorelick & Malathi, 1967; Wolfensberger, 1967a, pp. 343-344; Zuk, 1959).

Meyerowitz (1967a) found parents with children in special classes versus regular classes to have higher awareness of retardation in the first year. This greater awareness disappeared, however, by the end of the second year. Apparently, at the same time, Meyerowitz concluded that the mothers of retardates in regular classes were most inclined to see their children as deficient; next came the parents with children in special classes, while parents with normal children had the most favorable view of their offspring. The parents of the retarded had low expectations in regard to academic achievement but high expectations in regard to occupational achievement. The author stressed the sharp dichotomy drawn by these parents between scholastic achievement and occupational potential.

The detrimental effect of a retarded child on the family has recently been expressed with special poignance by Olshansky (1962, 1966) who indicates that mental deficiency is a family tragedy, and that most parents respond to the incident with "chronic sorrow." Families who wished to place their mongoloid child were apt to report that they were not able to give enough attention to their other children (12 out of 17), that the emotional bond between the parents was strained (7 out of 10), that their normal social activities were disrupted (15 out of 28), and that their other children were socially embarrassed (8 out of 13) (Kramm, 1963, p. 35). Wolfensberger (1967a, esp. pp. 340-341) cited a number of articles and studies most of which seemed to suggest that having a retarded child had a bad effect on the family. Other studies, however, showed no such effect. Wolfensberger concluded that the evidence was equivocal due to the lack of control over selection biases. Wolfensberger's conclusion was much the same in regard to the effect on siblings, except that in this case there seemed to be even less evidence and opinion.

Cummings, Bayley, and Rie (1966) compared mothers with retarded, chronically ill, neurotic, and healthy children. Mothers of retardates and neurotics showed higher levels of depression and difficulty in coping with anger directed toward the child and a lower sense of maternal competence. Mothers with retardates scored higher in preoccupation with the child. All of the deficiency groups ranked lower in enjoyment of the child, but only the neurotic group was significantly lower in deriving satisfaction from relationships with others. An article by Culver (1967), cited by Farber (1968b, p. 99), indicated that having a retarded child early in a marriage retarded the father's chances of upward mobility more than having a retarded child later in marriage.

Farber has been very active in the investigation of the effects of retardates on their parents and siblings, and has recently summarized relevant work by himself and others (Farber, 1968b; Farber & Ryckman, 1965). Farber and Ryckman concluded that the retarded child's siblings were affected adversely by the high degree of dependency of the retarded child. This dependency adversely affected the siblings' relationships with their mothers in that increased responsibility was given to the siblings for the care of the retarded child. He also concluded that a normal girl who interacts frequently with the retarded child generally has more tense family role relationships than a normal girl who interacts less frequently or not at all with her retarded sibling.

The possible pervasiveness of the influence of a retarded sibling is indicated by Farber and Jenne (1963) who related life goals to degree of interaction with the retarded sibling. The authors suggested that the sustained interaction with the retarded sibling comes to be regarded as a duty, and that the normal sibling internalizes welfare norms and turns his life career toward goals which require dedication and sacrifice. These frequent interactors were less concerned with life goals involving interpersonal relations. Parents rated the high interactors high in such traits as nervous, moody, stubborn, and angers easily. It might, of course, be that the higher interaction rate is caused by certain personality traits and value orientations rather than vice versa. The Farber and Jenne study is reminiscent of the position taken by Holt (1958) who said that families with retarded members gain in a spiritual and philosophical way, and of Tudor (1959) who said that caring for the retarded child provides excellent character training for the siblings. Also, Mahoney (1958) suggests that the retarded child can make a positive contribution to family cohesiveness if only by providing a scapegoat for other family members. In a study by Kramm (1963), 76% actually said that having a retarded child had been good for them.

2. The Question of Institutionalization

One way to deal with the effect of the retardate on his family is, of course, to place him in an institution. A physician or other person in a position to counsel a parent about what to do would, however, fail to find any helpful concensus among the experts. Stone (1967), for example, said that the literature did not yet provide consistent and reliable guides for a person who wished to counsel parents about whether to place their mongoloid child. It is, however, clear that in recent years the pendulum of opinion among experts has been swinging away from institutionalization. Some writers, in fact, are very critical of medical personnel (Wolfensberger, 1967a, pp. 369–375) who are apparently more inclined to encourage placement (Olshansky, Johnson, & Sternfeld, 1963). Milligan, while supporting home care and complaining about medical advice favoring placement, commented: "Many parents, of course, have resisted this advice and have had some very rewarding experiences [1965, p. 260]."

The ubiquitous bugaboo of selection artifacts, however, makes it difficult to decide whether or not institutionalizing the child is of any benefit to the rest of the family. The burdens—economic, emotional, and physical—of caring for a dependent retarded person at home would seem considerable; and although home care may save the taxpayers' dollars, it seems doubtful that home care is economical in a broader sense—considering that parents may be able to earn less money, pay less taxes, and render fewer community services, while requiring more social services as a consequence of the burden of care. One can make a case for institutionalization on such grounds as these, but several writers are counseling against placement apparently without any strong empirical rationale to counter this commonsense point of view.

Many writers of course are concerned that institutionalization may be bad for the child, but again satisfactory information (about the actual effects of institutional versus home living on the child) cannot be found. On a discursive basis it is quite possible to make a strong case either way. A case against placement was made by Tarjan (1966) who mentioned a shift from residential to community care, asserting that the need for institutions is being questioned by many who argue that the retarded could, and should, be cared for in the community. The preference for community care is also reflected in an article by Kirkland (1967).

The other point of view was developed by Edgerton and Sabagh (1962). While Edgerton and Sabagh conceded the possibility that institutional placement has its implications of rejection and humiliation in the so-called "stripping of the self," they pointed out that for the mental retardate life outside the institution may also be replete with instances of mortification, degradation, rejection, and humiliation. They argue further that for the mental retardate, life in the hospital may allow for some self-aggrandizement, which the outside world does not offer: (a) the presence of manifestly severely retarded patients may offer an opportunity for the higher grade retardate to make profitable comparisons of intellectual ability; (b) peer group relationships in the hospital in contrast to those outside the hospital may support an acceptable non-retarded conception of self; and (c) relationships with employees may encourage a more acceptable self-image. Farber (1968a, see especially pp. 208–216), in reviewing related literature, also leaves the impression that the institution offers the retardate not only an opportunity for social status but also an opportunity to avoid the employment he otherwise might have to undertake. Vogel, Kun, and Meshorer (1967) indicate that some studies suggest that institutionalization enhances cognitive development, while some suggest a debilitating effect and others show no effect.

Turning to the counseling of parents generally and in regard to institutionalization in particular, it is suggested that if experts convey the same attitudes to parents that they express in their articles, they may be contributing unnecessarily to the grief of these parents. Wolfensberger (1967a, pp. 350–353) says that the record of the handling of parents of the retarded by professionals is a sad one, and reviews a number of studies in support of this position. Many of the complaints are made by people in the field of retardation against medical practitioners, often in regard to the latter's tendency to encourage placement and in regard to a less than delicate communication of the diagnosis. Such concerns are not necessarily the same as those of the present writer, but these past criticisms indicate that the general issue of the behavior of professionals toward parents is a matter of long-standing and wide-spread concern.

The attitudes of some retardation experts, as expressed in their writings, may be summarized as follows: (a) a retarded child is a traumatic event (Abraham, 1958), which is almost certain to make for disappointment, grief, frustration, and anger (Wolfensberger, 1967a, p. 332), which precipitates a crisis (Farber & Ryckman, 1965; Mercer, 1966), which leads to needs for emotional support and life-long counseling (Appell, 1963; Begab, 1963), and which causes chronic sorrow (Olshansky, 1962). This chronic sorrow is not a neurotic manifestation—but a natural and understandable response (Olshansky, 1966), and failure to show grief may be a sign of pathology (Roos, 1963). (b) The parents must nonetheless accept, love, and cherish their child (Wolfensberger, 1967a, pp. 347–349) and in this process they can expect to have many rewarding experiences (Milligan, 1965, p. 260). (c) The parents should resist as unworthy any temptation to institutionalize the child because home care serves the welfare of the child, society, and perhaps even the family (Wolfensberger, 1967a, p. 331). Institutionalization may aggravate the parents' conflict as the decision to institutionalize is potentially emotionally self-destructive (Goodman, 1964) and a hazard to the mental health of the family unit (World Health Organization, 1954). Such a decision can have disastrous consequences for both child and family (Slobody & Scanlan, 1959), including feelings of guilt and self-recrimination (Giannini & Goodman, 1963). (d) Institutionalization is not a realistic way out in any case, since institutionalization can be a frightening experience (Milligan, 1965) which requires rather extensive preparation (Standifer, 1964), which is like a death without proper rites (Beddie & Osmond, 1955), and which apparently fails to dissipate the initial reactions of helplessness, grief, and guilt since follow ups done even after 15 years show emotional disturbance and unhappiness much in evidence (Thurstone, 1963).

Considering the infectiousness of attitudes and anxieties, it causes some concern to note that the comments of most of these several writers read like self-fulfilling prophecies of disaster. It is hoped that views such as the ones expressed above, whatever empirical veridicality they may have, will not be conveyed to parents.

It can be asserted with confidence that if institutionalization is a frightening experience for the parent, akin to a death without proper rites which is followed by years of emotional disturbance and unhappiness, it is only because the prevailing attitudes in the social milieu deem that it should be so. The experts who counsel the parents, of course, are going to be very influential members of this milieu.

IV. SUMMARY

I. Introduction

Social psychologists have paid very little attention to mental retardation and have produced no social psychology of mental retardation. Many articles by professionals concerned with retardation, however, are relevant from a social psychological point of view.

II. Retardation as a Social Problem

This paper offers an interpretation of retardation which stresses three variables: the genetic endowment of the population, the ability level of the population, and the demands of the society. Mental retardation is seen as a social problem which is destined to increase as the accelerating demands of society outdistance the ability of an ever-increasing percentage of the population. The recommended solution is the institution of one or more of several possible "eugenics" programs. In recommending such programs it is emphasized that retardation (and genius) does run in families, and that a phenotypically based program of birth control would, therefore, work—irrespective of whether the familial nature of the conditions is based on genetic or cultural factors or both.

III. The Mental Retardate in his Social Environment

A. *The Retardate's Social Success.* Mental ability is moderately related to popularity; this relationship is especially apparent when retarded children attend regular classes in which they must compete with average and superior children.

B. *The Retardate's Vocational Success.* Retardates who succeed vocationally are more intelligent than those who fail. Beyond this, little can be concluded. Employers have a moderate receptivity to retarded applicants.

C. *The Retardate's Self-concept.* Some evidence indicates that the retardate's self-concept is unfavorable and that his adjustment, generally, is poor, but there is no general agreement even on these points.

D. *The Public's View of the Mental Retardate.* Attitudes toward the retardate are at least moderately unfavorable. Those few attempts which have been made to change attitudes have generally been unsuccessful.

E. *The Retarded Child and His Family.* Experts present some evidence that a retarded child has some adverse impact on its family. They prefer home care over institutionalization. They manifest in their writings a constellation of attitudes that seem to concede having a retarded child to be a great tragedy while at the same time opposing any hope of adopting institutionalization as a solution. It is suggested that if such attitudes are expressed to the parents of retardates, the "chronic sorrow" expected by some experts will come about if only as a result of self-fulfilling prophecy.

REFERENCES

Abraham, W. *Barbara: A prologue.* New York: Rinehart, 1958.
Albizu-Miranda, C., & Matlin, N. Comments on professor Heber's paper. In H. A. Prehm, L. A. Hamerlynck, and J. E. Crosson (Eds.), *Behavioral research in mental retardation.* Eugene, Oregon: Rehabilitation Research and Training Center, University of Oregon, 1968. Pp. 23–30.
Albizu-Miranda, C., Matlin, N., & Stanton, H. R. The successful retardate. Unpublished manuscript, Hato Rey, Puerto Rico, 1966.
American Eugenics Society. Freedom of choice for parenthood. *Eugenical News*, 1953, 38, 25–31.
Appell, M. J. One community's approach: Planning for the mentally retarded. *Mental Retardation*, 1963, 1, 268–275.
Baldwin, W. K. The social position of the educable mentally retarded in the regular grades in the public schools. *Exceptional Children*, 1958, 25, 106–108.
Baller, W. R. A study of the present social status of a group of adults who, when they were in elementary schools, were classified as mentally deficient. *Genetic Psychology Monographs*, 1936, 18, 165–244.
Baller, W. R., Charles, D. C., & Miller, E. L. Mid-life attainment of the mentally retarded. *Genetic Psychology Monographs*, 1967, 75, 235–329.
Barnett, C. D. *Behavioral management of the institutionalized mentally retarded—a survey.* Atlanta: Southern Regional Education Board, 1964.
Beddie, A., & Osmond, H. Mothers, mongols, and mores. *Canadian Medical Association Journal*, 1955, 73, 167–170.
Begab, M. J. Some elements and principles in community planning. *Mental Retardation*, 1963, 1, 262–266, 304.
Beier, D. C. Behavioral disturbances in the mentally retarded. In H. A. Stevens & R. Heber (Eds.), *Mental retardation: A review of research.* Chicago: University of Chicago Press, 1964. Pp. 453–487.
Bialer, I. Relationship of mental retardation to emotional disturbance and physical disability. Paper presented at the International Conference on Social-Cultural Aspects of Mental Retardation, Nashville, June, 1968.
Bitter, J. A. Attitude change by parents of trainable mentally retarded children as a result of group discussion. *Exceptional Children*, 1963, 30, 173–177.
Bloom, W. Effectiveness of a cooperative special education vocational rehabilitation program. *American Journal of Mental Deficiency*, 1967, 72, 393–403.
Bobroff, A. A survey of social and civic participation of adults formerly in classes for the mentally retarded. *American Journal of Mental Deficiency*, 1957, 61, 127–133.
Brainerd, B. Increasing job potentials for the mentally retarded. *Journal of Rehabilitation*, 1954, 23, 4–6.
Butterfield, E. C. The role of environmental factors in the treatment of institutionalized mental retardates. In A. A. Baumeister (Ed.), *Mental retardation: Appraisal, education, and rehabilitation.* Chicago: Aldine, 1967. Pp. 120–137.

Charles, D. C. Ability and accomplishment of persons earlier judged mentally deficient, *Genetic Psychology Monographs*, 1953, **47**, 3-71.

Charles, D. C. Adult adjustment of some deficient American children. II. *American Journal of Mental Deficiency*, 1957, **62**, 300-304.

Charles, D. C. Longitudinal follow-up studies of community adjustment. In S. G. DiMichael (Ed.), *New vocational pathways for the mentally retarded*. American Rehabilitation Counseling Association symposium. Washington, D. C.: American Personnel and Guidance Association, 1966. Pp. 37-45.

Chennault, M. Improving the social acceptance of unpopular educable mentally retarded pupils in special classes. *American Journal of Mental Deficiency*, 1967, **72**, 455-458.

Clarke, A. D. B., Clarke, A. M., & Reiman, S. Cognitive and social changes in the feebleminded — three further studies. *British Journal of Psychology*, 1958, **49**, 144-157.

Clausen, J. Mental deficiency: Development of a concept. *American Journal of Mental Deficiency*, 1967, **71**, 727-745.

Cleland, C. C., & Chambers, W. R. Experimental modification of attitudes as a function of an institutional tour. *American Journal of Mental Deficiency*, 1959, **64**, 124-130.

Cleland, C. C., & Cochran, I. L. The effect of institutional tours on attitudes of high school seniors. *American Journal of Mental Deficiency*, 1961, **65**, 473-481.

Cleland, C. C., & Dingman, H. F. Dimensions of institutional life: Social organization, possessions, time and space. In A. A. Baumeister & E. Butterfield (Eds.), *Residential facilities for the mentally retarded*. Chicago: Aldine, 1970, in press.

Cohen, J. S. Employer attitudes toward hiring mentally retarded individuals. *American Journal of Mental Deficiency*, 1963, **67**, 705-713.

Collman, R. D., & Newlyn, D. Employment success of educationally subnormal ex-pupils in England. *American Journal of Mental Deficiency*, 1956, **60**, 733-743.

Collman, R. D., & Newlyn, D. Employment success of mentally dull and intellectual normal ex-pupils in England. *American Journal of Mental Deficiency*, 1957, **61**, 484-490.

Culver, M. Intergenerational social mobility among families with a severely mentally retarded child. Unpublished doctoral dissertation, University of Illinois, 1967.

Cummings, S. T., Bayley, H. C., & Rie, H. E. Effects of the child's deficiency on the mother: A study of mothers of mentally retarded, chronically ill and neurotic children. *American Journal of Orthopsychiatry*, 1966, **36**, 595-608.

Day, R. W. Genetic counseling and eugenics. In I. Phillips (Ed.), *Prevention and treatment of mental retardation*. New York: Basic Books, 1966. Pp. 177-198.

Dayan, M. Adaptive behavior and sociometric status among the mentally retarded. *American Journal of Mental Deficiency*, 1964, **68**, 599-601.

Delp, H. A., & Lorenz, M. Follow-up of 84 public schools special class pupils with IQ's below 50. *American Journal of Mental Deficiency*, 1953, **58**, 175-182.

Dentler, R. A., & Mackler, B. Mental ability and sociometric status among normal and retarded children: A review of the literature. *Psychological Bulletin*, 1962, **59**, 273-283.

Dentler, R. A., & Mackler, B. Effects on sociometric status of institutional pressure to adjust among retarded children. *British Journal of Social and Clinical Psychology*, 1964, **3**, 81-89.

Dexter, L. A. Towards a sociology of the mentally defective. *American Journal of Mental Deficiency*, 1956, **61**, 10-16.

Dexter, L. A. A social theory of mental deficiency. *American Journal of Mental Deficiency*, 1958, **62**, 920-928.

Dexter, L. A. A note on selective inattention in social science. *Social Problems*, 1959, **6**, 176-182.

Dexter, L. A. Research on problems of mental subnormality. *American Journal of Mental Deficiency*, 1960, **64**, 835-838.

Dexter, L. A. *The tyranny of schooling: An inquiry into the problem of "stupidity."* New York: Basic Books, 1964.

Diggs, E. A. A study of change in the social status of rejected mentally retarded children in regular classrooms. Unpublished doctoral dissertation, University of Colorado, 1964.

Dunn, L. C., & Dobzhansky, T. *Heredity, race, and society*. New York: New American Library, 1946.

Durling, D. The low intelligence quotient as economic index. *Journal of Juvenile Research*, 1931, **15**, 279-287.

Eagle, E. Prognosis and outcome of community placement of institutionalized retardates. *American Journal of Mental Deficiency*, 1967, **72**, 232-243.

Edgerton, R. B. A patient elite: Ethnography in a hospital for the mentally retarded. *American Journal of Mental Deficiency*, 1963, **68**, 372-385.

Edgerton, R. B. *The cloak of competence: Stigma in the lives of the mentally retarded*. Berkeley: University of California Press, 1967.

Edgerton, R. B. Anthropology and mental retardation: A plea for the comparative study of competence. In H. J. Prehm, L. A. Hamerlynck, & J. E. Crosson (Eds.), *A behavioral research in mental retardation*. Eugene, Oregon: Rehabilitation Research and Training Center in Mental Retardation, University of Oregon, 1968. Pp. 75-87.

Edgerton, R. B., & Sabagh, G. From mortification to aggrandizement: Changing self-conception in the careers of the mentally retarded. *Psychiatry*, 1962, **25**, 263-272.

Eliot, T. D. The bereaved family. *Annals of the American Academy of Political and Social Science*, 1932, **160**, 184-190.

Farber, B. *Mental retardation: Its social context and social consequences*. Boston: Houghton Mifflin, 1968. (a)

Farber, B. Sociological research in mental retardation. In H. J. Prehm, L. A. Hamerlynck, & J. E. Crosson (Eds.), *Behavioral research in mental retardation*. Eugene, Oregon: Rehabilitation Research and Training Center in Mental Retardation, University of Oregon, 1968. Pp. 93-109. (b)

Farber, B., & Jenne, W. C. Interaction with retarded siblings and life goals of children. *Marriage and Family Living*, 1963, **25**, 96-98.

Farber, B., & Ryckman, D. B. Effects of severely mentally retarded children on family relationships. *Mental Retardation Abstracts*, 1965, **2**, 1-17.

Fine, M. J., & Caldwell, T. E. Self evaluation of school related behavior of educable mentally retarded children: A preliminary report. *Exceptional Children*, 1967, **33**, 324.

Gardner, W. I. Personality characteristics of the mentally retarded: Review and critique. In H. J. Prehm, L. A. Hamerlynck, & J. E. Crosson (Eds.), *Behavioral research in mental retardation*. Eugene, Oregon: Rehabilitation Research and Training Center in Mental Retardation, University of Oregon, 1968. Pp. 53-68.

Giannini, M. J., & Goodman, L. Counseling families during the crisis reaction to mongolism. *American Journal of Mental Deficiency*, 1963, **67**, 740-747.

Ginzberg, E. The mentally handicapped in a technological society. In S. F. Osler & R. E. Cooke (Eds.), *The biosocial basis of mental retardation*. Baltimore: Johns Hopkins Press, 1965. Pp. 1-15.

Goldstein, H. Social and occupational adjustment. In H. A. Stevens & R. Heber (Eds.), *Mental retardation: A review of research*. Chicago: University of Chicago Press, 1964. Pp. 214-258.

Goodman, L. Continuing treatment of parents with congenitally defective infants. *Social Work*, 1964, **9**, 92-97.

Gorelick, M. C., & Malathi, S. Parent perception of retarded child's intelligence. *Personnel Guidance Journal*, 1967, **46**, 382-384.

Gorlow, L., Butler, A., & Guthrie, G. M. Correlates of self-attitudes of retardates. *American Journal of Mental Deficiency*, 1963, **67**, 549-555.

Greenbaum, J. J., & Wang, D. D. A semantic-differential study of the concepts of mental retardation. *Journal of General Psychology*, 1965, **73**, 257-272.

Guskin, S. L. Measuring the strength of the stereotypes of the mental defective. *American Journal of Mental Deficiency*, 1963, **67**, 569-575. (a)

Guskin, S. Social psychologies of mental deficiency. In N. R. Ellis (Ed.), *Handbook of mental deficiency*. New York: McGraw-Hill, 1963. Pp. 325-352. (b)

Guskin, S. L., & Spicker, H. H. Educational research in mental retardation. In N. Ellis (Ed.), *International review of research in mental retardation*. Vol. 3. New York: Academic Press, 1968. Pp. 217-218.

Guthrie, G. M., Butler, A., & Gorlow, L. Personality differences between institutionalized and non-institutionalized retardates. *American Journal of Mental Deficiency*, 1963, **67**, 543-548.

Guthrie, G. M., Butler, A., Gorlow, L., & White, G. N. Non-verbal expression of self-attitudes of retardates. *American Journal of Mental Deficiency*, 1964, **69**, 42-49.

Guthrie, G. M., Gorlow, L., & Butler, A. J. The attitude of the retardate toward herself: A summary of research at Laurelton State School and Hospital. *Pennsylvania Psychiatric Quarterly*, 1967, **7**, 24-34.

Haller, M. H. *Eugenics*. New Brunswick, N. J.: Rutgers University Press, 1963.

Harding, F. A., Singer, D. M., & O'Hara, J. Retarded in plastics industry. *Rehabilitation Record*, 1964, **5**, 16-17.

Hartley, E. L., & Hartley, R. *Fundamentals of social psychology*. New York: Knopf, 1952.

Heber, R. Personality. In H. A. Stevens & R. Heber (Eds.), *Mental retardation: A review of research*. Chicago: University of Chicago Press, 1964. Pp. 143-174.

Hegge, T. G. The occupational status of higher-grade mental defectives in the present emergency. *American Journal of Mental Deficiency*, 1944, **49**, 86-98.

Holt, K. S. The home care of severely retarded children. *Pediatrics*, 1958, **22**, 744-755.

Johnson, G. O. A study of the social position of mentally handicapped children in the regular grades. *American Journal of Mental Deficiency*, 1950, **55**, 60-89.

Johnson, G. O., & Kirk, S. A. Are mentally handicapped children segregated in the regular grades? *Exceptional Children*, 1950, **17**, 65-68.

Jones, R. L., Gottfried, N. W., & Owens, A. The social distance of the exceptional: A study at the high school level. *Exceptional Children*, 1966, **32**, 551-556.

Kahn, S. Retardates try social living. *Rehabilitation Record*, 1965, **6**, 20-22.

Katz, A. H. Some aspects of social research in mental retardation. *Slow Learning Child*, 1964, **11**, 3-11.

Kemp, T. Genetic-hygienic experiences in Denmark in recent years. *Eugenics Review*, 1957, **49**, 11-18.

Kennedy, R. J. R. The social adjustment of morons in a Connecticut city: Summary and conclusions, and Abstract of a Connecticut community revisited: A study of social adjustment of a group of mentally deficient adults in 1948 and 1960. In T. E. Jordan (Ed.), *Perspectives in mental retardation*. Carbondale, Ill.: Southern Illinois University Press, 1966. Pp. 339-358.

Kimbrell, D. L., & Luckey, R. E. Attitude change resulting from open-house guided tours in a state school for mental retardates. *American Journal of Mental Deficiency*, 1964, **69**, 21-22.

Kirkland, M. H. Institutions for the retarded: Their place in the continuum of services. *Mental Retardation*, 1967, **5**, 5-8.

Kleegman, S. J. Practical and ethical aspects of artificial insemination. In H. G. Beigel (Ed.), *Advances in sex research.* New York: Harper & Row, 1963. Pp. 112-118.
Kleegman, S. J. Practical and ethical aspects of artificial insemination. *Sociological Abstracts,* 1964, 12, 1047-1048.
Kniss, J. T., Butler, A., Gorlow, L., & Guthrie, G. M. Ideal self patterns of female retardates. *American Journal of Mental Deficiency,* 1962, 67, 245-249.
Kolstoe, O. P. An examination of some characteristics which discriminate between employed and not employed mentally retarded males. *American Journal of Mental Deficiency,* 1961, 66, 472-482.
Kramm, E. R. *Families of mongoloid children.* Washington, D. C.: U. S. Government Printing Office, 1963.
Kurtz, R. A. Implications of recent sociological research in mental retardation. *American Journal of Mental Deficiency,* 1964, 69, 16-20.
Laing, A. F., & Chazan, M. Sociometric groupings among educationally subnormal children. *American Journal of Mental Deficiency,* 1966, 71, 73-77.
Lapp, E. R. A study of the social adjustment of slow-learning children who were assigned part-time to regular classes. *American Journal of Mental Deficiency,* 1957, 62, 254-262.
Lerner, I. M. *Heredity, evolution, and society.* San Francisco: Freeman, 1968.
Lindesmith, A. R., & Strauss, A. L. *Social psychology.* New York: Holt, Rinehart & Winston, 1968.
Madison, H. L. Work placement success for the mentally retarded. *American Journal of Mental Deficiency,* 1964, 69, 50-53.
Mahoney, S. C. Observations concerning counseling with parents of mentally retarded children. *American Journal of Mental Deficiency,* 1958, 63, 81-86.
McAfee, R. O., & Cleland, C. C. The discrepancy between self-concept and ideal-self as a measure of psychological adjustment in educable mentally retarded males. *American Journal of Mental Deficiency,* 1965, 70, 63-68.
Mercer, J. R. Patterns of family crisis related to reacceptance of the retardate. *American Journal of Mental Deficiency,* 1966, 71, 19-32.
Meyerowitz, J. H. Parental awareness of retardation. *American Journal of Mental Deficiency,* 1967, 71, 637-643. (a)
Meyerowitz, J. H. Peer groups and special classes. *Mental Retardation,* 1967, 5, 23-26. (b)
Meyers, C. E., Sitkei, E. G., & Watts, C. A. Attitudes toward special education and the handicapped in two community groups. *American Journal of Mental Deficiency,* 1966, 71, 78-84.
Michal-Smith, H. Personality training in vocational education for the retarded child. *Journal of Exceptional Children,* 1951, 17, 108-110.
Miller, J. Postschool adjustment: A survey of fifty former students of classes for the educable mentally retarded. *Exceptional Children,* 1966, 32, 633-634.
Miller, R. V. Social status and socioempathic differences among mentally superior, mentally typical, and mentally retarded children. *Exceptional Children,* 1956, 23, 114-119.
Milligan, G. E. Counseling parents of the mentally retarded. *Mental Retardation Abstracts,* 1965, 2, 259-264.
Olshansky, S. Chronic sorrow: A response to having a mentally defective child. *Social Casework,* 1962, 43, 190-193.
Olshansky, S. Parent responses to a mentally defective child. *Mental Retardation,* 1966, 4, 21-23.
Olshansky, S. J., Johnson, G. C., & Sternfeld, L. Attitudes of some G P's toward institutionalizing mentally retarded children. *Mental Retardation,* 1963, 1, 18-20, 57-59.

Olshansky, S., & Schonfield, J. Parental perceptions of the mental status of graduates of special classes. *Mental Retardation*, 1965, 3, 16-20.
Peckham, R. Problems in job adjustment of the mentally retarded. *American Journal of Mental Deficiency*, 1951, 56, 448-453.
Perry, S. E. Notes for a sociology of prevention in mental retardation. In I. Phillips (Ed.), *Prevention and treatment of mental retardation*. New York: Basic Books, 1966. Pp. 145-176.
Phelps, W. R. Attitudes related to the employment of the mentally retarded. *American Journal of Mental Deficiency*, 1965, 69, 575-585.
Phillips, I. Children, mental retardation, and emotional disorders. In I. Phillips (Ed.), *Prevention and treatment of mental retardation*. New York: Basic Books, 1966. Pp. 111-122.
Piers, E. V., & Harris, D. B. Age and other correlates of self-concept in children. *Journal of Education Psychology*, 1964, 55, 91-95.
Quay, L. C. Academic skills. In N. R. Ellis (Ed.), *Handbook of mental deficiency*. New York: McGraw-Hill, 1963. Pp. 664-690.
Quay, L. C., Bartlett, C. J., Wrightsman, L. S., Jr., & Catron, D. Attitude change in attendant employees. *Journal of Social Psychology*, 1961, 55, 27-31.
Reed, E. W., & Reed, S. C. *Mental retardation: A family study*. Philadelphia: Saunders, 1965.
Report of the National Advisory Commission on civil disorders. New York: Bantam Books, 1968.
Ringness, T. A. Self concept of children of low, average, and high intelligence. *American Journal of Mental Deficiency*, 1961, 65, 453-461.
Robinson, H. B., & Robinson, N. M. *The mentally retarded child: A psychological approach*. New York: McGraw-Hill, 1965.
Roos, P. Psychological counseling with parents of retarded children. *Mental Retardation*, 1963, 1, 345-350.
Slobody, L., & Scanlan, J. Consequences of early institutionalization. *American Journal of Mental Deficiency*, 1959, 63, 971-974.
Smith, G. M. A study of a state employment counselors' attitudes toward and knowledge of the mentally retarded. *Dissertation Abstracts*, 1964, 25, 1014-1015.
Snyder, R. T. Personality adjustment, self-attitudes, and anxiety differences in retarded adolescents. *American Journal of Mental Deficiency*, 1966, 71, 33-41.
Snyder, R., Jefferson, W., & Strauss, R. Personality variables as determiners of academic achievement of the mildly retarded. *Mental Retardation*, 1965, 3, 15-18.
Southern Regional Council. *Hungry children*. 5 Forsyth St., N. W., Atlanta: Southern Regional Council, 1967.
Standifer, F. R. Pilot parent program: Parents helping parents. *Mental Retardation*, 1964, 2, 304-307.
Stevens, H. A. Overview. In H. A. Stevens & R. Heber (Eds.), *Mental retardation: A review of research*. Chicago: University of Chicago Press, 1964. Pp. 1-15.
Stone, N. D. Family factors in willingness to place the mongoloid child. *American Journal of Mental Deficiency*, 1967, 72, 16-20.
Strickland, C. G., & Arrell, V. M. Employment of the mentally retarded. *Exceptional Children*, 1967, 34, 21-24.
Tarjan, G. The role of residential care—past, present, and future. *Mental Retardation*, 1966, 4, 4-8.
Thurstone, J. R. Counseling the parents of mentally retarded children. *Training School Bulletin*, 1963, 60, 113-117.
Tudor, K. B. What to tell parents of a retarded child. *Lancet*, 1959, 79, 196-198.
United States Department of Health, Education, and Welfare. *The problem of mental retardation*. Washington, D. C.: U. S. Government Printing Office, 1966.

Vogel, W., Kun, K. J., & Meshorer, E. Effects of environmental enrichment and environmental deprivation on cognitive functioning in institutionalized retardates. *Journal of Consulting Psychology*, 1967, **31**, 570-576.

Wallin, J. E. W. New frontiers in the social perspective of the mentally retarded. *Training School Bulletin*, 1962, **59**, 89-104.

Warren, S. A., Turner, D. R., & Brody, D. S. Can education students' attitudes toward the retarded be changed? *Mental Retardation*, 1964, **2**, 235-242.

Windle, C. Prognosis of mental subnormals. *American Journal of Mental Deficiency*, 1962, **66**(Monogr. Suppl. 5).

Wolfensberger, W. Counseling the parents of the retarded. In A. A. Baumeister (Ed.), *Mental retardation: Appraisal, education, and rehabilitation.* Chicago: Aldine, 1967a. Pp. 329-400.

Wolfensberger, W. Vocational preparation and occupation. In A. A. Baumeister (Ed.), *Mental Retardation: Appraisal, education, and rehabilitation.* Chicago: Aldine, 1967b. Pp. 234-235.

World Health Organization. *The mentally subnormal child.* Geneva: WHO, 1954.

Zuk, G. H. Autistic distortions in parents of retarded children. *Journal of Consulting Psychology*, 1959, **23**, 171-176.

Mental Retardation in Animals

GILBERT W. MEIER

GEORGE PEABODY COLLEGE, NASHVILLE, TENNESSEE

I. Introduction 263
II. Genetic Factors 265
III. Prenatal Factors 267
    A. Hypoxia 270
    B. Ionizing Radiation 271
    C. Drugs 273
    D. Nutrition 276
    E. Maternal Emotion 278
    F. Prenatal Factors: Comment 280
IV. Perinatal Factors 281
    A. Hypoxia 281
    B. Other Birth Complications: Mode of Delivery 283
V. Postnatal Factors 284
    A. Hyperoxia 284
    B. Infantile Brain Damage 285
    C. Early Experience 290
    D. Drugs 292
    E. Nutrition 294
    F. Postnatal Factors: Comment 295
VI. Multivariate Analysis 296
VII. Conclusion 299
    References 300

I. INTRODUCTION

Research on behavioral defects—mental deficiency—in non-human subjects has moved by fits and starts, spurred by fads of causality, but halted by a persisting dilemma of conceptualization. The comparative investigator has not yet enjoyed the luxury of starting his explorations with a population of non-human mental defectives conveniently defined—or confined—by medical, social, or, even, legal criteria. Consequently, the dilemma of any comparative-behavioral study of mental deficiency is the prior establishment of a reasonable and adequate description of the phenomenon under investigation. More specifically, it is the finding of an acceptable operational definition, derived from human development and behavior, and capable of reformulation in analogous terms for a representative non-human species tolerant of laboratory existence and manipulation (see, also, Berkson, 1967a). Few, if any, research reports in this domain, however, offer a resolution of this dilemma, since rarely does the author of such a report reveal to the reader in explicit terms the definition used or the adequacy of the model chosen. Possibly, neither the clarity of thought nor the rigorous operational analysis existed prior to the initiation of the research. For that matter, the probability is small indeed that either the definition or the model exists now, or that either can be erected from present data and current methodology. Nevertheless, it is in this regard that the studies already completed reveal their greatest contribution as well as their most nagging handicap. A review of this research literature consistent with one delimitation of the field—mine—and one implicit resolution of this dilemma— also mine—may lead ultimately to the definition needed and the model desired.

Typically, the individual studies have begun with a statement of the etiology of mental deficiency and have followed with an attempt to verify that causal relation under laboratory conditions. Laboratory conditions being what they are, this maneuver has meant an imposition of the supposed agent, in a presumably relevant fashion, on one of a limited choice of species: commonly, the laboratory rat (*Rattus norvegicus*); occasionally the chick (*Gallus domestica*), the mouse (*Mus musculus*), cat (*Felis catus*), dog (*Canis familiaris*), guinea pig (*Cavia porcellus*), or monkey (*Macaca mulatta*, usually). Subsequently, the animal is examined for differences in behavior, especially of learned behavior, whether newly acquired or simply demonstrated under the testing conditions. Variants on this plan have been reported; in some of these reports greater regard is given to the occurrence of behavioral defects under natural conditions, or to the frequency of occurrence of deviant performance, or to the variety of extreme behaviors deemed relevant under laboratory conditions. Some have searched for behavioral homologues for symptoms of the totality of behavior of the mentally retarded human (e.g., Berkson, 1967b, 1968a). These, although provocative in their own right, have been truly exceptional and, as yet, without any real impact on the field as a whole.

As indicated, the comparative research has followed closely the fads and changing emphases regarding proposed etiological factors in mental deficiency. These factors have either been intrinsic to the developing organism, i.e., genetic influences, or to the environment in which that development occurs. Researches on the latter influences have dwelled on designated developmental periods, e.g., prenatal or prehatching, perinatal, neonatal, or infancy, and have been of the delayed consequences of manipulation of that environment as it directly or indirectly affects the organism. Only recently have we seen the research possibilities of the interaction between genetic and environmental factors and of the interaction of two or more experimental manipulations.

II. GENETIC FACTORS

The now classic studies relating heredity to adaptive behavior were shaped, first, by the growing sophistication in psychometrics represented by the mental test movement and, second, by the prevailing methodologies in plant and animal husbandry. Although not the first (cf. Fuller & Thompson, 1960, pp. 207–214), Tryon's effort (cf. 1946) to breed selectively laboratory rats for high and low levels of maze performance succeeded where those of his predecessors had failed. The two groups of laboratory rats, the maze-bright and the maze-dull, became increasingly dissimilar with each generation until at the eighth generation virtually no overlap in maze performance existed between the two populations. With continuing selection, further separation was minimal. When the two disparate groups were hybridized, the maze learning of the progeny closely resembled that of the initial population from which the first selection had been made generations earlier.

The conclusion regarding the fundamental nature of genetics and behavior drawn from Tryon's studies has been confirmed in the more recent study reported by W. R. Thompson (1954). In this study, the investigator responded to some of the criticisms regarding the generality of the definition of intellective performance used by Tryon (e.g., Searle, 1949) and to the genetic-selection limitations of those earlier efforts. Thompson used a multiple-test procedure, i.e., the many problems on the Hebb-Williams maze, which fits more clearly the pattern of human intelligence testing, and studied the selection trends in rats which were successively brother-sister inbred rather than selectively mated on the basis of individual performance as Tryon had done. As would be expected, differences in the high and low performing populations became evident in the second generation, and significantly so in the third generation. Little overlap occurred in performance in the two sublines from the fourth generation. Thus, Thompson showed that the more rapid reduction in genetic heterogeneity brought about by his inbreeding procedure hastened the development of discrete subgroups over that reported by Tryon.

Bignami (1964) reported that selective breeding can be used for the establishment of genetically distinct subgroups when criteria other than maze learning are used. He found that separate populations could be formed on the basis of speed of acquisition of a conditioned avoidance response.

The more recent trend in genetics-intelligence research has been with recognized breeds or strains of mammals, notably mice, rats, and dogs (cf. Fuller & Thompson, 1960, pp. 215-219; McClearn & Meredith, 1966, pp. 529-537). In the mouse studies, clearly the most numerous, marked strain differences in learning performance have been reported on a variety of tasks (cf. Collins, 1964; Meier & Foshee, 1963; Royce & Covington, 1960; Winston, 1963) and learning conditions (Bovet, Bovet-Nitti, & Oliverio, 1968, 1969). Henderson (1968a), for example, in an elegant analysis of strain contribution to the acquisition and extinction of a conditioned emotional response, demonstrated the feasibility of making precise genetic estimates of the variance in measured behaviors and the combining of genetic effects in hybridization. Others have shown that the optimal stimulus conditions for one strain may be less than optimal for a second, and vice-versa (Foshee, 1962; Oliverio, 1967). Retention of certain learned behaviors may also show significant differences (Henderson, 1968a). Some of the behavioral differences are complexly related to heterosis (Collins, 1964; Winston, 1964) and to sex and age at testing (Meier, 1964). Further, some of the differences can be associated with single gene loci (von Abeelen & Kroes, 1967; Denenberg, Ross, & Blumenfield, 1963; Winston & Lindzey, 1964). In another species of mouse, *Peromyscus maniculatus* rather than *Mus musculus*, development, reaction to early manipulation, and learning differences can be reasonably associated with ecological differences of the two subspecies compared (King & Eleftheriou, 1959).

Research with the rat in this area has been restricted by the absence of adequate genetic description and nomenclature, as well as by the limited inbreeding required for a meaningful classification of genetic subgroups. Nevertheless, learning differences between populations have been reported for conditioned avoidance responding (e.g., Broadhurst & Levine, 1963; Foshee, 1960; Tapp, 1964) and conditioned emotional responding (Singh, 1959). (The results reported by Tapp are particularly encouraging when placed in the context of the Tryon and Bignami studies. Tapp used Tryon's maze-bright and maze-dull sublines and found the other learning differences, conditioned avoidance responding, alluded to. Significant inter-problem correlations foster the hope that a more general definition of animal intelligence can be formulated, at least one with wider scope than used heretofore.) Other features to be considered are the relative performances of the maze-bright and maze-dull sublines selected by Tryon, which are now shown to be dependent upon procedural conditions of the learning test (McGaugh, Jennings, & Thomson, 1962; Rowland & Woods, 1961).

Similarly, the breed comparisons made by Fuller and Scott (1954) indicate that populations of dogs established by other criteria may perform significantly differently on laboratory learning tasks. Marked differences in performance dependent upon stimulus and reinforcement conditions are hardly surprising when the bases of the initial selections are considered. Somewhat in contrast with the few rat data available, rapid or slow learning depends as much upon the specific learning task as upon the particular breed. Again, this problem-specific behavioral characteristic is consistent with the purposes for which the particular breeds were established generations earlier.

III. PRENATAL FACTORS

Several years ago, immediately following the publication of Ashley Montagu's book, *Prenatal Influences*, several colleagues and I sat down to consider the possibility of preparing a sequel to Montagu's effort. Our intent, as we articulated it then, was to cover the laboratory or experimental researches in this area and give appropriate emphasis to the carefully contrived and controlled laboratory investigations in order to balance Montagu's review of clinic-derived data and speculations. As the discussion evolved one conclusion became increasingly evident: the laboratory-derived data were neither so abundant nor so unique in their theoretical orientations as would be necessary for the balance we sought. Still, these studies have provided confirmation of certain clinical postdictions under superior conditions of manipulative control and predictive conceptualization. Nevertheless, they have been woefully incomplete at both ends of the developmental continuum: on the analysis of the individual at the time of the experimental manipulation and, later, at the time of postnatal assessment of experimentally-induced change. The first has been virtually non-existent; the second, by virtue of the traditional time-sample approach, has been inadequate for the understanding either of the behavior change itself, or of the probable interactive influence of maturation and experience.

In the typical experiment consistent with this design, a design in accord with established teratological methodology (Runner, 1967; Wilson & Warkany, 1965), the avian embryo or mammalian fetus is exposed to the presumed action of the experimental treatment at a selected prehatching or prenatal age. The experimental treatment is chosen on the basis of clinic-derived speculations regarding regular, but infrequently, occurring syndromes, or of supposed confounding by secondary effects of widely used prophylactic procedures. Moreover, the research strategy relating temporal parameters to the prenatal influence has been equally stereotyped. With environmental manipulation, such as ionizing irradiation, hypoxia, and maternal stress, the duration of the experimental states has been limited, usually to a few minutes on a given day or to a given segment of the prenatal period. On the other hand, with nutritional and other biochemical agents, the developing organism has been maintained under the experimental conditions for the entirety of this period. [Exceptions to this last design are becoming more commonplace, although even here the proportion of the developmental period manipulated in a single experimental condition is still considerable. This may be an inevitable state of affairs because of the chemical nature of the agents used and the maternal and fetal physiologies (see Werboff & Gottlieb, 1963).] If discrete developmental stages are part of the experimental design, the selection is made on the basis of restricted knowledge of the ontogeny of the organism involved—typically a combination of extensive neuroanatomical, limited neurophysiological, and very sparse behavioral data—and of presumed comparability to the human developmental state in the particular clinic problem which gave rise to the experimental research. After the administration of the experimental treatment—and temporal and/or intensity factors are reasonable speculations, at best—the incubation or pregnancy is permitted to proceed to term. In the avian studies, the criterional examination of the treated subject begins shortly after hatching and continues for a few days or weeks thereafter. In the mammalian studies, the examination begins first tentatively after weaning but in earnest at near-adult ages. In other words, we are here discussing experimental researches founded on a seemingly endless series of assumptions of reasonableness, each without ready evaluation or verification.

In one such study, one in which I was deeply involved (Meier, Bunch, Nolan, & Scheidler, 1960), two pregnant rats were exposed to a single bout of a severe oxygen deficiency (2.91% equivalent oxygen) for 30 minutes (plus time for change of conditions), on each day of the 21 days of normal pregnancy. The females were then returned to their home cages to deliver their pups some days later. These offspring were examined much later, at 60 days of age and onward, for their acquisition of an operant response and of a simple visual discrimination habit, for their speed of locomotion, and for their rapidity in the solution of a complicated, multiple-unit water maze. The performances of these animals revealed that the prenatal oxygen deficiency—if such did actually occur to the fetuses as it did assuredly occur to their mothers—effected changes in the subsequent behaviors evaluated during early adulthood in a manner which reflected varying susceptibilities as related to age at the time of deprivation and to the sex of the conceptus.

In companion studies (Meier, 1958), groups of fertile chicken eggs were immersed in water saturated with pure nitrogen and thereby exposed to a condition of oxygen deprivation. The duration of this exposure, a median lethal exposure, varied exponentially with incubation age: from 240 minutes after 1 day of incubation to 20 minutes after 19 days. After hatching, the chicks were periodically examined in the 3 weeks that followed for adequacy of certain reflexive responses, acquisition of simple learned habits, and for the mastery of a multiple-unit maze. As in the mammalian studies, the particular pattern of performances was predictably related to developmental age at deprivation, such that each age group presented a characteristic pattern of behavior changes, each distinct from the other and from the normally-incubated, undisturbed, control chicks.

As stated to the consumer of these reports, the studies have corroborated and have made more explicit the hypotheses drawn from the clinic regarding prenatal manipulations and behavioral development. Often the reader is tantalized by the announcement that behavioral differences were noted in the absence of concommitent anatomical or biochemical differences—even though the author avoided even speculating on this seeming discrepancy (cf. Meier, 1968a). To the researcher himself, however, a number of imponderables of research strategy and interpretation loom large and often fully eclipse the data so laboriously gotten. Why did the particular manipulation *not* have the predicted long-range effect (e.g., Severs, Meier, Windle, Schiff, Monif, & Fabiyi, 1965)? Why did the predicted changes *not* appear in both the avian and mammalian subjects (e.g., Meier, 1959), or in the several strains of the species used (e.g., Weir & DeFries, 1964)? What was the immediate effect of the treatment upon the organism and its current behavior, and what is the position of that change in the causal chain by which the measured behavioral changes are produced (cf., Meier, 1968a)?

The first of these questions, the one dealing with specification of the clinical syndrome and the relevance of the experimental model, demands much additional data and theoretical analysis for a proper reply at some later date. The second, the one dealing with the problem of environment-embryo or maternal-fetus interaction, has been considered elsewhere by this author (Meier, 1961, 1962) among others, and should be relegated to our heritage of attitudes and orientations which guide the planning and execution of developmental research. The last question, the one dealing with the activity and reactivity potentials of the embryo-fetus and their relevance to prenatal manipulations and behavior sequelae, is part of the investigative domain of basic behavioral development. That domain has shown considerable rejuvenation in the last decade but still requires much care and cultivation.

The research design outlined above has been applied to a number of proposed etiological factors of mental deficiency, some at notable frequency and depth. These will be considered below.

A. Hypoxia

Among the many possible experimental manipulations available for study of behavioral teratology (Werboff, 1963), prenatal oxygen deprivation is unique in being without a clearly defined clinical counterpart. Nevertheless, theoretical interest in the possibility of its role in the causality of mental deficiency remains keen. The justification for this seeming paradox is the large number of mechanisms by which the fetal oxidative metabolism can be altered in the face of the difficulty of demonstrating the operation of any one of them in the context of the behavioral-developmental problems as seen in the clinic. Possibly, similar reasons are the bases for the relative lack of experimental efforts to elucidate predicted and possible relations between prenatal oxygen deficiency and subsequent behavior (cf. Meier, 1969a). For example, oxygen deprivation (hypoxia) to the pregnant mammal elicits many physiologic reactions, only one of which is deprivation to the fetus. Direct manipulation of the fetus to reduce its metabolism is procedurally difficult and not without its own indirect complications. To date, the latter technique has not been applied in a behavioral study. Despite the interpretive problems the former technique, i.e., manipulation of the fetus by way of deprivation of the pregnant female, has been applied in several attempts and the behaviors of the progeny examined.

As an initial effort in the experimental analysis of the effect of prenatal hypoxia upon postnatal behavior, Scheidler (1953) exposed pregnant laboratory rats to a condition of oxygen deprivation (6.2% equivalent O_2 for 120 minutes) at designated points during the second half of pregnancy. Samples of the offspring of the surviving females (12 of the 40 pregnant animals died during or immediately following hypoxia) were examined for their learning and relearning performances in a complex water maze and for their mastery of a brightness discrimination task. The significant differences in the behaviors of the offspring of the experimental (hypoxic) and of the control females suggested a trend between fetal age at deprivation and severity of postnatal deficit. The most marked behavioral differences, especially clear in the learning and retention of the maze pattern and in the transfer between the two problems, were observed in those animals presumably made hypoxic on the thirteenth day of gestation.

In a follow-up study, Meier *et al.* (1960) sampled a greater range of gestational ages. Corroborative differences in the behaviors of the two groups of offspring were observed: overall, the young born to the hypoxic mothers required the greatest number of trials and at longer swimming latencies for the mastery of the maze pattern. Moreover, the poorest performances were shown by those young exposed to the hypoxic conditions at about the fifteenth day of gestation. By contrast, however, those exposed at about the seventh day of gestation required the fewest number of trials and demonstrated the shortest latencies. Seemingly, two sensitive periods exist which are the resultants of the interaction of the deprivation conditions and the behavioral testing procedures.

Differences in activity and emotional behavior have also been described in both rats (Vierck, King, & Ferm, 1966) and mice (Vierck & Meier, 1963), but their pattern and significance for learning performance are far from clear.

A direct evaluation of the effect of oxygen deficiency on prenatal development is possible through the environmental manipulation of the fertile avian egg (cf. Grabowski & Paar, 1958). The passage of gases, specifically oxygen and carbon dioxide, can be curtailed by placing the egg in an oxygen-free aqueous medium at incubation temperature. Meier and Menzel (1955) followed such a procedure in exposing chick embryos to an LD_{50} condition at 4, 8, 12, 16, or 19 days of incubation. Behavioral tests applied in the first few days after hatching revealed deficiencies in the visually oriented behaviors of the experimental birds. Similar groups showed significant difficulties in the mastery of a version of the Hebb-Williams maze (Sundby, 1959). A more elaborate behavioral analysis of still other groups revealed profiles of test performances unique to each experimental group, each significantly different from the other. The most deviant profile was that of the group exposed to the deprivation conditions on the eighth day of incubation (Meier, 1958).

B. Ionizing Radiation

In the research on the behavioral sequelae of exposure to ionizing radiation, as elsewhere in the comparative research on mental retardation, the investigators have endeavored to estimate the possibility and, later, the probability of altered behavioral development subsequent to a medical accident or international holocaust. Fortunately, the likelihood of either occurring—either the unknowing or unwise exposure of the pregnant woman to a radiation source or nuclear explosion—has decreased greatly since the first behavioral reports appeared (Levinson, 1952; Tait, Wall, Balmuth, & Kaplan, 1952). Even though the pressures to understand a clinic problem have diminished, the usefulness of radiation as a tool in the analysis of structural-behavioral relations during fetal development must be recognized (Hicks, 1958). For a thorough coverage of the implications of prenatal exposure to ionizing radiation, as from a deep-therapy unit, the reader should consult Russell (1954), the reviews of behavioral research by Furchtgott (1956, 1963), and the research appraisal by Werboff (1964).

The initial research reports established the experimental procedure for the many which followed. In one (Levinson, 1952), pregnant rats were exposed to 300, 375, 450, or 600 r of X-radiation on Day 11, 13, 15, 17, or 19 of gestation. When tested on the Lashley III maze at 50 days of age (postnatal), the progeny of the females exposed to the highest radiation doses made the poorest performances, i.e., most errors, most trials to criterion, and longest running times. Further, those exposed to the radiation on Day 13 were the most severely affected. In the other report (Tait *et al.*, 1952) pregnant rats were exposed to 90 to 180 r of X-radiation at some point during the third and final week of pregnancy. The offspring of the irradiated females, tested during the second postnatal month, were significantly less efficient in the learning of a Lashley III maze than were the offspring of the non-irradiated controls. Those which were exposed to the radiation made significantly more errors than did the controls; fewer reached the pre-established criterion of mastery of the maze problem.

Subsequent investigations have tended to confirm these first efforts (e.g., Furchtgott, Echols, & Openshaw, 1958; Kaplan, 1962; Werboff, Goodman, Havlena, & Sikov, 1961a; Werboff, Havlena, & Sikov, 1962). These more recent reports have presented accounts of behavioral change following prenatal exposure to lesser amounts of radiation and with other behavioral measures and conditions, the general pattern of which is that the poorer performance is shown in those animals exposed prenatally on Day 15. Other age-response relations are not so clear, however. Werboff *et al.* (1962) noted superior maze performance in those animals exposed on Day 5 and Day 10, in addition to the inferior performance in those exposed later (Day 15). In that study behavioral differences were observed only in the female subjects; males showed no age-response relationship whatsoever. Persistent in these reports is the allusion to the altered emotionality, usually heightened, in those subjects born to irradiated females, the most lucid descriptions of which appear in the papers by Levinson and by Tait *et al.* This facet of the behavior of the experimental animals has been pursued in its own right (cf. Furchtgott, 1963) and now appears to be of such significance that some (most?) of the learning differences in mazes and conditioned avoidance devices can be explained on this intergroup difference alone (Deagle & Furchtgott, 1968).

The mechanism by which behavior changes are induced in the developing fetus by irradiation of the pregnant mammal is still moot (cf. Furchtgott, 1963, pp. 162-163; Meier, 1961, 1962). Chicks exposed to ionizing radiation (LD_{50}, 500-800 r) at 4, 8, 12, 16, or 19 days of incubation did not differ significantly from control birds when examined on a battery of behavioral tests during the first 3 weeks after hatching (Meier, 1959). These results are in sharp contrast with those reported for chicks exposed to an LD_{50} dose of hypoxia at comparable ages (Meier, 1958). Selective shielding of the pregnant rat during exposure may (Meier & Foshee, 1962) or may not (Sharp, 1961) support the conviction that the action of the irradiation is directly upon the adult female and that the subsequent radiation-induced biochemical and physiological changes then affect the fetus in the way revealed by the behavioral analyses. The issue is significant for its implications pertaining to prevention, prophylaxis, and predictions of long-range behavioral change and, therefore, requires empirical clarification.

C. Drugs

The Pharmacopeia is vast and the number of pharmacologic agents which could affect the course of pregnancy and fetal development is seemingly infinite. Nevertheless, spurred by the widespread use of drugs in modern society and the international tragedy following the use of one, thalidomide, a scrutiny of long-range effects has been urged. In this context the effects on fetal development, including behavioral development, of certain popularly used drugs have been assayed under laboratory conditions. Still, the number of studies published and the number of investigators committed to this endeavor are limited (cf. Werboff & Gottlieb, 1963; Young, 1967). (The distinction between biochemical-behavioral studies in which effects of drug manipulation are ascertained and those of the effects of nutritional manipulation is one of rationale and procedure. In the first, the level of a given biochemical within the living system is quantitatively increased or is introduced as a "foreign," i.e., not naturally occurring, substance. In the second, the level of a biochemical factor which does normally exist in that system is decreased either by limiting the normal process of ingestion or by making it selectively ineffectual through biochemical or metabolic antagonists.)

Dispensa and Hornbeck (1941) administered thyroid hormone to pregnant rats repeatedly throughout pregnancy. The investigators reported that the young born to these females learned the maze more rapidly than did the offspring of the control females or the offspring of another group of females which had been given an extract of the anterior pituitary gland.

More recently, Clendinnen and Eayrs (1961) found improved learning performance, in addition to striking cerebral cortical growth, in rats born to females given the purified anterior pituitary hormone, somatotrophin, during pregnancy. These enhanced learning performances, here and in the Dispensa and Hornbeck study, are unique to this literature on prenatal drug manipulation. Elsewhere, where behavioral differences are found, the nature of those differences suggests inferior performance by the treated animals.

Hamilton and associates (Hamilton, 1945; Hamilton & Harned, 1944; Harned, Hamilton, & Borrus, 1940; Harned, Hamilton, & Cole, 1944) reported depressed learning and problem-solving behaviors in rats born to females given sodium bromide, a widely used sedative at that time, during pregnancy. Similarly, Vincent (1958) reported deficient maze learning (more time, more errors, more trials to criterion) in the progeny of rats given repeated doses of ethyl alcohol during pregnancy. Moreover, the injections modified the motivational and emotional behaviors bidirectionally as related to the size of the doses of alcohol administered. More recently, Morra (unpublished manuscript) replicated Vincent's study with the addition of stress groups in an attempt to evaluate the influence of handling in Vincent's results. The pregnant rats were given ¾ cc saline placebo, ½ cc alcohol solution (about 24% ethyl alcohol in saline), or 2 cc alcohol solution on 5 consecutive days during the first half of gestation and exposed to a sound stressor (pulsing buzzer at about 95 dB) on 5 days during the middle of gestation, in a 2 × 3 factorial experimental design. Testing of the offspring of these females at 30, 45, and 60 days revealed significant effects of the sound stress upon emotionality but no effect of either the sound or the alcohol upon the behavioral preference for visual complexity. The efforts by Vincent and Morra were preceded by one of the oldest prenatal drug-behavior development investigations in the literature (Fletcher, Cowan, & Arlitt, 1916). In that study, Fletcher *et al.* introduced a small amount of 95% ethyl alcohol into the air chamber of chicken eggs at the start of incubation. In the testing program which followed hatching, the chicks developed in the alcoholic milieu showed certain difficulties in depth perception, overly long response times in the three maze situations, and an inability to master a discrimination task in a modified Yerkes apparatus. Simpler behaviors, e.g., reaction to light, pecking responses and accuracy, drinking reactions, did not differentiate the experimental and control groups. However, the conclusions drawn from the study were necessarily tentative, as some doubts were raised by the authors regarding the adequacy of the control conditions.

Consistent with this trend of comparative investigation following widespread drug usage and concern in the human population, Werboff and his colleagues at the Lafayette Clinic (Werboff & Dembicki, 1962; Werboff, Gottlieb, Dembicki, & Havlena, 1961b; Werboff, Gottlieb, Havlena, & Word, 1961c; Werboff & Kesner, 1963) examined the postnatal behaviors of offspring of female rats given repeated doses of a psychotropic drug or a distilled water placebo, during a designated portion of pregnancy. The drugs used included the antidepressants, iproniazid and isocarboxazid, and the tranquilizers, reserpine, chlorpromazine, and meprobamate. When tested in a Lashley III maze, only those animals born to mothers given meprobamate were significantly different (i.e., required more trials to reach criterion) from the water controls. In these studies by the Lafayette group, as in most cited on prenatal drug manipulation, marked differences were seen in many of the experimental groups in the levels of activity and of emotionality (see also, Hoffeld & Webster, 1965; Jewett & Norton, 1966). Although a general case could be made for the dismissal of the learning differences in most of these studies on the basis of the less subtle motivational and emotional differences, such a maneuver is not immediately possible in the instance with meprobamate (Werboff & Kesner, 1963).

The confounding of motivational-emotional factors in the analysis of learning performances is clearly demonstrated in the experimental reports by W. R. Thompson, Watson, and Charlesworth (1962), and by W. R. Thompson and Kano (1965). In the first report, the offspring of rats given doses of adrenaline on Days 7, 9, 11, and 13 of gestation were tested in an open field (50-60 days and 90-100 days), in a home cage-emergence situation (70-80 days), and in a simple water maze (120-150 days). The behavioral patterns were such that the authors could conclude," . . . Prenatal adrenalin injection, in the dosage used, produced heightened emotionality, improved performance in a learning situation motivated by fear, but possibly inferior retention [p. 20]." In the second report, rats maintained on a diet to which DL-phenylalanine and L-tyrosine were added (total: 10%) were mated after an initial adaptation period and the behaviors of their progeny observed. Behavioral tests (open-field activity, Hebb-Williams maze performance) were initiated at 5-40 days for emotionality and activity and at 50-60 days for maze adaptation and problem solving. Significant differences were evident between the offspring of the experimental and control mothers on all measures including the training to the maze situation, but not for problem solving. Presumably, the learning differences where they did exist, were the consequences of heightened emotionality in the experimental offspring.

As part of a broad program directed to the study of "biochemical lesions," Kerr, Chamove, Harlow, and Waisman (1968) fed pregnant rhesus monkeys an excess of L-phenylalanine for the entirety of the gestation period. In doing so, the investigators attempted to recreate in the laboratory the conditions of fetal phenylketonuria (PKU), which are presumed to exist in those human pregnancies wherein the level of phenylalanine in the maternal serum and of phenylketones in the maternal urine are abnormally high. The products of such pregnancies may be mentally retarded even though able to metabolize phenylalanine in a normal manner, in contrast with those children born with a genetically based metabolic error in the phenylalanine metabolism. During their pregnancies, the female monkeys showed significant elevations in serum phenylalanine and tyrosine (a degradation product of phenylalanine) and, thus, presented some of the features of the clinical syndrome. When tested at a year or more of age, the infants of these females were significantly retarded in their formation of object discrimination learning sets although undifferentiable from the control infants on the basis of other, simpler measures of learning performance. Nevertheless the investigators questioned the validity of their experimental model since the expected correlations between the measures of physical development and of learning performance and the levels of serum amino acids were lacking. [Thompson and Kano (1965) had also found no correlation between the measured behaviors and the amino acid levels in the pregnant females.] Kerr *et al.* concluded, "The etiology of mental retardation in patients with PKU, and in the monkeys reported in this study, is obscure. The circulating level of phenylalanine is certainly not the only factor involved . . . [p. 33]."

D. Nutrition

Behavioral research dealing with nutritional factors has had an uneven history, beginning with the very first experimental use of the laboratory rat. When vitamins were first recognized for their role in mammalian nutrition and, particularly, in early mammalian growth, a spate of reports appeared on the relation of prenatal deficiencies and postnatal behavior. More recently, with the identification of nutritionally based physical and educational disorders in the developing countries and in the more delimited dietary deficiencies in the impoverished populations in this country, a renewed interest in nutritional factors in behavioral development has been shown. Prominent in the latter-day investigations has been the concern with those factors involved in protein metabolism, whether in terms of total available protein or of the hormones and trace elements which are implicated in protein utilization (cf. Eichenwald & Fry, 1969; Hurley, 1968). The earlier research will not be reviewed here since much is of uneven quality and of limited value, methodologically or conceptually, when compared to the more recent studies which reflect the greater sophistication in behavioral, biochemical, and statistical technology. Instead, the reader is urged to consult a source such as Munn (1950, pp. 341–343).

With one exception, folic acid, a vitamin deficiency instituted prior to birth appears to be without effect on postnatal learning behavior in the laboratory animals studied (usually the rat). Whitley, O'Dell, and Hogan (1951) reported that the offspring of rat mothers deficient of folic acid since before mating were significantly inferior to the control animals in the mastery of a multiple unit maze at 8 to 10 weeks of age. The experimental offspring made significantly more errors and required significantly more trials to reach mastery of the 14-unit water maze (Stone pattern) than did the control offspring.

Another deficiency, that of pyridoxine (B_6), may lead to a greatly increased incidence of spontaneous convulsions (Daniel, Kline, & Tolle, 1942; Nelson & Evans, 1951) and a lowered seizure threshold to electroconvulsive shock (V. D. Davenport & Davenport, 1948) and to sound (Patton, Karn, & King, 1942). The postnatal age at first appearance is related to the developmental age when the dietary restriction was instituted (Daniel et al., 1942), and appears not to be confounded by changes in the adult female as could influence her offspring by way of her maternal behavior (Meier & Moss, 1960). In spite of these clear-cut changes in a certain form of early reactivity, no concordant changes have been detected in learning behavior as in avoidance conditioning, Dashiell maze performance, and the solution of the Krechevsky apparatus (Meier & McGanity, unpublished data). Thus, the effect of the deficiency is quite specific to the early neurologic disorders and is devoid even of possible interaction with early experience in the production of later performance differences.

The medical-legal complications instigated by convulsive disorders in infants maintained on a proprietary milk formula revived interest in B-vitamins, specifically pyridoxine, and behavioral development. Similarly, the recognition of the behavioral sequelae of presumed, prolonged protein deficiency, evident in the marasmus and kwashiorkor syndromes, suggested the need for laboratory research on protein metabolism and its implications for behavioral development. Cowley and Griesel (1959) maintained female rats on a low protein diet (about 14.5%) beginning at weaning (21 days). At 90 days of age, these animals were mated. The offspring of these were tested on a Hebb-Williams maze and compared with the offspring of females maintained on a control diet (about 21.3% protein). Although not different in exploratory behavior, the low-protein offspring were slower and less efficient in their overall performance in the maze. These behavioral differences existed only in the offspring of such mothers: the low- and high-protein females themselves could not be differentiated on the behavioral tests. In subsequent studies, these investigators (Cowley, 1967; Cowley & Griesel, 1963) showed that the prenatal dietary deficiency slowed behavioral development prior to weaning, that the learning performance deficit could not be corrected by "rehabilitation" procedures (i.e., change to the high-protein diet) at weaning, and that the severity of the behavioral deficit increased with each succeeding generation on the low-protein diet. Other data showed that although cross-fostering at birth had some ameliorative effect, however, when compared with the effect of the prenatal conditions, the postnatal dietary conditions were of secondary importance.

Especially provocative to theorizing on biochemical mechanisms in behavior modification through developmental manipulation (cf. Meier, 1968a, pp. 355–360) is the report of the post-hatching behavioral sequelae of altered specific protein balance during incubation (Kamrin, 1967). Kamrin induced an immune tolerant state in his chicks by way of parabiosis beginning during the second week of incubation and measured the approach-following and withdrawal-escape behaviors following hatching (up to 40 days). He noted that, on both measures, the experimental chicks were consistently more responsive to the testing situation and more differentiating of its uniquenesses.

Caldwell and Churchill (1966) looked at the prenatal influence of the dietary restriction of lipids to rats during the course of pregnancy. (All were maintained on a control diet prior to mating and after parturition.) The maze learning (Lashley III, 53 days of age) of the offspring of the females on the fat-free diet was compared with that of the offspring of the females maintained on the regular laboratory chow. The response latencies of the two groups were significantly different: the experimental animals were appreciably slower than the controls, especially on the second and third days of testing.

E. Maternal Emotion

A more recent concern is the possibility of maternal emotional factors influencing fetal development and, subsequently, postnatal behavior. Although much more nebulous for clinical and research analysis, the possibilities of this form of maternal-fetal interaction are much more numerous and the mechanisms more insidious than previously discussed factors (cf. Ferreira, 1965).

W. D. Thompson and Sontag (1956) exposed pregnant rats to audiogenic seizure episodes (twice daily) between the fifth and eighth day of gestation. When tested for behavioral differences (30 days and 60 days, general activity; 80 days, Lashley III water maze), the offspring of these females made more errors and required more trials to reach criterion than did the offspring of the control females. Other measures of these offspring (weights, litter size, activity) did not differentiate them from the controls. Nor were those animals which were cross-fostered at birth different in any way from those reared by their biologic mothers.

W. R. Thompson (1957) applied another form of prenatal stress, unavoidable exposure to the conditioned stimulus of an established conditioned stimulus-avoidance response relation, throughout the gestation period of pregnant rats. This form of maternal conflict during prenatal life modified the emotional behaviors of the offspring when measured at 30–40 and 130–140 days. It also increased the latency of response in the solution of a simple water maze at 130–150 days (W. R. Thompson *et al.*, 1962).

Conceptually consistent with the prenatal stress study, but methodologically in accord with the prenatal drug research, a follow-up investigation by W. R. Thompson, Goldenberg, Watson, and Watson (1963) provided additional data on prenatal-maternal influences upon behavioral development of the progeny as related to the intensity and timing of the prenatal manipulation. Learning and emotionality tests of young born to female rats given repeated administrations of one of two dose levels of adrenalin during the first, second, or third week of the 3-week pregnancy revealed significant group differences especially prominent in those animals born to females injected during the second trimester of gestation. Measures of open field activity, and of timing on the Hebb-Williams maze, were most sensitive to this form of prenatal stress. The authors concluded:

> In general, the experiment reported was successful in demonstrating some behavioral effects in offspring as a result of prenatal maternal stress. It was not successful, however, in affording a specification of those parameters responsible for the particular kind, magnitude, and direction of effects observed . . . The physiological effects of adrenalin may be too diffuse to allow the emergence of specific and well defined effects [p. 284].

Morra (1965, cf. also 1968), more recently, corroborated the effects of prenatal emotional stress on postnatal learning performances. He exposed pregnant rats, which had been differentially conditioned previously, to the conditioned stimulus (CS) of the avoidance conditioning situation daily for 10 trials per day between Days 1-11 and Days 9-19 of gestation. In addition to the usual tests of emotionality, the offspring of these females were presented with a learning situation, i.e., a simple spatial discrimination on Days 35-38 postpartum. The behaviors of the groups of animals were differentiated by level of stress to the mother (number of preconception conditioning trials) for both time and error measures, and by the period of pregnancy during which the CS was presented, and by the interaction between stress and period of pregnancy for the time scores. Differences were also observed in the emotional behaviors, consistent with the previously cited studies. [Such differences have been described in a number of studies on the behavioral effects of prenatal maternal stress.(cf. Ader & Plaut, 1968).]

Joffe (1965a, 1965b) maintained pregnant rats for 17 of the 22 days of gestation in a conflict situation (a variant of a passive-avoidance technique) in which the individual female was exposed to the approach-electroshock contingency for 23 of each 24 hours. The offspring of these females were cross-fostered at birth with those of females maintained in similar cages without the experimentally induced conflict. Subsequently, all young were tested for emotionality (open field test at 78-80 days) and for maze-learning performance (Hebb-Williams at 131-133 days). Joffe found significant differences in the maze learning of the two groups of offspring — the experimental animals made more errors — and some indication of an interaction effect on maze performances between sex of offspring and postnatal rearing condition.

F. Prenatal Factors: Comment

As stated at the outset of this section, the prenatal agents chosen and the research designs employed have reflected current clinical concerns and theoretical enthusiasms. In a very real sense the many efforts to evaluate the relationship between prenatal manipulation and postnatal behavioral development have been unqualified successes. They have made crystal clear the fragility of fetal life and the very intimate relationship between the life of the fetus and that of its mother; they have shown the continuing influence of the extrauterine and, even, extramaternal environment upon fetal development. No longer can we conceive of life *in utero* so fancifully as before when it was an existence of supreme stability and quiescence (cf. Arshavsky, 1968). The thought of a generation ago was "that the mammalian fetus, unlike lower organisms known to be subject to environmental influences, was unique in being protected from such influences by maternal inclosure [Mintz, 1958, p. 1]." Mercifully, this too is passing.

Still, these efforts present a serious limitation to the depth and scope of our appreciation of prenatal influences and the possibilities of extrapolation to human fetal life. Most of these studies were of influences on rodent, usually laboratory rat, development. The strictures that this methodologic myopia places on our understanding are well-recognized, especially in the area of drug and nutritional influences. Species and strain differences in drug response and nutritional requirements may be vastly greater than phyletic or anatomical similarities would suggest. Additionally, the rodent species make difficult an analysis of temporal factors in prenatal influences. Sixteen to 22 days, the range of gestation periods of the species used, tax even the finest procedures of subject manipulation and developmental scrutiny. Finally, the separation of connative and cognitive factors, no mean feat even at the human level (cf. Zigler, 1967), has so far defied the very best efforts with the laboratory mouse and rat. Clearly, we should turn to those species with behavioral repertoires much more nearly like our own for further elaboration of the manipulation-response relation intimated by the data cited here from rodent species. Moreover, these studies have shown the possibilities of certain extraembryonic influences on behavioral development. They have not, however, revealed the probabilities. Nor were they designed to do so. Only epidemiologic studies with humans can provide that information. Hopefully, this comparative research will be convincing of the urgency that these surveys be undertaken.

IV. PERINATAL FACTORS

A. Hypoxia

For well over a century the scientific and medical communities have toiled with the possible impact of difficult or prolonged delivery, neonatal hypoxia, and other complications of birth upon the subsequent behavioral and neurological development of the infant involved. Oxygen deficiency, for reasons of undisputed conceptual and methodologic simplicity, has been the perinatal complication scrutinized most carefully in comparative-experimental as well as in clinical research (cf. Meier, 1969a). In general, the pattern of comparative studies has been to take the mammalian fetus or infant (cat, dog, guinea pig, monkey, rat) and expose it to a degree of oxygen deprivation according to a predetermined criterion, e.g., total time in an atmosphere of low oxygen deprivation, set dose of drug which effects an impairment in oxygen metabolism; appearance of selected behavioral and/or physical signs following deprivation or asphyxiation. At some later date, usually when the infant reaches maturity, the experimental offspring are tested on one or more behavioral tasks and compared with other control offspring. Even though this experiment has been repeated many times, the causal relations remain uncertain still (Meier, 1968a).

Several have shown that under laboratory conditions long-term behavioral deficits can be produced by the exposure of newborn to an oxygen-deficient atmosphere (Berkson, 1968b; Cassin & Fregly, 1957; Hurder & Sanders, 1953; Meier, 1953; Meier & Bunch, 1950; Nolan, 1953). These investigators used a wide variety of learning tasks and testing situations which effectively covered the range of devices currently used with each of the species involved. In most of the studies differences were observed which suggested poorer acquisition and retention by the experimental animals when tested in early adulthood. Further, the magnitude of these differences was related to the severity of the neonatal deprivation conditions employed (Nolan, 1953).

Others have shown similar behavioral impairments following neonatal conditions modeled more closely after those of difficult or prolonged human parturition or after those advocated in certain obstetric practices. Among the first (Becker & Donnell, 1952; Richardson, 1954; Saxon, 1961a, 1961b; Saxon & Ponce, 1961; Windle & Becker, 1943) are those researchers who manipulated the fetus *in utero* or prior to the completion of the birth process, e.g., clamped the uterine vessels while the fetus remained intact, or surgically delivered the fetus but immersed it in a saline solution prior to the onset of respiration. In the second (Armitage, 1952; Becker, Boneau, Shearin, & King, 1964) are those who injected certain drugs, notably the barbiturates, into the pregnant mammal (rat) immediately prior to the expected date of normal delivery. As before, these investigators have reported difficulties in the mastery of appropriate learning tasks by the experimental animals long after they recovered from the immediate respiratory, neurologic, and/or locomotor sequelae of the deprivation experience.

Nevertheless, few if any of these behavioral differences in the neonatally deprived as contrasted with the control animals can be designated as simply differences in learning performance or learning capability, per se. Impressive differences in emotional and motivation behaviors have been reported for the cat (Meier, 1953), dog (Cassin & Fregly, 1957), and monkey (Saxon, 1961a, 1961b). In each instance, these latter differences were of such character and magnitude that the reported differences in learning performances are explicable on the basis of their contribution alone, without recourse to suppositions of primary learning deficiencies in the experimental animals. Moreover, the more complex the species studied, that is, the richer the behavioral repertoire of the species, the more difficult the definition of the behavioral deficit in learning constructs. This state of affairs is especially obvious in any comparison of the primate studies, including those on man (Meier, 1969b). Together, these studies suggest (1) our difficulty in defining the behaviors of the less-complex species in terms applicable to ourselves, and (2) our inability to sustain the more complex species either with or without the mother while excluding the confounding influence of the rearing processes (e.g., Sackett, 1968).

B. Other Birth Complications: Mode of Delivery

The significance of the birth process itself, despite wide-ranging theorizing in personality development, is first now being researched. In the behavioral sciences these efforts have been directed to an analysis of the effects of mode of delivery, specifically the differential influence of vaginal versus surgical delivery. The first such experimental analysis was in a brief report by Meier (1964) which revealed differences in level of activity and early, postnatal avoidance conditioning in rhesus monkeys delivered by surgical means about 1 week prior to expected parturition (168 days). The infants so delivered were less active, vocalized less, were less responsive to both the conditioned stimulus (tone: 3000 Hz) and the unconditioned stimulus (electroshock: 1 mA, to feet). In a more extensive analysis and report (Meier & Garcia-Rodriguez, 1966), surgically delivered infants showed both a poorer acquisition and retention of the avoidance response if the conditioning procedure was implemented within 12 hours of birth. If first conditioned 30 days later, surgically delivered infants revealed no differential effects related to their mode of delivery. Most impressive was the interaction between age at time of initiation of testing and repetition of the testing procedure. Other attempts to show differential effects of surgical and vaginal delivery (e.g., Grota, Denenberg, & Zarrow, 1966) have not revealed such differential effects of mode of delivery as reported by Meier and Garcia-Rodriguez. Rats delivered in this fashion showed no mode-of-delivery effects as reflected on tests of emotionality at maturity.

Significant differences exist between the rat and the primate studies in addition to the differences in species, age, and testing procedure. Most notable are the differences in the rearing procedures, now recognized but not understood. Moreover, the rejection and/or aggression directed to surgically delivered infants (only) by laboratory-reared primate mothers (Meier, 1965) illustrates fully the possibility of a mother-infant interaction which could exaggerate or ameliorate the long-range effects of the neonatal manipulation. *In toto*, these studies nicely frame the issues of the significance of the mammalian birth. For example, is the phenomenon uniquely mammalian? Is it best represented as a point or as an interval in time? How much more is it than a sharp increase in the behavioral opportunities available to the newborn? Is it a qualitative change in the repertoire as well? What are the significant changes in the parent which have meaning to the offspring? What are the significant changes, if any, in the sensory input to this organism? What are the significances of the obvious changes in offspring-parent interactions? Few of these questions have answers at present; most can evoke educated guesses, and little more. Slowly the picture is being drawn of a developmental event which is uniquely mammalian; which has both qualitative and quantitative values to the infant involved; which has a continuing involvement of both offspring and parent; and which endures for a considerable period in the intimate life between the two. The data suggest that the expression, "perinatal period," should be substituted for "birth" since the latter represents only a discontinuity and a conceptual midpoint. In the human, the total period encompassed is at least 4 weeks long and probably somewhat longer.

V. POSTNATAL FACTORS

A. Hyperoxia

Behavioral change induced by postnatal manipulation of available oxygen has not been seriously considered for experimentation (cf. Meier, 1969a). Postnatal states of oxygen deficiency, for example, are not widely recognized in the pediatric clinic for their epidemiological or behavioral relevance as distinct from similar states as they occur in adulthood. Moreover, the experimental literature on physiological, biochemical, and anatomical change tends to confirm this evaluation (Himwich, 1951). [A similar evaluation has been reached for postnatal ionizing radiation as well (cf. Levinson and Zeigler, 1959; Furchtgott, 1963). That the developmental trends for the two variables, hypoxia and X-radiation, are believed to be converse enhances immeasurably the historical significance of the prenatal period.] Nevertheless, at least one writer (Windle, 1967) sees the respiratory complications leading to a chronic hypoxia in the infant within the nursery as a causative factor in certain profound neurologic disorders, notably cerebral palsy, which may have implications for a more generalized behavioral retardation.

On the other hand, pressures from the clinic to study experimentally induced states of hyperoxia are acute. With the utilization of high oxygen concentrations in instances of prematurity and of postnatal respiratory distress produced by a variety of means, and in the recent introduction of the hyperbaric chamber into the nursery for the alleviation of such disorders has come the realization of potential adverse effects of such practices, viz., retrolental fibroplasia and blindness. The question of the uniqueness of the retina in its sensitivity to a superabundance of oxygen has not yet been resolved satisfactorily. Moreover, we hear from behaviorally oriented writers (Glavin, 1966; Rimland, 1964) that such hyperoxic conditions are correlated with exaggerated behavioral inadequacy in childhood, specifically infantile autism. Greenbaum and Gunberg (1963; cf. also Greenbaum & Gunberg, 1962), in an unpublished study, reported equivocal results, that is, a curvilinear relation between degree of hyperoxia and extent of behavioral change and, therefore, failed to clarify the issues. They exposed infant rats to one of two degrees of hyperoxia (50% and 75%) for one of two durations (10 and 20 days, postpartum) and tested adult behaviors on measures of timidity, sexual responsiveness, and maze learning (Hebb-Williams). Significant differences in maze performance were found between the experimental groups: those animals exposed to 50% oxygen for 10 or 20 days or to 75% oxygen for 10 days were poorer performers (more errors) than were those exposed to the 75% oxygen for 20 days. The latter could not be differentiated from the controls. Less striking differences were seen on the test of sexual responsiveness and on post-testing adrenal weights. The pattern, however, was not one of consistency. These claims and these data provide strong cases for a complex causative relation between hyperoxia and behavioral defect which awaits experimental confirmation.

B. Infantile Brain Damage

Experimentation on infantile brain damage as it influences behavior and behavioral development need not be rationalized: its relevance to clinical theorizing and practice is self-evident. Of all the possible etiological factors of postnatal origin, early brain damage—usually defined as cerebral cortex damage—has had the longest and least controversial history. When doubts have arisen they have pertained to the relative significance of this factor in the epidemiology of mental retardation or to the probable mechanisms by which the damage is inflicted. Clearly, the effects of cortical damage inflicted upon the adult are much too serious and much too obvious to question meaningfully the validity of any claim regarding its role in the infant. The adult relation affords the prototype for the rationale of the childhood behavioral syndrome; it affords the logic and the methodology for the experimental research, as well. This research, however, has justified the enthusiasm but has failed to support the fundamental assumptions of brain-behavior relationships. Instead, it provided new directions in which profitable theorizing might go. Clearly, circumscribed brain lesions in the mammalian infant need not—and usually do not—modify behavior in either a qualitative or quantitative manner comparable to analogous lesions in the adult. The changes induced by infantile damage may be categorically distinct from that of the adult, much more minor than in the adult, or beyond the detectability of existing testing techniques.

The research has evolved conceptually from the general and all-encompassing to the specific and detailed while shifting the anatomical focus from the cerebral neocortex to the archicortex and brainstem structures. [For an up-to-date review and appraisal of this work, the reader is directed to Isaacson (1968). For aspects of some of the earlier work in which acute as well as chronic changes are considered, see Cruikshank (1954).] In the first studies, e.g., Tsang (1937a), broad lesions were inflicted on the weanling rats (22 days old) and maze-learning measured when the subjects were young adults (90 days and later). Postoperative behavioral decrement was inversely related to age at surgery. Recent replications (e.g., Peeler, 1962) yielded the same conclusion: extensive neonatal cortical damage outside the primary sensory and motor areas has minimal effect as compared with similar adult damage on the acquisition of a maze solution, a non-specific task.

The researches with specific cortical sensory areas and modality-related testing procedures yielded similar conclusions of little or no effect of the neonatal damage. Thus, Benjamin and Thompson (1959) reported only minimal tactile discrimination deficits in cats which had suffered removal of the somesthetic cortex (areas I and II) shortly after birth (5 days). In clear contrast with cats exposed to a comparable insult while adult, these infantile-lesioned animals were within the normal range of discrimination performance on all except the most difficult tasks. Likewise, Scharlock, Tucker, and Strominger (1963) reported that infantile destruction of the auditory cortex (auditory areas I, II, and Ep) was without effect on subsequent discrimination of differences in temporal and frequency patterns (also see Záhlava & Mysliveček, 1964). Comparable adults were, as a group, unable to master even the easier discrimination, that of temporal patterns. Wetzel, Thompson, Horel, and Meyer (1965) and Tucker and Kling (1966) concurred for infantile lesions in the visual cortex (also see Tsang, 1937b). The infant operates had no difficulty in visual placing or in the mastery of visual discrimination problems, although they did show some initial difficulty in visually-guided locomotion. The latter, however, was transient. Adult operates were seriously impaired on all discrimination tasks. In sum, in each instance in which sensory loci and related discrimination performance were evaluated, differences between infantile operates and controls may exist on only the most subtle discriminations—if at all—unlike the generally deficient discrimination behavior of the adult operates. The only dissent to this conclusion appeared in the study of visual discrimination by Doty (1961) in which defective behavior was reported following lesions inflicted later in infancy (2 months rather than 4 days) or with lesions enlarged to include portions of the striate cortex.

Infantile damage to non-primary cortical areas may have significant effects on subsequent behaviors if tested for transfer of training facility at a later age rather than for overall learning capability—as on a maze—or for discrimination performance. Harlow and his associates at the University of Wisconsin (Harlow, Blomquist, Thompson, Schiltz, & Harlow, 1968) realized significant learning-to-learn deficits in monkeys which suffered bilateral frontal lobectomies or topectomies during early infancy. These animals, tested on a multiple problem, object discrimination procedure when about 200 days of age, were unexpectedly slow in establishing the learning set even though their object discrimination learning on single tasks could not be differentiated from intact or normal controls, nor was their performance on a delayed response task distinguishable. The Wisconsin researchers began with the hypothesis "that there is a relation between the amount of loss in an ability consequent to cortical damage and the stage of maturation of the ability that depends on the integrity of the cortical area subjected to lesion [p. 118]." Their earlier data on delayed response learning supported such a view (Harlow, Akert, & Schiltz, 1964). Their more recent effort provided neither corroboration nor rejection, for that matter; it did provide additional data to underscore the contribution of age-related variables to any concept of cerebral localization.

Although supporting the Wisconsin studies on infantile damage and delayed response learning, Kling and Tucker (1968) reported behavioral deficiencies on delayed alternation tasks in frontal monkeys lobectomized shortly after birth. Further, they noted inferior delayed response learning in those animals in which the lesions were extended to include the frontal lobe and the caudate nucleus. In some instances the infant operates performed at least as poorly as did the adult operates. By contrast, combination lesions in the frontal and parietal cortex together resulted in sparing of performance on both the object discrimination and the delayed response tasks.

[This picture of infantile frontal lobe injury and delayed response performance is not without contradiction. V. E. Thompson (1966), for example, was unable to differentiate infantile, young juvenile, and adult operates (cats; frontal gyrus, bilateral) on a rather unique testing procedure; he could distinguish all from their litter-mate controls. The explanation for the discrepancy offered by this study is not immediately available; age and testing differences are the most likely possibilities.]

Others of the data reported by Kling (1962, 1965, 1966) supported the initiating hypothesis of the Harlow et al. (1968) study. Bilateral amygdaloidectomy in adult cats and monkeys produced profound changes in affective (aggressive, sexual), oral, and conditioning behaviors. Comparable lesions in the infant (2–10 weeks) were without such sequelae, although lesions inflicted after this age produced the adult syndrome. The only consequence of the earlier lesions was the possible increase in maturation rate of certain behaviors during the pre-adult period. Conceivably, the earlier damage was without effect on the designated behaviors because of the temporal dysjunction between the stage of behavioral maturation and of the relevant cerebral structures at the time of the operation.

Elsewhere, damage to the archicortex, specifically hippocampus, reveals even more clearly the complex relation between the age at insult and the testing parameters. Isaacson, Nonneman, and Schmaltz (1968) destroyed bilaterally the hippocampus in neonate, 6-week infant and adult cats, and tested them later for runway performance, brightness discrimination, and the acquisition of complex operant schedules. From the behaviors observed, the investigators concluded:

> (1) For some problems, destruction of the hippocampus in the neonate produces less behavioral debilitation than that at later ages [p. 76]; (2) . . . The degree of impairment shown by animals with lesions made early in life is specific to the task [p. 77]; (3) . . . Even though neonatal damage to the hippocampus may lessen, or even eliminate, a particular deficit usually caused by lesions in adulthood, this does not imply that the behavior of the neonatally damaged is like that of normal animals [p. 77].

They summarized as follows:

> The results of destruction of the hippocampus . . . should not be evaluated as some unitary trend toward "normal behavior" but rather as a trend toward a different pattern of behavior than that produced by lesions made later in life [p.77].

Differences in exploratory behavior of possible relation to general learning behaviors were described by Peeler and Andy (1969a, 1969b) in kittens (from about 7 days to 5½ months) which had suffered lesions to the anterior septal region between 3 to 7 days after birth. The order of these differences was not that anticipated with the traditional orientation: the operates showed more exploratory behavior, qualitatively and quantitatively, at an earlier age than did their litter-mate controls. Conceivably, the septal lesions hastened behavioral development. Peeler and Orlando, on the other hand, preferred a different interpretation in which behavioral maturation is viewed as the resultant of an interaction between two or more systems. In this instance, the destruction meant the premature removal of certain inhibitory processes.

Foshee, Meier, and Andy (1969) inflicted bilateral lesions (electrolytic; about 70% destruction) in the inferior colliculi within the first 24 hours after birth (either vaginal or surgical). Immediate behavioral changes observed in the first 3 months seemed not to be related to brain damage, per se, but to the operative procedures by which the infant was delivered and the brainstem damage inflicted. Later, examinations in a free-field situation when the subjects were about a year of age indicated greater exploratory behavior in the operates than in the sham-operate controls. The latter demonstrated greater emotionality in this situation. When observed at 2½ to 3½ years of age, the operates continued to show certain locomotor difficulties (in a few cases) but very little stereotypy. The controls, by contrast, showed most of the self-manipulation and locomotor repetition typically seen in isolate-reared rhesus monkeys. (All of the animals were isolate-reared for the first year.) This study, begun as a behavioral analysis of specific anatomical defects usually associated with neonatal asphyxia (Ranck & Windle, 1959; cf. Towbin, 1969 for a newer and more complicating picture), raised the possibility that an activation system had been violated surgically, reducing the behavioral arousal typically elicited by removal from isolation-rearing conditions. In the absence of the recognizably bizarre behaviors the operate animal appeared "more normal" (i.e., more like the feral-reared) than did the sham operate controls.

Returning to the original problem, the supposition of localized brain damage in mental retardates or in children with certain learning handicaps, we find the data from these experiments perplexing. Nowhere do we see the generalized learning deficits comparable to inferior scholastic performance as we had expected from our knowledge of the behavior of the adult brain-injured. In non-human subjects whatever decrement in performance observed is task-specific and, possibly, modality-specific as well. Brainstem and other forms of subcortical damage may have other significant effects, especially on emotional behaviors, but none which is uniquely and categorically relevant to learning disorders.

Nevertheless, this research area has made more numerous and more persistent methodological advances than any other cited in this review, without exception. The participating researchers have come to appreciate the contributions and collaboration of investigators in allied fields, particularly neuroanatomy, neurohistology, and neurosurgery; have employed experimental designs which not only make their analyses more powerful, but more relevant to the theorizing on brain-behavior relations; and have adopted sophisticated behavioral testing procedures readily with an eye to greater sensitivity, reliability, and psychological significance. How much of this growth is attributable to the rather unique relation the problem bears on clinical concerns and theories is probably debatable. That such at attribution can be made and sustained is unquestioned. The reciprocal advantage of this state of affairs is that the patent relevance of the research presents a real and continuing pressure to make the clinical concepts of behavioral retardation meaningful to experimental analysis and to specify experimentally the behavioral processes and the anatomical and developmental variables implicated. It has made untenable the classical search for simplistic correlates of generalized defective adaptive behavior.

C. Early Experience

Early postnatal experience, that is, behavioral interaction with the early postnatal environment, has an appreciable effect on subsequent behavioral development and, ultimately, on the nature of the adult behavior. This statement is now a truism in psychology recognized by theorist and researcher alike (cf. Beach & Jaynes, 1954; Hunt, 1961; Newton & Levine, 1968; W. R. Thompson, 1955, 1960). Questions that remain deal with the meaningful specification of the early experience and the qualification of the behaviors which are modifiable and are, indeed, modified by this form of manipulation. What are the qualitative, quantitative, and temporal parameters of the experiences which lead to long-range behavioral effects? What are the species and other genetic limitations? What are the social complications, that is, what are the implications of the concurrent behaviors of parents or parental surrogates, sibling, litter-mates, or age-peers? What are the implications of the maturational age of the infant at the time of this specific experience? What are the possible confounding features of the testing procedures? Do they vitiate any single-factor interpretation of the observed behavioral differences? These and possibly other questions have been asked of the reported data and of the interested researchers (e.g., Mirsky, 1968), but they need to be reiterated here. Each has considerable bearing on our topic, viz., the comparative investigation of mental deficiency and its etiological factors. We must be concerned about cross-species generality, the social influences, and, finally, the relation of the reported modified behavior to the ultimate level of learning performance.

Here, as always in any operational designation of a comparative model for abnormal behavior with a view to the researching on programmed or experimentally induced deviates, e.g., "mentally retarded" animals, the selection of control conditions is critical. To the methodological purist the conditions of usual colony rearing and maintenance of laboratory subjects are logically defensible, if not preferable. To the systematist however, whose interest is the "larger world" with all of its phylogenetic and ontogenetic relations, some abstract notion of natural conditions dictates that the proper controls are those which exist for the feral-reared. The significance of this difference in orientation is more than procedural and, therefore, is not limited to the machinations by which research is done. In the context of the research on long-range behavioral influences of environmental manipulation during early postnatal life, the logic of the control group provides the interpretive base for the behavioral relations reported. Moreover, it provides the basis for comprehending the seeming contradiction between those studies on rodents and other readily produced laboratory subjects, and those on laboratory primates, for example, which demand considerable experimenter attention for the production and maintenance of the individual subject. In the former, manipulation during pre-adult periods tends to enhance learning performance (fewer trials to criterion and/or shorter response latencies on conditioning and maze learning tasks) whereas maintenance with restricted environmental input, e.g., visual experience limited to mother and litter-mates, impairs such learning performances as compared with animals reared under enriched conditions or, even, under the control conditions (viz., standard laboratory procedures). By contrast, those behavioral differences which are reported in the primate studies indicate that any laboratory rearing procedure leads to defective behavior, especially of connative rather than cognitive behavior, when these animals are compared with feral- or socially reared controls. (See Bronfenbrenner, 1968; Denenberg, 1966; and Haywood, 1967 for general theoretical reviews.) Conceivably, the disparity in the results reported for the two groups of laboratory species reflect only a fundamental lack in our understanding of the variables in animal husbandry and, more importantly, of the variables actually effective in each of these studies (Meier & Schutzman, 1968; Sackett, Porter, & Holmes, 1965). Still, the ready extrapolation to the human species, in which our ignorance of factors in early development is at least as great, is premature and potentially distracting. Even though the differences in the results reported in these studies may only be relative and dependent upon the behaviors of the animals chosen for comparative purposes, the application to human rearing practices is often absolute and categorical.

No less significant in our estimation of the applicability of the data from the comparative studies on early experience and intellectual development is the cross-species relevance of the behavioral measures used and our capability as observers and theorists to specify behavioral homologues. Without doubt our capability to recognize these identities in animals with limited behavioral repertoires or which are phyletically remote from *Homo sapiens* is limited. Our ability to manipulate these animals is, similarly, limited by our anthropocentric view by which we focus on and recognize those variables of human significance. That ability is also limited by those critical methodologic variables reflected in species-typical developmental and motivational trends. Thus, tests of learning performance in laboratory rats are routinely confounded by influences of age-at-testing and/or motivational-emotional parameters of the testing situation (cf. Henderson, 1968b). Thus, multiple-problem, object discrimination performance may not be biased by infantile-juvenile social isolation in monkeys or chimpanzees after the experimenter has coaxed the subject to learn "to play the game" in a Wisconsin General Test Apparatus (R. K. Davenport, Rogers, & Menzel, 1969; Harlow, Harlow, & Schiltz, 1968b) even though a laboratory rat reared with mother and siblings under relatively impoverished stimulus conditions is slow to reach criterion on a two- or three-dimensional object discrimination task in a Grice Apparatus (Meier & McGee, 1959) or in the mastery of a closed-field maze (Denenberg, Woodcock, & Rosenberg, 1968b). Which species has a learning handicap? Both? Neither?

Major reviews of the comparative literature may be identified by theoretical orientation and by species used and/or considered particularly relevant, e.g., Fuller (1967) on dogs, Haywood and Tapp (1966) on rodents, Meier (1968b) on cats, and Sackett (1969) on monkeys. Nevertheless, the conclusion from these reviews, collectively, is the conclusion given here: whereas early environmental manipulation does have marked effects on subsequent behavioral development, temporal, maturational, species-genetic, and evaluative factors loom as the major deterrents to the reaching of any consensus on the nature of those effects. In short, the territorial claim has been recognized but the description of the significant features awaits further exploration.

D. Drugs

Repeatedly through this review, we have seen that negative or nonconfirmatory data may have the strongly salutary effects of clarifying the research model, of promoting growth of relevant research procedures and technologies, of sharpening the conceptualizations of the overall problem, and of raising significant issues, in this case, on behavioral development. The research on postnatal—and the post-drug—effects of induced high serum levels of phenylalanine, experimental phenylketonuria (PKU), presents still another instance of such a state of affairs. Certainly, this is the message conveyed by a thorough review and critique of the literature. From one such review by Karrer and Cahilly (1965), the reader gains the impression that in spite of the concentrated research activity on this model of phenylpyruvic oligophrenia, a consensus is nowhere in sight. The one trend that does appear to be emerging from the welter of studies indicates that an early age of onset of the experimental treatment is necessary for sustained behavioral effects. In the rat this age is newborn; in the monkey, probably late fetus. Elsewhere, one sees problems of methodologic, pharmacologic, comparative, and metric origin. The contradictory reports of the nature and permanence of the behavioral sequelae—a dilemma not resolved by investigations published since the Karrer-Cahilly review (e.g., Polidora, Cunningham, & Waisman, 1966; Schalock & Klopfer, 1967a, 1967b)—are, in reality, attempts at the resolution of one or several of these problems suggested by individual researchers. Moreover, where careful behavioral and biochemical analysis of the individual subject is permitted, as in the rhesus monkey, the confounding influence of differential motivation and differential early handling is made manifest, and therefore cannot be lightly dismissed (Waisman & Harlow, 1965; Young, 1967).

A feature not seriously considered in the PKU studies is the possibility of a performance deficit produced by the long period of inhibition of activity and reactivity induced in the animals through the experimental treatment. Effectively, so it seems, the high loads of phenylalanine given to the animals from birth to adolescence or from weaning to adolescence, create a condition of sensorimotor deprivation for these animals not fundamentally different from that created environmentally in other studies. That such a possibility is real is demonstrated by the investigations of learning differences during late adolescence and adulthood displayed by animals maintained on minimal levels of tranquilizers throughout infancy (e.g., Meier & Huff, 1962). Conceivably, the subjects in the PKU studies were maintained in a form of sensory isolation through the drug period the effectiveness of which depended upon the developmental period as well as upon the duration and depth of the drugged state.

In sum, we must recognize that although the research on the behavioral consequences of early pharmacologic manipulation is provocative in the extreme, the overall endeavor is just beginning (Young, 1967). Necessarily, present conclusions are tentative and long-term relations, speculative. Moreover, the methodologic considerations which obtain for psychopharmacologic research generally are greatly exacerbated by the variable time, by virtually every facet of the developing organism not the least of which is behavioral growth itself. That these developmental schedules are only dimly known and that those which are known are devoid of comparative (i.e., cross-species) relevance increases greatly the burdens of the researcher in developmental psychopharmacology. To the researcher in this area, however, positive results—administration of drug A during infancy leads to altered learning performance during adulthood—is sufficient encouragement to continue to the eventual achievement of reasoned hypotheses and meaningful drug-development-behavior relationships. Hopefully, the existence of positive results, e.g., the influence of propylthiouracil on the development of senorimotor functions in the cat (Berkson, 1968b) and of maze-learning behaviors in the rat (Essman, Mendoza, & Hamburgh, 1968); the discrimination learning deficits in rats following administration of reserpine during the first 6 weeks of postnatal life (Meier & Huff, 1962); the mitigation of the extrastimulation effects of an enriched environment by the concurrent administration of chlorpromazine (Doty, Doty, Wise, & Senn, 1964) during the first 10 weeks in the postnatal life of the laboratory rat, will provide sufficient inducement for others to join the endeavor.

E. Nutrition

The relations between nutrition during early postnatal development and learning has been the subject of a number of recent scholarly reviews (Coursin, 1967; Witkop, 1967). The compilation by Scrimshaw and Gordon (1968) is particularly noteworthy for its breadth of coverage and excellence of organization. The frequency with which these have appeared underscores the current popular concern with such fundamental problems in all human communities (cf. Cravioto, 1968; Eichenwald & Fry, 1969). Nevertheless the diversity as well as the vigor of these research efforts, especially those with laboratory subjects, make a simple summary of findings trivial. One can do little more than state that the nutritional-behavioral development relations are varied, or that the nutritional influence, albeit profound at times, is generally insidious.

Consistent with this prevailing widespread lay interest, the most spectacular recent research deals with the manipulation (usually reduction) of the major dietary constituents, notably the proteins and occasionally the carbohydrates, rather than with the vitamins as was typical of the earlier nutritional-behavioral investigations (cf. Munn, 1950, pp. 341–343). The latter are still very much a matter of keen concern (e.g., Coursin, 1968), but the significance of the contributions has diminished relatively in the face of the changing trends and political-economic pressures. The principal clinical disorders explored in these studies are kwashiorkor and marasmus, nutritional syndromes associated with early weaning and abrupt changes from high protein to high carbohydrate diets, disorders reported with alarming regularity in the developing nations. The replication of these phenomena in the laboratory has realized the feasibility of experimental analysis. Nováková (1966) weaned litters of rats at varying postnatal ages, from 15 to 30 days, and found significant differences in the acquisition and retention of classically conditioned appetitive responses at 8 and 12 months, respectively. Those pups weaned at the earliest ages showed the slowest rates of acquisition and poorest retention. Nováková conjectured that the differences in behavior were attributable to the sudden change of diet occasioned by the early weaning with its cessation of breast milk. The ambiguity of data such as these has been discussed fully by Barnes (1967). Other interpretations exist, the most immediate of which emphasize the non-nutritive aspects of the mother-infant relationship (cf. Ader, 1962).

By manipulating the infantile diet directly (low protein, high fat; low protein, low fat; control, restricted intake; control, ad libitum intake), Barnes and his associates (Barnes, 1968; Barnes, Moore, Reid, & Pond, 1968) were able to effect marked differences in shuttle-box performance in pigs, especially in the extinction of the avoidance response, which was still evident 9 months or so after the termination of the experimental diet (2 months) and rehabilitation on standard chow. Moreover, these behavior differences appeared in the context of marked variations in physical dimensions — evident even between the two control groups — but without attendant differences in motivational characteristics of the experimental and control animals. These differences are unique when contrasted to behavioral analysis of analogous dietary restrictions to adult animals (e.g., Griffiths & Senter, 1954).

[Not to be overlooked in these studies of early nutritional manipulation, especially of rodent populations with their unique maintenance problems, is the possible influence of differential motivational processes at the time of the behavioral assessment. For a review and a critique, see Barnes (1967).]

F. Postnatal Factors: Comment

Even though unsupported by empirical fact, the conviction persists nonetheless that postnatal manipulations are less real, "softer," and without substantive base in the integrity of the organism. That is, the changes induced by postnatal manipulations are more transient, more subject to other manipulations or corrective procedures and are, therefore, of less significance to the behavioral character of the involved organism, much less to subsequent generations of which he is parent or grandparent. Although unfortunate, this belief prevails even though rarely made explicit. Its basis — whatever it might be — is undoubtedly augmented by the choice of experimental subject, the laboratory rat. This creature with its conveniently short life cycle and its absurdly simple demands for daily sustenance reduces to an equal absurdity the experimenter's concern about its behaviors and the possibilities of subtle but long-range effects.

A small reversal in this trend has come with the popularization of the early experience studies. Although the nature of the induced behavioral change is still debated, these efforts have vindicated the philosophical and clinical suppositions of others interested in behavioral development. Moreover, they have made precious to all the infantile existence. They have not, however, been convincing that this period merits the necessary detailed comparative analysis of the behavioral repertoire and the organism-environment factors which alter it, even to a state of behavioral insufficiency. We have equated postnatal change with learning (and prenatal, with genetics) which is impermanent and, therefore, erasable. Consequently, in the comparative study of mental retardation, the unfounded dichotomy persists: congenital versus acquired, prenatal or neonatal versus postnatal. Other postnatal variables exist outside the learning mode; these should be studied for their possible role in mental retardation.

VI. MULTIVARIATE ANALYSIS

In the mind of this reviewer, the most meaningful studies for the larger understanding of behavior are those in which the investigator eschews the conventional single cause or single variable approach but elects, instead, to look at two or more simultaneously and to seek possible interactions among them. The application of such a multivariate orientation to the comparative investigation of mental retardation is of recent origin and, therefore, offers few examples of its potency. Nevertheless, encouragement for wider, or even routine, application comes from reports in other disciplines and in other fields of behavioral study. Runner (1967), for example, has described remarkably diverse consequences of prenatal drug states in the laboratory mouse which vary not only with the peculiarities of the drug used but also with the specifics of the particular strain of mouse. Similarly, W. R. Thompson and Olian (1961) and DeFries and Weir (DeFries, 1964; DeFries, Weir, & Hegmann, 1967; Weir & DeFries, 1964) described differential effects on emotional behavior of rats and mice, respectively, induced by the uniqueness of genetic strain and the nature of the prenatal maternal stress. Joffe (1965b) showed that this differential effect could be transmitted through the postnatal, preweaning interaction between female and foster-offspring. The avoidance performance of young adult rats was related to the preconceptual stress experiences of the foster mother rather than to the particular genetic origin; emotional behaviors were related to that origin rather than to the foster-mother interaction.

Lucey and his associates (Lucey, Hibbard, Behrman, Esquivel de Gallardo, & Windle, 1964) offered a non-human primate model of the developmental disorder kernicterus, which satisfies the biochemical, neuroanatomical, and neurological criteria by which the condition is known in the human infant. Asphyxiating the infant rhesus monkey to a subclinical level (i.e., no detectable brain damage) and then maintaining the infant on high levels of bilirubin for 48 hours, they subsequently observed the localized deposition of the biochemical in the cerebrum, especially in the basal ganglia but also within the neurones in the cortex, and the appearance of opisthotonus with concurrent abnormalities in the electroencephalogram. One must wonder about the behavioral sequelae of such a preparation, since the search for them was not part of this particular research program of studies. After the disappearance of the jaundice and the more severe neurological symptoms, will the infant show patterns of behavioral development which could be compared only with those of the mental defective? [Rozdilsky's report (1966) of a similar state produced in infant kittens following the repeated administration of bilirubin alone without the prior neonatal asphyxiation raises important questions of species specifics of a non-behavioral nature which the behavioral scientist must contemplate in his comparative investigations.]

An excellent example of this mode of research is the study by Schwarz (1964) in which adult maze performance was related to neonatal brain damage and to stimulus complexity of the rearing environment. Schwarz ablated posterior cortical tissue bilaterally in infant rats (within 24 hours of birth) and maintained them thereafter, along with their sham operate controls, in a standard laboratory environment or in an enriched environment until about 95 days of age. When the rats were about 135 days of age, he presented them with a series of problems on the Hebb-Williams maze and found the expected depressing effects of both the ablation and the stimulus impoverishment of the standard environment. More importantly, however, Schwarz observed the interaction between the surgery and the rearing procedures: the enriched environment appeared to offset the effects of the neonatal brain damage whereas the impoverished environment exacerbated the effects of the cortical loss.

Berkson (1968b), in his study of behavioral maturation in kittens, noted that the effectiveness of the propylthiouracil in the production of the sensorimotor defects observed was complicated by the rearing conditions of the kittens described. Hand-rearing the kittens tended to exaggerate the effects seen in the kittens reared by their natural mothers. [In a parallel experiment, Kling and Green (1967) noted that mother-rearing infant monkeys following neonotal amygdalectomy had no effect whatsoever on the sequence of behaviors observed elsewhere in brain-damaged infants, that is, the infants could not be differentiated from the intact controls.]

Simeonsson and Meier (unpublished study) observed a strain-prenatal treatment interaction in their study of prenatal irradiation. Female mice of the C57BL/6 and BALB/c strains were exposed to a low dose rate (1 r/hr) of gamma radiation (Co_{60}) during Days 3–5 to Days 18–20 (total: 15 days or 360 r) of their pregnancy. The offspring produced were tested for open-field behavior, avoidance conditioning, and water-maze performance at about 105 days of age. The differences between the groups indicated that the magnitude of the prenatal irradiation effect was strain-dependent and was particularly clear in the BALB/c animals in the open field. An interaction between the major factors was especially marked in the avoidance conditioning, with the experimental BALB/c's being exceptionally high performers and the others being more nearly alike. The overall effect of the prenatal irradiation seemed to be one of emphasis of the peculiar strain-specific behaviors. (This genetic-treatment interaction was evident in the morphologic changes, as well.) The genetic implication was even more striking in a third strain, the 129, which was excessively responsive to any form of prenatal manipulation, including that necessary for the irradiation control procedures.

In some instances, these multivariate studies have had the effect of depicting, more or less sharply, procedural complications or flaws in other comparative-developmental researches. Thus, sex (Meier & Schutzman, 1968), strain (Henderson, 1968b), and cross-fostering (Bovet-Nitti, Oliverio, & Bovet, 1968; Oliverio, Satta, & Bovet, 1968), as well as strain and cross-fostering together (Ressler, 1966) have been shown to be significant variables in the strategies of experimentation on early experience and its influence upon the learning process.

Perhaps the most ambitious and, therefore, the most complex program of multifactor studies is that undertaken by Denenberg and his associates at Purdue University. In one study, these investigators (Denenberg, Karas, Rosenberg, & Schell, 1968; also see Denenberg & Whimbey, 1968; Whimbey & Denenberg, 1967) related pre-conception-maternal manipulation, infantile handling, infantile housing, and post-weaning housing to several measures of emotional and learning behavior recorded when the subjects were adult (220 days of age, and later). Expectedly, an analysis of variance of the multiple behavioral measures revealed many significant terms, including those for the major factors as well as for certain interactions. The researchers concluded that "the results establish that significant 'individual differences' can be created by experimental means independent of any contribution from genetic variance." Presumably these effects were both predictable as well as stable. Moreover, the temporal persistence of the influence of some of these effects is impressive, indeed. Whimbey and Denenberg (1967) first sought behavioral difference in their rats more than 6 months after the termination of the last experimental treatment—and they found those effects! Even more striking are the reports by Ressler (1966) and by Denenberg and Rosenberg (1967) in which behavior change was reliably traced to manipulations of the grandparent of the observed animal.

In short, the results of these multivariate studies are too unique or too novel, too complex or too confusing to be readily assimilated into the research endeavor under review here. Nevertheless they do offer the attraction of closer approximation to the real world in which many variables are operative simultaneously. This is the world in which the typical mammal develops—and from which the mentally retarded arises.

VII. CONCLUSION

At the outset of this review, I suggested that the absence of a conceptual model of mental retardation from a comparative perspective was, and is, the major stumbling block to effective research on behavioral retardation, i.e., learning deficits in non-human animal experimental subjects. A re-consideration of the studies cited, with their procedural strengths and weaknesses, and with their findings of statistically significant—or non-significant—differences in behavior in the experimental and control groups, suggests an equally serious deterrent to effective comparative research in this domain: the failure of those committed to a non-comparative approach to research or to the intervention in a clinical population, to carefully evaluate such data as are reviewed here. That is, many accept differences—or non-differences—as practically significant without regard to methodological and/or conceptual considerations. Recall the Head Start-type project in which no heed is given to dietary insufficiencies, even in those projects in geographic areas or in those segments of our population in which such deficiencies are known to exist, and when such deficiencies have been reliably related to inferior intellectual performance. Or, consider the sought-for improvement in intelligence following early intervention when studies on other primates discourage such ambitions, or at least the interpretation of any behavioral improvement in intellectual terms, i.e., IQ scores. Or, weigh the emphasis on a localized "minimal brain damage" incurred at birth when the laboratory data, such as reviewed here, indicate that those neurological deficits which are presumed to exist in the clinical population are completely without serious consequence in the experimental, non-human population. Or, finally, reflect on the undying preference for simplistic causal relations. Like a bad habit, the tendency endures whereby causal relations are limited to single variables acting in isolation, unimpeded by the interaction with other variables, even those which are known to be operative at that developmental period and under those environmental circumstances. Still, as will be concluded from a quick review of the publication dates, alone, of the references cited herein, progress in the comparative research on mental retardation has been exponential — and positive.

REFERENCES

Ader, R. Social factors affecting emotionality and resistance to disease in animals: III. Early weaning and susceptibility to gastric ulcers in the rat. A control for nutritional factors. *Journal of Comparative and Physiological Psychology*, 1962, **55**, 600–602.

Ader, R., & Plaut, S. M. Effects of prenatal maternal handling and differential housing on offspring emotionality, plasma corticosterone levels, and susceptibility to gastric erosions. *Psychosomatic Medicine*, 1968, **30**, 277–286.

Armitage, S. G. The effects of barbiturates on the behavior of rat offspring as measured in learning and reasoning situations. *Journal of Comparative and Physiological Psychology*, 1952, **45**, 146–152.

Arshavsky, I. A. Adaptive and homeostatic mechanisms in the development of physiologically mature and immature organisms. In G. Newton & S. Levine (Eds.), *Early experience and behavior*. Springfield, Ill.: Thomas, 1968. Pp. 299–337.

Barnes, R. H. Experimental animal approaches to the study of early malnutrition and mental development. *Federation Proceedings*, 1967, **26**, 144–147.

Barnes, R. H. Behavioral changes caused by malnutrition in the rat and pig. In D. C. Glass (Ed.), *Environmental influences*. New York: Rockefeller University and Russell Sage Foundation, 1968. Pp. 52–60.

Barnes, R. H., Moore, A. U., Reid, I. M., & Pond, W. G. Effects of food deprivation on behavioral patterns. In N. S. Scrimshaw and J. E. Gordon (Eds.), *Malnutrition, learning, and behavior*. Cambridge, Mass.: M.I.T. Press, 1968. Pp. 203–217.

Beach, F. A., & Jaynes, J. Effects of early experience upon the behavior of animals. *Psychological Bulletin*, 1954, **51**, 239–263.

Becker, R. F., Boneau, C. L., Shearin, C. A., & King, J. E. Behavioral alterations of young rats with a history of oversedation at birth. *Neurology*, 1964, **14**, 510–520.

Becker, R. F., & Donnell, W. Learning behavior in guinea pigs subjected to asphyxia at birth. *Journal of Comparative and Physiological Psychology*, 1952, **45**, 153–162.

Benjamin, R. M., & Thompson, R. F. Differential effects of cortical lesions in infant and adult cats on roughness discrimination. *Experimental Neurology*, 1959, **1**, 305–321.

Berkson, G. Aspects of a comparative psychology of mental deficiency. *American Journal of Mental Deficiency*. 1967, **72**, 10–15. (a)

Berkson, G. Abnormal stereotyped motor acts. In J. Zubin & H. F. Hunt (Eds.), *Comparative psychopathology*. New York: Grune & Stratton, 1967. Pp. 76–94. (b)

Berkson, G. Development of abnormal stereotyped behaviors. *Developmental Psychobiology*, 1968, **1**, 118–132. (a)

Berkson, G. Maturation defects in kittens. *American Journal of Mental Deficiency*, 1968, **72**, 757–777. (b)

Bignami, G. Selection for fast and slow avoidance conditioning in the rat. *Bulletin of the British Psychological Society*, 1964, **17**, 5A.

Bovet, D., Bovet-Nitti, F., & Oliverio, A. Memory and consolidation mechanisms in avoidance learning of inbred mice. *Brain Research*, 1968, **10**, 168–182.

Bovet, D., Bovet-Nitti, F., & Oliverio, A. Genetic aspects of learning and memory in mice. *Science*, 1969, **163**, 139–149.

Bovet-Nitti, F., Oliverio, A., & Bovet, D. Effects of cross-fostering on avoidance learning and freezing behavior of DBA2J and C3H/He inbred mice. *Life Sciences*, 1968, **7**, 791–797.

Broadhurst, P. L., & Levine, S. Behavioural consistency in strains of rats selectively bred for emotional elimination. *British Journal of Psychology,* 1963, **54,** 121-125.
Bronfenbrenner, U. Early deprivation in mammals: A cross-species analysis. In G. Newton & S. Levine (Eds.), *Early experience and behavior.* Springfield, Ill.: Thomas, 1968. Pp. 627-764.
Caldwell, D. F., & Churchill, J. A. Learning impairment in rats administered a lipid free diet during pregnancy. *Psychological Reports,* 1966, **19,** 99-102.
Cassin, S., & Fregly, A. R. Neurological sequelae of experimental anoxia in newborn dogs. *Federation Proceedings,* 1957, **16,** 20.
Clendinnen, B. G., & Eayrs, J. T. The anatomical and physiological effects of prenatally administered somatotrophin on cerebral development in rats. *Journal of Endocrinology,* 1961, **22,** 183-193.
Collins, R. L. Inheritance of avoidance conditioning in mice: A diallel study. *Science,* 1964, **143,** 1188-1190.
Coursin, D. B. Relationship of nutrition to central nervous system development and function: Overview. *Federation Proceedings,* 1967, **26,** 134-138.
Coursin, D. B. Vitamin deficiencies and developing mental capacity. In N. S. Scrimshaw & J. E. Gordon (Eds.), *Malnutrition, learning, and behavior.* Cambridge, Mass.: M.I.T. Press, 1968. Pp. 289-299.
Cowley, J. J. Behavioural studies in rats following rehabilitation from low protein diets. In J. Kuhnau (Ed.), *Proceedings of the seventh international congress.* Vol. 1. *Nutrition and health.* New York: Macmillan (Pergamon), 1967. Pp. 338-341.
Cowley, J. J., & Griesel, R. D. Some effects of low protein diet on first filial generation of white rats. *Journal of Genetic Psychology,* 1959, **95,** 187-201.
Cowley, J. J., & Griesel, R. D. The development of second-generation low-protein rats. *Journal of Genetic Psychology,* 1963, **103,** 233-242.
Cravioto, J. Nutritional deficiencies and mental performance in childhood. In D. C. Glass (Ed.), *Environmental influences.* New York: Rockefeller University and Russell Sage Foundation, 1968. Pp. 3-51.
Cruikshank, R. M. Animal infancy. In L. Carmichael (Ed.), *Manual of child psychology.* (2nd ed.) New York: Wiley, 1954. Pp. 186-214.
Daniel, E. P., Kline, O. L., & Tolle, C. D. A convulsive syndrome in young rats associated with pyridoxine deficiency, *Journal of Nutrition,* 1942, **23,** 205-216.
Davenport, R. K., Rogers, C. M., & Menzel, E. W., Jr. Intellectual performance of differentially reared chimpanzees: II. Discrimination-learning set. *American Journal of Mental Deficiency,* 1969, **73,** 963-969.
Davenport, V. D., & Davenport, H. W. Brain excitability in pyridoxine-deprived rats. *Journal of Nutrition,* 1948, **36,** 263-275.
Deagle, J., & Furchtgott, E. Passive avoidance in prenatally X-irradiated rats. *Developmental Psychobiology,* 1968, **1,** 90-92.
DeFries, J. C. Prenatal maternal stress in mice: Differential effects on behavior. *Journal of Heredity,* 1964, **55,** 289-295.
DeFries, J. C., Weir, M. W., & Hegmann, J. P. Differential effects of prenatal maternal stress on offspring behavior in mice as a function of genotype and stress. *Journal of Comparative and Physiological Psychology,* 1967, **63,** 332-334.
Denenberg, V. H. Animal studies on developmental determinants of behavioral adaptability. In O. J. Harvey (Ed.), *Experience, structure, and adaptability.* New York: Springer, 1966. Pp. 123-147.
Denenberg, V. H., Karas, G. G., Rosenberg, K. M., & Schell, S. F. Programming life histories: An experimental design and initial results. *Developmental Psychobiology,* 1968, **1,** 3-9. (a)

Denenberg, V. H., & Rosenberg, K. M. Nongenetic transmission of information. *Nature*, 1967, **216**, 549-550.

Denenberg, V. H., Ross, S., & Blumenfield, M. Behavioral differences between mutant and nonmutant mice. *Journal of Comparative and Physiological Psychology*, 1963, **56**, 290-293.

Denenberg, V. H., & Whimbey, A. E. Experimental programming of life histories: Toward an experimental science of individual differences. *Developmental Psychobiology*, 1968, **1**, 55-59.

Denenberg, V. H., Woodcock, J. M., & Rosenberg, K. M. Long-term effects of preweaning and postweaning free-environment experience on rats' problem-solving behavior. *Journal of Comparative and Physiological Psychology*, 1968, **66**, 533-535.

Dispensa, J., & Hornbeck, R. T. Can intelligence be improved by prenatal endocrine therapy? *Journal of Psychology*, 1941, **12**, 209-224.

Doty, L. A., Doty, B. A., Wise, M. A., & Senn, R. K. Effects of postnatal chlorpromazine on discrimination in rats. *Perceptual and Motor Skills*, 1964, **18**, 329-332.

Doty, R. W. Functional significance of the topographical aspects of the retino-cortical projection. In R. Jung & H. Kornhuber (Eds.), *The visual system: Neurophysiology and psychophysics.* Berlin: Springer, 1961.

Eichenwald, H. F., & Fry, P. C. Nutrition and learning. *Science*, 1969, **163**, 644-648.

Essman, W. B., Mendoza, L. A., & Hamburgh, M. Critical periods of maze acquisition development in euthyroid and hypothyroid rodents. *Psychological Reports*, 1968, **23**, 795-800.

Ferreira, A. J. Emotional factors in prenatal environment: A review. *Journal of Nervous and Mental Diseases*, 1965, **141**, 108-118.

Fletcher, J. M., Cowan, E. A., & Arlitt, A. H. Experiments on the behavior of chicks hatched from alcoholized eggs. *Journal of Animal Behavior*, 1916, **6**, 103-137.

Foshee, D. P. Quality of the conditioned stimulus and strain of subjects as variables in avoidance learning (CAR). Unpublished master's thesis, Vanderbilt University, 1960.

Foshee, D. P. Strain responsiveness to stimulus quality: An arousal dimension in avoidance learning (CAR). Unpublished doctoral dissertation, Vanderbilt University, 1962.

Foshee, D. P., Meier, G. W., & Andy, O. J. Neonatal brain damage in monkeys and behavioral development. Paper presented at the meeting of the Southeastern Psychological Association, New Orleans, March 1969.

Fuller, J. L. Early deprivation and later behavior. *Science*, 1967, **158**, 1645-1652.

Fuller, J. L., & Scott, J. P. Heredity and learning ability in infrahuman mammals. *Eugenics Quarterly*, 1954, **1**, 28-43.

Fuller, J. L., & Thompson, W. R. *Behavior genetics.* New York: Wiley, 1960.

Furchtgott, E. Behavioral effects of ionizing radiations. *Psychological Bulletin*, 1956, **53**, 321-334.

Furchtgott, E. Behavioral effects of ionizing radiations: 1955-61. *Psychological Bulletin*, 1963, **60**, 157-199.

Furchtgott, E., Echols, M., & Openshaw, J. W. Maze learning in pre-and neonatally X-irradiated rats. *Journal of Comparative and Physiological Psychology*, 1958, **51**, 178-180.

Glavin, J. P. Rapid oxygen change as possible etiology of RLF and autism. *Archives of General Psychiatry*, 1966, **15**, 301-309.

Grabowski, C. T., & Paar, J. A. The teratogenic effects of graded doses of hypoxia on the chick embryo. *American Journal of Anatomy*, 1958, **103**, 313-348.

Greenbaum, M., & Gunberg, D. L. The effect of neonatal hyperoxia on sexual arousal and emotionality in the male rat. *Animal Behaviour*, 1962, **10**, 28-33.

Greenbaum, M., & Gunberg, D. L. Effects of multiple stress on behavior. (1.) A further study of the effects of neonatal hyperoxia on adult behavior in the rat. Terminal Progress Report on U.S. Public Health Service Grant M-4527 (CL), 1963.

Griffiths, W. J., Jr., & Senter, R. J. The effect of protein deficiency on maze performance of domestic Norway rats. *Journal of Comparative and Physiological Psychology*, 1954, **47**, 41-43.

Grota, L. J., Denenberg, V. H., & Zarrow, M. X. Normal versus caesarian delivery: Effects upon survival probability, weaning weight, and open-field activity. *Journal of Comparative and Physiological Psychology*, 1966, **61**, 159-160.

Hamilton, H. C. The effect of the administration of sodium bromide on the behavior of the offspring: IV. Emotionality (timidity) and experimentally induced seizures. *Journal of Psychology*, 1945, **19**, 17-30.

Hamilton, H. C., & Harned, B. K. The effect of the administration of sodium bromide to pregnant rats on the learning ability of the offspring: III. Three table test. *Journal of Psychology*, 1944, **18**, 183-195.

Harlow, H. F., Akert, A. K., & Schiltz, K. A. The effects of bilateral prefrontal lesions on learned behavior of neonatal, infant, and preadolescent monkeys. In J. M. Warren & K. Akert (Eds.), *The frontal granular cortex and behavior*. New York: McGraw-Hill, 1964. Pp. 126-148.

Harlow, H. F., Blomquist, A. J., Thompson, C. I., Schiltz, K. A., & Harlow, M. K. Effects of induction age and size of frontal lobe lesions on learning in rhesus monkeys. In R. L. Isaacson (Ed.), *The neuropsychology of development: A symposium*. New York: Wiley, 1968. Pp. 79-120. (a)

Harlow, H. F., Harlow, M. K., & Schiltz, K. A. Effects of social isolation on learning by rhesus monkeys. Paper presented at the Second International Congress of Primatology, Atlanta, July 1968. (b)

Harned, B. K., Hamilton, H. C., & Borrus, J. C. The effect of bromide administration to pregnant rats on the learning ability of offspring. *American Journal of the Medical Sciences*, 1940, **200**, 846.

Harned, B. K., Hamilton, H. C., & Cole, V. V. The effect of the administration of sodium bromide to pregnant rats on the learning ability of the offspring. II. Maze-test. *Journal of Pharmacology and Experimental Therapeutics*, 1944, **82**, 215-226.

Haywood, H. C. Experiential factors in intellectual development: The concept of dynamic intelligence. In J. Zubin & G. A. Jervis (Eds.), *Psychopathology of mental development*. New York: Grune & Stratton, 1967. Pp. 69-104.

Haywood, H. C., & Tapp, J. T. Experience and the development of adaptive behavior. In N. Ellis (Ed.), *International review of research in mental retardation*. Volume 1. New York: Academic, 1966. Pp. 109-151.

Henderson, N. D. A genetic analysis of acquisition and retention of a conditioned fear in mice. *Journal of Comparative and Physiological Psychology*, 1968, **65**, 325-330. (a)

Henderson, N. D. The confounding effects of genetic variables in early experience research: Can we ignore them? *Developmental Psychobiology*, 1968, **1**, 146-152. (b)

Hicks, S. P. Radiation as an experimental tool in mammalian developmental neurology. *Physiological Reviews*, 1958, **38**, 337-356.

Himwich, H. E. *Brain metabolism and cerebral disorders*. Baltimore: Williams & Wilkins, 1951.

Hoffeld, D. R., & Webster, R. Effect of injection of tranquilizing drugs during pregnancy on offspring. *Nature*, 1965, **205**, 1070-1072.

Hunt, J. McV. *Intelligence and experience*. New York: Ronald Press, 1961.

Hurder, W. P., & Sanders, A. F. The effects of neonatal anoxia on the maze performance of adult rats. *Journal of Comparative and Physiological Psychology*, 1953, **46**, 61-63.

Hurley, L. S. Approaches to the study of nutrition in mammalian development. *Federation Proceedings*, 1968, **27**, 193-198.

Isaacson, R. L. *The neuropsychology of development: A symposium*. New York: Wiley, 1968.

Isaacson, R. L., Nonneman, A. J., & Schmaltz, L. W. Behavioral and anatomical sequelae of the infant limbic system. In R. L. Isaacson (Ed.), *The neuropsychology of development: A symposium.* New York: Wiley, 1968. Pp. 41-78.

Jewett, R. E., & Norton, S. Effect of tranquilizing drugs on postnatal behavior. *Experimental Neurology*, 1966, **14**, 33-43.

Joffe, J. M. Emotionality and intelligence of offspring in relation to prenatal maternal conflict in albino rats. *Journal of General Psychology*, 1965, **73**, 1-11. (a)

Joffe, J. M. Effect of foster-mothers' strain and pre-natal experience on adult behaviour in rats. *Nature*, 1965, **208**, 815-816. (b)

Kamrin, B. B. The effect of the immune tolerant state on early behaviour of domestic fowl. *Animal Behaviour*, 1967, **15**, 217-222.

Kaplan, S. J. Behavioural manifestations of the deleterious effects of pre-natal X-irradiation. In *Effects of ionising radiation on the nervous system*, Vienna: International Atomic Energy Agency, 1962. Pp. 225-241.

Karrer, R., & Cahilly, G. Experimental attempts to produce phenylketonuria in animals: A critical review. *Psychological Bulletin*, 1965, **64**, 52-64.

Kerr, G. R., Chamove, A. S., Harlow, H. F., & Waisman, H. A. "Fetal PKU:" The effect of maternal hyperphenylalaninemia during pregnancy in the rhesus monkey (*Macaca mulatta*). *Pediatrics*, 1968, **42**, 27-36.

King, J. A., & Eleftheriou, B. E. Effects of early handling upon adult behavior in two subspecies of deermice, *Peromyscus maniculatus*. *Journal of Comparative and Physiological Psychology*, 1959, **52**, 82-88.

Kling, A. Amygdalectomy in the kitten. *Science*, 1962, **137**, 429-430.

Kling, A. Behavioral and somatic development following lesions of the amygdala in the cat. *Journal of Psychiatric Research*, 1965, **3**, 263-273.

Kling, A. Ontogenetic and phylogenetic studies on the amygdaloid nuclei. *Psychosomatic Medicine*, 1966, **28**, 155-161.

Kling, A., & Green, P. C. Effects of neonatal amygdalectomy in the maternally reared and maternally deprived macaque. *Nature*, 1967, **213**, 742-743.

Kling, A., & Tucker, T. J. Sparing of function following localized brain lesions in neonatal monkeys. In R. L. Isaacson (Ed.), *The neuropsychology of development: A symposium.* New York: Wiley, 1968. Pp. 121-146.

Levinson, B. Effects of fetal irradiation on learning. *Journal of Comparative and Physiological psychology*, 1952, **45**, 140-145.

Levinson, B., & Zeigler, H. P. The effects of neonatal X-irradiation upon learning in the rat. *Journal of Comparative and Physiological Psychology*, 1959, **52**, 53-55.

Lucey, J. F., Hibbard, E., Behrman, R. E., Esquivel de Gallardo, F. O., & Windle, W. F. Kernicterus in asphyxiated newborn rhesus monkeys. *Experimental Neurology*, 1964, **9**, 43-58.

McClearn, G. E., & Meredith, W. Behavioral genetics. *Annual Review of Psychology*, 1966, **17**, 515-550.

McGaugh, J. L., Jennings, R. D., & Thomson, C. W. Effect of distribution of practice on the maze learning of descendants of the Tryon maze bright and maze dull strains. *Psychological Reports*, 1962, **10**, 147-150.

Meier, G. W. Delayed effects of natal anoxemia on behavior and electroencephalographic activity. Unpublished doctoral dissertation, Washington University, St. Louis, 1953.

Meier, G. W. Prenatal anoxia in relation to behavioral phenomena in other animals. In W. F. Windle (Ed.), *Neurological and psychological deficits in asphyxia neonatorum.* Springfield, Ill.: Thomas, 1958.

Meier, G. W. Behavioral irradiation effects in the developing chick. *Psychological Reports,* 1959, 5, 3-9.

Meier, G. W. Prenatal anoxia and irradiation: Maternal-fetal relations. *Psychological Reports,* 1961, 9, 417-424.

Meier, G. W. In defense of "Prenatal anoxia and irradiation: Maternal-fetal relations." *Psychological Reports,* 1962, 11, 27-31.

Meier, G. W. Differences in maze performances as a function of age and strain of housemice. *Journal of comparative and physiological Psychology,* 1964, 58, 418-422.

Meier, G. W. Maternal behaviour of feral- and laboratory-reared monkeys following the surgical delivery of their infants. *Nature,* 1965, 206, 492-493.

Meier, G. W. In search of the engram: In the nursery. In G. Newton & S. Levine (Eds.), *Early experience and behavior.* Springfield, Ill.: Thomas, 1968. Pp. 338-364. (a)

Meier, G. W. Use of cats in behavioral research. In W. I. Gay (Ed.), *Methods of animal experimentation.* Volume 3. New York: Academic Press, 1968. Pp. 125-173. (b)

Meier, G. W. Hypoxia. In E. Furchtgott (Ed.), *Pharmacological and biophysical agents and behavior.* New York: Academic Press, 1969, in press. (a)

Meier, G. W. Comments on Sackett's "Innate mechanisms, rearing conditions, and a theory of early experience effects in primates." In M. R. Jones (Ed.), *The prediction of behavior: Early experience.* Coral Gables: University of Miami Press, 1969, in press. (b)

Meier, G. W., & Bunch, M. E. The effects of natal anoxia upon learning and memory at maturity. *Journal of Comparative and Physiological Psychology,* 1950, 43, 436-441.

Meier, G. W., Bunch, M. E., Nolan, C. Y., & Scheidler, C. H. Anoxia, behavioral development, and learning ability: A comparative-experimental approach. *Psychological Monographs,* 1960, 74, (1, Whole No. 488), 1-48.

Meier, G. W., & Foshee, D. P. Indirect foetal irradiation effects in the development of behaviour. In *Effects of ionizing radiation on the nervous system.* Vienna: International Atomic Energy Agency, 1962. Pp. 245-259.

Meier, G. W., & Foshee, D. P. Genetics, age, and the variability of learning performances. *Journal of Genetic Psychology,* 1963, 102, 267-275.

Meier, G. W., & Garcia-Rodriguez, C. Continuing behavioral differences in infant monkeys as related to mode of delivery. *Psychological Reports,* 1966, 19, 1219-1225.

Meier, G. W., & Huff, H. W. Altered adult behavior following chronic drug administration. *Journal of Comparative and Physiological Psychology,* 1962, 55, 469-471.

Meier, G. W., & McGee, R. K. A re-evaluation of the effect of early perceptual experience on discrimination performance during adulthood. *Journal of Comparative and Physiological Psychology,* 1959, 52, 390-395.

Meier, G. W., & Menzel, E. W., Jr. Prenatal oxygen deprivation and subsequent specific behavior dysfunctions. *Science,* 1955, 122, 419-420.

Meier, G. W., & Moss, M. H. Maternal behavior and progeny development of pyridoxine-deprived albino rats. *Journal of Comparative and Physiological Psychology,* 1960, 53, 480-482.

Meier, G. W., & Schutzman, L. H. Mother-infant interactions and experimental manipulation: Confounding or misidentification? *Developmental Psychobiology,* 1968, 1, 141-145.

Mintz, B. *Environmental influences on prenatal development.* Chicago: University of Chicago Press, 1958.

Mirsky, I. A. Communication of affects in monkeys. In D. C. Glass (Ed.), *Environmental influences.* New York: Rockefeller University and Russell Sage Foundation, 1968. Pp. 129-137.

Morra, M. Level of maternal stress during two pregnancy periods on rat offspring behaviors. *Psychonomic Science*, 1965, **3**, 7-8.

Morra, M. Prenatal sound stimulation on offspring visual variation seeking. *Psychonomic Science*, 1968, **12**, 201-202.

Munn, N. L. *Handbook of psychological research on the rat.* Boston: Houghton Mifflin, 1950.

Nelson, M. M., & Evans, H. M. Effect of pyridoxine deficiency on reproduction in the rat. *Journal of Nutrition*, 1951, **36**, 263-275.

Newton, G., & Levine, S. *Early experience and behavior.* Springfield, Ill.: Thomas, 1968.

Nolan, C. Y. The effect of natal anoxemia on the ability to learn a multiple unit maze. Unpublished doctoral dissertation, Washington University, St. Louis, 1953.

Nováková, V. Weaning of young rats: Effect of time on behavior. *Science*, 1966, **151**, 475-476.

Oliverio, A. Effects of different conditioning schedules based on visual and acoustic conditioned stimulus on avoidance learning of two strains of mice. *Journal of Psychology*, 1967, **65**, 131-139.

Oliverio, A., Satta, M., & Bovet, D. Effects of cross-fostering on emotional and learning behavior of different strains of rats. *Life Sciences*, 1968, **7**, 799-806.

Patton, R. A., Karn, H. W., & King, C. G. Studies on the nutritional basis of abnormal behavior in albino rats. II. Further analysis of the effects of inanition and vitamin B_1 on convulsive seizures. *Journal of Comparative Psychology*, 1942, **33**, 253-258.

Peeler, D. F., Jr. The performance of the adult albino rat as a function of cerebral injury and the age of its occurrence. Unpublished master's thesis, Vanderbilt University, 1962.

Peeler, D. F., Jr., & Andy, O. J. The effect of limbic system lesions on the development of fear. Paper presented at the meeting of the Southeastern Psychological Association, New Orleans, February 1969. (a)

Peeler, D. F., Jr., & Andy, O. J. The effect of limbic system lesions on the development of investigatory and play behavior. Paper presented at the meeting of the Midwestern Psychological Association, Chicago, May 1969. (b)

Polidora, V. J., Cunningham, R. F., & Waisman, H. A. Phenylketonuria in rats: Reversibility of behavioral deficit. *Science*, 1966, **151**, 219-221.

Ranck, J., & Windle, W. F. Brain damage in the monkey, Macaca mulatta, by asphyxia neonatorum. *Experimental Neurology*, 1959, **1**, 130-154.

Ressler, R. H. Inherited environmental influences on the operant behavior of mice. *Journal of Comparative and Physiological Psychology*, 1966, **61**, 264-267.

Richardson, J. W. Effects of neonatal anoxia on maze learning in rats. *Proceedings of the Society for Experimental Biology and Medicine*, 1954, **86**, 341-343.

Rimland, B. *Infantile autism: The syndrome and its implications for a neural theory of behavior.* New York: Appleton-Century-Crofts, 1964.

Rowland, G. L., & Woods, P. J. Performance of the Tryon bright and dull strains under two conditions in a multiple T-maze. *Canadian Journal of Psychology*, 1961, **15**, 20-28.

Royce, J. R., & Covington, M. Genetic differences in the avoidance conditioning of mice. *Journal of Comparative and Physiological Psychology*, 1960, **53**, 197-200.

Rozdilsky, B. Kittens as experimental model for study of kernicterus. *American Journal of Diseases of Children*, 1966, **111**, 161-165.

Runner, M. N. Comparative pharmacology in relation to teratogenesis. *Federation Proceedings*, 1967, **26**, 1131-1136.

Russell, L. B. The effects of radiation on mammalian prenatal development. In A. Hollaender (Ed.), *Radiation biology.* Vol. I. *High energy radiation.* Part 2. New York: McGraw-Hill, 1954. Pp. 861-918.

Sackett, G. P. Abnormal behavior in laboratory-reared rhesus monkeys. In M. W. Fox (Ed.), *Abnormal behavior in animals*. Philadelphia: Saunders, 1968. Pp. 293-331.

Sackett, G. P. Innate mechanisms, rearing conditions, and a theory of early experience effects in primates. In M. R. Jones (Ed.), *The prediction of behavior: Early experience*. Coral Gables: University of Miami Press, 1969, in press.

Sackett, G. P., Porter, M., & Holmes, H. Choice behavior in rhesus monkeys: Effect of stimulation during the first month of life. *Science*, 1965, 147, 304-306.

Saxon, S. V. Effects of asphyxia neonatorum on behavior in the rhesus monkey. *Journal of Genetic Psychology*, 1961, 99, 277-282. (a)

Saxon, S. V. Differences in reactivity between asphyxial and normal rhesus monkeys. *Journal of Genetic Psychology*, 1961, 99, 283-287. (b)

Saxon, S. V., & Ponce, C. G. Behavioral defects in monkeys asphyxiated during birth. *Experimental Neurology*, 1961, 4, 460-469.

Schalock, R. L., & Klopfer, F. D. Phenylketonuria: Enduring behavioral deficits in phenylketonuric rats. *Science*, 1967, 155, 1033-1035. (a)

Schalock, R. L., & Klopfer, F. D. Induced phenylketonuria in rats: Behavioural effects. *Journal of Mental Deficiency Research*, 1967, 11, 282-287. (b)

Scharlock, D. P., Tucker, T. J., & Strominger, N. L. Auditory discrimination by the cat after neonatal ablation of temporal cortex. *Science*, 1963, 141, 1197-1198.

Scheidler, C. H. The effects of prenatal anoxemia on learning of white rats. Unpublished doctoral dissertation, Washington University, St. Louis, 1953.

Schwarz, S. Effect of neonatal cortical lesions and early environmental factors on adult rat behavior. *Journal of Comparative and Physiological Psychology*, 1964, 57, 72-77.

Scrimshaw, N. S., & Gordon, J. E. (Eds.) *Malnutrition, learning, and behavior*. Cambridge, Mass.: M.I.T. Press, 1968.

Searle, L. V. The organization of hereditary maze-brightness and maze-dullness. *Genetic Psychology Monographs*, 1949, 39, 279-325.

Severs, J. L., Meier, G. W., Windle, W. F., Schiff, G. M., Monif, G. R., & Fabiyi, A. Experimental rubella in pregnant rhesus monkeys. *Journal of Infectious Diseases*, 1965, 116, 21-26.

Sharp, J. C. Effects of fetal x-irradiation on maze-learning ability and motor coordination in albino rats. *Journal of Comparative and Physiological Psychology*, 1961, 54, 127-129.

Singh, S. D. Conditioned emotional response in the rat: I. Constitutional and situational determinants. *Journal of Comparative and Physiological Psychology*, 1959, 52, 574-578.

Sundby, E. A. The effects of prenatal anoxia on learning behavior of the chick. Unpublished master's thesis, Vanderbilt University, 1959.

Tait, C. D., Jr., Wall, P. D., Balmuth, M., & Kaplan, S. J. Behavioral changes following radiation; II. Maternal behavior and maze performance. *USAF School of Medicine, Special Report*, 1952, 12 pp.

Tapp, J. T. Strain differences in the acquisition of a conditioned emotional response. *Journal of Comparative and Physiological Psychology*, 1964, 57, 464-465.

Thompson, V. E. Neonatal orbitofrontal lobectomies and delayed response behavior in cats. *Dissertation Abstracts*, 1966, 26, 6882.

Thompson, W. D., Jr., & Sontag, L. W. Behavior effects in the offspring of rats subjected to audiogenic seizure during the gestational period. *Journal of Comparative and Physiological Psychology*, 1956, 49, 454-456.

Thompson, W. R. Influence of prenatal maternal anxiety on emotionality in young rats. *Science*, 1957, 125, 698-699.

Thompson, W. R. The inheritance and development of intelligence. In D. Hooker & C. C. Hare (Eds.), *Genetics and the inheritance of integrated neurological and psychiatric patterns*. Baltimore: Williams & Wilkins, 1954. Pp 209-231.

Thompson, W. R. Early environment — its importance for later behavior. In P. H. Hoch & J. Zubin (Eds.), *Psychopathology of childhood*. New York: Grune & Stratton, 1955. Pp. 120-139.
Thompson, W. R. Early environmental influences on behavioral development. *American Journal of Orthopsychiatry*, 1960, **30**, 306-314.
Thompson, W. R., Goldenberg, L., Watson, J., & Watson, M. Behavioural effects of maternal adrenalin injection during pregnancy in rat offspring. *Psychological Reports*, 1963, **12**, 279-284.
Thompson, W. R., & Kano, K. Effects on rat offspring of maternal phenylalanine diet during pregnancy. *Journal of Psychiatric Research*, 1965, **3**, 91-98.
Thompson, W. R., & Olian, S. Some effects on offspring behavior of maternal adrenalin injection during pregnancy in three inbred mouse strains. *Psychological Reports*, 1961, **8**, 87-90.
Thompson, W. R., Watson, J., & Charlesworth, W. R. The effects of prenatal maternal stress on the offspring behavior in rats. *Psychological Monographs*, 1962, **76**, (38, Whole No. 557).
Towbin, A. Mental retardation due to germinal matrix infarction. *Science*, 1969, **164**, 156-161.
Tryon, R. C. Individual differences. In F. A. Moss (Ed.), *Comparative psychology*. (Rev. ed.) New York: Prentice-Hall, 1946. Pp. 330-365.
Tsang, Y. Maze learning in rats hemidecorticated in infancy. *Journal of Comparative Psychology*, 1937, **24**, 221-254. (a)
Tsang, Y. Visual sensitivity of rats deprived of visual cortex in infancy. *Journal of Comparative Psychology*, 1937, **24**, 255-262. (b)
Tucker, T. J., & Kling, A. Differential effects of early vs. late brain damage on visual duration discrimination in the cat. *Federation Proceedings*, 1966, **25**, 207.
Vierck, C. J., Jr., King, F. A., & Ferm, V. H. Effects of prenatal hypoxia upon activity and emotionality of the rat. *Psychonomic Science*, 1966, **4**, 87-88.
Vierck, C. J., Jr., & Meier, G. W. Effects of prenatal hypoxia upon locomotor activity of the mouse. *Experimental Neurology*, 1963, **7**, 418-425.
Vincent, N. M. The effects of prenatal alcoholism upon motivation, emotionality, and learning in the rat. *American Psychologist*, 1958, **13**, 401.
von Abeelen, J. H. F., & Kroes, H. W. Albinism and mouse behaviour. *Genetica*, 1967, **38**, 419-429.
Waisman, H. A., & Harlow, H. F. Experimental phenylketonuria in infant monkeys. *Science*, 1965, **147**, 685-695.
Weir, M. W., & DeFries, J. C. Prenatal maternal influence on behavior in mice: Evidence of a genetic basis. *Journal of Comparative and Physiological Psychology*, 1964, **58**, 412-417.
Werboff, J. Research related to the origins of behavior. *Merrill-Palmer Quarterly*, 1963, **9**, 115-122.
Werboff, J. Prenatal irradiation: Effects on the development of the central nervous system and postnatal behavior. *Science*, 1964, **144**, 84-86.
Werboff, J., & Dembicki, E. L. Toxic effects of tranquilizers administered to gravid rats. *Journal of Neuropsychiatry*, 1962, **4**, 87-91.
Werboff, J., Goodman, I., Havlena, J., & Sikov, M. R. Effects of prenatal x-irradiation on motor performance in the rat. *American Journal of Physiology*, 1961, **201**, 703-706. (a)
Werboff, J., & Gottlieb, J. S. Drugs in pregnancy: Behavioral teratology. *Obstetrical and Gynecological Survey*, 1963, **18**, 420-423.
Werboff, J., Gottlieb, J. S., Dembicki, E. L., & Havlena, J. Postnatal effect of antidepressant drugs administered during gestation. *Experimental Neurology*, 1961, **3**, 542-555. (b)

Werboff, J., Gottlieb, J. S., Havlena, J., & Word, T. J. Behavioral effects of prenatal drug administration in the white rat. *Pediatrics*, 1961, 27, 318-324. (c)

Werboff, J., Havlena, J., & Sikov, M. R. Effects of prenatal X-irradiation on activity, emotionality, and maze-learning ability in the rat. *Radiation Research*, 1962, 16, 441-452.

Werboff, J., & Kesner, R. Learning deficits of offspring after administration of tranquilizing drugs to the mothers. *Nature*, 1963, 197, 106-107.

Wetzel, A. B., Thompson, V. E., Horel, J. A., & Meyer, P. M. Some consequences of perinatal lesions of the visual cortex in the cat. *Psychonomic Science*, 1965, 3, 381-382.

Whimbey, A. E., & Denenberg, V. H. Experimental programming of life histories: The factor structure underlying experimentally created individual differences. *Behaviour*, 1967, 29, 296-314.

Whitley, J. R., O'Dell, B. L., & Hogan, A. G. Effect of diet on maze learning in second-generation rats. Folic acid deficiency. *Journal of Nutrition*, 1951, 45, 153-160.

Wilson, J. G., & Warkany, J. *Teratology. Principles and techniques.* Chicago: University of Chicago, 1965.

Windle, W. F. Asphyxia at birth, a major factor in mental retardation: Suggestions for prevention based on experiments in monkeys. In J. Zubin & G. A. Jervis (Eds.), *Psychopathology of mental development.* New York: Grune & Stratton, 1967. Pp. 140-147.

Windle, W. F., & Becker, R. F. Asphyxia neonatorum: An experimental study in the guinea pig. *American Journal of Obstetrics and Gynecology*, 1943, 45, 183-200.

Winston, H. D. Influence of genotype and infantile trauma on adult learning in the mouse. *Journal of Comparative and Physiological Psychology*, 1963, 56, 630-635.

Winston, H. D. Heterosis and learning in the mouse. *Journal of Comparative and Physiological Psychology*, 1964, 57, 279-283.

Winston, H. D., & Lindzey, G. Albinism and water escape performance in the mouse. *Science*, 1964, 144, 189-191.

Witkop, C. J., Jr. Genetics and nutrition. *Federation Proceedings*, 1967, 26, 148-151.

Young, R. D. Developmental psychopharmacology: A beginning. *Psychological Bulletin*, 1967, 67, 73-86.

Záhlava, J., & Mysliveček, J. Complex evaluation of higher nervous activity in dogs after perinatal destruction of auditory cortex. *Activitas Nervosa Superior*, 1964, 6, 40-41.

Zigler, E. Familial mental retardation: A continuing dilemma. *Science*, 1967, 155, 292-298.

Audiologic Aspects of Mental Retardation

LYLE L. LLOYD

GALLAUDET COLLEGE, WASHINGTON, D.C.[1]

I. Introduction and Historic Perspective 311
II. Incidence of Hearing Impairment 313
III. Methodologic and Intermethod Research 334
    A. Puretone Audiometry 335
    B. Behavior Observation Audiometry (BOA) 342
    C. Speech Audiometry 345
    D. Special Procedures 351
IV. Intramethod Research 354
    A. Puretone Audiometry 354
    B. Speech Audiometry 358
    C. Other Procedures 358
    D. Drugs 359
V. Habilitation 360
VI. Summary and Conclusions 361
    References 363

I. INTRODUCTION AND HISTORIC PERSPECTIVE

The major research contributions on the Audiologic Aspects of Mental Retardation have been made during the past decade. The lack of research in this area prior to the 1950's and 1960's may be rationalized when one considers the recent development of audiology as a profession during the 1940's. The paucity of earlier research may also be rationalized in terms of a previous custodial philosophy and the care of the retarded which has only recently changed to a more habilitative philosophy. However, these rationalizations are not justification when one considers: (1) the effect of sensory deprivation, such as hearing impairment, on the language and mental development of an individual, (2) the common etiologic factors of some hearing impairments and organically caused mental retardation, (3) the high prevalence of physical impairments including abnormal ear canals and middle ear structures found

[1]*Present address:* Mental Retardation Research and Training Committee, National Institute of Child Health and Human Development, National Institutes of Health, Bethesda, Maryland.

among the retarded, and (4) the number of hearing impairments that may be related to poor self-help skills and upper respiratory conditions found among many retarded patients.

The observation that hearing impairment was common among mentally retarded individuals was made by several early writers (e.g., Scheidemann, 1931, p. 189; A. F. Tredgold, 1908, pp. 102–103). With the advent of the electronic audiometer, developed during the 1920's and 1930's, there were numerous hearing surveys of various populations; however, only a few of these early surveys related to the problem of mental retardation. The few early surveys (e.g., Burt, 1937; Madden, 1931; Sterling & Bell, 1930; Waldeman, Wade, & Aretz, 1930, p. 114) yielded inconsistent findings as a result of many variables such as acoustic environment, equipment calibration, sample selection, mental tests, hearing impairment criteria, and screening procedures. Although the committee on the deaf and hard of hearing of the 1930 White House Conference recommended "a survey of children classed as mentally deficient or retarded to ascertain, by means of adequate scientific hearing tests, whether their hearing is normal [Wilber, 1931, p. 322]," such a study was not reported until the late thirties. Abernathy's (1938) doctoral dissertation was the first audiometric report of a relatively large sample of mentally retarded patients. He attempted to investigate the hearing levels of retarded persons regarded as having "average hearing ability." Unfortunately Abernathy's pioneering investigation was not followed up until Birch and Matthews (1951) reported the first audiometric survey of an institution for the retarded. Since the Birch and Matthews study there have been numerous reports on the incidence of hearing impairment among the retarded.

The early work directed toward determining the incidence of hearing impairment may be considered as the first of four major phases of audiologic research with the retarded. The problems encountered in testing some retarded patients resulted in attempts to develop more powerful audiologic assessment procedures. The attempts to develop improved methodologies included numerous inter-method comparison studies and may be considered as the second major phase of audiologic research with the retarded. Although it would seem logical to investigate reliability or conduct intra-method studies prior to inter-method studies, this was not the case. The intra-method reliability, which may be considered the third major phase of audiologic research, was primarily conducted during the 1960's. The fourth phase of audiologic research, which is concerned with habilitation, is just beginning. This chapter reviews these four phases in order of their chronology. Although the review refers to "the retarded" as a population it is assumed that the reader understands the heterogeneity of this population.

II. INCIDENCE OF HEARING IMPAIRMENT

In the first major audiometric study of the retarded, Abernathy (1938) attempted to investigate the hearing levels of retarded persons regarded as having "average hearing ability." He started with an institutional population of 512 individuals who met his criteria of age range of 9 to 20 years and an IQ of 20 to 69. Forty-nine individuals were eliminated because of a history of hearing problems. The remaining 463 subjects were given an otologic examination which eliminated another 32 subjects because of observable ear pathology. The 81 subjects eliminated because of history and/or otologic examination is a higher figure than would be expected in a normal population. Of the 431 subjects assumed to have "average hearing ability" and given audiometric tests, 373 presented data that were essentially average, 5 showed gross deviations in hearing level, and 53 subjects could not be tested or did not provide reliable data. The proposed normative aspects of Abernathy's study are no longer of significance since he was using the old Western Electric 2-A audiometer and most current audiologic data are obtained in terms of either the 1951 ASA or the 1964 ISO references.[1] It is of interest to note that data on 22 subjects retested approximately 9 months later indicated a fair degree of reliability.

Thirteen years later Birch and Matthews (1951) published the first audiometric survey of an institution. They reported an extremely high incidence of hearing loss. Since 1951 there have been 35 published reports of incidence figures based upon 31 studies. The pertinent information from these reports is summarized in Table I. Inspection of Table I reveals considerable variation in percentage figures reported. Such inter-study variation may be accounted for by many factors, including subject selection variables, audiometric variables, and hearing-loss criteria. These factors must be considered in the interpretation of the 35 reports.

---

[1]Currently, research and case study data are reported in sound pressure level (SPL) or more frequently in hearing level (HL). HL is based on biological normative references for each frequency. Most puretone data on the retarded are based on the 1951 ASA reference thresholds, with some more recent reports based upon the 1964 ISO reference thresholds. The relationship between these two references for HL are shown below:

Frequency (Hz or cps)	125	250	500	1000	2000	4000	8000
1951 ASA (in dB SPL)	54.5	39.5	25	16.5	17	15	21
1964 ISO (in dB SPL)	45.5	24.5	11	6.5	8.5	9	9.5
Difference (in dB)	9	15	14	10	8.5	6	11.5

For a more detailed discussion of reference thresholds the reader is referred to Davis and Kranz (1964; Davis, 1965).

TABLE I
AUDIOMETRIC STUDIES OF THE MENTALLY RETARDED (1951–PRESENT) REPORTING FIGURES ON THE
INCIDENCE OF HEARING LOSS AND/OR TESTING DIFFICULTIES

Investigators	N	CA (years-months)	MA (years-months)	IQ	Techniques (freq. range, cps or Hz)	Hearing loss criteria dB re: ASA 1951	Hearing loss (%)
Birch & Matthews (1951)	247	10 to 19	Mdn = 7-0	Mdn = 49	Standard pure tone screening at 15 dB with thresholds for failed freq. (512 to 8,192)	Ciocco-Palmer categories[a] and functioning class[b]	
						(2) I–II	10.1
						(3) I–III	7.3
						(4) I–IV	5.3
						(5) I–(V, VI, VII, VIII)B[b]	3.6
						(6) III–III B[b]	1.6
						(7) (V, VI, VII, VIII) C[b] (V, VI, VII, VIII)	4.9
						(8) IV–IVC[b]	4.5
						(9) II–IIIC[b]	4.5
						(10) II–IIC[b]	4.0
						(11) III–IVC[b]	2.8
						(12) III–(V, VI, VII, VIII)C[b]	2.0
						(13) II–IVC[b]	1.6
						(14) II–(V, VI, VII, VIII)C[b]	1.6
						(15) IV–(V, VI, VII, VIII)C[b]	1.6
						Total	55.4
						B and C[b]	32.7
Schlanger (1953a)	74	8 to 16 M = 12-1	M = 6-8	Above 40	Standard (125 to 12,000)	Binaural speech loss A.M.A. 4–10% or greater	30
Schlanger (1953b)	62	6-11 to 16-7	3-7 to 10-11	39–77	Standard (125 to 12,000)	% not given but several reported as "unreliable" 20 dB or more in four freq. in one or both ears	32

As reported in a secondary source: Schlanger (1961, p. 7)

AUDIOLOGIC ASPECTS OF MENTAL RETARDATION

Also reported as			As reported in a secondary source: Schlanger & Gottsleben (1956, p. 487)	Ciocco-Palmer[c]	
Foale & Paterson (1954)	118	DNG	DNG M = 66		32
	100	10 to 19	Standard with a "yes" response (Freq. not given but assumed to be 512 to 8,192)	(2) I–II	4
				(3) I–III	13
				(4) I–IV	3
				(5) I–(V, VI, VII, VIII)	2
				(6) III–III	0
				(7) (V, VI, VII, VIII) (V, VI, VII, VIII)	6
				(8) IV–IV	1
				(9) II–III	1
				(10) II–II	0
				(11) III–IV	1
				(12) III–(V, VI, VII, VIII)	1
				(13) II–IV	0
				(14) II–(V, VI, VII, VIII)	0
				(15) IV–(V, VI, VII, VIII)	1
				Total	33

[a] *Group I*: Good hearing for all tones. All tones are heard at an intensity equal to or less than 20 dB (decibels). *Group II*: Slight loss for auditory frequencies of the middle range (256 to 1024 cycles). These tones are heard at an intensity between 25 and 35 dB. All other tones are heard as in I. *Group III*: Slight loss for high tones. Tones of 2048; 4096; and 8192 cycles are heard between 20 and 30 dB. All other tones heard as in I. *Group IV*: Marked high tone loss of the abrupt type. Tones of 2048; 4096; and 8192 cycles heard only at an intensity greater than 30 dB. All other tones heard as in I. *Group V*: Marked high tone loss with involvement of low and middle tones. The curves slope downward from left to right and correspond to the high tone loss of the "gradual" typed discussed by Crowe and others. All tones except those of 64 and 128 cycles are heard only at an intensity greater than 20 dB. The impairment for high tones is greater than that for middle tones. *Group VI*: Moderate loss for all tones. Thresholds are between 25 and 45 dB. *Group VII*: Marked loss for all tones. Thresholds are between 45 and 65 dB. *Group VIII*: Extreme loss for all tones. No tone is heard at an intensity less than 55 dB. Here are included cases in which the child did not respond to any tone, even at the maximum intensity of the audiometer. (Ciocco & Palmer, 1941).

[b] Class B and C impairments which may be noticed by patients in ordinary life activities (Birch & Matthews, 1951, p. 391).

[c] See footnote 2 for the Ciocco-Palmer categories. Although Foale and Paterson do not specify their reference levels, it should be noted that since this was a British study, they may have used a British audiometer that may have been calibrated on British Standard #2497 (1954) rather than on the 1951 ASA or its approximate equivalent. Therefore, their use of this classification may be misleading.

TABLE I (Cont'd.)

Investigators	N	CA (years-months)	MA	IQ	Techniques (freq. range, cps or Hz)	Hearing loss criteria dB re: ASA 1951	Hearing loss (%)
P. W. Johnston & Farrell (1954)	270	M = 13-2	DNG	M = 61	Not given but all got audiograms (250 to 6000)	Impairment noticed by patient in ordinary life activities	13
						20 dB or greater at two or more freq. in either ear upon retest.	24
						Additional S's could not cooperate in testing because of low IQ	
Bradley et al. (1955)	30	*High group* 7-11 to 13-6 M = 10-4	3-4 to 9-58 M = 7-3	54-79 M = 67	(250 to 8000) Alternate ear Standard Both of the above	Greater than 20 dB loss at two freq. Same Same	43 30 20
	30	*Middle group* 7-8 to 12-4 M = 8-1	2-8 to 6-0 M = 4-9	34-50 M = 44	Alternate ear Standard	Same Same	47 33
						Not possible to test	13.3
Schlanger & Gottsleben (1956)	210	*S's below 20 years* M = 13.9 ±3.6	M = 7.8 ±3.0	DNG	Hand raising and/or ear choice (125 to 12,000)	II Slight[a]	12.4
						III Moderate	5.2
						.1 Conductive	17.1
						.2 Perceptive and	2.9
						.12 Mixed	0.5
						IV (Hard of hearing)	10.5
						V (deaf)	
						VI (Non-testable)	
						II through V above	38.1

AUDIOLOGIC ASPECTS OF MENTAL RETARDATION

	288	S's above 20 years
		M = 39.6 M = 7.8
		± 15.0 ± 3.0
			DNG	Same	II Slight — 15.3
					III Moderate
					  .1 Conductive — 4.5
					  .2 Perceptive and .2 Mixed — 27.2
					IV (Hard of hearing) — 8.3
					V (Deaf) — 1.4
					VI (non-testable) — 20.8

	498 = Totals for both groups above			Same	II through V above — 56.7 II through V above — 48.8 VI above (non-testable) — 16.5
Schlanger & Gottsleben (1957)	This is a second report of the Schlanger & Gottsleben (1956) study reported above				
Irwin, Hind, & Aronson (1957)	20	9 to 38	DNG	(500, 1000 & 4000) GSR	% HL not investigated — 25 % Inadequate CR or "Emotional Upset" (EU), i.e., no response
				Standard	No voluntary response or EU — 15
				Both standard and GSR	EU — 10

[a] II Slight Loss. Tests at 20–30 dB for two or more frequencies in one or both ears outside speech frequency range. III Moderately severe loss in one or both ears but hearing aid prescription not warranted as residual hearing is adequate for communication. 1 – Conductive loss. 30 dB or more for frequencies 125, 250, 500, 1000 Hz in air conduction test. Bone conduction results usually give improved readings. 2 – Perceptive loss. 30 dB or more from 2000 to 12000 Hz and including frequencies 3000, 4000, 6000, and 8000 Hz, air conduction. Approximately same bone conduction readings of 2000, 3000, 4000 Hz. .12 Mixed loss. Both low and high frequencies depressed. Any combination of .1 or .2. However, one ear is sufficiently intact for speech reception. IV Hard of Hearing. Loss in both ears greater than 30 dB but with residual hearing. Interferes with the hearing of speech. V Deaf in one or both ears. No response in affected ear(s) at any frequency at maximum output of audiometer. VI Invalid responses to audiometric testing – "nontestable" (Schlanger & Gottsleben, 1956, p. 488).

TABLE I (Cont'd.)

Investigators	N	CA (years-months)	MA (years-months)	IQ	Techniques (freq. range, cps or Hz)	Hearing loss criteria dB re: ASA 1951	Hearing loss (%)
Schlanger (1957)	(general information)			DNG	DNG	Hearing impaired	35
						Untestable	16
Kodman et al. (1958a)[e]	84	Young group 7 to 19 M=15-4	M=6-8	M=53-1	Standard ear choice and/or various modifications. Screened at 20 dB then thresholds (250 to 8000)	30 dB or greater at one or more freq. in either ear	19
	105	Old group 20 to 64 M=38-7	M=6-4	M=48	Same	Same	24
	208 = Total of both groups above ("old" and "young") plus 19 "untestable" S's					Same	21
		"untestables" 1 to 4	M=2.4	M=25.5		Non-testable	9
Melmer (1958)	87	7-5 to 21-4 M=14-1	2-6 to 8-0 M=4-4	25-64 M=38	as reported in a secondary source: Wiley & Jacobs (1965) (500 & 2000) GSR Speech audiometry	Not investigated % HL not investigated but 33% (n=10) were untestable	37
Kodman et al. (1959)	31						
Siegenthaler & Krzywicki (1959)[f]	396	School group 14-46 M=21-7	DNG	44-84 M=42	Standard and/or play Screened at 15 dB then threshold (250 to 4000)	(1) Handicapping loss; better ear average 20 dB or more (500–1000–2000)	6.6
						(2) Significant loss: unilateral average 20 dB or more (500–1000–2000)	5.8

Study	N	Age	IQ	MA	Method	Criterion	%
	242	Non-school group 22-47 M=35	DNG	24-82 M=51	Same	(3) Non-significant loss: any freq. 20 dB or more in either ear (250–4000)	5.1
							17.5
						(4) Any of the above	
						(5) Non-testable with audiometer	2.5
						(1) Same as 1 above	15.7
						(2) Same as 2 above	7.9
						(3) Same as 3 above	8.7
						(4) Same as 4 above	32.3
						(5) Same as 5 above	5.0
Rittmanic (1959)	638 = Totals for the above two groups						
	25	Less than 10 years	DNG	DNG	Individual pure-tone (250 to 8000)	Same as 4 above	23
	297	10–19				Greater than 15 dB. Two or more freq. in one or both ears	.4
	244	20–29			Same	Same	19.8
	245	30–39			Same	Same	25.0
	196	40–49			Same	Same	43.2
	137	50–59			Same	Same	57.1
	76	60+			Same	Same	61.7
	Total = 1220[g]	6 to 80			Same	Same	84.2 / 40.5
Wolfe & MacPherson (1959)[h]	26	5-4 to 12-3	1-8 to 3-11	30–129 23–57	Threshold: descending techniques (250 to 4K)	20 dB	% of HL varied considerably from method to method, pre-test to post-

[e]Techniques, some of the results, and some suggestions were also discussed by Kodman et al. (1958b).
[f]This study also provides data for 294 ears (147 girls) on the pattern with degree of hearing loss according to Carhart's 1945 classification system.
[g]Selected on the basis of ability to respond reliably to individual pure tone screening.
[h]This study was designed to evaluate audiometric techniques and audiometric training and not to investigate the incidence of hearing loss.

TABLE I (Cont'd)

Investigators	N	CA (years-months)	MA	IQ	Techniques (freq. range, cps or Hz)	Hearing loss criteria dB re: ASA 1951	Hearing loss (%)
					Blinking light[i]	test, N of S's completing each procedure, etc. But authors estimate (p. 77), "The true incidence of significant hearing loss for the sample.... somewhere between five percent and ten percent"	
					Ear choice		
					Pediacoumeter[i]		
					PGSR		
					Modified SRT		
					Screening: (500 to 6000)	20 dB 1st Test	
					Otometer-toy car[i]	15 dB 2nd Test	
					Otometer-traffic light[i]	Each method was unsuccessful for several children – the N (and %) varied from pre-test to post-test and	
					PGSR	from method to method	
Feinmesser et al. (1959) Roy (1959)	305	Public schools as reported in dsh Abstracts, 1960, p. 13 "Adults"		30–104		Hearing loss Untestable	8.7 37 8.5
Atkinson (1960)	110	8 to 16	DNG	46–80	as reported in a secondary source: Wiley & Jacobs (1965) (500 to 2000)		
	59	DNG	Non-institutionalized		Standard	Two freq. at 20 dB or more in poorer ear	8.5 5.7
					Eye puff	Same	
					Four-choice force-choice	Same	1.9
	51	DNG	Institutionalized		Bekesy	Same	86.0
					Standard	Same	2.0
					Eye puff	Same	0.0

Study	N	Age	IQ	Method	Criterion	Result	%
MacPherson (1960)				Four choice force-choice Bekesy	This Ph.D. Thesis is the same study as that reported above as Wolfe & MacPherson (1959)	Same Same	21.5 64.9
Rigrodsky et al. (1961)	325	5 to 71	DNG	Standard and/or "conditioning techniques" (250 to 8000)	Below 25 to borderline	20 dB or greater for any two freq. in one ear[j] Of the 25% Conductive loss = 11% Perceptive loss = 44% Mixed loss = 45% Untestable	25 6
Gaines (1961)	92	8 to 18	Institutionalized 50-80	Standard and instrumental "train test" conditioning (250 to 8000)	Poorer than 20 dB in one or more freq. in either or both ears	Conventional test Train test Both tests	27.17 31.5 15.2
Schlanger (1961)[k]	199[l]	M=15-7	M=5-1	M=36	(500 to 4000)[m]	Failure to respond to two	

[i] These techniques may be considered as various forms of instrumental conditioning procedures like the peep show, slide show and/or COR methods.

[j] This article also gives a summary of the types of hearing loss according to the intellectual levels of functioning and summary of the incidence of hearing loss according to the etiological classification code of the American Association of Mental Deficiency. The authors report they used the criterion established by Schlanger and Gottsleben (1956) to determine the distribution of the various types of hearing loss but then summarize the system as follows: "According to this system a conductive loss is 20 decibels or greater for frequencies 250, 500, 1000 cycles per second. A perceptive loss was a depression of the frequencies 2000, 4000, 8000 cycles per second. A mixed loss was a depression of both low and high frequencies. [Rigrodsky et al., 1961, p. 36]." It should be noted that the audiometric configuration can provide high misleading data relative to the conductive-perceptive classification scheme, and that the authors did not mention the most critical single item in such a classification system, i.e., the air-bone relationship.

[k] Data are also provided on the type (neural, conductive or mixed) and degree of hearing impairment for ears (p. 67) and subjects (p. 68).

[l] These subjects were selected from 400 or the basis of suitability for audiometric testing.

[m] The technique(s) used for the incidence figures is not specified.

TABLE I (Cont'd.)

Investigators	N	CA (years-months)	MA	IQ	Techniques (freq. range, cps or Hz)	Hearing loss criteria dB re: ASA 1951	Hearing loss (%)
155 of the above (excluding 44 because of testing problems)		DNG	DNG	DNG	Standard play Ear choice GSR SRT	or more freq. at 30 dB or more in either ear	32
					Same	Same	42
Schlanger (1962)[n]	199[l]	M = 15-7	M = 5-1	M = 36.4	Same	Same approximately	33[n] 9[n]
						20 dB or greater in one or both ears. N = 101	
Pantelakos (1963)	537	DNG Murdock, N. C. School (state institution)	DNG	DNG	(250 to 8000) Ear choice Hand	Group II. A. Slight hearing loss in one or both ears for one or more freq. (20–30 dB) Type:[o] 1. Perceptive $N = 19$ 2. Conductive $N = 6$ 3. Mixed $N = 2$ B. Hearing normal to 30 dB in low and mid tones with moderate to marked high tone loss. $N = 10$ Group III. Moderately severe hearing loss in one or both ears (30–60 dB)	6.8 6.0

Study	N	Population	%	Method	Results

LaCrosse & Bidlake (1964)	384	Institutionalized	Moderate 8.17%; Very severely retarded 8.53%	Instrumental conditioning (250, 750, 1000, 1500, 2000, 4000 & 8000)	Type:[o]
					  1. Perceptive $N = 14$
					  2. Conductive $N = 15$
					  3. Mixed $N = 3$ — 2.6
					Group IV. Severe hearing loss (60 to over 100 dB)
					Type:[o]
					  1. Perceptive $N = 10$
					  2. Conductive $N = 2$
					  3. Mixed $N = 2$
					  $N = 2$ — .4
					Group V. Deaf in one or both ears at any freq. at maximum output of audiometer and tuning forks.
					Group VI. Untestable or invalid responses. $N = 16$ — 3.0
					Total $N = 101$ — 18.8
					30–20 dB with special emphasis on 1500 and 4000 cps — 7.55
					Unreliable — 7.81

Webb et al. (1964)	369	DNG Institutionalized		(500, 1000 & 2000)	Poorer than 20 dB in

[n] This article mainly concerns "the effects of training upon audiometry," and cites data previously reported (Schlanger, 1961). It should also be noted that it seems that based upon 65 subjects selected from the original 199 Schlanger (1962, p. 274) states, "The decrease in incidence from screening to final testing was from 35% to approximately 9% of the 199 subjects."

[o] Type of loss was not defined audiometrically but was determined by otolaryngology residents. Data are also provided on the types of pathology.

TABLE I (Cont'd.)

Investigators	N	CA (years-months)	MA	IQ	Techniques (freq. range, cps or Hz) pure tone audiometry[p]	Hearing loss criteria dB re: ASA 1951	Hearing loss (%)
	1093		Mt. Pleasant			either ear at one or more test freq.	25
						Less than two observable responses at 20 dB	24
Schlanger & Christensen (1964)[q]	53	15-8	5-0	M = 36	Standard (500 to 4000)	Failure to respond to two or more freq. at 30 dB or poorer in either ear	32
McIntire, Menolascino, & Wiley (1965)	60 Testable of the total N below	DNG	DNG	DNG (Mongoloids)	DNG	DNG	
						"Severe Hearing Sensitivity Loss"	1.7
						"Mild Hearing Disorder"	6.7
						Total	8.4
	86	DNG	DNG	Moderate to profound retardation (Mongoloids)	DNG	Hearing loss total from above	5.8
						"not ascertainable" or "not testable"	30.2
Wiley & Jacobs (1965)	87 Functional	DNG	DNG	Mildly retarded	Puretone (500, 1000, 2000) and/or speech audiometry	Unilateral loss	7
						Bilateral loss (<30 dB)	6
						Bilateral loss (>30 dB)	0
						Questionable results	8
	43 Organic	DNG	DNG		Same	Unilateral loss	9
						Bilateral loss (<30 dB)	0
						Bilateral loss (>30 dB)	2
						Questionable results	9
	Total = 130	DNG	DNG		Same	Unilateral loss	8
						Bilateral loss (<30 dB)	4
						Bilateral loss (>30 dB)	1

AUDIOLOGIC ASPECTS OF MENTAL RETARDATION   325

Study	N	Age	?	IQ	Method	Criterion / Results	%
Lloyd & Reid (1965)[p]	608 (total institutional population)	6 to 25	DNG	MI-I to V borderline normal to "untestable"	(Octaves 250–8000 plus 6000) Standard ear choice play, and/or slide show	Questionable results Poorer than 15 dB in either or both ears at one or more freq.	8 21.9
						Difficult-to-Test (DTT) — were not responding after 3 sessions	22.9
	469		Same as above but excluding those classed as DTT		Same	Poorer than 15 dB in either or both ears at one or more freq.	29.6
Glovsky (1966)	38	12.8 to 52.8	3.2 to 52.8 M=30.9 (Mongoloid)	19 to 71 M=36	(Octaves 250–8000) "Conditioning" Key tapping with a musical toy then puretones	Same but criteria based on 500, 1000 & 2000 Better ear Average loss 15 dB or more	10.23
						20 dB or poorer at any two freq. in one ear	
						Conductive[s]	2.6
						Perceptive[s]	52.6
						Mixed[s]	
						"Could not be conditioned"	21
Michigan Department of Health (1966)	688	12.6	DNG	M=64 from Public Sch. Spec. Classes	(Octaves 500–8000) various standard and/or play	15 dB or more at one or more freq.	11

[p] They present additional data on other testing procedures, such as EEG and behavior observation audiometry (which they call the PALI), but percentage of hearing loss figures are not given for any of these other methods which were used with small samples of subjects.

[q] This article mainly concerns "the Effects of Training upon Audiometry," and cites data previously reported (Schlanger, 1961, 1962).

[r] Lloyd and Reid (1965) is the preliminary report on the population at Parsons (Kansas) State Hospital and Training Center as of February, 1965 and was presented to a conference in March (see Lloyd & Frisina, 1965). Later Lloyd and Reid (1967) made a more detailed report of the population at Parsons as of September 1965.

[s] Although the author reports using the criterion established by Schlanger and Gottsleben (1956) to determine the various types of hearing loss, his restatement of the criterion, like Rigrodsky et al. (1961), gives audiometric configuration factors rather than the critical factor of air-bone relationship. Again it should be noted that audiometric configuration can provide misleading data relative to type of hearing loss.

TABLE 1 (Cont'd.)

Investigators	N	CA (years-months)	MA	IQ	Techniques (freq. range, cps or Hz)	Hearing loss criteria dB re: ASA 1951	Hearing loss (%)
Dansinger & Madow (1966)	967	6 to 85	DNG[t]	DNG[t]	Verbal auditory screen for children	27 dB or poorer ($N=143$) "Untestable"	14.7
	857	Same as above but "for whom there were valid tests"[t]				27–35 dB in better ear 10.1	11.3
						39–43 dB in better ear 2.5	
						47 dB or more in better ear 4.1	
Lloyd & Reid (1967)	638 (total institutional population)	6 to 22	DNG	MI & AB -I to -IV	(Octaves 250–8000 plus 6000) Standard ear choice play and/or slide show	Poorer than 15 dB in either ear at one, or more, freq. ($N=138$)	22[u]
					Same as above	DTT ($N=156$)	24[u]
	482	Same as above but excluding those classed as DTT				Based upon air-bone gap an otologic exam ($N=138$)	
						Conductive ($N=60$) 43%[u]	
						Sensori-neural ($N=41$) 30%[u]	
						Mixed ($N=25$) 18%[u]	
						Undetermined ($N=12$) 9%[u]	
					Same tech. as above (Octaves 250–8000 plus 6000)	Poorer than 15 dB in either, or both, ear at one, or more, freq.	29[u]
					Same	Poorer than 15 dB in either ear at one, or more, freq.	24[u]

				(Octaves 250–8000 plus 6000)	Poorer than 25 dB in either ear at one, or more, freq. 19^u
				(Octaves 250–4000)	Poorer than 15 dB in either ear at one, or more, freq. 20^u
				Same	Poorer than 15 dB in each ear at one, or more, freq. 13^u
				(4000 only)	Poorer than 15 dB in either ear 18^u
				(Octaves 500, 1000, and 2000)	Average threshold of 15 dB, or poorer, for the three freq. in either ear 16^u
				Same	Average threshold of 15 dB, or poorer, for the three freq. in the better ear 10^u
Fulton & Giffin (1967)	2290 (of a total institutional population of 2483)	0-6 to 87 M = 25	DNG	Borderline to profound	Average poorer than 25 dB re ISO 1964 (or about 15 dB ASA) for puretone. DNG for speech and informal techniques ($N = 629$) 27.4^v Could not test, unclassified, and non-ambulatory 9.6 Of the 629 hearing impaired, Degree was: 26 to 45 dB ISO 64.5%^{v}

---

^{t}They included patients that could identify the pictures but excluded those "already diagnosed as deaf" and those that "were total care residents, profoundly retarded . . . and adults that could not perform routine tasks." There are data for sex and age groups and other hearing loss criteria.

^{u}A further breakdown of the data is provided according to AB, MI, and sex.

^{v}Considerable data are provided on functioning level, detailed otologic diagnosis, surgical intervention.

TABLE 1 (Cont'd.)

Investigators	N	CA (years-months)	MA	IQ	Techniques (freq. range, cps or Hz)	Hearing loss criteria dB re: ASA 1951	Hearing loss (%)
Nober (1968)	1074	1 to 90	DNG[w]	DNG[w]	(Octaves 500 to 4000 plus 6000) Group screening Hand raising	46 to 75 dB ISO 25.6%[v] 76 dB ISO or more 9.8%[v] Type based on otologic exam and audiometric data was: Conductive 6.2%[v] Sensori-neural 26.7%[v] Mixed 4.5%[v] Undifferentiated 62.6%[v] 30 dB ISO at any freq.[w]	46
	639	1 to 90	"Conducted when feasible"		(Same) Individual screening Ear choice Hand raising "Yes", "No" verbal response	Same[w]	45
	1884	1 to 90	Attempted with "lower level patients" unable to participate in, or failed the group screening		Warblet reflex Screening (3K)	80 dB SPL[w]	46
	324 (648 ears)	1 to 90	"Extremely low level patients"		(Octaves 250–4000 plus 6000) AC thresholds	Average of 500, 1000 & 2000 *dB re ISO right ear[w] left ear[w]*	
			Patients who failed individual screening usually				

Study	N	CA	MA	Screening procedure	dB range	n	Type of loss	%
Total =	3747			referred to as DTT				
Fulton & Lloyd (1968)	79 (Total institution population of Mongoloids)	1 to 90 7-11 to 27-2 M = 15-3 Rome (N.Y.) State School	DNG[w] DNG M = 30.5[x]	DNG[w] Ascending-descending pulsating-tone Earchoice, hand raising and other responses Various combinations of the above (500, 1000 & 2000) Relatively conventional procedures plus TROCA	0–30 31–50 51–70 71–90 90+	n = 104, n = 128 n = 106, n = 86 n = 42, n = 40 n = 16, n = 19 n = 26, n = 21	DNG[w] Type of loss based upon otologic exam and air-bone gap. Degree is based on average in better ear. Conductive 26–45 dB ISO (n = 16) 45–65 dB ISO (n = 1) Sensori-neural 26–45 dB ISO (n = 4) 46–65 dB ISO (n = 3) Mixed 26–45 dB ISO (n = 4) 46–65 dB ISO (n = 3) DTT even with TROCA and behavior observation procedures	21.5[x] 8.9[x] 8.9[x] 2.5[x]

[w] The three screening procedures are for pass-fail rather than determination of hearing impairment, per se. Although DNG is stated for many of the subject description tables, it should be noted that several tables are provided grouping results according to AAMD Etiologic Classifications, CA, MA, and previous diseases.
[x] Data are also presented according to AB and MI level, and more detailed otologic diagnosis and disposition.

The chronological age (CA), mental age (MA) and general behavior of the subjects selected as a sample are critical variables affecting the obtained results. Such factors are related to the type of hearing impairment and degree of testing success expected in the general population as well as in a sample of retarded persons. Sampling errors could be a major source of error in the percentage figure obtained if small samples of less than 50 to 100 subjects are used since the expected incidence of hearing impairment in the general population is small (approximately 4% depending upon the criteria employed). Unfortunately, many investigators based their incidence figures upon relatively small samples of readily testable and cooperative (in some cases relatively high-level) subjects.

Audiometric techniques (including instructions, response mode, behavior modification procedures, and stimuli), acoustic environment, experience (and training) of the audiologist (or examiner), audiometric calibration, amount of time used, etc., are critical variables affecting the obtained results. These factors have varied considerably from study to study. In some cases these variables have not been specified while others have been lax in controlling these variables.

The hearing-loss criteria have varied from a relatively lax criterion of "poorer than 15 dB in either or both ears at one or more frequencies" for seven frequencies from 250 to 8000 Hz to a relatively stringent criterion of "failure to respond to two or more frequencies at 30 dB or poorer in either ear" for a frequency range of 500 to 4000 Hz. As one would expect, the studies which used less stringent criteria, in general, showed a higher percentage of hearing loss than did the studies which used more stringent criteria. In 1958 Kodman discussed the inconsistencies due to differences in criteria and recommended using "the criterion of a 30 dB or greater loss at one or more frequencies in either ear [Kodman, 1958, p. 676]." In light of more recent data, a less stringent criterion seems appropriate (Darley, 1961, p. 31; Eagles, Wishik, Doerfler, Melnick, & Levine, 1963; Lloyd, 1966b).

Considering the inter-study variations and the above mentioned factors, it is apparent from the data in Table I that there is general agreement in finding a higher incidence of hearing impairment among the mentally retarded than would be expected from a non-retarded sample of the same age. The studies employing sample sizes of 200 or more all found a high incidence of hearing impairment (Birch & Matthews, 1951; Dansinger & Madow, 1966; Fulton & Giffin, 1967; P. W. Johnston & Farrell, 1954; Kodman, Powers, Philip, & Weller, 1958; LaCrosse & Bidlake, 1964; Lloyd & Reid, 1965, 1967; Michigan Department of Health, 1966; Nober, 1968; Pantelakos, 1963; Rigrodsky, Prunty, & Glovsky,

1961; Rittmanic, 1959; Roy, 1959; Schlanger & Gottsleben, 1956; Siegenthaler & Krzywicki, 1959; Webb, Kinde, Weber, & Beedle, 1964; Wiley & Jacobs, 1965). A few of the studies presented in Table I reported relatively low incidence figures for their samples, but they used highly selective and/or extremely small samples. Two studies of retarded children in public school programs corroborated the general finding with institutionalized retardates that, in general, there is a higher incidence of hearing impairment among the retarded than the non-retarded (Feinmesser, Baubergertell, & Bilski-Hirsch, 1959; Michigan Department of Health, 1966).

Although there is agreement among the larger sample studies, some writers (e.g., Atkinson, 1960; LaCrosse & Bidlake, 1964; Schlanger, 1961) have questioned such findings of a greater incidence of hearing loss among the retarded than among the non-retarded and have suggested that puretone audiometry is not a reliable and valid estimate of the retardate's auditory sensitivity. The puretone data reported by some investigators may be questioned if the audiometric variables were not carefully controlled, but when such variables are controlled there is no a priori reason to question the puretone data obtained from the retarded. The audiometric variables were controlled in several of the major studies presented in Table I. For example, Lloyd and Reid (1967) reported data obtained by a staff experienced in working with the retarded using audiometric procedures demonstrated to be reliable (Lloyd, 1965a; Lloyd & Melrose, 1966b; Lloyd, Reid, & McManis, 1968a) in an appropriate acoustic environment, with equipment monitored for calibration. The puretone data were collected as part of a complete audiologic assessment procedure within the framework of an on-going audiology program which facilitated the cross checking of the data. In addition to intra- and inter-audiometric procedure checks, the audiometric data were checked against otologic findings and other outside criteria, such as speech and language performance. Such reliability and validity checks are an essential part of an audiologic assessment program and are critical in the consideration of incidence reports.

The high incidence figure based on the larger and more carefully controlled audiometric studies is corroborated by otologic reports. Otologists (Fulton & Giffin, 1967; Hilson, 1966; Kimmich, 1965; Kock & Serra, 1962; Pantelakos, 1963; Sprinkle, Fitz-Hugh, Harden, & Waldren, 1965) have provided information on the otologic aspects of mental retardation. Kimmich's paper was a general discussion paper while the other five papers presented rather detailed otologic data. These papers, combined with a preliminary report on otologic findings in one institution (Nudo, 1965), and several incidence studies that concerned themselves with otologic examinations as a part of the determination of the type of hearing impairment (Fulton & Lloyd, 1968; Lloyd & Reid, 1967; Michigan Department of Health, 1966) indicate considerably more otologically abnormal ears among the retarded than one would expect to find in the general population. The audiologic-otologic studies reveal many conductive impairments which may partially relate to the abundance of young subjects. However, age cannot totally account for the large number of conductive impairments. It would appear that limited self-care skills and habits significantly contributed to conductive impairments. Often the retarded have cerumen which is so severely impacted that cerumenalitic agents and general anesthesia are required for removal. Perforated tympanums, suppurative middle and external ear conditions, and scarred and disrupted tympanums from prior active pathologies are common. It was also noted that the retarded demonstrate a higher proportion of congenital middle-ear anomalies than the normal population (Fulton & Giffin, 1967; Fulton & Lloyd, 1968; Nudo, 1965; Pantelakos, 1963).

In addition to the audiologic-otologic studies, there are a priori reasons to assume a higher incidence of hearing impairment among the retarded (Lloyd, 1965a, 1965c; Lloyd & Frisina, 1965; Lloyd & Reid, 1967; Lloyd & Young, 1969). Lloyd & Reid (1967) discussed the logic of their data and the generally high incidence of hearing impairment as follows:

> Lloyd (1965a, 1965c) and Lloyd and Frisina (1965) have previously cited several reasons why they felt it reasonable to assume a higher incidence of hearing impairment among the retarded than is usually found among the non-retarded. These reasons included the high number of sensori-neural pathologies (including brain damage) and congenital anomalies that are etiologically related to MR, along with the frequently poor self-care skills (or habits). Considering the organic causes of MR and viewing the auditory system as an integral part of the sensori-neural systems, it is apparent that there is a higher probability of hearing impairment among the retarded. Rubella, mumps, and influenza during the first trimester of pregnancy and kernicterus are often cited as causes of congenital brain damage and subsequent retardation (Goldberg, Foster, Segerson, and Baumeister, 1963; Kodman, 1963; Krugman, 1965; Levine, 1951; Masland, Sarason, and Gladwin, 1958; Pasamanick and Lilienfeld, 1955; President's Panel, 1962; Tredgold and Soddy, 1963; Yannet, 1962). These four conditions are also frequently cited as common causes of congenital hearing problems (Davis and Silverman, 1960; Krugman, 1965; Levine, 1951; Newby, 1964). Similarly, meningitis may cause MR and sensori-neural hearing problems. The probability of a second defect or problem in the person with any congenital anomaly or physical weakness is higher than it is for the individual without the first anomaly or weakness (Miller and Miller, 1959; Myklebust, 1958; Pasamanick and Lilienfeld, 1955). Anthropmetric data has demonstrated that institutionalized MR patients diverge considerably from physical normality (Benda, 1960; Goldberg, et al., 1963; Mosier, Grossman, and Dingman, 1965). Therefore, the retarded with organic etiologies may frequently have sensori-neural or conductive hearing impairments of related origin.

Any group that has a high incidence of diseases and infections (especially the upper respiratory type), such as children with Down's Syndrome (Benda, 1960), has an increased probability of related conductive hearing impairments such as otitis media. Since poor self-care frequently results in hearing problems and may compound the effects of such conditions, there is an increased probability for the retarded, as a result of cultural deprivation and other cultural-familial causes, to have hearing impairments related to the factors causing the retardation.

Furthermore, since sensory deprivation (such as a hearing impairment) may, in and of itself, cause retardation (Heber, 1961; Kodman, 1963; President's Panel, 1962), the finding of a relatively high incidence of hearing loss among the retarded seems plausible [Lloyd & Reid, 1967, pp. 754–756].

The literature in general, research data in particular, and logic clearly demonstrate that hearing impairment is a major problem among the retarded. The magnitude of this problem has major programmatic implications. Attempts at the habilitation of many retarded persons is questionable unless audiologic services are included in the programming. The audiology program must include comprehensive diagnostic and (re)habilitative services. A minimum of service should include at least: (1) a puretone screening of all persons seen for differential diagnosis, (2) audiologic assessment and otolaryngologic examination depending upon screening results, (3) appropriate habilitation, and (4) some systematic rescreening (and hearing conservation) procedures. Audiology must have a functional relationship with otologic (and other medical) services as well as the non-medical habilitation services. The habilitative program must include direct services (e.g., auditory training, hearing aid guidance, language therapy, speech therapy, and lip reading), and indirect services. Much of the communicative and educational effects of hearing impairment can be alleviated by providing the retarded individual's parents, teachers, therapists (e.g., music, occupational, physical, and recreational) and, in the case of institutional programs, the patient care staff (e.g., nurses and aides) with appropriate audiologic information and assistance in coping with hearing impairments.

The data and logic presented should provide sufficient justification for audiologic services in all programs for the retarded; therefore, there is no longer a need to survey the incidence of hearing impairments among the retarded in general. However, there is a need to investigate the specific types of hearing impairment found within specific diagnostic categories of mental retardation. Down's Syndrome is the only specific diagnostic category to be researched. These investigations indicate patients with Down's Syndrome have a high incidence of conductive impairments which may be related to: (1) upper respiratory tract infections involving the sinuses and middle ear (tympanic cavity), (2) poor drainage of the sinuses and middle ear due to abnormal skull development, and (3) congenital anomalies directly affecting the transmission capacity of the outer and middle ear (Fulton & Lloyd, 1968; Hilson, 1966; Kock & Serra, 1962; Yannet, 1964).

The audiologic aspects of other diagnostic categories should be investigated. Of particular interest would be those conditions that could result in retardation and/or hearing impairment. Clinical reports indicate hearing deviations associated with various physiologically caused retardation including Albright's Hereditary Osteodystrophy, Bielschowsky-Jansky Disease, Hurler's Syndrome, Spielmeyer-Vogt Disease, Oculo-Cerebro-Renal Syndrome, Ring-Chromosome 18, Sanflippo Syndrome, Tay-Sachs Disease, Trisomy 13-15, Turner's Syndrome, and phenylketonuria (Bochenek & Kus, 1958; Gellis & Feingold, 1968; Little, 1962; Richards, 1950, Richards & Rundle, 1959; Volk, 1964), but to date there have not been any controlled audiologic-otologic studies of the type and degree of hearing impairment in these syndromes. Through gaining a fuller understanding of such conditions this research could have major implications for program development and preventive medicine.

The high incidence of congenital ear anomalies found among the retarded (Fulton & Giffin, 1967; Fulton & Lloyd, 1968; Nudo, 1965; Pantelakos, 1963) has research implications for audiologists. Audiologic and otologic data should be related to embryonic development. Furthermore, the retarded offer exceptional opportunities for the investigation of the auditory system relative to its parent central nervous system (CNS) by relating auditory behavior to known CNS involvements of known etiologies. Institutionalized retarded populations would include a high proportion of subjects with known brain damage. Non-institutional programs would offer similar opportunities. Such investigation would require collaboration with medical fields such as genetics, neurology, and otolaryngology. Improved audiology services in both residential and non-residential programs for the retarded would enhance research in these areas.

The need for audiology services is apparent, but a limited survey of 142 state institutions indicates there is a definite lack of organized audiologic and otologic programming for the retarded (Fulton & Reid, 1967). This investigation should be replicated in expanded scope to include both residential and non-residential programs. Additional data are needed relative to the barriers to developing audiology programs.

II. METHODOLOGIC AND INTERMETHOD RESEARCH

In addition to a high incidence of hearing impairment many of the studies reported in Table I indicate many "untestable," "non-testable," and difficult-to-test subjects. The use of the term "difficult-to-test," rather than such terms as "untestable" and "non-testable," is preferred as a point of basic philosophy. Difficult-to-test assumes the individual is testable when the appropriate methods are utilized, and that the untestability lies with the examiner and/or procedure and not necessarily with something inherent in the individual. This does not imply that the appropriate method has been developed for each individual. The testing difficulties encountered in testing some retarded individuals resulted in attempts to improve audiometric procedures and a number of intermethod comparisons.

Except for material or tangible reinforcement operant conditioning audiometry (TROCA) procedures (see: Lloyd, Spradlin, & Reid, 1968b) the methodologic research has involved the application of procedures developed for testing children and other non-retarded individuals. These procedures have been discussed elsewhere (e.g., Davis & Silverman, 1960, pp. 228–240; Frisina, 1963; Giolas, 1969; Goldstein, 1963; Hogan, 1969; Lloyd, 1966a; Lloyd & Young, 1969; Newby, 1964, pp. 185–201; Price, 1969). Most of the methodology studies with the retarded have employed puretone stimuli to test auditory sensitivity with only limited research relative to speech audiometry and special procedures for differential diagnosis of site of lesion.

A. Puretone Audiometry

Audiometry is based upon basic stimulus-response relationships. When the primary question is one of auditory sensitivity puretone stimuli are desirable because they can be accurately specified and controlled (other types of stimuli will be considered in subsequent sections). Audiometric procedures have developed using both operants and respondents. Procedures involving operant or "voluntary" responses are frequently referred to as behavioral audiometry while procedures involving respondent or reflexive responses are frequently referred to as electrophysiologic audiometry. The primary advantage of behavioral over electrophysiologic audiometry is that behavioral audiometry provides an index to the basic *functional* relationship between a person and his environment in terms of auditory input, and an output.

1. BEHAVIORAL AUDIOMETRY

The preponderance of audiometric research, both with the retarded and the non-retarded, has involved behavioral audiometry. For a general discussion of behavioral audiometry the reader is referred to Frisina (1963, pp. 137–152) and Lloyd (1966a).

The ear choice and modified ear choice methods (Atkinson, 1960; Bradley, Evans, & Worthington, 1955; Curry & Kurtzrock, 1951; Lloyd, 1965a; MacPherson, 1960; Schlanger, 1961; Wolfe & MacPherson,

1959), a four-choice-forced-choice procedure (Ickes, 1960), and play audiometry (Barr, 1955; Bradshaw, 1961; Lloyd, 1965a; Lloyd & Melrose, 1966a, 1966b; Schlanger, 1961; Webb et al., 1964) have been successfully used with many retarded individuals. These procedures have been most successful with mildly and moderately retarded or those in the measured intelligence (MI) level $-1, -2, -3$ and in some cases MI = -4 (the MI classification scheme is presented by Heber, 1961). The frequent success of play audiometry, which includes high probability behavior and a pleasurable activity for most children, coupled with social reinforcement, demonstrates the effectiveness of positive reinforcement. Furthermore, the use of simple straight forward responses in such procedures increases the likelihood of obtaining puretone data from retarded persons.

Several investigators have focused upon instrumentation and various forms of reinforcement in developing procedures to obtain data from more severely retarded subjects (MI level -4 and -5). The reinforcement devices and items used with the retarded include *electrical toys* (D'Asaro & Grey, 1964; Fulton, 1962; Fulton & Graham, 1966; Wolfe & MacPherson, 1959), *trains* (Gaines, 1961), *edibles* (Bricker & Bricker, 1969; LaCrosse & Bidlake, 1964; Lloyd, 1968; Lloyd et al., 1968b; Meyerson & Michael, 1960, 1964; Spradlin & Lloyd, 1965; Spradlin, Lloyd, Hom, & Reid, 1968), *liquids* (Bricker & Bricker, 1969), *slides and film strips* (Lloyd, 1965c; Weaver, 1965), *assorted trinkets* (Meyerson & Michael, 1960, 1964), *toys* (Knox, 1960), and *lights* (MacPherson, 1960; Wolfe & MacPherson, 1959). In general, these were successful with many retardates including several that could not be tested with other procedures. Some investigators concluded that their instrumentation provided equal or better thresholds and a high success rate; while, in fact, it was the application of basic reinforcement principles that produced success. In these procedures the success frequently resulted from having an activity or item that was truly reinforcing to particular individuals while activities or items used in other procedures did not have such reinforcing properties. The success of these procedures also resulted from reinforcing only desired responses to the discriminative stimulus (S^D), and the immediacy of the reinforcement. It should be noted that the lack of success with standard hand raising, ear choice, and play procedures frequently results from the following: (1) the play activity and the behavior of the examiner do not have reinforcing properties for the particular subject, (2) human error in administering play and social reinforcement at inappropriate times, and/or (3) latency of administering reinforcement. These factors may have relatively little influence on testing reasonably intelligent, cooperative subjects, but they are of major importance in attempting to test the severely retarded individual. Basic operant principles and their application to audiometry are discussed in greater detail elsewhere (e.g., Lloyd, 1966a, 1968; Lloyd et al., 1968b; Spradlin, 1965; Spradlin, Locke, & Fulton, 1969).

The application of operant principles has resulted in considerable success with many severely and profoundly retarded, but there is a need for further investigation of behavior modification in audiometry. Some of the initial research was done with continuous reinforcement (CRF) (Lloyd et al., 1968b) while other studies have used fixed ratio (FR) schedules (Bricker & Bricker, 1969; Meyerson & Michael, 1960, 1964; Spradlin et al., 1969), but there has not been any systematic research comparing the maintaining of stimulus control at threshold level with different reinforcement schedules. Based upon clinical observation and logic, the primarily descending method of threshold searching is recommended (Lloyd, 1966a; Lloyd et al., 1968b), but systematic research in this area is also lacking. The one investigation that compared the descending with the ascending method failed to find any differences (Spradlin et al., 1969), but further research is needed since the study used subjects that were previously trained with TROCA, and the two methods varied from the typical clinical procedure. Bricker and Bricker (1969) investigated the use of light alone, light and tone, and tone alone as the S^D in the initial training phases of TROCA and, in general, concluded the tone alone was the most efficient procedure, except that tone alone as the S^D could present problems with severely, hearing-impaired subjects. Considerable research is needed in this area of the initial S^D and stimulus shifting in TROCA procedures.

The TROCA procedure primarily uses positive reinforcement of appropriate responses and a mild punishment (time out) for false positives or error responses, but other operant approaches have not been applied to audiometry. Spradlin et al. (1969) reported pilot or demonstration projects using escape avoidance and conditioned suppression procedures which show promise as audiometric procedures, but there is a need for extensive research on the application of other operant procedures.

Research is also needed on the relative merits of one-manipulandum (Lloyd et al., 1968b) and two-manipulanda (Meyerson & Michael, 1960) procedures and on the application of operant procedures to audiometric procedures other than puretone threshold testing.

The puretone audiometry considered above have been primarily concerned with air conducted stimuli, but the basic puretone test frequently includes bone conducted stimuli and a need to mask one ear while obtaining thresholds for the other ear. Bone conduction and masking procedures are routinely employed by many audiologists working with the mentally retarded (Lloyd & Reid, 1967), but only two investigations (Barber, 1967; Schlanger, 1961) have reported specific bone conduction data, and no research has focused specifically on masking with the retarded. Barber (1967) and Barber and Rose (1969) found no significant differences in reliability and transducer placement (forehead vs. mastoid) obtained from 10 retarded and 10 non-retarded subjects. Schlanger (1961, 1962) and Schlanger and Christensen (1964) used bone conduction testing as one of several relatively conventional audiometric techniques in an investigation of the effects of listening training with 199 retarded subjects. They found that, in general, if the subject was capable of responding to standard puretone techniques he was also capable of responding to bone conduction techniques.

There is no a priori reason for the retarded to present any unique problems in bone conduction audiometry. It is possible that infants and selected clinical groups that have incomplete ossification of the cranial bones, or other gross head and skull deviations, may have different normative thresholds and variations in interaural attenuation values for bone-conduction stimuli. But excluding such specific transmission differences a different manner of stimulus presentation (namely a bone receiver) from the conventional earphone presentation should not pose any special behavioral or responding problems if the examiner is aware of the basic aspects of bone conduction as previously discussed by others (e.g., von Bekesy, 1960; Carhart, 1950; Hirsh, 1952; Hood, 1957; Studebaker, 1962a, 1962b, 1964, 1967; Zwislocki, 1953). Although bone conduction and masking research with retarded subjects is limited there does not seem to be major research needs in this area of audiology.

2. Electrophysiologic Audiometry

Although most retarded individuals can be tested with behavioral audiometry, the problems presented by some individuals have resulted in the use of electrophysiologic or neurophysiologic audiometry. Electrophysiologic audiometry does not require a voluntary or operant response by the subject. Furthermore, electrophysiologic audiometry does not require any cooperation from the subject except that he must be reasonably quiet during testing. For a general discussion of electrophysiologic audiometry the reader is referred to Frisina (1963, pp. 152–158) and Goldstein (1963). This section will consider the various types of electrophysiologic audiometry in terms of the frequency of use with the retarded.

Electrodermal responses (EDR) of the autonomic nervous system (ANS) have been used to test the retarded more than other forms of respondents. The use of EDR's in audiometry is currently referred to as electrodermal audiometry (EDA), but it has also been referred to as galvanic skin response (GSR) and psychogalvanic skin response (PGSR) audiometry.

Fourteen studies have involved the use of EDA with retarded subjects (Barr, 1955; Baumeister, Beedle, & Urquhart, 1964; Baumeister, Hawkins, & Kellas, 1965; Collmann, 1959; Fulton, 1962; Graham, 1969; Irwin, Hind, & Aronson, 1957; Kodman, Fein, & Mixson, 1959; N. L. Lamb & Graham, 1968; MacPherson, 1960; Moss, Moss, & Tizard, 1961; Schlanger, 1961; Webb et al., 1964; Wertz, 1961). In general these studies demonstrated the clinical feasibility of EDA with some retarded individuals even in the severely and profoundly retarded range (e.g. MI = −4 and −5). However, the data indicate EDA is no more effective—and frequently much less effective—than behavioral audiometry. Also EDA was demonstrated as less effective with retarded than with non-retarded subjects. These findings, coupled with the unpleasantness and complications of using a noxious stimulus such as an electric shock, contraindicate the clinical use of EDA with the retarded unless vastly improved EDA methods can be developed. Other forms of electrophysiologic audiometry offer greater research promise.

Through the use of computer analysis, electroencephalic responses (EER), or electroencephalographic (EEG) responses have been used to assess auditory sensitivity. This technique is referred to as electroencephalic audiometry (EEA) or cortical evoked response audiometry. EEA is still in the experimental or developmental state, with the preponderance of the research reported during this decade, and few audiologists are prepared to use EEA clinically. Recently EEA studies involving retarded subjects were reported (Hogan, 1966; Hogan & Graham, 1967; Nodar, 1967, 1968; Price & Goldstein, 1966; Rose, 1967; Rose & Rittmanic, 1969; Webb et al., 1964).

Several investigators reported the use of EEA with children, but the first report of its use with the retarded appeared in 1964. Webb et al. (1964) attempted to test 20 retardates using three visual methods of evaluating EERs without the aid of computer analysis. They found poor test-retest reliability. Since they were unable to clearly identify responses at their lower levels of signal presentation they rejected EEA, as employed within the limits of their project, as a screening device. Subsequent EEA studies using computer analysis have been more encouraging. For example, Price and Goldstein (1966) demonstrated good agreement between EEA and behavioral audiometry results on 70 children including many retardates. They did not report the data for the retarded children separately. Other investigators have focused more on the retarded (Hogan,

1966; Hogan & Graham, 1967; Nodar, 1968; Rose, 1967; Rose & Rittmanic, 1969).

Hogan (1966; Hogan & Graham, 1967) obtained a longer latency of EERs but a similar waveform (amplitude and phase) from retarded adults when compared to those of normal adults obtained by L. E. Lamb and Graham (1967) using the same EEA recording technique. However, fewer retardates exhibited detectable EERs; Hogan felt the lower number of observed EERs could be due to abnormal EER patterns rather than a reduced responsiveness. Nodar (1967, 1968) found no difference between the EERs including the latency of response of 10 young adult retardates and 5 non-retarded adults. His data for retardates were in better agreement with L. E. Lamb and Graham's (1967) data for non-retarded than with Hogan and Graham's (1967) data for retarded adults.

Rose and Rittmanic (1969) found 71% of 35 retarded males (CA: 21-51 years) yielded EEA and behavioral thresholds at 1000 Hz with ±5 dB agreement for the two methods. Although all subjects gave behavioral thresholds of 30 dB HL or better, one subject failed to give EERs at any level. The fallacy of using EEA results as the ultimate in the assessment of hearing is demonstrated by a recent case reported by Rose (1967). He reported being unable to obtain EERs at levels as low as behavioral audiometry indicated on a retarded girl. Assuming the behavioral responses valid he conditioned EERs to sound by initially pairing a light with the tone.

The limited EEA research with the retarded demonstrates the potential of using EEA with the retarded but before such potential can be realized further research is indicated. There is a need to investigate the relationship between EEA and behavioral thresholds. Although the effect of drugs on the EER of non-retarded has been investigated there is a need for further research in this area using both retarded and non-retarded subjects. Also the effect of neurological pathology upon the EER to various auditory stimuli needs to be explored.

Although EEA has potential it should not be considered the answer to testing the difficult-to-test patient. In addition to the cost of equipment, cost of professional time, and need for further basic research on the parameters of EEA, the time a patient is required to remain quiet is a major limitation in the use of EEA with many uncooperative subjects. The use of drugs and anesthesia, behavior modification, and telemetry offer three possible solutions to this problem. In addition to needing further data about the effect of drugs and anesthesia on the EER this solution is costly and introduces a risk factor. Behavior modification may be time consuming but it offers added benefits in that the investment to train the patient to be quiet during the test could be extended to behavioral audiometry, other examinations, and habilitative procedures. Telemetry has been used in animal research to record physiologic functions while affording the animal freedom of movement. Reneau and Mast (1968) are developing wearable telemetric EEA instrumentation to transmit the auditory signal to the subject as well as transmit the EER to the analyzing equipment, but further work is needed before this procedure is clinically applicable.

Further EEA research may also lead to the use of response patterns to obtain diagnostic information in addition to auditory sensitivity.

Responses of the autonomic nervous system (ANS) can be used in audiometry. The conditioning of EDRs of the sweat gland have the most common application of ANS responses to audiometry. However, heart rate, heart rate variability, pulse pressure, pulse rate, pulse volume, pupil dilation, pupil constriction, respiration rate, and respiration amplitude are all ANS functions that are relatively accessible to the audiologist, but he has made little use of such respondents. For a discussion of the use of ANS functions in audiometry the reader is referred to Hogan (1969). In general, there is a need for considerable research before ANS functions have major clinical applicability. Therefore it is reasonable that, except for the EDA studies reported above, only one investigation has involved ANS functions and retarded subjects. Butterfield (1962) noted considerable variability in the heart rate of the three retarded subjects she found sufficiently cooperative to participate in the study. She obtained positive responses from her two non-retarded subjects but failed to obtain positive responses from the three retarded subjects. Butterfield used the same basic procedure as Zeaman and Wegner (1956), which has two basic methodological problems. First, the subjects were advised to expect an electric shock at some time during the experiment, but no shock was presented. Therefore, the heart rate responses could have been responses to fear of shock and levels of intellectualizing about shock and/or the unconditioned response to the auditory signal. Second, the subjects were asked to affirm the presence of the test tone. Therefore, responses may have related to the tone or to the physical activity of the verbal response. Because of these methodological questions Butterfield's (1962) negative findings should not discourage future research on using ANS responses to obtain audiometric data from the retarded. Actually this study serves to highlight the need for investigation of the basic variables of ANS responses to auditory stimulation, then to use such respondents in developing auditory assessment procedures, and then to apply ANS audiometry procedures to the assessment of the retarded. Hogan (1969) proposed such research, including the multiple recording of ANS variables, and has initiated such a program in an institutional setting.[2] ANS audiometry should receive considerable attention in the near future.

B. Behavior Observation Audiometry (BOA)

Research indicates most individuals can be tested with behavioral audiometry using operant behavior. Furthermore, the future development of electrophysiologic audiometry offers considerable promise for use with individuals who are untestable with the above-mentioned behavioral audiometry procedures. Whenever there is a hearing impairment such procedures should be employed to obtain information for each ear, using earphones and the bone conduction transducer. However, audiologists are sometimes faced with individuals who appear untestable with such procedures because of time limitations, and/or the examiner's limited skill with such procedures. Also, there are cases in which a screening of low and high frequency auditory sensitivity is more expedient than the conventional puretone screening tests. In such cases the audiologist may get a gross index of auditory sensitivity by using sound field behavior observation audiometry (BOA). In general, BOA refers to the presentation of various auditory stimuli to a subject while the examiner(s) attempts to observe the overt responses of the subject to these sounds. The responses may be operants and/or respondents but they must be reliably and temporally related to the auditory signals. There is considerable variation in the application of BOA (viz., auditory stimuli, stimulus controls, test situations, responses observed, response and observer reliability, response criteria). For a more detailed discussion the reader is referred to numerous other sources (e.g., Darley, 1961, pp. 21–25; Downs, 1962, 1967; Frisina, 1963, pp. 130–137; Ewing, 1943, 1957; Ewing & Ewing, 1944; Hardy, Dougherty, & Hardy, 1959; Lloyd & Frisina, 1965, pp. 275–278; Lloyd & Young, 1969, pp. 11–13; J. Miller, DeSchweinitz, & Goetzinger, 1963; K. P. Murphy, 1961, 1962; Newby, 1964, pp. 185–189).

Although BOA is used clinically, very little has been published relative to its use with the retarded per se.

Webb *et al.* (1964) provide a rather detailed discussion of their attempt to develop a BOA screening technique. Subsequently Beedle, Webb, Kinde, and Weber (1966) presented a brief journal report of the project. They presented tape-recorded speech and non-speech sounds at three different levels (20, 40, and 60 dB re .0002 dyne/cm^2 [*sic*]) to var-

[2] Personal communication.

ious groups of institutionalized retarded children. The final report (Beedle et al., 1966) included only 30 subjects representing 6 subgroups. These investigators only got moderately high correlations of agreement for both intra-observer (0.63–0.80) and inter-observer (0.58–0.80) judgment of responses when they accepted any *change* in behavior as a response. Statistical analysis revealed no significant interactions for type of stimuli, level of presentation, or subgroups. Analysis did reveal a significant difference within subjects and between subgroups for level of presentation. Therefore the investigators state the "technique did discriminate mentally retarded subjects with a known hearing loss [$n = 6$] from mentally retarded subjects with normal hearing. [Beedle et al., 1966, p. 681]."

Waldon (1965) reported a BOA procedure employing the filtered cries of a baby as a successful technique with an initial sample of 24 mentally retarded subjects under 12 years of age. Interestingly, he also reported that he obtained puretone threshold data with play audiometry but was not able to obtain reliable results with EDA. He later reported similar BOA results with a total sample of 52 subjects (Waldon, 1968). Although Waldon stresses the initial success, he indicates his "results are not conclusive." Furthermore, as of this date, other investigators have not replicated his success with his procedure.

Nober (1968) reported the use of BOA with 1884 retardates. His stimulus was a 3000 Hz frequency modulated tone (warble tone) presented at 70, 80, 90, and 100 dB SPL. He used five observers with three agreements necessary to determine a positive response to sound. The observers also considered type and degree of response. Nober (1968, p. 36) reports "periodic retests showed excellent agreement among the examiners as a collective group and for independent examiner." However, it should be noted that only 60% of 200 subjects were classed the same on retesting, and test-retest phi coefficient correlations were only 0.67 for males and 0.17 for females.

In considering the variety of stimuli used in BOA, Bradshaw (1961) obtained comparable thresholds for puretones and filtered environmental sounds from a group of 20 retarded subjects. The environmental sounds were filtered to control the frequency range of the stimuli but were still recognizable as meaningful sounds. Although such environmental sounds may be used in BOA, Bradshaw's study should not be considered as a comparison of BOA to the more conventional puretone audiometry since the response to both types of stimuli involved a common play audiometry procedure. Another project (Ryan & Stewart, 1965; Watkins, Stewart, & Ryan, 1966) demonstrated the use of animal sounds as another type of stimuli. They used tactile reinforcement of correct response; therefore, the procedure was more like conventional audiometry than BOA.

At two conferences on the audiologic assessment of the retarded, BOA was discussed (Fulton & Lloyd, 1969; Lloyd & Frisina, 1965). Although there are differences of opinion about the use of BOA the following generalizations seem appropriate:

(1) The more conventional speech and puretone procedures are preferable to BOA.

(2) If BOA procedures are to be used clinically, there is a need to objectify the procedures and better quantify the stimuli and results. Particular attention needs to be devoted to improving test-retest, intra-observer, and inter-observer agreement in judging the BOA responses of severely retarded subjects.

(3) When forced to use BOA, in general, the audiologist should view the results as gross information for initial program planning, until more definitive audiometric data can be obtained.

Based on the work of K. P. Murphy (1961, 1962) it seems that as BOA procedures are improved they may be incorporated as an index of development as well as an audiometric screening procedure. Improved developmental listening norms could be useful in differential diagnosis.

C. Speech Audiometry

Speech audiometry is a critical part of any complete audiologic assessment. While puretone threshold data provides a valid index of a patient's auditory sensitivity, and the basic functional relationship of the patient to his acoustic environment, speech audiometry provides a more valid index of the patient's auditory reception of verbal stimuli in communication. The routine audiologic assessment should include some type of speech reception threshold (SRT) and supra-threshold speech discrimination data. The SRT usually refers to the level, in decibels, at which the subject can respond correctly to 50% of the verbal stimuli. Although an SRT may be obtained with any verbal stimuli, spondee (equal stress, two-syllable) words are the stimuli used by most audiologists for this measure. When spondee words are used the SRT may be more appropriately referred to as a "spondee threshold." The supra-threshold speech discrimination measures are usually obtained with monosyllabic words and are expressed in the percent of words, presented at a given level, to which the subject correctly responded. General discussions of speech audiometry are provided elsewhere (e.g., Davis & Silverman, 1960, pp. 181–194; Giolas, 1969; Newby, 1964, pp. 106–132).

Although speech audiometry is a critical part of the typical audiologic assessment, relatively little speech audiometry research has been conducted with the retarded. The majority of the publications in this area have been concerned with speech thresholds.

1. SPEECH RECEPTION THRESHOLDS (SRT)

In the first study to report speech audiometry data on retarded subjects, Meyerson (1952, 1956) used spondee words and a point-to-the-picture response to test the hearing of 20 slow or mentally retarded first grade children as a minor part of the development of his verbal audiometric test (VAT) for children. Although the 20 could perform the task, several children with normal auditory sensitivity for puretones had poor VAT scores. Also, the slow children performed poorer on the VAT than a comparison group of intellectually normal children. Statistical analysis led to the conclusion that "It is practically certain, therefore, that hearing for spondaic words is positively related to intellectual level. [Meyerson, 1956, p. 128]." His data may have resulted from specific linguistic factors, such as familiarity of the words and/or vocabulary level of the subjects, rather than "intellectual level." Numerous studies have demonstrated familiarity as a significant variable in speech audiometry with non-retarded subjects (e.g., Hutton & Weaver, 1959; Oyer & Doudna, 1960; Tillman & Jerger, 1959). Vocabulary has also been demonstrated as a relevant variable with non-retarded subjects (e.g., Brooks & Goetzinger, 1966; Farrimond, 1962).

More recently 13 reports representing 8 different investigations have, in general, demonstrated the feasibility of SRT measures with groups of retarded subjects (Clausen, 1966; Dansinger & Madow, 1966; Kodman et al., 1959; Lloyd, 1965a; Lloyd & Melrose, 1966a, 1966b; Lloyd & Reid, 1966; Lloyd, Reid, & McManis, 1967; MacPherson, 1960; Schlanger, 1961, 1962; Schlanger & Christensen, 1964; Wolfe & MacPherson, 1959). Two studies (Dansinger & Madow, 1966; Schlanger, 1961, 1962; Schlanger & Christensen, 1964) used both dissyllables and monosyllables while the others all used spondaic dissyllables. Some of the studies involved verbal responses while others used point-to-the-picture responses.

Lloyd (1965a; Lloyd & Melrose, 1966a, 1966b) compared the verbal and point-to-the-picture responses of 40 normal-hearing retarded children (MI −2 & −3) with procedures that were demonstrated reliable. There was a small but statistically significant difference between the thresholds obtained with these two methods, with the verbal response resulting in a slightly lower (better) threshold. Although this mean difference of less than 3 dB is probably not of clinical significance, it offers interesting theoretical possibilities as follows:

> This difference is hard to account for if one considers the developmental order of learning speech later than gestural (non-verbal) communication. The only plausible explanation would be that, for these Ss, a simple vocal recall, or echoic, response of spondaic words was easier than the identification of a picture that represented a spondaic word. The motor response of pointing to a picture representing a word might have required a more complex CNS function than would the motor response of repeating a word. In other words, the CNS function for the picture SRT may have been complicated by the need for association and by the need to involve non-acoustic systems (visual scanning, visual identification, and association) as well as the motor act of pointing.
>
> The relative difficulty of the repeat-the-word as differed from the point-to-the-picture responses might also be considered in terms of how much originality or initiative was required. When each stimulus and response is a unit, the picture identification test required the child to initiate something new in the response, i.e., S was not just mimicking the examiner's model, but he was required to make his own response on the basis of information carried in the examiner's model or in the stimulus. The repeat-the-word test did not require S to initiate a response on the basis of the stimulus input but simply required echoing or mimicking a model (or the stimulus word). The reasoning behind this interpretation of the data is supported by the pattern of linguistic development in children. [Lloyd & Melrose, 1966a, pp. 212-213.]

A replication study (Lloyd et al., 1967) with 24 normal-hearing moderately retarded children (MI −3) failed to corroborate the previously reported statistically significant difference between the two methods. The difference between the two studies cannot be accounted for as a methodological factor. It was hypothesized the difference resulted from subject differences since mentally retarded subjects, even in the same CA and MI range, represent a wide range of behavior.

Although response mode differences may not be of clinical significance, further research should be pursued with particular reference to subject differences as a differential diagnostic tool. In addition to different response modes such research could employ modified speech stimuli.

The relationship of SRT's and puretone thresholds has been of interest to several investigators. Such speech and puretone data interpretation must be pursued with caution because of (1) differences in normative reference thresholds and energy distributions of the two different types of stimuli, (2) methodological variations, (3) individual differences in end organ processing of the stimuli, and (4) individual differences in linguistic background and skill as well as CNS processing of information.

Although Meyerson (1952, 1956) found his retarded subject did poorly on the verbal audiometric test, Schlanger (1961, 1962) and Clausen (1966) obtained lower SRT's than puretone thresholds and suggested speech audiometry as a method of choice over puretone audiometry. In addition to their data, these investigators based their recommendation on: (1) a theory that retardates operate on a low arousal level and have an inability to direct attention to a stimuli for any length of time, and (2) an assumption that speech stimuli are more meaningful to retardates. Generalization of these assumptions is limited since retardation includes a wide spectrum of behavior. Some subjects may not have the particular neurophysiologic dysfunction associated with "arousal." Also, in many cases with language retardation and communication problems words may be relatively meaningless.

In considering the assumptions made about the meaningfulness of various stimuli, it should be noted that K. P. Murphy (1962) found type of stimuli was not as important in eliciting responses from normal infants as the source. The infants responded more frequently to puretones coming from a speaker hidden in a doll than they did to noisemakers (assumed to produce meaningful sounds) they could not see.

As Sheridan (1958) pointed out in her discussion of the use of speech stimuli to test mentally retarded children, speech audiometry provides additional or specific information and is not a substitute for puretone data.

The previously mentioned study of 40 normal-hearing retardates found significantly lower puretone thresholds than SRT's using either response mode (Lloyd, 1965a; Lloyd & Melrose, 1966a). When reference thresholds are considered in this carefully controlled study, the findings are in general agreement with Meyerson's (1952, 1956) findings with the VAT and with numerous data on non-retarded subjects (e.g., Tillman & Jerger, 1959). Lloyd and Melrose (1966a, p. 212) state,

An assumption that speech stimuli were more meaningful to retardates than pure-tone stimuli and, therefore, provided a better estimate of the auditory sensitivity, was not supported by the data of the present study. Actually, it would seem that the auditory sensitivity of retardates, with their language retardation and verbal communication difficulties, could best be evaluated with non-verbal stimuli such as pure tones. The present findings were consistent with such an assumption, and were in general agreement with the findings of Meyerson (1956), who found that many slow learning children who had passed a puretone screening test failed the verbal audiometric test. Our data for MR children were consistent with the findings of Farrimond (1962), who found that adults with below-average vocabularies gave significantly poorer performances on sentence speech tests than adults with above-average vocabulary ability ($p \leq .05$) even though their pure-tone hearing . . . was similar.

Correlations are frequently used to report inter-method comparisons. Table II summarizes the four studies (Clausen, 1966; Kodman et al., 1959; Lloyd, 1965a; Schlanger, 1961) reporting puretone-speech threshold correlations. Most of the correlations are moderately high and all are statistically significant. However, the common variance reflected by these correlations is modest, indicating that although there is a positive relationship between the thresholds, the predictive value of one type of threshold for another is limited. In general, these correlations for retarded subjects are slightly lower than those of non-retarded subjects (e.g., Chaiklin & Ventry, 1963; Graham, 1960).

The moderate positive puretone-speech correlations for retardates and the difference between such correlations for retarded and non-retarded subjects may be considered in light of a number of methodological and subject selection factors and are considered elsewhere (Lloyd,

TABLE II
Correlations between Puretone and Speech Reception Thresholds for Four Studies. All Correlations were Statistically Significant

Investigators and type of puretone measure	N	Speech reception threshold		
		Type not spec'd	Repeat the word	Point to the picture
Kodman et al. (1959)				
EDR @ 500 Hz	31	.74	—	—
EDR @ 2000 Hz	31	.64	—	—
Schlanger (1961)				
Average threshold (frequency not specified—assumed to be PTA)				
Standard (hand-raising)				
Initial test	49	—	—	.76
Final test	47	—	—	.80
Lloyd (1965a; Lloyd & Melrose, 1966a)				
PTA (threshold average of 500, 1000, and 2000 Hz)				
Standard (hand-raising)	40	—	.66	.67
Modified ear-choice	40	—	.81	.77
Play (block-dropping)	40	—	.71	.67
Slide-show	40	—	.72	.60
Clausen (1966)				
Average threshold (frequency not specified—assumed to be PTA)				
Variety of "standard" procedures				
right ear				
8–10 year olds	68	.34	—	—
12–15 year olds	105	.55	—	—
20–24 year olds	103	.39	—	—
left ear				
8–10 year olds	68	.48	—	—
12–15 year olds	105	.34	—	—
20–24 year olds	103	.40	—	—

1965a, pp. 64-70), but one factor should be considered here. The lower correlations for the retarded samples may reflect the verbal language retardation present in most retardates.

The data obtained from retardates indicate puretone and speech thresholds have predictive value for each other, but the predictive value is not as great as it is for non-retarded subjects. The audiologist may use puretone and speech thresholds for corroboration, but he should adjust his corroborative judgments relative to the language disadvantage many retarded subjects have in speech audiometry. The puretone-speech correlation for retarded subjects does not appear sufficient to allow the use of one measure in lieu of the other. It should be noted that acceptance of SRT's as an index of auditory sensitivity have frequently led to the misdiagnosis and underestimating of hearing impairment (e.g., Ross & Matkin, 1967; Sheridan, 1944). Both high frequency and low frequency hearing impairments of communicative significance can remain undetected if the examiner depends upon verbal screening tests. Therefore, it is concluded that puretones are the best stimuli to assess basic auditory sensitivity while speech stimuli are useful in corroborating the basic puretone data and for providing data about the subject's threshold level for the understanding of verbal communication.

2. SUPRA-THRESHOLD SPEECH DISCRIMINATION

SRT's provide an index of a subject's reception of verbal communication, but supra-threshold data better approximates the typical verbal communication situation. Although supra-threshold speech discrimination is, or at least should be, attempted in the typical audiologic assessment of the retarded, only three investigators reported data on such measures with the retarded (Fulton, 1967b; Katz, 1969; Myatt & Landes, 1963).

Myatt and Landes (1963) developed four, 20-word monosyllable discrimination tests with a point-to-the-picture response. They gave the test (at 50 dB SL) to four groups of 20 normal-hearing children each, as follows: (1) normals (CA = 4-3 to 4-10), (2) speech-defectives (CA = 3-7 to 6-10), (3) educable mentally retarded (EMH, IQ = 50 to 70; CA = 6-5 to 15-0) and (4) trainable mentally retarded (TMH, IQ = 25 to 50; CA = 5-2 to 15-6). The TMH group scored significantly poorer than the others. Test score and IQ correlations were computed for the EMH and TMH groups. The moderate, but significant, correlation of 0.51 for the TMH group and the nonsignificant correlation of 0.03 for the EMH group led the authors to conclude that intelligence is a factor for subjects with IQ below 50 but that above 50 IQ intelligence does not affect achievement on this discrimination test. Of the three groups with similar scores, the EMH group had the smallest number of errors.

In considering the reasons for this, a study of the curricula to which this group was exposed showed that these children were very much "picture-oriented." Concepts are given pictorial representations rather than abstract explanations. Therefore, the EMR child habitually responds to pictorialization and is well suited to the use of a picture test. [Myatt & Landes, 1966, pp. 361-362].

Fulton (1967b) administered four forms of the CID W-22 speech discrimination lists to 25 normal-hearing retardates. Since a verbal response was required only subjects with articulation test scores of at least 90% were used. Fulton (1967b, p. 358) concluded:

Subjects performed equally as well or better on initial as on later presentations; there was no necessity to establish an adaptation plateau. A significant positive correlation [$r = .46$] was found between total discrimination scores and Peabody Picture Vocabulary Test raw scores.

This finding relative to vocabulary is in agreement with previous findings for non-retarded (e.g., Brooks & Goetzinger, 1966; Farrimond, 1962). The finding is also in agreement with Schlanger's (1961, 1962) finding of a relationship between SRTs and Peabody Picture Vocabulary Test results of retarded subjects. It is difficult to interpret the findings, but the results seem inconclusive relative to familiarity as a factor in the speech discrimination of retarded subjects. Further investigation of the role of familiarity and other linguistic parameters of speech stimuli in speech discrimination testing with the retarded is indicated.

From the limited data reported and clinical observation, it is apparent that current speech discrimination procedures developed for the non-retarded are applicable for many retarded individuals, but considerable research is needed in this area. In addition to the role of linguistic parameters, methodological research is needed on such aspects as the use of: (1) various response modes, (2) open message set vs. limited message set, (3) reinforcement, and (4) speech stimuli other than monosyllabic words. As improved procedures are developed investigation of the types of speech discrimination errors made by retardates should be conducted. As modified speech discrimination procedures are developed for use with the retarded, attention should be given to methods of obtaining auditory, visual, and combined (auditory-visual) data.

Katz (1969) has reported the use of staggered spondaic word (SSW) tests with 34 retarded subjects (MI = -1 through -4). In the SSW test, different words are presented to each ear in a staggered manner so the final syllable of one word and the initial syllable of the other word are presented at the same time. Although the SSW test is not the typical auditory discrimination test, it is presented in this section since it involves suprathreshold speech discrimination. This is a preliminary report and the significance of the findings are inconclusive, but it does demonstrate the use of a complex auditory discrimination procedure with the retarded. Katz (1969, p. 36) states "It appears that the SSW test is providing diagnostic information despite the presence of severe retardation. Experience thus far indicates that the procedure may be more difficult to subjects below 35 IQ." It is also of interest that two master theses found MI had no significant effect upon the SSW test performance of elementary school children (Brunt, 1965; Turner, 1966).

3. COMFORTABLE AND UNCOMFORTABLE LEVELS

Frequently the audiologist attempts to audiometrically determine what a patient considers his most comfortable levels (MCL) and uncomfortable levels (UCL) for listening to speech. The MCL and UCL have value in habilitative planning especially in considering the use of amplification devices. MCL and UCL measures have been used clinically with retardates, but research in this area has not appeared. There is a need for such research. In developing improved MCL procedures one might adapt Lindsley's conjugate arrangement of consequences for determining preferences (e.g., Lindsley, 1962; Nathan, Schneller, & Lindsley, 1964). The conjugate arrangement uses the patient-control of level or modified method of adjustments used in the Bekesy audiometer, which has already been successfully employed to obtain MCL data from non-retarded subjects (Kopra & Blosser, 1968).

D. Special Procedures

Puretone and speech audiometry considered in the preceding sections are part of the "typical audiologic assessment" necessary to provide basic auditory sensitivity and other data critical to evaluating communication problems. The audiologist can also provide considerable information for the differential diagnosis of site of lesion and pseudohypacusis through the use of special audiometric procedures. These procedures have been used clinically with retarded patients, but relatively little research in this area has involved retarded subjects.

1. DIFFERENTIAL DIAGNOSIS OF SITE OF LESION

The differential diagnosis of site of lesion is a medical decision, but modern otologic diagnosis is dependent upon audiometric data. The differentiation between conductive (outer and/or middle ear) and sensori-neural (cochlear and/or retro-cochlear) components of a hearing impairment can be made with great accuracy by just using the relationship between bone-conducted and air-conducted puretone data. The more specific differential diagnosis of site of lesion within the conductive or sensori-neural categories is dependent upon special audiologic procedures and data. General discussion of such procedures (e.g., acoustic impedance measurements, ABLB, Bekesy, distorted speech tests, SISI, Tone Decay) are provided elsewhere (e.g., Fulton, 1969; Jerger, 1962; Katz, 1969; L. E. Lamb & Norris, 1969; Newby, 1964, pp. 161-184). To date, only a limited amount of research with these special procedures used with retarded subjects has appeared (Atkinson, 1960; Fulton, 1967b; Fulton & Reid, 1968; Hollis & Fulton, 1968; Katz, 1969; L. E. Lamb & Norris, 1969; Young, 1968; Young & Estes, 1967).

Bekesy audiometry has become a common tool in the differential diagnosis of site of lesion. The procedure is frequently used with children, but the first report of its use with retarded subjects was by Atkinson in 1960. Unfortunately Atkinson found significantly poorer thresholds by the Bekesy procedure than any of the three other methods he used. In general, more recent investigations (Fulton, 1966, 1967b; Fulton & Reid, 1968; Young, 1968) have obtained good Bekesy intra-test agreement indicating reasonable reliability and inter-test agreement between Bekesy and conventional puretone data showing a degree of concurrent validity. These three investigations demonstrate the feasibility of Bekesy audiometry with many retarded subjects. Two of these investigations (Fulton, 1967b; Fulton & Reid, 1968) considered variables such as attenuation rate, recording pen excursion size, and continuous vs. interrupted stimuli, and found that most subjects performed as one would expect non-retarded subjects to respond. These investigators found, at least for MI levels -1, -2, and -3, that MI level was not a major factor in Bekesy results, in general. However, Fulton (1966) reported obtaining measurable Bekesy results from only 25% of his 40 more severely retarded subjects (MI $= -4$) even with 30 minutes of pre-training.

There is still a need for further investigation of the use of Bekesy audiometry with the retarded. Modification of the response switch and the application of behavior modification methods seems indicated. Hollis and Fulton (1968) have described a modification of the Bekesy audiometry modified from Blough's (1958) two-button response system. Such modifications offer promise of obtaining diagnostically meaningful Bekesy results from more retarded subjects.

Bekesy audiometry is the special differential diagnostic procedure that has been most investigated with the retarded. Use of the SISI and tone decay tests with the retarded have not been reported extensively, but with careful attention to training and instructions these procedures could be used with many retarded subjects. The selective operant conditioning of specific responses could be used in training a subject to the tasks required in such test. There has been one report of the successful use of a relatively complete diagnostic battery with a retarded patient with a left hemispherectomy (Hodgson, 1967).

As was indicated in the previous section Katz (1969) has already demonstrated the applicability of using the SSW test with retarded subjects. Other types of competing message and distorted speech tests could be developed for use with the retarded. Current procedures could be modified to use non-verbal responses. Further research is needed in this area.

Research involving retarded subjects with known CNS pathology would help to refine retro-cochlear site of lesion procedures for use with the non-retarded.

Three investigations (L. E. Lamb & Norris, 1969; Young, 1968; Young & Estes, 1967) have demonstrated the feasibility of acoustic impedance measurements with the retarded. They all used relative impedance, as measured with the Madsen Electronics Acoustic Impedance Meter, and demonstrated the clinical reliability of this particular type of impedance measure. Although absolute impedance measurement, as obtained by the Grason-Stadler, Zwislocki, Acoustic Bridge, may be a better measurement in some cases of middle ear pathology, it requires patient cooperation to maintain a good seal during measurement. Furthermore, the abnormally small ear canals found in many retardates may pose additional problems with the absolute measurement. These two problems are minimized with relative measurements. However, investigation of the use of absolute as well as relative impedance measurements with retarded subjects seems warranted. A major advantage of impedance measurement with the retarded is that these measurements do not require a voluntary response from the subject. In addition to the value of impedance measurements in differentiating conductive pathologies, such measurements may prove beneficial as an indirect measure of recruitment, which is of significance in diagnosing cochlear pathology. Inconsistency between impedance results and puretone audiometry may also prove of value in detecting pseudohypacusis. An extensive discussion of acoustic impedance measurement is provided elsewhere (e.g., L. E. Lamb & Norris, 1969).

2. Pseudohypacusis

During the past 20 years there have been major advances in the sophistication of audiometric procedures for detecting pseudohypacusis, referred to as functional, non-organic, or psychogenic hearing loss. General discussions of these special procedures (e.g., Delayed Feedback

Tests, Doerfler-Stewart Test, EDA, Lombard Test, Shifting Voice Test, Stenger Test) are presented elsewhere (e.g., Chaiklin & Ventry, 1963; Goldstein, 1966; Newby, 1964, pp. 139–161). These procedures can be used with the retarded but to this reviewer's knowledge research involving these procedures and retarded subjects has not been reported. Most of these procedures would require little, or no modification for use with the retarded in general. Further clinical use and possible demonstration activity in this area are needed.

IV. INTRAMETHOD RESEARCH

The reliability of audiometric measures obtained from retarded subjects has been questioned by some investigators while others have pointed out that the retarded are not innately unreliable. It would seem that if reliability was questioned that intramethod research should have preceded intermethod comparisons but this was not the case. Basic reliability research was not reported until 10 years after the incidence and intermethod studies started to appear.

There have been 16 reports of 12 different intramethod studies of puretone and speech audiometry (Bradley *et al.*, 1955; Fulton, 1962, 1967a; Fulton & Graham, 1964, 1966; Kopatic, 1963; Lloyd, 1965a; Lloyd & Melrose, 1966b; Lloyd & Reid, 1966; Lloyd *et al.*, 1968a; MacPherson, 1960; Schlanger, 1961, 1962; Schlanger & Christensen, 1964; Wolfe & MacPherson, 1959; Young, 1968). Three of the intramethod studies did not produce basic reliability data because of various experimental design and methodological factors (Bradley *et al.*, 1955, MacPherson, 1960; Schlanger, 1961, 1962; Schlanger & Christensen, 1964; Wolfe & MacPherson, 1959).

All of the audiometric reliability studies with retarded subjects have involved institutionalized retardates. Most of the basic reliability studies have been with puretone audiometry and speech audiometry.

A. Puretone Audiometry

Kopatic (1963) administered puretone tests to 47 retarded adult females (mean IQ= 64) four times at several week intervals. Unfortunately, he did not specify such critical variables as audiologic or otologic status of the subjects, testing environment, number of examiners, training of examiners, experience of examiners, procedure, instruction, response mode and threshold criterion. Retest resulted in generally lower thresholds. His first-second test correlations were 0.62 for the right ear and 0.63 for the left ear while his third-fourth test correlations were 0.82 and 0.88, respectively. He concluded

For purposes of validity, objectivity and reliability of pure tone audiometry with the mentally handicapped, it is necessary to obtain several audiograms before the retarded subject's hearing capacity can be ascertained [Kopatic, 1963, p. 135].

This recommendation has not been supported by subsequent research that attended to the above mentioned variables.

Tables III and IV summarize the findings of the major test-retest reliability studies using puretone procedures with the retarded. In general, the correlation coefficients presented in Table III indicate good relative consistency within the groups. The moderate correlations found by Fulton (1967a) probably reflect the use of a 15 minute time limit. The other studies reported in Table III did not impose such a time limit.

TABLE III
Test-retest Correlations of Mentally Retarded Subjects for Five Studies that used Relatively Conventional Puretone Procedures

	500 Hz	1000 Hz	2000 Hz	4000 Hz
Lloyd (1965a; Lloyd & Melrose, 1966b)				
$MI = -2$ & -3, $n = 40$				
Standard (hand-raising)	.84	.81	.85	—
Modified ear-choice	.88	.86	.87	—
Play (block dropping)	.88	.85	.81	—
Slide show	.83	.88	.82	—
Fulton & Graham (1966)				
$MI = -2, -3$ & -4, $n = 34$				
COR	.81	.41	.71	—
Fulton (1967a)				
$MI = -1$ & -2, $n = 65$	.39	.49	.63	.50
$MI = -4$ & -5, $n = 69$	.75	.78	.77	.82
Lloyd et al. (1968a)				
right ear				
$MI = -2$ & -3, $n = 12$	.94	.95	.95	.93
$MI = -4$ & -5, $n = 12$	.86	.97	.95	.84
left ear				
$MI = -2$ & -3, $n = 12$	.98	.93	.85	.95
$MI = -4$ & -5, $n = 12$	.84	.79	.92	.90
Young (1968)				
$MI = -2$ & $MI = -3$, $n = 40$	.75	.78	.74	—

Note: The AAMD classification of measured intelligence (MI) is presented elsewhere (Heber, 1961). The Lloyd (1965a; Lloyd & Melrose, 1966b), and Young (1968) data are from normal subjects while the other three studies are with clinical samples, which included hearing impaired subjects.

Correlations are commonly used in reporting reliability in psychometry but are less commonly used to report audiometric reliability. One problem is that a restricted range and/or skewed distribution, as frequently occurs in audiologic research, tends to restrict the correlation. Therefore the correlations reported by Lloyd (1965a; Lloyd and Melrose, 1966b) and Young (1968) may be depressed because they use normal hearing subjects. Another problem with correlations is that it reflects how well individuals within a group preserve their relative standing and is therefore an index of relative consistency. In audiometric reliability the question is how does a subject vary around his own "true threshold" or what is his absolute consistency? Other procedures such as standard error of estimate, actual data plots, or the actual amount of test-retest agreement would prove more meaningful in reporting audiometric reliability. In audiometry a ±5 dB variation is accepted as clinical tolerance or clinical error with non-retarded subjects (Currier, 1943; Meyers & Harris, 1949; Witting & Hughson, 1940). Therefore the percentage of subjects with ±5 dB, or better, test-retest agreement is probably the best functional analysis of audiometric reliability.

Table IV summarizes the four studies that have reported puretone reliability in percentage of subjects with the clinically acceptable ±5 dB, or better, agreement. In general, the percent of retarded subjects with ±5 dB agreement is comparable to that previously reported on non-retarded subjects (Currier, 1943; Witting & Hughson, 1940). The purpose of the investigation and a number of audiometric variables should be considered in reviewing these studies. For example, Fulton and Graham's (1964) data reflect a relationship between adaptive behavior, or functioning level, and percentage of ±5 dB repeatability, but it should be noted that they used limited time and did not impose a response criterion prior to threshold searching. Therefore, the low percentage of ±5 dB agreement by lower level subjects actually reflects difficulty in testing the subject with the particular method rather than a lack of basic reliability with appropriate procedures. The subsequent study by Fulton (1967a) still reflects agreement under a 15 minute time limit, but fails to show a reliability-functioning level relationship since a response criterion was employed.

Considering test-retest variations that can result from hearing fluctuations related to pathology, Lloyd (1965a; Lloyd & Melrose, 1966b) first investigated the basic reliability of normal-hearing retardates and then investigated reliability with a clinical sample including hearing-impaired retardates (Lloyd et al., 1968a). Special attention was given to the critical audiometric variables previously mentioned. The results of these two studies coupled with the data from Fulton (1962), Fulton and

TABLE IV
The Percent of Mentally Retarded Subjects Indicating ±5 dB Test-retest Agreement or Better for Four Studies that used Relatively Conventional Puretone Procedures

	500 Hz	1000 Hz	2000 Hz	4000 Hz
Fulton & Graham (1964)				
AB I, $n = 7$	—	100	—	—
AB II, $n = 14$	—	64	—	—
AB III, $n = 15$	—	47	—	—
AB IV, $n = 15$	—	0	—	—
Lloyd (1965a; Lloyd & Melrose, 1966b)				
MI = -2 & -3, $n = 40$				
Standard (hand-raising)	93	95	95	—
Modified ear-choice	95	93	93	—
Play (block-dropping)	100	98	95	—
Slide-show	88	95	93	—
Fulton (1967)				
MI = -1 & -2, $n = 65$	71	66	74	69
MI = -3 & -4, $n = 69$	63	75	81	68
Lloyd et al. (1968a)				
right ear				
MI = -2 & -3, $n = 12$	75	83	84	75
MI = -4 & -5, $n = 12$	67	75	83	42
left ear				
MI = -2 & -3, $n = 12$	100	92	67	92
MI = -4 & -5, $n = 12$	92	83	67	75

NOTE: The AAMD classifications of adaptive behavior (AB) and measured intelligence (MI) are presented elsewhere (Heber, 1961). The Fulton and Graham (1964) study includes three subjects and 15 subjects in AB groups III & IV, respectively, that did not complete the tests and were therefore not counted as having ±5 dB agreement. The Lloyd (1965a; Lloyd & Melrose, 1966) study used normal hearing subjects while the other three studies used clinical samples covering a range of auditory sensitivity (from Lloyd & Young, 1969).

Graham (1964, 1966), and Young (1968) are in general agreement. When tested by an experienced qualified audiologist,[3] using appropriate audiometric procedures (including instructions, demonstration, response mode, response criteria, threshold criteria, and behavior modification considerations) and calibrated equipment in an appropriate acoustic environment, retardates generally can be expected to provide relatively reliable and valid puretone thresholds. Naturally, the audiolo-

---

[3] In general, a "qualified audiologist" may be defined as a person holding the American Speech and Hearing Association Certificate of Clinical Competence in Audiology.

gist will need to use appropriate intra- and inter-test checks as well as nonaudiometric information to make reliability and validity judgments about thresholds of retardates just as he would with non-retarded subjects or patients. Also, this does not imply that all retarded subjects will provide reliable puretone threshold data. However, it does imply that the retardates, in general, do not have inherent biologic or etiologic differences that make them innately unreliable on puretone measures.

B. Speech Audiometry

The first basic reliability study of speech audiometry was completed in 1965 (Lloyd, 1965a; Lloyd & Melrose, 1966b). This study found normal-hearing retarded children ($N = 40$; mean CA = 12-6 years; MI = -2 & -3) were reliable on both the "say-the-word" and the "point-to-the-picture" spondee threshold procedures. Subsequently, spondee threshold reliability was also demonstrated with a clinical sample of retarded children ($N = 24$; MI = -2 & -4, Mean CA = 13-0; MI = -3 & -4, Mean CA = 14-11 years) including hearing impaired subjects (Lloyd & Reid, 1966) and another sample of normal-hearing retarded children ($N = 24$; MI = -3; Mean CA = 14-9 years) (Lloyd et al., 1967) Later Young (1968) demonstrated basic spondee threshold reliability using both response modes with a sample of normal-hearing retarded adults ($N = 40$; CA 21 to 36 years; MI = -2 & -3).

One study has also demonstrated the reliability of monosyllable (W-22) word discrimination using a verbal response on 25 normal-hearing retarded children (Mean CA = 14-11 years) with no major articulation errors (Fulton, 1967b).

C. Other Procedures

Fulton (1967b) attempted to investigate the reliability of Bekesy audiometry with a large sample ($N = 153$) of retardates representing a wide range of age, hearing ability, and four MI levels ($-1, -2, -3$ & -4). On the basis of the Bekesy results he was able to obtain on 134 subjects, he concluded that for most retarded subjects repeated Bekesy tracings should show approximately a ± 10 dB agreement, and that valid and reliable Bekesy results were not necessarily limited to subjects of the higher MI levels. Young's (1968) study of 40 normal-hearing retarded adults (MI = -2 & -3) also demonstrated reasonably reliable Bekesy results with retardates.

As indicated in the section on special tests, relative acoustic impedance measures have also been demonstrated as a reliable procedure with many retarded subjects (L. E. Lamb & Norris, 1969; Young, 1968;

Young & Estes, 1967). Dugas and Baumeister (1968) found 18 retarded males (mean CA = 20-7 years; MI = −2) more variable on judgments of difference limens (DL) for intensity with and without a light distractor than 18 male college students.

In general the basic reliability of puretone, speech, and selected special audiometric procedures used with several groups of retarded subjects has been demonstrated when appropriate attention was given to the critical audiometric variables. These data are not in agreement with the statement that "the retarded" are innately unreliable on audiometric procedures. Although most retarded subjects included in these studies demonstrated reliability, some retarded subjects may give unreliable data with our current tests and level of skill. In addition to control of the critical audiometric variables, appropriate skill and knowledge are required in making reliability judgments about audiometric data obtained from each retarded subject just as they are with non-retarded subjects. Although basic reliability has been demonstrated, it still seems appropriate to report reliability data on procedures and subjects used in inter-method comparison research. Reliability data should also be provided on modified and new procedures as they are applied to various retarded samples.

D. Drugs

Tranquilizers or relaxing drugs may be used to control behavior during testing. Also, at the time for an audiologic assessment, many retarded subjects may be on medication for various other reasons. The data on permanent changes in auditory function due to certain antibiotics seems conclusive, and limited data on temporary changes due to certain relaxing drugs are also reported for non-retarded subjects (e.g., Cawthorne & Ranger, 1957; Fulton, 1969; Katz, 1969; Leach, 1962; Lloyd & Young, 1969; McGee, 1968, Price, 1969). Considering the possible temporary and permanent effect of drugs on audiometric performance and the frequency of using drugs with the retarded plus the possible use of drugs for the physiologic control of behavior during testing, the effect of drugs on the auditory performance of retardates should be a major area of investigation. However, to this reviewer's knowledge there has only been one major investigation (Nudo, 1967) and a pilot investigation in this area (Katz, 1969).

Nudo (1967) investigated the effects of Trilafon (perphenazine) on puretone and speech audiometry with 41 institutionalized retardates (CA = 12-43 years) with normal hearing and various types of hearing loss. He found small but statistically significant improvements in some of the threshold measures. The pilot investigation reported by Katz (1969) was inconclusive. Considerable research is needed to improve the interpretation of audiometric data obtained from retardates on medication. Extensive research is also needed before audiologists start to make use of drugs to control behavior during testing.

V. HABILITATION

The incidence studies have clearly demonstrated that hearing impairment is a major problem among the retarded. This means medical and nonmedical (e.g., communicational, educational, social, vocational aspects) programming for the audiologic aspects of mental retardation should be a major concern to program administrators. Unfortunately, in general, these areas have been neglected.

The area of medical habilitation was considered in a previous section on incidence (Section II), and will not be reviewed at this point. The major needs for research, service, and demonstration in this area are apparent.

The area of nonmedical habilitation was also briefly discussed in a previous section, but further literature will be considered in this section. Most of the literature is of a discussion nature, with a limited number of case studies, and only a few "research papers."

Some of the incidence studies stressed follow-up and a total programmatic approach including audiometric screening, audiologic assessment, otologic examination, otologic habilitation, and aural (re)habilitation phases (e.g., P. W. Johnston & Farrell, 1954, 1957; Lloyd & Reid, 1967; Rittmanic, 1959; Schlanger & Gottsleben, 1956; Siegenthaler & Krzywicki, 1959). Additional discussions of specific aural (re)habilitation programs have also been presented (e.g., Barber, 1968; Barnes, 1967; Bissell, Blue, & Stevens, 1965; Huffman, 1967; James, 1967; Lloyd, 1967; Miltenberger, 1967; Moore, Miltenberger, & Barber, 1969; Rittmanic, 1966; Silverman, 1967; Snyder, 1965; Stuckless & Burrows, 1967). In general, these programmatic discussions have emphasized the need for both direct clinical services to the retarded patient and indirect services by working with others working with the retarded. Specific classroom considerations and other suggestions for working with the hearing-impaired retardate have been presented stressing "indirect services" (e.g., Glovsky & Rigrodsky, 1963; P. W. Johnston & Farrell, 1954, 1957; Lloyd, 1966c; Lloyd & Burrows, 1967; Luszki, 1964; McCoy & Lloyd, 1967). There have been several case study reports that have demonstrated benefits of aural (re)habilitation with retarded patients (Hartman, 1958; Rittmanic, 1959; Schlanger & Gottsleben, 1957; Snyder & Lloyd, 1967; E. C. Murphy, 1964; Taylor, 1968).

There have been numerous references to the multiply handicapped deaf, including the diagnostic and habilitative (and/or educational) problems of the mentally retarded deaf (e.g., Abruzzo & Stehman, 1961; Anderson, Stevens, Stuckless, 1966; Connor, 1963; Costello, 1966; Johnson, 1964; W. A. Johnston, 1968; Keir, 1965; Leshin & Stahlecker, 1962; Mangan, 1964; Minski, 1957; Mitra, 1969; Monaghan, 1964; Nelson, 1961; Ramger, 1957; Schunhoff & MacPherson, 1951; Sellin, 1964; Warren & Kraus, 1963).

Although there have been many references to the aural (re)habilitation of the hearing-impaired retardate, research in this area is lacking. There have been two studies involving auditory training with specified listening activities for retarded subjects (Christensen & Schlanger, 1964; MacPherson, 1960; Schlanger, 1961, 1962; Schlanger & Christensen, 1964; Wolfe & MacPherson, 1959). These investigations are encouraging in that they demonstrated improved listening behavior at the end of the program, but the programs involved general listening activities and were not designed for specific hearing-impaired subjects. Candland and Conklyn (1962) reported a pilot study in which they successfully used the "oddity problem" and positive reinforcement approach to teach four congenitally deaf retarded subjects to read. Unfortunately, the extension of this pilot project has not appeared. There is a major need for research of this type. There is a need to apply behavior modification and programming principles to improve the hearing-impaired retardates' skills in specific areas such as auditory speech reception, language, speech, and visual speech reception. Research is also needed on the application of these principles to other areas of aural rehabilitation such as hearing aid orientation. There is also a need to explore different methods of communication for the retarded-deaf.

In summary, it is clear that aural (re)habilitation of the hearing-impaired retardate is the area that has been most neglected by researchers. Although continued research is needed in some areas of audiometry the major thrust of investigation should be in the field of (re)habilitative audiology.

VI. SUMMARY AND CONCLUSIONS

Within the past twenty years a sizeable amount of literature has been addressed to the "Audiologic Aspects of Mental Retardation." In reviewing this body of literature it is assumed that the "retarded" are not a homogeneous group of individuals. Therefore, the findings with one group of retarded subjects have only limited generalization to other retarded subgroups. In general, the audiologic sophistication reflected in the literature has improved with time. This chapter has reviewed this body of literature in a chronological sequence within the structure of four major phases, or areas, of activity.

The first phase, determination of the incidence of hearing impairment among the retarded, revealed that the retarded have a significantly higher incidence of hearing impairment than is found in the general population. This finding stresses the need for increased audiologic programming, including aural (re)habilitation. Except for the possibility of exploring specific subgroups of retardation there appears to be little need for further research in this area.

The second phase, methodological and intermethod comparison research, resulted from the problems encountered testing some retarded subjects. This research has resulted in improved audiologic assessment procedures for the retarded. However, there is still need for considerable research in the development of improved methodologies and the application of audiologic methodologies that are currently available.

The third phase of investigation includes a number of reliability and intramethod comparison studies. Research in this area has demonstrated considerable reliability of many of the audiologic procedures used with many retarded individuals. However, further research in this area is definitely warranted.

The fourth and most limited phase is concerned with the (re)habilitation of the hearing impaired retardate. Although program needs have been stressed there have not been any major research or demonstration projects in this area. Research and demonstration projects in this area should receive top priority during the next few years.

In conclusion, it appears the general summary statements of a national conference on "The Audiologic Assessment of the Mentally Retarded" held in 1965 are still appropriate. Therefore the "general conclusions" of the conference are presented as a conclusion to this review chapter.

In addition to the specific summary statements presented above . . . , there are several generalized conclusions that may be drawn from the papers presented along with the scheduled and unscheduled discussions of the week. These generalized conclusions are as follows:

1. There is a need for increased audiologic services for the retarded. It is obvious that audiologists can provide considerable information to assist in the total medical and non-medical habilitation of the retarded; however, relatively few institutions and other programs for the retarded are adequately staffed with qualified audiologists.
2. Although the qualified audiologist with his current armamentarium can enhance the total habilitation program for the retarded, it is apparent that audiology as a profession needs to develop more effective assessment procedures in order to provide relevant data on the many DTT (or the untestable by currently used methods) subjects.
3. In addition to the need for more powerful tests, to facilitate the audiologic assessment of the previously untestable or DTT child, a major need exists to utilize (and in

some cases adapt) currently available supra-threshold tests in the determination of site of lesion of auditory pathologies among the retarded.
4. If properly developed, institutions for the retarded provide an excellent setting for basic research in the areas of audition and the communicative processes. MR institutions could also provide an optimal setting for applied research especially in the area of test development.
5. Institutions that develop a strong audiology program under the direction of a qualified audiologist provide an exceptional clinical training facility.
6. The research data and clinical experiences obtained in institutions for the retarded have widespread implications for improved audiology services in nonretarded populations. The most immediate applications are related to other DTT populations of children, but the underlying data and clinical skills are pertinent to audiology in general [Lloyd & Frisina, 1965, pp. 282-284].

REFERENCES

Abernathy, E. B. Auditory acuity of feeble minded children. Unpublished doctoral dissertation, Ohio State University, 1938.

Abruzzo, A. M., & Stehman, V. A. (Project Directors). The identification and vocational training of the institutionalized retarded-deaf patient (Part I Diagnostic Study). Office of Vocational Rehabilitation, RD 800S, Washington, D.C., 1961 (Michigan Department of Mental Health, Research Report No. 43).

Anderson, R. M., Stevens, G. D., & Stuckless, E. R. Provisions for the education of mentally retarded deaf students in residential schools for the deaf. Cooperative Research Project No. 32-48-1110-5008, U.S. Office of Education, University of Pittsburgh, 1966.

Atkinson, C. J. Perceptive and responsive abilities of mentally retarded children as measured by several auditory threshold tests. Cooperative Research Project No. 176 (6471), U.S. Office of Education, Southern Illinois University, 1960.

Barber, P. S. Oscillator placement in bone conduction testing with selected groups of children. Unpublished master's thesis, Northern Illinois University, 1967.

Barber, P. S. Diagnosis and habilitation of suspected hearing problems in young mentally retarded children. Paper presented at the meeting of the American Association of Mental Deficiency. Boston, May 1968.

Barber, P. S., & Rose, D. E. Bone conduction oscillator placement in testing hearing of selected groups of children. *American Journal of Mental Deficiency*, 1969, 73, 666-672.

Barnes, G. H. A team-teaching-project approach with the multiple handicapped deaf. *Report of the proceedings of the 43d meeting of the convention of American instructors of the deaf.* West Hartford, Conn.: American School for the Deaf, 1967. Pp. 276-280.

Barr, B. Pure tone audiometry for preschool children. *Acta Oto-Laryngologica, Supplementum*, 1955, 121.

Baumeister, A., Beedle, R., & Urquhart, D. GSR conditioning in normals and retardates. *American Journal of Mental Deficiency*, 1964, 69, 114-120.

Baumeister, A., Hawkins, W. F., & Kellas, G. The interactive effects of stimulus intensity and intelligence upon reaction time. *American Journal of Mental Deficiency*, 1965, 69, 526-530.

Beedle, R. K., Webb, C. E., Kinde, S. W., & Weber, B. A. A behavior observation technique of hearing screening of institutionalized mentally retarded children. *American Journal of Mental Deficiency*, 1966, 70, 675-682.

Benda, C. E. *The child with mongolism.* New York: Grune & Stratton, 1960.

Birch, J. W., & Matthews, J. The hearing of mental defectives: Its measurement and characteristics. *American Journal of Mental Deficiency*, 1951, **55**, 384-393.

Bissell, N. E., Blue, C. M., & Stephens, L. M. Audiology services in a day school for SMR children. Paper presented at the meeting of the American Association of Mental Deficiency, Miami Beach, June 1965.

Blough, D. S. A method for obtaining psychophysical thresholds from the pigeon. *Journal of the Experimental Analysis of Behavior*, 1958, **1**, 31-43.

Bochenek, A., & Kus, J. Case of congenital hearing impairment with retinitis pigmentosa and mental deficiency. *Otolaryngologica Polska*, 1958, **12**, 181-186.

Bradley, E., Evans, W. E., & Worthington, A. M. The relationship between administration time for audiometric testing and the mental ability of mentally deficient children. *American Journal of Mental Deficiency*, 1955, **60**, 346-353.

Bradshaw, A. W., A new approach to auditory testing with the mental retardates. Unpublished master's thesis, Vanderbilt University, 1961.

Bricker, W. A., & Bricker, D. D. A comparison of four variations of operant audiometry with low-functioning children. *American Journal of Mental Deficiency*, 1969, **73**, 981-987.

Brooks, R. S., & Goetzinger, C. P. Vocabulary variables and language skills in the PB discrimination of Children. *Journal of Auditory Research*, 1966, **6**, 357-370.

Brunt, M. A. Performance on three auditory tests by children with functional articulation disorders. Unpublished master's thesis, University of Pittsburgh, 1965.

Burt, C. *The backward child*. New York: Appleton-Century, 1937.

Butterfield, G. A note on the use of cardiac rate in the audiometric appraisal of retarded children. *Journal of Speech and Hearing Disorders*, 1962, **27**, 378-379. (Forum)

Candland, D. K., & Conklyn, D. H. Use of the oddity problem in teaching mentally retarded deaf-mutes to read: A pilot project. *Training School Bulletin*, 1962, **59**, 38-41.

Carhart, R. Clinical application of BC audiometry. *A.M.A. Archives of Otolaryngology*, 1950, **51**, 798-808.

Cawthorne, T., & Ranger, D. Toxic effect of streptomycin upon balance and hearing. *British Medical Journal*, 1957, **1**, 1444-1446.

Chaiklin, J. B., & Ventry, I. M. Functional hearing loss. In J. Jerger (Ed.), *Modern developments in audiology*. New York: Academic Press, 1963. Pp. 76-125.

Christensen, N. J., & Schlanger, B. B., Auditory training with the mentally retarded. *Mental Retardation*, 1964, **2**, 290-293.

Ciocco, A. A., & Palmer, C. E. The hearing of school children: A statistical study of audiometry and clinical records. *Monographs of the Society for Research in Child Development*, 1941, 7, No. 3, 3-4.

Clausen, J. Threshold for pure tone and speech in retardates. *American Journal of Mental Deficiency*, 1966, **70**, 556-562.

Collmann, R. D. The galvanic skin response of mentally retarded and other children in England. *American Journal of Mental Deficiency*, 1959, **63**, 626-632.

Connor, L. E. Research in the education of the deaf in the United States. *Volta Review*, 1963, **65**, 523-534.

Costello, P. M. The dead end kid. *Volta Review*, 1966, **68**, 639-643, 714.

Currier, W. D. Office noises and their effect on audiometry. *A.M.A. Archives of Otolaryngology*, 1943, **38**, 49-59.

Curry, E. T., & Kurtzrock, G. H. A preliminary investigation of the ear-choice technique in threshold audiometry. *Journal of Speech and Hearing Disorders*, 1951, **16**, 340-345.

Dansinger, S., & Madow, A. A. Verbal auditory screening with the mentally retarded. *American Journal of Mental Deficiency*, 1966, **71**, 387-392.

Darley, F. L. (Ed.) Identification audiometry. *Journal of Speech and Hearing Disorders, Monograph Supplement*, 1961, **9**, 1-68.

D'Asaro, M. J., & Grey, H. A. A comparison of two methods of audiometric threshold determination in neurologically handicapped and normal children. *Asha,* 1964, **6,** 411. (Abstract)

Davis, H. The ISO zero-reference level for audiometers. *Archives of Otolaryngology,* 1965, **81,** 145–149.

Davis, H., & Kranz, F. International audiometric zero. *Journal of the Acoustical Society of America,* 1964, **36,** 1450–1454.

Davis, H., & Silverman, S. R. (Eds.) *Hearing and deafness.* New York: Holt, Rinehart & Winston, 1960.

Downs, M. P. Audiometry in children. *International Audiology,* 1962, **1,** 268–270.

Downs, M. P. Organization and procedures of a newborn infant screening program. *Hearing and Speech News,* 1967, 27–36.

Dugas, J. L., & Baumeister, A. A. A comparison of intra-subject variability in auditory difference limens of normals and retardates. *American Journal of Mental Deficiency,* 1968, **73,** 500–504.

Eagles, E. L., Wishik, S. M., Doerfler, L. G., Melnick, W., & Levine, H. S. Hearing sensitivity and related factors in children. *Laryngoscope,* 1963, June. (Special Issue)

Ewing, I. R. Deafness in infancy and early childhood. *Journal of Laryngology and Otology,* 1943, **58,** 137–142.

Ewing, I. R. Screening tests and guidance clinics for babies and young children. In A. W. G. Ewing (Ed.), *Educational guidance and the deaf child.* Manchester, Eng.: Manchester University Press, 1957. Pp. 21–43.

Ewing, I. R., & Ewing, A. W. G. The ascertainment of deafness in infancy and early childhood. *Journal of Laryngology and Otology,* 1944, **59,** 309–333.

Farrimond, T. Factors influencing auditory perception of pure tones and speech. *Journal of Speech and Hearing Research,* 1962, **5,** 194–204.

Feinmesser, M., Baubergertell, L., & Bilski-Hirsch, R. A hearing survey in the public schools of Jerusalem. *Israel Medical Journal,* 1959, **18,** 59–63. (*Deafness Speech and Hearing Abstracts,* 1960, 1, 13, Abstract.)

Foale, M., & Paterson, J. W. The hearing of mental defectives. *American Journal of Mental Deficiency,* 1954, **59,** 254–258.

Frisina, D. R. Measurement of hearing in children. In J. Jerger (Ed.), *Modern developments in audiology.* New York: Academic Press, 1963. Pp. 126–166.

Fulton, R. T. Psychogalvanic skin response and conditioned orientation reflex audiometry with mentally retarded children. Unpublished doctoral thesis, Purdue University, 1962.

Fulton, R. T. Bekesy audiometry with the mentally retarded. Paper presented at the meeting of the American Association on Mental Deficiency, Chicago, May, 1966.

Fulton, R. T. Standard puretone and Bekesy audiometric measures with the mentally retarded. *American Journal of Mental Deficiency,* 1967, **72,** 60–73. (a)

Fulton, R. T. Task adaptation and word familiarity of W-22 discrimination lists with retarded children. *Journal of Auditory Research,* 1967, **7,** 353–358. (b)

Fulton, R. T. Bekesy audiometry. In R. T. Fulton & L. L. Lloyd (Eds.). *Audiometry for the retarded: With implications for the difficult-to-test.* Baltimore: Williams & Wilkins, 1969, Pp. 57–96.

Fulton, R. T., & Giffin, C. S. Audiological-otological considerations with the mentally retarded. *Mental Retardation,* 1967, **5,** 26–31.

Fulton, R. T., & Graham, J. T. Puretone reliability with the mentally retarded. *American Journal of Mental Deficiency,* 1964, **69,** 265–268.

Fulton, R. T., & Graham, J. T. Conditioned orientation reflex audiometry with the mentally retarded. *American Journal of Mental Deficiency,* 1966, **70,** 703–708.

Fulton, R. T., & Lloyd, L. L. Hearing impairment in a population of children with Down's Syndrome. *American Journal of Mental Deficiency*, 1968, **73**, 298–302.

Fulton, R. T., & Lloyd, L. L. (Eds.) *Audiometry for the retarded: With implications for the difficult-to-test*. Baltimore: Williams & Wilkins, 1969.

Fulton, R. T., & Reid, M. J. A survey of audiologic/otologic programs of 142 state institutions for mentally retarded. Parsons Demonstration Project Report. No. 72, Parsons (Kansas) State Hospital and Training Center, 1967.

Fulton, R. T., & Reid, M. J. Bekesy audiometry with the retarded. Parsons Demonstration Project Report No. 83, Parsons (Kansas) State Hospital and Training Center, 1968.

Gaines, J. A. L. A comparison of two audiometric tests administered to a group of mentally retarded children. Unpublished master's thesis, University of Nebraska, 1961.

Gellis, S. S., and Feingold, M. *Atlas of mental retardation syndromes*. Washington, D.C.: U.S. Government Printing Office, 1968.

Giolas, T. G. Speech audiometry. In R. T. Fulton & L. L. Lloyd (Eds). *Audiometry for the retarded: With implications for the difficult-to-test*. Baltimore: Williams & Wilkins, 1969. Pp. 32–56.

Glovsky, L. Audiological assessment of a mongoloid population. *Training School Bulletin*, 1966, **63**, 27–36.

Glovsky, L., & Rigrodsky, S. A classroom program for auditorally handicapped mentally deficient children. *Training School Bulletin*, 1963, **60**, 56–69.

Goldberg, B., Foster, D. B., Segerson, J. A., & Baumeister, J. Congenital malformations in the mentally retarded. *Bulletin of the Menninger Clinic*, 1963, **27**, 275–290.

Goldstein, R. Electrophysiologic audiometry. In J. Jerger (Ed.), *Modern developments in audiology*. New York: Academic Press, 1963. Pp. 167–192.

Goldstein, R. Pseudohypacusis. *Journal of Speech and Hearing Disorders*, 1966, **31**, 341–352.

Graham, J. T. Evaluation of methods for predicting speech reception threshold. *Archives of Otolaryngology*, 1960, **72**, 347–350.

Graham, J. T. The effect of signal magnitude on frequency of response in galvanic skin response audiometry. *American Journal of Mental Deficiency*, 1969, in press.

Hardy, J. B., Dougherty, A., & Hardy, W. G. Hearing responses and audiologic screening in infants. *Journal of Pediatrics*, 1959, **53**, 382–390.

Hartman, B. T. Study of therapeutic and functional values of hearing aids for the mentally handicapped. *American Journal of Mental Deficiency*, 1958, **62**, 803–809.

Heber, R. A manual on terminology and classification in mental retardation. *American Journal of Mental Deficiency*, 1961, (Monogr. Suppl.).

Hilson, D. The abnormally shaped ear. *Developmental Medicine and Child Neurology*, 1966, **8**, 210–212.

Hirsh, I. J. *The measurement of hearing*. New York: McGraw-Hill, 1952.

Hodgson, W. R. Audiological report of a patient with left hemispherectomy. *Journal of Speech and Hearing Disorders*, 1967, **32**, 39–45.

Hogan, D. D. The use of the summing computer in analyzing the auditory evoked cortical responses of mentally retarded adults. Unpublished doctoral dissertation, Purdue University, 1966.

Hogan, D. D. Autonomic responses as supplementary hearing measures. In R. T. Fulton & L. L. Lloyd (Eds.), *Audiometry for the retarded: With implications for the difficult-to-test*. Baltimore: Williams & Wilkins, 1969. Pp. 238–262.

Hogan, D. D., & Graham, J. The use of the summing computer for analyzing auditory evoked responses of mentally retarded adults. *Journal of Auditory Research*, 1967, **7**, 1–13.

Hollis, J. H., & Fulton, R. T. Bekesy audiometer modification for Blough threshold techniques. Parsons Demonstration Project Report No. 84, Parsons (Kansas) State Hospital and Training Center, 1968.

Hood, J. D. The principles and practice of BC audiometry. *Proceedings of the Royal Society of Medicine*, 1957, **50**, 689-697.

Huffman, J. M. The hospital improvement program for the mentally retarded deaf minors at Sonoma State Hospital. *Report of the proceedings of the 43d meeting of the convention of American instructors of the deaf.* West Hartford, Conn.: American School for the Deaf, 1967. Pp. 270-272.

Hutton, C., & Weaver, J. PB intelligibility and word familiarity. *Laryngoscope*, 1959, **69**, 1443-1450.

Ickes, W. K. A clinical application of an accuracy indicator for testing hearing. Unpublished doctoral dissertation, Southern Illinois University, 1960.

Irwin, J. V., Hind, J. E., & Aronson, A. E. Experience with conditioned GSR audiometry in a group of mentally deficient individuals. *Training School Bulletin*, 1957, **54**, 26-31.

James, W. C. A hospital improvement program for mentally retarded deaf children at Sonoma State Hospital. *Report of the proceedings of the 43d meeting of the convention of American instructors of the deaf.* West Hartford, Conn.: American School for the Deaf, 1967. Pp. 272-276.

Jerger, J. F. Hearing tests in otologic diagnosis. *Asha*, 1962, **4**, 139-145.

Johnson, R. K. The institutionalized mentally retarded deaf. *Report of the 41st meeting of the convention of American instructors of the deaf.* Gallaudet College, June 1963. Washington, D.C.: U.S. Government Printing Office, 1964. Pp. 568-573.

Johnston, P. W. & Farrell, M. J. Auditory impairment among resident school children at the Walter E. Fernald State School. *American Journal of Mental Deficiency*, 1954, **58**, 640-643.

Johnston, P. W., & Farrell, M. J. An experiment in improved medical and educational services for the hard of hearing children at the Walter E. Fernald State School. *American Journal of Mental Deficiency*, 1957, **62**, 230-237.

Johnston, W. A. Let's educate multiply handicapped children. *Teacher Deaf*, 1968, **66**, 115-119.

Katz, J. Differentional diagnosis of auditory impairments. In R. T. Fulton & L. L. Lloyd (Eds.), *Audiometry for the retarded: With implications for the difficult-to-test*. Baltimore: Williams & Wilkins, 1969. Pp. 97-124.

Keir, E. H. Communication problems of the mentally retarded deaf child. In J. D. Van Pelt (Ed.), *Proceedings of the 4th interstate conference on mental deficiency.* Melbourne: Australian Group for the Scientific Study of Mental Deficiency, 1965. Pp. 43-50.

Kimmich, H. M. Otologic aspects of mental retardation: Implications for diagnostic audiology. In L. L. Lloyd & D. R. Frisina (Eds.), *The audiologic assessment of the mentally retarded: Proceedings of a national conference.* Parsons, Kansas: Speech and Hearing Department, Parsons State Hospital and Training Center, 1965. Pp. 119-136.

Knox, E. C. A method of obtaining pure tone audiograms in young children. *Journal of Laryngology and Otology*, 1960, **74**, 475-479.

Kock, C., & Serra, M. Mongolism and alterations of acoustic and vestibular function. *Archives of Italian Oto-rhinolaryngology*, 1962, **70**, 45-61.

Kodman, F. Sensory processes and mental deficiency. In N. R. Ellis (Ed.), *Handbook of mental deficiency*, New York: McGraw-Hill, 1963.

Kodman, F., Jr. The incidence of hearing loss in mentally retarded children. *American Journal of Mental Deficiency*, 1958, **62**, 675-678.

Kodman, F., Fein, A., & Mixson, A. Psychogalvanic skin response audiometry with severe mentally retarded children. *American Journal of Mental Deficiency*, 1959, **64**, 131-136.

Kodman, F., Powers, T. R., Philip, P. P., & Weller, G. M., An investigation of hearing loss in mentally retarded children and adults. *American Journal of Mental Deficiency*, 1958, **63**, 460-463 (a).

Kodman, F., Jr., Powers, T. R., Weller, G. M., & Philip, P. P. Pure tone audiometry with the mentally retarded. *Exceptional Children*, 1958, 24, 303-305 (b).

Kopatic, N. J. The reliability of pure tone audiometry with the mentally retarded: Some practical and theoretical considerations. *Training School Bulletin*, 1963, 60, 130-136.

Kopra, L., & Blosser, D. Effects of method of measurement on most comfortable loudness level for speech. *Journal of Speech and Hearing Research*, 1968, 11, 497-508.

Krugman, S. Rubella: A new light on an old disease. *Journal of Pediatrics*, 1965, 67, 159-161.

LaCrosse, E. L., & Bidlake, H. A method to test the hearing of mentally retarded children. *Volta Review*, 1964, 66, 27-30.

Lamb, L. E., & Graham, J. Influence of signal variables on evoked responses to sound. *Journal of Speech and Hearing Research*, 1967, 10, 257-267.

Lamb, L. E., & Norris, T. W. Acoustic impedance measurement. In R. T. Fulton & L. L. Lloyd (Eds.), *Audiometry for the retarded: With implications for the difficult-to-test*. Baltimore: Williams & Wilkins, 1969. Pp. 164-209.

Lamb, N. L., & Graham, J. T. GSR audiometry with mentally retarded adult males. *American Journal of Mental Deficiency*, 1968, 72, 721-727.

Leach, W. Ototoxicity of neomycin and other antibiotics. *Journal of Laryngology and Otology*, 1962, 76, 774-790.

Leshin, G., & Stahlecker, L. Academic expectancies of slow-learning deaf children. *Volta Review*, 1962, 64, 599-602.

Levine, E. S. Psychoeducational study of children born deaf following maternal rubella. *American Journal of Diseases of Children*, 1951, 86, 199-209.

Lindsley, O. R. A behavioral measure of television viewing. *Journal of Advertising Research*, 1962, 2, 2-12.

Little, S. W. Suspected hearing defects in phenylketonuria. *Archives of Otolaryngology*, 1962, 75, 515-518.

Lloyd, L. L. A comparison of selected auditory measures on normal hearing mentally retarded children. Unpublished doctoral dissertation, University of Iowa, 1965. (a)

Lloyd, L. L. The new audiology program at Parsons State Hospital and Training Center. *Hearing News*, 1965, 33, 5-7, 12. (b)

Lloyd, L. L. Use of the slide show audiometric technique with mentally retarded children. *Exceptional Children*, 1965, 32, 93-98. (c)

Lloyd, L. L. Behavioral audiometry viewed as an operant procedure. *Journal of Speech and Hearing Disorders*, 1966, 31, 128-136. (a)

Lloyd, L. L. Comments on "dilemmas in identification audiometry." *Journal of Speech and Hearing Disorders*, 1966, 31, 161-165. (b)

Lloyd, L. L. Helping your retarded patients with hearing impairments. *Journal of Psychiatric Nursing*, 1966, May-June, 255-259. (c)

Lloyd, L. L. Programming for the audiologic aspects of the mentally retarded. Paper presented at the annual meeting of the CEC, St. Louis, March 29, 1967.

Lloyd, L. L. Operant conditioning audiometry with retarded children. In E. F. Waldon (Ed.), *Differential diagnosis of speech and hearing problems of mental retardates*. Washington, D.C.: Catholic University of America Press, 1968. Pp. 103-121.

Lloyd, L. L. & Burrows, N. L. Audiologic considerations for teachers of the retarded. *Education and Training of the Mentally Retarded*, 1967, 2, 155-163.

Lloyd, L. L., & Frisina, D. R. Introduction to the March audiology conference. In L. L. Lloyd & D. R. Frisina (Eds.), *The audiologic assessment of the mentally retarded: Proceedings of a national conference*. Parsons, Kansas: Speech and Hearing Department, Parsons State Hospital and Training Center, 1965. Pp. 7-16.

Lloyd, L. L., & Melrose, J. Inter-method comparisons of selected and audiometric measures used with normal hearing mentally retarded children. *Journal of Auditory Research*, 1966, 6, 205–217. (a)

Lloyd, L. L., & Melrose, J. Reliability of selected auditory responses of normal hearing mentally retarded children. *American Journal of Mental Deficiency*, 1966, 71, 133–143.(b)

Lloyd, L. L., & Reid, M. J. The percent of hearing impaired and difficult-to-test patients at Parsons State Hospital and Training Center. A special report presented to the March Audiology conference, 1965. In L. L. Lloyd & D. R. Frisina (Eds.), *The audiologic assessment of the mentally retarded: Proceedings of a national conference.* Parsons, Kansas: Speech and Hearing Department, Parsons State Hospital and Training Center, 1965.

Lloyd, L. L., & Reid, M. J. The reliability of speech audiometry with institutionalized retarded children. *Journal of Speech and Hearing Research*, 1966, 9, 450–455.

Lloyd, L. L., & Reid, M. J. The incidence of hearing impairment in an institutionalized mentally retarded population. *American Journal of Mental Deficiency*, 1967, 71, 746–763.

Lloyd, L. L., Reid, M. J., & McManis, D. L. The effect of response mode on the SRT's obtained from retarded children. *Journal of Auditory Research*, 1967, 7, 219–222.

Lloyd, L. L., Reid, M. J., & McManis, D. L. Pure tone reliability of a clinical sample of institutionalized MR children. *American Journal of Mental Deficiency*, 1968, 73, 279–282.(a)

Lloyd, L. L., Spradlin, J. E., & Reid, M. J. An operant audiometric procedure of difficult-to-test patients. *Journal of Speech and Hearing Disorders*, 1968, 33, 236–245.(b)

Lloyd, L. L., & Young, C. E. Puretone audiometry. In R. T. Fulton & L. L. Lloyd (Eds.), *Audiometry for the retarded: With implications for the difficult-to-test.* Baltimore: Williams & Wilkins, 1969. Pp. 1–31.

Luszki, W. A. Application of deprivation concepts to the deaf retarded. *Mental Retardation*, 1964, 2, 164–170.

MacPherson, J. R. The evaluation and development of techniques for testing the auditory acuity of trainable mentally retarded children. Unpublished doctoral dissertation, University of Texas, 1960.

Madden, R. The school status of the hard of hearing child. *Teachers College Contributions to Education*, 1931, No. 499.

Mangan, K. R. A state program of services for the mentally retarded deaf child. *Report of the proceedings of the 41st meeting of the convention of American instructors of the deaf.* Gallaudet College, June 1963. Washington, D.C.: U.S. Government Printing Office, 1964. Pp. 565–568.

Masland, R. L., Sarason, S. B., & Gladwin, T. *Mental subnormality: Biological, psychological and cultural factors.* New York: Basic Books, 1958.

McCoy, D. F., & Lloyd, L. L. A hearing aid orientation program for mentally retarded children. *Training School Bulletin*, 1967, 64, 21–30.

McGee, T. M. Ototoxic antibiotics. *Volta Review*, 1968, 9, 667–671.

McIntire, M. S., Menolascino, F. J., & Wiley, J. H. Mongolism—some clinical aspects. *American Journal of Mental Deficiency*, 1965, 69, 794–800.

Melmer, P. E. The speech characteristics of a selected group of institutionalized mentally retarded children of school age. Unpublished master's thesis, University of Nebraska, 1958.

Meyers, C. K., & Harris, J. D. The inherent stability of the auditory threshold. Medical Research Laboratory (New London) Progress Report No. 3, Bu Med. Project NM-003-021, 1949.

Meyerson, L. Hearing for speech in children: A verbal audiometric test. Unpublished doctoral dissertation, Stanford University, 1952.

Meyerson, L. Hearing for speech in children: A verbal audiometric test. *Acta Oto-Laryngologica, Supplementum*, 1956, 128.

Meyerson, L., & Michael, J. L. The measurement of sensory thresholds in exceptional children: An experimental approach to some problems of differential diagnosis and education with special reference to hearing. Cooperative Research Project No. 418, U. S. Office of Education, Department of Health, Education and Welfare, University of Houston, Houston, Texas, 1960.

Meyerson, L., & Michael, J. L. Assessment of hearing by operant conditioning procedures. *Report of the proceedings of the international congress on education of the deaf and of the 41st meeting of the convention of American instructors of the deaf.* Gallaudet College, June 1963. Washington, D.C.: U.S. Government Printing Office, 1964. (Senate Document No. 106, 88th Congress, 2nd Session.)

Michigan Department of Health. Vision and hearing screening in selected classes for the mentally retarded — City of Detroit. U.S. Department of Health, Education and Welfare (Welfare Administration, Children's Bureau), 1966.

Miller, J., DeSchweinitz, L., & Goetzinger, C. P. How infants three, four, and five months of age respond to sound. *Exceptional Children*, 1963, 30, 149-154.

Miller, J. B., & Miller, C. A. Acoustically handicapped children: A ten year summary. *Journal of the Kansas Medical Society*, 1959, 60, 343-348.

Miltenberger, G. Hearing aid evaluation program for the mentally retarded at the Dixon State School. Paper presented at the meeting of the American Association of Mental Deficiency, Denver, May 1967.

Minski, L. *Deafness, mutism and mental deficiency in children.* New York: Philosophical Library, 1957.

Mitra, S. B. A descriptive study of institutional educational programs for the mentally retarded deaf. Unpublished doctoral dissertation, The Catholic University of America, 1969.

Monaghan, A. Educational placement for the multiply handicapped hearing impaired child. *Volta Review*, 1964, 66, 383-387.

Moore, E. J., Miltenberger, G. E., & Barber, P. S. Hearing aid orientation in a state school for the mentally retarded. *Journal of Speech and Hearing Disorders*, 1969, 34, 142-145.

Mosier, H. D., Grossman, H. J., & Dingman, H. F. Physical growth in mental defectives: A study in an institutionalized population. *Pediatrics*, 1965, 36 (Suppl.).

Moss, J. M., Moss, M., & Tizard, J. Electrodermal response audiometry with mentally defective children. *Journal of Speech and Hearing Research*, 1961, 4, 41-47.

Murphy, E. C. A future for a profoundly deaf and mildly retarded child. In J. Oster (Ed.), *International Copenhagen congress on the scientific study of mental retardation.* Copenhagen: Statens Andssvageforsorg Falkoner Alle 11, 1964. Paper 162, pp. 847-848.

Murphy, K. P. Development of hearing in babies. *Hearing News*, 1961, 29, 9-11.

Murphy, K. P. Development of hearing in babies — a diagnostic system for detecting early signs of deafness in infants. *Child and Family*, 1962, 1, 16-17.

Myatt, B. D. & Landes, B. A. Assessing discrimination loss in children. *Archives of Otolaryngology*, 1963, 77, 359-362.

Myklebust, H. R. The deaf child with other handicaps. *American Annals of the Deaf*, 1958, 103, 496-509.

Nathan, P. E., Schneller, P., & Lindsley, O. R. Direct measurement of communication during psychiatric admission interviews. *Behaviour Research and Therapy*, 1964, 2, 49-57.

Nelson, M. Identification and training of institutionalized and retarded deaf patients. *Journal of Speech and Hearing Research*, 1961, 4, 398.

Newby, H. A. *Audiology.* (2nd ed.) New York: Appleton-Century-Crofts, 1964.

Nober, E. H. *The audiometric assessment of mentally retarded patients.* Syracuse: Syracuse University Division of Special Education, 1968.

Nodar, R. H. An investigation of auditory evoked responses of mentally retarded adults during sleep. Unpublished doctoral dissertation, Purdue University, 1967.

Nodar, R. H. An investigation of auditory evoked responses of mentally retarded adults during sleep. *Journal of Electroencephalography and Clinical Neurophysiology*, 1968, **25**, 73-76.

Nudo, L. Comparison by age of audiological and otological findings in a state residential institution for the mentally retarded: A preliminary report. In L. L. Lloyd & D. R. Frisina (Eds.), *The audiologic assessment of the mentally retarded. Proceedings of a national conference.* Parsons, Kansas: Speech and Hearing Department, Parsons State Hospital and Training Center, 1965. Pp. 137-163.

Nudo, L. The effects of frelofon on certain audiological measures obtained from an institutionalized population with normal hearing acuity, conductive hearing losses and sensori-neural hearing losses. Unpublished doctoral dissertation, University of Illinois, 1967.

Oyer, H. J., & Doudna, M. Word familiarity as a factor in testing discrimination of hard-of-hearing subjects. *Archives of Otolaryngology*, 1960, **72**, 351-355.

Pantelakos, C. G. Audiometric and otolaryngologic survey of retarded students. *North Carolina Medical Journal*, 1963, **24**, 238-242.

Pasamanick, B., & Lilienfeld, A. M. Association of maternal and fetal factors with development: I. Abnormalities in the prenatal and paranatal periods. *Journal of the American Medical Association*, 1955, **159**, 155-160.

President's Panel. *A proposed program for national action to combat mental retardation.* Washington, D.C.: Superintendent of Documents, 1962.

Price, L. L. Cortical evoked response audiometry. In R. T. Fulton & L. L. Lloyd (Eds.), *Audiometry for the retarded: With implications for the difficult-to-test.* Baltimore: Williams & Wilkins, 1969. Pp. 210-237.

Price, L. L., & Goldstein, R. Averaged evoked responses for measuring auditory sensitivity in children. *Journal of Speech and Hearing Disorders*, 1966, **31**, 248-256.

Ramger, C. M. A course of study in science for the slow deaf learner. Unpublished master's thesis, San Francisco State College, 1957.

Reneau, J., & Mast, R. Telemetric EEG audiometry instrumentation for use with the profoundly retarded. *American Journal of Mental Deficiency*, 1968, **72**, 506-511.

Richards, B. W. Congenital double athetosis, deaf mutism, and mental deficiency: 5 cases. *Journal of Mental Science*, 1950, **96**, 280-284.

Richards, B. W. & Rundle, A. J. A familial hormonal disorder associated with mental deficiency, deaf mutism and ataxia. *Journal of Mental Deficiency Research*, 1959, **3**, 33-35.

Rigrodsky, S., Prunty, F., & Glovsky, L. A study of the incidence, types and associated etiologies of hearing loss in an institutionalized mentally retarded population. *Training School Bulletin*, 1961, **58**, 30-44.

Rittmanic, P. A. Hearing rehabilitation for the institutionalized mentally retarded. *American Journal of Mental Deficiency*, 1959, **63**, 778-783.

Rittmanic, P. A. A state-wide speech and hearing program for the mentally retarded and mentally ill. *Asha*, 1966, **8**, 182-187.

Rose, D. The absence of evoked responses to high level acoustic stimulus. Paper presented at the annual convention of the American Speech and Hearing Association, Chicago, November 1967.

Rose, D., & Rittmanic, P. The use of the evoked response computer in testing the mentally retarded. *Archives of Otolaryngology*, 1969, **88**, 495-498.

Ross, M., & Matkin, N. D. The rising audiometric configuration. *Journal of Speech and Hearing Disorders*, 1967, **32**, 377-382.

Roy, R. Incidence and severity of hearing loss of institutionalized mentally retarded adults of various intelligence levels. Unpublished master's thesis, University of Nebraska, 1959.

Ryan, M. D., & Stewart, J. H. The use of textured pictures as a reinforcement in meaningful sound identification audiometry. In L. L. Lloyd & D. R. Frisina (Eds.), *The audiologic assessment of the mentally retarded: Proceedings of a national conference*. Parsons, Kansas: Speech and Hearing Department, Parsons State Hospital and Training Center, 1965.

Scheidemann, N. V. *Psychology of exceptional children*. New York: Houghton Mifflin, 1931.

Schlanger, B. B. Speech examination of a group of institutionalized mentally handicapped children. *Journal of Speech and Hearing Disorders*, 1953, **18**, 339–349. (a)

Schlanger, B. B. Speech therapy with slow learning children. Unpublished Report, Division of Mental Hygiene, State Department of Public Welfare, Madison, Wisconsin, 1953. (b)

Schlanger, B. B. The speech and hearing program at the Training School. *Training School Bulletin*, 1957, **53**, 267–272.

Schlanger, B. B. The effects of listening training on the auditory thresholds of mentally retarded children. Cooperative Research Project No. 973 (8936), U.S. Office of Education, 1961.

Schlanger, B. B. Effects of listening training on auditory thresholds of mentally retarded children. *Asha*, 1962, **4**, 273–275.

Schlanger, B. B., & Christensen, N. J. Effects of training upon audiometry with the mentally retarded. *American Journal of Mental Deficiency*, 1964, **68**, 469–475.

Schlanger, B. B., & Gottsleben, R. H. Testing the hearing of the mentally retarded. *Journal of Speech and Hearing Disorders*, 1956, **21**, 487–493.

Schlanger, B. B., & Gottsleben, R. H. Testing the hearing of the mentally retarded. *Training School Bulletin*, 1957, **54**, 21–25.

Schunhoff, H. T., & MacPherson, J. R. What about the deaf or hard-of-hearing mentally deficient? *Training School Bulletin*, 1951, **48**, 72–75.

Sellin, D. F. The mentally retarded, hearing-handicapped learner: Implication for teacher education. *Volta Review*, 1964, **66**, 258–261.

Sheridan, M. D. High-tone deafness in school children simulating mental defect. *British Medical Journal*, 1944, **ii**, 272–274.

Sheridan, M. D. Simple clinical hearing tests for very young or mentally retarded children. *British Medical Journal*, 1958, **ii**, 999–1004.

Siegenthaler, B., & Krzywicki, D. F. Incidence and patterns of hearing loss among an adult mentally retarded population. *American Journal of Mental Deficiency*, 1959, **64**, 444–449.

Silverman, S. I. Speech and language therapy with hearing impaired, multiple handicapped mentally retarded children. Paper presented at the meeting of the American Association of Mental Deficiency, Denver, May 1967.

Snyder, H. J. Communication programming for the mentally retarded. *Pennsylvania Psychiatric Quarterly*, 1965, **5**, 20–27.

Snyder, H. J., & Lloyd, L. L. The habilitation of two severely retarded deaf girls. Paper presented at the meeting of the American Association on Mental Deficiency, Denver, May 1967.

Spradlin, J. E. Operant principles applied to audiometry with severely retarded children. In L. L. Lloyd & D. R. Frisina (Eds.), *The audiologic assessment of the mentally retarded: Proceedings of a national conference*. Parsons, Kansas: Speech and Hearing Department, Parsons State Hospital and Training Center, 1965.

Spradlin, J. E., & Lloyd, L. L. Operant conditioning audiometry (OCA) with low level retardates: A preliminary report. In L. L. Lloyd & D. R. Frisina (Eds.), *The audiologic as-*

sessment of the mentally retarded: Proceedings of a national conference. Parsons, Kansas: Speech and Hearing Department, Parsons State Hospital and Training Center, 1965. Pp. 45-58.

Spradlin, J. E., Lloyd, L. L., Hom, G. L., & Reid, M. J. Establishing tone control and evaluating the hearing of severely retarded children. In G. A. Jervis (Ed.), *Expanding concepts in mental retardation: A symposium from the Joseph P. Kennedy, Jr. Foundation.* Springfield, Ill.: Thomas, 1968. Pp. 170-180.

Spradlin, J. E., Locke, W. J., & Fulton, R. T. Conditioning and audiologic assessment. In R. T. Fulton & L. L. Lloyd (Eds.), *Audiometry for the retarded: With implications for the difficult-to-test.* Baltimore: Williams & Wilkins, 1969. Pp. 125-163.

Sprinkle, P. M., Fitz-Hugh, G. S., Harden, G., & Waldren, D. Incidence of hearing loss and otolaryngologic disorders in consecutive admissions to a state mental hospital. *Virginia Medical Monthly,* 1965, 92, 124-129.

Sterling, E., & Bell, E. Hearing of school children as measured by the audiometer and as related to school work. *Public Health Reports, U.S.,* 1930, 20, 1129.

Stuckless, E. R., & Burrows, N. L. Teaching methods with the mentally retarded deaf. Paper presented at the meeting of the American Association of Mental Deficiency, Denver, May 1967.

Studebaker, G. A. On masking in BC testing. *Journal of Speech and Hearing Research,* 1962, 5, 215-227. (a)

Studebaker, G. A. Placement of vibrator in BC testing. *Journal of Speech and Hearing Research,* 1962, 5, 321-331. (b)

Studebaker, G. A. Clinical masking of air- and bone-conducted stimuli. *Journal of Speech and Hearing Disorders,* 1964, 29, 23-35.

Studebaker, G. A. Inter-test variability and the air-bone gap. *Journal of Speech and Hearing Disorders,* 1967, 32, 82-86.

Taylor, A. P. Learning in moderately retarded deaf adults: An attempt at a structured approach. Paper presented at the meeting of the American Association of Mental Deficiency. Boston, May 1968.

Tillman, T. W., & Jerger, J. E. Some factors affecting the spondee threshold in normal-hearing subjects. *Journal of Speech and Hearing Research,* 1959, 2, 141-146.

Tredgold, A. F. *Mental deficiency.* Baltimore: William Wood, 1908.

Tredgold, R. F., & Soddy, K. *Tredgold's textbook of mental deficiency (subnormality).* (10th ed.) Baltimore: Williams & Wilkins, 1963.

Turner, L. A normative study on the SSW test for various age groups. Unpublished master's thesis, University of Kansas, 1966.

Volk, B. W. (Ed.) *Tay-Sachs disease.* New York: Grune & Stratton, 1964.

von Bekesy, G. *Experiments in hearing.* New York: McGraw-Hill, 1960.

Waldeman, J. L., Wade, F. A., & Aretz, C. W. *Hearing and the school child.* Washington, D.C.: Volta Bureau, 1930.

Waldon, E. F. Testing of infants: Implications for audio-reflexometry. In L. L. Lloyd & D. R. Frisina (Eds.), *The audiologic assessment of the mentally retarded: Proceedings of a national conference.* Parsons, Kansas: Speech and Hearing Department, Parsons State Hospital and Training Center, 1965. Pp. 171-191.

Waldon, E. F. Techniques for determining hearing thresholds of mentally retarded children. In E. F. Waldon (Ed.), *Differential diagnosis of speech and hearing problems of mental retardates.* Washington, D.C.: Catholic University of America Press, 1968. Pp. 122-150.

Warren, S. A., & Kraus, M. J. Deaf children, mental retardation and academic expectations. *Volta Review,* 1963, 65, 351-352, 383.

Watkins, E. O., Stewart, J. H., & Ryan, M. D. A novel hearing test for retardates with mental ages below four years. *American Journal of Mental Deficiency,* 1966, 71, 396-400.

Weaver, R. M. The use of filmstrip stories in slide show audiometry. In L. L. Lloyd & D. R. Frisina (Eds.), *The audiologic assessment of the mentally retarded: Proceedings of a national conference.* Parsons, Kansas: Speech and Hearing Department, Parsons State Hospital and Training Center, 1965. Pp. 71-88.

Webb, C. E., Kinde, S. W., Weber, B. A., & Beedle, R. K. Procedures for evaluating the hearing of the mentally retarded. Cooperative Research Project No. 1731, U.S. Office of Education, Central Michigan University, 1964.

Wertz, T. L. An investigation of the use of GSR audiometry with a selected group of mental retardates. Unpublished master's thesis, West Virginia University, 1961.

Wilber, R. L. (Chn.) *The White House conference on child health and protection.* New York: Century, 1931.

Wiley, J., & Jacobs, G. The incidence and characteristics of hearing loss in an institutionalized, mildly retarded population. In L. L. Lloyd & D. R. Frisina (Eds.), *The audiologic assessment of the mentally retarded: Proceedings of a national conference.* Parsons, Kansas: Speech and Hearing Department, Parsons State Hospital and Training Center, 1965. Pp. 155-163.

Witting, E. G., & Hughson, W. Inherent accuracy of a series of repeated clinical audiograms. *Laryngoscope,* 1940, **50**, 259-269.

Wolfe, W. G., & MacPherson, J. R. The evaluation and development of techniques for testing the auditory acuity of trainable mentally retarded children. Cooperative Research Project No. 172. U.S. Office of Education, University of Texas, 1959.

Yannet, H. Classification and etiological factors in mental retardation. In J. H. Rothstein (Ed.), *Mental retardation: Readings and resources.* New York: Holt, Rinehart & Winston, 1962.

Yannet, H. Mental retardation. In W. E. Nelson (Ed.), *Textbook in pediatrics* (8th ed.) Philadelphia: Saunders, 1964. Pp. 1232-1243.

Young, C. E. An investigation of intra- and inter-test relationships between selected auditory measures on normal hearing mentally retarded adults. Unpublished doctoral dissertation, Oklahoma State University, 1968.

Young, C. E., & Estes, J. An investigation of acoustic impedence measurements in an adult mentally retarded population. Paper presented at the meeting of the American Association of Mental Deficiency, Denver, May 1967.

Zeaman, D., & Wegner, N. Cardiac reflex to tone of threshold intensity. *Journal of Speech and Hearing Disorders,* 1956, **21**, 71-75.

Zwislocki, J. Acoustic attenuation between the ears. *Journal of the Acoustical Society of America,* 1953, **25**, 752-759.

Author Index

Numbers in italics refer to the pages on which the complete references are listed.

Abernathy, E. B., 312, 313, 335, *363*
Abraham, W., 254, *256*
Abruzzo, A. M., 361, *363*
Adams, H. B., 70, *101*
Ader, R., 280, 295, *300*
Akert, A. K., 287, *303*
Albizu-Miranda, C., 231, 238, 246, *256*
Alexander, D., 207, *224*
Allen, G., 121, 122, *147*
Allen, J., 206, *224*
Allen, L., *190*
Allen, R. M., 212, *221*
Alper, A. E., 154, *189*, 209, 216, 217, *221*
Anders, T. R., 23, 25, *31*
Anderson, J. E., 173, 174, *189*
Anderson, R. M., 361, *363*
Andy, O. J., 288, 289, *302, 306*
Appell, M. J., 254, *256*
Aretz, C. W., 312, *373*
Armitage, S. G., 282, *300*
Aronson, A. E., 317, *367*
Arrell, V. M., 244, *261*
Arshavsky, I. A., 280, *300*
Arlitt, A. H., 274, *302*
Arthur, G., 152, *189*
Asher, E. J., *189*
Atchison, C. O., 218, *221*
Atkinson, C. J., 320, 331, 352, *363*
Atkinson, R. C., 6, *31*

Baldwin, W. K., 239, 240, *256*
Balla, D., 121, 122, *144*
Baller, W. R., *189*, 243, *256*
Balmuth, M., 272, *307*
Balvin, R. S., 108, *145*
Barber, P. S., 338, 360, *363, 364*
Barclay, A., *189*, 203, 220, *221, 223*
Barnes, G. H., 360, *363*

Barnes, R. H., 295, *300*
Barnett, C. D., 83, *100*, 136, *145*, 249, *256*
Baroff, G. S., 215, 216, 218, *222*
Barr, B., 336, 339, *363*
Barrett, B. H., 66, *100*
Bartlett, C. J., 213, *222*, 249, *261*
Baubergertell, L., 320, 331, *365*
Baumeister, A. A., 113, 129, 130, 132, 133, 136, *144*, 213, *222*, 339, 359, *363, 365*
Baumeister, J., 332, *366*
Bayley, H. C., 251, *257*
Bayley, N., 49, 50, *101, 189*
Beach, F. A., 290, *300*
Beck, H. S., 219, *222*
Becker, R. F., 282, *300, 309*
Beddie, A., 254, *256*
Beedle, R. K., 113, *144*, 323, 331, 336, 339, 342, 343, *363, 374*
Begab, M. J., 254, *256*
Begg, T. L., 203, *227*
Behrend, E. R., 119, *145*
Behrman, R. E., 296, *304*
Beier, D. C., 245, *256*
Bell, A., 152, *189*
Bell, E., 312, *373*
Belmont, I., 213, 216, 217, 219, 220, *222*
Belmont, J. M., 7, *31*, 138, 139, 144, *145*
Benda, C. E., 332, 333, *363*
Benjamin, R. M., 286, *300*
Bensberg, G. J., Jr., 208, 216, 217, *222, 227*
Benton, J., *190*
Berko, M. J., 218, *222*
Berkson, G., 264, 282, 294, 297, *300*
Berman, P. W., *189*
Bialer, I., 246, *256*
Bidlake, H. A., 323, 330, 331, 336, *368*
Bignami, G., 265, *300*
Bijou, S. W., 212, *222*
Bilodeau, E. A., 64, *101*

375

Bilski-Hirsch, R., 320, 331, *365*
Birch, H. G., 213, 216, 217, 219, 220, *222*
Birch, J. W., 203, 205, 207, *222*, 312, 313, 314, 315, 330, *364*
Bissell, N. E., 360, *364*
Bitter, J. A., 249, *256*
Bitterman, M. E., 119, *145*
Blake, K. A., 125, 127, 130, *146*
Bloom, B. J., 173, *189*
Bloom, W., 244, *256*
Blomquist, A. J., 287, *303*
Blosser, D., 351, *368*
Blough, D. S., 352, *364*
Blue, C. M., 360, *364*
Blumenfield, M., 266, *302*
Bobroff, A., 244, *256*
Bochenek, A., 334, *364*
Boice, R., 116, *145*
Bolles, M. M., 124, *145*
Boneau, C. L., 282, *300*
Borkowski, J. G., 129, *145*
Borrus, J. C., 274, *303*
Bousfield, A. K., 93, *101*
Bousfield, W. A., 93, *101*
Bovet, D., 266, 298, *300*
Bovet-Nitti, F., 266, 298, *300*
Bower, G., 6, *31*
Bradley, E., 316, 335, 354, *364*
Bradshaw, A. W., 336, 343, *364*
Brainerd, B., 240, *256*
Brengelmann, J. C., 199, 218, *222*
Bricker, D. D., 336, 337, *364*
Bricker, W. A., 336, 337, *364*
Briggs, G. E., 125, 127, *145*
Broadbent, D. E., 2, 6, *31*
Broadhurst, P. L., 99, *101*, 266, *301*
Brody, D. S., 250, *262*
Bronfenbrenner, U., 291, *301*
Brooks, R. S., 345, 350, *364*
Brunt, M. A., 351, *364*
Bryant, P. E., 140, *145*
Budoff, M., 202, *222*
Bunch, M. E., 268, 271, 282, *305*
Burnett, C. T., 10, *32*
Burrows, N. L., 360, *368*, *373*
Burt, C., 40, 66, *101*, 312, *364*
Butler, A. J., 199, 216, *225*, 245, 246, 247, *259*, *260*
Butterfield, E. C., 249, *256*
Butterfield, G., 341, *364*

Cahilly, G., 292, *304*
Caldwell, D. F., 278, *301*
Caldwell, T. E., 246, *258*
Candland, D. K., 361, *364*
Carhart, R., 338, *364*
Carleton, F. O., 206, 216, *222*, *226*
Carlton, T., 211, *222*
Carrier, N. A., 210, *222*
Cassell, R. H., 82, *101*, 127, 130, *145*
Cassin, S., 282, *301*
Castaneda, A., 210, *222*
Catron, D., 249, *261*
Cattell, P., 152, *189*
Cattell, R. B., 57, 70, *101*
Cawthorne, T., 359, *364*
Chaiklin, J. B., 348, 354, *364*
Chambers, W. R., 249, *257*
Chamove, A. S., 276, *304*
Chapanis, A., 154, *189*
Charles, D. C., *189*, 243, *256*, *257*
Charlesworth, W. R., 275, 279, *308*
Chazan, M., 241, *260*
Chennault, M., 240, *257*
Christensen, N. J., 324, 338, 345, 354, 361, *364*, *372*
Churchill, J. A., 41, *105*, 278, *301*
Ciocco, A. A., 315, *364*
Clarke, A. D. B., 152, 154, *189*, 242, *257*
Clarke, A. M., 138, *148*, 152, 154, *189*, 242, *257*
Clausen, J., 132, 133, *145*, 234, *257*, 345, 346, 347, 348, *364*
Cleland, C. C., 241, 247, 249, *257*, *260*
Clendinnen, B. G., 274, *301*
Cochran, I. L., 249, *257*
Cohen, J., 213, *222*
Cohen, J. S., 244, *257*
Cole, V. V., 274, *303*
Collins, R. L., 266, *301*
Collmann, R. D., 154, *189*, 203, *222*, 243, *257*, 339, *364*
Conklyn, D. H., 361, *364*
Connor, L. E., 361, *364*
Conrad, H. S., *190*
Conry, J., 35, 37, 42, 43, *102*
Cooper, G. D., 70, *101*
Costello, P. M., 361, *364*
Coursin, D. B., 294, *301*
Covington, M., 266, *306*
Cowan, E. A., 274, *302*

AUTHOR INDEX

Cowley, J. J., 277, 278, *301*
Cravioto, J., 294, *301*
Crissy, O. L., 154, *189*
Croskery, J., 121, 122, *147*
Crowne, D. P., 198, *226*
Cruse, D., 137, *145*
Cruikshank, R. M., 286, *301*
Culver, M., 251, *257*
Cummings, S. T., 251, *257*
Cunningham, R. F., 293, *306*
Currier, W. D., 356, *364*
Curry, E. T., 335, *364*
Curti, M., 50, *101*
Cutts, R. A., 214, *226*

Daniel, E. P., 277, *301*
Dansinger, S., 326, 330, 345, *364*
Darley, F. L., 330, 342, *364*
D'Asaro, M. J., 336, *365*
Daston, P. G., 70, *101*
Davenport, H. W., 277, *301*
Davenport, R. K., 292, *301*
Davenport, V. D., 277, *301*
Davidson, K., 210, *225*
Davis, A., 55, *101*
Davis, H., 313, 332, 335, 344, *365*
Davis, L. J., Jr., 203, *222*
Day, R. W., 234, *257*
Dayan, M., 239, *257*
Deagle, J., 273, *301*
Dean, R. F. A., 51, *102*
DeFries, J. C., 269, 296, *301*, *308*
deLabry, J., 116, 124, *149*
Delp, H. A., 244, *257*
Dembicki, E. L., 275, *308*
Denenberg, V. H., 266, 283, 291, 292, 298, 299, *301*, *302*, *303*, *309*
Denny, R., 108, 112, 116, *145*
Dentler, R. A., 239, 241, *257*
DeSchweinitz, L., 342, *370*
Deutsch, M. R., 216, *226*
Dever, R., 35, 37, 42, 43, *102*
Dexter, L. A., 230, 231, 232, *257*, *258*
Diamond, F. R., 108, *145*
Diamond, S., 108, *145*
Diggs, E. A., 239, 240, *258*
Dingman, H. F., 213, *222*, 241, *257*, 332, *370*
Dispensa, J., 273, *302*
Dixon, J. C., 124, *148*

Dobzhansky, T., 234, *258*
Doerfler, L. G., 330, *365*
Doll, E. A., 152, *189*
Donnell, W., 282, *300*
Dooley, M. D., 220, *223*
Doppelt, J. E., 206, 209, *222*, *225*
Doty, B. A., 294, *302*
Doty, L. A., 294, *302*
Doty, R. W., 287, *302*
Doudna, M., 345, *371*
Dougherty, A., 342, *366*
Downs, M. P., 342, *365*
Dugas, J., 24, *31*
Dugas, J. L., 359, *365*
Duncan, C. P., 135, *145*
Dunn, L. C., 234, *258*
Durling, D., 243, *258*

Eagle, E., 242, 243, *258*
Eagles, E. L., 330, *365*
Earhart, R., 154, *189*
Eayrs, J. T., 274, *301*
Echols, M., 272, *302*
Eckland, B. K., 40, *101*
Edgerton, R. B., 36, *101*, 229, 232, 235, 240, 241, 243, 246, 253, *258*
Eells, K., 55, *101*
Eichenwald, H. F., 277, 294, *302*
Eimas, P. D., 117, *145*
Eleftheriou, B. E., 266, *304*
Eliot, T. D., 250, *258*
Ellis, N. R., 2, 5, 10, 20, 22, 24, 25, *31*, 74, 83, *100*, *101*, 132, 133, 136, 137, 138, 139, 144, *144*, *145*, *146*
Engel, A. M., 152, *189*
Erickson, M. T., 154, *189*
Erlenmeyer-Kimling, L., 40, *102*
Esquivel de Gallardo, F. O., 296, *304*
Essman, W. B., 294, *302*
Estes, J., 352, 353, 359, *374*
Eustis, R. S., 152, *189*
Evans, H. M., 277, *306*
Evans, W. E., 316, 335, 354, *364*
Ewing, A. W. G., 342, *365*
Ewing, I. R., 342, *365*

Fabiyi, A., 269, *307*
Fagan, J. F., III, 128, 130, *145*
Farber, B., 232, 233, 234, 241, 250, 251, 253, 254, *258*

Farrell, M. J., 316, 330, 360, *367*
Farrimond, T., 345, 347, 350, *365*
Fein, A., 318, 345, 347, 348, *367*
Feingold, M., 334, *366*
Feinmesser, M., 320, 331, *365*
Feldhusen, J. F., 210, *223*
Ferm, V. H., 271, *308*
Ferreira, A. J., 279, *302*
Fine, M. J., 246, *258*
Finley, C. J., 207, 209, 216, 217, *223, 226*
Fisher, G. M., 199, 200, 205, 206, 207, 209, 212, 213, 216, 220, *223, 224, 226*
Fishler, K., 154, *189*
Fitz-Hugh, G. S., 331, *373*
Fletcher, J. M., 274, *302*
Floor, L., 154, *190*
Foale, M., 315, *365*
Foshee, D. P., 266, 273, 289, *302, 305*
Foshee, J. G., 108, *148*
Foster, D. B., 332, *366*
Francey, R. E., 203, *223*
Franken, R. E., 210, *226*
Frazeur, H. A., 218, *224*
Frederiksen, J., 96, *103*
Fregly, A. R., 282, *301*
Friedman, E. C., 220, *223*
Frisind, D. R., 325, 332, 335, 338, 342, 344, 363, *365, 368*
Fry, P. C., 277, 294, *302*
Fuller, J. L., 40, *102*, 265, 266, 267, 292, *302*
Fulton, R. T., 327, 329, 330, 331, 332, 334, 336, 337, 339, 344, 349, 350, 352, 354, 355, 356, 357, 358, 359, *365, 366, 373*
Furchtgott, E., 272, 273, 284, *301, 302*
Furth, H. G., 121, 122, 126, 129, *147*

Gagné, R. M., 51, *102*
Gainer, W. L., 209, 216, *223*
Gaines, J. A. L., 321, 336, *366*
Gallagher, J. J., 216, 219, *223, 224*
Gamlin, P., 131, 133, *147*
Garcia-Rodriguez, C., 283, *305*
Gardner, W. I., 246, *258*
Gates, A. I., 74, *102*
Geber, M., 51, *102*
Gellis, S. S., 334, *366*
Giannini, M. J., 254, *258*
Gibson, J. B., 42, *105*
Giffin, C. S., 327, 330, 331, 332, 334, *365*

Ginzberg, E., 234, *258*
Giolas, T. G., 335, 344, *366*
Girardeau, F. L., 137, *145*
Gladwin, T., 47, *104*, 332, *369*
Glasman, L. D., 93, 94, 95, *102*
Glavin, J. P., 285, *302*
Glovsky, L., 321, 325, 330, 360, *366, 371*
Goetzinger, C. P., 342, 345, 350, *364, 370*
Goldberg, B., 332, *366*
Goldenberg, L., 279, *308*
Goldstein, H., 233, 235, 240, 242, *258*
Goldstein, R., 335, 338, 339, 354, *366, 371*
Gonzalez, R. C., 119, *145*
Goodman, I., 272, *308*
Goodman, L., 254, *258*
Gordon, J. E., 294, *307*
Gorelick, M. C., 250, *259*
Gorlow, L., 245, 246, 247, *259, 260*
Gottesman, I. I., 34, 40, *102*
Gottfried, N. W., 249, *259*
Gottlieb, J. S., 268, 273, 275, *308, 309*
Gottsleben, R. H., 315, 316, 317, 321, 331, 360, *372*
Goulet, L. R., 78, 82, 85, 92, *102*, 203, *221*
Grabowski, C. T., 271, *302*
Graham, J. T., 336, 339, 340, 348, 354, 356, 357, *365, 366, 368*
Graliker, B. V., 154, *189*
Green, P. C., 297, *304*
Greenbaum, J. J., 248, *259*
Greenbaum, M., 285, *302*
Grey, H. A., 336, *365*
Griesel, R. D., 277, *301*
Griffiths, W. J., Jr., 295, *303*
Grossman, H. J., 332, *370*
Grota, L. J., 283, *303*
Guertin, W. H., 152, *189*
Guilford, J. P., 51, *102*
Gunberg, D. L., 285, *302*
Guskin, S. L., 235, 245, 246, 248, *259*
Guthrie, G. M., 245, 246, 247, *259, 260*
Gynther, M. D., 114, *145*

Haller, M. H., 237, 238, *259*
Hamburgh, M., 294, *302*
Hamilton, H. C., 274, *303*
Harden, G., 331, *373*
Harding, F. A., 244, *259*
Hardy, J. B., 38, *102*, 342, *366*

AUTHOR INDEX

Hardy, W. G., 342, *366*
Harlow, H. F., 276, 287, 292, 293, *303*, *304*, *308*
Harlow, M. K., 287, 292, *303*
Harmon, H. H., 152, *190*
Harned, B. K., 274, *303*
Harris, D. B., 246, *261*
Harris, J. D., 356, *369*
Harter, S., 116, *145*
Hartley, E. L., 229, *259*
Hartley, R., 229, *259*
Hartman, B. T., 360, *366*
Havighurst, R. J., 39, 55, *101*
Havlena, J., 272, 275, *308*, *309*
Hawkins, W. F., 129, 130, 136, 137, *144*, *145*, 339, *363*
Haworth, M. R., 199, 219, *225*
Haywood, H. C., 291, 292, *303*
Headrick, M. W., 112, 118, *146*, *147*
Heal, L. W., 108, 114, 116, 117, 118, 121, 122, 124, 125, 139, 140, *146*
Hearn, C. B., Jr., 81, *105*, 136, *148*
Hebb, D. O., 2, 6, *31*
Heber, R., 35, 37, 42, 43, *102*, 194, *226*, 245, *259*, 333, 336, 355, 357, *366*
Hegge, T. G., 244, *259*
Hegmann, J. P., 296, *301*
Henderson, E. M., 51, *101*
Henderson, N. D., 266, 292, 298, *303*
Hermelin, B., 65, *104*, 121, 122, *147*
Herrick, V. E., 55, *101*
Hewson, L. R., 220, *224*
Hibbard, E., 296, *304*
Hicks, S. P., 272, *303*
Higgins, C., 70, *102*
Hilson, D., 331, 334, *366*
Himwich, H. E., 284, *303*
Hind, J. E., 317, *367*
Hirschenfang, M. P., *190*
Hirsh, I. J., 338, *366*
Hirsh, N. D. M., 154, *189*
Hiskey, M. S., 201, 203, *224*
Hoakley, Z. P., 152, *190*, 218, *224*
Hodgson, W. R., 353, *366*
Hoffeld, D. R., 275, *303*
Hogan, A. G., 277, *309*
Hogan, D. D., 335, 339, 340, 341, *366*
Holland, J. M., 129, 130, 136, *144*
Hollis, J. H., 352, *366*
Holmes, H., 291, *307*

Holowinsky, I., 154, *190*
Holt, K. S., 252, *259*
Hom, G. L., 336, *373*
Honzik, M. P., 41, *102*, *190*
Hood, J. D., 338, *366*
Hope, R., 5, 10, 20, 22, *31*
Horel, J. A., 286, *309*
Hornbeck, R. T., 273, *302*
Horne, B. M., 154, *189*
House, B. J., 78, 79, *105*, 115, 116, 117, *146*, *148*, 154, 156, 167, *191*, 208, 227
Huff, H. W., 293, 294, *305*
Huffman, J. M., 360, *367*
Hughes, R. B., 218, *224*
Hughson, W., 356, *374*
Hull, C. L., 2, *32*
Hunt, J. McV., *190*, 290, *303*
Huntley, R. M. C., 40, *102*
Hurder, W. P., 282, *303*
Hurley, L. S., 277, *303*
Hutton, C., 345, *367*

Ickes, W. K., 335, *367*
Irwin, J. V., 317, *367*
Isaacson, R. L., 286, 288, *303*
Iscoe, I., 86, *102*, *104*, 126, 129, *146*

Jacobs, G., 324, 331, *374*
James, W. C. A., 360, *367*
Jarvik, L. F., 40, *102*
Jastak, J., 212, *224*
Jaynes, J., 290, *300*
Jefferson, T. W., 212, *221*
Jefferson, W., 247, *261*
Jenne, W. C., 251, *258*
Jennings, R. D., 267, *304*
Jensen, A. R., 38, 39, 40, 55, 56, 69, 70, 73, 74, 75, 77, 82, 83, 84, 85, 86, 90, 96, *102*, *103*
Jerger, J. F., 345, 347, 352, *367*, *373*
Jewett, R. E., 275, *304*
Joffe, J. M., 280, 296, *304*
Johnson, B. M., 113, *146*
Johnson, G. C., 252, *262*
Johnson, G. O., 125, 127, 130, *146*, 239, 240, *259*
Johnson, J. T., Jr., 112, 114, 121, 122, *146*

Johnson, R. K., 361, *367*
Jones, H. E., 40, *103*, *190*
Jones, R. L., 249, *259*
Jones, R. W., 136, 137, *145*, *146*
Johnston, P. W., 316, 330, 360, *367*
Johnston, W. A., 361, *367*

Kaback, G. R., 210, 216, *224*
Kagan, J., 51, *103*
Kahn, S., 240, *259*
Kamrin, B. B., 278, *304*
Kano, K., 275, 276, *308*
Kaplan, O., 152, *190*
Kaplan, S. J., 272, *304*, *307*
Karas, G. G., 298, *301*
Karn, H. W., 277, *306*
Karrer, R., 132, 133, *145*, 292, *304*
Kaspar, J. C., 154, *190*, 202, *227*
Katz, A. H., 229, *259*
Katz, E., 211, *224*
Katz, J., 349, 350, 351, 352, 353, 359, *367*
Keir, E. H., 361, *367*
Kellas, G., 339, *363*
Kemp, T., 235, *259*
Kennedy, R. J. R., 243, 244, *259*
Kenny, J. T., 199, 218, *222*
Kephart, N. C., 152, 154, *190*
Kern, W. H., 124, *146*
Kerr, G. R., 276, *304*
Kesner, R., 275, *309*
Kilman, B. A., 199, 200, 207, *223*, *224*
Kimbrell, D. L., 249, *259*
Kimmich, H. M., 331, *367*
Kinde, S. W., 323, 331, 336, 339, 342, 343, *363*, *374*
King, C. G., 277, *306*
King, F. A., 271, *308*
King, J. A., 266, *304*
King, J. E., 282, *300*
Kirk, S. A., 239, 240, *259*
Kirkland, M. H., 253, *259*
Klausmeier, H. J., 210, *223*
Kleegman, S. J., 237, *260*
Kline, O. L., 277, *301*
Kling, A., 286, 287, 288, 297, *304*, *308*
Klopfer, F. D., 293, *307*
Knights, R. M., 210, *224*
Kniss, J. T., 247, *260*
Knobloch, H., 51, *103*
Knox, E. C., 336, *367*

Koch, C., 331, 334, *367*
Kock, R., 154, *189*
Kodman, F., 318, 332, 333, 345, 347, 348, *367*
Kodman, F., Jr., 318, 319, 330, *367*, *368*
Kolstoe, O. P., 243, *260*
Kopatic, N. J., 354, *368*
Kopra, L., 351, *368*
Koski, C. H., 112, *147*
Kounin, J. S., 120, 121, 122, 124, 144, *146*
Kral, P. A., 118, *146*
Kramm, E. R., 250, 251, 252, *260*
Kranz, F., 313, *365*
Kraus, M. J., 361, *373*
Kraus, M. J., Jr., 218, *227*
Krechevsky, I., 120, *146*
Kroes, H. W., 266, *308*
Krugman, S., 332, *368*
Krzywicki, D. F., 318, 331, 360, *372*
Kuhlmann, F., 152, *190*, 211, *224*
Kurtz, R. A., 229, *260*
Kurtzrock, G. H., 335, *364*
Kun, K. J., 253, *262*
Kus, J., 334, *364*
Kushlick, A., 34, 37, *103*

LaCrosse, E. L., 323, 330, 331, 336, *368*
Laing, A. F., 241, *260*
Lam, R. L., 219, *222*
Lamb, L. E., 340, 352, 353, 358, *368*
Lamb, N. L., *368*
Landes, B. A., 349, 350, *370*
Lapp, E. R., 240, *260*
Lawrence, E. M., 41, *103*
Leach, W., 359, *368*
Leahy, A. M., 41, *103*
Lehtinen, L. E., 137, *148*
Lerner, I. M., 236, *260*
Leshin, G., 361, *368*
Lessler, K., 218, *224*
Levin, J., 199, 217, *226*
Levin, J. R., 89, *104*
Levine, E. S., 332, *368*
Levine, H. S., 330, *365*
Levine, M., 120, *146*
Levine, S., 266, 290, *301*, *306*
Levinson, B., 272, 284, *304*
Lighthall, F., 210, *225*
Lilienfeld, A. M., 332, *371*

AUTHOR INDEX

Lindesmith, A. R., 229, *260*
Lindsley, O. R., 351, *368, 370*
Lindzey, G., 266, *309*
Lipman, R. S., 135, 136, *146*
Little, S. W., 334, *368*
Lloyd, L. L., 325, 326, 330, 331, 332, 333, 334, 335, 336, 337, 338, 342, 344, 345, 346, 347, 348, 354, 355, 356, 357, 358, 359, 360, 363, *366, 368, 369, 372*
Lobb, H., 113, 131, 133, *146, 147*
Longstreth, L. E., 120, *147*
Loos, F. M., 220, *224*
Lorenz, M., 244, *257*
Lucey, J. F., 296, *304*
Lucito, L. J., 216, *224*
Luckey, R. E., 249, *259*
Luria, A. R., 108, 131, 133, *147*
Luszki, W. A., 360, *369*
Lynch, S., 86, 89, *104*
Lynn, R., 131, *147*

Macfarlance, J. W., *190*
Mackay, P. B., 112, *147*
Mackler, B., 239, 241, *257*
MacPherson, J. R., 319, 321, 335, 336, 339, 345, 354, 361, *369, 372, 374*
Madden, R., 312, *369*
Madison, H. L., 242, *260*
Madow, A. A., 326, 330, 345, *364*
Magaret, A., 214, 215, *224, 226*
Mahoney, S. C., 252, *260*
Malathi, S., 250, *259*
Malpass, L. F., 210, *222, 224*
Mangan, K. R., 361, *369*
Mark, S., 210, *224*
Marshall, F. B., 50, *101*
Masland, R. L., 47, *104*, 332, *369*
Mast, R., 341, *371*
Mateer, F., 112, *147*
Matkin, N. D., 349, *371*
Matlin, N., 231, 238, 246, *256*
Matthews, J., 312, 313, 314, 315, 330, *364*
Maxwell, E., 206, *224*
Maxwell, J., 38, *104*
McAfee, R. O., 247, *260*
McCandless, B. R., 210, *222*
McClearn, G. E., 266, *304*
McCoy, D. F., 360, *369*
McCulloch, T. L., 205, *225*
McGaugh, J. L., 267, *304*

McGee, R. K., 292, *305*
McGee, T. M., 359, *369*
McGurk, F. C. J., 56, *104*
McIntire, M. S., 324, *369*
McManis, D. L., 85, *104*, 129, 130, *147*, 331, 345, 346, 354, 356, *369*
McNemar, Q., 81, *104*, 201, 202, 206, 209, 213, 215, *224*
Meier, G. W., 266, 268, 269, 270, 271, 273, 277, 278, 281, 282, 283, 284, 289, 291, 292, 293, 294, 298, *302, 304, 305, 307, 308*
Mellone, M. A., 201, *225*
Melmer, P. E., 318, *369*
Melnick, W., 330, *365*
Melrose, J., 331, 336, 345, 346, 347, 348, 354, 355, 356, 357, 358, *369*
Mendoza, L. A., 294, *302*
Menolascino, F. J., 324, *369*
Menzel, E. W., Jr., 271, 292, *301, 305*
Mercer, J. R., 254, *260*
Meredith, W., 266, *304*
Merrill, M. A., 72, 75, *105*, 194, 197, 202, 204, 210, *226*
Meshorer, E., 253, *262*
Meyer, P. M., 286, *309*
Meyerowitz, J. H., 239, 240, 250, *260*
Meyers, C. E., 213, *222*, 248, *260*
Meyers, C. K., 356, *369*
Meyerson, L., 336, 337, 345, 346, 347, *369, 370*
Michael, J. L., 336, 337, *370*
Michal-Smith, H., 244, *260*
Milgram, N. A., 121, 122, 126, 129, *147*
Miller, C. A., 332, *370*
Miller, F. J., 189, 243, 256
Miller, G. A., 30, *32*
Miller, J. B., 244, *260*, 332, 342, *370*
Miller, J. B., 332, *370*
Miller, R. V., 239, *260*
Milligan, G. E., 254, *260*
Miltenberger, G., 360, *370*
Minogue, B., 152, *190*
Minski, L., 361, *370*
Mintz, B., 280, *305*
Mirsky, I. A., 290, *305*
Mitra, S. B., 361, *370*
Mixson, A., 318, 345, 347, 348, *367*
Moffitt, A., 131, 133, *147*
Mogel, S., 207, *225*
Mohan, P. J., 210, *226*

Monaghan, A., 361, *370*
Monif, G. R., 269, *307*
Moore, A. U., 295, *300*
Moore, D., 207, *224*
Moore, E. J., 360, *370*
Morra, M., 279, *306*
Mosier, H. D., 332, *370*
Moss, J. M., 339, *370*
Moss, M., 339, *370*
Moss, M. H., 277, *305*
Munn, N. L., 277, 294, *306*
Murphy, E. C., 360, *370*
Murphy, K. P., 342, 344, 347, *370*
Myatt, B. D., 349, 350, *370*
Myklebust, H. R., 332, *370*
Mysliveček, J., 286, *309*

Nale, S., 199, *224*
Nathan, P. E., 351, *370*
Neff, W. S., 38, 39, *104*
Nelson, M., 361, *370*
Nelson, M. M., 277, *306*
Neugarten, B. L., 39, *102*
Newby, H. A., 332, 335, 342, 344, 352, 354, *370*
Newlyn, D., 154, *189*, 203, *222*, 243, *257*
Newman, J. R., 220, *224*
Newton, G., 290, *306*
Nober, E. H., 328, 330, 343, *370*
Noble, C. E., 81, *104*
Nodar, R. H., 339, 340, *371*
Nolan, C. Y., 268, 271, 282, *305*, *306*
Nonneman, A. J., 288, *304*
Norman, D. A., 6, *32*
Norris, T. W., 352, 353, 358, *368*
Norton, S., 275, *304*
Nováková, V., 295, *306*
Nowakiska, M., 154, *190*
Nudo, L., 331, 332, 334, 359, *371*

O'Connor, N., 65, *104*, 121, 122, 133, *147*, *148*
O'Dell, B. L., 277, *309*
Oden, M., 44, *105*
Ogdon, D. P., 211, *224*
O'Hara, J., 244, *259*
Ohlrich, E. S., 114, *147*
Olian, S., 296, *308*
Oliverio, A., 266, 298, *300*, *306*

Olshansky, S. J., 248, 251, 252, 254, *260*, *261*
Openshaw, J. W., 272, *302*
Orton, K. D., 210, *222*
Osborne, R. T., 73, *104*, 206, *224*
Osmond, H., 254, *256*
Owens, A., 249, *259*
Owens, E. P., 213, *226*
Owens, W. A., *190*
Oyer, H. J., 345, *371*

Paar, J. A., 271, *302*
Palermo, D. S., 210, *222*, *224*
Palmer, C. E., 315, *364*
Pantelakos, C. G., 322, 330, 331, 332, 334, *371*
Pasamanick, B., 51, *103*, 332, *371*
Paterson, J. W., 315, *365*
Patton, R. A., 277, *306*
Peckham, R., 240, *261*
Peeler, D. F., Jr., 286, 288, *306*
Penney, R. K., 121, 122, *147*
Perry, S. E., 230, 238, *261*
Peterson, L. R., 2, *32*
Peterson, M. J., 2, *32*
Phelps, W. R., 245, *261*
Philip, P. P., 318, 319, 330, *367*, *368*
Phillips, I., 245, *261*
Piers, E. V., 246, *261*
Pinneau, S., 162, *190*
Pitts, V. A., 218, *227*
Plant, W. T., 154, *190*
Platt, J. R., 111, *148*
Plaut, S. M., 280, *300*
Plenderleith, M., 121, 122, *147*
Polidora, V. J., 293, *306*
Ponce, C. G., 282, *307*
Pond, W. G., 295, *300*
Porter, M., 291, *307*
Poull, L. E., 154, *190*
Powers, T. R., 318, 319, 330, *367*, *368*
Prehm, H. J., 78, 79, 92, *104*
Price, L. L., 335, 339, 359, *371*
Prunty, F., 321, 325, 330, *371*
Pryer, M. W., 83, *100*, 136, 137, *145*
Pryer, R. S., 128, 130, *147*
Purseglove, E. M., 202, *222*

Quay, H. C., 213, *226*
Quay, L. C., 241, 249, *261*

AUTHOR INDEX

Ramger, C. M., 361, *371*
Ranger, D., 359, *364*
Ranck, J., 289, *306*
Rapier, J. L., 78, 88, *104*
Rautman, A. L., 214, *224*
Razran, G., 130, 131, *147*
Reed, E. W., 44, 46, 48, 53, *104*, 234, 236, 238, *261*
Reed, S. C., 44, 46, 48, 53, *104*, 234, 236, 238, *261*
Reger, R., 154, *190*
Reid, I. M., 295, *300*
Reid, M. J., 325, 326, 330, 331, 332, 333, 334, 335, 336, 337, 338, 345, 346, 352, 354, 356, 360, *366*, *369*
Reid, W. B., 207, *224*
Reiman, S., 152, 154, *189*, 242, *257*
Reneau, J., 341, *371*
Ressler, R. H., 298, 299, *306*
Rhone, D. E., 210, *226*
Richards, B. W., 334, *371*
Richardson, J. W., 282, *306*
Rie, H. E., 251, *257*
Rigrodsky, S., 321, 325, 330, 360, *366*, *371*
Rimland, B., 60, 61, *104*, 285, *306*
Ringness, T. A., 246, *261*
Riopelle, A. J., 119, *147*
Risley, T. R., 209, *223*
Rittmanic, P. A., 319, 331, 339, 340, 360, *371*
Roberts, J. A. F., 35, *104*, 201, *225*
Robinson, H. B., 68, *104*, 233, 234, *261*
Robinson, N. M., 68, *104*, 233, 234, *261*
Roden, A., 83, *103*
Rogers, C. M., 292, *301*
Rohrs, F. W., 199, 219, *225*
Rohwer, W. D., Jr., 82, 85, 86, 87, 88, 89, 90, 100, *103*, *104*
Roos, P., 254, *261*
Rose, D. E., 338, 339, 340, *363*
Rosen, R., 154, *190*
Rosenberg, K. M., 292, 298, 299, *302*
Ross, L. E., 108, 112, 114, 116, 117, 121, 122, 124, 139, 140, *146*, *147*
Ross, M., 349, *371*
Ross, R. T., 154, *190*
Ross, S., 266, *302*
Rossi, E. L., 92, *104*
Rowland, G. L., 267, *306*
Roy, R., 320, *372*

Royce, J. R., 266, *306*
Rozdilsky, B., 297, *306*
Rundle, A. J., 334, *371*
Runner, M. N., 267, 296, *306*
Rushton, C. S., *190*, 203, *225*
Russell, L. B., 272, *306*
Ryan, M. D., 343, *372*, *373*
Ryckman, D. B., 251, 254, *258*

Sabagh, G., 253, *258*
Sackett, G. P., 283, 291, 292, *307*
Sadnavitch, J. M., 201, 203, *224*
Sandercock, M. G., 199, 216, *225*
Sanders, A. F., 282, *304*
Sanders, B., 108, 116, 117, 121, 122, 124, 139, 140, *146*, *147*, 148
Sarason, S. B., 47, *104*, 210, *225*, 332, *369*
Satter, G., 218, *225*
Satz, P., 207, *225*
Saxon, S. V., 282, *307*
Scanlan, J., 254, *261*
Scarr, E. H., 201, 203, *225*
Schalock, R. L., 293, *307*
Scharlock, D. P., 286, *307*
Scheidemann, N. V., 312, *372*
Scheidler, C. H., 268, 270, 271, *305*, *307*
Schell, S. F., 298, *301*
Schiff, G. M., 269, *307*
Schlanger, B. B., 314, 315, 316, 317, 318, 321, 322, 323, 324, 325, 331, 335, 336, 338, 339, 345, 346, 347, 348, 350, 354, 360, 361, *364*, *372*
Schiltz, K. A., 287, 292, *303*
Schmaltz, L. W., 288, *304*
Schneider, B., 199, 217, *226*
Schneller, P., 351, *370*
Schonfield, J., 248, *261*
Schulman, J. L., 154, *190*, 202, *227*
Schunhoff, H. T., 361, *372*
Schutzman, L. H., 291, 298, *305*
Schwarz, S., 297, *307*
Scott, J. P., 267, *302*
Scott, K. G., 2, *32*, 108, *148*
Scott, M. S., 2, *32*
Scrimshaw, N. S., 294, *307*
Searle, L. V., 265, *307*
Seashore, H., 209, 217, *225*
Segerson, J. A., 332, *366*

Sellin, D. F., *372*
Semler, I. J., 86, *102, 104,* 113, 126, 129, 146, *148*
Sen, A., 138, *148*
Senn, R. K., 294, *302*
Senter, R. J., 295, *303*
Serra, M., 331, 334, *367*
Severs, J. L., 269, *307*
Sharp, H. C., 199, *225*
Sharp, J. C., 273, *307*
Shearin, C. A., 282, *300*
Sheridan, M. D., 347, 349, *372*
Shields, J., 35, 64, *104, 105*
Shiffrin, R. M., 6, *31*
Shotwell, A. M., 199, 200, 205, 206, 209, *223, 225, 226*
Shuey, A. M., 65, *105*
Siegel, D. S., 108, *148*
Siegel, L., 208, 216, *226*
Siegenthaler, B., 318, 331, 360, *372*
Sikov, M. R., 272, *308,* 309
Silverman, S. I., 360, *372*
Silverman, S. R., 332, 335, 344, *365*
Silverstein, A. B., 154, 167, *190,* 194, 202, 205, 206, 207, 208, 209, 210, 211, 220, *223, 225, 226*
Singer, D. M., 244, *259*
Singh, S. D., 266, *307*
Sitkei, E. G., 248, *260*
Sivers, C., 70, *102*
Slater, E., 35, *105*
Sloan, W., 152, *190,* 199, 208, 214, 216, 217, *222, 226, 227*
Slobody, L., 254, *261*
Smith, G. M., 245, *261*
Snyder, H. J., 360, *372*
Snyder, R. T., 245, 247, *261*
Soddy, K., 332, *373*
Sokolov, E. N., 130, 131, *148*
Sontag, L. W., 279, *307*
Spain, C. J., 132, 133, *144*
Spaulding, P. J., 203, *226*
Speer, G. S., 212, *226*
Spence, K. W., 111, 117, *148*
Sperrazzo, G., 70, *105*
Spicker, H. H., 235, 245, 246, *259*
Spitz, H. H., 135, 136, *146, 148*
Spradlin, J. E., 335, 336, 337, *369, 372, 373*
Sprague, R. L., 213, *226*

Sprinkle, P. M., 331, *373*
Stacey, C. L., 199, 206, 216, 217, *222, 226*
Stahlecker, L., 361, *368*
Stallings, L., 154, *190*
Standifer, F. R., 254, *261*
Stanley, J. C., 110, *148*
Stanton, H. R., 231, 246, *256*
Steggerda, M., 51, *101*
Stehman, V. A., 361, *363*
Stephens, L. M., 360, *364*
Stephens, M. W., 198, *226*
Sterling, E., 312, *373*
Sternfeld, L., 252, *262*
Sternlicht, M., 208, 211, 216, *226*
Stevens, G. D., 361, *363*
Stevens, H. A., 194, *226,* 238, 242, *261*
Stevenson, H. W., 116, 121, 122, 124, 125, *148*
Stewart, J. H., 343, *372, 373*
Stockwin, A. E., *190,* 203, *225*
Stone, N. D., 252, *261*
Strauss, A. A., 137, *148,* 152, 154, *190*
Strauss, A. L., 229, *260*
Strauss, R., 247, *261*
Strickland, C. G., 244, *261*
Strominger, N. L., 286, *307*
Stuckless, E. R., 360, 361, *363, 373*
Studebaker, G. A., 338, *373*
Sundby, E. A., 271, *307*
Suzuki, N., 89, *104*

Taft, L. T., 219, 220, *222*
Tait, C. D., Jr., 272, *307*
Talland, G. A., 61, *105*
Tapp, J. T., 266, 292, *303, 307*
Tarjan, G., 253, *261*
Taylor, A. P., 360, *373*
Taylor, G. A., 74, *102*
Terdal, L. G., 134, *148*
Terman, L. M., 44, 72, 75, *105,* 194, 197, 202, 204, 210, *226*
Thompson, C. I., 287, *303*
Thompson, C. W., 152, *190,* 214, 215, *224, 226*
Thompson, J. M., 207, 209, 216, 217, *223, 226*
Thompson, R. F., 286, *300*

AUTHOR INDEX

Thompson, V. E., 286, 287, *307*, *309*
Thompson, W. D., Jr., 279, *307*
Thompson, W. R., 40, *102*, 265, 266, 275, 276, 279, 290, 296, *302*, *307*, *308*
Thomson, C. W., 267, *304*
Thorndike, R. L., *190*
Throne, F. M., 154, *190*, 202, *227*
Thurstone, J. R., 254, *261*
Tillman, T. W., 345, 347, *373*
Tizard, B., 132, 133, *148*
Tizard, J., 339, *370*
Tolle, C. D., 277, *301*
Towbin, A., 289, *308*
Tredgold, A. F., 312, *373*
Tredgold, R. F., 332, *373*
Tryon, R. C., 265, *308*
Tsang, Y., 286, *308*
Tucker, T. J., 286, 287, *304*, *307*, *308*
Tudor, K. B., 252, *262*
Turner, D. R., 250, *262*
Turner, L. A., 351, *373*
Tyler, L. E., 38, 68, *105*
Tyler, R., 55, *101*

Underwood, B. J., 86, *105*
Unell, E., 124, *149*
Urquhart, D., 113, *144*, 339, *363*

Vanderhost, L., 216, 217, *227*
Ventry, I. M., 348, 354, *364*
Vernon, P. E., 51, *105*, *190*
Vierck, C. J., Jr., 271, *308*
Vincent, N. M., 274, *308*
Vogel, W., 132, 133, *148*, 253, *262*
Volk, B. W., 334, *373*
vonAbeelen, J. H. F., 266, *308*
vonBekesy, G., 338, *373*

Wade, F. A., 312, *373*
Waisman, H. A., *189*, 276, 293, *304*, *306*, *308*
Waite, R., 210, *225*
Waldeman, J. L., 312, *373*
Waldon, E. F., 343, *373*
Waldren, D., 331, *373*
Wall, P. D., 272, *307*
Wallace, W. P., 86, *105*

Wallin, J. E. W., 247, *262*
Walters, C. E., 51, *105*
Walton, D., 203, *227*
Wang, D. D., 248, *259*
Warkany, J., 267, *309*
Warren, S. A., 154, *189*, 218, *227*, 250, *262*, 361, *373*
Watkins, E. O., 343, *373*
Watson, J., 275, 279, *308*
Watts, C. A., 248, *260*
Waugh, N. C., 6, *32*
Weaver, J., 345, *367*
Weaver, R. M., 336, *374*
Weaver, T. T., Jr., 124, *148*
Webb, A. P., 199, 209, 216, *227*
Webb, C. E., 323, 331, 336, 339, 342, 343, *363*, *374*
Weber, B. A., 323, 331, 336, 339, 342, 343, *363*, *374*
Webster, R., 275, *303*
Wechsler, D., 72, 73, *105*, 196, 197, 209, 217, *227*
Wegner, N., 341, *374*
Weir, M. W., 269, 296, *301*, *308*
Welch, D. B., 10, *32*
Weller, G. M., 318, 319, 330, *367*, *368*
Werboff, J., 268, 270, 272, 273, 275, *308*, *309*
Wertz, T. L., 339, *374*
Wesman, A., 209, *225*
Wetzel, A. B., 286, *309*
Whatley, R. G., 154, *190*
Wheeler, L. R., 154, *191*
Whimbey, A. E., 298, 299, *302*, *309*
White, D., 154, *191*
White, G. N., 245, *259*
White, S. H., 51, 99, *105*
Whitley, J. R., 277, *309*
Wilber, R. L., 312, *374*
Wiley, J. H., 324, 331, *369*, *371*
Wilkins, W. L., 70, *105*
Willerman, L., 41, *105*
Williams, W. C., 154, *189*
Wilson, J. G., 267, *309*
Windle, C., 242, *262*
Windle, W. F., 269, 282, 284, 289, 296, *304*, *306*, *307*, *309*
Winston, H. D., 266, *309*
Wise, M. A., 294, *302*

Wishik, S. M., 330, *365*
Witkop, C. J., Jr., 294, *309*
Witting, E. G., 356, *374*
Wolfe, W. G., 319, 335, 336, 345, 354, 361, *374*
Wolfensberger, W., 133, *148*, 233, 250, 251, 252, 253, 254, *262*
Woodall, C. S., 154, *191*
Woodcock, J. M., 292, *302*
Woods, P. J., 267, *306*
Word, T. J., 275, *309*
Worthington, A. M., 316, 335, 354, *364*
Wright, C., 204, 205, *227*
Wright, L., 81, *105*, 136, *148*
Wrightsman, L. S., Jr., 249, *261*

Yaeger, J. A., 112, 121, 122, 124, *147, 148*
Yannet, H., 332, 334, *374*
York, M. W., 70, *101*
Young, C. E., 332, 335, 342, 352, 353, 354, 355, 356, 357, 358, 359, *369, 374*
Young, F. M., 218, *227*
Young, M., 42, *105*
Young, R. D., 273, 293, *309*
Yudin, L. W., 207, *227*

Záhlava, J., 286, *309*
Zarrow, M. X., 283, *303*
Zeaman, D., 78, 79, 80, 81, *105*, 115, 116, 117, *146, 148*, 152, 156, 167, *191*, 208, *227*, 341, *374*
Zeigler, H. P., 284, *304*
Zigler, E., 2, *32*, 116, 121, 122, 124, 125, *144, 148, 149*, 281, *309*
Zubek, J. P., 152, *189*
Zuk, G. H., 250, *262*
Zwislacki, J., 338, *374*

Subject Index

Abilities,
  equal, inhibition deficits and, 109-110
  hierarchy of, 51-61
    intelligence tests and, 54-57
    Levels I and II, 53-54
      correlation between, 61-64
      evidence for, 66-97
      "fluid" and "crystallized" intelligence and, 57-58
      focus of attention and, 60-61
      relationship to mental retardation of, 64-66
      socioeconomic status and, 58-60, 62-63, 86-91
Abstraction, inhibition deficits and, 143
Adjustment, vocational, 242-244
Administration, intelligence tests and, 210-213
Age,
  changes in IQ and, 165-167
  chronological, *see* Chronological age
  intelligence measurement and, 208-209
  mental, *see* Mental age
Animals,
  genetic factors in mental retardation and, 265-267
  perinatal factors in mental retardation and, 281-284
    hypoxia and, 281-283
    mode of delivery and, 283-284
  postnatal factors in mental retardation and, 284-296
    comment on, 295-296
    drugs and, 292-294
    early experience and, 290-292
    hyperoxia and, 284-285
    infantile brain damage and, 285-290
    nutrition and, 294-295
  prenatal factors in mental retardation and, 267-281
    comment on, 280-281

    drugs and, 273-276
    hypoxia and, 270-271
    ionizing radiation and, 271-273
    maternal emotion and, 278-280
    nutrition and, 276-278
Anxiety, intelligence measurement and, 210
Associative clustering, abilities and, 91-97
  social class differences in, 93-97
Associative learning, *see* Learning, associative
Attention,
  focus of, 60-61
  inhibition and, *see* Inhibition deficits
Attitudes,
  public's view of retardate and, 247-250, 255
  change in attitude and, 249-250
  vocational success and, 244-245
Audiology, 311-374
  habilitation and, 360-361
  historical aspects of, 311-312
  incidence of hearing impairment and, 313-334
  intramethod research and, 354-360
    drugs and, 359-360
    puretone audiometry and, 354-358
    speech audiometry and, 358
  methodologic and intermethod research and, 334-354
    behavior observation audiometry and, 342-344
    puretone audiometry and, 335-342
    special procedures and, 351-354
    speech audiometry and, 344-351

Behavioral audiometry, 335-338
Behavior observation audiometry, 342-344
Binet, *see* Stanford-Binet Intelligence Scale
Birth complications, 283-284
Brain damage, infantile, 285-290

387

388 Subject Index

CA, *see* Chronological age
Child, retarded, family and, 250–256
Chronological age, inhibition deficits and, 110–111
Classical conditioning, 113–115
Clustering, associative, abilities and, 91–97
Conditioning,
   classical, 113–115
   instrumental, 115–116
      negative cues and, 116–119
Cues,
   distraction and, 137–141
   negative, 116–119
Cultural differences, memory processes and, 28
Cultural-familial retardation, 35–37

Delay effect, memory processes and, 21–23
Delivery, mode of, 283–284
Development, cognitive, abilities and, 68–69
Differentiation, inhibition deficits and, 113–119
   classical conditioning and, 113–115
   instrumental conditioning and, 115–116
   negative cues and, 116–119
Difficulty, memory processes and, 13–20
Digit span, abilities and, 74–78
Discrimination,
   speech, supra-threshold, 349–351
   transfer suppression and, 120–125
Distraction, 136–141
   cues external to learning task and, 137–139
   novel cues embedded in training task and, 139–141
Drugs,
   audiology and, 359–360
   postnatal, 292–294
   prenatal, 273–276

Early experience, 290–292
Education, familial mental retardation and, 97–101
Electrophysiologic audiometry, 338–342
Emotion, maternal, 278–280
Encoding, inhibition deficits and, 143
Environment,
   abilities and, 64
   familial mental retardation and, 38–49

   social, 239–255
      public's view of retardate and, 247–250, 255
      retardate's self-concept and, 245–247, 255
      retardate's social success and, 239–242, 255
      retardate's vocational success and, 242–245, 255
      retarded child and his family and, 250–256
Ethnicity, intelligence measurement and, 209–210
Extinction, inhibition deficits and, 111–113

Factor analysis, intelligence measurement and, 213–214
Familial mental retardation, 33–105
   diagnosis and taxonomy of, 33–37
      cultural-familial retardation and, 35–37
      diagnostic categories and, 34–35
   evidence for Level I–Level II hypothesis and, 66–97
      associative learning and intelligence and, 78–85
      free recall and associative clustering and, 91–97
      general observations and, 66–68
      memory span and, 71–78
      paired-associate learning and, 85–86
      psychometric, 68–71
      rote learning, IQ, and socioeconomic status and, 86–91
   implications for education and, 97–101
   social class and, 37–51
      genetic and environmental factors and, 38–49
      motoric precocity and later intelligence and, 49–51
   theory of, 51–66
      correlation between Level I and Level II abilities and, 61–64
      hierarchy of abilities and, 51–61
      relationship of Levels I and II abilities to retardation and, 64–66
Family, retarded child and, 250–256
   impact of child on family and, 250–252
   institutionalization and, 252–254

SUBJECT INDEX

Genetics, *see also* Heredity
  mental retardation in animals and, 265–267
  social class and, 38–49
Goodness of fit, 168–169
Growth, intelligence and, *see* Intelligence growth

Habilitation, audiology and, 360–361
Handicap, physical, intelligence measurement and, 211–212
Hearing, *see* Audiology
Heredity, *see also* Genetics
  abilities and, 64
Heterogeneity, familial retardation and, 69–71
Hyperoxia, postnatal, 284–285
Hypoxia,
  perinatal, 281–283
  prenatal, 270–271

Individual differences, inhibition deficits and, 141–144
Inhibition, proactive and retroactive, 125–130
Inhibition deficits, 107–149
  attention to stimulus input and external inhibition and, 130–141
    distraction in instrumental learning and, 136–141
    orienting reflex and, 130–133
    satiation phenomena and, 133–136
  definitions and rationale of, 107–111
    contrast groups and assessment of inhibitory deficits and, 109–111
  individual differences in learning processes and, 141–144
    abstraction and, 143
    encoding and, 143
    response inhibition and, 141–142
    rigidity and, 143–144
    stimulus inhibition and, 142–143
  learned responses and internal inhibition and, 111–130
    differentiation and, 113–119
    extinction and, 111–113
    transfer suppression and, 119–130
Input, *see* Stimulus input

Institutionalization,
  length of, intelligence measurement and, 208–209
  retarded child and his family and, 252–254
Instrumental conditioning, 115–116
  negative cues and, 116–119
Intelligence,
  associative learning and, 78–85
  "fluid" and "crystallized," 57–58
  social class and, 49–51
Intelligence growth, 151–191
  age-changes in IQ by level and, 165–167
  cross-sectional growth, by level and, 162–163
  determination of constant measure of retarded intelligence and, 167–174
    empirical equation and, 167–168
    goodness of fit and, 168–169
    interpretation of parameters and, 169–171
    reliability and constancy compared to IQ, 172–173
    reliability of constant and IQ over time, 173–174
    simplification of equation and, 171–172
    values of, 177–188
  diagnostic categories and, 163–165
  growth curve and, 159–161
  semi-longitudinal growth, by level and sex and, 163
  semi-longitudinal MA growth, by level and, 161–162
  semi-longitudinal method and, 156–159
  subject population and, 156
Intelligence measurement, 193–227
  administration and scoring of tests and, 210–213
    physically handicapped subjects and, 211–212
    pseudo-retarded subjects and, 212–213
    range of testing and, 210–211
    severely retarded subjects and, 211
  constant measure of retarded intelligence and, 167–174
  descriptions of tests and, 194–197
    Binet, 194–195

WISC and WAIS, 196-197
diagnostic applications of tests and, 218-221
  Binet and, 218-219
  WISC and WAIS and, 219-221
factor analyses and, 213-214
item analyses and pattern analyses and, 214-218
  Binet and, 214-215
  WISC and WAIS and, 215-218
nonintellectual factors and, 207-210
  age and length of institutionalization and, 208-209
  anxiety and, 210
  ethnicity and, 209-210
  sex and, 209
reliability of tests and, 201-204
  alternate-form, 202
  internal consistency and, 202-204
  test-retest, 201-202
short forms of tests and, 204-207
  Binet, 204-206
  WISC and WAIS, 206-207
validity of tests and, 197-201
  authors' positions and, 197
  comparisons among tests and, 198-201
  reviewer's position and, 197-198
Intelligence quotient,
  abilities and, 68-69, 86-91
    memory span and, 74-78
  age-changes in, 165-167
  reliability and constancy of, 172-174
Intelligence scales, 54-57, *see also* Intelligence measurement
IQ, *see* Intelligence quotient
Item analysis, 214-218
  Binet and, 214-215
  WISC and WAIS and, 215-218

Learning,
  associative, familial mental retardation and, 78-85
  discrimination, transfer suppression and, 120-125
  inhibition and, *see* Inhibition deficits
  instrumental, distraction and, 136-141
  paired-associate, familial mental retardation and, 85-86
  rote, abilities and, 86-91

Learning processes, individual differences in, 141-144
Learning rate, abilities and, 68-69
Lesion, diagnosis of site of, 351-353

MA, *see* Mental age
Memory processes, 1-32, *see also* Recall
  experimental studies and, 8-28
    cultural differences and, 28
    delay effect and, 21-23
    graduated difficulty and, 13-20
    interpolated recall and, 25
    motivational effects and, 26-27
    presentation rate and, 8-12
    rehearsal and, 20, 24-26
  experimental task and, 3-5
  theory and, 5-7
Memory span, familial mental retardation and, 71-78
  interaction of digit span, IQ, and socioeconomic status and, 74-78
  short-term memory and, 74
Mental age,
  abilities and, 68-69
  inhibition deficits and, 109-110
  semi-longitudinal growth of, 161-162
Mental retardation,
  familial, *see* Familial mental retardation
  genetic factors in, 265-267
  multivariate analysis of, 296-299
  perinatal factors in, 281-284
    hypoxia and, 281-283
    mode of delivery and, 283-284
  postnatal factors in, 284-296
    comment on, 295-296
    drugs and, 292-294
    early experience and, 290-292
    hyperoxia and, 284-285
    infantile brain damage and, 285-290
    nutrition and, 294-295
  prenatal factors in, 267-281
    comment on, 280-281
    drugs and, 273-276
    hypoxia and, 270-271
    ionizing radiation and, 271-273
    maternal emotion and, 278-280
    nutrition and, 276-278

SUBJECT INDEX 391

Motivational effects, memory processes and, 26–27
Motoric precocity, social class and, 49–51

Nonintellective factors, intelligence measurement and, 207–210
Nutrition,
  postnatal, 294–295
  prenatal, 276–278

Orienting reflex, *see* Reflex, orienting

Paired-associate learning, *see* Learning, paired-associate
Pattern analysis, 214–218
  Binet and, 214–215
  WISC and WAIS and, 215–218
Precocity, motoric, social class and, 49–51
Presentation rate, memory processes and, 8–12
Pseudohypacusis, 353–354
Pseudo-retardation, intelligence measurement and, 212–213
Psychometrics, familial mental retardation and, 68–71

Radiation, ionizing, prenatal, 271–273
Recall, *see also* Memory processes; Memory span
  free, abilities and, 91–97
  interpolated, 25
Reflex, orienting, inhibition deficits and, 130–133
Rehearsal, memory processes and, 20, 24–26
Reliability, constant measure of retarded intelligence and, 172–174
  intelligence scales and, 201–204
    alternate-form, 202
    internal consistency and, 202–204
    test-retest, 201–202
Response, learned,
  differentiation and, 113–119
  extinction and, 111–113
  inhibition deficits and, 141–142
  transfer suppression and, 119–130
Rigidity, inhibition deficits and, 143–144
Rote learning, *see* Learning, rote

Satiation phenomena, 133–136

  neural, 135
  reactive, 135–136
  stimulus, 134–135
Scoring, intelligence tests and, 210–213
Self-concept, 245–247, 255
Semi-longitudinal method, 156–159
Sex,
  growth of intelligence and, 163
  intelligence measurement and, 209
Social class,
  associative clustering and, 93–97
  genetic and environmental factors and, 38–49
  motoric precocity and later intelligence and, 49–51
Social environment, *see* Environment, social
Social psychology, 229–261
  retardate in his social environment and, 239–255
    public's view of retardate and, 247–250, 255
    retarded child and his family and, 250–256
    self-concept and, 245–247, 255
    social success and, 239–242, 255
    vocational success and, 242–245, 255
  retardation as social problem and, 230–239, 255
Social success, 239–242, 255
Socioeconomic status, abilities and, 58–60, 62–63, 86–91
  memory span and, 74–78
Speech audiometry, 344–351, 358
  comfortable and uncomfortable levels and, 351
  speech reception thresholds and, 345–349
  supra-threshold speech discrimination and, 349–351
Stanford-Binet Intelligence Scale,
  description of, 194–195
  diagnostic applications of, 218–219
  item analysis and pattern analysis and, 214–215
  short form of, 204–206
Status, socioeconomic, *see* Socioeconomic status
Stimulus, inhibition deficits and, 142–143
Stimulus input,

distraction in instrumental learning and, 136–141
  cues external to task and, 137–139
  novel cues embedded in task and, 139–141
  orienting reflex and, 130–133
  satiation phenomena and, 133–136
    neural, 135
    reactive, 135–136
    stimulus, 134–135
Suppression, *see* Transfer suppression

Threshold,
  speech discrimination and, 349–351
  speech reception and, 345–349
Transfer suppression, 119–130
  discrimination learning and, 120–125
  proactive and retroactive inhibition and, 125–130
Validity, intelligence scales and, 197–201
  authors' positions and, 197
  comparisons among tests and, 198–201
  reviewer's position and, 197–198
Vocational success, 242–245, 255
  employer receptivity and, 244–245
  variables predicting successful adjustment and, 242–244

WAIS, *see* Wechsler Adult Intelligence Scale
Wechsler Adult Intelligence Scale, description of, 196–197
  diagnostic applications of, 219–221
  item analysis and pattern analysis and, 215–218
  short form of, 206–207
Wechsler Intelligence Scale for Children description of, 196–197
  diagnostic applications of, 219–221
  item analysis and pattern analysis and, 215–218
  short form of, 206–207
WISC, *see* Wechsler Intelligence Scale for Children

RC
570
I 5
v.4
1970

APR 15 1976